IN GOD'S NAME

IN GOD'S NAME

Examples of preaching in England
from the Act of Supremacy to
the Act of Uniformity

1534-1662

Chosen and edited,
with an introduction and annotations, *by*

JOHN CHANDOS

HUTCHINSON OF LONDON

HUTCHINSON & CO (PUBLISHERS) LTD

3 *Fitzroy Square, London* WI

London Melbourne Sydney Auckland
Wellington Johannesburg Cape Town
and agencies throughout the world

First published 1971

*This book has been set in Bembo type, printed in Great Britain
on antique wove paper by Alden & Mowbray Ltd at the Alden Press, Oxford,
and bound by Wm. Brendon of Tiptree, Essex*

ISBN 0 09 105930 5

Obscurata diu populo bonus eruet atque
Proferet in lucem speciosa vocabula rerum
Quae priscis memorata Catonibus atque Cethegis
Nunc situs informis premit et deserta vetustas

HORACE, *Epistles* I. ii. 115

CONTENTS

* Only those Sermon titles asterisked are the preachers' own.

PART TWO: *Jacobean*

ix

PART THREE: *Carolean and Civil Wars*

ILLUSTRATIONS

For my daughter, Angela

FOREWORD

The reconnaissance for the following expedition was a series of illustrated talks which I broadcast in 1966, in the Third Programme of the B.B.C. The broadcasts were not intended as a preparative for a larger work, but the exercise convinced me that the content of English preaching, over the period covered, deserved a fuller display than it had been possible to give in the talks, or than it had received, as a whole, at any time.

The largest collections of sermons published were mid- and late-Victorian products. Excess of modesty was not a Victorian critical defect, and these anthologies are laden with the contributions of contemporary divines (and the precursors of the nineteenth-century spirit like Wesley), while examples from earlier times, when the English pulpit was vigorously, sometimes dangerously, alive, were either not rediscovered or, when they were, were likely to be reburied as unsuitable for general exhibition on the grounds of indelicacy (or worse), eccentricity, or irrelevance to the nineteenth-century standards of propriety. This tendency was not present in the labours of scholars-for-scholars, such as Corrie's edition of Latimer and the Homilies, Eden's edition of Taylor, Bliss's edition of Laud, and of course the publications of learned societies like the Camden and the Harleian. But these publications had a limited circulation at the time and both they and the more popular productions have long been out of print.

The Victorian sermons as a whole have not worn well. As literature, they are, with few exceptions, grandiose shams. As historical documents they are sometimes significant, but more often than not they merely confirm the decadence, full of genteel platitudes, to which the medium had sunk. But to follow preaching into the seventeenth and sixteenth centuries is to find the pulpit, though drenched in blood and bigotry, superstition and intolerance, yet in the thick of the melée, in the van of controversy, leading and influencing, and enduring a high rate of casualties, as some of the examples in this book will testify. Another reason for my pursuing the subject as far as I have is that English preaching contains an underworked—perhaps the only remaining underworked—vein of English literature. That it has been relatively sequestered from investigation is due in part to the eclipse of God, and the transcendental authority which He implies, in the firmament of portents which has guided man's movements during the past century. No star has shone in revelation over the buried treasure of the pulpit; and contemporary products strewing the surface have given no indication of the riches below.

The scarcity of surviving copies of many of the originals has been another dissuasive; and it was this consideration which resolved me to produce an annotated collection, as well as an illustrated study.[1] My object has been to provide, in one book, enough examples of English preaching of sufficient substance to give the reader a solid portion to chew on, even at the risk of indigestion, rather than a fleeting savour of the fare. Limitations of space have required me to make internal cuts in some of the material; and, while in principle I regret this, in practice, I have not found that these reductions diminish the quality, or impoverish the meaning of the passages. Larger cuts are indicated by a space between lines together with an asterisk; smaller cuts by a series of dots or ellipses. No one could be more keenly aware than I am of the imperfections of my efforts; but, before I submit myself to the just charges of omission and commission from critics whose favourite voice is missing or whose least favoured seems too prominently featured, I must declare the principles which have guided me in the choice of material. First, of course, *merit*: no collection of sermons which omitted examples of Latimer in the sixteenth, or Taylor in the seventeenth century, could be regarded as a valid representation. Second, *accessibility*: part of the object of the assembly was to show together, in a manageable form, examples of influential preaching not otherwise readily accessible. Third, *historical interest*: the 'Fast Sermons' of the Long Parliament make a claim upon our attention in excess of any literary merit they possess. Fourth, *curiosities*, including parody: to be complete, the picture of the place of preaching in the life of the community requires the recoil of irreverence and satire, as well as the drive of ardour and piety.

In accommodating these various demands, sacrifices and concessions have been necessary. The space accorded to Donne has been modified by the consideration that he has been handsomely served as recently as 1960 in an edition of his collected sermons by Potter and Simpson.[2]

1. *The Sword in the Mouth* (work in progress, 1971).
2. *The Sermons of John Donne* (ed. George R. Potter and Evelyn M. Simpson), 1952–62.

Conversely, in allocating space to Thomas Adams, account has been taken of the obstacles to obtaining a copy of his works at all. The sermons of Crashaw and Lushington in this book have been given almost in their entirety; the former for the special interest of the subject it treats, the latter for the uniqueness of its nature. In decisions such as these, whatever the reputations involved, one must in the last resort be true to one's personal judgement. As I find John Owen, Sibbs and Farindon well-nigh unreadable, they are excluded despite their undoubted influence in their lifetimes.

The number of footnotes has been kept down to such elucidations as I felt a reader had a right to expect, and I was capable of providing. Here, in addition to offering my own footnotes, I have made use, when they seemed helpful, of the footnotes of my learned predecessors in this field, especially of Corrie's and Eden's. All of these I have checked, and I am responsible for any error or inaccuracy of theirs which I may have permitted to survive. Some of the Latin abbreviations favoured by the close fellowship of Victorian classical scholarship reduce their references to a point where they might mystify, before they inform, the modern reader. Not all readers educated in Latin have necessarily read Plutarch's *De Conjugalia Praecepta*, and those who have may well know it rather as *Nuptialia Praecepta*; it therefore seemed to me something short of sufficient to refer to the work as *Conj. Praec.* Most of the older classical references have, accordingly, been expanded. I have accepted with reluctance my publishers' advice that inclusion of the keys to Biblical quotations which I had compiled would overload the book. Bearing in mind that excessive Biblical quotation was a vice of seventeenth century preaching and that efficient concordances are today generally accessible, I hope that serious students of the texts will experience no difficulty in identifying any scriptural reference which has not been specifically distinguished.

Allusions and quotations in the text extend over an area of such diversity that I have preferred not to adhere to one uniform method of citation. In general, in the case of modern or rare books I have furnished page numbers or signs of particular editions; but with much-published classics I judged it more practical to give verse or chapter and line or paragraph references.

In addition to revising previous, and furnishing new, footnotes, I have provided a linking commentary for the several items of the collection. The Introduction is addressed primarily to students already conversant with the subject and the period under consideration. Not without some misgivings I have, in the main, left the orthography in its original state. There were strong arguments for and against the possible alternatives. In the end obsolete letters have been amended, and archaic forms like the ligature, the 'thorn' and the horizontal stroke, removed. But punctuation has been altered only when it might have impaired the meaning, and the original spelling, variable as it is, has been retained (except where it was an obvious mistake), as the expression of the organic mutations of language, which it is part of the function of this book to display in motion.

In the course of producing the present work I have received help from more people than may be conveniently named. But certain debts must be acknowledged. Professor H. R. Trevor-Roper has been unfailingly generous whenever I sought his advice. Dr. Valerie Pearl has given me valuable information concerning London politics in the Civil Wars. In reading my proofs, Dr. J. W. Blench has brought to my aid an unsurpassed knowledge of English sermons in the period covered. Sir Maurice Bowra and Professor Owen Chadwick have been kind enough to answer questions I have put to them on topics as disparate as Cyclopic lore and the thought of John Cassian. Mr. Sears McGee, of Yale University, has feasted me upon the manna of his own research. Dr. L. Goldstein has led me in giving chase to the occasional elusive term, pursuit of which I might otherwise have abandoned. My thanks are tendered, for patient co-operation, to the Keeper of Printed Books at the British Museum and to his staff in the North Library; also to the librarians of the Dr. Williams Library, the Lambeth Palace Library, the Bodleian Library and Cambridge University Library. Above all I must acknowledge with gratitude my obligation to Mr. Julian Roberts, Assistant Keeper of Printed Books at the British Museum, who has placed at my service his mastery of 16th and 17th century bibliography.

INTRODUCTION

When Richard Hooker said, 'Things are preached not in that they are taught, but in that they are published',[1] he put a divining finger on the nature of the process which was to grow into the first strategic exercise in popular communications in the history of England. Preaching and the preacher's stage, the pulpit, had long previously been operative on several levels, but so far removed from each other at their extremities, as to hold no mutual communication. At the top of the pyramid of mediaeval preaching was the recondite university preaching of complex arguments of theology and philosophy, complemented by the practice of syllogistic disputation. At the bottom, the base and broadest part of society, was the unco-ordinated distribution of simple, colloquial moral *exempla*, by the itinerant, cosmopolitan friars who toured Christendom and circulated news and gossip, as well as mythology and divinity.

One intention of the founders of the preaching orders of friars was to reinforce psychologically the authority of the church and state, in that order of priority, on the supposition that the two would be (except for normal domestic bickering) for ever united. But a weapon, once created, may be used for other ends than those it was designed to serve. The Lollard movement at Oxford demonstrated that rebellion against higher authority could come from educated defectors within the church itself, even from the very friars whom the church had trained as her protectors in the arts of public speaking and persuading the multitude.

The mouths of Lollardy were silenced, where necessary consumed by fire, and its adherents driven underground with cruelties inspired by fear. But a hundred years later, when Henry VIII asserted his right to divorce his first wife, and the English crown's right to divorce the papacy, it was to the pulpits, notwithstanding their dangerous antecedents, that he turned for an instrument by which popular sentiment could be roused and controlled to his advantage. It became obligatory for every parish priest to preach against the claims of papal supremacy and to support the independence of the English crown and church.

1. *Works* (Oxford, 1888), Vol. II, Bk, V, Ch. XIX.

Again, the initiators of these policies were too preoccupied with immediate tactical conflicts to foresee the ultimate harvest which would be reaped from scattering in fallow ground the seeds of licensed dissent. Henry himself seems to have supposed, at least at first, that he could activate an avalanche, and thereafter arrest its motion. Preaching rapidly shaped in England into a weapon of war, the outward and visible assertion of 'protestant'—equated with 'patriotic'—reform. For protestant zealots, preaching became a way of life and, not without significance, a highly conspicuous and illustrious one; for some it enlarged almost to obsession in the battle against threats, real or imaginary, from 'the enemy', Satan's emissary on earth, the antichrist, enthroned in Rome.

The circulation of hot eloquence turned into a lively but wayward servant to the government. The habit of publicly criticizing foreign ruling authorities was one which, as it gained muscle and confidence, showed an indisposition to accept subsequent guidance or restraint, or to remain confined within the limits of the task which it had been enlisted to perform. No one appreciated better than Elizabeth I the dangers inherent in allowing the pulpits to become free dispensaries of any inflammable doctrine which a fiery tongue might ignite (seditiously or zealously) and it was not the least of her achievements that she succeeded, over a long reign, in bridling the ambitions of her parliament for a larger share of government, and in subduing their potential channels of access to the ear of the country, the pulpits, to reluctant obedience or ineffectuality. Church and state, authorities spiritual and temporal, were still deemed unseparated and inseparable; the church was as secular in application as she was ecclesiastical in principle; the bulwark of the eminence from which control was claimed over thought, education, and, therefore, *publication*.

But even a sovereign as intuitively skilful as Elizabeth in making subjects who were not free, feel free, found herself unable to maintain a stable relationship between the crown-controlled church and the expanding desire to self-expression of a rival, secular virility. Towards the end of her reign, especially, signs of impatience began to show through the loyalty of her parliaments. With the death of Elizabeth and the withdrawal of her moral strength, restraint was less broken through than overrun by concurrent tidal excitations over an area so broad that it was never again brought under uniform or secure control.

Archbishop Laud very nearly did impose a settlement; the nearness to success of his campaign to suppress lecturers, and the feoffee system of subsidy by private and voluntary subscription which produced them—the frontline soldiers of the Puritan cause—before swords were actually drawn tends to be disregarded in the light of the dramatic *dénouement* of 1640–1. Had Strafford not fallen into a trap by returning to London when and how he did, immediate events would certainly have followed a different course, one which could hardly have failed to modify the pattern which followed. But, in the events which did occur, the pulpit became a strong-point from which great influence could be exercised upon the issue. The conflict which the pulpits inspired and dominated led to victories in the field as militarily as decisive as the most optimistic challengers could have hoped for, but they proved like the devil's promises, which, though kept precisely, produce very different consequences from those savoured in anticipation by the beguiled human transactors. The relationship between the sword and the pulpit in the civil war was so intimate that it is impossible to separate one from the other. The pulpit created and sustained the morale and discipline which purchased victory for men with no tradition of arms, over men whose status and pride was mounted on a distinctive competence to bear arms.[1]

It was also the first application of the weapon of oral communications in social conflict, the more remarkable because the medium had been in the control, though unexploited, of the other side. But the medium, like the apprentice sorcerer's spells, began to take over and race out of control. As soon as the opposition of the common enemy was crushed, the verbal swordsmen did not sheath their weapons, they turned them upon each other; 'saints' battered 'saints' with denunciations and invective from rival pulpits. The first begetters of the 'Good Old Cause' were shocked to find that many of those whom they had counted of their number, who had shared with them the reproachful name of 'Puritan' and had contributed substantially to the victory over the 'malignants' were 'Puritans', or, as they would have put it, 'godly' and 'well affected', only in a

1. There were, of course, 'gentlemen' fighting in both armies; but as the first war progressed, so did the number and achievements on the parliamentary side of men of relatively humble origins, who would not, in the ordinary course of their lives in time of peace, have carried or known the use of a sword (i.e. Hewson, Harrison, Packer, Berry) and Cromwell later spoke frankly on the problem of cultivating a fighting spirit in men untrained to arms (see *Letters and Speeches*, ed. Carlyle, Vol. iv, pp. 59–61; 1897 edn.).

negative sense, and either wished to go further than the socially conservative Presbyterians deemed righteous or, worse, to travel on the tidal opportunities of the civil war in different directions altogether from those already decreed by the senior 'saints'. Whereas the Presbyterian idealists had striven to 'purify' the church of 'idolatry', 'superstition', 'heresy' and, above all, of hierarchal court-control, their erstwhile allies against the prelacy now showed themselves minded to 'purify' the country of *all ecclesiastical dominion*. Worse still, many men in the victorious army revealed themselves as not authentic Calvinists at all, but turbulent and licentious Antinomians, masquerading in 'Puritan' disguise, and using the sharp verbal hooks they had picked up from Calvinism to fish for carnal 'liberties' and 'refreshments' in God's name. They learnt from their superiors to meet cant with cant. When the army Levellers mutinied for causes which were economic and political–revolutionary, they described themselves as 'A faithful remnant . . . that hath not yet bowed their knees to Baal.'[1] Pressing for acceptance of their demands for arrears of pay and relief from foreign service, they declared, 'We are now resolved not to dally with our God.' The first leaders had aimed to reform and *strengthen* the church; the followers, no longer, in the hour of victory, prepared to follow, revealed themselves as rivals for power, purposing to disarm the church, break her as a magisterial institution, and let her decline into impotent fragments. The word 'liquidate' was not then current in political converse, but that was what, in its post-Marxian sense, the radical Independent and sectary preachers designed. 'The Presbyterians called the Independent churches whore', observed the irrepressible William Erbury, 'and the Independents called them whore again; and I say they are all whores together.'[2]

In forming the events of this extraordinary period from 1601 (but mainly from 1629) to 1660, full of violence and rupture and sharp changes in society, the pulpit enjoyed a dramatic apotheosis of influence, then fell almost as precipitously into decadence, to re-emerge at the end of the cycle with a new and polished identity, tamed and diluted to a level of genteel decorum.

Preaching harboured the seeds of its decay in its own popularity; it truly 'went to seed' as it changed from the public promotion of eminent

---

1. *The Levellers (falsely so called) Vindicated or the case of the Twelve Troops . . .* (1649).
2. William Erbury's testimony before 'the Committee of Plundered Ministers'; *Clarke Papers*, ii. 233.

minds, into the promiscuous amplifying of every common theologaster
and loud-mouthed malcontent with a taste for haranguing his equals,
or, for that matter, his superiors. When preaching declined in force, it
sank less under repression than disrepute, and from its reconstitution
at the Restoration, in a style as passionless as it was polite, it gradually
became a conventional decoration of the orthodox Church-of-England
Sunday. When we join Pepys, strolling from church to church, tasting
sermons and ogling fine women in the congregations to whet his thirst
for drinking a morning draught of wine with his friends, we are in
a new world, one which only began to fall into unmistakable decay in
relatively recent times. Puritan, apocalyptic evangelism, and 'fundamen-
talism' did persist, at first in the underground world of secret conventicles, and later, as toleration ceased to be presumed dangerous, in the
strained earnestness of English nonconformity. But, with the passive
acceptance, in 1662, of the Act of Uniformity, the age when pistols
were drawn upon offending preachers, when murder and affrays were
perpetrated in the shadow of the pulpit, when 'pulpits did like beacons
flame'[1] and a surplice was the most dangerous garment a man could
own, passed out of English spoken history, to hiss and splutter only
as a curious relic of ancient bigotries, in anachronistic pockets of survival,
like Tennessee, the hinterland of North Carolina, and the northern
counties of Ireland. We have, of course, since, nourished other and
newer bigotries of our own, which is part of the reason why the passions of the Reformation and of the English Civil Wars have remained
perpetually alive as subjects for study and relevant to successive
generations. Another reason for the attention which the period commands is our primary and particular concern here: it was the first time
that political resistance to the crown government used the broadcasting
of the spoken word to appeal, not to a landed élite or an enfranchised
minority only, but to the population at large.

Much thought and energy have been devoted to the task of identifying and defining the causes of this most seminal of conflicts, the
English Civil Wars, and contemporary voices will be heard upon the
theme in the company assembled below, seldom perhaps expressing a
view of the wood, but taking close account at least of the trees in front
of the speakers' noses; and, as it is profitable sometimes to remember,
no trees, no wood. Other voices speak on what still seems to me an
imperfectly resolved paradox: the spontaneous collapse, without a

1. *A Dose for Chamberlain* (1660).

shot fired, or a blow struck, of the most feared and respected fighting force of the age.

There is, of course, no lack of hypotheses proffered as solutions to the latter problem, and I myself will subscribe to one of them. There was, in the nature of the Puritan complex, an unhealing schism between, on one side, the *ideal individualism* of each just man living by his conscience and the *word* in direct and sufficient communication with God, and, on the other, the *vocational apostolicism* requiring the enlightened elect to dominate their society and impose, if need be by force, a godly discipline to repress sin and repel Satan. The latter of these uneasy sibs militated in practice to encourage hard work now, as well as faith-in-glory later. But, to remain effectively united, the Puritan complex needed a solid corporeal enemy to externalize Satan; it needed crises, and heroes to meet them; heroes perpetually declaring a state of emergency. This was a condition too inflexible in its epitonic tension to be capable of unbroken continuity. But Puritan eschatology could not modify its posture without compromising its identity; to an authentic Puritan, to relax meant to collapse, to betray the withholding from himself of God, and his own fate as preterition. The collapse of the Puritan complex in England was not a failure caused by death at the roots, but a withering and decaying of branch and leaf in a psychic climate too relaxing to favour their character. The roots remained vital and, at irregular intervals, regenerative. A variety of grafts have since produced strange and polymorphic fruit which would have seemed monstrous growths to the sixteenth- and seventeenth-century sowers of *the word* as the seed of life eternal. The same roots of Puritan evangelism have shown themselves capable of nourishing *flora* as incongruous as W. E. Gladstone and D. H. Lawrence, prophets and reformers both, and preachers most of all, perhaps, in the sense Lamb meant when, Coleridge having enquired, 'Did you ever hear me preach?', he answered, 'Damn, I never heard you do anything else.'

Puritan preaching, fascinating as it is, must not be allowed to monopolize the subject, for the story of English preaching in the period we are covering is not merely the sum of the Puritan contributions. The Puritans did not, in fact, produce most of the preachers of the highest quality, despite the currency of that notion in circles of respectable scholarship. The most accomplished exponents of public discourse tended to be conservative Anglicans such as Hammond, Byam, Lushington, Steward and Obidah Rogers. The evidence exists for all to see who are willing to dig a little, enquire into the university reputations of the time, or simply to turn a few of the following pages. The most enduring literary artificers of the pulpit, John Donne and Jeremy Taylor, were also faithful, although, being artists, idiosyncratic servants of the church. Their commitment was not the result of a narrow view or rigid temperament, but of a mistrust of the nature and probable consequences of demotic aspirations to power, shared by most educated gentlemen of the times from Bacon to Hobbes. The danger lay in the possibility of insubordination by the amorphous multitude, men, in the words of Bacon, 'full of savage and unreclaimed desires and profits, of lusts, of revenge . . .'. As long as such as these 'gave ear to precepts, to laws, to religion, sweetly touched with eloquence and persuasion of books of sermons, of harangues', so long was 'society and peace maintained'; but if these instruments were silent, 'so that sedition and tummult make them not audible all things dissolve into anarchy and confuision'.[1] Already by 1615, Thomas Adams, Puritan in his Presbyterian[2] sympathies, was concerned lest exertions for church reform should be made a pretext for inciting social disorder, 'for experience tells us', he warned, 'that where slouth refuseth the ordinary pains of getting, there lust hunts for it in the unwarrentlable paths of wickedness and you shall find that if ever occasion should put such power into their hands they would be ready to pilfer your goods, fire your house and cut your throats'.[3]

Of course social situations and moral problems were not cast in uniform black and white. Unemployment, desperate poverty and hunger could not be cured, especially after the economic depressions of the twenties, by a simple increase in the will to work of the workless, and Adams, with pastoral experience of London and the country, knew it better than most. He was signalling an early warning of a threat of trouble to come to the masters. He had no personal economic stake to protect in the pattern of society; a poor man when he spoke, he was to become a poorer one before he died, and he probably endured consider-

1. Francis Bacon, *The Advancement of Learning*; *Works*, ed., Spedding and Heath, 6 Vols. (1657), Vol. 3, p. 302.

2. The word 'Presbyterian' to denote a church reformation party was not yet in general use in England at the time when Adams was preaching this cautionary message, but its application here is, if anticipatory, a convenient, and in no degree misleading description of the non-separating, socially conservative Puritans who later became the Presbyterian party, religious and political.

3. *The White Devil*; *Works* (1629), p. 42.

able hardship in his old age,[1] but he was never *naïf* enough to suppose that the suffering of poverty and injustice was an education likely to breed moral superiority, or that members of the wretched multitude, invested with power, would behave better than, or as well as, their masters. He too lived in suspicious dread of the multitude and the savage anarchy which he feared would follow if they were unbridled and ran wild. When, at the end of the Civil War, the 'base men' and those of the 'middling sort' (which were still pretty low in the social scale) were at last, as Bacon had uneasily anticipated, able to raise their voices from the captured pulpits and army printing-presses, the ferocity of their feelings, as they demanded a share of the good things, was still served up with an unctious scriptural dressing.

'You powers of earth, or Lord Esau the Elder brother, because you have appeared to rule the Creation, first take notice, That the power that sets you to work is selvish Covetousness and an aspiring Pride, to live in glory and ease over Jacob, the meek Spirit; that is the Seed that lies hid in and among the poor Common People, or younger Brother, out of whom the blessings of Deliverance is to rise and spring up to all Nations.'[2]

Later, even direct threats of violence and pillage were circulated from pulpits and tracts as pious, 'godly' duties. For the imminently ferocious Fifth Monarchists, all that was to be done was to be done 'only for the glory of Christ and primitive purity', but the maintaining of Christ's power is presented as indivisible from the obligation to 'destroy human powers', and this turns out to mean taking from 'great personages who have too much', for distribution, of course, to the just and needy. To a twentieth-century mind this may seem a proposition moderate and reasonable enough, but little consonance was to be expected between the principles devoutly expressed and the actions ferociously performed. The naked revolutionary force which was animating the left wing of the Puritan complex flashes to the surface in the ominous words preached to sanctify violence and extremity of every kind; 'poverty judgeth the law and justifieth itself'.[3]

It must be conceded, in fairness to the fanatics who did resort in fury to lawless violence, that peaceable measures by prospective social

1. Two sermons, 'God's Anger'; 'Man's Comfort' (published posthumously, 1653) are dedicated 'To the most honourable and Charitable Benefactors . . .' who dispensed charity to him 'in this my necessitous and discrepit old age . . .'.
2. *The True Levellers Standard Advanced* (1649), p. 9.
3. *Denus Petition to the Lord General* (1651), p. 4.

reformers to improve the conditions of the poor, when they were attempted, received little sympathy or encouragement from above. The Diggers, the one genuinely temperate and creative party of radicals, were, with the aid of the pulpits, harried and persecuted out of existence; and the pulpits were manned by Puritan, not Anglican, preachers. It must therefore be understood, that if the best Anglican[1] preachers were the most accomplished public speakers, by sophisticated standards of oratory, they were not the most successful during the crucial years of the late thirties and early forties. They were comparatively few, and the very superiority of their talents was often inappropriate to the conditions. One is reminded of T. S. Eliot's observation that minds of a second order are necessary for a rapid circulation of ideas. What drew and affected large congregations, and what the Puritans provided, were not classical rhetoricians, performing as for their equals, but shrewdly provocative demagogues, with 'swords in their mouths', pumping emotion from professional bleeding-hearts, and whipping their hearers into a lather of ecstasy with affluent promises. The Puritans also enjoyed the advantage of ground and initiative. Whereas the Anglican preachers were, from the beginning, on the defensive, striving to preserve, tranquillize and repair, the Puritans were engaged in the much easier task of fanning and agitating disaffection; their preachers were more numerous, with a higher *average* standard and had the aggressive energy of pioneers; they felt they had nothing to lose and incalculable benefits to gain; above all, in the late Jacobean and Caroline temperature of heteroclitic fever, they enjoyed the further advantage of telling substantial and actively discontented minorities what *they wanted to hear*. In the words, again, of Richard Hooker, 'He that goeth about to persuade a multitude that they are not as well governed as they ought to be shall never want attentive and favourable hearers.'[2]

The Puritan movement first glorified and professionalized, and then debased and debauched, the pulpit. By the time of the Restoration, preaching, being thought of as inseparable from Puritans, was a compromised medium. Anglican preaching only came into its own as a weapon when the loyal Episcopalian clergy fell from power, and in

---

1. Again, the term 'Anglican' was not in contemporary use to describe what I identify here: English orthodox Episcopalian clergy who asserted principles of sacerdotalism against the Puritan campaign for a reformed 'preaching ministry'.

2. *Ecclesiastical Polity*, Bk 1, para. 2.

poverty and persecution and banishment showed what they were made of, which was, in most cases, very tough stuff indeed. They found, as their adversaries had done, a position of militant opposition to be, if tenable, the most favourable pulpit, and, when the defeated Cavaliers returned to power by the paradoxically smooth and pacific progress which so mystified contemporary foreign observers, the new Tory-to-be ascendency, lay and clerical, resolved that preaching must be given, not merely a new look, but a new, milder nature, graceful and literate, but *harmless*; they recognized, as one of their number put it, that 'it was the pulpit that supplied the field with swordsmen and the parliament house with incendiaries',[1] and they resolved that never again should the pulpit be allowed to menace the peace and security of the government established; never, at least, so long as that government was their own. It seldom did do so again, less by reason of any measures taken to tame it, although measures were taken—thirty-nine of them—than of an irregular but progressive decline in the force of religious passion in the lives of men. The process, gradual, and interrupted by spasmodic evangelical agitations[2] which camouflaged the abatement of the ancient fires, was far advanced before its entelechy was conceded. It was not until the second half of the nineteenth century that, as Julia Wegewood put it, 'for the first time in history since Christianity existed it was possible to ignore Christianity'.[3]

It is no part of my commission to ask whether the spirit of Christianity is dead, dying or merely, in general, dormant, or whether it is passing through an intermediate stage in the process of absorption and transmogrification. My concern is limited to the expression of the spirit of 'protestant' Christianity in the English language, during a period when men were willing to kill in God's name, which is always a sure, if uncomfortable, token of life and, what was more difficult, to strive to persuade or compel other men to live as God had confided in his elect that they ought to do, notwithstanding God's will in all things being pre-ordained, inexorable and unalterable in the smallest particular.

The sequel in action of much of what was preached may not have

1. Robert South, *Sermons*, (1865 edn) 1. 429.

2. One example only of many: the reformed Puritan, Joseph Glanvill, as conforming Rector of the Abbey Church, Bath, complained pitiously after 1666 of harassment by Puritan sectary 'fanaticks' who seemed to have reverted at Bath to the spirit of 1643. (See W. A. S. Glanvill-Richards, *Records of the Anglo-Norman House of Glanville*, pp. 78–80. 162.)

3. *Contemporary Review*, Vol. lxxii, p. 457.

been entirely (to use a favourite Puritan term) 'edifying', but neither would the discrepancy be a symptom peculiar to Christianity, in any of its mutations. Lucretius had not enjoyed the benefits of Christian enlightenment when he observed *Tantum religio potuit saudere malorum*.[1] To follow that view would be to beg, or disregard, the question of the origin of responsibility for cause and effect in religion; to treat its appearance as a self-contained donative, rather than as a still imperfectly understood and mysterious strand in the natural history of man. Hostility to 'religion' is itself an impressive tribute to the force of the passions which have been mobilized in God's name and, even to those of us for whom the proper study of mankind remains man, the words which surged and spurted with such furious urgency from our ancestors' pulpits may still have a message of value to impart, even if it is not quite what the original speakers intended it to be.

1. *De Rerum Natura*, i, 101.

I

TUDOR

ROGER EDGEWORTH

When Henry VIII took the decision to break with Rome and national-
ize the Church of England he prepared the country with a succession
of paralysing blows upon the privileges and, above all, the *wealth* of the
church, which left the English prelacy in no doubt of who was their
master, in this world at least. In 1531 he declared the entire body of the
English clergy guilty of treason by the law of *praemunire* and their
pardon was bought by payment to the crown by a sum equivalent to
many millions of pounds today. The following year he abolished papal
'first fruits', the payment of a newly appointed bishop's first year's
revenue, to Rome. There could be little doubt of the end to which all
these measures were directed and Sir Thomas More prudently asked
to be relieved of the Great Seal.

But by far the most important part of the preparation was not Henry's
and was not planned. Without it nothing would have been possible,
nor probably attempted by a monarch with a keen Tudor nose for
practicalities. It was the gradual, spontaneous preparation of mind
for separation from Rome which had been taking place in England's
Protestant underworld for the past century. Ever since, in 1381, the
Peasant Revolt had reminded the secular arm that religious and political
grievances could be dangerously interactive, open manifestations of
heresy had been put down with rigorous severity. But out of public
sight, all over England, in East Anglia in particular, the Lollard spirit of
evangelical rebellion remained alive and smouldering, only awaiting a
favourable wind to burst into flame again.

It was Henry's intention to emancipate himself from the control
of Rome and, in the name of reform, to plunder the endowed religious
orders. It was no part of his intention to change his religion. A faithful,
a superstitious, Catholic, he needed the support of the reforming
party to realize his personal and political ambitions. He underrated the
gathering momentum behind the drive he was liberating, just as the
first reformers themselves underrated the degree of dissolution their
acts would initiate. Both thought they could release the genie from its
bottle, put it to work to serve their chosen purpose—and no more—

3

and then return it securely to the bottle. Neither foresaw a loss of control at the top, a fragmentation into rabid rival sects, with nothing in common but intolerance of each other and, of course, the claim to an exclusive special relationship with the Almighty.

After Henry had been proclaimed Supreme Head of the Church in 1531, Cranmer, his newly appointed Archbishop, and the one man Henry seems to have trusted absolutely, began to 'tune the pulpits', the principal instruments for shaping public opinion, and in 1533 preachers were ordered, in all references to the Pope, to degrade him to the rank of a Bishop. But other influences from the continent were soon feeling their way into England, the thin edge of the Calvinistic wedge entering in the form of books,[1] and the results were already to be seen in the growing violence of controversy between laymen, as well as priests, a do-it-yourself divinity which was to be a characteristic of the confusion to come.

In 1536 the Catholic north of England rose in revolt against the attack on their whole way of life, but it was tricked into defeat and Henry VIII proceeded on his way, crushing and squeezing dry the remaining monasteries. Assets might be freely liquidated but doctrine was to remain solid; and, to check the progress of already perceptible heresy, the Six Articles were introduced, confirming the Catholic Faith as obligatory and imposing severe penalites for their denial. The Protestants did not revolt. Nothing had been taken from them. The luckier ones were already doing well out of the division of monastic spoils. They were not getting what they wanted fast enough; but at this stage they felt that time was on their side; they could afford a policy of passive resistance and, wherever possible, of group infiltration of church order.

The first voice in this survey of preaching from the Act of Supremacy to the Restoration, is not a new protestant voice. A very traditional, conservative Englishman and priest stands, worried and disapproving, on the brink of incalculable changes. In the voice of Roger Edgeworth we hear the misgivings of the old order, religious and social, at the prospect of the changes being canvassed in the name of reform. He is too seasoned and too realistic to idealize an imperfect past, but he fears the consequence of spurious zeal in ignorant men masquerading as enlightenment, the loss of mutual respect between the social orders,

1. *Treatise declaring and shewing dyuers causes that pyctures and ymages are in no wise to be suffered in Churches*. Translated from the Latin of Strasbourg preachers. 1535.

the abandonment of tried stabilizing, traditional forms, the encouragement of muddled pretensions in the uneducated. Of all Tudor preachers whose words have survived, Edgeworth brings us, with the freshest immediacy, the savour and style of English domestic, and especially English country life in the middle of the momentous sixteenth century.

Of Idolls and Images[1] (c. 1540)

Domine verba vitae eternae habes. O Lord God, thou hast the wordes of everlasting life. The wordes be good because they be the wordes of God, although I do not understand them. Thus ordering yourselves in the study of holy scripture you do lyke good men, and lyke gods seruauntes, and God wyll be good Lorde vnto you. *Et non dabit ineternum fluctuationem iusto.* And wyll not suffer you finallye for euer to fleete and wauer inconstantlye, running from one opinion to an other, from one illusion to an other, thou shalt stay thy selfe by the ancour of faythe, and that shall keepe thee from the rocks, that be perelous heretikes. For if thou fleete and wauer tyll thou fal on one of them, thou shalt have suche a crash of false doctrine and leude vnderstandyng that thou shalt not avoyde shypwracke, thou shalte not come to the porte of safe knowledge, ne to the port of ease, quietnes, and caulmenes euerlasting in heauen, if thou be made by suche false doctrine to erre in the essentiall and necessarye pointes of thy belefe.

Therefore in your learnynge see that you vse charitie with humilitie and lowlynesse of hart, and then you shall shewe your selfe that your learnynge is the true science gyuen of the holye goste, of whyche we now entreate. And by the same gift you shall as well know what you shal beleue, as to iudge and dyscerne the thynges that you shall beleue, from the thinges that you shall not beleue, And also you may ascende to so hyghe knowledge, that you shall be able to declare the articles of your faythe, and to induce and perswade other men to beleue, and also to conuince and ouercome countersayers, and such as woulde impugne the faith, Althoughe it be not gyuen to all menne to ascende vnto so hyghe a degree of science. And because I spoke euen nowe of Images and Idolles, I woulde you shoulde not ignorauntlye confounde and abuse those termes, takynge an Image for an Idolle, and an Idolle for an Image, as I haue hearde manye doe in thys citye, as well of the fathers and mothers (that shoulde be wyse) as of theyr babies and chyldren that haue learned foolyshnesse of theyr parentes. Nowe at the dissolocion of

1. *Sermons* (1557 edn.), The Fourth Sermon: fol. xli–fol. xliiii.

Monasteries and of freers houses many Images haue bene caryed abrod, and
gyuen to children to playe wyth all. And when the chyldren haue theym in
theyr handes, dauncynge theim after their childyshe maner, commeth the
father or the mother and saythe: What nasse, what haste thou there? the
childe aunsweareth (as she is taught) I haue here myne ydoll, the father laugh-
eth and maketh a gaye game at it. So saithe the mother to an other, Iugge, or
Thommye, where haddest thou that pretye Idoll. John our parishe clarke
gave it me, saythe the childe and for that the clarke muste have thankes, and
shall lacke no good chere. But if thys follye were onelye in the insolent
youthe, and in the fonde unlearned fathers and mothers, it myght soone be
redressed. But youre preachers that you so obstinatelye folow, more leaninge
to the vulgar noyse and common erroure of the people, then to profounde
learnyng they bable in the pulpittes that they hearethe people reioyce in.

   And so of the people they learne their sermons, and by their sermons they
indurate[1] their audyence and make the people stubbourne and harde to be
perswaded to science, contrarye to theyr blinde ignoraunce, as well in this
point of Images and Idolles, as in manye other like. They would haue that this
latine worde *Imago* signifieth an Idole, and so these new translations of the
english bibles hath it in all places, where the translatours would bring men to
beleue that to set vp Images, or to haue Images is idolatrye, And therefore
where the scriptures abhorreth idols, they make it Images, as though to haue
imagerie, were idolatrie, that God so greatly abhorreth. But you must under-
stande and knowe that an Image is a thinge kerued, or painted, or cast in a
moulde, that representeth and signyfyeth a thing that is in dede, or that hath be
or that be in dede. And so speaketh our Sauiour Christ of an Image, when
the Pharisies send their disciples wyth Herodes seruauntes, to aske hym thys
question: whether it were lawfull for the Jewes to paye tribute to the
Emperour or not: He called them Hipocrites, and bad them shewe him the
coyne or money that was vsually payde for the tribute. They brought him a
denere, wee call it a peny. He asked them: *Cuius est Imago hec et superscriptio
Mat. xxii.* Whose is this Image & the scripture about? They answered: the
emporours. Note here (good frendes) that Christ asked not *cuius est idolum
hoc?* Whose is this idole? for he knewe it was none, but that it was an
image, as is the Image of our soueraigne Lord the king vpon his money
coyned in London, in Bristow, or in other places, whiche no man that hath
witte woulde call an Idole. For Saynte Paule sayth, *i. Cor. viii. Scimus quia
nihil est Idolum in mundo, & quod nullus est deus nisivnus.* We knowe that an
ydole is nothinge in the worlde, and that there is no God but one.[2] Where the
blessed Apostle referreth muche vnto science in this matter of ydoles, and of
meat offered vnto them, and spoke to them that were learned, and shoulde
haue conning to discerne in this mater: sayinge in the beginninge of that.

1. Harden.   2. Verse 4.

viii. Chapiter. *Scimus quoniam omnes scientiam habemus.* We knowe, for all we haue science and conninge to iudge of these meates that be offered to Idoles, what know we? *Scimus quia nihil est Idolum in mundo & quod nullus est deus nisi vnus.* We haue this science, and this we know, that an Idole is nothinge in the worlde, and that there is no God but one. An ymage is a similitude of a naturall thinge, that hath be(en), is, or may be. An ydole is a similitude representing a thing that neuer was nor maye be. Therefore the ymage of the crucifixe is no ydole, for it representeth and signifieth Christ crucified, as he was in dede. And the Image of Saint Paule with the sworde in his hande, as the signe of his martirdome is no Idole, for the thinge signified by it, was a thinge in dede, for he was beheaded with a sworde in dede: but an Idole is an ymage that signifieth a monster that is not possible to be, as to signifie a false God whiche is no God in dede. For as S. Paule sayde, *There is no God but one*: As the Image of Jupiter set vp to signifie the god Jupiter, is a false signifier, & signifieth a thinge of nothinge for there is no God Jupiter. And the Image of *Venus* to signifye the goddes *Venus* is nothinge, for that is signified by it, is nothynge, for there is no she goddes *Venus*: As in a lyke speakynge we say *Chimera* is nothing, because the voyce is sometyme putte to signifie a monster, hauinge a head lyke a Lion, with fyre flamynge out of his mouth, and the bodye of a goate, and the hynder parte lyke a serpente or a dragon, there is no suche thynge, althoughe the poetes faine suche a monster, therefore the voice *Chimera* is a false signifier, and that is false is nothinge, therefore we say *Chimera* is nothinge but *Chimera* signifiynge a certayne mountayne in the countrey of *Licia*, flaminge fyre out of the toppe of it, bredynge and hauyng Lions nyghe about the hier part or toppe of the same hyl, and downewarde aboute the mydle parte, hauynge pastures where breadeth goates or such other beastes, and at the fote of it marshes or moyste grounde breadynge serpentes: such an hyl there is in the sayde countrey, and of the diuers disposition of the partes of the sayd hyll, the fiction of the forsayd monster is ymagened, whiche is nothynge, and therefore so we say that *Chimera* is nothing, but the same vocable put to signify the hyl in *Licia* aforesayd is somwhat, and a true signifier, for it signifieth a thinge that is in dede as appeareth by *Pomponius Mela, lib. i.* and *Soline Cap. lii.*[1] with their expositours, and euen so it is true that Paule sayth that an Idole is nothing, for there is none suche thinge as is signified by it, there is no God *Saturne*, there is no God *Iupiter*, there is no Goddes *Venus*, but I saye more, that yf a man coulde carue or paynte an Image of *Iupiters* soule burnynge in the fyre of hell, or lykewise an Image of *Venus* soule there burnynge; If Saynte Paule had sene suche a pycture or ymage, he woulde neuer haue called it an ydole, or a

1. Pompionus Mela: Roman geographer who flourished during the reign of Claudius. Caius Julius Solinus, grammarian, historian, fl. *c.* A.D. 250. Refers to his *Collectanea Rerum Memorabilium.*

thynge of nothinge, for it shoulde signifie a thing that is in dede, for *Iupiters*
soule is in hel in dede, and so is *Venus* soule, and other lyke taken for Goddes
made of mortall men.[1] After this maner good frendes, you must by science
and connyng, learnedly speake of Images and Idoles, and not to confounde
the wordes, or the thinges signified by them, takyng one for an other. And
by this you maye perceaue, that when you will arrogantly of a proude hearte
medle of maters aboue your capacitie, the holy goste withdraweth his gyfte
of science frome you, and that maketh you to speake you can not tell what,
for the holy goste will not inspyre his gyftes but vpon them that be humble
and lowlye in hearte. And because I sayde heretofore, that this gyfte of
science as it is here taken, extendeth to mecanical science, and handy craftes.
This appeareth by the text. *Exo. xxxi*. when the holy tabernacle shoulde be
made in deserte, almyghty God prouided an artificer and workeman for
the same nonce called *Beseleel*[2] sonne of *Huri*, sonne of *Hur*, of the tribe of
Iuda. I haue filled him (sayth God) with the spirite of God *Sapientia, intelligen-
tia, & scientia in omni opere*. I haue geuen him sapience, by whiche he might wel
discerne and iudge of the thinges that god woulde haue made, in so much that
he was able to teach others the thinges that he knewe by goddes reuelation
and instruction. And this properly perteyneth to the gyfte of *Sapience*, as I
haue sayd afore. I haue fylled hym with the spyryt of *intelligence* or wyttines,
and fine and cleare perceyuinge and understanding, by which he may more
perfitly pearce and enter with his wit into the thinges that be taught him,
then he should haue done if he had lacked the sayd gyft of *intelligence*. I haue
also (sayth God) fulfilled *Beseleel* with the gifte of science. Of whiche
speaketh Christ oft in a sermon of the holy goste after this maner. When
Moyses made the tabernacle in wyldernes, he had nede then not onelye of
doctryne and learnynge, but also of the gifte of a mayster craftes man, to
knowe howe he should sew togither fyne clothes and sylkes of precious
colours, and howe to weaue them, plat them, and shape them together, And
howe he should cast golde and other metalles necessary for the ceremonies
there to be vsed, and howe to polyshe precious stones, and also to frame the
timber for the same tabernacle. For there and such other purposes almighty
God gaue him and to his workeman *Beseleel*. the spirite of science, that they
mighte frame all suche thinges accordingely. And euen so in your occupations and handy craftes, when you exercise your selues diligentlye and
trulye withoute slouth, withoute disceate, gile, or sutteltie in all your exercise,
ordering your selues to your neighbour, as you would be ordered yourself, so
longe youre occupation, exercise, and laboure is adnexed and ioyned with
charitie, and semeth plainely to come of the holy gooste: for without charitie

1. It was a mediaeval commonplace to treat pagan gods and goddesses, not as fictions,
but as demons or human impostors who would be punished for pretending to divinity.
2. Belzaleel, the son of Uri.

this gifte of science comminge of the holy gooste will not be, no more then other vertues infused. And contrarye, lyke as euerye good thinge hath an enemie, or at the leaste wise an ape or a counterfeiter, as fortitude or manlines hath folyshe hardines or rashe boldenes, which semeth manlines and is not so, so hath science or conninge, gile or sutteltie, whiche counterfeiteth conning, and is no true conninge, in as muche as it is withoute Charitie, and also withoute iustice. *Cicero ex platone. i. offic. Sciencia que est remota a iusticia calliditas potius quam cientia est appelanda.* Science remoued from iustice is rather to be called wylynes then science. And to this purpose, it is necessarye that you seruauntes do youre dutye to youre maysters obedientlye with feare and quakynge, in simplicitie and playnes of hearte, as unto Christe, not seruinge to the eye, as to please man, but like the seruauntes of Christ, doinge the will of God with hearte and all. *Ephe. vi.* not deceauing your maisters by your idlenes, or els beinge occupied about your owne busines, when your master thinketh that you be in his labours. And lykewyse you maysters do you to youre seruauntes, instructynge them in theyr occupations, for whiche they came to your seruyce, according to the truth that theyr parentes and frendes hath put you in, that they maye get them lyuynge and yours with truth & iuste dealynge and honestye, and medle not to muche with other mens occupations that you cannot skyll on, leaste whyle ye be so curious in other mens matters not perteininge to your lerning, you decaye as well in your owne occupation, as in the other, so fallynge to penurye, extreme pouertye, and very beggery. For when a tayler forsakynge his owne occupation wyll be a marchaunt venterer, or a shomaker to become a groser, God sende him well to proue. I have knowen manye in this towne, that studienge divinitie, hath kylled a marchaunt and some of other occupations by theyr busy labours in the scriptures, hath shut up the shoppe windowes, faine to take Sainctuary, or els for mercerye and groserye, hath be fayne to sell godderds[1] steanes,[2] and pitchers, and suche other trumpery. For this I shall assure you, that althoughe diuinitie be a science verye profitable for the soule health, yet small gaynes to the purse, or to the worlde aryseth by it. Not that I intende to reproue the studye of scriptures, for I extoll it and prayse it above all other studye, so that it be vsed as I have sayde afore, with modestye and charitie, with longanimitie[3] and easye sufferaunce, tyll God sende them a true instructour, not infected with wylful and newfangled heresyes: From whiche I pray god to defende you all, and sende you teachers indued with such science as may instructe you in the truth, by whiche you may attayne to ioyes everlastynge. Amen.

1. Godderd (or goderd): a drinking cup.   2. Stean: a vessel, usually of clay.
3. Patience.

HUGH LATIMER

Henry had been dead only a year but already much had happened at court. The left wing of the reforming party had made a rapid advance and consolidation of gains; the mass outlawed, auricular confession discouraged, the forms of worship of many centuries swept away as idolatry. The majority of people did not welcome or trust the change, but they were unresolved and divided—the Reformation divided not only friends but families—and the reformers, like all effective iconoclasts were dedicated men. The chief popular spokesman for Cranmer's measures was Hugh Latimer,[1] formerly Bishop of Worcester, and he accumulated a full record of his principal sermons, thanks in part to the devotion of his Swiss servant Augustine Bernher who wrote them down and preserved them.

The compelling vigour of the man and the homely simplicity and fervour of his preaching are celebrated in the tributes of his contemporaries. He affected the lives of many; some, like Bradford, permanently, and he fearlessly exposed the abuses of the times, despite the hostility of the newly enriched. His personality can only be surmised, but his words, as vital as the day he uttered them, testify that here was

1. Hugh Latimer, 1485–1555. Born at Thurcaston near Leicester, son of a countryman with a smallholding (see p. 16). Educated at Cambridge, he was made a fellow of Clare College in 1510, while still an undergraduate. Having already taken holy orders he was appointed a university preacher, and preaching proved to be his life's vocation. At first a perfectly orthodox Roman Catholic priest—he preached an attack on Melancthon—he later came enduringly under the influence of Thomas Bilney and with him began to move deeper into the reformed doctrines which relied for salvation upon faith, denying the efficacy of pilgrimages, good works, the intercession of Our Lady and the saints, and above all prayers for the dead. He found favour with Henry by approving his divorce from Catherine, and was appointed chaplain to Anne Boleyn; then disfavour and imprisonment for urging reformations which were no part of Henry's plans (see p. 3). Consecrated Bishop of Worcester in 1535 he resigned in 1539 and resisted all subsequent proposals for his reinstatement. His influence was at its height in the reign of Edward VI and ended with the young king's death in 1553 and the accession of Mary. Choosing to remain, though he could have escaped, he was arrested in April 1554, examined at Oxford, and after being held for a year in the common jail condemned as a heretic and sentenced to be burned. He met his death at the stake outside Balliol College with a cheerful heroism unsurpassed in the annals of religious martyrdom, and suffered in company with his former colleague Ridley.

the gifted herald of a great language soaring to maturity. The tools he
already uses could do almost anything, and very soon would do almost
everything realizable by language within the compass of contemporary
human knowledge. What is interesting here is that, reformer though
he is, Latimer has even more urgent matters to raise than doctrine.
There are occasional simple admonitions, especially to beware 'idolatry'
and superstition and, now and again, the conventional fulmination
against Rome; but, although the Protestant establishment is by no
means yet firmly secured, Latimer feels too shamed and embarrassed
by the social consequences of the Reformation to dwell upon victory,
such as it was. Something has gone seriously wrong with their aims.
The righteous have triumphed, but what are the fruits? Is life any
better? As far as Latimer can see it is grimly worse:[1] the rich richer and
less charitable, the poor poorer and less hopeful, the wicked bolder and
more successful. Monasteries have been emptied of their idle treasure,
but the resources have not gone to relieve the distressed; they have
merely been diverted into the coffers of secular tyrants without even
a nominal obligation to succour the needy. In the country, small men,
ruined by the enclosures, are being reduced to beggary; in London the
destitute famish and freeze to death in the streets. Amidst this cruel
welter of opportunism and corruption Latimer yearns for the 'good
old days' when England was more Christian and neighbourly. Then
he seems abashed, as if he had fallen into a trap, for he remembers that
in those better days 'old England' was also 'Catholic England'. The
contingency is not, of course, spontaneous. This is an accomplished
public speaker making an effect. But it is also the genuine perplexity
and uneasiness of a man too honest to deny what his eyes see, even when
it is unfavourable to his allegiance.

---

1. *Seventh Sermon preached before King Edward VI*, see p. 13.

Sermon of the Plough[1]

preached at the Shrouds at St. Paules
Crosse on January 18th. 1548

Nowe what shall we saye of these ryche citizens of London? What shall I saye of them? shal I cal them proude men of London, malicious men of London, mercylesse men of London. No, no, I may not saie so, they wil be offended wyth me than. Yet must I speake. For is there not reygning in London, as much pride, as much coueteousnes, as much crueltie, as much oprrission, as much supersticion, as was in Nebo? Yes, I thynke and muche more to. Therefore I saye, repente O London. Repent, repente. Thou heareste thy faultes tolde the, amend them amend them. I thinke if Nebo had had the preachynge yat thou haste: they wold haue conuerted. And you rulers and officers be wise and circumspect, loke to your charge and see you do your dueties and rather be glad to amend your yll liuyng then to be angrye when you are warned or tolde of your faulte. What a do was there made in London at a certein man because he sayd, and in dede at that time on a iust cause. Burgesses quod he, nay butterflies. Lorde what a do there was for that worde. And yet would God they were no worse then butterflies. Butterflyes do but theyre nature, the butterflye is not couetouse, is not gredye of other mens goodes, is not ful of enuy and hatered, is not malicious, is not cruel, is not mercilesse. The butterflye gloriethe not in hyr owne dedes, nor preferreth the tradicions of men before Gods worde; it commitment teth not idolatry nor worshyppeth false goddes. But London can not abyde to be rebuked suche is the nature of man. If they be prycked, they wyll kycke. If they be rubbed on the gale: they wil wynce.[2] But yet they wyll not amende theyr faultes, they wyl not be yl spoken of. But howe shal I speake well of them. If you could be contente to receyue and folowe the worde of god and fauoure good preachers, if you coulde beare to be toulde of youre

1. 1548 edition. Sig BI*r*–BVIII*r* probably preached on a wet day: the 'Shrouds' was a covered area beside the cathedral church, where a large concourse of people could hear a sermon preached in the open air and receive some protection from the rain. Stow, *Survey of London* (ed. Strype 1745), Bk iii, p. 644.

2. This is typical of many examples which might be cited of the roots in popular preaching from which Shakespeare's (and of course his contemporaries') imagery derived. 'If you prick us, do we not bleed? if you tickle us do we not laugh?', etc. *Merchant of Venice*, ii, 1.

faultes, if you coulde amende when you heare of them: if you woulde be
gladde to reforme that is a misse: if I mighte se anie suche inclinacion in you,
that leaue to be mercilesse and begynne to be charytable I would then hope
wel of you, I woulde then speake well of you. But London was neuer so yll as
it is now. In tymes past men were full of pytie and compassion but nowe
there is no pitie, for in London their brother shal die in the streetes for colde,
he shall lye sycke at theyr doore between stocke and stocke.[1] I can not tel what
to call it, and peryshe there for hunger, was there any more vnmercifulnes in
Nebo?[2] I thynke not. In tymes paste when any ryche man dyed in London,
they were wonte to healp the pore scholers of the vniuersitye wyth exhibition.
When any man dyed, they woulde bequeth great summes of money to-
warde the releue of the pore. When I was a scholer in Cambridge my selfe, I
harde verye good reporte of London and knewe manie that had releue of the
rytche men of London, but nowe I can heare no such good reporte, and yet I
inquyre of it, and herken for it, but nowe charitie is waxed colde, none
helpeth the scholer nor yet the pore. And in those days what dyd they whan
they helped the scholers? Mary they maynteyned and gaue them liuynges
that were verye papists and professed the popes doctrine and nowe that the
knowledge of Gods word is brought to lyght, and many earnestelye studye
and laboure to set it forth now almost no man healpeth to maynteyne them.
Oh London London, repente repente, for I thynke God is more displeased
wyth London then euer he was with the citie of Nebo. Repente therfore
repent London and remember that the same God liueth nowe yat punyshed
Nebo, euen the same god and none other, and he wyl punyshe synne as well
nowe as he dyd then, and he will punishe the iniquitie of London as well as
he did then of Nebo. Amende therfore and ye that be prelates loke well to
your office, for right prelatynge is busye labourynge and not lordyng.
Therfore preache and teach and let your ploughe be doynge, ye lordes I saye
that liue lyke loyterers, loke well to your office, the ploughe is your office
and charge. If you lyue idle and loyter, you do not your duetie, you folowe
not youre vocation, let your plough therfore be going and not cease, that the
ground maye brynge foorth fruite. But nowe me thynketh I heare one saye
vnto me, wotte you what you say? Is it a worcke? It is a labour? how then
hath it happened that we haue had so manye hundred yeares so many vn-
preachinge prelates, lording loyterers and idle ministers? Ye would haue me
here to make answere and to showe the cause thereof. Nay thys land is not
for me to ploughe, it is to stonye, to thorni, to harde for me to plough. They
haue so many thynges yat make for them, so many things to laye for them
selues that it is not for my weake teame to plough them. They haue to lay for

1. Between door-posts.
2. Nebo: a city in Reuben, east of Jordan. *Thus saith the Lord of Hosts, the God of
Israel. Woe unto Nebo! for it is spoiled.* Jeremiah. 48:1.

them selues longe customes Cerimonyes, and authoritie, placyng in parliamente and many thynges more. And I feare me thys lande is not yet rype to
be ploughed. For as the saying is, it lacketh wethering this geare lacketh
wetheringe at leaste way it is is not for me to ploughe. For what shall I loke
for amonge thornes but prickyng and scrachinge? what among stones but
stumblyng? What (I had almost sayed) among serpenttes but stingyng? But
thys muche I dare say, that sense lording and loytrying hath come vp,
preaching hath come downe contrarie to the Apostells times. For they
preached and lorded not. And nowe they lorde and preache not.

For they that be lordes wyll yll go to plough. It is no mete office for them.
It is not semyng for their state. Thus came vp lordyng loyterers. Thus crept
in vnprechinge prelates, and so haue they longe continued.

For howe many vnlearned prelates haue we now at this day? And no
meruel. For if the plough men that now be, were made lordes they woulde
cleane gyue ouer ploughinge, they woulde leaue of theyr labour and fall to
lordyng outright, and let the plough stand. And then bothe ploughes not
walkyng nothyng shoulde be in the common weale but honger. For euer
sence the Prelates were made Loordes and nobles, the ploughe standeth, there
is no worke done, the people sterue.

Thei hauke, thei hunt, thei card, they dyce, they pastyme in theyr prelacies
with galaunte gentlemen, with theyr dauncinge minyons, and with theyr freshe
companions, so that ploughinge is set a syde. And by the lordinge and
loytryng, preachynge and ploughinge is cleane gone. And thus if the ploughe-
men of the countrey, were as negligente in theyr office, as prelates be, we
shoulde not longe lyue for lacke of sustinaunce. And as it is necessarie for to
haue thys ploughinge for sustentacion of the bodye: so muste we haue also
the other for the satisfaction of the soule, or elles we canne not lyue longe
gostly. For as the bodie wasteth and consumeth awaye for lacke of bodily
meate: so doeth the soule pyne a way for default of gostly meate. But there
be two kyndes of inclosynge to lette or hinder boeth these kyndes of ploughe-
inge. The one is an inclosinge to let or hinder the bodily ploughynge, and the
other to lette or hynder the holiday ploughyng, the church ploughinge. The
bodylye plougheyng, is taken in and enclosed thorowe singulare commoditie.
For what man wyll lette goe or deminishe hys priuate commoditie for a
commune welth? and who wyll susteyne any damage for the respecte of a
publique commoditie? The other plough also no man is diligent to sette
forward, nor no man wyll herken to it, but to hinder and let it, al mennes
eares are open, yea and a greate meany of this kynde of ploughmen which
are very busie and woulde seme to be verie good worckmen. I feare me some
be rather mocke gospellers then faythful ploughmen. I knowe many my
selfe that professe the gospel, and lyue nothyng there after. I knowe them,
and haue bene conuersaunt wyth some of them. I knowe them, and I speake it

wyth an heauy herte, there is as litle charitye and good liuinge in them as in any other, accordyng to that which Christe sayed in the Gospel to the greate numbre of people that folowed hym, as thoughe they had had an earneste zeale to his doctrine, wher as in deede they had it not. *Non qui vidistis signa, sed quia comedistis de panibus*.[1] Ye folowe me (sayth he) not because ye haue seene the sygnes and myracles that I haue done, but because ye haue eaten the breade and refreshed your bodyes. Therefore you folowe me, so that I thynke manye one nowe a dayes professeth the gospel for the lyuynge sake, not for the loue they beare to gods word. But they that wil be true ploughmen muste worke faythfullye for Goddes sake, for the edifiynge of theyr bre-therne. And as diligentelye as the husband man plougheth for the susten-tacion of the bodye: so diligently muste the prelates and ministers labour for the fedinge of the soule: boeth the ploughes muste styll be doynge, as mooste necessarye for man. And wherefore are magistrates ordayned, but that the tranquillitie of the commune weale maye be confirmed limiting both ploughes.

But nowe for the defaulte of vnpreaching prelates me thinke I coulde gesse what myghte be sayed for excusynge of them: They are so troubeled wyth Lordelye lyuynge, they be so placed in palacies, couched in courtes, ruffe-lynge in theyr rentes, daunceynge in theyr dominions, burdened with am-bassages, pamperynge of theyr panches lyke a monke that maketh his Jubilie, mounchynge in their maungers[2], and moylynge in their gaye manoures and mansions, and so troubeled wyth loyterynge in theyr Lorde-shyppes: that they canne not attende it. They are otherwyse occupyed, som-me in the Kynges matters, some are ambassadoures, some of the pryuie counsell, some to furnyshe the courte, some are Lordes of the Parliamente, some are presidentes, and some comptroleres of myntes. Well, well.

Inflation of Prices and Decay of Standards

first sermon preached before King Edward VI
on 8th March 1549

We of the cleargye had to much, but that is taken away. And nowe we haue to little. But for myne owne part, I haue no cause to complaine, for I thanke God and the kyng. I haue sufficient, and God is my iudge I came not to craue of anye man, any thyng, but I knowe theim that haue to litle. There

1. Not because ye saw the miracles, but because ye did eat of the loaves—John vi: 26.
2. Manger, in jocular-satirical sense.

lyeth a greate matter by these appropriacions[1] greate reformacions is to be had in them. I knowe wher is a great market Towne with diuers hamelets and inhabitauntes, wher do rife yereli of their labours to the value of. l. [fifty] pounde, and the vicar that serueth (being so great a cure) hath but. xii. or. xiiii. markes by yere, so that of thys pension he is not able to by him bokes, nor geue hys neyghboure dryncke, al the great gaine goeth another way. My father was a Yoman, and had no landes of his owne, onlye he had a farme of. iii. or iiii. pound by yere at the vttermost, and here vpon he tilled fo much as kepte halfe a dosen men. He had walke for a hundred shepe, and my mother mylked. xxx. kyne, He was able and did find the king a harnesse, wyth hym selfe, and hys horsse, whyle he came to ye place that he should receyue the kynges wages. I can remembre, yat I buckled hys harnes, when he went vnto Blacke heeath felde.[2] He kept me to schole, or elles I had not bene able to haue preached before the kinges maiestie nowe. He maryed my systers with v. pounde or. xx. nobles a pece, so that he broughte them vp in godlines, and feare of God.

He kept hospitalitie for his pore neighbours. And sum almess he gaue to the poore, and all thys did he of the sayd farme. Wher he that now hath it, paieth. xvi. pounde by yere or more, and is not able to do any thing for his Prynce, for himselfe, nor for his children, or geue a cup of drincke to the pore. Thus al the enhansinge and rearing goth to your priuate commoditie and wealth. So that where ye had a single to much, you haue that: and syns the same, ye haue enhansed the rente, and so haue encreased an other to much. So now ye haue doble to muche, whyche is to to much. But let the preacher preach til his tong be worne to the stompes, nothing is amended. We haue good statutes[3] made for the commen welth as touching comeners, enclosers, many metinges and Sessions, but in the end of the matter their commeth nothing forth.[4] Wel, well, thys is one thynge I wyll saye vnto you, from whens it commeth I knowe, euen, from the deuill. I knowe his intent in it. For if ye bryng it to passe, that the yomanry be not able to put their sonnes to schole (as in dede vniuersities do wonderously decaye all redy) and that they be not able to mary their daughters to the auoidyng of whoredome, I say ye plucke saluation from the people and vtterly distroy the realme. For by yomans sonnes, the fayth of Christ is, and hath bene mayntained chefely. . . .

1. 'Appropriacions': the 'Reformation' was already generating its own make of abuses; church tithes had been appropriated to the crown and thence, as impropriations, dispensed to various secular hands; little remained for parish incumbents. See Blackstone, Bk 1, Ch. xi, para. 5; cf. Kennet, *Cases of Impropriations* (1704), pp. 18 *et seq.*

2. Where the Cornish rebels were defeated in 1497.

3. Latimer would have had in mind 4 Henry VII c. 19, 7 Henry VII c. 1, 25 Henry VIII c. 13, and Henry VIII c. 22.

4. In 1548 a Royal Commission was appointed to redress grievances caused by arbitrary enclosures of common land, but its operations were blocked by powerful vested interests. See Strype, *Ecclesiastical Memorials* (Oxford, 1822), ii, 145 *et seq.*; 348 *et seq.*

A Cure for Violence and Corruption

the sixth sermon preached before King Edward VI
the 12 daye of April 1549

I do not knowe what ye call chaunce medley in the lawe, it is not for my
studye. I am not a scholar in scripture in gods boke, I study that I knowe
what voluntary murder is before God. If I shall fall out with a man, He
is angry with me, and I wyth hym, and lackyng opportunitie and place, we
shall put it of for that tyme; in the meane season I prepare my weapon, and
sharpe it agaynste a nother tyme, I swell and boyle in thys passion towardes
hym. I seke hym, we medle together, it is my chaunce by reason my weapon
is better then his, and so furth, to kyl him, I geue hym his dethes stroke, in my
vengeaunce and anger.

Thys call I voluntarye murder in scripture, what it is in the lawe I can not
tell.[1] It is a greate synne, and therefore I call it voluntarye. I remember what
a greate Clarke[2] wrytteth of thys.

Omne peccatum adeo est Voluntarium ut nisi sit voluntarium non sit peccatum.

Euerye synne (sayeth he) is so voluntarye, that if it be not voluntarye, it can
not be called synne. Synne is no actuall synne, if it be not voluntarye. I would
we woulde all knowe oure faultes, and repente, that that is done, is done, it
can not be called backe agayne. God is mercifull, the Kynge is mercifull,
heare we maye repente, thys is the place of repentaunce. When we are gone
hence, it is to late then to repent. And let vs be content wyth such order as
the magystrates shall take. But suer it is a perillous thing to beare wyth anye
suche matter. I toulde you what I hard saye, I woulde haue no mans honestye
empayred by me tellynge. I harde saye syns of a nother murder, that a
Spanyarde shoulde kyll an Englisheman, and ronne hym thorowe wyth hys
swerde: they saye he was a tall man. But I here it not that the Spanyarde was
hanged for hys laboure. If I had, I woulde haue tould you it to. They fell out,
as the tale goeth, about a whore. O Lord what whordom is vfed nowe a
dayes. As I here by the relacion of honeste men, whyche tell it not after a
worldlye sorte, as thoughe they reioysed at it, but heuely, wyth heuy hertes,

---

1. Formal *duelling* had not yet come into fashion in England, but brawls and affrays
were a common occurrence and a social problem.

2. St. Augustine, *De Vera Relig.* cap. xiv. 27. Latimer paraphrases—often inaccurately
—rather than quotes, Latin texts. Augustine wrote: 'Nunc vero usque odeo peccatum
voluntarium malum est, ut nullo modo sit peccatum si non sit voluntarium.'

howe God is dyshonored by whoredome in thys cytie of London. Yea the
bancke,[1] when it stode, was neuer so commune. If it be true that is toulde, it
is maruayle yat it doeth not sincke, and that the earth gapeth not and
swalloweth it vp. It is wonderfull that the citye of London doeth suffer
such whordom vnpunished. God hath suffered long of hys great lenitie,
mercye, and benyngnitye, but he wyl punishe sharply at length, if we do
not repente. There is sum place in London, as they saye, *immunitie, impunitie.*[2]
What should I call it? a preueledged place for whoredome. The Lorde Mayer
hath nothynge to do there, the Sheriffes, thei can not medle wyth it. And
the queste, they not enquire of it, and there men do brynge theyr whores,
yea other mennes wyues, and there is no reformacion of it.

There is suche dysynge howses also, they saye, as hath not bene wonte to
be, where yong Gentlemenne dyse away their thrifte, and where dysynge is,
there are other folyes also.

For the loue of God lette remedye be hadde, lette vs wrestle and stryue
agaynste synne?

Menne of Englande in tymes paste, when they woulde exercyse theym
selues (for we must nedes haue some recreation, oure bodyes canne not
endure wythoute some exercyse) they were wonte to goo a brode in the
fyeldes a shootynge,[3] but nowe is turned in to glossyng,[4] gullyng,[5] and whor-
ing wythin the housse.

The arte of shutynge hath ben in tymes past much estemed in this
realme, it is a gyft of God that he hath geuen vs to excell all other nacions
wyth all. It hath bene goddes instrumente, whereby he hath gyuen vs manye
victories agaynste oure enemyes. But nowe we haue taken vp horynge in
tounes, in steede of shutyng in the fyeldes. A wonderous thynge, that so
excellente a gift of God shoulde be so lytle estemed. I desyer you my Lordes,
euen as ye loue the honoure, and glory of God, and entende to remoue his
indignacion, let ther be sente fourth some proclimacion, some sharpe
proclimacion to the iustices of peace, for they do not their dutye. Iustices now
be no iustices, ther be manye good actes made for thys matter already. Charge
them vpon their allegiaunce yat this singular benefit of God maye be

1. The Bank-side in Southwark.

2. The precinct of St. Martin le Grand, a place of sanctuary before the Reformation,
continued to be treated as an area protected by privilege long after the immunity of
sanctuary had ceased to be officially recognized. A. F. Kemp, *Historical Notices of the
Church of St. Martin le Grand.*

3. The literary classic of archery had been written only four years before the preaching
of this sermon, but in *Toxophilus* Ascham was performing an act of piety, not answering
a living demand. Archery was still honoured in sentiment, as part of a glorious past but
its popularity with the youth of the country had been waning for some time. See Acts,
Henry VIII 33. c. 9; also Stow, *Survey of London* (ed. Strype), Bk. 1, p. 302 *et seq.*

4. Glossing: drinking.   5. Gulling: cheating.

practised, and that it be not turned into bollyng, glossyng and whoryng wythin the townes, for they be negligente in executyng these lawes of shuting. In my tyme, my poore father, was as diligent to teach me to shote, as to learne anye other thynge, and so I thynke other menne dyd theyr children. He taughte me how to drawe, how to laye my bodye in my bowe, and not to drawe wyth strength of armes as other nacions do, but with strength of the bodye. I had my bowes boughte me accordyng to my age and strength as I encreased in them, so my bowes were made bigger, and bigger, for men shal neuer shot well, excepte they be broughte vp in it. It is a goodly art, a holsome kynde of exercise, and much commended in phisike. Marcilius Phicinus[1] in hys boke *de triplici uita* (it is a greate while sins I red hym nowe) but I remember he commendeth this kinde of exercise, and sayth, that it wrestleth agaynst manye kyndes of diseases. In the reuerence of God, let it be continued. Let a Proclamation go furth, chargynge the Iustices of Peace, yat they se suche Actes and statutes kept, as were made for this purpose. I wyl to my matter. I entend this day to entreate of a pece of scripture, written in the begynynge of the. v. Chapter of Luke. I am occasioned to take thys place by a boke, sent, to the Kynges May[e]stye that deade is, by Mayster Poel.[2] It is a texte, that he doeth great lye abuse, for the supremitye. He rackes it, and vyolentes it, to serue for the mayntenaunce of the byshop of Rome. And as he did enforce the tother place, that I entreated of last, so dyd he inforce thys also, to serue hys matter. The storye is thys.

Our Sauioure Christe was come nowe to the bancke of the water of Genezareth.

The people were come to hym and flocked aboute hym to here hym preache. And Iesus toke a boote that was standynge at the poole, it was symonnes bote, and wente into it. And sittyng in the bote he preached to them that were on the bancke. And whan he had preached and taught them he spake to Simon and bade hym launch out fourther into the depe, and lose hys nettes, to catche fyshe. And Symon made aunswere, and sayed. Mayster, we haue labored all nyght, but we caught nothing howe be it at thy commaundement because thou byddest vs, we wyll go to it agayne. And so they dyd, and caught a greate draught, a miraculus draught so muche that the net bracke, and they called to theyr fellowes that were bye, for they had. ii. botes to come to healpe them, and they came and filled both theyr botes so full, that they were nygh drounynge. Thys is the storye: That i maye declare thys texte so, that it may be to the honoure of God and edificacion of youre soules and myne boeth. I shall desier you to healpe me wyth your prayer in the whiche. etc.

1. Marsilio Ficino, *De Vita*, lib. ii, cap. 4. Exercise is commended, but not archery in particular.
2. *Pro ecclesiasticae unitatis defensione* (1537).

Factum est autem. (Sayth the text) *cum turba irrueret in eum.*[1] Sayncte Luke telles the storye, and it came to passe, when the people presed vpon him, so that he was in perill to be cast into the pond they rushed so faste vpon hym and made such throng to him. A wonderous thynge, what a desyre the people had in those dayes to heare oure sauioure Christe preache, and the cause may be gathered of the latter end of the chapter that went before. Oure Sauioure Christ had preached vnto them, and healed the sycke folkes of suche diseases and maladies as they had and therefore the people woulde haue retayned hym styll. But he made them aunswere, and sayed.

Et aliis ciuitatibus oportet me euangelisare regnum dei, nam in hoc missus sum. I must preache the kyngedome of god to other cyties also, I muste shewe them my fathers wyll: for I came for that purpose. I was sente to preache the worde of God. Our Sauioure Christ sayed, howe he muste not tarye in one place, for he was sent to the worlde to preache euerye where. Is it not a meruaylous thyng, that oure vnpreaching prelates can read thys place, and yet preach no more then they do. I maruayle, that they can go quyetlye to bed, and se how he allureth them with hys example, to be diligente in theyr office. Here is a godly lesson also howe oure Sauioure Christe fled from glory. Yf these ambiciouse parsons, that climbe to honoure by bywal[k]es inordinatly, would consider this example of Iesus christ, they shold come to more honour then they do: for when thei seke honour by such bywalkes, thei come to confucion honour foloweth them that fle from it. Our sauiour Christ, gat hym a waye erlye in the mornynge, and went vnto the wildernes. I woulde they woulde folowe thys example of Christe, and not seke honoure by suche by walkes as they do. But what dyd the people? when he had hyd hym selfe, they smelled him out in the Wylldernes, and came vnto hym, by flockes, and folowed hym a greate nombre. But where reade you that a greate nomber of scribes and Pharises, and Byshoppes followed hym.

1. And it came to pass, that, as the people pressed upon him to hear the word of God, he stood by the lake of Gennesaret,

And saw two ships standing by the lake: but the fishermen were gone out of them, and were washing *their* nets.

And he entered into one of the ships, which was Simon's, and prayed him that he would thrust out a little from the land. And he sat down, and taught the people out of the ship.

Now when he had left speaking, he said unto Simon, Launch out into the deep, and let down your nets for a draught.

And Simon answering said unto him, Master, we have toiled all the night, and have taken nothing: nevertheless at thy word I will let down the net.

And when they had this done, they inclosed a great multitude of fishes: and their net brake.

And they beckoned unto *their* partners which were in the other ship, that they should come and help them. And they came, and filled both the ships so that they began to sink.—Luke v:1-7.

There is a doctour that wryteth of thys pla[c]e, his name is Doctoure Gorrham, Nycolas Corrham[1] I knewe hym to be a schoole Doctoure a greate while a go, but I neuer knewe hym to be an enterpreter of scripture til nowe of late: he sayeth thus, *maior deuocio in laicis Vetulis quam in clerics, etc.*[2] There is more deucion fayeth he, in laye folke, and olde Wyues, These symple folke, the vulger people, then in the clarkes[3] they be better affecte to the worde of God, then those, that be of the cleargye. I maruayle not at the sentence, but I maruayle to fynd such a sentence in such a doctor. Yf I shoulde saye so much, it would be sayed to me, that it is an euyll byrd that defiles hys owne nest, and *Nemo laeditur nisi a seipso.* There is no man hurte, but of hys owne selfe. There was veryfied the sayinge of oure Sauioure Christe Whiche he spake in an other place. *Vbicunque fuerit cadauer, ibicongregabuntur aquilae.*[4] Wheresoeuer a deade carion is, thither wil ye e[a]gles gather. Our sauiour christ compares hymselfe to a deade carion, for where the carion is, there wyl the Egles be, and though it be an euyl smel to vs. and stynckes in a mans noose yet it is a swete smel to the Egles, they wyl seke it out. So the people sought oute Chryst, they smelt hys fauour, he was a swete smell to them. He is *Odor uitae ad uitam,*[5] the smel of life to life. Thei flocket about him lyke Egles. Christ was the carrion, and the people were the Egles.

Thei had no pleasure to heare the Scribes and the Pharises thei stancke in their nose, their doctrine was unsauery, it was but of Lolions[6] of decimations of Anets feade, and Cummyn and suche gere. There was no comfort in it for soore consciences, there was no consolation for woundes soules, there was no remedye for synnes, as was in Christes doctryne. Hys doctryne eased the burden of the soule, it was swete to the common people, and sower to ye Scribes. It was such comforte and pleasure to them, that thei came flockyng aboute hym. Wherefore came thei? *Vt audirent uerbum dei,*[7] it was a good commyng. They came to heare the word of God. It was not to be thought

---

1. Nicholas Gorham, or Corrham, or Nicholas de Gorrain (died 1400) wrote commentaries on the New Testament and sermons which, although he had been a Dominican, were freely quoted by Protestants. See William Cave, *Scriptorum Historia Literaria* (1740). Appendix 86.

2. As usual Latimer's Latin has run wild. Gorham's text reads, 'Nam in laicis et vetulis quamque major reperitur denotio quam in clericis.' *Commentaria* (Cologne, 1537) f. 327.

3. An interesting amendment was introduced into the 1603 edition, when the Puritan rank and file in the church had begun their struggle to oust the episcopal hierarchy: 'clarkes' was changed to 'great clarkes'.

4. Matt. xxiv: 28.

5. The savour of life unto life. 2 Cor. ii: 16.

6. Infelix lolium: 'a vicious grayne, called ruie of darnell, which commonlye groweth amonge wheat'. Sir Thomas Elyot, *Bibliotheca* (1550).

7. To hear the word of God. Luke v: 1.

that they came all of one mynde to here the worde of God. It is lykely that in so grat a multitude, some came of curiositie, to here some nouelles, and some cam smelling a swete sauour, to haue consolation and comfort of Gods word for we cannot be saued without heringe of the worde. It is a necessarye waye to saluation.

We can not be saued wythout fayeth, and fayth commeth by hearynge of the worde. *Fides ex auditu*[1] And howe shal they heare wythout a preacher? I tel you it is the fotesteppes of the ladder of heauen, of oure saluacion. There must be preachers if we loke to be saued. I toulde you of thys gradacion before in the tenth of the Romaynes. Consider it well. I had rather ye shoulde come of a naughtye mynde, to heare the worde of God, for noueltye, or for curiositie to heare some pastime, then to be awaye. I had rather ye shoulde come as the tale is by the Gentel-woman of London one of her neyghbours mette her in the streate, and sayed mestres whether go ye, Mary sayed she, I am goynge to S. Tomas of Acres[2] to the sermon, I coulde not slepe al thys laste nyght, and I am goynge now thether, I neuer fayled of a good nap there, and so I had rather ye should a napping to the sermons, than not to go at al. For with what mind so euer ye come, thoughe ye come for an ill purpose, yet peraduenture ye maye chaunce to be caught or ye go, the preacher maye chaunce to catche you on hys hoke. Rather then ye should not come at al, I would haue you come of curiositie, as Saynte Augustyne came to heare Sainct Ambrose. When Saynte Augustyne came to Myllane, (he telles the storye hym selfe in the ende of his boke of confessions) he was very desirous to here S Ambrose, not for anye loue he had to the doctrine that he taughte, but to here his eloquence, whether it was so greate, as the speache was, and as the brute went. Wel, before he departed Saynte ambrose caught hym on hys hoke and conuerted hym[3] so, that he became of a Maniche, and of a platoniste a good christian, a defender of christes religion, and of the fayeth afterwarde. So I woulde haue you come to sermones. It is declared in many mo places of scripture, howe necessarye preachynge is, as thys. *Euangelium est potentia dei, ad salutem omni credenti*.[4] The preachynge of the Gospel, is the power of god to euery man that doth beleue. He meanes gods word opened, It is the instrument, and the thing wherby we are saued. Beware beware ye diminishe not thys office, for if ye do, ye decaie goddes power to al that do beleue. Christe sayeth consonaunte to the same. *Nisi quis renatus fuerit e supernis, non potest uidere regnum dei.*

1. Faith cometh by hearing. Rom. x:17.
2. Hospital and chapel in Cheapside dedicated to St. Thomas of Acre, where Thomas Becket was born. Stow, op. cit., Bk iii, p. 555.
3. Augustine, *Confessions*, lib. v, cap. xiii–xiv.
4. The gospel of Christ: for it is the power of God unto salvation to every one that believeth. Rom. 1:16.

Except a man be borne a gayne from a boue, he can not se the kyngdome of God.[1] He muste haue a regeneracion: and what is this regeneracion? It is not to be Christened in water (as these fyre brandes expound it) and nothyng elles. Howe is it to be expounded then? saynct Peter sheweth. That one place of Scripture declareth another. It is the circumstance, and collacion of places that make scripture playne. *Regeneramur autem* (sayeth Sayncte Peter) and we be borne a gayne. Howe? *Non ex semine mortali, sed immortali.*[2] Not by a mortall seade, but by an immortall. What is this immortall seade? *per sermonem dei uiuentis.* By the word of the liuyng God, by the worde of God preached and opened. Thus commeth in oure newe byrth. Here you maye se how necessarye thys offyce is to oure saluacion This is the thynge that the deuill wrastleth most agaynste, it hath bene all hys studye to decaye thys office, he worketh agaynste it as muche as he can, he hath preuailed to much, to much in it. He hath set vppe a state of vnpreachynge prelacye in this Realme this. vii. c. (seven hundred) yere, A state of vnpreachyng prelacy He hath made vnpreachynge prelates. He hath styrred vp by heapes to persecute thys office in the title of heresy he hath sturred vppe the Magistrates to persecute it in the title of sedicion.

*

It followeth in the texte. *Sedens docebat de naui* (He taught the people out of the ship) He taught sittyng. Preachers be lyke, were sitters in those daies, as it is written in a nother place. *Sedent in cathedra mosi.* They sette in the chayer of Moses.[3]

I woulde oure preachers woulde preache sittynge, or standynge, one waye, or other. It was a godly pulpit that our Sauiour Christ hadde gotten hym here. An olde rotten bote. And yet he preached hys fathers wyll, hys fathers message out of thys pulpyt. He regarded the people more then the pulpit. He cared not for the pulpit, so he myght do the people good. In dede it is to be commended for the preacher to stand, or sit, as the place is, but I would not haue it so supersticiously esteemed, but that a good preacher may declare ye worde of god sitting on a horse, or preching in a tre. And yet if this shold be done, ye vnpreaching prelattes would laughe it to skorne.

And though it be good to haue the pulpit set vp in churches, that the people may resort thither, yet I woulde haue it so supersticiously vsed, but that in a prophane place the worde of God might be preached some times, and I woulde not haue the people offended wyth all, no more, then they be with out Sauioure Christes preachyng out of a bote.

1. John iii:3.
2. Being born again, of corruptible seed, but of incorruptible, by the word of God, which liveth and abideth for ever. 1 Pet. i:23.
3. Matt. xxiii:2. Luke iv:3.

And yet to haue pulpetes in churches it is very well done to haue them, but
they woulde be occupied, for it is a vayne thyng to haue them as they stand
in many churches. I harde of a Byshop of Englande that wente on visitacion
and (as it was the custom) when the Byshop shoulde come and be runge into
the toune[1] the greate belles clapper was fallen doune, the tyall was broken, so
that the Byshop coulde not be runge into the toune. Ther was a greate matter
made of thys, and the chiefe of the paryshe ware muche blamed for it in the
visitacion. The Byshop was some what quicke wyth theym, and signified
that he was muche offended. They made theyr aunsweres, and excused
them selues, as well as they coulde, it was a chaunce, sayd they, that ye clapper
brake and we coulde not get it amended by and by, we must tarrye til we
can haue done it. It shall be amended as shortelye as maye be. Amonge the
other there was one wyser then the rest, and he commes to me the Bishop.
Whi mi Lord, sayth he, doth your lordship mak so grat matter of the bell,
that lacketh hys clapper? here is a bell, sayeth he, and poynted to the pulpit,
that hath lacked a clapper thys. xx yeres. We haue a parson, that setteth out
of thys benefice fiftye poundes euerye yere, but we neuer se hym. I warrant
you the Byshop was an vnpreachyng prelate. He could fynde faute wyth the
bel, that wanted a clapper, to ryng hym into the toune, but he could not fynd
any faut wyth the parson that preached not at his benefice. Euer thys office of
preachynge hath bene least regarded, it hath skante hadde the name of
goddes seruyce. They must synge *Salue festa dies* aboute the churche, that no
man was the better for it, but to shewe theyr gaie cotes, and garmentes. I
came once my selfe to a place, ridyng on a iornay home warde from London,
and I sente worde ouer nyghte into the toune that I would preach there in the
morninge because it was holy day, and me thought it was an holye dayes
worcke, The church stode in my waye, and I toke my horsse, and my com-
panye, and went thither, I thoughte I shoulde haue founde a greate com-
panye in the churche, and when I came there, the churche dore was faste
locked.

I tarried there halfe an houer and more, at last the keye was founde, and
one of the parishe commes to me and sayes. Syr thys is a busye daye wyth vs,
we can not heare you, it is Robyn hoodes daye. The parishe are gone a
brode to gather for Robyn hoode, I praye you let them not. I was
fayne there to geue place to Robyn hoode, I thought my rochet shoulde haue
bene regarded, thoughe I were not, but it woulde not serue, it was fayn to
geue place to Robyn hoodesmen. . . .

1. It was an ancient custom to ring the church bells in honour of a Bishop at his visitation. Brand, *Popular Antiquities* (1904 edn.), p. 41.

Indiscipline and Superstition

the seventh sermon preached before King Edward VI
on 19th April, 1549

I neuer sawe surely so lyttel discipline as is nowe a daies. Men wilbe maysters, they wyl be maysters, and no Disciples. Alas where is thys disciplyne nowe in England. The people regarde no discipline, they be without al order. Wher thei shuld geue place, they wyll not stur one inch, yea, wher magistrates shold determyne matters, they wyl breake into the place, before they come, and at theyr commynge not moue a whitte for them. Is this discipline? Is thys good order? Yf a man say any thyng vnto them, they regarde it not. They that be called to aunswere wyll not aunswere directlye, but skoffe the matter out. Men the more thei knowe, the worsse they be, it is truely sayed.

Sciencia inflat,[1] knowledge maketh vs proude and causeth vs to forget all, and set a waye discipline. Suerlye, in Poperye they had a reuerence, but now we haue none at all, I neuer sawe the lyke. Thys same lacke of the feare of God, and discipline in vs, was one of the causes that the father woulde not heare hys sonne. Thys payne suffered our sauioure Christ for vs, who neuer deserued it. Oh what it was, that he suffered in thys gardeyn, til Iudas came. The doloures, the terroures, the sorrowes that he suffered, be vnspeakable, He suffered partelye, to make amendes for oure synnes, and partelye, to geue vs example, what wee shoulde do in lyke case.

What comes of thys gere in the ende? Wel, nowe he prayeth agayne, he resorteth to his father agayne. *Angore correptus, prolixius orabat*,[2] He was in sorer paines, in more anguishe, then euer he was, and therefore he prayeth longer, more ardentlye, more faruentelye, more vehementelie, then euer he did before.

Oh Lorde, what a wonderfull thynge is thys, thys horroure of death is worsse then death it selfe, more ugsome, more bytter then anye bodylye death. He prayeth nowe the thyrde tyme. He dyd it so instauntlye, so feruently, that it brought out a bloudy sweate, and suche plentye that it dropped downe euen to the grounde. Ther issued out of hys precious bodye droppes of bloude. What a paine was he in, when these bloudy droppes fell so abundantlye from hym. Yet for all that, how vnthankefull do we shewe

1. Knowledge puffeth up. 1 Cor. viii:1.
2. And being in agony (et factus in agonia) he prayed more earnestly. Luke xxii:44.

oureselues toward hym that dyed only for oure sakes, and for the remedy of oure synnes. Oh what blasphemye do we commit daye by daye, what litle regard haue we to his blessed passion thus to sweare by goddes bloude, by Christes passion. We haue nothynge in no pastime, but gods bloude, gods woundes. We continually blaspheme his passion in haukyng, hunting, dising, and cardinge. Who would thynke he shoulde haue suche enemyes a monge those that professe hys name.

What became of hys blud that fell downe trowe ye? was the bloude of Hales[1] of it (wo worthe it). What a do was it to brynge thys out of the kynges heade, thys greate abhominacion of the blould of hales could not be taken a great whyle out of his mynde. You that be of the court, and especially ye sworne chapleynes be ware of a lesson that a greate man taught me at my fyrst comming to the courte; he tolde me for good wyll, he thoughte it well. He saye vnto me. You must beware howe soeuer ye do that ye contrari not the Kynge, let hym haue hys sayinges, follow hym, go wyth hym[2]. Mary out vpon thys counsayle, shall I saye, as he sayes. Saye youre conscience, or eles what a worme shal ye fele gnawynge, what a remorse of conscience shall ye haue, when ye remembre howe ye haue slacked your dutye. It is a good wyse verse. *Gutta cauat lapidem, non ui sed soepe cadendo.* The droppe of raine maketh a hole in the stone, not by violence, but by ofte fallynge. Lykewyse a Prynce muste be turned not violentlye, but he must be wonne by a lytle and a lytle. He muste haue hys dutye tolde hym, but it muste be done wyth humblenes, wyth request of pardon, or els it were a daungerous thynge.

Vnpreacheynge Prelates haue bene the cause, that the bloud of Hales did so long blynd the Kynge. Wo worthe that suche an abhomynable thyng, shuld be in a Christen realme, but thankes be to God it was partly redressed in the Kynges dayes that dead is, and much more nowe. God graunte good wil, and power to go forwarde, yf ther be any suche abhomynacion behinde, that it may vtterly be rooted vp.

1. One of the most notorious and profitable pre-Reformation shrinal frauds. Said to be the Saviour's blood, miraculously preserved at the Abbey of Hales, in Gloucestershire, it was discovered to be 'coloured honey', but Henry VIII relinquished his belief in the 'relic' only slowly and reluctantly.

2. Henry had tendered financial offerings to the Boxley Rood in Kent, a bearded image of Christ crucified, which could be manipulated to move its eyes and lips, to foam at the mouth and shed tears.

BERNARD GILPIN[1]

From all accounts Bernard Gilpin must have been one of the most satisfactory priests ever to take orders. After an academic career of glittering distinction, no eminence in the church was beyond his reach; but he refused the bishopric of Carlisle and the provostship of Queen's College, Oxford, preferring to spend most of his life vicar of a rural parish, far from London and the court, near Durham. His reputation for integrity attracted many gifts and bequests and he dedicated his wealth, like himself, to his pastoral duties. His house, 'as large as a Bishop's palace', was made to perform the function resigned by the monasteries and became a place of sanctuary and shelter for the poor and distressed. Gilpin himself travelled and worked unremittingly among his parishioners and beyond them, preaching; nursing; distributing food, alms, clothing. He fought the battles of the injured poor. He founded a grammar school.

It was inevitable that such a man should be hated by a few as well as loved by many. Virtue to some is as provocative as vice to others. But there seems to have been a wonderful grace about the man which pierced the hearts of even the most worldly acquisitive and converted adversaries into disciples. One story, fact or fancy, is a microcosm of his life's reputation.

Gilpin's friend Pilkington was succeeded as Bishop of Durham by Richard Barnes who quickly confirmed his reputation for being ill-disposed to Gilpin by suspending him from preaching. Presently, however, the new bishop summoned Gilpin to Chester-le-Street where he had assembled the diocesan clergy in full synod and also his brother the Chancellor of the cathedral, of whom it was said that it was difficult to tell whether he was more lustful or covetous. On being required to preach without notice Gilpin protested that he was unprepared, but the bishop insisted, saying that everyone knew that he was able to preach

1. Bernard Gilpin 1517–1583, born at Kentmer Hall, Westmorland. Queen's College Oxford, 1533, B.A. 1539; M.A. 1541. Fellow of Christ Church. Life, in Latin, by George Carleton, Bishop of Chichester, 1628; English translation, 1629. Life of Bernard Gilpin, by William Gilpin, 1753. Also Charles Collingwood's *Memoirs of Bernard Gilpin*, 1884; Strype's *Life and Acts of Edward Grindal*, 1710; Wood's *Fasti* (ed. Bliss), i, 129.

without warning. Whereupon Gilpin climbed into the pulpit and, although he noted that there were clerks in the church taking down carefully in writing all that he said, delivered a stinging denunciation of the crimes and abuses which were tolerated in the diocese, sparing none of the guilty, least of all the bishop.

When it was over Gilpin's friends surrounded him anxiously and warned him that he had put a sword into the bishop's hand to slay him. After they had all dined together the bishop accompanied Gilpin to his house and on entering seized his hand, exclaiming, 'Father Gilpin, I acknowledge you are fitter to be Bishop of Durham than I am myself parson of this church of yours. I ask forgiveness for errors past. Forgive me, father. I know you have hatched up some chickens that now seek to pick out your eyes;[1] but so long as I shall live Bishop of Durham be secure, no man shall injure you.'

In 1558, the third year of the Marian frenzy of Protestant persecution, Gilpin was denounced in London and a pursuivant despatched to Durham to bring him before Bonner. On the journey south Gilpin broke his leg and the delay caused by the accident probably saved his life. By the time the party reached London Mary was dead and there was nothing to fear from any Catholic prelate any more. It was Bonner now, who, snubbed by the queen, was heading for his last imprisonment and death.

The sermon, part of which follows, is the only sermon of Gilpin's to have survived, and we are lucky to have even this one, for clearly he was not interested in publishing and preserving his sermons when they had served their workaday pastoral purpose. The only reason this may have been published is that it was preached at court before the king (only a year before Edward's death) and was much noted. So much that his uncle, Cuthbert Tunstall, Bishop of Durham, advised him to travel for a time, and he spent the next few years in Paris and Louvain before returning to a north country parish. During this time abroad he insisted, against Tunstall's advice, on resigning his benefice.

Gilpin does not wander discursively in his address, nor buttonhole his auditory for a matey chat like Latimer. He chooses his points, shapes his discourse to their exposition and stays with them till they have transfixed his targets. '. . . there was one Barrabas, S. Mathewe calleth

1. Barnes was probably alluding here to Hugh Broughton, whom Gilpin had discovered wandering the roads, a clever but penniless and unemployed youth, sent to Oxford and educated, and who later intrigued against his benefactor.

him a notable theef, a gentleman theef, such as rob now a daies in velvet coates ...' leading to, without letting go of the image of a 'common thief', insolent in his finery, 'There be so many mighty Nemrothes in England, mightie hunters that hunt for possessions & Lordships, that pore men are daily hunted out of their livings ....'.

It is not surprising that this sermon, preached at court before an assembly of insatiable, newly ennobled Barabases, provoked resentment.

The New Oppressors
Antichrists of the Reformation

A Godly Sermon preached in the Court at Greenwich
on the first Sunday after Epiphanie, 1552[1]

Nowe forsomuch as the greatest parte of the world haue at this day forsaken their fathers businesse, applying their own, and are altogether drowned in sinne: For, *The whole head is sicke & the whole heart is heauy. From the sole of the foote to the head, there is nothing whole therein &c.* And as Saint Paule saith. *All seeke their owne, & not that which is Iesus Christes.* And I am here ascended into the high hill of Sion, the highest hill in all this realme. I must needes as it is giuen me in commission, *Cry aloud & spare not: lift vp thy voice like a trumpet & shew my people their transgressions.* I must crye vnto all estates aswell of the Ecclesiasticall ministerie, as of the ciuill gouernaunce, with the vulgare people. But for somuch as example of holy scriptures with experience of Christs church in all ages hath taught vs that the fall of Priestes is the fall of the people, and contrariwise the integrity of them is the preservation of the whole flocke: And the ministers as Christ faith, *being the light of his mysticall body, if the lighte be turned into darkenesse, there must needes followe great darknesse in the whole body.* I think it conuenient to begin with them which seeme to haue brought blindnes into the whole body, making men to forget their heauenly fathers businesse. They which shoulde haue kept the candle still burning: these will I chiefly examine in the businesse which Christe so earnestly committed to all pastors before his ascension: when he demaunded thrise of Peter if he loued him, and euery time vpon Peters confession,

1. Published 1581, pp. 12–19 and 46–56.

enioyned him, straightly to feede his lambes & sheepe. Wherein we haue the true triall of all ministers,who loue Christ, who apply this businesse. But to consider how it hath ben forgotten in the church many yeares, it mighte make a Christians harte to bleede. He that wrote the generall Chronicle of all ages: when he commeth to the time of Iohn the 8. and Martin the seconde, Byshops of Rome about 600 years agoe, the conferring golden ages going before with the iniquitie of that time: when through ambition, avarice & contention, the office of setting forth Goddes word was brought to an vtter contempt & troden vnder foote. In token whereof the Byble was made the Bishops footestoole, he falleth to a sudden exclamation & complaineth thus with the lamentable voice of the prophet Ieremy *Helas, Helas, O Lorde God: Howe is the golde become so dimme? How is the goodly colour of it so sore changed? O moste vngratious time* (faith he) *wherein the holy man faileth* (or is not) *all truethes are diminished from the sonnes of men: there are no Godly men left, the faithfull are worne out among the children of men.* In that time as it appeareth both by this hystory and others, ambition & gredy auarice taught ministers to seek & contest for liuings, who might climb the highest by vtter contempt of their office, and of our heauenly fathers businesse: And so to make Christe his *flock a ready pray for the diuel who go thabout like a roaring Lyon seeking whome he may deuour.* Then the Bishop of Rome abusing alwaies Peters keyes to fill Iudas Satchels, dispensed with all prelates (that brought any mony) from obeing of Christes commission giuen to Peter, Feede, Feede, Feede, my Lambs and my sheepe, and stretched it so largely, that in steade of feeding Christe his Lambes and sheepe, he allowed them to feede Hawks, Hounds, and Horses (I will not say) Harlottes. Then in steede of *Fishers of men*, he made them to become fishers of benefices & fat liuinges. He brought preaching into such a contempt, that it was accompted a greate absurdity for a Cardinall to preach, after he had once bestred his Moile. But let vs see after, how this euill encreased. S. Bernard in his time aboute 200 yeares after lamented, that when it seemed the open persecution of Tyrants & Heretikes was ceased in the Church, then an other persecution farre worse, and more noisome to Christes gospell did succeede, when the ministers, Christes owne friends by pretence, were turned into persecutors. *My louers & my friendes stande aside from my plague, & my kinsmen stand afar off.* The iniquitie of the Church (Sayeth Bernard) began at the elders. *Heu, Heu, Domine Deus, &c. Alas, alas, O Lorde God, they are the formost in persecuting of thee, whiche are thought to loue the chiefest place or preheminence in the Churche.* This complaint with much more to long to be rehearsed, made Saint Bernard in his time against the Prelates of Rome, nothing afraide in the fame place (for obscuring of Christe his Gospell) to cal them Antechristes, and for murthering of silly soules redeemed with Christ his pretious bloude, he maketh more cruell persecutors of Christe, then the Iewes, whiche shed his bloud. If the iniquitie of Rome 400. yeares agoe, was so great, & since hath not a little increased, it was high time that God should open the eyes of some Christian princes to see the great abuses and enormities of Romish Byshoppes, and to deliuer Christes gospell out of captiuity, & to bring down his hornes, whose pride (if he mighte haue had successe in his tiranny) began to ascend with Lucifer aboue the starres. It is not many years agoe, that a champion of his named *Pelagius*,[1] writing against *Marcilius Paduanus*,[2] in defence of Rome, hath not bene ashamed to leaue in writing, that the pope, *quodamodo*, after a sort doth participate both natures, the Godhead and manhod with Christ: and that he may not be iudged of the Emperour, because he is not a meere man, but as a God vpon earth, & God (saith he) may not be iudged of man. What intollerable blasphemy is this? If I had not read it my selfe, I could scarsly beleeue any such blasphemy to pro-ceede from him which professeth Christ. Doe you not perceiue plainely the hissing and poyson of the old serpent, when he tempted our first parents, & promised they should become like Gods? A vile wretched creature, wormes meate, forgetting his estate, must become a God vppon earth. Such Gods shall followe *Iupiter*, *Mars*, and *Venus*, into the pit of damnation. But some will say, what should we speake so much of the Byshop of Rome, is he not gone? his power taken away? If preachers would let him alone, the people would sone forget him. Truly for my part, if I had that gift, strength & calling, I had rather (though I were sure to smarte therefore) speake against his enormities in Rome, then to speake of them here. And I thinke no man beareth (at least I am sure no man ought to bear) any malice or euill will against his person, in speaking against his vice and iniquitie. *Wee fight not (Saith Sainte Paul) against flesh and bloud, but we fight against the prince of darkesse*. . . .

O with what glad hearts & cleare consciences might noble men go to rest, when they had bestowed the whole day in hearing Christe himselfe complain

1. Alverus Pelagius, Roman Catholic exegist, successively Bishop of Coronea and Silves; he published *De Planctu Ecclesiae libre II* (Ulm. 1474), a sweeping justification of papal supremacy. Gilpin treats him more seriously than his subsequent co-religionists were to do. In the *Dictionnaire de Théologie Catholique* (Paris, 1903) there is no mention of Alvarus Pelagius. Students of the Counter-Reformation are referred to a useful study, N. Iung, *Un Franciscan Théologian du pouvoir pontifical au XIVe siecle, Alvaro Pelayo* etc. (Paris, 1931).

2. Marsilius of Padua: the most radical and the boldest 14th-century precursor of the Protestant Reformation. Employed, with Jean Jardien, by the Emperor Louis of Bavaria, to attack the authority of Pope John XXII, Marsilius produced (*c.* 1326) *Defensio Pacis*, in which he asserted that, while God was the ultimate source of all power, his authority was expressed on earth through the *people*, and further, that St. Peter received no more authority than any of the other disciples and neither he nor any other disciple was appointed head of the Church. It was the first expression of the momentous challenge to the Papacy, which Luther, deeply influenced by Marsilius, would a century later, drive to a climax.

in his members & redressing his wrongs. But alas for lacke hereof poore people are driuen to seeke their right among the lawyers: And there as the prophet Ioel faith, Looke what the Caterpillers had left in their robbery & oppression at home, all that doth the greedie Locustes, the lawyers, deuour at London. They laugh with the monie which maketh others to weepe, & thus are the poore robbed on euerie side without redresse, and that of such as seeme to haue authoritie therto. When Christe suffered his passion there was one Barrabas, S. Mathewe calleth him a notable theef, a gentleman theef, such as rob now a daies in veluet coates, and other two obscure theeues and nothing famous. The rusticall theeues were hanged and Barrabas was deliuered: Euen so nowe a dayes little theeues are hanged that steale of necessitie, but the great Barrabasses haue free liberty to rob & to spoil without al measure in the middest of the citie. The poore pyrate said to Alexander, we rob but a few in a ship, but thou robbest whole cuntries and kingdomes. Alas silly pore members of Christ, how you be shorn, oppressed, pulled, haled to & fro on euery side, who can not but lament, if his heart be not of flint? There be a number euery terme, & many continually, which lamentably complain for lack of Iustice, but all in vaine. They spende that which they had left, and many times more, whose il successe here causeth thousandes to tarry at home beggers and leese their right, & so it were better, them here to sel their coats: for this we see, be the poor mans cause neuer so manifest a truth, the rich shal for mony find 6. or 7. counsellers shall stande with subtelties and sophismes to cloak an euill matter & hide a knowne trueth. A pitteous case in a christian common wealth. Alas that euer manifest falshood should be mainteined, where the God of trueth ought to be honored. But let them alone, they are occupied in their fathers business, euen the prince of darknesse. *You are of your father the diuel*: Yet I cannot so leaue them I must needes cry on Gods behalfe, to his patrons of Iustice, to you most redoubted prince, whom God hath made his minister for their defence: with all those whom god hath placed in authoritie vnder you. Looke vpon their misery, for this is our heauenly fathers businesse to you apointed by his holy word. When I come among the people, I call vpon them, as my duety is, for seruice, duty and obedience vnto their prince, to all magistrates, to their Lordes, and to al that be put in authoritie ouer them, I let them heare their owne faultes. But in this place my duty is & my conscience vppon Gods word bindeth me, seeing them so miseraby, so wrongfully, so cruelly intreated on euery side, in Gods behalfe to pleade their cause, not by forme of mans lawe, but by Gods word, as an intercessor. For as they are debters vnto you & other magistrates of loue, fear, seruiue, & obedience vnder God: So you are again debters vnto them of loue, protection of Iustice & equitie, mercy & pitie. If you denie them these, they must suffer, but god shal reuenge them. *He standeth* (saith Dauid) *in the congregation of Gods, & as iudge among gods.* Take heede all you that be counted as Goddes, Gods ministers vppen earth, you haue one God iudge ouer you, which as he in the same Psalme sharply rebuketh vngodly rulers for accepting of persons of the vngodly: so he telleth faithfull christian magistrates, their true duties & businesse in plaine words, *Defend the pore & needy, see that such as be in necessite haue right, deliuer the outcast & pore, saue them from* the hands *of the vngodly.* Heare haue all noble men & christian magistrates most liuely set forth to them their heauenly fathers businesse, wherein he woulde haue them continually occupied: woulde to God the whole Psalm were grauen in their hartes. Truely for lacke that this businesse is not applied, but the pore despised in all places, it hath giuen such boldnesse to couetous cormorantes abrode, that now their robberies, extortion & open oppression, hath no end nor limits, no banks can keepe in their violence. As for turning poore men out of their holdes, they take for no offence, but saie *Their lande is their owne, and forget altogether that the earth is the Lords, & the fulnesse thereof.* They turne them out of their shrouds[1] as thicke as mice. Thousandes in England through such begge nowe from dore to dore, which haue kept honest houses. These crie daily to God for vengeance, both against the greate Nemrothes workes thereof, and their mainteners. There be so many mighty Nemrothes in England, mightie hunters, that hunt for possessions & Lordships, that pore men are daily hunted out of their liuings: there is no couert nor denne can keep them safe. These Nemrothes haue such quick smelling houndes, they can lye at London and turne men out of their farms and tenements, a hundred, some 200, miles of. O Lord, when wicked Achab hunted after Nabothes vineyard, he could not (though he were a king) obteine that pray, till cursed Iesabel (as women many times haue shrewde wittes) til she tooke the matter in hand: So hard a thing it was in those dayes to wring a man from his fathers inheritaunce, which now a meane man will take in hande. And nowe our valiant Nemrothes can compasse the matter without the helpe of Iesabel, yet hath England euen now as great a number of Iesabels, which to mainteine their intolerable pride, their golden heads, wil not sticke to put too their wicked hands. O Lord what a number of such oppressors worse then Achab are in England, which *sell the poore for a paire of shoes,* of whome if God shoulde serue but 3. or 4. as he did Achab, to make the dogs lap the bloud of them, and their wiues & their posteritie, I thinke it would cause a great number to beware of extorsion, to beware of oppression, & yet escaping temporall punishment, they are certein by Gods' word, their bloud is reserued for hel-houndes, Cerberus and his companie: which they nothing feare. A pittifull case and great blindnesse, that hearing Gods word, man shoulde feare more temporall punishmente, then euerlasting. Yet hath Englande had of late some terrible examples of Gods wrath in soudeine and straunge deathes of such as ioyne feelde to feelde and house to house. Greate

1. In this context, 'sheds', 'weak, insubstantial' shelters.

pittie they were not cronicled to the terror of other which feare neither god nor man, so hardened in sinne, that they seeke not to hide it, but rather are such as glorie in their mischefe: which maketh me oftentimes remember a writer in our time, Musculus[1] vpon Sainte Mathews gospel, which meruelled much at the subtile and manifold working of Satan, howe he after the expelling of superstition and hypocrisie, trauelleth most busilie to bring in open impietie. That wher as before, hipocrits, men feared men and not God, now a great number, feare neither God nor man. The moste wicked are counted most manlike, and innocencie is holden for beastlines: yet may wee not say hipocrisie is expelled, for as many of these Achabs as signifie they fauour Gods word by reading or hearing it, or with praier honouring him (as Christe saith) *with their lippes, their heartes beeing farre from him*, they are as detestable hypocrites as euer was couered in cowle or cloister. . . . What their painted friend ship is, and howe of Christ it is esteemed, S. Augustine setteth forth by an apt similitude: *Euen as* (saith he) *a man shuld come to embrace thee, to kisse & honour thee vpward, & beneath with a paier of shoes beaten full of nailes, tread vpon thy bare foote, the heade shall despise the honour done unto it, and for the foote that smarteth, say, why treadest thou vppon mee? So when fained Gospellers honour Christe our heade, sitting in haeuen and oppresseth his members in earthe, the heade shall speake for the feete that smarte, and say, Why treadest thou on me?* Paule had a zeale towards God, but he did tread vpon Christes feete on earth, for whom the head cried forth of heauen, *Saul, Saul, why persecutest thou me?* Although Christ sitteth at the right hande of his father, yet beth in earth, he hungereth in earth, he suffereth al calamities here on earth, he is many times euill intreated here no earth. Wold to god we could beare away this briefe and shorte lesson, that what we doe to his members vpon earth we do to him: it would bring men from oppression, to shew mercy, without whiche no man can obteine mercie. If they would remember how the rich gluttone was damned in hel, not as we read for any violence, but for not shewing mercie, they might soone gather howe sharpe iudgement remaineth for them, which are not only vnmerciful, but also violently adde thereunto oppression: who are so farre from mercie? a great number their hearts will serve them to destroy whole townes, they would wish all the people destroyed to have all the field brought into a sheep pasture.

1. It is not clear whether this allusion is to Wolfgang or Andreas Musculus.

JOHN BRADFORD

In the company of unusual men who qualified for martyrdom in the Marian persecutions, John Bradford, a Lancastrian, born near Manchester about 1510, was the most extraordinary.[1] A lawyer by training and a shrewd man of business, he had been a useful servant to Sir John Harrington, treasurer of the King's Camps and Buildings, until the unhappy day for his master when he heard Latimer preaching against corruption, and the sermon so worked upon him that, by his knowledge of the ways and means employed, he compelled Harrington to disgorge the excess of what he had lately amerced from the crown. Fox depicts Bradford as much loved and intrepid. To Fox, all prominent Protestants were lovable and heroic, especially if they were martyred. But in this case there is confirmation from other sources of these qualities. In 1548 he went to St. Catherine Hall, Cambridge, and took Holy Orders. His impact as a preacher was immediate; he was made one of the king's few itinerant chaplains with licence to preach anywhere. The vivid eloquence of his imagery at its best redeems his fervour from vulgarity if not always from monotony. If his ecstasy had not been authentic it must have been insufferable, and those nearest to him were most devoted to him. On the friendliest evidence of his contemporaries it seems probable that he would have been classified by modern psychological medicine as 'a suitable case for treatment'. Thomas Sampson describes how among friends he would sit rapt and silent for long periods thinking of Jesus and 'sometimes at this silent sitting plenty of tears should trickle down his cheeks'.[2]

Soon after the accession of Mary he was arrested; not, however, at the instance of Bourne, as Fox inventively suggests. After trial and condemnation for heresy he spent more than a year in the Tower, though such was his gaoler's confidence in him that he was allowed out on parole to visit the sick. Then, on Saturday June 29th, 1555, the keeper's wife ran into his room 'seeming much troubled and almost

1. A reverent, but not seriously inaccurate, biographical essay by Aubrey Townsend introduces his edition of Bradford's works: *The Writings of John Bradford* (1848–53).
2. John Bradford, *Two Notable Sermons* (1574, 1581, 1599 edns), Preface.

windless, said, "O Master Bradford I come to bring you heavy news."
"What is that?" said he. "Marry," Quoth she, "Tomorrow you must
be burned and your chain is now a-buying." "I thank God for it,"
he said, "The Lord make me worthy thereof." ' Next day he was taken
out and burned at Smithfield, together with John Leaf. Almost his last
words reported were, "Be of good comfort, brother, for we shall have
a merry supper with the Lord this night."

Sermon of Repentance[1]

Adam in Paradyse transgressed greuously as the paynful punishment, which
we al as yet doe feele, proueth, yf nothinge else.

Thoughe by reason of his synne he displeased God sore, and ran away from
God, for he woulde have hyd him selfe, yes he would haue made God the
causer of his synne, in that he gaue hym such a mate, so farre was he from
askinge mercy; yet all this not withstandinge, God turned hys fearce wrath,
nether upon him, nor Eue, which also requyred not mercye, but upon the
serpente Sathan; promysing unto them a sede[2] Jesus Christe, by whom they
at the length shoulde be delyuered: In token whereof, though they wer
caste out of Paradyse, for theyre nurture, to serue in sorow, which woulde
not serue in ioye, yet he made them apparell to coure theyr bodies, a visible
sacramente and token of his invisible loue & grace concerning theyr soules.

Yf God was so merciful to Adam, whych so sore brake hys comaundement,
and rather blamed God, then asked mercy, troweste thou oh man, that he
wyll not be mercyful to the, whiche blameste thyselfe and desyrest pardon. To
Cayn he offered mercy, yf he woulde haue asked it: What haste done sayeth
God? the voyce of thy brothers bloude cryeth unto me, out of the earthe.
Oh mercyfull Lord (shuld Cayn haue sayd) I confesse it. But halas he dyd
not so: And therfore sayd God, Now, that is, in that thou desyrest not mercy,
now I say: be thou accursed. Lo to the reprobate he offered mercy, and wil he
denye it thee which arte hys chylde.

Noah dyd not he synne and was dronken: Good Lot also both in Sodome
dissembled a lyttle wyth the Angels, prolonginge the tyme, & out of Sodome
he fell very foule: as did Judas and the Patriarchs, agaynste Joseph, but yet I
wene they found mercy.

Moyses, Myriam, Aaron, though they tombled a little, yet recaued they

----

1. The text is that of the first edition, 1553.   2. Seed.

mercye: yea the people in the wylderness often synned & displeased God so that he was purposed to haue destroyed them: let me alone sayth he to Moyses, that I maye destroye them, but Moyses dyd not lette hym alone, for he prayed styll for them, and therefore God spared them. Yf the people were spared through Moyses prayer, they not praying with him, but rather, worshipping theyr golden calfe, eatinge, drinkinge, and makinge ioly good cheare: why shouldeste thou doubte, whether God wyll be mercyfull to thee: hauyinge as in dede thou hast, one muche better then Moyses to pray for thee and with thee, euen Jesus Christ who sytteth on the right hand of his father and prayeth for us, being no lesse faithful in his fathers house the church then moses was in the Sinagoge. Dauid the good kynge, had a foule soyle, when he committed whoredom with hys faythful seruantes wyfe Bethsabe, where unto he added also a mischeuous murder, causing her husband hys most faythfull souldier Urye to be slayne with an honest company of his most valiaunt men of warre, and that with the swearde of the uncircumsised. In this hys synne thoughe a great whyle he laye a slepe (as many do now a dayes, god geue them wynne waking) thinking that by hys sacrifices he offered, all was well, God was content: yet at length when the Prophet by a parable had opened the poke and brought hym in remembraunce of his owne synne in such sorte, then he gaue judgement agaynst hymself, then quaked he, his sacryfices hadde no more taken awaye his sines, then our Syr Johns[1] trentalles,[2] and wagging of his fyngers ouer the heades of such as lye a slepe in theyr synnes, out of the which when they are awaked, they wyl well se, it is nether masse, not mattens, nor crossying wyll serue; then (I say) he cryed out sayinge, *peccaui domino*, I haue synned sayeth he agaynst my Lorde, and good god whiche hath donne so muche for me, I caused in dede Urye to be kylled, I haue synned, I haue sinned, what shall I dooe? I haue

1. 'Sir' was commonly used as a form of address for priests of all ranks, but especially for those who had not graduated as Master of Arts at a university *c.* 1360: 'Sere biscop ta god kepe' (*Cursor Mundi* 27450). 1471: 'Item, to Sir John Cerne to say a trentall mass for me, 2s 6d.' (In *Somerset Wills*, pub. 1900). It began to be applied ironically; then satirically, as in the present instance, where 'Sir John' signifies ignorant, superstitious priests in general *c.* 1546: 'The most ragged ronnagate and idle idiot among them, is no less than a syr, which is Lord in Latin as Sur John . . .' (John Bale, *Image of Both Churches*, ii, f. VI, 1550 edn.); 1595: 'Well preacht sir Iacke . . .' (Robert Green, *George a Greene*).

2. Trental, trentall (or trentae), of a 'months mind': trentuale, trentena, terntenarius, tricenarium, trigesimale, trigintale, etc.—different names for the same thing—an office of thirty masses for the dead. See du Cargne (sometimes catalogued Englished as 'Ducargne', or under Fresne, Charles du), *Lexicon Manuale ad Scriptores Mediiae et Infamae Latinitatis*. In *Compendium Redactum*, ed. Migne. (Paris, 1870). Trentals are not heard of as a practice until the eighth century and their origin is obscure; they may possibly have been inspired by Gregory the Great who said (*Dialogues*, IV, 55) that he once ordered a priest to offer up sacrifice for thirty days consecutively for the soul of a monk who had broken his rule.

synned and am worthye of eternall dampnation. But what sayth God by his Prophete: *Dominus* (sayth he) *transluit peccatum tuum non morieris*, the Lorde hath taken awaye they synnes, thou shalt not dye.

*

Jesus Christ gaue hys life for our euylles and by his death delyuered us, Oh then, in that he lyveth now and cannot dye, wille he foresake us? His hearte blood was not too deere for us when we asked it not: what can be nowe to dere for us askyng it? Is he a changling? is he mutable as man is? can he repent hym of his gyfts? Did he not foresee our falls? Payde not he therefore the pryce? Becaue he sawe we shulde fall sore, therefore would he suffer sore. Yea, if his sufferings hadde not been enough, he would yet once more come agyne. God the Father, I am sure, yf the death of hys Sonne incarnate wold not serue, woulde himselfe and the holy Ghost also become incarnate, and dy for us. This death of Christ therefore loke on as the very pledge of Gods love towards the, whosoeuer thou art, how deep soever thou hast sinned. See, Gods hands are nayled, they cannot strike thee; his feete also, he cannot run from thee: his armes are wide open to embrace the, his heade hanges down to kyse the, his very harte is open so that therein see, toote,[1] looke, spie, pepe and thou shalt se nothyng therein but loue, loue, loue, loue to the: hide thee therefore, lay thy head there with the Evangeliste.

*

Therefore dearely beloued I beseche you to consider this geare and deceaue not your selues. Yf you be not Christes, then pertain you to the deuyl, of which things the fruites of the fleshe doeth assure you, as whoredom, adultry, uncleanes, wantonnes, ydolatri, witchcraft, enuie, strife, contention, wrathe, sedicion, murthers, dronkenes, glottonie, blasphemy, slouthfulnes, ydlenes baudy talking, sclaunderinge, etc. Yf these apples growe oute of the apple trees of your hearts, surely, surely the deuyl is at Inne[2] with you: you are his byrdes whom, when he hath wel fed you, he wyl broch you and eate you, chaw you, and champ you, world without ende in eternall wo and miserie. But I am otherwyse perswaded of you al: I trust you be al Christes Jesus his people and children, yea bretheren by fayth.

As ye see your sinnes in Gods lawe and tremble, syghe, sorow, & sob for the same, euen so you see his great mercies in his Gospell and free promises, and therefore are glad, merrie, and ioyfull for that you are accepted into Gods fauer, haue your sinnes pardoned & are endued with the good spirit of God even the seal & signe manuel of your election in Christe before the beginning of the world.

1. Peer.   2. Lodging with.

THE BOY BISHOP

The religious issues which had divided the country since the death of Henry VIII and the rapid acceleration of reform sprang, for an informed minority, from differences of doctrine, but, for a larger and broader-based part of the population, the differences were of palpable practice. Those who deemed themselves equipped to argue predestination and the precise status of the Virgin Mary might wrangle and, as we have heard from Edgeworth, so novel and strong was the attraction that addicts neglected their livelihood and beggared themselves to do so. But the majority of people were more concerned for the forms and customs of worship. Catholic England had been a land of frequent festivals and celebrations, with music, processions, mumming, pilgrimages, miracle plays and a host of traditional customs requiring group participation to actualize the themes of their faith. In these celebrations the laity joined as much as the clergy.

To the emergent Puritan mind such practices were blasphemous relics of an idolatrous past which must be trampled on and atoned for, and their appearance could provoke violence. This ascetic drive (which had always existed in the church in one form or another) had been active long before the breach with Rome. In the *Summa Predicantium*[1] the Dominican John Bromyard expresses a pious dread of the coming of Spring; for then, with the soft and balmy air and young bursting leaves and birdsong, the thoughts of men and women turned to the merry greensward, May games and revelry, whither they would go with heads rose-garlanded for feasts and shows. For the preacher, he says, this is a time of gloom. All the good work of the Lenten shrift and the sermon threatens to be undone. There were priests too who preached against the ancient institution of the Miracle play.

'. . . an erthly seruant dar not taken in play and in bourde that that her erthly lord takith in ernest, myche more we shulden not maken our play and bourde of thos myraclis and wekis that God so ernestly wrought to us . . .'.[2]

---

1. Sections *Munditia* and *Chorea*. Quoted by G. R. Owst, *Literature and the Pulpit in Medieval England* (Oxford, 1951 edn.), p. 393.
2. From a volume of Homilies formerly in the church of St. Martin-in-the-Fields. Re-

Both the Dominican and that anonymous puritan priest, writing in the fifteenth century, were a zealous minority. The objects and practices which, in the mid-sixteenth century, the reformers laboured to abolish, the generality of England still cherished as the familiar and comforting furniture of their and their ancestors' lives. Thus, except in certain revolutionary areas, the familiar old patterns of worship and celebration persisted tenaciously against the impatient programme of reform. The accession of Mary gave the religious conservatives a further respite, and so, in the middle of the century, many of the old profane 'pagan' customs were still alive and active. At this time Thomas Becon, Cranmer's chaplain, being an honest man and no martyr, thought it prudent policy to disappear for a spell and went into hiding in the Peak District, where he was shocked to find that 'all the religion of the people consisted in hearing masses and matins'.

Of all the fanciful celebrations which adorned the calendar of the old order, none provided more sport, and ultimately provoked more criticism, than the reign of the Boy Bishop at Childermass.

As December approached, in large abbeys and in cathedrals a little boy was chosen from among the choristers on the merits of good looks or popularity, or perhaps seniority, to be Boy Bishop at the Feast of the Innocents. During the allotted period, which varied from place to place, the boy was attired and treated, and conducted himself as Bishop; and was accorded, in public at least, nothing less than canonical obedience. After going in solemn procession on the eve of Innocents Day, arrayed in the vestments of a bishop and attended by his fellow choristers, dressed as canons and prebends, he conducted a service in the cathedral, the upper seats in the choir being reserved exclusively for him and his party. He pronounced prayers, he dispensed blessings; there is evidence that, at least in some places, he said mass, or part of the mass; and he *preached*. Afterwards, when the juvenile party went on a tour of the 'bishop's' diocese, the real fun began. He might go in procession through the streets, accompanied by singers and dancers collecting gifts from the public. Two independent observations on the practice will illustrate the diversity which was struggling in England to find resolution.

'Wheras heretofore dyvers and many superstitious and chyldish obsercances have been used . . . in many and sundry parts of the realm . . . children being strangelie decked and apparyled to counterfeit priests, bishops and women,

produced in W. L. Hazlitt, *English Drama and the Stage under the Tudors and Stuarts, 1547–1664* (1869).

and so be ledde with songs and daunces from house to house blessing the
people and gathering money, and boys do sing masse and preache in the
pulpit with such unfitting and inconuenient usages. [1]

'What merry work it was here in the days of our holy fathers (and I know not
whether in some places it may not so still) that, upon St. Nicholas, St.
Katherine, St. Clement and Holy Innocents day, children were wont to be
arrayed in chimeras, rochets, surplices, to conterfeit bishops and priests, and
to be led with songs and dances from house to house, blessing the people
who stood grinning in the way to expect that ridiculous benediction, yea,
that boys in the holy sport were wont to sing masses and to climb into the
pulpit and preach (no doubt learnedly and edifyingly) to the simple auditory.'[2]

The institution was of considerable antiquity and its hermeneutic
purpose was to recall to the adult laity Christ's admonition concerning
the sacredness of childish innocence, and the necessity to be born again
and become as little children if they would be saved.

According to early Christian writers,[3] the tradition had its origin in
an episode involving the Bishop Alexander, who one day as he walked
by the sea shore at Alexandria saw children playing at religious ceremonies, and went to them intending to reprove them, until he found
that the proceedings were being perfectly correctly conducted under the
directions of a little boy called Athenasius.

The nearness of the date to the Roman feast of Saturnalia (December
16th–23rd), the slaves' holiday, suggests that its origins were even older.
During this period, Lucian[4] tells us, no public function or public
business was permitted. Nothing was lawful save drinking, playing,
making imaginary kings, mixing servants with masters: a time of
unlimited licence.

In Christian England official merry-making began on Christmas Day
and continued for the three following days, the Feast of St. Stephen,
of St. John the Evangelist, and of the Holy Innocents and Feast of the
Circumcision. Previously the Boy Bishop had been elected on December 6th, the day sacred to St. Nicholas. According to Moreri, in *Le
Dictionnaire Historique* St. Nicholas was Bishop of Myra in the fourth
century. He seems to have been an infant of precocious piety for it is

1. Proclamation, Henry VIII, July 22nd, 1541.
2. Dr. George Hall, *The Triumph of Rome* (1655) p. 26.
3. Rufinus, *Historia Ecclesiastica*, I, 14; Socrates, *Historia Ecclesiastica*, I, 15; Athanasius,
Orations (Bright's edition), Biographical Introduction, pp. 2–3.
4. *Saturnalia* 'TA ΠΡΟΕ ΚΡΟΝΟΝ' ('Conversations with Cronos').

said that he fasted regularly in his cradle. He began to become a subject of veneration after his remains had been brought from Myra in Lycia to Bari in the year 1087[1] and his special association with schoolboys derives from a spectacular miracle attributed to him.[2] The story goes that three brothers, travelling from a distant country to school in Athens, stopped *en route*, on their father's instruction, at Smyrna, to obtain the bishop's blessing. Unfortunately they chose for their residence the establishment of a villainous innkeeper who murdered them, dismembered their bodies and marinated the several parts in a tub of brine, intending to pass them off for sale as pickled pork. But the bishop saw the entire transaction in vision, hastened to the place and charged the innkeeper with the crime. The innkeeper, overcome by the shock of discovery, confessed all. St. Nicholas then did whatever a saint does when he performs a miracle, and the boys leapt out of the tub whole and alive and embraced their benefactor thankfully. It is not related whether the innkeeper was punished or compensated, or simply left hoping for better luck next time.

By the thirteenth century the cult was established in most of Christian Europe. In England, as elsewhere, the character and tone of the event varied widely according to the tastes and interests of the prelate within whose authority the festival was organized, and of the prebend in charge of the choristers' education and discipline. In some places the

1. Hone, *Ancient Mysteries* (1823), p. 193.
2. St. Nicholas was also the patron saint of town clerks and of spinsters. In *Contes Populaires* (Rouen 1834), p. 129, Plaquet recalls the lines which French girls used to recite:

> Patron des Filles, St. Nicholas
> Mariez nous, ne tardez pas.

His particular patronage of unmarried maidens began with another act of benevolent intervention by which he is said to have saved two virtuous girls from a career of prostitution, and which inspired the tradition of giving children (and later, by extension, adults) presents in the name of St. Nicholas at Christmas. Two girls whose father was too poor to provide them with a dowry were about to adopt a life of prostitution, when St. Nicholas came to their aid with a purse of gold sufficient to marry them both respectably. But mindful of the admonition of St. Matthew (6:1-3) 'Take heed that you do not your righteousness before men, to be seen of them . . .' and ' . . . when thou doest alms, let not they left hand know what thy right hand doeth . . .', St. Nicholas did not wish his identity as donor to be known. Therefore he came by night and threw the purse through an open window into the father's chamber. In imitation of which parents from at least the thirteenth century used, on Christmas Eve, to leave gifts for their children to find, and when asked whence they came, said St. Nicholas had left them. At a later date the Dutch settlers in America shortened the name Sankt Nikolas to Sankt Klaus, and the rest of America made Santa Claus of it. Cf. Hampson, *Medii Aevi Kalendrum* (1861), i, 66-7.

affair might become a mere frolic of clowning and ribaldry which could, and sometimes did, lead to rowdy disorder and brawls.[1] The boys in procession were protected from interference from louts by threat of anathema, a penalty which could strike terror into conditioned hearts, however brutish; but the evidence suggests that the boys were well, perhaps too well, able to look after themselves. At Salisbury in 1449 the precentor, Nicholas Upton, tried to persuade the chapter to nominate three approved candidates, Thacham, Kynton and Boke-binder, for election; but the chapter refused to interfere with the tradition of free elections. The records of the previous year explain Upton's concern. In 1448 there had been a brawl involving the choir, in which the 'bishop's vicar' had killed a servant of one of the canons. Thereafter the boys were forbidden to carry staves and the vicar ordered to exclude from the proceedings ridiculous representations, shouting, lewd secular songs and disorderly behaviour.

There were also foundations like York Minster where the festival was maintained with a considerable expenditure of money and planning, and the local magnates took a benevolent pride in the event.

The York *Compatus* for 1396 lists the several disbursements made to meet approved expenses.[2] Personal items for the Boy Bishop himself: a torch, a cap, linen gloves, knives, spurs, the making of a tailored gown to his measure, also an overcoat of lambs' wool, and silk cope and sleeves. The Great Supper on the eve of Innocents Day cost 15s. and the fare included lord's bread, veal and mutton, sausages, ducks, chickens, woodcock and plover, field fare (venison and hare), small birds, wine, mustard, candles, flour, fuel—and 6d. for the cook.

In the solemn service held on Innocents Day the 'Bishop' said a prayer, *Diffusa est gratia labiis tuis*. Then, *Deus qui salutis aeternae*, and *Pax vobis*. After the *Benedicamus Domino* he sang *Cum mansuetudine humilitate vos ad benedictionem* and the chorus answered *Deo Gratias*. Finally he sang Compline and pronounced *Benedicat vos omnipotens Deus pater, et filius, et spiritus sanctus*.

After these onerous obligations to the great assembly were ended, it was time for the Boy Bishop and his escort to set off in cavalcade on a tour of the diocese. It is not clear whether on their travels there was any

1. In France the occasion soon became known as the Feast of Fools, but it survived until 1721.
2. J. G. Nicholas and Edward F. Rimbault, *Boy Bishops*, Camden Miscellany, Vol. VII, (1845).

disciplinary supervision by an accompanying adult, but we know that, after only a few miles, the bishop's hat needed repair.

For the boys the tour was not only a delightful spell of outdoor freedom, lasting a full month (till the beginning of February), but a very profitable exercise; for, at each of the great secular houses or religious foundations where they called, they were received with hospitality and gifts. From the Countess of Northumberland the little prelate received 20s. and a gold ring, at Bridlington a noble from the Prior and 3s. 4d. from the Prior of Watton. After stopping at Beverley for a new girth, which cost 1d., he received 6s. from Sir Stephen de Scrope, and 11s. from the Prior of Drax. From the Abbot of Selby and the Prior of St. Oswald he received a noble apiece. Lady Marmion at Tanfield bestowed a noble, a gold ring and a silk purse, and Lady Darcy, the Lady of Harlsay, gave half a noble.

Thus replenished, they breakfasted on bread and ale and meat and stopped for some sport at Allerton, where there was 'Baiting'.

It was also an occasion for the bishop to dispense largesse to various attendants (perhaps he felt it prudent) and to buy more wine. They received handsome presents from the city dignitaries of York, and altogether, after every expense had been paid, they were provided with liberal pocket money for some time to come.[1]

For the Boy Bishop the most testing moment of the reign was the delivery of the sermon to the great assembly in the Cathedral. Certain of the cleverer boys, who had been recipients of the forced cultivation of a superior education might have acquitted themselves unassisted with a precocious fluency. But, in general, the occasion was considered too important to be left to the fancy of the lad himself, and it was customary for the sermon to be written by one of the cathedral prebends. Of the many sermons devised for Boy Bishops over the centuries only two in English have survived.

The first, which falls within the reign of Henry VII, is jocular, rib-nudging stuff, designed to raise laugh after laugh. The little bishop first intercedes in prayer for the Archbishop of Canterbury and for 'the right reverend father and worshipful Lord my brother the Bishop of London . . .'. He requests the prayers of the congregation for himself that he may never be troubled by Jeremiah's vision of the 'waken rod' from which he has suffered in the past. He wishes that his master, whom

---

1. At the end of this visitation, when all expenses were paid, the Boy Bishop could declare a profit of £2 0s. 6½d., a substantial sum at the end of the fourteenth century.

he sees present, may make away with himself and that all his other teachers may be promoted to be perpetual fellows of the famous college of the King's Bench, and may end their lives in that holy way called Via Tiburtina.[1] He then expatiates conventionally upon the negligence of rulers, spiritual and temporal, the prevalence of sin, the cruelty of schoolmasters, and upon the written law and the law of grace.

This was routine stuff, but with our second and only other example in English,[2] by the sheerest of historical accidents, we strike gold.

The sermon 'pronownsyd' at Gloucester Cathedral by John Stubs 'Querester', the Boy Bishop in 1558, was one of the last, perhaps the last, of its kind to be heard in England. It was the final year of Mary Tudor's reign, and with her passing many old customs also passed away. New brooms became vigorously busy, cleansing the church of idolatry, and the author of the sermon himself fell an early victim, being deprived of the Rectory of Shenington in Gloucester the following year as a papist. His name was Richard Ramsay (B.D. 1539, Wood, *Fasti* i.110) who was admitted Vicar of Wellan in Somersetshire in 1546 and occupied the sixth prebendal stall in Gloucester Cathedral. His duties may have included supervision of the choir. Ramsay accepts the obligation imposed by the traditional hermeneutic purpose of the sermon, which was to recall to the adult laity Christ's monition upon the sacredness of childish innocence, and the necessity to be born again and become as little children if they would be saved. In writing words to be spoken by a child to an adult auditory he avoids the two tempting shoals of frivolity and portentousness. The language is taut and elegant, nicely calculated to sound strange and arresting in the mouth of a little boy, yet never so loaded with learning and sophisticated allusions as to seem ridiculous and unreal. The jokes are not too many and never broad. They are carefully placed to brace and sharpen the attention of the congregation to the essential seriousness of the exhortation which, forming and reforming in successive images, runs through the discourse. Christ preaches rebirth and purity of heart, as of an innocent child: but where are such children to be found? The preacher searches the city of Gloucester in vain, and does not neglect the choir itself. This leads to the domestic pleasantry of the occasion, when he singles out

1. Be hanged at Tyburn.
2. A Latin sermon by Erasmus, *Concio de Puero Jesu*, written for a Boy Bishop of St. Paul's School, may be found in the folio edition of his works, published in Rotterdam in 1704.

among his companions a cherubic little figure in the choir whose character and record must have been known to everyone present, who 'looks as though butter would not melt in his mouth', but 'if you know as much as I do . . .'

The general effect is strikingly modern. To make it entirely contemporary in its application, all one need do is reduce the emphasis on the importance of corporal punishment and add a line or two in reprobation of psycho-analysts as accessories of juvenile delinquency.

Of young 'John Stubs' who delivered the sermon nothing more is known, though it may be presumed that he was a handsome boy with a good singing voice. It has been suggested that he was the same John Stubbs who lost his hand for objecting to Queen Elizabeth's projected marriage with the Duke of Anjou. An attractive notion, but the author of the *Gaping Gulf* matriculated at Corpus Christi College, Cambridge, on November 12th, 1555, three years before the occasion of the delivery of this sermon, to which we now return, in Gloucester Cathedral, in 1558.

RICHARD RAMSAY

The Sermon of the Boy Bishop[1]

Pronownsyd by John Stubs, Querester, on Childermass day, at Gloceter, 1558

Quiescite agere perverse, discite bene facere, "Cease to do evill and learn to do well." Who that observes the first part is an innocent, if he cease to do evill; who that observes the 2. part is a just man, if he learne and practise to do well.

The same is expressed by the prophete David in these wordes, *Declina a malo, et fac bonum,* "Shon the evill, and do the good." The shonning of evill belonges to the innocent; the doing of good belonges to the just man. The first is expressyd agayne by the vertuose man Tobie, saying to his son, *Quod oderis tibi fieri hoc alteri unquam ne feceris,* "What thing thow wold not have

1. Cotton MS. Vespasian A XXV 173-9. Camden Miscellany, Vol. VII (1845).

done to thy selfe that thyng never do unto other." Mark this part for the innocent. The other part is expressyd by our Saviour hymselfe, Luc. 6. saying, *Prout vultis ut faciant vobis homines et vos facite illis similiter*, "Evyn as yow desire that other should do to yow, do yow the same good unto them." Lykewise marke this part for the rightuose man.

Now compare yow the ij. partes togyder, and se how far or how nere yow are to the kyngdom of heavyn. If yow have both these partes of right-uosness yow are very nere to the kyngdom, and the kyngdom is nere unto yow. Yf yow have but the first part only, which standeth by innocency, then are yow halfe the way to the kyngdom. Yf yow have nother the one part nor the other, and hold yow ther, then are yow from the kyngdom so farr as thei that shall never cum ther: therfor loke well unto it; and remembre the wordes of our Saviour, that except yow wilbe convertyd and chaungyd, and becum lyke unto litill childer, yow shall not entre into the kyngdom of heavyn. And this I have said as touching the first part for yow that be the elders.

Now for yow childer, both boys and wenches, that beare the name of childer, I gather this lesson of the wordes of our Saviour, that it is for yow most necessary to kepe the innocency of your childhod, and other vertues proper unto that tendre age, and not to learn the vices and evill qualities of your elders, leste yow lose the kyngdom which is appoynted unto yow by name. And tyme it is to call upon yow this to do; for not only I, but the world, do se in yow that yow and the very litill ones that follow yow do grow nowadayes so fast owt of this innocent state that it is wonder to me to se amonge yow so many childer in years, and so few innocentes in maners. I am not very old my selfe to speake by experience; but I have hard say of my elders that a child was wont to continew an innocent untill he was 7. years old, and untill 14. years he was provyd to be of such vertue and honest nurture that he deservyd the love and prayse of all people; and now we shall not fynd such a one at 7. as was then at 14, nor at 5. as was then at 7, nor scant at 3. as was then at 9. or x. years old: this is great odes, but is this a good hearyng? Tell me, yow boys, yow childer, yow litill ones, are yow not ashamyd of your partes that yow are so sone corruptyd? so sone ripe, and so sone rottyn? so late innocentes, and so sone lewd lads? deservyng nother love nor prayse of any honest person. What yow are I kan not tell; but, a my honestie, I am both ashamyd of it and sory for it, that yow should so slandre the name of childer, and deceive your elders, which have an eye unto yow to note and folow your maners, as thei are advertysed by the wordes of Christ.

Good people, yow know your charge by the wordes of Christ how that yow must of necessitie be convertyd if yow will enjoy the kyngdom of heavyn, and how yow are sent to these childer to take example of your conversion to the better; and I have partly exhortyd yow here unto; and now the childer that should be for your example are so evill maneryd for the most part, and so vitiosly corruptyd in ther maners, that I will not wish yow to folow them, except it be upon great choyse and great discrecion; and yet some I must appoynt unto yow for example.

But wher shall I fynd them? In the citie? I dare not warrant yow to folowe the childer of the citie, no not the yongest of all, if thei be ones owt of ther mothers' handes and kan run abowt the streates and speake all thinges perfittly; for thei have be scolyd at home that of them as yong as thei are yow may learne as evill properties as yow have all redy of your own; yea and perhapps the same which the child learnyd of yow before, as to swere with a grace, as som termes the othes that cum from the hart, with a stomake to curse bitterly, to blaspheme, to lye, to moke ther elders, to nykname ther aequalls, to knowledge no dutie to ther betters, and such other many mo. Thei go to scole in the open streates one with an other. I will not wysh yow to folow such.

Which then? The childer that go to scole in the grammer scoles under a master? A man wold think yea, because thei are scoles set up purposly for the good educacion of childer, as well in good nurture as in good learning; but yet I dare not warant yow to folow the childer of the grammer scoles, for, how so ever it happ, nurturyd thei are as evill or rather worse then the other. Yf yow will have a profe herof, mark ther maners in the temple, and at the table; mark ther talkes and behavior by the wayes at such tymes and houres as thei leave scole and go home to ther meales, specially on holydays and campos dayes,[1] when thei are sett a litill at libertie. I will say no more; but mark them, for I have lost my mark except yow find the most of them most ongracious grafftes, ripe and redy in all lewd libertie. I will not wish yow to folow such.

Which then? The queresters and childer of the song-scole? Beware what yow do: for I have experience of them more then of the other. Yt is not so long sens I was one of them myself but I kan remember what shrewness was used among them, which I will not speake of now,[2] but I kan not let this passe ontouched how boyyshly thei behave themselves in the church, how rashly thei cum into the quere without any reverence: never knele nor cowntenaunce to say any prayer or Pater noster, but rudely squat down on ther tayles,[3] and justle wyth ther felows for a place; a non thei startes me owt of the quere

1. Campus day: a day of outdoor recreation and field sports.
2. An afterthought. He had already 'spoken' more and crossed it out. The erased passage reads 'what fyghting, lying, mooching and forging of false excuses was among them that, where thei are brought specially to serve God in the Church, they do nothing lesse in the church than serve God.
3. 'which lak twyngging', erased.

agayne, and in agayne and out agayne, and thus one after an other, I kan not tell how oft nor wherfor, but only to gadd and gas abrode, and so cum in agayne and crosse the quere fro one side to another and never rest, withowt any order, and never serve God nor our Lady with mattyns or with evynsong, no more then thei of the grammer scoles; whose behaviour is in the temple as it were in ther scole ther master beyng absent, and not in the church God being present. I will not wysh you to folow such.

Which then? Here is a company afore me of childer, semely in sight, most like unto innocentes, specially one litill one in the mydes, which puts me in mynd of the child which Jesus callyd unto hym and set in the myd of his disciples when they were at bate who should be chefe among them; the child had prayse of Jesus's own mouth for his meke behaviour and nurture, so much that Jesus said of him, *Quique se humiliavit sicut parvulus, iste intrabit in regnum celorum*, "Who so that meke and humble hym selfe as this child doth here before yow, he shall entre into the kyngdom of heaven." Such a one this litill one in the mydes here appereth to be that he myght be thought worthy to be sett in the mydes for an example unto yow of pure childhode, mekness, and innocency. Loke in his face and yow wold think that butter wold not melt in his mouth; but, as smothe as he lokes, I will not wysh yow to folow hym if yow know as much as I do. Well, well! all is not gold that shynes, nor all are not innocentes that beare the face of childer.

Now I se non other choyse but that I must leave the boys and the childer that are ripe in witt and speche, and must poynt yow to the litill ones which yet run on ther mother's hand, onable of them selfes to run strongly abrode, as yet onrype in witt and onperfitt in speche: sett your eye upon such and observe in them the true vertues of a child for your example, for such I dare warant yow. As for the residue, I dare not warant yow, except it be one among a C., whom yow must chewse with great observacion and discrecion.

Here is a great lake and small choyse among so many childer: and where is the falte? wher is the great falte? Evyn in yow that are ther parents, ther fathers, mothers, and ther scolemasters.

Where is the great falte? Evyn in the parentes, fathers, mothers and scolemasters, which do nother teach ther childer good, nother yet chastice them when thei do evill; when thei lye and swere as I have hard some do, Good Lord, how abominably! and curse with plages and pestilence and murrens upon ther felows, brothers, and sisters, evyn ther parentes standyng by and hearing them; and yet not a word of correction, notwithstandyng thei have a great care and charge upon their childer as thei know ther folies, and shall gyve a straight accompte for them unto allmyghtie God. And what is the matter? a folysh affection and a fond opinion in the parentes, which very fondly seke the love of ther child that knoweth not what love or dutye meaneth, and that he may say "I am father's boy" or "I am mother's boy," and "I love father (or mother) best;" to wyn this word, and the love of the child, the parentes contend who shall make most of the child, and by these means no partye dare displease hym, say he or do he never so ongraciously, but both parties dandill hym and didill hym and pamper hym and stroke his hedd and sett hym a hye bence, and gyve hym the swetyst soppe in the dish evyn when he lest deserve it: this marrs the child, it makes hym to thynke he does well when he do stark nought.

There are very fond fathers in this poynt, and many mo fond mothers. Dyd you never here, yow fond mothers, what the wise Salomon saith, *Qui parcitur virgae odit filium,* "Thei that spare the rodd do hate the child:" and yet yow that never use the rod wyll say that yow do it for love toward your child. The wyse man sayth such love is hatered; therfor it must nede be a fond love that you beare toward your childer in this poynt, specially in such mothers as when ther childer do a falt, and never so many faltes, which will not ones touch the child, but take the rod and beate the quyssion or the forme and after borne the rodd and say thei spare not the rodd. O fond, fond mothers! what falt have the quyssion don to be bettyn? what falt have the rodd don to be brent? Your child have done the falt, why do not he smart of the rodd? Why do you spare the child? What hurt kan the rodd do to your child? Ys it not an old and a tru saying, *The rodd breakes no bones?* But you have such a fond tendrenes that yow kan not fynd in your hart to beat your tendrelyng, for if he should wepe yow must wepe to for company. Well, I wyll take upon me now to be a prophete in this matter, that such mothers shall wepe here after to see the ontowardness of such childer, when the childer will not wepe with the mothers for company as yow mothers do now with them.

The fathers are as fond agayne on the other part: "Nay, (say thei,) yf I should beate my child, and kepe hym undre and in awe now, I should kill his corage in his youth, and take away his hart that he shall never be bold when he is a man." Mary! that is the very thyng that is meanyd in all good edu-cacion, to discorage youth utterly as touching vice and vicious maners, and to bolden and corage them in all probitye and vertue, and vertuose maners. To lake a stomake and boldness in vice is no lake nor disprayse, but prayse and profitt withall; but, yf your desire be to have them stowt in evill demaner, yow shal be the first that shall have experience of that stowtness; for, after a litill time, thei wil be so styfe and stubborn against yow that yow shall not be able to rule them yf yow wold, and, in conclusion, they will contempne yow, and sett yow at nought above all other persons. This is the retorne of such fond tendreness; as experience teacheth by the example of thowsands which have ben brought up so choysely, tendrely, and dangerosly. Well, to be breffe, if yow will know the resolucion of this opinion for stowtness, and for [the end] of such corrupt educacion, rede yow the boke of the son of

Syrac, cap. 30. Ther you shall find the matter playn ynowgh agaynst yow, and I wold now recyte it unto yow if it were not to long for this short tyme.

Now, farewell yow fathers and mothers: yow have your lesson. I must have a word or ij. with the scolemaisters, which, at some of your handes, take your childer in cure to teach and nurture them, as well in vertue as in prophane learnyng.

Therfor I say now to yow scolemasters, that have the youth under your handes to make or marr, marr them not by your neglygence, but make them to God ward with your diligence. Remembre that Allmyghtie God regardeth the litill ones, and wold not have them to be led from hym by yow, but by yow to be brought unto hym; and this he will require at your handes, as well as at the parentes, for your scole is your cure, and yow shall give accomptes for every scoler in your scole for the tyme beyng; and yow owght to regard them all as your childer, and your selfes as their fathers, for Quintilian, the flower of scolemasters, termeth you to be *tertios parentes*, the thred parentes to the child which yow have under your cure for good educacion; for, as the carnall parentes by caranalitye do fascion the body, so the scolemaster do or owght to fascion the soule of the child by good educacion in learnyng of good nurture and vertue; and therefore the scholemaster that so doth is cowntyd to be the 3. parent to the child, yea, and the most worthiest parent of the 3, in as much as the good fascionyng of the soule by nurture and vertue is better then the best fascionyng of the body by nature; and so the scolar will regard his scolemaster for ever if he have at his handes such educacion that he fele hym selfe the better, otherwise he will contempne hym of all men, evyn as the child brought up in stoutness will most contempne the father and mother. Yow scolemasters have a good order in your scoles for breaking Priscian's head[1] or syngyng out of tune. I wold yow wold take the same order for breakyng of God's comandementes and ontunynge of Godes harpe, which soundeth in all his wordes. Yf a scoler of the song scole syng out of tune, he is well wrong by the ears or else well beatyn. Yf a scoler in the gramer scole speak false Lattyn or Englysh forbyddyn, he is takyn withall of one or the other and warnyd custos to be beatyn. I wysh that yow wold take the like order for the evill behaviour of your scolers, that, if any be takyn with a word of blasphemy, with a word of ribaudry, with a manifest lye, and such talke or dedes as are contrary to the laws of God and the holye Churche, let them be first warnyd custos, or wrong by the ears for it, and after be correctyd as the custos is usyd. Other good orders devise of

---

1. 'breaking Priscian's head', to construe faultily. Priscian (Priscianus) surnamed Caesarienis, the grammarian, flourished in the first half of the sixth century. His treatises, especially his eighteen-volume *Commentariorum Grammaticorum*, were in universal use as text books in the Middle Ages.

your selves for the good purpose, as yow wyll avoyd the reproche of synfull negligence both before God and man.

Perhaps some will think hert in ther myndes that I am very bold to fynd so many faltes with so many parties—fathers, mothers, scolemasters, childer, scolers, and no scollers; and take upon me to reforme my elders, I beyng so yong in age as I am, and to reprove other wherin I am not all clere my selfe, as some will judge that knew me in my childhode. Well! if we all amend we shalbe never the worse; and I confesse to them that I was sumtyme, as yet the most of them are, shrewd ynough for one; but I paid well for it, and have now left it, and I may now alledge for my self the wordes of S. Pawl, *Cum essem parvulus, sapiebam ut parvulus, cogitabam ut parvulns, loquebar et parvulus: nunc autem factus sum vir evacuavi ea quoe erant parvuli:* 'When I was a chyldysh boy, my discrecion was therafter, my wordes and dedes were therafter, the fansys and desires of my hart were therafter; but, now that I have cum to be a man, I have cast of all boy's touches," that is to say, all shrowdness of childhood, as I wold all yow had don, retayning the puritie of your childhood, that it may [endure] with yow togyther with age and years, and no doubt that will cause you to grow unto honestie and worshippe (as you see in me this day), and also bring yow to the honor and felicitie of the kingdom, which is promised to pure and innocent childer; and, so being, I wold wysh yow to have many folowars, yea, all this holl audience present, that, as thei folow yow in your puritie and innocency, so thei may entre with yow into the kyngdom of everlastyng glorye throwghe the intercession of the holy and blessyd Innocentes, who are the occasion of this my simple collacion this day, and through the merittes of our Saviour Jesus Christ, unto whom, with the Father and the Holy Gost, be all prayse honor, and glory, for ever and ever! Amen.

Deo Gratias

HOMILIES

It has been a problem to decide where to place the following passages from the collection 'Certayne Sermons ...', assembled under the general editorship of Cranmer and first published in 1547, because new editions continued to appear at short intervals for the next ninety-five years and belong as much to the Elizabethan[1] and Jacobean church as they do the early Edwardian.

I have therefore, in their case, varied a generally consistent chronological order and placed them at the beginning of Elizabeth's reign, when they were much needed and much used. The disturbing break in continuity and the sharp fluctuations in ecclesiastical policy, which ensued after the breach with Rome, discouraged able university graduates from taking holy orders, and there was a serious shortage of competent and reliably orthodox preachers in a clergy whose ranks included near illiterates and infants. To supply a basic ration of approved instruction, Cranmer commissioned a team of divines to produce a set of sermons suitable for general use by clergy with pastoral responsibilities. To serve this purpose the Homilies are, in design, carefully simple, and in intent, unequivocally didactic, and they cover the principal subjects upon which a parish priest was expected to address his flock, at suitable intervals, in instruction or remonstrance. It has already been noted that the larger, though insufficiently organized, part of the population was Catholic in sympathy and resented the 'reforms' which were being forced into the churches on the initiative of the new establishment. The latest Catholic revolt—in the west this time—had given the government a fright, and one of the sermons was designed to reassure the wavering and uneasy, and rally them to the Protestant cause. '. . . *God's vengeance hath been and is daily provoked, because much*

1. *Certain Sermons appointed by the Queen's Majesty to be Declared and Read by all parsons ... every Sunday and holyday in their Churches for the better understanding of the simple people* (1582).

NB. The following version, which is predominantly an Elizabethan text, has benefited wherever the meaning seemed to need clarifying by my being able to refer to the syntheses of previous texts, one edited by G. E. Corrie (Cambridge, 1850), and the other by John Griffiths (Oxford, 1859).

wicked people pass nothing to resort to the church, either for that they are so blinded, that they understand nothing of God and godliness, and care not with what devilish example to offend their neighbours; or else for that they see the church altogether scoured of such gay gazing sights, as their gross fantasy was greatly delighted with: because they see the false religion abandoned, and the true restored, which seemeth an unsavoury thing to their unsavoury taste; as may appear by this, that a woman said to her neighbour, "Alas, gossip, what shall we now do at church, since all the saints are taken away, since all the goodly sights we were wont to have are gone, since we cannot hear the like piping, singing, chanting, and playing upon the organs, that we could before." [1]

Another sermon was aimed to cushion the shock felt by some on being confronted for the first time with the Bible in the vernacular. Much has been written, especially by evangelical exegetists, on the marvellous joy and enlightenment which free access to holy scripture in English brought to the people. This was true in the case of the converted, who had been inducted gradually within a reformist family or work-group, to a diet of biblical text, but it was by no means the whole picture. Other people, sufficient in number to pose a problem, were appalled or disgusted or worse, moved to hilarity, by the naked text of the Old Testament, and the record therein of what seemed to them scandalous and disreputable acts, perpetrated by men whose names they had been brought up, in their innocence, to revere. To restore such to reverence for the scripture and allay their misgivings, a hopeful corrective was produced entitled *An Information For Them which take offence at certain places in the holy scripture*. It is a revealing document.

'*The great utility and profit that Christian men and women may take if they will be hearing and reading the holy scripture, dearly beloved, no heart can sufficiently conceive much less is my tongue able to express. Wherefor Satan, our old enemy . . . doth what he can to drive the reading of them out of God's church. And for that end he hath always stirred up, in one place or another, extreme enemies unto God and his infallible truth to pull with violence the book out of the people's hand . . . pretending most untruly that the much hearing and reading of God's word is an occasion of heresy and carnal liberty.*'

The author tackles early in the sermon a divine promise which evidently had been the occasion of infectious mirth. *I will break the horns of the ungodly, and I will make David's horn to flourish.*

---

1. Op. cit. 'The second part of the Homilie of the place and time of prayer'.

The author goes on, more warily than comfortably, to engage the subject of 'Moab's Washpot', which had been found to provoke ribald comment, and after that, no more happily, to try to show why the startling abundance of the holy prophets' sexual activities was not illicit. In ancient times, he explains, the word *concubine* did not bear the opprobrious connotations which it does in our modern sixteenth century. In these far off, holy times, the word concubine meant . . . *concubine*.

Of Washpots and Concubines[1]

In the 132. Psalme, it is sayde, I will make Dauids horne to florishe. Here Dauids horne signifieth his kingdome. Almightie God therefore by this manner of speaking, promiseth to giue Dauid victorie ouer all his enimies, and to stablishe him in his kindgome, spite of all his enimies. And in the threescore Psalme it is writen: *Moab* is my washpotte, and ouer *Edom* will I cast my shoe, &c. In that place the Prophete sheweth howe gratiously God hath dealt with his people the children of Israel, giuing them great victories vpon their enimies on euery side. For the *Moabites* and *Idumeans*, beeing two great nations, proude people, stout and mightie, God brought them vnder, and made them seruantes to the Israelites, seruantes I say, to stoupe downe, to pull of their shoes, and washe their feete. Then *Moab* is my washpot, and ouer *Edom* will I caste out my shoe, is, as if he had sayde, The *Moabites* and the *Idumeans*, for all their stoutnesse against vs in the wildernesse, are now made our subiectes, our seruantes, yea underlinges to pull of our shoes, and washe our feete. Nowe I pray you, what vncomely manner of speach is this, so vsed in common phrase among the Hebrues? It is a shame that Christian men should be so light headed, to toy as ruffians doe of such manner speaches, vttered in good graue signification by the holy ghost. More reasonable it were for vaine men to learne to reuerence the sourine of Gods wordes then to gaud at them to their damnation. Some again are offended to heare that the godly fathers had many wiues and concubines, although after the phrase of the scripture, a concubine is an honest name, for euery concubine is a lawfull wife, but euery wife is not a concubine. And that ye may the better vnderstande this to be true, ye shall note that it was permitted to the

1. Op. cit.: 'The First Part of the Information of Certain Places of Scripture', Sig. N1ᵛ, N2ʳ.

fathers of the olde Testament, to haue at one time moe wiues then one, for what purpose ye shall afterwarde heare. Of which wiues some were free women borne, some were bonde women and seruantes. Shee that was free borne, had a prerogatiue aboue those that were seruantes and bond women. The free borne woman was by mariage made the ruler of the house vnder her husbande, and is called the mother of the housholde, the maistres or the dame of the house, after our manner of speaking, and had by her mariage an interest, a right, and an ownership of his goods vnto whom she was maried. Other seruantes and bonde women were giuen by the owners of them, as the maner was then, I will not say alwayes, but for the most parte, vnto their daughters at that day of their mariage, to be handmaydens vnto them. After such a sorte did Pharao king of Egypt giue vnto *Sara* Abrahams wife, *Agar* the Egyptian to be her mayde. So did *Laban* giue vnto his daughter *Lea*, at the day of her mariage, *Zilpha*, to be her handmayde. And to his other daughter *Rachel*, he gaue another bondmayde, named *Bilha*. And the wiues that were the owners of their handmaydes, gaue them in mariage to their husbandes, vpon diuers occasions. *Sara* gaue her mayde *Agar* in mariage to Abraham. *Lea* gaue in like manner her mayde *Zilpha* to her husbande Jacob. So did *Rachel* his other wife giue him *Bilha* her mayde, saying vnto him, Goe in vnto her, and shee shall beare vpon my knees: which is, as if she had sayde, Take her to wife, and the children that she shall beare, will I take vpon my lappe, and make of them as if they were mine owne. These handmaydens or bondwomen, although by mariage they were made wiues, yet they had not this prerogatiue to rule in the house, but were still vnderlinges, and in subiection to their maisters, and were neuer called mothers of the housholde, maistresses, or dames of the house, but are called sometimes wiues, sometime concubines. The pluralitie of wiues, was by a speciall prerogatiue suffered to the fathers of the olde Testament, not for satisfying their carnall and fleshly lustes, but to haue many children, because euery one of them hoped, and begged oft times of God in their prayers, that that blessed seede, which God promised should come into the worlde to breake the Serpents head, might come and be borne of his stocke and kinred.

Nowe of those which take occasion of carnalitie and euill life, by hearing and reading in Gods booke, what God had suffered, euen in those men whose commendations praysed in the scripture: As that Noe, whome Saint Peter calleth the eight(h) preacher of righteousnesse, was so drunke with wine, that in his sleepe he vncouered his owne priuities. The just man Lot was in like manner drunken, and in his drunkennes lay with his owne daughters, contrary to the law of nature. . . .

Lechery and *Carnal Delectation:* these were never far from the surface of the preacher's mind and seldom far from his tongue; and luridly foul apparitions they are made in the manifold pictures painted by his zeal. Despite the lawfulness, in principle, of enjoying carnal exercise within wedlock, sexual appetite was, in practice, invariably presented by the moral prelectors as an infective and corrupting monster which, when secured within the sanitary bounds of wedlock, was better starved into abject impotence.

Since the foundation of the church, censorious asceticism has provoked a casualty so ubiquitously recurrent, that scholars seem to have reached a tacit agreement to treat its causes, in distinction from its effects, as an imponderable mystery beyond the competence of human enquiry. An investigation in depth of the nature and origins of the obsession with and revulsion from the vitality of the flesh, which has characterized our cultural antecedents, has yet to be undertaken. At the stage in time of the second half of the sixteenth century which here concerns us, we find horrendous denunciations and remonstrances still being handed down, from generation to generation, virtually unchanged and unchallenged since they were launched upon the world, by penitentiary ascetics, as different otherwise from each other as Origen and Tertullian.

Within the frame of a small authoritarian society this repressive drive was in perpetual conflict with the alternating adversaries of rowdy brute bawdiness and the erotic disguises and bleeding-heart romanticism of courtly love. The resultant chafe of friction and frustration might produce sudden, unpremeditated acts of rage and violence; or it might nurse patiently the consolations of old, secretly planned stratagems of envy or revenge. *Deception, Injury, Revenge:* these made a popular syndrome in folklore as well as in the more sophisticated literature of Bocaccio and Ariosto, the favourite themes of ballads, broadsheets and chap-books which the Elizabethan dramatists assumed as a legacy and raised to a new sombre grandeur of their own.

The preacher divided responsibility for carnal sin and its consequential evils, unequally between the sexes.

'In the woman wantonly adorned to capture souls, the garland upon her head is a single coal or firebrand of hell to kindle men with that fire; so too the horns of another, so the bare neck, so the brooch upon the breast, so with all the curious finery of the whole of their body. What else could it seem or could be said of it save that each is a spark breathing out hell fire, which this wretched incendiary of the Devill breathes so effectually . . . that, in a single day, by her dancing or her perambulation through the town, she inflames with the fire of lust it may be, twenty of those who behold her, damning the souls whom God has created and redeemed at such cost for their salvation.'[1]

Meanwhile, men, knights and courtiers, in insolent mockery of the preacher, disport themselves in the streets, in the church itself as he preaches (for the church was the favourite recruiting ground for the amorous) in fashions of blatant incitant indecency; for 'they wear garments so short that they scarcely hide their private parts', and worse, are shaped to reveal and exaggerate and thrust out conspicuously the male member with intent to provoke lasciviousness in the beholder.[2]

There is nothing unusual in the correlation of sexual and sartorial offences. The two were deemed mutually encouraging and as we see from the approaching Tudor Homilies on *Whoredom and Uncleanness*, *Excess of Apparel*, and *Contention*, despite the passage of more than a century and the process of an alleged reformation, the substance of the discourse is not significantly changed from that which the Dominican Bromyard and Master Rypon[3] of Durham, among others, were delivering in the previous century.

Of Whoredom and Uncleanness[4]

Although there want not (good Christian people, great swarms of vices worthy to be rebuked (unto suche decay true godlinesse and virtuous living bow come) yet above other vices the outragious seas of adulterie (or breaking of wedlock) whoredome, fornification and vncleannesse, haue not onely brast

1. John Bromyard, *Predicantium*. Quoted in Owst, op. cit., Chap. VII, 'The Preaching of Satire and Complaint', p. 395.
2. Robert Rypon, Sermon, Harl. MS. 4894. Quoted in Owst, op. cit., p. 404.
3. The cod piece, reviled by Master Rypon, would persist in a variety of forms for the next three hundred years, and attract no less varied kinds of attention. 'His cod piece seems as massy as his club . . .', *Much Ado about Nothing*, III, iii; in 1659, in a satire on the gallant of the day, it is lamented that there remains nothing left for him to do with his cod piece except to leave it open.
4. Op. cit., I sig., G2ᵛ, G5ʳ, G5ᵛ, G8ʳ.

in, but also ouerflowed almost the whole worlde, vnto the great dishonour
of God, the exceeding infamie of the name of Christe, the notable decay of
true religion, and the vtter destruction of the publike wealth, and that so
abundantly, that through the customable vse thereof, this vice is growen into
such an height, that in a maner among many, it is counted no sinne at all,
but rather a pastime, a dalliaunce, and but a touche of youth: not rebuked, but
winked at: not punished, but laughed at. Wherefore it is necessarie at this
present, to intreate of the sinne of whoredome and fornication, declaring
vnto you the greatnesse of this sinne, and howe odious, hatefull, and abominable it is, and hath alway been reputed before God and all good men, and
how grieuously it hath beene punished both by the lawe of God, and the
lawes of diuers princes. Againe, to shew you certaine remedies, whereby ye
may (through the grace of God) eschew this most detestable sinne of whoredome and fornication, and leade your liues in all honestie and cleannesse,
and that ye may perceiue that fornication and whoredome are (in the sight
of God) most abhominable sinnes, ye shall call to remembrance this commandement of god, Thou shalt not commit adulterie: by the which word
adulterie, although it be properly vnderstande of the vnlawfull commixtion
or ioining together of a married man with any woman beside his wife, or of a
wife with any man beside her husband: yet thereby is signified also all vnlawfull vse of those partes, which be ordeined for generation. And this one
commandement (forbidding adulterie) doth sufficiently paint and set out
before our eies, the greatnesse of this sinne of whoredome, and manifestly
declareth howe greatly it ought to bee abhorred of all honest and faythfull
persons. And that none of vs shall thinke himselfe excepted from this commandement, whether we bee olde or young, married, or vnmarried, man or
woman, heare what God the Father saith by his most excellent Prophet
Moses, There shal bee no whore among the daughters of Israel, nor no
whoremonger among the sonnes of Israel.

*

And surely if we would weigh the greatnes of this sinne, and consider it in
the right kinde, we shoulde finde the sinne of whoredome, to be that most
filthy lake, foule puddle, and stinking sinke, whereunto al kinds of sinnes and
euils flowe, where also they haue thir resting place and abiding.

For hath not the adulterer a pride in his whoredome? As the wise man
saith, They are glad when they haue done euill, and reioice in thinges that
are starke nought. Is not the adulterer also idle, and delighteth in no godly
exercise, but only in that his most filthy and beastly pleasure? Is not his minde
plukt, and vtterly drawen a way from all vertuous studies, and fruitefull
labours, and onely giuen to carnall and fleshly imagination? Doeth not the
whoremonger giue his mind to gluttonie, that he may be the more apte to

serue his lustes & carnal pleasures? Doeth not the adulterer giue his minde to
couetousnesse, and to polling and pilling[1] of other, that he may be the more
able to mainteine his harlots and whores, and to continue in his filthy and
vnlawefull loue? Swelleth he not also with enuie against other, fearing that
his pray should be allured and taken away from him Againe, is he not
yrefull, and replenished with wrath and displeasure, euen against his best
beloued, if at any time his beastly and deuilishe request be letted? What
sinne, or kinde of sinne is it that is not ioined with fornication and whoredome? It is a monster of many heads: it receiueth all kindes of vices, and
refuseth all kindes of vertues. If one seuerall sinne bringeth damnation, what
is to bee thought of that sinne, which is accompanied with all euills, and
hath waiting on it whatsoeuer is hatefull to God, damnable to man, and
pleasant to Satan?

Great is the damnation that hangeth ouer the heades of fornicatours and
adulterers. What shall I speake of other incommodities, which issue and
flowe out of this stinking puddle of whoredome. Is not that treasure, which
before al other is most regarded of honest persons the good fame and name
of man & woman, lost through whordome? What patrimonie or liuelode,
what substance, what goodes, what riches doth whoredome shortly consume
and bring to nought? What valiauntnes and strength is many times made
weake, and destroyed with whoredome? What wit is so fine, that is not
doted and defaced thorow whoredome? What beautie (although it were
neuer so excellent), is not disfigured through whoredome? Is not whoredome
an enimie to the pleasant floure of youth, and bringeth it not gray heares
and olde age before the time? What gift of nature (although it were neuer so
precious) is not corrupted with whoredome? Come not the french
pocks, with other diuers diseases, of whoredome? From whence come so
many bastardes and misbegotten children, to the high displeasure of God,
and dishonour of holy wedlocke, but of whoredome? Howe many consume
al their substance and goods, & at the last fall into suche extreme pouerty, that
afterwarde they steale, and so are hanged, through whoredome? What
contention and manslaughter commeth of whoredome? Howe many maidens
be defloured, howe many wiues corrupted, howe many widowes defiled
through whoredome? Howe much is the publique and common weale
impouerished, and troubled through whoredome? Howe much is Gods
worde contemned and depraued through whoredome and whoremongers?
Of this vice commeth a great parte of the deuorses which (now adaies) be so
commonly accustomed & vsed by mens priuate authoritie, to the greate
displeasure of God, & the breache of the most holy knott and bonde of
matrimonie. For when this most detestable sinne is once crept into the
breast of the adulterer, so that he is intangled with vnlawfull and vnchast

1. 'Poll', 'pill': both words mean to plunder.

loue, streightwaies his true and lawfull wife is despised, her presence is abhorred, her company stinketh, and is loathsome, whatsoever she do this dispraised: there is no quietnesse in the house, so long as she is in sight: therefore to make short tale, she must away, for her husbande can brooke her no longer. Thus through whoredome, is the honest and harmelesse wife put away, and an harlot received in her steed: and in like sort, it happeneth many times in the wife towards her husbande. O abhomination.

*

Let us nowe heare certaine lawes, which the ciuill Magistrates deuised in their countries, for the punishment thereof, that we may learne howe uncleannesse hath ever beene detested in al wel ordred citties and common wealthes, and among all honest persons. The lawe among the *Lepreians* was this, that when any were taken in adultery, they were bounde and caried three daies thorow the Citie, and afterwarde as long as they liued, were they despised, and with shame and confusion counted as persons voide of all honestie. Among the *Locrensians* the adulterers have both their eyes thrust out. The *Romans* in times past, punished whoredome, sometime by fire, sometime by sworde. If any man among the *Egyptians* hadde beene taken in adulterie, the lawe was, that he shoulde openly in the presence of all the people bee scourged naked with whippes, vnto the number of a thousande: stripes, the woman that was taken with him hadde her nose cutte off, whereby she was knowne euer after, to be a whore, and therefore to bee abhorred of all men. Among the *Arabians*, they that were taken in adulterie, hadde their heades striken from their bodyes. The *Athenians* punished whoredome by death in like maner. So likewise, did the barbarous *Tartarians*. Among the *Turkes* euen at this day, they that bee taken in adulterie, both man and woman are stoned streight waye to death, without mercie. Thus wee see what godly actes were deuised in times past of the high powers, for the putting awaye of whoredome, and for the mainteining of holye matrimonye, or wedlocke, and pure conuersation. And the authours of these actes were no Christians, but the Heathen: yet were they so inflamed, with the loue of honestie and purenesse of life, that for the mainetenance and conseruation or keeping up of that, they made godly statutes, suffering neither fornication or adulterie to raigne in their Realmes unpunished. . . .

Of Excess of Apparel[1]

... He that is ashamed of base and simple attire, will be proude of gorgious apparell, if hee may get it. We must learne therefore of the Apostle S. Paul both to vse plentie, and also to suffer penurie, remembering that we must yeelde accountes, of those thinges which wee have receyued, vnto him who abhorreth all excesse, pride, ostentation, and vanitie, who also vtterly condemneth and disaloweth what so euer draweth vs from our duetie towardes God, or diminisheth our charity towardes our neighbours & children, whome we ought to loue as ourselues. The fourth and last rule is, that euery man beholde and consider his owne vocation, in as much as God hath appoynted every man his degree and office, within the limittes whereof it behoueth him to keepe him selfe. Therefore all may not looke to weare like apparell, but euery one according to his degree, as God hath placed him. Which, if it were obserued, many one doubtlesse shoulde be compelled to weare a russet coate, which now ruffeleth in silkes and veluettes, spending more by the yeere in sumptuous apparell, then their fathers receiued for the whole reuenue of their landes. But alaw nowe a dayes how many may we beholde

---

1. Op. cit., sig. Ii iv^v–Ii viii^r. Costly 'vanity', especially extravagence of attire, provides the most persistent refrain in the preaching of social satire from the twelfth century till well into the seventeenth. It seemed to the preacher to be the outward and visible sign of worldly sinfulness, and a provocation to a host of other temptations. It was deemed a vice of the greatest antiquity, beginning in effect at the moment when Eve adopted clothing, and in the *Book of the Knight of Latour Landry* we are told that Noah's flood itself was ordained as a punishment for the 'pride and disguysing that was among women'. An impression of the unbroken continuity of attitude may be gained by comparing the homily with a few words of an anonymous thirteenth-century preacher.

'Now also the comyn peple is hie stied into the synne of pride. For now a wrecchid cnave, that goth to the plou and to carte, that hath no more good but serveth from yer to yer for his lifelode, there-as sumtyme a white curtel and a russet gown wolde have served suchon ful wel, now he muste have a fresch doublet of fyve schillynges or more the price; and above, a costli gowne with bagges hangynge to his kne, and irideld [pleated] under his girdil as a new ryven roket [kind of surplice or vest of linen], and a hood on his heved, with a thousand ragges on his tipet; and gaili hosid an schood as thouw it were a squyer of cuntre; a dagger harneised with selver bi his gurdel, or ellis it were not worth a pese.' *Speculum Laicorum* (Add MSS. 41323, fols. 101b-2) quoted by Owst, op. cit., p. 369.

The admonitions of St. Bernard were commonly in use. See *Sermones in Cantica,* xxxiii. 15. 16.

occupied wholly in pampering the fleshe? taking on care at all, but onely howe to decke them selues, setting their affection altogether on worldelye brauerie, abusing Gods goodnesse, when he sendeth plentie, to satisfie their wanton lustes, hauing no regarde to the degree wherin God hath placed them. The Isralites were contented with such apparell as God gaue them, although it were base and simple: And God so blessed them, that their shooes and clothes lasted them fourtie yeres, yea, and those clothes which their fathers had worne, their children were contented to use afterward. But we are neuer contented, and therefore we prosper not, so that most commonly he that ruffleth in his Sables, in his fine furred goune, corked slippers, trime buskinnes, and warme mittons, is more ready to chill for colde, then the poore labouring man, which can abide in the feelde all the day long, when the North winde blowes, with a fewe beggerly cloutes about him. We are loth to weare such as our fathers haue left us, wee thinke not that sufficient of good enough for us. Wee must haue one gowne for the day, another for the night, one long, another shorte, one for Winter, another for Sommer, one through furred, another but faced, one for the working day, another for the holie day, one of this colour, another of that colour, one of Cloth, another of Silke or Damaske. We must haue chaunge of apparell, one afore dinner, another after, one of the Spanishe fashion, another Turkie: and to be briefe, neuer content with sufficient. Our Sauiour Christ bad his disciples they should not haue two coates: but the most men, farre vnlike to his schollers, haue their presses so full of apparell, that many knowe not howe many sortes they haue. Which thing caused Saint James to pronounce this terrible curse against such wealthy worldlinges, Goe to yee riche men, weepe & howle on your wretchednesse that shall come vpon you, your riches are corrupt, and your garmentes are moth eaten, ye haue liued in pleasure on the earth, and in wantonnesse, ye haue nourished your heartes, as in the day of slaughter. Marke I beseech you, saint James calleth them miserable, notwithstanding their richesse and plentie of apparell, forasmuch as they pamper their bodies, to their owne destruction. What was the riche glutton the better for his fine fare and costly apparell? Did not he nourish himselfe to be tormented in hell fire? Let us learne therefore to content our selues, having foode and rayment, as Saint Paul teacheth, least desiring to be enriched with aboundaunce, we fall into temptations, snares, and many noysome lustes, which drowne men in perdition and destruction. Certainely, such as delight in gorgious apparell, are commonlie puffed vp with pride, and filled with diuers vanities. So were the daughters of Sion and people of Jerusalem, whom Esai the Prophete threatneth, because they walked with streatched out neckes and wandering eyes, mincing as they went, and nicely-treading with their feete, that almightie God would make their heades baulde, and discouer their secret shame. In that day, saith he, shall the Lorde take away the ornamente of the slippers, and the caules, and the rounde attires, and the sweete balles, and the braceletes, and the attires of the heade, and the sloppes, and the head bandes, and the tablettes, and the eareringes, the ringes, and the mufflers, the costly apparell, & the vailes & wimples, and the crisping pinne, and the glasses, and the fine linnen, and the hoodes, and the lawnes. So that almightie God would not suffer his benefites to be vainely & wontonly abused, no not of that people whome he most tenderly loued, and had chosen to him selfe before all other. No lesse truely is the vanity that is vsed among us in these dayes. For the proude and hautie stomacks of the daughters of Englande, are so maintayned with diuers disguised sortes of costly apparell, that as *Tertullian* an auncient father saith, there is lefte no difference in apparell betweene an honest matrone and a common strumpet.[1] Yea many men are become so effeminate, that they care not what they spende in disguising them selues, euer desiring newe toyes, and inuenting newe fashions. Therefore a certaine man that would picture euery conntreyman in his accustomed apparell, when he had painted other nations, he pictured the Englishe man all naked, and gaue him cloth under his arme, and badde him make it him selfe as he thought best, for he changed his fashion so often, that he knew not how to make it.[2] Thus with our phantasticall deuises, wee make our selues laughing stockes to other nations, while one spendeth his patrimonie vpon pounces and cuttes, another bestoweth more on a dauncing shirte, then might suffice to buye him honest and comely apparell for his whole bodye. Some hang their reuenues about their neckes, ruffling in their ruffes, and many a one ieopardeth his best ioynt, to maintaine him selfe in sumptuous raymente. And euery man, nothing considering his estate and condition, seeketh to excell other in costlie attire. Whereby it commeth to passe, that in aboundaunce and plentie of all thinges, we yet complaine of wante and penurie, while one man spendeth that which might serue a multitude, and no man distributeth of the aboundaunce which hee hath receiued, and all men excessively waste that which should serue to supplye the necessities of other. There hath beene very good prouision made against such abuses, by diuers good and wholsome lawes, which if they were practised as they ought to bee of all true subiects, they might in some part serue to diminish this raging and riotous excesse in apparell. But alas, there appeareth amongest us litle feare and obedience either of God, or man. Therefore must we needes looke for Gods fearefull vengeaunce from heauen, to overthrowe our presumption and pride, as hee ouerthrewe Herode, who in his royall apparell, forgetting God, was smitten of an Angell, and eaten by of wormes. By which terrible example, God hath taught vs that wee are

1. 'Video et inter matronas atque prostibulas nullum de habitu discremen relictum', Tertullian, *Apolog. Adversus Gentes*, cap. VI.
2. See Andrew Bord. *The fyrst boke of the Introduction of Knowledge* ... (1542), Ch. I.

but wormes meate, although we pamper our selues neuer so much in gorgeous apparell.

Here we may learne that which Jesus the sonne of Sirach teacheth, not to be proud of clothing and rayment, neither to exalt our selues in the day of honour, beacuse the workes of the Lorde are wonderfull, and glorious, secrete, and unknowen, teaching vs with humblenesse of mind, euery one to be mindefull of the vocation whereunto God hath called him. Let Christians therefore endeuour them selues to quench the care of pleasing the fleshe, let vs vse the benefites of God in this world, in such wise, that we be not too much occupied in prouiding for the body. Let vs content our selues quietly with that which God sendeth, be it neuer so litle. And if it please him to sende plentie, let vs not ware proude thereof, but let vs vse it moderately, aswell to our owne comforte, as to the reliefe of such as stande in necessitie. Hee that in aboundance and plentie of apparell, hideth his face from him that is naked, despiseth his owne flesh, as Esai the Prophet saith. Let vs learne to knowe our selues, and not to despise other, let vs remember that we stande all before the maiestie of almightie God, who shall iudge vs by his holy worde, wherein hee forbiddeth excesse, not onely to men, but also to women. So that none can excuse them selues, of what estate or condition so euer they be. Let vs therefore present our selues before his throne, as *Tertullian* exhorteth, with the ornamentes which the Apostle speaketh of, Ephesians the vi. Chapter, hauing our loynes girte about with the veritie, hauing the breste plate of righteousnesse, and shodde with shoes prepared by the Gospel of peace. Let vs take vnto us simplicitie, chastitie, and comlinesse, submitting our neckes to the sweete yoke of Christ. Let women bee subiect to their husbandes, and they are sufficiently attired, saieth *Tertullian*.[1] The wife of one *Philo* an heathen Philosopher, beeing demaunded why she ware no golde: she answered, that she thought her husbandes vertues sufficient ornamentes.[2] How much more ought Christian women, instructed by the word of God, to content them selues in their husbandes? Yea, how much more ought euery Christian to content him selfe in our saviour Christ, thinking him selfe sufficiently garnished with his heauenly vertues. But it will be here obiected and said of some nice and vaine women, that all which we doe in painting our faces, in dying our heare, in embawming our bodies, in decking vs with gay apparell, is to please our husbandes, to delight his eyes, and to retayne his loue towardes vs. O vaine excuse, and most shamefull aunsweare, to the reproch of thy husbande. What couldest thou more say to set out his foolishnesse, then to charge him to be pleased & delighted with the deuils tire? Who can paint her face and curle her heare, and chaunge it into an unnaturall colour, but therein doth worke reproofe to her maker, who made her? As though she could make her selfe more

1. *De Cult Fem.* II, 13.   2. Stobaeus. *Florilegium*, lxxiv, 54.

comely then God hath appoynted the measure of her beautie. What doe these women, but goe about to refourme that which God hath made? not knowing that all thinges naturall is the worke of God, and thinges disguised and vnnatural be the workes of the deuil. And as though a wise and Christian husband should delight to see his wife in such painted and florished visions, which common harlotes mostly doe vse, to traine therewith their louers to naughtinesse, or as though an honest woman could delight to be like an harlot for pleasing of her husband. Nay, nay these be but vaine excuses of such as goe about to please rather others then their husbandes. And such attires be but to prouoke her to shewe her selfe abroad, to entice others: a worthy matter. She must keepe debate with her husbande to maintaine such apparell, whereby she is the worse huswife, the seldomer at home to see to her charg, and to neglecte his thrifte, by giuing greate prouocation to her houshoulde to waste and wantonnesse, while shee must wander abroade to shewe her owne vanitie, and her husbandes foolishnesse. By which her pride, she stirreth vp much enuie of others which bee so vainely delighted as shee is. Shee doeth but deserue mockes & scornes, to set out all her commendation in Jewish and Ethnicke apparell, and yet brag of her Christianity. She doth but waste superfluously her husbandes stocke by such sumptuousnesse, and sometimes is the cause of much briberie, extortion, and deceite, in her husbandes occupying, that she may be the more gorgiously set out to the sight of the vaine worlde, to please the deuils eyes, and not Gods, who giueth to euerie creature sufficient and moderate comelinesse, wherwith we should be contented if we were of God. What other thing doest thou by those meanes, but prouokest other to tempt thee, to deceiue thy soule, by the baite of thy pompe and pride? What els doest thou, but settest out thy pride, and makest of the vndecent apparell of thy body, the deiuls net, to catch the soules of them which beholde thee? O thou woman, not a Christian, but worse then a Panim, thou minister of the deuill: Why pamperest thou that carren fleshe so high, which sometime doeth stincke and rotte on the earth as thou goest? Howe so euer thou perfumeth thy selfe, yet can not thy beastlynesse be hidden or ouercome with thy smelles and sauours, which doe rather defourme and mishape thee, then beautifie thee. What meant Salomon to say, of such trimming of vaine women, when he sayd, A faire woman without good manners and conditions, is like a Sowe which hath a ring of golde upon her snout? but that the more thou garnishe thy selfe with these outwarde blasinges, the lesse thou carest for the inwarde garnishing of thy minde, and so doest but defoule thy selfe by such aray, and not beautifie thy selfe? Heare, heare, what Christes holy Apostles doe write, Let not the outwarde apparell of women (saith Saint Peter) be decked with the brayding of heare, with wrapping on of golde, or goodly clothing: but let the mind, and the conscience, which is not seene with the eyes, be pure and cleane, that is, saieth he, an acceptable and an excellent thing before God. For so the olde anncient holy women attired themselues, & were obedient to their husbandes. . . .

Of Contention and Brawling[1]

It has beene declared vnto you in this Sermon against strife and brawling, what great inconuenience commeth thereby, specially of such contention as groweth in matters of religion: and how when as no man will giue place to another, there is none ende of contention and discorde: and that vnitie which God requireth of Christians, is vtterly thereby neglected and broken: and that this contention standeth cheefely in two pointes, as in picking of quarrelles, and making of frowarde aunsweres. Nowe ye shall heare Saint Paules wordes, saying, Dearely beloued, auenge not your selues, but rather giue place vnto wrath, for it is written, vengeaunce is mine, & I wil reuenge, saith the Lord. Therefore if thine enemie hunger, feede him, if he thirst, give him drinke: bee not ouercome with euill, but ouercome euill with goodnesse. All these be the wordes of Saint Paul, but they that bee full of stomacke, and set so much by themselues, that they may not abide so much as one euill worde to be spoken of them, peraduenture will say: If I be reuiled, shall I stande still like a Goose, or a foole, with my finger in my mouth? Shal I be such an ideote and disarde[2], to suffer euerie man to speake vpon mee what they list, to raile what they list, to spewe out all their venime against mee at their pleasures? Is it not conuenient that he that speaketh euill, should be aunswered accordingly? If I shall use this lenitie and softnesse, I shall both increase mine enimies frowardnes, and prouoke other to doe like. Such reasons make they that can suffer nothing, for the defence of their impacience. And yet if by frowarde aunswering to a frowarde person, there were hope to remedie his frowardnesse, he shoulde lesse offende that so shoulde aunswere, doing the same not of ire or malice, but onely of that intent, that hee that is so frowarde or malitious, may be reformed. But he that can not amend an other mans faulte, or can-not amend it without his owne fault, better it were that one should perish, then two. Then if he can not quiet him with gentle wordes, at the least let him not folow him in wicked & vncharitable words. If he can pacifie him with suffering, let him suffer, and if not, it is better to suffer euill, then to doe euill, to say well, then to say euill. For to speake well against euil, commeth of the spirite of God: but to render euill for euill, commeth of the contrarie spirite. And he that can not

1. Op. cit., Sig H4ʳ, H4ᵛ, H5ʳ, H5ᵛ. The text quoted is the second part of the Sermon.
2. Variant of 'dizzard': blockhead.

temper nor rule his owne anger, is but weake and feeble, and rather more like a woman or a childe, then a strong man. For the true strength and manlines is to ouercome wrath, and to dispise iniuries, and other mens foolishnes. And besides this, hee that shall dispise the wrong done vnto him by his enimie, euerie man shall perceiue that it was spoken or done without cause: where as contrarie, he that doth fume and chafe at it, shall helpe the cause of his aduersarie, giuing suspition that the thing is true. And in so going about to reuenge euill, wee shewe our felues to bee euill, and while we will punish and reuenge an other mans follie, we double and augment our owne follie. But many pretences find they that be wilfull, to colour their impacience. Mine enimie, say they, is not worthie to haue gentle wordes or deedes, being so full of malice or frowardnesse. The lesse hee is worthie, the more arte thou therefore allowed of God, and the more arte thou commended of Christ, for whose sake thou shouldest render good for euill, because hee hath commaunded thee, and also deserued that thou shouldest so doe. Thy neighbour hath peraduenture with a worde offended thee: cal thou to thy remembrance with how many words and deeds, how greeuously thou hast offended thy Lorde God. What was man, when Christ dyed for him was he not his enemie, and vnworthie to haue his fauour and mercie? Even so, with what gentlenesse and patience doeth he forbeare and tollerate and suffer thee, although he is dayly offended by thee? Forgive therefore a light trespasse to thy neighbour, that Christ may forgiue thee many thousandes of tres-passes, which art euery day an offender. For if thou forgiue thy brother, being to thee a trespasser, then hast thou a sure signe and token, that God will forgiue thee, to whom al men be debters and trespassers. How wouldest thou haue God mercifull to thee, if thou wilt be cruell vnto thy brother? Canst thou not finde in thine heart to do that towards another that is thy fellow, which God hath done to thee, that art but his seruant? Ought not one sinner to forgiue another, seeing that Christ which was no sinner,[1] did pray to his father for them that without mercie and dispitefully put him to death? Who, when he was reuiled, did not vse reuiling words againe, and when he suffered wrongfully, he did not threaten, but gaue all vengeance to the iudgement of his father which iudgeth rightfully. And what crakest thou of thy heade, if thou labour not to be in the body? Thou canst be no member of Christ, if thou follow not the steppes of Christ: (who as the Prophete saith) was ledde to death like a Lambe, not opening his mouth to reuiling, but opening his mouth to praying for them that crucifyed him, saying, Father, forgiue them, for they can not tell what they doe. The which example, anone after Christ, Saint Steven did folow, & after S. Paul: We be euill spoken of (saith he) and wee speake well: we suffer persecution, and

1. A notable aberration, 'Christ which was a sinner', in 1582 edn: repeated 1587 edn. No comment by Corrie or Griffiths.

take it patiently: Men curse vs, and we gentlie entreate. Thus S. Paul taught that he did, and he did that he taught. Blesse you (saith he) them that persecute you; blesse you, and curse not. Is it a great thing to speake well to thine aduersarie, to whom Christe doeth commaund thee to doe well? Dauid when Semei did call him all to naught, did not chide againe, but saide patiently. Suffer him to speake euill, if perchaunce the Lorde will haue mercie on mee. Histories bee full of examples of Heathen men, that tooke verie meekely both opprobrious and reprochful wordes, and iniurious or wrongfull deedes. And shall those heathen excell in patience vs that professe Christe, the teacher and example of all pacience? *Lisander*, when one did rage against him, in reuiling of him, he was nothing mooued, but saide, Goe to, go to, speake against me as much and as ofte as thou wilt, and leaue out nothing, if perchaunce by this meanes thou maist discharge thee of those naughtie thinges, with the which it seemeth that thou art full laden. Many men speake euill of al men, beause they can speake well of no man. After this sort, this wise man auoideth from him, the reprochfull words spoken vnto him, imputing and laying them to the naturall sicknesse of his aduersarie. *Pericles* when a certaine scoulder, or rayling felowe did reuile him, he aunsweared not a worde againe, but went into a gallerie and after towardes night, when he went home, this scoulder folowed him, raging still more and more, because he sawe the other to set nothing by him: and after that he came to his gate (being darke night) *Pericles* commanded one of his seruantes to light a torch, and to bring the scoulder home to his owne house[1]. Hee did not onely with quietnesse suffer this brauler patiently, but also recompenced an euill turne with a good turne, and that to his enimie. Is it not a shame for vs that professe Christ, to be worse then heathen people, in a thing cheefely perteyning to Christes religion? shall philosophie perswade them, more then Gods worde shall perswade vs? shall naturall reason preuaile more with them, then religion shall with vs? shall mans wisedome leade them to those thinges, wherevnto the heauenly doctrine can not lead vs? What blindnesse, wilfulnesse, or rather madnes is this? *Pericles* being prouoked to anger with manie villanous wordes, aunswered not a word. But we, stirred but with one litle word, what foule work doe we make? How do we fume, rage, stampe, and stare like mad men? Many men, of euery trifle will make a great matter, and of the sparke of a litle worde will kindle a great fyre, taking all thinges in the worst part. But howe much better is it, & more like to the example and doctrine of Christ, to make rather of a great fault in our neighbour, a small fault, reasoning with our selues after this sorte, He spake these wordes, but it was in a sodaine heate, or the drinke spake them, and not hee, or hee spake them not against me, but against him whom he thought me to be.

1. Plutarch, *Pericles* V. Cf. *Apothegmata Laconica*.

EDWARD DERING

Anyone who approaches early Elizabethan sermons expecting to find in them a foretaste of the great feast of language to come, is in for a disappointment. There was little friendly communication between the pulpit and the stage, and no longer common ground, for the lively mediaeval tradition, sustained by the friars, of teaching by colourful *exempla* and anecdotes was in eclipse. In the new 'Protestant' style words were for reproof and amendment, and were not at first encouraged to explore reality beyond that strict commission. In the previous two decades there had been a steep decline in the quality and even quantity of recruitment to the priesthood. The stalwart leaders of the first wave of reform were dead or growing old; meanwhile the fluctuation in doctrine and policy of the recent past had had an unsettling and discouraging effect upon potential ordinands. Careful fathers and ambitious sons saw in the prospect of the ministry only inadequate means, unstable conditions and even, given another change of fashion in theology, mortal danger. In the words of a contemporary,

haue youe not sene how manie learned men haue bene put to trouble of late, within these 12 or 15 years, and all for declaringe their opinions in things that haue arisen in controversie? haue you not seene whan one opinion hathe ben set furthe, and who so ever saide against it were put to trouble, and shortly after that, whan the contarie was furthered and set furthe, weare not the other, that prospered before, put to trouble for seyinge theire mynedes against the latter opinions and so neither part escaped the business; either first or last he came to it, of whether side so euer he was, except it were some wise fellows that could change their opinions as the more and stronger parte did chaunge theirs.[1]

Why, he asks, should a father cast his son into this hazardous confusion. Why should a young man go to university at all? 'A man will rather put his childe to that seience that may bring him to a better fruiete than this, or what scholar shall haue courage to studie to this ende?'

The situation was worse than a mere shortage of priests. 'The whole order of presthode', said Cuthbert Scott, '. . . is so ronne into contempte,

1. *A Discourse of the Common Weal of this Realm of England*, c. 1549. Lambrade MS., ed. Elizabeth Lamond (1893).

that it is now nothing else but a laughing stock for the people.'[1] Some of those appointed for convenience, as cheap incumbents, by holders of rights of presentation, were no more than negatively incompetent, a deficiency which time and improved selection could make good; but others were showing an embarrassingly independent irreverence for authority. The unprepared minds of the ignorant and the vulgar were being dangerously inflamed and deluded—so it seemed to the custodians of orthodox learning—by the heady wine of biblical translation, causing the discipline and control of their superiors to be recklessly challenged. The problem extended beyond the issue of insubordinate clergy, to the growth of the phenomenon (noted earlier with misgivings by Edgeworth) of presumptuous laymen who boldly contradicted their betters, provoked mischievous conventicles, and even dared unlawfully to *preach*, with the insolent complacency of men who feel they enjoy the advantage of a direct 'person to person' line of communication, in the vernacular, with Almighty God.[2]

This was a by-product of his programme which Tyndale may not have foreseen, when he boasted to a critic, '. . . ere many years I will cause a boy that driveth the plough shall know more of the scripture than thou dost'. But it was one with which both his and his adversaries' successors had to grapple. These promiscuous secondary growths were particularly galling to members of the English Calvinist left wing, for they felt that it was on the tide of *their* Reformation that such a subversive rabble of babbling mountebanks had sailed in and landed upon the holy ground previously reserved, and paid for, by the true elect.

With the death of Mary they had hastened back from exile, hoping and expecting, with impatient righteousness, that the new queen would invest their party with secular power sufficient to enforce the submission of the profane, the carnal and the idolatrous of all types, after the model of the 'godly', all-pervading social discipline favoured in Geneva. But

---

1. *Two Notable Sermons Lately Preached at Paul's Crosse* (1544), sig Gi^r.

2. An early example of a layman's disciplinary public recantation by one William Warde, in 1544, at St. Paul Cross, is characteristic of many others which were to follow. 'Good people, ye shall understand that wanting . . . both experience, wytte and learning I have dyverse tymes in alehouses and uncomlie and unmeate places taken upon me to bable and talke and rangle of the Scripture which I understood not yea and to expound it after my own folyshe fantasie chieflie these tymes when I haue not ben myne owne man but over come with Ale.' Quoted in M. Maclure, *Pauls Cross Sermons* (Toronto, 1958), p. 16, from *Fox's Acts and Monuments*.

the queen had different notions of the form the Church of England should assume under her rule and so had her primate.[1]

One of the most gifted members of the Protestant left, within the church, was Edward Dering. Matthew Parker called him 'the most learned man in England'; he was not the wisest, as the archbishop himself was to discover. Dering lacked in particular the kind of sensitive realism, so acutely developed in the woman who was his sovereign, which could nicely appreciate what, and how much, in prevailing conditions might effectively be attempted at a given time. He could have learnt a useful lesson from old Latimer, too: 'a prince . . . must have his duty told him but it must be done with humbleness'.[2]

Dering's general unacceptability by others for the praetorian role in which he had cast himself suggests that, gifted as he was, he lacked authentic humility or charm, qualities by grace of which, words and acts which would be offensive from one man may become acceptable from another.

On February 25th, 1569, when he was twenty-nine years old and a fellow of Christ's College, Cambridge, Dering preached a sermon before the queen. From what we know of his record we may surmise that his tone probably matched his words, and his words amounted to a peremptory demand that the queen promote forthwith a policy of radical reform, the first move of which would be the curtailment of the episcopal authority of his own superiors in the church. Some of the reforms he advocated were just and due; nobody knew it better than the queen; but it was an inopportune occasion to denounce, in personal terms, the practice of patrons reserving part of the revenues of their benefices; the means by which a useful part of Her Majesty's own income was raised.[3]

1. 'God keep us from such a visitation as Knox has attempted in Scotland', Parker, C.S.P.D, November 6th 1559.

2. See above, p. 25. *The Seventh Sermon Preached before King Edward VI, on April 19th, 1548.*

3. Elizabeth's appropriations reached such a scale that patient old Parker had to remonstrate with her over her calculated delays in appointing bishops to the vacant northern sees, so that meanwhile she could divert into her own purse the gross annual diocesan receipts. But here again she knew what she was doing. The practice of levying unofficial tax upon ecclesiastical appointments within her patronage did not stop. As late as 1597 she charged Thomas Bilson an annuity of £400 a year for the bishopric of Winchester (see W. H. Frere, *The English Church in the reigns of Elizabeth and James* (1904), p. 203), and after the death of Richard Cox, the Bishop of Ely, in 1581, she sequestered his estates for the next fourteen years.

On the Duties of a Prince

A sermon preached before Her Majestie, on the 25th
day of February, 1559, by Master Edward Dering.

*Psalms 78. 70 He chose David his seruant also and took him
from the sheepfolds euen from behind the ewes great with young
took he him: to feede his people and Jacob and his inheritance in
Israel. So he fed them according to the simplicity of his heart, and
guided them by the discretion of his hands.*

A miserable Common-wealth it must needes be, and far separated from God
and his mercies, that hath blind leaders, who cannot leade themselues. Who
so feareth the Lord, will surely looke vnto it, that he maintaine no such
offences within his kingdom, nor nourish any such sores within the body of
his Countrey. If a man be once called to the Ministry, let him attend vpon
his flocke, and feed them as his duty bindeth him, with the foode of life, or
let him bee remooued. Christ sayed, *Pasce, pasce, pasce,* Feed, feed, feed. This
charge he hath giuen, euen as we loue him, so to see it executed. Say what
we will say, and the more we say it, the more impudently we shall lye, if
we say we loue him, while wee keepe not his commaundements. Would to
God we were wise to vnderstand it. Christ said, *They are the salt of the earth,*
and what shall be done with them, if they can season nothing? Christ sayd,
they are the light of the world, and what heapes of miseries shall they bring
with them, if they themselues bee darke? Christ said, *they be the watchmen*:
and what case shall the Citty be in, if they doe nothing but sleepe, and delight
in sleeping? Who seeth not these incurable sicknesses, that can see any thing?
They are the Pastors, and howe hungry must the flocke be, when they haue
no foode to giue them? They are the Teachers, and howe great is the ignoraunce, where they themselues know nothing? They are the Euangelists or
messengers of glad tydings: howe little hope haue they, and what slender
faith, whose messengers cannot tell what the Lord sayth?

The Lord enlarge within your Maiesty, the bowels of mercy, that you
may once haue pitty vpon your pore subiects. This cogitation made Paule
the Apostle say to Timothy, (a paynefull father vnto a carefull childe;) *I
charge thee before God, and before the Lord Iesus Christ, that shal iudge the quicke
and dead at his appearance, and in his kingdome: preach the worde, been instant in
season, and out of season, reproue, rebuke, exhort, &c.* Of all miseries wherewith
the Church is grieued, none is greater than this: that her Ministers be ignorant,
and can say nothing. What could Ieroboam do more than this, to strengthen

all his Idolatry, then to make him Priestes of the lowest of the people? What could haue made Asa (being otherwise religious) so soone to haue turned away from the service of God, sauing only he suffered his people to be without a Priest, which could teach them the word of God? What plague did God threaten greater against a rebellious people, than that hee would take away from them their true Prophets? When were the peoples sinnes so ripe to procure vengeance, as when their preachers were dumb dogs and could not bark? And what I beseech you is our condition better? Or what be many ministers of our time & Country, other then dumbe dogs? Surely as Ahiiah[1] said of the people of Israel, so wee may say of our Ministers: haue we not made vs Priests like the people of our Country? whosoeuer commeth to consecrate with a yong Bullock, and seauen Rams, the same may be a Priest for them that are no Gods. And so surely if we serued Baal, a great number of our Priestes at this day were tollerable. But if we serue the Lord, what do they with that function they cannot skill of? Let them returne againe to their old occupation. And yet this is but one euill: and if we were reformed, yet much still were amisse. If I would declare vnto your Maiesty al the great abuses that are in your ministerie, I should leade you along in the Spirite, as God did the Prophet Ezechiel: and after many intollerable euils, yet I shall say still vnto you, behold you shall see moe abhominations then these.

I would first leade you to your Benefices, and beholde some are defiled with impropriations, some with sequestrations, some loaden with pensions, some robbed of their commodities. And yet behold more abhominations then these. Looke after this vpon your Patrons, and loe, some are selling their Benefices, some farming them, some keepe them for their Children, some giue them to Boyes, some to seruing men, a very few seeke after learned Pastors. And yet you shall see more abhominations then these. Looke vpon your ministerie, and there are some of one occupation, some of another some shake-Bucklers[2], some Ruffians, some Hawkers and Hunters, some Dicers and Carders, some blind guides, and cannot see, some dumbe dogs and wil not barke. And yet a thousand more iniquities haue now couered the Priest-hood. And yet you in the meane while that all these whordoms are committed, you at whose hands God will require it, you sit still and are carelesse, let men doe as they list. It toucheth not be like your common-wealth, and therefore you are so well contented to let all alone. The Lord increase the gifts of his holy spirit in you, that from faith to faith you may grow continually, till that you be zealous as good King Dauid, to worke his will. If you know not how to reforme this, or haue so little counsel (as mans hart is blinded) that you can deuise no way, aske counsaile at the mouth of the Lord, and his holy wil shal be reuealed vnto you.

1. Abijah, 2 Chron. xiii:9.
2. Nickname for a serving man.

To reforme euil Patrones, your Maiesty must strengthen your lawes, that they may rule as wel high as lowe. For as Esdras sayed once, so may I boldly say now: The handes of the Princes and Rulers, are chiefe in this trespasse. If you wil haue it amended, you must prouide so, that the highest may be afraid to offend.

To keepe backe the ignorant from the Ministery, whom God of his goodnesse hath not called to such a function, take away your authority from the Bishops, let them not thus at their pleasure make Ministers in their Closset, whome soeuer it pleaseth them. To stop the inconueniences that grow in the Ministery by other(s), who say they are learned and can preach, and yet do not, that are (as I sayd) dumbe dogs, and will not barke, bridle at the least their greedy appetites, pull out of their mouthes those poysoned bones, that they so greedily gnaw vpon. Take away dispensations, Pluralities, Totquots[1], Non residences, and such other sinnes. Pull downe the Court of Faculties, the mother and nurse of all abhominations. I tell you this before God, that quickneth all things, and before our Lord Iesus Christ, that shall iudge the quick and the dead, in his appearance, and in his kingdome: amend these horrible abuses, and the Lord is on your right hand you shall not be remoued for euer. Let these things alone, and God is a righteous God, hee will one day call you to your reckoning. The God of al glory open your eyes to see his high kingdome, and enflame your heart to desire it.

The third thing that I sayd in this place was to be noted, was of Dauid himselfe, how faithfully hee executed that whereunto he was called. The Prophet sayth: *He fed them in the sincerity of his heart, and guided them with the discretion of his hands.* An excellent vertue, and meet for King Dauid, that was a man according to the hart of God. He knew that obedience was better then sacrifice, and that Gods people were neuer better ruled, then when their Princes brought into captiuity their owne vnderstanding, and in simplicity of hart were obedient onely to the wisedome of almighty God.

He had too good experience of his owne wisedome, and had tryed it often how it made him to rebell: therefore to please God effectually, hee walked in his simplicity. O that our Christian Princes had so great measure of Gods holy Spirite: how many and grieuous burthens should then be taken from vs, that now Christian eyes & eares can hardly beholde and heare? how many sinnes should be extinct and buried, that now vaine policy doth maintaine and strengthen? The time is past, and I wil say no more.

Nor did he. The queen had his licence to preach suspended forthwith. His ability caused him to be given further chances, but he seems

1. A 'Totquot' was a dispensation permitting the recipient to hold as many ecclesiastical benefices as he could obtain. The curate's stipend, usually, was pathetically inadequate.

to have been a compulsive quarreler and even alienated Matthew Parker. He died at the age of thirty-seven, probably from tuberculosis.

THOMAS DRANT

Thomas Drant[1] in contrast to the rigorous Dering was, in effect, a euphuist, but, as he anticipated Lyly, we should more properly call him a *guevarist*. He would certainly have read Antonio de Guevara's *Libro Aurea*, either in the court preacher's Spanish original or in Berners' or North's translations.[2] He was one of the most prominent exponents of this, the 'florid' style of rhetoric, during its brief flourish between novelty and decay. In the following passage he exercises the resources of his school with evident, self-conscious satisfaction: parison in the first paragraph (. . . to gather up lilies is to gather up men . . .): paromeon (forming out of 'That Christ should gather hys sheepe . . .'): then a sally into polyptoton with variation on the use of 'tyme': antithesis and apostrophe extended into partnerships of stichomithia. The slender stalk of the sermon's content is bowed to near breaking under the weight of layer upon layer of ornamental tropes. When he reproves the court gallants for sartorial vanities, it is difficult to conceive who is more over-dressed, the people he rebukes or the language he rebukes them in. Solomon, of course, cannot be kept out of the business, for his name is a cue for a summary of the current extravagancies of the import trade in garments for the well-dressed man-about-town. Here and there a stroke of fancy shines, like the evocative 'the huffe of your ruffe', to the court peacocks, or the comic-poignant 'knobbed gout'. But these bright points are choked and overlaid by a surfeit of allusive *tableaux*, designed to display the preacher's range of virtuosity. Drant was preoccupied by 'wit', in the prime contemporary sense of 'stylized ingenuity' as an end in itself; and no doubt he was talking above the heads of the general congregation to a minority of *avant-garde* men of letters and academic rhetoric-tasters. But the movement could not evolve; it

1. Thomas Drant. Born in Lincolnshire; died 1578. St. John's College, Cambridge, 1558. B.A. 1560. Composed English, Latin and Greek verse for Queen Elizabeth on the visit to Cambridge, 1564. Domestic chaplain to Grindal, divinity reader St. Paul's. B.D. 1569. Prebend of Fiales in the church of Chichester, Rector of Shinfold in Sussex; Archdeacon of Lewes, 1569.
2. Published as *The Diall of Princes* (1557).

was sterile and would become, like prolonged feats of jugglers and acrobats, more difficult to improve than interesting to watch.

A further maturation of language, fertilized by the accidents of genius, would be needed to give—and then only in two quite separate and curiously singular cases—the sublimation capable of breathing life back into the corpse of poetic oratory. But Jeremy Taylor and John Donne were not born when Drant preached this sermon. Shakespeare was six years old.

O Men, O Lilies

A Sermon preached at St. Marie Spittle,
on Tuesday in Easterweek, 1570[1]

'And to gather up Lilies.'

Of gathering of Lilies, many thinges may be spoken many wayes. And what Lilies do signifie in this place, I am to say as before: that when the beloved goeth down into his spicery to be fed in the Orchardes and to gather Lilies, is no more but that he goeth to be refreshed in the earth. Howbeit the fathers have made a further processe in this matter, and some yelde one sense, and some an other. But for my selfe I would not for anything rehearse opinions upon opinions, and notes upon opinions, and exhortations uppon notes, for that would be now long and werisome: onely I will say something of one exposition which Rabbi Jarhi and S. Barnard do seeme to embrace: that is, to gather up Lilies, is to gather up men: and yet even in this one exposition resteth to be handled that Christ is a gatherer, and men be flowers. If Christ be a gatherer, then he is no disperser. In deede it is meete that the shepeheard should gather his sheepe, and the hen her chickins, and the husbandman the graine into the barne. Even to the Prophet Ezechiel sayth: That Christ should gather hys sheepe out of all landes, and gather them into their owne land. So doth he himselfe say with an affection of most deepe love: O Jerusalem, Jerusalem, how often would I have gathered thee together, as the henne gathereth her chickins under her wing, and thou wouldest not. And as Lilies grow dispersed here one, and there one: so good men grow rare and thinne. And as Christ picketh Lilies from among thornes (for they growe among thornes): so picked he Abraham from the thornes of Chaldae, Job from the Hussites, Hiram from the Tirians, Naaman from the Syrians, the Ninivites from the Assirians. Lilies growe rare, and good men grow rarer: Lilies

1. *Two Sermons* (1570).

amongest thornes, and good men amongest thornes. And as the gathering of Lilies and men be like: so men and Lilies be very like. I will speake a thyng of marvellous troth: A man is but a Lily, the pride and glory of a man is but the pride and glory of a Lilie. Salomon is a Lilie, King Salomon is a Lilie, King Salomon in hys glory is a Lilie, Sonnes of vanitie to whom it is delightfull to have fethers to daunce in your toppes as bigge as Ajax shieldes, to have your heades turkish and your backes spanish, your wastes italian, and your feete Venetian, with such a world of hosen glory about your loynes, Sonnes (I say) of vanitie, ye are but Lilies, Salomon in all his glory is but a Lily. Salomon in his worst workeday apparell, is better than the best of you all. Salomon in his best holiday apparell, is not so brave as a Lily: ye therefore in the huffe of your ruffe are nothing comparable to a Lily, no not to a field Lily. Daughters of vanitie, and dames of delicacy, ye thinke it fine and featous[1] to be called roses, primroses, and Lilies: and indeede it is true, in respectes you are roses, primroses and Lilies. When ye have gotten all upon your heades and backes which Englishe soyle doth yelde, and many a marchant hath fetched full farre, when all your taylors have broken their braines about contriving of formes, and fashions, yet then are ye nothing so tricksy trim as the Lily. The best of ye all in all your best bravery, is not lyke to a field Lily, which hapely tomorrow is pluckt up, and flung into the fornace. Pricke and prune your selves to the day of doome, ye will never be like to the field Lily. For the Lily of this our fleshe is not so goodly gay, as the Lily of grasse: otherwise and in many imperfections we are very perfect, and true Lilies. The Lily of grasse shooteth up for a time, but then he layeth downe his toppe, and is made even to the floore. The Lily of fleshe florisheth for a time, but then by honering death he is taught to poer upon the ground, and to let down his top like a Lily. The wrath of winter doth conquer and kill the Lily of grasse: there be moe then many occasions to vanquish, and kill the Lily of flesh. Barnard sayth that there is a worme that eateth up the roote of the Lily of grasse: Ech Lily of flesh hath his worme and consumer. Julius Caesar, Hercules, and Mahomet have the falling sicknesse, Mecaenas hath a three yeres agew, Orestes hath the frensie, Spensippus hath the palsey, Heraclitus and Aristarcus the dropsy, Marcus Crassus the stuffing in the head, Hieroboam the withered arme, Lazarus and Job, biles and botches, Aristotle an evill stomacke, Euripides purtifaction of lounges, Coruinus the lethargie, Anacrion lacke of sleepe. Agesilaus and Ptolomeus the gout, Naaman and Mary the leprossie. But what do I say that every Lily of flesh hath his worme and consumer, sithens I may truley say that every part of every Lily of flesh hath his diverse worms and consumers. The head hath the Apoplexia, the Epilepsia, and the turnabout sicknesse, the eyes have the Opthalmia and the Migrim, the necke hath the Palsey and the convulsion, the nose hath the Polipus, the

1. Featous: handsome.

pallat hath the vuula[1], the gumes have the canker, the teeth have the toothach, the throate hath the angine, the toung hath blisters and swelling, the stomacke hath the motive cause of the cardiacall passion, and murthering rewmes (the studentes sicknesse), the sides have colickes stitches, a prickling pleurisies, the reines have the stone, the legges have dropsies and crampes, the feete and handes have the knobbed gout. Besides that the Lily of flesh hath wormes of mynde and wormes of conscience, many wormes and sore wormes. The Lily of grasse hath hys own worme, and the Lily of flesh hath hys thousand wormes: the Lily of grasse can not live from that one worme, but will be smitten of it nor the Lily of the flesh shall scape all these wormes. Agayne, all the grasse Lilies are dead and gone that have growen on the face of the earth and all flesh Lilies are dead that lived uppon this earth, Abraham Gods frend, and Noah that walked wyth God, Aaron full of dignitie, and Moses full of authoritie, holy Melchisedech, and just Job, strong Sampson, and huge Ogge, vaunting Goliah and disdainfull Senacharib, fayre Absolon, and sweete lovely Jonathan, wife Salomon, rich Cresus, and wealthy Crassus, lucky Pompey, victorious Julius, riall Augustus, and triumphant Emelius, all these have had a tyme like a Lily, and dyed in time like a Lily. They have had the spring of their budding, and the sommer of their blossoming, they have likewise come to the Autume of their parching, and the winter of theyr perishing. O all ye, ye men that drawe breathe under the cope of the skies, ye spring up like lilies, and goe downe like Lilies; ye florish like Lilies and deflower like Lilies. Pindarus seyd thryse, Mammea, Mammea, Mammea. Jeremy cried thryse Earth, Earth, Earth; so I, Lilies, Lilies, Lilies; and then a second time, Lilies, Lilies, Lilies; and, for that I would have it remembered I crye again, Lilies, Lilies, Lilies; and then thus, O Men, O Lilies, O Men, O Lilies, O Men, O Lilies. O field of Grasse, O Flowers of Decaye; Yet came Christ among such Lilies to gather up such fleting flowers of flesh, and to be conversant among his spicery.

One may wonder whether that last paragraph, at least, did not provoke levity in the congregation. There is no doubt that euphuism had them rolling in the aisles a quarter of a century later, when Shakespeare parodied its fly-blown pretensions. Into a short rally between Holofernes, Sir Nathanial and Dull, he packs a varied assortment of the jargon, including the favourite devices, paronomasia and homoeoteluton.

SIR NATHANIAL

Very reverend sport, truly and done in testimony of a good conscience.

1. Uvula.

HOLOFERNES

The deer was, as you know, sanguis in blood: ripe as a pomewater, who now hangeth like a jewel in the ear of the coelo, the sky, the welkin, the heaven, and anon falleth like a crab on the face of terra, the soil, the land, the earth.

SIR NATHANIAL

Truly, Master Holofernes, the epithets are sweetly varied, like a scholar at the least; but sir, I assure ye it was a buck of the first head.

HOLOFERNES

Sir Nathanial, Haud credo.

DULL

'Twas not a haud credo, 'twas a pricket.

HOLOFERNES

Most barbarous intimation. Yet a kind of insinuation, as it were in via, in way of explication; farce, as it were, replication, or rather, ostentare, to show, as it were, his inclination, after his undressed, unpolished, unpruned, untrained, or rather unlettered, or ratherest unconfirmed fashion, to insert again my haud credo for a deer.[1]

1. *Love's Labour's Lost*, Act IV, Scene II.

JOHN BRIDGES[1]

It is something of a relief to descend from euphuism and come to earth on a simple sermon for plain people by John Bridges. Not that this preacher was 'simple' in any limiting sense; he had travelled much, lived in Italy and translated the pervasive works of Machiavelli. But he was a man rooted in the ways of the old pre-Reformation church, and he would have been unlikely to preach that which might make a secular congregation discontented with anything but their own faults. Likeness will be found to Ramsay and Edgeworth, though he is not as stylish as either. The sermon is interesting for its allusions to the origins of the word 'cockney' and to the unflattering reflections upon Londoners by the rural and provincial English, who regarded metropolitans with a mixture of envy and scorn. Children are found to be as spoilt and ungrateful as ever, and servants are insubordinate and dishonest. But who corrupts them?

The Effects of Example

A Sermon preached at Paule's Cross on Monday in Whitsun weeke, Anno Domini 1571, entreating on this sentence,

Sic Deus dilixet mundum ut daret unigentium filium suum, ut omnibus qui credit in eum non pereat, sed habeat vitam aeternam. John 3.16

Many fathers and mothers now a days complain of the disobedience, wilfullnesse, and lacke of loue in their children, more than they had wont to do. What is the cause hereof; first this is a general obseruation (although in

1. John Bridges. Died 1618. Pembroke Hall, Cambridge. B.A. 1556, M.A. 1560; Fellow 1556; D.D. Cantab. 1575. He took part in the Martin Marprelate controversies, and was a strongly anti-Puritan, right-wing member of the Church of England.

particulers it be not altogether true) that the parents loue is greter to his child, than the childs loue is to his parents, whereof the townsmen of *Gaunt* set vp a monument. For wher as, on a time they had condemned a father and his sonne, for certain notorious crimes committed: on muche entreatie made to the senate for them, it was at length graunted, that but one of them shoulde die, and that on this condition, that the one shoulde do the execution on the other, and he that executed the other shoulde him selfe escape, agree on the matter as they could which of them should suffer: The sonne being asked, refused to die for the father, and had rather execute his father than his father shold execute him. The father being demaunded, was content to suffer death him self of his sonnes hand, though his sons vnnaturalnesse did greue him, rather than he wold put his sonne to death. Wheruppon this monument was erected for a perpetuall memorie, the pictures of bothe father and sonne, the son behedding his father, engrauen in marble, and this poesie writen vnderneth, *Amor descendit non ascendit.* Loue descendeth but not ascendeth. And so the ryuers course descendeth but not ascendeth: A stone naturally descendeth, not ascendeth. And the scripture commendeth many fathers vnto vs, that ful entierly haue loued their sons, but few sons like Isaac, Joseph and Tobie, are commended vnto vs, for the like loue againe vnto their fathers. This naturall loue wrought not in the vnnaturall sonne Absalon, but it wrought so deepe in the father Dauid, that he cryed out againe, *Absalon fili mi, fili mi, Absalon fili mi &c.* O Absalon my sonne, my son Absalon, my sonne, woulde to God I myghte die for thee, O Absalon my sonne, my sonne. The seconde reason of the sonnes disobedyence, is the fathers cockeryng.

And that was the cause of Dauids weepyng, and Absalons destruction, euen hys fathers indulgence. Thys destroyed Hely[1] and his sonnes also: And hathe broughte many foolyshe fathers to their graue with heauinesse, and hath brought many sonnes to the Gallowes wyth wretchednesse. Remember the Fable of the chylde that bitte of his mothers nose,[2] when hee went to hanging, bicause she would not bite his breche with a good rod, when he went to filching. A great many mothers nowe a dayes can not abide to haue their children beaten, and a number of fathers as wise as the mothers: the Schoolemaster that shoulde fetche bloudde of theyr chylde, Oute alas, it were a pityfull syghte. But were it not a more pitifull syghte to see howe myserablye the one destroyeth the other? they thinke it loue, it is more than mortall hatrede, this foolyshe cockeryng of theyr chyldren. Whiche if they feele not in the miseries of this life, wherby repentance may saue the soule, howesoeuer the body abye the follie of this hatefull cockering loue: if not: yet after this life, the father and mother may mete the sonne in helle, and there repeate those heauie and horrible curses that Gregorie tels of, Cursed be the houre sayth the father, that euer thou wast borne, Cursed be the tyme,

1. Eli, see 1 Sam. 4:12–19. 2. Aesop's *Fables.*

sayeth the sonne, that euer thou begattest me: and thus the one shall curse & ban the other, and al bicause of this their cursed cockering. O ye fathers and mothers, especially you of this noble citie of London, shame not youre Citie, vndoe not youre children and youre selues also.

We are thorough out all the Realme called cockneys that are borne in London, or in the sounde of Bow bell, this is your shame, recouer this shame: as god be praised ye do, more than euer was wont to be done. It had wont to be an olde saying, that fewe or none but were vnthrifts, and came to nothing, that were cockneys borne, for so are we termed abroade. But God be praised, this is nowe a false rule, and hath ben a good while since, chiefly since the Gospels light hath shined on this noble citie, it hath brought for the many worthy gouernors, notable preachers, godly pastors, wise counselors, pregnant wits, graue students, welthy citizens, and is ful of maruellous [sic] towardes youth God blesse them, and I trust will euery day more and more so blesse this renoumed citie, that where before, for wanton bringing vp it hath bene (althoughe in other thyngs famous inoughe, yet in this poynt of our births place, a speck of blushing, a terme of cockney, a note of nipping vs) It shall hereafter (by Godly education) be a thing to glory in, that we borne in sutche a glorious citie, as not only God hath made the hed of other in welth and honor, but also a myrror of other in godlinesse and religion. And that this may be, loue your children but hate cockering. Read and reade ouer twentie times, and write it in steele and iron as Job saith, that is, graue it in youre memorye that woorthie chapter (in this pointe) the thirtie chapter of Jesus the sonne of Syrach, and there thou shalt see, what the cockering of the chyld, will bring bothe father and chylde vnto, and what the contrary.

The third cause of childrens disobedience is the yll ensample of their parentes: soone crookes the tree that good camocke[1] will bee. It soone prickes wil be a thorne: the yong cockrel will learne easily to crow as he heareth the old cocke: A great many suche crauen cockes there are, that crowe full yll fauoredly, and teach their cockrels to do the same scarse ere they be out of the shell. We are prone inough, and to prone of our selues to all vice, without a teacher, and alas shall the father and mother teache it them? nay it is no meruaile, how coulde the olde Crabbe teache the yong Crab to goe, but a byas. They haue nousled vp them selues in all wickednesse, and so they teache their children, so that as it were they clayme hel by inheritance. It is a world to see how soone wee are decked vp to be proude, or ere we knowe what pride meaneth. What a laughter and sport it is to the parentes, to se their yong chyld do any vnhappy touch....

We reade of greate loue that seruauntes haue borne theyr maysters, that maisters againe haue born theyr seruantes, the one hath suffred death to saue the other. This was a notable loue: Where are suche maisters and seruantes

1. A crook-stick used in ball games.

now become? nay it is now the old prouerbe vp & downe, trim tram, such
maister, suche man suche cuppe, suche couer, neyther barrell better herring,
bothe maister and man may go in a line together, for a great many of men
and maisters now a dayes. In many places where I come, I heare the maisters
complaine of their seruantes stubbornesse and vnfaithfull dealing, of their
seruantes dissolutenesse, and lacke of awe. But the maister seeth not howe
God punisheth hym with his owne rodde, howe his owne selfe is the cause
hereof. He would haue his seruant all for lucre, all on the pennie, all for
aduauntage, neyther to care ought howe he cometh by it, swering and staring,
cursing and banning, euen to deceaue his owne father: on my faith and
honestie it cost me thus much, hauing in deede neither faith nor honestie to
sweare by, and therfore it were the lesse matter, if he appealed only to his
false faithe and litle honestie: But he spareth not to take to witnesse the
righteous iudgements of almightie God that seeth his falshod, and yet will he
not spare to say, now as God shall saue me, as God shall iudge me, thus and
thus it stands me in, and yet it stands him not in half the money, yea often
times the bier shall haue it for the third penie that the seller asketh. O mercifull God, what an order is this among Christians? And no nation noted for this
horrible abusage more than englishmen. We think we should not thriue if
we should not vse this curset kind of bargayning. We counte it almost nothing now adaies, it is growne into sutche a cusstome, euery seconde worde
to be poudred with an othe for credit, yea to blaspheme God & his dredfull
iudgementes, to renounce God and the benefite of our saluation, and that for
a little credite, or for a paltrie gaine: Cursed be that gaine that winneth such
a losse, that body and soule is lost, to the which al the winning of the wide
world were but a trifle. Cursed be that credite, that to retaine his estimation
with an harde beleuyng man, will not stycke to blaspheme and renounce his
part of God. But thou louedst cursing and cursing will come vppon thee.
Tushe a poynt, sayeth his mayster, that fingreth the gaine, *Iura periura
secretum prodere noli*, Sweare (hooreson) and forsweare, bewray not my
mistery. This is a mystery with a very mischefe, that the couetouse maister
without all conscience teacheth his man. Is this the waie to thriue? Haue these
menne (I will not saie any feare of God for they haue none) *Non est timor dei
ante oculos eorum*. But haue they any opinion there is a God? No truely, they
saie in their harts with the foole ther is no God. For if they thought there
were, they durst not thus abuse him. And therefore the master careth not for
the seruants instruction, how he should come to the knowledge of God? but
with his seruant would haue all daies alike Sabbaoth day and other. And
neuer passeth whether his seruant here, know, or beleue God & his word or
no. The seruant now being without all knowledge like a beast, and his
master without all conscience like a dyuell: he hath as litle conscience to
deceaue his master, as his master wold haue him haue to decaue others. And

hence cometh so many stubborn knaues, saucie marchants, crafty varlets, priuie theeves, ruffianlye cutters, ryottous prentices, and all the wicked sort of suche vnfaithfull seruantes among artificers and marchants, that deceiue so many other men, make their maysters bankruptes, and bring them selues to miserye. And thoughe the principall faulte herein, bee in the maister that complayneth on his seruant, yet is not this a bolster to the seruant, whose dewtye is, thoughe not to assent to theire mayster in wickednesse, yet in euery rightefull thng, to obey honour and loue their master with all seruice, truth and diligence: If they doe not, either they shall neuer be masters themselues, or be like wise punished in their seruants. Behold the faithful seruise of Abraham's man and how god blessed his iorny, and his master made him the garde of all he had.

HENRY SMITH[1]

With Henry Smith we come to the most eloquent and the most praised—(the miracle and wonder of his age)[2]—of orators in the Elizabethan church. He leant moderately towards the Puritan complex but it was sufficient for him to be suspended by Aylmer, the Bishop of London, on information laid. He was later restored by the help of that remarkably tolerant new eminence, Lord Burghley. His theme is the familiar one, the dreadful and unrelieved poverty which remained the open running sore of society.

The Poor Man's Tears

The Lawgiver's answer to the laywer's question.

Luke. 10. 25. And behold, a certain lawyer stood up and tempted him saying, Master, what shall I do to inherit eternal life.

Tears are the last thing that man, woman, or child can move by; and where tears move not, nothing will move. I therefore exhort you by the lamentable tears which the poor do daily shed through hunger and extreme misery, to be good unto them, to be charitable and mercifull unto them, and to relieve those whom you see with misery distressed.

The Scripture saith, *Give to every one that asketh:* God gave herbs and other food unto every living thing. Every Commonwealth that letteth any member in it to perish for hunger, is an unnaturall and uncharitable Commonwealth. But men are now-a-days so full of doubts, through a covetous desire to themselves, that they cannot abide to part with any thing to the poor, notwith-

1. Henry Smith, 1550–91. Born in Leicestershire. Queens' College, Cambridge, 1573; then, after private study, matriculated Lincoln College, Oxford, 1575. B.A. 1578, entering the ministry although heir to a considerable fortune. He collected his sermons only late in life. Posthumous publication 1592 and 1631. Reprint 1860.

2. Wood, *Athenae Oxoniensis*, ed. Bliss, i, 603.

standing that God hath promised he will not forget the work and love which you have shewed in his name to the poor and distressed.

Some will say for their excuse, that they are overcharged by giving to a number of persons; and therefore they cannot give to so many beggars: for by so doing they might soon become beggars themselves. David answered this objection very well, and saith thus, *I never saw the just man forsaken, nor his seed beg his bread:* whereby he meant, that in all the time that he had lived, (and the like for any man living the years of *David*) he scarcely ever saw, that upon an upright heart in giving, a man was brought to beggery.

There are a number that will deny a poor body a peny, and plead poverty to them, though they seem to stand in never so great extremes; when in a far worser sort they will not stick immediately to spend ten or twenty shillings. The rich worldling makes no conscience to have ten or twenty dishes of meat at his table; when in truth the one half might sufficiently satisfie nature, the rest run to the relief of the poor; and yet in the end he might depart better refreshed with one dish then commonly he is with twenty. Some will not stick to have twenty coats, twenty houses, twenty farms, yea twenty Lordships, and yet go by a poor person whom they see in great distresse, and never relieve him with one peny, but say, God help you, I have not for you. There are Lawyers that will not stick to undo twenty poor men, and Merchants that make on conscience to eat out twenty others, that have their hundreds out at usury, their chests crambed full of crowns, and their coffers full of golden gods, or glistering angels, that will go by twenty poor, miserable, hungry, impotent and distressed persons, and yet not bestow one peny on them: and though they do most shamefully ask it, yet can they most shamefully deny it, and refuse to perform it.

The people of this world can very easily find a staff to beat a dog; they are never without excuses, but ready to find delaies, and very pregnant to devise new shifts to keep in their alms. Now will I shew you reasons why we should give. God faith, *Whoso giveth to the poor, lendeth to the Lord, and shall be sure to find it again,* and receive for the same an hundred-fold. And again, *Blessed is he that considereth of the poor and needy; the Lord shall deliver him in the day of trouble.* Hereby appeareth that we shall receive our alms again, except we doubt whether God's word be true or no. For confirmation whereof, the Prophet *David* saith, *The testimonies of God are true and righteous.* And God speaks by the mouth of the Prophet *Esay,* saying, *The word is gone out of my mouth, and it shall not return.* The promise which God made to *Sara* was found true; his promise made to the children of *Israel* was found true; his promise to *Joshua* in the overthrowing of his enemies was found true. God promiseth *David* his Kingdome, to *Solomon* he promised wisedome; to *Pharaoh* he threatned destruction by water, to *Saul* the losse of his kingdome, and to *Solomon* the dividing of his Kingdom: all which and far more proved true. Then let us not doubt of God's promises, but fear his judgements; for from time to time they have been found true and just. Let us consider that we must die, and leave our goods we know not to whom: then, while we are here, let us distribute thereof unto the poor, that we may receive our reward in the kingdome of heaven. God saith by *S. Luke, O fool, this night will I fetch away thy soul, and then that which thou hast got who shall possesse it?* Here is a question worth the noting, and meet for rich men to consider: especially such as hoord up wealth, and have no regard to the relief of the poor. Do they think that the wealth which they have gathered together will come to good after their decease? No, it will melt and consume away like butter in the Sun. The reason is, because they would not doe as God hath commanded them, in distributing part of that to the poor which was lent them by the Lord.

The children of God in the 6. of the *Apocalyps* cry out, *How long, O Lord, thou that art holy and true, dost thou not judge and revenge our bloud upon those that dwell on the earth?* Whereby appeareth that God exerciseth good men, and those whom he loveth in the troubles of this world, which we account *long*; yet is their time but short, although their trouble makes it seem long. But these I say ought to be content, and all those that do trust in God must be content to relieve one another for a time, since after a short time we shall doubtlesse find the fruits of our alms again. Short is man's life while we are in this world: *David* compareth it to a *vapour*, to a *bubble*, to *wind*, to *grasse*, to a *shadow*, to *smoak*, and every fading thing that consumeth in a moment. *Esay* compareth it to the *removing of a Tabernacle*; and *Job* to an *Eagle's wing*, or a *weaver's shuttle*. So that our life is but short; and after a few days, though you think them many, whatsoever you mercifully bestow upon the poor here on earth, you shall certainly find the same again both in heaven and on earth. *Solomon* in the 21. of the *Proverbs* saith, *He that stoppeth his ear at the cry of the poor, shall cry himself, and not be heard. The bread of the needy is the life of the poor; he that keepeth it from them is a man of bloud.* S. *Paul* saith, No man giveth but he that hath received. And an ancient Father of the Church doth charge the rich with wast, for which they shall surely answer. Art thou not (saith he) a robber in keeping another man's substance, and to recon it as thine own? It is the bread of the hungry which thou dost detain, the coat due to the naked thou lockest in thy house, the shoes that appertain to the barefoot lie drying in thy house, and the gold which should relieve the poor lies cankering in thy coffers. Which saying, as it teacheth the liberality due unto the poor; so it blameth the careless rich, that account all to be their own, and will part with nothing, keeping to themselves more then is sufficient. But to such Saint *James* saith, that at the latter day the mite in the crums, the moaths in the garments, and the rust in the gold, shall fret them like cankers. *Ambrose* saith, It is no greater sin to take from him that rightly possesseth, then, being able, not to give him that wanteth.

The right rich man, that duly deserveth that name, is not known by his possession, by his costly fare, and costly building, by his sumptuous palace, by his plate, jewels and substance, but by considering the poor and needy. Whereof *Austine* saith thus, The rich are proved by the poverty of others. So that still the Scriptures and Fathers prescribe not an indifferency, but a necessity, not pleasure, but upon duty, that the poor and needy should be considered and relieved.

Where is the large liberality become that in times past was rooted in our fore-fathers? They were content to be liberall, though they applied it to evil purposes. The successours of those which in times past gave liberally to maintain Abbots, Friers, Monks, Nuns, Masses, Dirges, Trentals, and all Idolatry, seeing the abuses thereof, may now bestow it to a better use, namely to foster and feed the poor members of Christ.

The world is as great as it hath been, the people now are more rich then they have been, and more covetous then they have been: yea, they have more knowledge then ever they had, yet they want the desire they have had to become liberal, and seem therein most wilfully ignorant.

The extortioner can spare nought unto the poor, for joyning house to house, and land to land, though he have the poor man's curse for it. The Prophet *Esay* saith, the extortioner doeth no good to the poor, but daily seeketh to root them forth of doors. The pride of apparel maketh us forget the patches of the poor; our costly fare, their extreme hunger; and our soft lodging, their miserable lying.

O how liberal were people in times past to maintain superstition! and now how hard-hearted are they grown, not to keep the poor from famishing! Will ye make a scorn of the poor and needy? The poor now perisheth by the rich men, and no man considereth it. This is not the right duty of faithfull Christians: this ought not to be the fruits of our profession: neither is this the mercy which we learn by the Word.

Therefore towards the relief of the poor, I say, give, and give gladly: for the bread that is given with a stony heart is called stony bread, though necessary to be taken by the poor, to slake hunger; yea, it is but sour bread. Such a giver, in my opinion, is next kinsman unto Satan: for he gave *Christ* stones in stead of bread; but this man giveth Christians stony bread. The Wise man saith, Lay up thy alms in the hands of the poor: and know that in the end, what thou keepest thou shalt lose; but that thou givest to the poor shall be as a purse about they neck. For as this life waxeth old, and our days passe away, so shall this vain self pass away from us: neither shall riches help in the day of vengeance; but the corruption abideth, which fretteth like a canker. Then what shall it profit to get all the world? and when the world forsaketh us, that shall be most against us that best we loved while we were in the world. Let every man therefore perswade himself, that his soul is better then those subtle riches; the possession whereof is variable and uncertain, for they pass from us much more swiftly then they came unto us: and albeit we have the use of them even till the last day, yet at length we must leave them to others. Then, ere you die, lay them forth for the profit of your poor brethren. Learn to forsake the covetous world, before it forsake you: and learn counsel of our Saviour *Christ*, who adviseth you to *make friends of the wicked Mammon*.

We see daily that every one is good to the poor, (as we commonly say) but they will give them nought but words. Then I say, great boast and small roast makes unsavoury mouths. Yet if words will doe any good, the poor shall not want them: for it doth cost nothing to say, Alas! good soul, God help thee, God comfort thee, I would I were able to help thee: and such commonly will say so that have store of wealth lying by them. Such still wish well unto themselves in wishing themselves able: but of such wishing and such wishers I say as a beggar said to a Bishop who made the like answer, that if such wishes were worth but one half-peny to the poor, I doubt they would not be so liberal. I with you (good brethren) leave wishing, and fall to some doing. You lock up, and will not lose: you gather together even the devil and all; and why? because you would fain hatch the Cockatrice egge; you nurse up a canker for your selves; you keep the pack that shall trouble your voiage unto God, as *Christ* saith, *O how hard shall it be for a rich man to be saved! it shall be easier for a Camell to go through a needle's eye.* This he saith not, because no rich man shall be preferred; but because the mercilissee rich man shall be damned. We are admonished to liberality by sundry natural examples. The clouds, if they be full, do yield forth their rain: much rain is a burthen to clouds, and much riches are burthens to men. It is said of *Abraham*, *Gen.* 13.12. that he was burthened with gold: yet *Abraham* was a good man, but it burthened his head to be busied with the cares of gold. Again, to eat much, to drink much, and to rest much, is a burthen to the soul, though it be pleasant to the body: and in *Luke* 12.19. it appeareth, that abundance of riches maketh one to *eat* much, *drink* much, and rest much: then, were it not for the covetous minds of those that have much, they might impart to the poor one part of that which they daily spend in superfluity. It this be not amended, I let you to understand, that the poor must cry, and their voice shall be heard, their distresse considered, and your venegance shall be wrought. I tell you troth, even in *Jesus Christ*, that the poor have cried into the Lord, and he hath heard them. With speed therefore open your ears; if not to man, yet to *Christ*, who continually commandeth us to give and bestow upon the poor and needy. *Give, and it shall be given you*, saith he by *Luke*; and setteth before our eyes the example of the poor widow's mite; as also the example of a covetous rich man, who demanding how he might obtain eternal life, was answered thus by him, *Go sell all thou hast, and give to the poor;* not that it is necessary for every man so to doe, or that a man cannot be saved without he doe so; but thereby teaching him particularly to loath the world, and generally seek means for the daily cherishing and the refreshing of the poor. Do not continually feed your equals, for that is offensive: but when you may spare to spend and banquet your selves, then call the poor and impotent, and refresh your poor distressed neighbours and brethren: and when *Dives* hath dined, let *Lazarus* have the crums. And still remember the saying of Saint *Matthew, Blessed are the mercifull, for they shall obtain mercy.*

To conclude, (beloved in the Lord) let me intreat you rich men to consider it is your duty to remember the poor, and their continual want: you that eat till you blow, and feed till your eyes swell with fatnesse, that tast first your course meats, and then fall to finer fare, that have your severall drinks for your stomack, and your sorts of wine for your appetite, impart some of your superfluity unto the poorer, who, being comforted by you, will doubtlesse pray for you, that God would blesse you and yours, and increase your store a thousand fold. . . .

RICHARD BANCROFT[1]

In the latter years of Elizabeth's reign religious feelings were growing impassioned. It was apparent to the ecclesiastical establishment that the Puritan movement was intent upon undermining the episcopacy and taking over the church. The queen herself did not favour the Puritan penetration of the church, which she equated with a threat to authority, and that, in the end, meant *her* authority; but, as usual, she did not wish to be personally embroiled in the contest. Her method was to appoint to the crucial see of London a strong man whose opinions on the issue she knew and approved. She chose Richard Bancroft. In 1588 this future Archbishop of Canterbury had preached a sermon at Paul's Cross which had spread resentment and consternation in Puritan circles and marked him out as the movement's most formidable enemy.

A Warning Against Puritans

A sermon preached at Pauls Cross on the 9th February,

1588

The Doctrine of the Church of *England*, is pure, and holy: the government thereof, both in respect of her Majesty, and of our Bishops is lawfull, and godly: the booke of Common-Prayer containeth nothing in it contrary to the Word of God.

All those points have bene notably approoved, and maintained not onely against the Papists, but likewise against some other schismatikes, and you your selves with great joy, and comfort have in time past imbraced them accordingly. If any of you now, my brethren, be otherwise affected, the fault

1. Richard Bancroft, 1544–1610. Archbishop of Canterbury. Christ's College Cambridge. B.A. 1556. Licensed University preacher. D.D. 1585; Bishop of London 1597. Played a leading part on the side of the episcopacy in the Martin Marprelate controversies, and was chiefly responsible for the detection and arrest of John Penry and his collaborators.

is in your selves: for they remaine (as the nature of truth requireth) to be as they were before: but you through your rashness in following of every spirit, are growen to a wonderfull newfanglenes: and are in deed become meere changelings. *Quemadmodum eadem terra stat recte valentibus, quæ vertigine correptis videtur moveri*: As the same Earth (saith *Greg. Naz.*) appeareth immooveable to those that are in health, which to the giddy doth seeme to turne about: so you, my brethren, by following the perswasions of false Prophets (who, as *Irenæus* saith; *De iisdem non semper easdem sententias habent*: Of the selfe same things have not alwaies the same opinions) are drawen to an unjust mislike of the Church; *Et amantes vel non amantes, haud eadem de eisdem judicatis*: And according to your love, or hate your judgments upon the selfe same things do vary, and alter.

See, I pray you, what dislike is able to worke; and therefore take heed of those who shall indevour, through lies, and slanders, to make the truth, and the preachers thereof odious, and hatefull unto you. For as the Apostle writeth; *Æmulantur vos non bene, sed excludere vos volunt, ut, illos æmulemini*: They are jealous over amisse, even for their owne purpose, and commodity: yea they would exclude you from the Doctrine you have received at our hands, and from the affection, and love, which you once bare unto us, that ye might altogether love them, and follow their devises.

And that is the end of their railings, and libelling. *Mos semper fuit hæretuorum, quorum doctrinam non possunt confutare, illorum vitam in odium adducere*: It hath alwaies bene the manner of heretikes, to bring their lives into hatred, whose Doctrine they cannot confute. Knowing that by the contempt of the one, doth easily ensue the dislike of the other.

Howbeit, they will pretend that the zeale of Gods glory doth moove them unto such bitternes, against the present estate or Religion, and against the chiefe maintainers of it, and that for conscience sake, and for the glory of Sion they are driven to use such more than tragicall outcries. But *Bernard* will not suffer them to hide their malice under these maskes, who writing against certain schismatikes in his time, saith, *Allii quidem nude atque irreverenter, uti in buccam venerit, virus evomant detractionis*:[1] Some do plainely, and irreverently, even as it comes into their stomacke, spue out the poyson of their slanders. Many others there be, who cover their malice more cunningly, nay more hypocritically, as though all they said proceeded of meere love, and Christian charity, of whom it followeth, *Videas alta præmitti suspiria: sicque quadam cum gravitate et tarditate, vultu mæsto, demissis superciliis et voce plangenti egredi maledictionem, et quidem tanto persuasibiliorem, quanto creditur ab his qui audiunt corde invito et magis condolentis affectu, quam malitiose proferri*.[2] You shall see

1. Bernard, *Cantica Canticorum*. Sermon 24.4. Bancroft's Latin has been restored to conformity with St. Bernard's.
2. Ibid.

some, that after they have set divers great sighes, and groanes, will presently with great gravity, and drawing out ot their words, with a heavy countenance, with casting downe their heads, and with a pittifull voyce, breath out malediction, the which men do rather beleeve, because it seemeth by such their hypocriticall dealing, rather to proceed of a sorrowfull compassion, than of malice, and hatred. But dearly beloved, take heed of these spirits. Where you finde these conditions, beleeve not, I pray you, any such protestations.

Furthermore, you shall have some that will come unto you with a long tale, protesting that they cannot refraine their teares; with the ancient men in *Ezra*, to see the foundation of our new Temple not to be answerable (as they say) to the beauty of the old. And herein they thinke they should be very acceptable unto you: whereas in truth the crying of these aged men, was a great discouragement to the builders, and one of the principall lets, why the worke went no better forward:[1] and the Prophet *Aggæus* was sent from God to reproove them for it; allowing nay, preferring in some respects, the new building, which then they had in hand, before the other, which some so much affected.

So as, deerely beloved, when you heare the like cries, in any wise beleeve them not; but rather shout aloud for joy (as there it is likewise noted) in that you have lived to see your Temples purged from the leaven of Popery, and to flourish, as they do, with the sincerity, and truth of Christian Religion.

They will furthermore (the better to creepe into your harts) pretend great humility, and bitterly exclaime against the pride of Bishops as though they affected nothing else by their desired equality, but some great lowlines, and to prostrate themselves at your feete for your service: whereas in deede they shoote at greater superiority, and preeminence, then ever your Bishops did use of challenge unto them: and would no doubt tyrannize by their censures over both Prince, and people at their pleasure, in most untollerable, and popelike manner. As partly you may gather by the premisses, and partly furthermore understand in that not onely they do use the very same arguments for the soveraigne authority of their presbyteries (against the Prince) in causes Ecclesiasticall: that the Pope doth for his principality in the same (and none other so far as I can read, or I thinke can be shewed by any) but do likewise make to all our arguments for her Majesties supremacy against them, the very same answers, (if not word for word, yet alwaies in effect) that *Harding, Stapleton, Dorman*, and *Saunders*[2] have made to the same arguments, used by Bishop *Iewell*, Bishop *Horn*, Master Nowell, and others to the same

1. Ezra 3 and 4.
2. Thomas Harding, Thomas Stapleton, Thomas Dorman and Nicholas Sanders: members of a group of English (mainly Wykhamist) Roman Catholic controversialists, who left England after the accession of Elizabeth, and conducted polemical warfare against Bishop Jewel.

purpose, and against the Pope. I cannot stand to enter into any particular examples of this matter, onely I thought it necessary at this time to advertise you of it (take his advantage thereof who list) that you might the better beware of such kinde of spirits.

You have heard them, I am sure, greatly exclaime against our Bishops livings, as though they had too much, thereby to perswade you with what simple allowance they could content themselves: and yet (as you have heard) they reckon all the livings of the Church too little for themselves: condemn-ing you of the laity, who eyther have or would have part with them, for cormorants, *Dionysians*[1], and for such wicked traitors against the Church, as *Iudas* was against Christ.

They would gladly seeme to be very godly, zealous, and religious: and yet notwithstanding, if you will rely upon Saint *Iames* his opinion, and judge of them by the usage of their tongues, in their immodest speeches, and libelling, you shall finde their profession thereof to be full of so great vanity, as that particularly it may be verified almost of everyone of them: *Hujus vana est religio.*

If they set foorth a booke of Common Prayer, then caution is made that nothing be done contrary to any thing set downe in the same. If they decree any thing in their synods (yea though it be in civill matters) against an act of Parleament, that treason is not treason, yet if you withstand them, you are foorthwith accursed: or as touching Church causes, except it should so fall out, that they do erre in their determinations, and that in some great matter of faith, all men must stand unto their orders, decrees lawes, and constitu-tions.

But on the other side, if the Church indeed, upon sufficient grounds shall eyther publish a booke, or command any thing to be observed, though that which is commanded have bene determined of, not onely by provinciall or nationall synods, but by all the generall councels in effect, which were held before the tyranny of popery: yet (as Saint *Bernard* saith in the like case) *Hærent ad singula quæ insunguntur, exigunt de quibusque rationem, male suspicantur de omni præcepto, nec unquam libenter acquiescunt, nisi cum audire contigerit quod forte libuerit:* they sticke at all things which are injoined, they require the reason of every thing, they suspect amisse of every precept, and will never willingly hold themselves contented but when they heare that, which peradventure doth please them. . . .

1. Like Dionysius (elder or younger), Tyrant of Syracuse, 4th century B.C., notorious for cruelty.

THOMAS PLAYFERE[1]

Thomas Playfere was reputed one of the most graceful public speakers among the learned men of the universities in the latter part of the reign of Elizabeth. He held various academic appointments at Cambridge, including that of Lady Margaret Professor of Divinity from 1596. He appears to have been a man of intense feelings. On November 4th, 1602, Chamberlain wrote to Carleton, 'Dr. Playfer the Divinity reader is crazy for love . . .'[2] and the words seem to have been no exaggeration, for by 1606 he was declared insane, and remained so (although he continued to occupy the Chair of Divinity) until his death. The subject of *The Pathway to Perfection* is the importance of cultivating humility before God.

The Pathway to Perfection[3]

Truth it is, we may remember, both that we haue done ill, to amend it, & also that we haue done well, to continue it. For the first, *Chrysostome* saith, Nothing doth so well helpe vs forward in a good course, as the often remembrance of our sins. Whereas in the bitternes of our soules we call to remembrance the dayes of old, which we haue passed away in sin. Whereupon the Psalmist particularly intituleth the eight & thirtieth Psalm, a *Memorandum*, or a Remembrance, because he made it when he called to remembrance his sinnes, which he had in former time committed. And generally *Baruch* saith to vs in this sort: Remember well what you haue done, & as it came in your hearts to turne away from God, so now striue with your selues tenne times more to turne againe vnto him. Thus did *Paul*, remembring hee

1. Thomas Playfere, 1561?–1609. Matriculated St. John's College, Cambridge. Lady Margaret Foundation B.A. 1579. M.A. 1583. B.D. 1590. D.D. 1596. University appointments included medical lecturer, examiner in rhetoric, senior fellow, senior dean 1598, principal lecturer 1600. Inner Temple 1594. Lady Margaret Professor of Divinity 1596. Chaplain to King James I.

2. *C.S.P.D.* cclxxxxv, 48.   3. First preached 1595; first published 1599.

had once beene a persecutor, he did repent him of it, and made amends for it, and was afterward ten times more zealous to saue the wicked, then before he had beene to destroy the godly. For the second, another sayth: O what heauenly comfort doe they inwardly feele, which are delighted with the remembrance of vertue past, with the fruition of ioy present, with the expectation of felicity to come? This threefold cord of comfort, as it can neuer be broken, so it must alwaies be drawne forth at length, that he which is iust, may be still more iust: that he which is strong, may be still more strong. Thus did *Dauid*, remembring he had once slain a *Beare*, he did not repent him of it, but gathered strength and courage by it, and was afterward more bold to combate with a mighty Gyant, then before he had been to deale with an eluish[1] Beare. Therefore as they which leape, the further they go backward to fetch their run, the further they leape forward, when they haue runne: so here we may looke back a little, & remember both what we haue done ill, to amend it, and also what we haue done well, to continue it. Otherwise, the remembrance eyther of vices or vertues, is so farre from putting vs any whit forward, that it casteth vs quite backeward. For as *Marke* the Eremite witnesseth, The remembrance of former sinnes is enough to cast him downe altogether, who otherwise might haue had some good hope. Our sins, and *Elies* sonnes are alike. *Elie* hearing his sonnes were slaine, whom he himselfe had not chastised and corrected as he ought, fell downe backward, and brake his necke. And so all they that remember and hearken after their former sinnes, which they should haue mortified and killed, fall downe backward, and turne away from God. For this is the difference betweene the godly and wicked. Both fall. But the godly fall forward vpon their faces, as *Abraham* did when hee talked with God: the wicked fall backward vpon the ground, as the Iewes did when they apprehended Christ. Hee that remembers his sinnes, to be sorry for them, as *Abraham* did, fals forward vpon his face: but he that remembers his sinnes, to reioyce in them, as the Iewes did, falles backward vpon the ground. Wherefore if thou bee vpon a mountaine, looke not backward againe vnto Sodom, as *Lots* wife did: if thou be within the Arke, flie not out againe into the world, as *Noahs* Crow did: If thou be well washed, returne not againe to the mire, as the Hogge doth: If thou be cleane purged, runne not againe to thy filth, as the Dogge doth: If thou be going towards the land of Canaan, thinke not on the flesh-pots of Egypt: If thou bee marching against the hoast of Midian, drinke not of the waters of Harod: If thou be vpon the house top; come not downe: If thou haue set thy hand to the plough, looke not behinde thee: remember not those vices which are behinde thee. No, nor those vertues neyther. For as *Gregorie* writeth: The remembrance of former vertues doth many times so besot and inueigle a man, that it makes him like a blinde Asse fall downe into a ditch. When *Orpheus*

1. In the sense of 'intractable', unmanageable.

went to fetch his wife *Eurydice* out of hell, hee had her granted to him, vpon condition that hee should not turne backe his eyes to looke vpon her, till hee had brought her into heauen. Yet hauing brought her forward a great way, at length his loue was so excessive, that he could not containe any longer, but would needs haue a sight of her. Wherupon forthwith he lost both her sight and her selfe, shee suddenly againe vanishing away from him. This is a Poeticall fiction: neuerthelesse it serueth very fitly to this purpose to admonish vs, that if we haue any vertue, which is to be loued, as a man is to loue his wife, yet we must not bee so blind in affection, as to dote too much vpon it, or to stand in admiration of our seules for it, or to be alwaies gazing and wondring at it, left by too much looking vpon it, & by too well liking of it, and by too often remembring it, we lose it: because indeed hee that remembers his vertues, hath no vertues to remember. Seeing hee wants humility, which is the mother-vertue of all vertues. For this is the difference betweene the godly and the wicked: Both remember vertues. But the godly remember other mens vertues, the wicked remember their owne vertues. They remembring their owne vertues, make them ensamples to imitate: these remembring their owne vertues, make them miracles to wonder at. Therefore the godly remembring they haue some one or other little vice in them, are humbled, though they haue very many great vertues: But the wicked remembring they haue some one or other little vertue in them are proud, though they haue very many great vices. Wherefore though thou haue conquered Kingdomes, yet crake[1] not of it, as *Senacherib* did: though thou hast built Babel, yet brag not of it, as *Nabuchadonozer* did: though thou haue a great people, yet number them not, as *Dauid* did: though thou haue rich treasure, yet shew them not, as *Ezechias* did: though thou haue slaine a thousand Philistins, yet glory not in it, as *Samson* did: though thou haue built seuen Altars, yet vaunt not of it, as *Balack* did: though thou giue almes, yet blow not a Trumpet, though thou fast twice a weeke, yet make no words of it, (remember it not but) *Forget that which is behind.*

If thou wilt be *Perfect, Sell all that thou hast, and follow me,* sayth our Sauiour. Sell all that thou hast. Or if no man will buy it, giue it. Or if no man will take it, *Forget* it. *Themistocles* sayd, he had rather learne the art of forgetfulnesse, then of memory. That is, as I vnderstand it, rather Diuinity, then Phylosophy. For Philsophy is an Art of memory, but Diuinity is an Art of forgetfulnesse. Therefore the first lesson that *Socrates* taught his Scholler was, *Remember.* For he thought that knowledge is nothing else but a calling of those things to remembrance which the mind knew, before it knew the body. But the first lesson that Christ teacheth his Scholler is, *Forget.* Hearken O daughter (sayth he) and see, Forget thine owne country and thy fathers

1. Crake (a variant of 'crack'), still used in Suffolk dialect: to boast, brag. See above, p. 68.

house. So that fayth is that faire *Helena*, which drinks to vs in a cup of *Nepenthes*, and saith, Be of good cheere, there shall be no more sorrow, neyther crying, neyther death, neyther paine, for the first things are past. And the water of the Word of God is that fountaine *Lethe*, which when we come to drinke of it, speaks to vs (as it were) in this sort: *Remember not the former things, neyther regard the things of old.* For as they which dye cloth, doe not immediately change one contrary into another, but first turne a white into an azure, and then make a puke of it: So we can neuer hold colour, as a good puke, except first our white be turned into an azure: that is, as *Lyrinensis* saith, except first we do well to *Forget* that, which we did ill to get, except first we do happily vnlearne that, which wee did vnhappily learne. And like as they which worke in wax, cannot frame any new impression in it, till the old be defaced: so the image of *Cæsar*, the Prince of the world the diuell must first bee defaced, before the Image of Christ can bee formed in vs. For this Image of Christ (as *Clemens* testifieth) is seene onely in them, which *Forget* the hill of *Helicon*, and dwell in mount *Syon*. Wherefore though thou haue had a bloody issue twelue yeeres, yet thine issue being now stopt, *Forget* all bloodinesse: though thou haue had a crooked body eighteene yeeres, yet thy body being now straightned, *forget* all crookednesse: though thou haue had blind eyes, yet thine eyes being now cleared, forget all blindnesse in seeing the truth: though thou haue had deafe eares, yet thine eares being now opened, *forget* all deafnesse in hearing the Word: though thou haue had a dry hand, yet thy hand being now restored, *forget* all drynesse and niggard-linesse with men: though thou haue had a lame foot, yet thy foote being now recured, *forget* all limping and haulting with God: though thou haue been dead and buried in the graue foure dayes, as *Lazarus* was, yet being now reuiued, *forget* all deadnesse in sin: though thou haue bin possessed and tor-mented with seuen diuels, as *Mary Magdalen* was, yet being now deliuered, renounce the deuill & all his workes: and *forget* all thy wicked works which are behinde thee. Yea and all thy good works also. For if thou *forget* them, then will God remember them. The Patriark *Abraham* was content for Gods pleasure to sacrifice his sonne *Isaac*. But as soone as hee had done, he *forgets* it. Therefore God remembers it, and sets downe euery seuerall circumstance of it. By mine owne selfe haue I sworn (saith the Lord) because thou hast don this thing. There is the general. But what thing? The perticular followes. And hast not spared; yea not thy seruant, but thy sonne: nay, not onely thy sonne, but thine onely sonne: *and hast not spared thine onely sonne*: therefore I wil surely blesse thee. That good woman gaue Christ louing and friendly enter-tainement. But as soone as she had done, she *forget* it. Therefore Christ re-members it, and amplifies it from point to point. He turned to the woman and said to *Simon*, Seest thou this woman? when I came to thy house, thou gauest me no water for my feet: but she hath washed my feet with the teares of her eyes, and wiped them with the haires of her head. Thou gauest me no kisse: but she since the time, I came in, hath not ceased to kisse my feet. My head with Oile thou didst not anoint, but shee hath anointed my feet with ointment. Lo, see how true it is which I said before, that if we remember our good works, then God will forget them: but if we *forget* them, then God will remember them: yea and he will reward them when we haue forgotten them. If we wage warre with God, and thinke to ouercome him with ten thousand of our good deeds, then wil he like a puissant Prince, bring forth into the field a huge Army of our sinnes, twenty thousand of our sins against vs, & with twenty thousand of our sins will easily ouerthrow ten thousand of our good deeds, and so finally confound vs. But if on the other side we can be content to *forget* all our good workes, and to strow our best garments, and our most flowrishing branches at Christs feet: and to cast downe our very crownes before the throne of the Lambe, then he will be a right Lamb indeed, he will not fight with vs, but he will crowne vs with honour & glory. Almighty God appointed his people not to sheare the first borne of the sheep. The first born of the sheep are the best of our good workes. These we must not sheare, nor lay naked and open to the view and knowledge of all men, but *forget* them, and hide them vnder the fleece of silence, and keepe them secret to our selues.

RICHARD HOOKER[1]

'There is in them such seeds of eternity, that if the rest be like this, they shall last till the last fire shall consume all learning.' These words, uttered in an age of religious intolerance, are remarkable forasmuch as they are not the conventional praise of one partisan for the apologetics of a fellow-traveller, but the words of Pope Clement VIII upon reading the first writings of a humble English 'heretic' priest.

Richard Hooker brought a spirit of tolerance and a light of enquiring humanism into the attrite broadsides of rigid absolutes and scurrilous abuse exchanged by religious adversaries in the sixteenth century. He declared that every kind of knowledge and experience was not only admissible, but necessary to the fulfilment of the destiny ordained for man in the nature of his being. The Scriptures were holy and a general guide to the supernatural will; but they were not intended to be every-thing, since man was not a prisoner without initiative. They did not provide inflexible rules for every occasion; they did not absolve men from the God-sent duty of thinking actively and judging fresh situations afresh, in the light of Christian principles. There was no one absolute form of a Christian church; one form might be more temporally suitable in one set of circumstances than another; by which token, though the English church, within this catholicity, had its lawful inde-pendence, the church of Rome was also a true Church of Christ and a sanctified church. These were courageous words for an English clergy-man to use in the prevailing atmosphere of hatred and recrimination. Hooker was a Christian existentialist; everything he wrote was perme-ated by the affirmation of the duty of perpetual revision and correction in

1. Richard Hooker, 1554–1600. Born in or near Exeter. Admitted Corpus Christi, Oxford, 1567. M.A. 1577, subsequently Fellow. After taking holy orders was given the mastership of the Temple through the influence of Whitgift. In 1591, at his own request he was allowed to withdraw to the quiet living of Boscombe, six miles from Salisbury, and it was here he finished the first four books of the *Laws of Ecclesiastical Polity*, the seminal masterpiece of his works. The year after their publication in 1594 he removed to the living of Bishopsbourne, near Canterbury, where he died in 1600 'of a cold caught in a passage of water betwixt London and Gravesend'. An important part of his unpub-lished writings was said to have been destroyed by his wife's Puritan relations (see Izaak Walton's *Life*).

the light of expanding knowledge and experience. He taught that the present was not a substitute for the past, nor the past a dead corpse that could be buried and treated as if it had never been, for the past was alive within us and might not without danger be denied or ignored; 'reformation' could mean correction but not denial. His learning was cyclopaedic; he took (making scrupulous acknowledgement) from every quarter, and the sum of the parts greatly exceeded the whole, for they were sublimated by the majesty of his organization and insight. Like his contemporary, Shakespeare, Hooker was a creative eclectic of the highest order. He provided, against a coming day of trouble, the precious common ground of a rational centre, upon which temperate episcopalians and latitudinarians could converge, and by virtue of which, after the wracking conflicts of the following century, the Church of England was delivered from the alien rigour of Calvinism.

Hooker's prose flows with the seeming-effortless, architectonic variety of disciplined invention, in which similia appear, like artifacts in settings true to their nature, each attesting its authenticity with an air of its presence being unrehearsed, yet inevitable, however brief its function. He was never a 'popular' preacher; his thought was too exacting, and his preaching unhelped by any technic of rhetoric. Of 'mean stature', he spoke in a quiet, undramatic, probably monotonous voice, with his eyes fixed on one spot. One had to listen with care for the words to do their office.

Approaching them now at a remove of centuries, the sermons are occasionally surprising for the startling shock which Hooker can administer when he chooses. In *A Remedy Against Sorrow and Fear* he first relaxes the reader with the conventional imagery of Christ crucified, a concept of suffering clothed in reassuring garments of familiar propriety: God is suffering, but graciously, with dignity and resignation; a *Raphael* Christ, enduring more in sorrow of spirit than pain of flesh. Then, in an instant, the familiar drooping divinity on the cross is suddenly and hideously altered; in the turn of a single word the figure changes from Christ the God, transcending brief humanity, to Christ the man, convulsing the wreck of his body in incontinent carnal agony, struggling and 'roaring' like any tortured animal. Hooker's studied and sparing use of shock has an interesting similarity to E. M. Forster's method of lifting a situation to prominence by introducing, without warning, a sudden violent outrage in the context of established restraint and seeming security.

The passage which follows is chosen for the tempering quality which Hooker brought to an area of white-hot controversy, without sacrificing the integrity of his criticism either of the Roman admission of a doctrine of merit and supererogation, or of the Puritan Calvinists' insistence upon the exclusivity of the elect. He declines to embrace one, merely because he rejects the other. The majestic comprehensiveness of this thought, perplexing and enraging, at the time, to zealots of both sides, generated a light, by means of which the Church of England went on to confirm her independence without betraying her catholicity.

Justification and Works[1]

But we say our salvation is by Christ alone, therefore howsoever, or whatsoever wee adde vnto Christ in the matter of salvation, we overthrow Christ. Our case were very hard, if this argument so vniversally meant, as it is proposed, were sound and good. We our selues doe not teach Christ alone, excluding our owne faith, vnto iustification; Christ alone, excluding our own works, vnto sanctification; Christ alone, excluding the one or the other vnnecessarie vnto salvation. It is a childish cavill wherewith in the matter of iustification our adversaries do so greatly please themselues, exclaiming that wee tread all Christian vertues vnder our feet, and require nothing in Christians but faith, because wee teach, that faith alone iustifieth: whereas by this speech we never meant to exclude either hope, or charitie from being alwaies ioined as inseparable mates with faith in the man that is iustified; or workes from being added as necessarie duties required at the hands of every iustified man: but to shew, that faith is the only hand, which putteth on Christ vnto iustification; and Christ, the only garment, which being so put on, covereth the shame of our defiled natures, hideth the imperfections of our workes, preserveth vs blameles in the sight of God, before whom otherwise, the weaknesse of our faith were cause sufficient to make vs culpable, yea to shut vs from the kingdome of heaven, where nothing that is not absolute, can enter. That our dealing with them bee not as childish as theirs with vs, when wee heare of salvation by Christ alone, considering that [alone] as an exclusiue particle, we are to note, what it doth exclude, & where. If I say, such a iudge only, ought to determine such a case, all our sanctification cannot be

1. A Learned Discourse of Iustification, Works & How the foundation of faith is overthrowne (delivered 1591 and published 1613).

accomplished without them. The doctrine concerning them is a thing builded upon the fitnes which is in it to serve his turne; in us no such thing. Touching the rest, which is laid for the foundation of our faith, importeth farther; that by him we are called; that we have redemption, remission of sins through his blood, health by his stripes; iustice by him; that he doth sanctify his church, & make it glorious to himself; that entrance into ioy shall be given us by him, yea all things by him alone. Howbeit not so by him alone as if in us, to our vocation, the hearing of the Gospell; to our iustification, faith; to our sanctification, the fruits of the spirit; to our entrance into rest, perseverence in hope, in faith, in holinesse, were not necessary.[1]

Then what is the fault of the Church of Rome? Not that shee requireth workes at their handes which will bee saved: but that she attributeth unto workes a power of satisfying God for sin; yea a vertue to merite both grace here, and in heaven glorie. That this overthroweth the foundation of faith, I grant willingly; that it is a direct denying therof, I utterly denie.[2] What it is to hold, and what directly to deny, the foundation of faith, I have already

1. I have amended the punctuation of this passage to make it more readily apprehensible to a modern eye; but it may still be desirable to add, that the imperative point of catholic doctrine here being made is that, while Christ is alone and wholly responsible for our salvation, we join with our Saviour in a unity of *active* experience, in as much as he works *within* us as subjects, not *upon* us as objects. The authorities on which this argument rests are as follows: 1 Gal. 5:8; 1 Pet. 2:9; Eph. 1:7; Isa. 53:11; Jer. 23:6; Eph. 8:6; Matt. 35:23; Thess. 2:14; Gal. 2:16; Gal. 5:23; Thess. 2:15.

2. Hooker is refusing to join in the popular Protestant reproach of Rome for renegation of faith; he is objecting only to a misinterpretation of doctrine conducive to an erroneous emphasis upon human endeavour as a principal cause of salvation. His criticism was one approved by the more discerning and far-sighted theologians of the Church of Rome. Readers who might wish to pursue this aspect of Catholic doctrine are referred in particular to Robert Bellarmine's *Disputationes de Controvertiis Christianae Fidei*, 3 vols. (Rome, 1581), as well, of course, for the Anglican view, to Hooker's *Laws of Ecclesiastical Polity*, the best modern edition of which is in his *Works* (Oxford, 1888). For the Calvinist position, Calvin's own *Institutes* are indispensable. Calvinist Puritanism in England, synchronous with Hooker, is best represented by Thomas Cartwright, *A Second Admonition to Parliament* (1572); the controversy which provoked it, *An Admonition to Parliament*, by John Field and Thomas Wilcox, will sharpen the focus of the view when read in conjunction with the establishment's reply, Whitgift's *An Answer to a Certain Libel intitled an Admonition to Parliament* (1572). Walter Travers's rather rare *Ecclesiasticae Disciplinae* (La Rochelle, 1574) would be worth reading if only because its author was the abrasive sand to Hooker's oyster. Travers's work was translated (probably by Cartwright) as *A ful and plaine declaration of Ecclesiastical Discipline* (1574) and provided the material for *A Directory of Church Government*, reprinted, with an introduction by Peter Lorimer, in 1872. Everything written by William Perkins is relevant to Puritan Calvinism as a whole, for the influence of 'our wonder', as Phineas Fletcher called him in his *Miscellanies*, 'living though dead', was far-reaching and enduring in England and America. The 'complete' editions are far from complete, and Perkins must be sought out piecemeal; perhaps the best collection is the 1608 edition in 3 volumes. Modern studies, although useful as guides, are not substitutes for the primary material.

opened. Apply it particularly to this cause, and there needes no more adooe. The thing which is handled, if the forme under which it is handled be added thereunto, it showeth the foundation of any doctrine whatsoever. Christ is the matter whereof the doctrine of the Gospell treateth; and it treateth of Christ as of a Saviour. Salvation therefore by Christ is the foundation of Christians. As for works, they are a thing subordinate, no otherwise than because things incident to the determination thereof, besides the person of the Iudge, as laws, depositions, evidences, &c. are not hereby excluded; persons are not excluded from witnessing herein, or assisting, but only from determining & giving sentence. How then is our salvation wrought by Christ alone? Is it our meaning that nothing is requisit to mans salvation but Christ to saue, & he to be saved quietly without any more adoe? No; wee acknowledge no such foundation. As we haue receiued, so wee teach, that besides the bare and naked worke, wherein Christ without any other associate finished al the parts of our redemption, & purchased salvation himselfe alone: for conveiance of this eminent blessing vnto vs, manie things are of necessity required, as to be knowne & chosen of God before the foundation of the world; in the world to bee called, iustified, sanctified; after wee haue left the world, to bee receaued vnto glory; Christ in every of these hath somwhat, which hee worketh alone. Through him according to the eternall purpose of God, before the foundation of the world, borne, crucified, buried, raised, &c. we were in a gracious acceptation knowne vnto God, long before we were seene of men: God knew vs, loved vs, was kind to vs in Iesus Christ; in him we were elected to be heires of life. Thus farre God through Christ hath wrought in such sort alone, that our selues are meere patients, working no more then dead & senselesse matter, wood, or stone, or yron, doth in the artificers hands, no more then the clay when the potter appointeth it to be framed for an honourable use: nay, not so much; for the matter wherevpon the craftsman worketh, hee chooseth being moved by foundation; therefore the doctrine, which addeth vnto them the power of satisfying or of meriting, addeth vnto a thing subordinated, builded vpon the foundation, not to the very foundation it selfe: yet is the foundation by this addition consequently overthrowne, for as much as out of this addition it may be negatiuely concluded; He which maketh any worke good, and acceptable in the sight of God, to proceede from the naturall freedome of our wil; he which giueth vnto any good workes of ours, the force of satisfying the wrath of God for sin, the power of meriting either earthly or heavenly rewards; he which holdeth workes, going before our vocation, in congruity to merite our vocation, workes following our first, to merit our second iustification, and by condignitie our last reward in the kingdome of heaven; pulleth vp the doctrine of faith by the roots; for out of every (one) of these the plaine direct deniall thereof may bee necessarilie concluded. Not this only, but what other heresie is there, that doth not raze the very foundation of faith by consequent? How be it, we make a difference of heresies accounting them in the next degree to infidelitie, which directly denie any one thing to be, which is expressly acknowledged in the articles of our beliefe; for out of any one article so denied, the deniall of the very foudation it selfe is streight way inferd. As for example; if a man should say, *There is no Catholike Church*, it followeth immediatly therevpon, that this Iesus whom we call the Saviour, is not the Saviour of the world; because all the Prophets beare witnesse, that the true Messias should *shew light vnto the Gentils*,[1] that is to say, gather such a church as is Catholicke, not restrained any longer vnto one circumcised nation. . . .

1. Acts 26: 23.

JOHN DOD[1]

It seems somewhat hard that an honest man should be best remembered by a parody of himself, but that has been the fate of John 'Decalogue' Dod. Junior at Cambridge by a few years to Perkins, whom he long outlived, Dod acquired, as a fellow of St. John's College, a reputation for good scholarship and better life. However he seems to have had a sense of playfulness somewhat irregular in a Puritan divine of the period, and he was noted for the ingenuity of his sermonical divisions.

Whether the parody is pure invention, or cultivated from a germ of fact is not known; but the story goes that at Cambridge Dod was wont to preach very strongly against the prevalence of drunkenness amongst what he called the 'malt-worms' of the university; and, one evening, as he was walking homewards through the countryside, his progress was observed by a party of undergraduates emerging from a tavern, who decided there and then to amuse themselves with their critic. Accordingly they lay in wait for Dod at a lonely spot on the footpath and barred his way, declaring that he should not have liberty to proceed until he had preached them a sermon on a text of their choosing, and the text of their choice was the word MALT. His pulpit should be a hollow tree trunk which stood hard by. Finding no way open but to comply, Dod ascended into the tree trunk and addressed his auditory as follows.

1. John Dod, 1549?–1645. Born at Shotlidge, nr. Malpas; youngest of seventeen. Jesus College, Cambridge, scholar and Fellow. Suspended from the living of Hanwell in 1604 and then silenced even by Archbishop Abbot; he was deemed intractably non-conformist. Later at the Rectory of Fawsley, he was troubled by royalist troops, who plundered his house. Publications include *Two Sermons* (1602), *Ten Sermons* (1633). See Fullers's *Church History* ed. Brewer (Oxford, 1845), VI, 305–8; *Worthies*, I, 181; Neale's *Puritans*, III, 270; Taylor's *Memorials* (1875); *Old Dod's Sayings* (1680).

An Unprepared Sermon on *Malt*[1]

Beloved, let me crave your reverend attention: I am a little man, come at a short warning, to preach a short sermon, from a short subject to a thin congregation, in an unworthy pulpit. Beloved, my text is Malt. Now, there is no teaching without a division. I cannot divide my text into sentences, because there are none; nor into words, it being but one; nor into syllables, it being but a monosyllable. Therefore I must divide it into letters, which I find in my text to be four: M, A, L, T. M, my beloved, is moral, A, allegorical, L, literal, and T, theological. First, the moral teaches such as you drunkards good manners: wherefore, M, my masters, A, all of you, L, listen, T, to my text. Secondly the allegorical is when one thing is spoken of and another meant; the thing spoken of is malt, the thing meant is the oil of malt, properly called strong beer; which you, gentlemen, make M, your meat, A your apparel, L, your liberty, and T, your treasure. Thirdly, the literal sense hath ever been found suitable to the theme, confirmed by beggarly experience: M, much, A, ale, L, little, T, thought. Fourthly, the theological is according to the effects that it worketh, which are of two kinds: the first in this world, the second in the world to come. The effects that it worketh in this world are M, murder, A, adultery, L, looseness of life, and T, treason. In the world to come the effects of it are M, misery, A, anguish, L, lamentation, and T, torment. And the appliation of my text is this: M, my masters, A, all of you, L, look for, T, torment.

After that it seems only fair to offer a specimen of authentic Dod[2]. By those who were in sympathy with his independent position Dod was much admired as a preacher. Indeed, while he was still at Cambridge, a visiting body of Oxford scholars, hearing him preach, and pronouncing him 'fecitously solid' tried to lure him to an Oxford fellowship, but he declined the honour and remained loyal to Cambridge.

1. The sermon has survived in a variety of versions of which this is a reduction to what seems the earliest version. See in particular *Sermon on the word Malt by the Rev. John Dod* (1777).

2. See below, p. 189.

WILLIAM BARLOW[1]

When, on Sunday, February 8th, 1601, Robert Devereux, Earl of Essex, aged thirty-three, rode out of his London house at the head of a party of armed men, made his bid, and failed, to capture the person of the sixty-four-year-old Queen and arrest her advisers, it was deemed necessary, on conviction of treason, to exact the death penalty. Even if his intentions had been no more than he averred—to change Her Majesty's counsellors and summon parliament—alive, he would have remained, as he himself admitted, a resort for discontented men of both extremes, Papist and Puritan. These were the potentially explosive elements which it had always been the crown's domestic policy to keep dispersed and unled. But Essex personally had been a popular hero to the citizens of London,[2] and it was judged advisable, that any lingering sympathy might be quenched, to present a persuasively unfavourable account of the earl's actions to the people without delay. The preacher selected for this commission was William Barlow, a discreet, ambitious, orthodox divine, averse to the Puritan element and approved of by the queen.

Familiar as Barlow was with the mobility of court intrigue, he felt embarrassment as he mounted the pulpit at Paul's Cross, a few days after he had attended Essex on the scaffold, because, from that same pulpit, he had on an earlier occasion preached an oration in fulsome praise of the living man whom, in death, he was now come to denounce. But, meticulously briefed by Cecil, he knew his duty and addressed himself to the appointed task.

---

1. William Barlow, d. 1613. Bishop of Lincoln. St. John's College, Cambridge, B.A. 1583-4; M.A. 1587. Fellow of Trinity Hall, 1590; B.D. 1594; D.D. 1599. Bishop of Rochester, 1605; Bishop of Lincoln, 1608.

2. After the execution the headsman was attacked by the crowd and had to be rescued by the Sheriff (John Nichols, *The Progresses of Queen Elizabeth*. III, 550).

On the Beheading of the Earl of Essex

A sermon preached at Paule's Crosse on the first
Sunday in Lent, 1601

One thing I cannot omit, which much mooued me against him, (though I honoured him as much as any follower of his, who carieth with him a good subiects hart) which perhaps you knowe not, namely his strange Apologie of himselfe vnto Maister Deane of Norwiche, sent vnto him by the Lordes for his soules good, the next day after his arraignement, who vrging him to acknowledge his offences, the late Earle vtterly denied, *That in any thing he had done he was guiltie of offending Almighty God.* But because I promised to giue you nothing of report, I call to minde the very speeche he vttered vnto my Lordes Grace of Canterburie in Lambeth house, the night of his apprehention. Oh, my Lord, saith the Archbishop, I am sorie to see this day, & that you haue so farre forgot your selfe: the Earle replyed smilingly, *that the sinceritie of my conscience and the goodnesse of my cause dooth comfort me*: this speech argues he thought himselfe not guiltie of *offending God.* As if a good intention, we will suppose it so, dooth make the action good. The Canon Lawyers say, that God loues Aduerbes better then Adiectiues, he cares not how good *quam bonum,* but *quam bene,* how well, and by what good meanes it is done which we intend. The iustifying of an ill execution vpon a good purpose and meaning, is the vtter subuersion of all religion and policie: an opinion forged at the fire of hell, and hammered at the Anuile of the Popes faculties. The same Deane asking him why he refused to come to the Lords, being sent for by the appointment of her Maiestie, he answered that, by Scripture, and thus reasoneth, *Dauid refused to come to Saul when he sent for him: Ergo I might lawfully refuse to come to Queene Elizabeth.*

Here a diuine cannot be patient, to see Gods word alleadged in despight of Gods ordinance, thus the deuil delt with Christ *Math. 4,* in quoting a place of scripture to iustifie the breaking of his neck. And *Clement* the Frier who killed *Henry* the third the French king, reasoned thus with himselfe for his bloudy murther out of Gods booke, *Ehud* killed king *Eglon,* therefore I may kill *Henry, Eglon* was a king, so is *Henry.* What then? *Eglon* signifieth a Calue and *Henrie* is a Calvenist, *Ergo* I may kill him by authority of scripture. It is recorded by *Mercurius Gallobelgicus*[1] in his first booke. Let Papists lay these grounds, and make these proofes, I am sory that any, who caries the name

1. Translated by R. Booth and published in 1614.

of a Protestant, should argue thus. It is the speach of *Salomon, He that wrings his nose, fetcheth out bloud.* Which *Gregory* fitly applies, that he which wresteth the scripture from the true sence, bringeth forth either an herisie or a phrensie, it is that which the learned call *Glossa viperine* when an interpretation like a Viper, eates out the bowels of the text. For, God be thanked, there is no semblance of this example makes for his refusall. Because *Saule* was reiected by God, but Queene *Elizabeth* is the chosen and the beloued of God, which from heauen by his prouidence ouer her, as in shielding her from many, so from this *Presumptuous* attempt, he hath demonstratiuely shewed. *Dauid* by a Prophet, at Gods appointment was anoynted king, so was not he. But I vrge this no further because it is not within his confession verball or written, to which I promised to stand, yet to shew you how farre he was gone that way, the word he vsed to vs of *Leprosie,* makes that good which he spake in a passion to the Deane, *If you knew how many motions haue beene made to me to do my best to remooue such euills as the common wealth is burthened with, you would greatly wounder.* It seemes the contagion is spred. To which the Deane replying, that extraordinary attempts must haue extraordinary warrants, and willed him to shew his authority, his answer was, that *He was Earle Marshall of England and needed no other warrant.* Yet that was not so, because he was sequestred from it long before. But his conclusion peremptory *what should I* (saith he) *reason with you vpon this point, seeing we holde not one principle,* which was, *that hee might remooue euils from the land,* for that was it which from the beginning to the end he held, as by complaint to vs of *some things to be reformed,* he insinuated. Indeede the wise man saith *Prou. 25. Remooue the wicked from the King, and his throne shall be established in iudgement:* but who must remooue them, and by what meanes? he there sheweth by similitude, *as the drosse must be taken from the siluer:* The Gold finer must do it, by the fire; so iust authority and lawfull meanes; the first ouer Kings is Gods alone, as before I proued, otherwise, as S. *Augustine* speaketh of impatient world-lings, *Nisi homini Deus placuerit Deus non erit,* vnlesse God please men, he shall be no God: so in this case of discontented subiects, except the prince please them, she shall be no prince, and all shall be accompted wicked who satisfie not their humors. Belooued, see here what it is, when it pleaseth God to leaue a man to himselfe; or as the Earle sayd of himselfe, *to be carried away and puffed vp with vanitie and wordly loue,* in his first speach vppon the scaffolde.

This stifnesse of his, both at the barre, and with the Deane, my associate and my selfe hearing, not vnderstanding of his repentance, we agreed betweene vs, fearing he would so haue dealt with vs, to haue beate him downe, and to haue wounded his hart with the dreadfull iudgementes of God: yet afterwarde to haue raysed him agayne with the comfortable promises of the gospell: but when we came vnto him, we found him more open to reueale, then became vs to inquire, and more resolute himselfe, then we, vpon the suddayne, could haue made him, and we more welcome a great deale then we expected: for he most hartely desired *God so to blesse vs as our comming did comfort him:* and so fell into expressing the memorie of this his purposed mischeife, with such detestation and remorse, that I, fearing as the Apostle speaketh of that Corinthian, *2.Cor.2.7* that he should be ouercome with ouermuch heauinesse, layd before him the comfortable speach of *S. Paul,* that Christ Iesus came into the world to saue sinners, though a man were *peccatorum maximus, 1.Tim.1.17.* but sayth *Doctor Montford* vnto him, who had beene at his araignment: I wounder your Lordshippe thus guiltie to your selfe, could be so confident at the barre, it offended many of your very good friends: yea, but now saith the late Earle, *I am become another man,* the cause thereof he ascribed *to the worke of Gods spirite within him;* and *the meanes to his chaplain Maister Ashton who was there* present with vs; for *he,* as he said to the honourable the Lord Keeper and the rest, *hath plowed vp my hart,* as he said to vs, *hath brought me down and humbled me.* And then he tolde vs he *had satisfied the Councell with his voluntary confession vnder his owne hand subscribed with his name, wherin though I haue,* said he, *detected many (already apprehended) yet I hold it my duty to God and the Realme to cleare my conscience.* For some three or foure dayes before his execution he made meanes by maister *Warbarton* one of her Maisties gentlemen Pencioners, to haue some *conference with three or foure of the Lordes of her Maiesties Counsell, wishing also if it pleased her Maiestie, that maister Secretary Cecill might be sent with them:* wherevpon the Lord Keeper, Lord Treasurer, & the Lord Admiral, taking Maister Secretary with them, came vnto him, to whome he clearely laide open the whole proiect and purpose, penitently confessed it, expressed his harty sorrow for his confidence at his araignment, asked forgiuenes of the Lord Keeper, &, by him, of the rest whom he caused in his house to be imprisoned: particulerly and vehemently in christian charitie desired Maister Secretary to forgiue him that great iniury which at the Barre in his passion, by vniust calumniation, he had cast vpon him, and of them also he requested forgiuenes whom he had challenged for his enimies, & had charged with such great, but false imputations. (All which, in grosse and general, he confessed to vs, forgiuing and asking forgiuenes) & so after an entire reconciliation with teares on both sides shed, he moued two requestes, the one very earnest, the other most necessary: the first was, *it would please them to moue her maiestie that he might die priuately within the Tower;* the reason thereof he expressed vnto vs in the morning of his execution, of which anone. The second was, *that he might haue libertie to set downe in writing what in worde he had confessed to them, and other things which either at the barre he had denied, or should then occure to his memory.* The confession it selfe filles foure sheetes of paper, euery worde in his owne hand, and his name at the end, which my selfe haue seene, and will shew vnto you so much as is fit: the preface thereof I haue transcribed for your sakes, and this it is, *Since that God of his mercie hath opened mine eyes, and made me see my sinne, my offence, and so touched my hart as I hate it both in my selfe and others, I will as God shall inable my memorie, set downe how far we all are guiltie, and where, and by what degrees our sinne, this offence grew.* The cheife, and the briefe is this, his purpose *of surprising the court with a power;* the places allotted to foure persons, *S. Christopher Blunt* the gate with a company; *S. Iohn Dauis* the hal a third to master the guard by seazing the halberts; *S. Charles Dauers* to possesse the priuie chamber with another companie; all this confest by himselfe, and the rest vnder their handes.

Here now imagine with your selues what affrighting euen the rumour thereof had beene to a prince of that sex, a Lady Queene, in a time of peace, and the peace so long by her meanes continued; in her owne court and chamber; the prouerbe is, *Leues loquntur, ingentes stupent,* that sleight feares make women shrike, but if they be great and sodayne, they cast them into a swoune; and I doubt if in that case she should have swounded, they would haue taken it for death, and haue bestowed little paynes to fetch her againe. But resistance beeing made, as it is not possible but there would, there must needes be bloud shed: now thinke you what an horror would this haue beene to her gratious nature, to haue seene bloud running in her chambers?

Then looke to the commanders, two of thy principall, stiffe and open Papists, and the fourth, by report, affected that way, what danger to her person, to religion, to the Realme they may gesse, who haue reade the libelles of *Bozius, Reynolds, Gifforde,*[1] and others of that church, writing

1. 'Reynolds', 'Gifforde', supposed Roman Catholic sympathizers or contrivers with Essex: but in fact, although Essex was an obvious magnet for all discontented men, the earl and his circle had mainly been the resort of the extreme Puritan faction; it was even rumoured that after his arrest he would be rescued by the London 'preachers', a synonym for 'Puritans' (CSPD, February 18th, 1601, Vol. CCLXXVIII, p. 584). There was no one consistent official attitude towards the Roman Catholics; attitudes varied according to their zone of origin, and fluctuated according to prevailing circumstances. Bancroft's (like the Queen's) opposition to the Papists, was political rather than doctrinal, and he was repeatedly reproached by Puritan sympathizers, including members of the Privy Council, for showing indulgence and leniency towards captured priests (see Henry Foley, *Records of the English Province of the Society of Jesus* (1877, etc.) I, 8, 23, 24). His force was reserved for the Jesuits, whom he regarded as subversive political agents (ibid., 147) and he worked with some success to sow discord between them and the secular priests. Since the execution of Mary Stuart and the despatch of the Armada, Roman Catholicism could be cast in the role of scapegoat for all displays of domestic discontent, not otherwise conveniently accountable. The names which Barlow (speaking on the instructions of Bancroft) threw to the populace to gnaw on were, as Catholics, a mixed, and as conspirators, an unlikely bunch. 1. 'Bozius' is a printer's corruption of de Boissie, the French Ambassador to England, who had been present at the trial of the earls, and was subsequently accused of having 'sent back a letter very slanderously taxing both the proceeding and the Justice of the condemnation', copies of which were 'spread about the

slaunderously of her Maiesties person, blasphemously of our religion; and basely of our Realme and policie. You may remember the state of Israel, when they were forced to sharpen their axes and tooles, and haue no weapons but from the *Philistines.1.Sam.13*. And such a slavery and misery, assure your selues, had ours been for Prince and religion, if we had stoode to the courtesie of armed Papistes and their reformation. Perhaps you will say, that this was but like the grouth of a Tadstoole, *Oritur, moritur*, a nights conceit, but vanished in the morning. Yea, but himselfe voluntarily confessed to vs, that *it was plotting and deuising not long after hee laye in the Lorde Keepers house:* euen then when he protested that he had made a diuorce betweene the worlde and himselfe; But he meant no hurt to the Qeenes person, say you. Surely that hee protested both in his confession to the Lords and to vs, and writeth it, *that when he sent the Articles to Drury house be considered of, by his complices, he put in that caueat still, that as little bloud might be shed as could, and that the Queenes owne person might receiue no harme.* And we will beleeue it. Marry the question is first, whether it had beene in his owne power at the time of their rage and in hot bloud to haue kept her safe? certainely, as we obiected to him, hee *which could not*, as him selfe, to vs confessed, *restraine them from murthering the Queenes subiects when he stood vpon his defence in his house*, they beeing but a few, must not thinke hee could haue stayed them in the Court, the obiect of their reuenge. For beeing many, and many of them needy, what Rapine would haue satisfied them? beeing youthfull, and lustfull, what Rapes woulde haue stanched them? being discontented and reuengefull, what bloud would haue glutted them? and the chiefe of them Popish and armed, would they not haue said, which comes euen now to my minde, as that bloudy *Story* once saide; What doe we pruning the boughes and branches, let vs strike at the roote.

For mine owne part, I professe, I woulde trust neuer a Papist in the world, if he might haue her at that vantage. God be thanked that this is but an

French court'. It subsequently received wider circulation, reaching even the 'Palgrave' to the indignation of the English Protestant Left. De Boissie denied authorship and the Queen diplomatically accepted his word. (See *Memorials of affairs of State in the reigns of Queen Elizabeth and James I from the papers of Sir Ralph Winwood* (3 vols., 1725), I, 296, 316, 329). 2. William Reynolds (or Rainolds): Roman Catholic brother of John Reynolds (the Calvinist theologian and President of Corpus Christi College), professor of Divinity and Hebrew at the English College at Rheims; his activities were mainly directed to doctrinal controversy. 3. Gilbert Gifford: English Roman Catholic 'double-agent', but one who was in practice too shrewd to try to double-cross his real employer, Francis Walsingham, the Protestant Puritan head of the English secret service. Gifford's skill in gaining Mary Stuart's confidence and then betraying her correspondence, paved her way to the scaffold. For Barlow to fulminate against Gifford's Roman Catholic perfidy was as appropriate as it might have been for *Pravda* to fulminate against Kim Philby's British Imperialist perfidy, before that battered, but unbowed, serpent had shed his true-blue skin.

imagination, for had it come *ab imagine ad rem*, from a purpose to an effect; *God knowes*, saith he himselfe to vs, *what daunger and harme it had wrought to the Realme.*

But in this point of *the Queenes safetie*, what thinke you of *summoning a Parlament*, which foure or fiue vnder their hands, and himselfe also hath confessed. Who should haue called it, she or they? It is a controuersie betweene vs and the Papists, whether the Emperour or the Pope, haue the absolute authoritie of calling a Councell, but it was neuer made question, that I can read, in England who hath authoritie to call a Parlament, either the Prince or the Peeres. Among the Spaniards and French they may, saith *Bodin*[1], but *apud Anglos*, in the Realme of England, *nec admitti possunt conuentus, nec dimitti absque Principis edicto*, without the Princes warrant it cannot either be sumoned or dissolued. Why, she should haue done it; how? voluntarily or by force? the first we may not imagine that she would so soone yeeld; if the second, where is the safety of her person? vnlesse you count that safety for a Prince to be a prisoner to her subiects. God forbid we should haue felt the Issue of this, nay *God be thanked* saith he to vs, *that it was preuented.* And withall gaue God like thankes *that he had made him this example to be iustly spewed out of the land.* Which word *Spewed* he inforced with a violence, arguing himselfe thereby to be, vnto this Realme, as a surfet vnto the stomack, both a burthen and a danger. He saw himselfe a burthen in this charge of souldiers, beeing a burthen to the Cittie and countrie, which but for him had now been spared: he felt himselfe a burthen, as it seemed, to vs by longing and desiring, which oft he did, that the time of execution were come. A danger he confessed himselfe to be in these words of his, which I pray you obserue, *he knew that the Queene could not be in safetie so long as he liued vpon the earth.* I will stretch nothing to farre, but yet marke this, if her safety were so vncertain, he being a prisoner in the Tower, what could her safety haue beene when he was possessed of her court with an armed power?

But why do I eyther amplifie by circumstance, or inforce by argument the haynousnesse and daunger of this plot? if I had the tongue of men and Angels, I could not better, nor would in more bitter tearmes expresse it, then himselfe hath done in foure epithetes or adiunctes in his prayer to God, or in his speach to the Lordes, or in both vpon the Scaffolde: desiring God to forgiue him *his great sinne, his bloudy sinne, his crying sinne, his infectious sinne:* why these wordes, for none of them is, as *Basil* speaketh, ἀργον ῥῆμα an idle worde. First, *great* in comparison of his other sinnes, which he on the Scaffold laide out in odious termes against himselfe his *delicta iuuentutis*, not that they were little sinnes, for vnto us, in his Chamber, he confessed that *sometimes in the Fielde encountring the enemye, beeing in any danger the weight of his sinnes lying heauie vpon his conscience, being not reconciled to God, quelled his spirits, and*

1. Jean Bodin, *Republica Libri Sex* (Paris, 1586), lib. 1, cap. viii (De iure maiestatis).

made him the most timorous and fearefull man that might be. But this sinne exceeded them all, euen that which we obiected to him in his chamber, and he acknowledged, which the Schoolemen call *Vactans conscientiam,* so wasting and spoiling his conscience, as that not one good thought was left in his hart. That sinne which *Moses* calleth the sinne with an high hand *Nomb.33.* himselfe called it, a *Presumptuous sinne.* Secondly, *great* in it selfe, because as the *Nabis* in *Egipt*[1] is a beast shaped of many beasts; and *Hannibals* armie in *Liuie,* was *collunies omnium gentium,* the miscellan of all nations; so this his offence and treason, the compound of all the famous rebellions eyther in Gods booke, or our owne land: (which himselfe in other words scatteringly expressed:) consisting of *Abners* discontment, of *Corahs* enuie, of *Absalons* popularity, of *Sheba,* defection, of *Abimelechs* faction, and banding his familie and allyes, of *Hamans* pride and ambition: in pretence small, all one with that of *Henrie* Duke of Lancaster, against *Richard* the second, *remoouing certaine which misled the King.* In pretence originall, that of *Kettes* and *Tylers* for the King, as they in your citty cryed in that insurrection *for the Queene, for the Queene.*

The second worde was *his bloudy sinne.* It should haue beene no *drye rebellion,* for how could it be? in that he who could hardly represse the rage of his owne people from murthering the honourable counsellers in his owne house, they beeing the men not aymed at in shew of their *reformation,* should not be able to stay their armed fury in the place designed for the execution of their intent. But here you of the citie will say, it should not haue beene bloudy to vs, he loued vs well: be it so; yet I will tell you his opinion vttered of you the very nyght of his apprehension, and his beeing in Lambeth house, in the hearing of the Lord Archbishop, of the Lord Admirall, of the Lord of Effingham, and diuers other, and my selfe among the rest, *That you were a very base people: that he trampled vp and downe your city without any resistance: that he would vndertake with foure hundreth men of his choise to haue ouerrunne your citie: that he passed many of your lanes and chaines baraccadoed* (it was his worde) *without one blow offered at him, in his returne from Ludgate to Queenehith.* Againe, what his conceipt was of your loue to him, his owne speeches shall testifie, wherby he argued that you were both a daunger to his body and his soule: in the first, I telling him that his relieng vpon the peoples plausibilitie

1. No divinity or demon of animal form called 'Nabis' exists in the records of classical Egyptian antiquity. But the name appears, with variant spelling, on gnostic semi-precious-stones, of later, Graeco-Roman times, often in connection with the word 'Chnoubis', and probably charged with magical significance. Such amulets were syncristic and cosmopolite, and circulated throughout the empire. The word 'nabis' is sometimes found on stones in company with the figures of hybrid monsters (e.g. part serpent, part lion), which may have caused Barlow's misunderstanding. See Campbell Bonner, *Studies in Magical Amulets* (1950), pp. 53–57, 182, 199; Arm and Delatte and Phillippe Derchain, *Les Intailles magique Greco-egyptienne* (Paris, 1964), no. 77, 78.

spurred him on, but now they had deceived him. *True* (sayth he) *a mans friendes will fayle him;* and addes to that a very diuine speech, *All popularitie and trust in men is vayne, whereof my selfe haue had late experience.* Thus he accompted your loue at the best to be but vanitie, or as he sayd in the prophet, an *Aegiptian* reede, which eyther breaketh & fayleth him that leaneth on it or pearceth his hand to his hurt: in-sinuating hereby, that, had he not trusted vpon you, he would not haue ventured so farre: and thus you seemed by his wordes to haue indaungered his body, as beeing a remote motiue to that his action. Then the request which he so *earnestly made vnto the Lordes for his priuate death within the tower,* was principally because of you: for in the morning he confessed *himselfe much bound to God, and her maiestie that he should die thus priuately, because he feared, least if it had beene publike, your acclamations should haue houen him vp* (for this he much doubted in himselfe euen in that small companie which was there, and therefore *desired God still to graunt him an humbled spirite: and requested vs if we eyther see his countenance, eye, or tongue wander, that we would interrupt him*) *and so haue withdrawne his minde from God, and haue beene a temptation vnto him:* and thus he tooke your loue to him, but as a danger to his soule: but thinke you it had not been vnto you a *bloudy* day, if it had beene effected what they purposed: now heare and tremble; beeing asked what he meant by taking the *tower of London,* sithence his principall proiect was for the court? he answered, *that he meant it should haue beene a bridle, to your citie,* marke that worde, *a bridle* hath raines and a bit: so that if you had made an head for him agaynst the Queene (which I hope you would not) he would haue giuen you the raines, you should haue gone on without any restraint to haue beene rebels to your prince and country: but if you had vnited your force against him as good subiects (and as I am fully perswaded you would) they are his owne wordes, *if happely the Citie should haue misliked his other attempt,* then you should taste of the Bit. They call it the playeng of the Bit in the horse mouth: but I beleeue the playing of the Ordinance from the Tower would haue fetcht both your houses downe, and your *bloud* out.

The third word, *his crying sinne,* which word is borrowed from *Gen. 19* Where the sinnes of Sodom are said to cry vp to heauen, namely, to fetch down vengeance from God, so intollerable they were, and one of those sinnes was *pride;* which, I was bold to tell him, was the ground of all this action, and he tooke it very well. This also argued, that there was *bloud* in this sinne, for the first crying sinne we read of was *Caines* murther *Gen. 4.* The last word was *his infectious sinne,* the meaning thereof he explaned to vs in our conference with him (which I named before) that *it was a leaprosie which had infected far and neare.* Which vnfoldeth both the greatnesse of the danger, and argueth that the contagion of the sinne is not gone with him. Doctor *Montford* asked him if there were not an oth taken by them for secrecie and resolution. He vtterly denied that: how durst you trust each other being so many said we? His answere was *that they were firmly perswaded each of others faithfulnesse mutually, as any one of them could be of his owne hart to himselfe.* Now then. the time beeing more then spent, conferre these points together, all out of his owne wordes, and beginne with the last first, they are thirteene in all.

1. This conspiracie thus banded.
2. The offence *contagiously*, and generally dispersed.
3. His sinne crieng to God for present vengeance.
4. A sinne bloudy in execution, if effected.
5. Great in selfe, the compound and mixture of all rebellions.
6. His life a daunger to that Queene.
   marke that
7. Himself a surfet to the realme, to be spewed out justly.
8. Articles propounded, disputed, concluded so long together aguynst the state.
9. The court surprised with an armed power, and the Queene mured up with her owne vassalles.
10. A parlament to be summoned.
11. The Chiefe places of the court at the commaund of Papists armed and attended, neyther with the welthiest, nor the contendedest men.
12. The Command of the tower a bridle to you of this city.
13. His hard opinion and censure of your basenesse and unfaithfulnesse to the Queene.

And then judge you with what safty to the Queene's person; with what peace to the law; with what hope of the Gospels continuance could this man have lived, if he had beene remitted: and thinke with your selues whether you may not iustlye conclude that it was the most dangerous plotte that euer was hatched within this land. What now remains—but to conclude with my text, Giue unto Caesar the things of Caesar, oure most gracious Soueraigne, I meane, honour her, obey her, feare her, but aboue all pray for her, that she being the light of this land may shine among us as long as the two great lights of heauen, the sonne and the moone endureth. This God grant for his mercie sake. Amen.

2
JACOBEAN

SAMUEL COLLINS

For Barlow, his service to the crown had a sequel not without irony. Bishop though he was, and further rewarded though he would be, the queen never received him in her presence therafter. The sight of him, says Manningham, might have reminded her of Essex. It might also have reminded her of herself. The death of the impulsive young man whom, in a cruel and familiar Tudor syndrome, she had loved and indulged, frustrated and killed, was the prelude to her own death. She had outlived her time and the faithful servants who had made it triumphant. She did not even appreciate the quality of the late literary harvest which confers immortality upon her reign. The old fury was out of touch with the changing tastes and wishes of the people. Suggestive talk of more 'freedom' offended her authoritarian spirit as a menace to order and social cohesion. In her latter days, only the reverence still felt for her personally bridged the gulf between the throne and a succession of restive parliaments; while her private life was a scene of irascible eccentricities and acts of petty violence. In ever more frequent fits of rage, she would fling about the room, stabbing the arras with an old sword; then came the day when she no longer had the strength to move, but only to sit (she refused to lie down) propped up on pillows; in which posture, surrounded by her council, about three o'clock in the afternoon of March 22nd, 1603, she 'departed this lyfe, mildly, like a lamb, easily like a ripe apple from the tree, *cum leue quadam febre absque gemitu*'.[1]

The disappearance of the queen and, with her, the respectful restraint which her credit had commanded, suddenly exposed forces of discontent formerly under subjection. A dissident element, the so-called 'Puritan' shoal of the population, began to assert, with mounting vehemence, that the Protestant reforms requisite to 'righteousness' had not yet been fulfilled. Theological issues of free will and predestination apart, the actual service of the church still smacked of the old religion, ceremonious, formal, symbolistic; that is to say, *idolatrous*. The word idolatry was then as emotionally provocative,

1. Manningham's *Diary*, March 1602.

as charged with irrational prejudice, as the words communist and fascist are today. The counter-word of abuse, Puritan, also cannot be avoided because, inadequate and imprecise though it is as a classification, it was the word of the times, and the only word to describe the amorphous anti-ritualistic Protestant left wing, which was united by no single party or constructive programme (though the Presbyterians fancied themselves for this appointment) but only by a negative and iconoclastic intolerance of certain practices of worship which still prevailed in the church. The issues concerned the disputed propriety of vestments, whether a table was an altar or a table, and where it should be placed; the objections to canonical prayers (in effect the Book of Common Prayer); the alleged sinfulness of liturgical music and all 'representation', with paramount emphasis laid on the Bible as the sole and absolute authority for doctrine. From the latter belief grew the compulsive evangelical cultivation of *preaching*, which became identified in the early years of the new century as the essential characteristic of Puritan fervour. At this stage in the history of religious 'non-conformity', nothing was further from the Puritan mind than tolerance. The Presbyterians wished to substitute their form of compulsory order for the prevailing episcopal rule, while already multiplying independents, though dissenting from Presbyterian principles, agreed that first worship must be purged of its devilish and blasphemous practices.

The Puritan complex was not a majority but, like all energetic and vociferous minorities, it was able to seem so, sometimes, to the real majority whose main desire was for a quiet life.

To a member of the academic élite, like Samuel Collins,[1] Provost of King's College, Cambridge, and Regius Professor of Divinity, the content of popular Puritan agitation would have been fatuous if it had not been contagious. But early in the new reign he observed that, behind the earnest cant and the solecisms, there was a real and dangerous excitation among uneducated men which might overturn the traditions and laws of the established church. This meant to him nothing less than a threat to order and security, in particular to the integrity of scholarship which had recently begun to recover from the devastations of

1. Collins, Samuel, 1576–1651. Born at Eton where he was educated, being the son of the Vice Provost. 1591 Scholarship to King's College, Cambridge, proceeded B.A., M.A. Chaplain to Archbishop Bancroft. 1610 Vicar of Braintree, Essex. D.D. 1612. Regius Professor of Divinity, Cambridge, 1617. Friend of Sir Henry Wotton. Deprived of his chair and benefices during the civil war.

'reform'. In this sermon preached at St. Paul's Cross he satirizes the zealots who dictate, in their domestic life, a manner of worship, not only to their wives and families but to their servants and apprentices, and brow-beat their neighbours; yet suppose themselves to be absolved from any obligation to respect the higher authority of their sovereign over them.

The caustic quality of Collins's mind is celebrated in an anecdote concerning accusations, made against him by his enemies at Cambridge, of simony and corruption. Archbishop Williams, who investigated the charges, dismissed them as 'groundless, inspired by the resentment of Collins's biting wit upon the Fellows'. Collins was reputed the most fluent latinist of his age; but in this sermon he is addressing a very mixed London congregation, and he conceals his learning as well as any Puritan could wish.

Preaching Charlatans

A sermon preached at Paul's Cross on November 1st.,
All Souls Day, 1607

If any of you should commaund your seruant, or your son, to carry a Bible with them to Church vpon the Sondaies, vnder paine of your heauie displeasure if they did not, doe you think it were a law that might be broken, or no? A law doubtless it were, as being taxed with punishment vppon the offendor. Your selues would think it fit to be kept, not fit to be broken. And yet it is in matter of Gods seruice and Religion. For, let no man deceiue himself my deere brethren, not willingly misconster vs; there was none of vs euer placed so much Religion in a garment, as you doe in a Booke. And yet Christ neuer badde it, and it is left free; for all sinne not, you must think, that come to Church without their Bibles, though they can read.

Winde your selues now out of this net, as well as you can, which is no net, but a sounde and substantial confutation, specially you that delight in ambush, as *the twelue reasons*, and intortled[1] Syllogismes. Or, if you say that Christ commanded vs to search the Scriptures; well, though that doth not enforce, that wee should carrie them to the Church, to euerie Lecture, or sermon, with vs; yet, let the former supposition hold, but in *Lidleyes prayer Booke*, or *Bradfords Meditations*, or some such like, and then see what you can

1. Entwined.

say to it; whether you will allowe your seruant or your sonne to crosse your commandement in such a respect or not. Neither againe maie you except that the bringing of the Bible helpes to edifie, the ceremonies not: for the ceremonies edifie too in their place and order (I will not now compare them with a lay mans Bible) and the question is not so much touching edification (if you mark it) as whether they may be vrged vppon the consciences of beleeuers by lawe, though they be neuer so apt in themselues to edifie.

How then is it my deare Brethren and sisters of this Cittie? may your prentises be constrained, your children compelled, by your priuate law giuing authoritie, thus and thus to demeane themselues in Gods seruice & worship, without anie disparagement to the supreame Law-giuer, and may not they whose iurisdiction is so farre greater than yours, attempt the same ouer them that they gouerne? Maie the Housholder do this in his house, and not the king in his kingdomes? Maie the father and the mother, and not Gods Lieftenaunt and Deputie generall? Naie, maie the *Pædant* in his flock and not the *Prince?*

For to say the father commands but a few, and the maister a fewe, the King all the Ministers & Preachers of the Land, is an opposition more fit for you to make than for me to remoue, or rather so vnfit for me to remoue, that indeed it is not fit for you to make: the kings authoritie iustly stretching farther, why? because the limits of his Realms are wider; and if he allow you to be kings in your housholds, you must allow him to be a housholder in his kingdom, at the least.

Again, to say that the one are Ministers and Preachers, the other but children & seruants, is as vain. For, if christian libertie must not be infringed in binding ministers & preachers, no more may it be infringed in binding children, and seruants; & if Ecclesiasticall Canons wrong the priuiledge that came by Christs blood, so do domesticall: we know no such prerogatiue of one aboue another in these kind of causes, euery mans conscience is as free and as vntouchable as anothers before God, one price was paid for all.

. . . While the good man sleeps the enemy is not idle, but sowes his tares very industriously. Mischance is nimble, & one *Ate* outstrips they say a hundred *Litæ*. I could wish, our men would imitate their diligence; but by al means they must beware of their pestilence. Who knowes not what hath bin the wonted argument of their sermons? railing against our seruice book, & defacing praier, to take vp the time forsooth in preaching; like the hedge-hog that draue his Host out of dores. For so praier lets in preaching: & by it we can do, if we can do any thing. Yet as *Cæsar* drowned *Bibulus*[1] his Consul-ship, so they make one of them to liue by the spoile & wrack of another,

1. Calpernius Bibulus, appointed Consul with Julius Caesar: the stubborn ineffec-tuality of his opposition to Caesar's agrarian legislation provoked the pleasantry that this was the consulship of Julius and Caesar.

preaching by praying; though the Church be the house of praying not of preachinh, properly so instiled by God himselfe. Then their squibbing at the Prelacie, yea & glancing somtimes at the soveraign authority: which I haue heard, to my great grief, with mine own ears in this Citie, when time was; not without the great applause of the seduced multitude. And now no dumb dogges I warrant you, but (which is worse) barking afore they espie a thief, yea biting true men that com in their way: whose legs would bee broken, or their hamstrings cut, by the custom of old *Rome*, for being so fierce by day; wheras they are set to watch the night, & the Capitoll to giue them maintenance for such a seruice only, & no otherwise. They tell vs of rigor, & persecution, & hard measure: but it is they with their tongue, not the church with hir hand, that is the persecutor. *Hagar* beats *Sara*, & not *Sara Hagar*, though you would think it otherwise when you read the story; because *Hagar* is the male part, as hauing gotten a great belly (these being ful & desirus to vent, like a vessel stuft with new wine, as *Iob* saies): *Sara* doth but as a mistress should (& so the Church) striking when shee is prouoked. And shall these paines bee mentioned to their praise, which a mean seuerity wil not serue to chastice? They delighted in bitterness, let it come vnto them; their theme was cursing, let them inherit it; be it as water vnto their bowels, and as the girdle to their loines, that they are girt withall. They tel vs, they haue laied their axe to the Prelacie to hew it down: but if it chance to swerue & hit the striker, let such a man know that it coms of the Lord. This I haue spoken of the matter of their sermons: but now if I should enter to entreat of their form. the day would fail me. Be it conceiued in a word, The most of them haue made Gods offerings to stinke, like the sons of *Eli*, & the pulpits to lose much of their antient estimation & credit, that they held in former times, by the vndiscreet handling of their business. *Aristotle.* was wont to say, it was the reward of a lier not to be belieued when he told truth: so, many men of worth are the worse thought on for their vnworthines. To omit other faults, so reckless & so dissolute they are in their preaching, that now it is become a law among them as it was among the *Tarentines, nemo de nobis,* let him be no body in the faction, that brings a studied or a premeditate sermon. That were to ty the Holy Ghost to an inkhorn, turn the cock & it will run well enough of it selfe, (I think I speak their own Prouerbs:) & there are som worse, as when they say they bring sermons of Gods own making, because they took no pains in the penning; with others mo, that for honesty sake must be concealed. Thus they tell vs of labor, & labor, in their preaching; and when all comes to all, they hold it no preaching, if it be laborious. *Alex* would be painted by none by *Apelles,* grauen by none but *Lysippus,* one an excellent painter the other an excellent caruer: these can allow any to handle the word, to touch the misterie with vnwasht hands, δικοτρίξων διμοτρίξας as S. *Basil* saies, base fellows, and (more then so) a degree belowe baseness it self. And therfore no maruaile, if anie thing be counted good enough for our Order, when they haue counted any body fit enough for the labour.

But to let go this, because they will saie this is to preach in the euidence of the spirit, and in all demonstration of power and authoritie (though God knowes there is great difference between the two) what think you of that, that they challenge to themselues a conuerting power, (I speak no more than I know by good proof) and deny to others a conuerting ministration? In the latter whereof they are not so iniurious against charitie toward men, as in the former hainous in excess of pride and impiety towards God. Certainly, my deare brethren, if we could conuert others, we would first begin with the conuersion of our selues: but because no man conuerteth himself; therfore, it is most true, he cannot conuert another. *Turn vs Lord and we shall be turned*, saies the Prophet himself, though he could preach no doubt sufficiently: and our Sauiour likewise, *You haue not chosen me*, but *I haue chosen you*.

Latimer preaching to King Edward VI and his court

The burning of Latimer and Ridley

John Hales

Thomas Adams

Lancelot Andrewes

John Donne

St. Paul's Cross and the Shrouds

William Chillingworth

Christopher
Love

" .... this is a
lovely Dogge
with a thin pair
of chops"
(*see p472*)

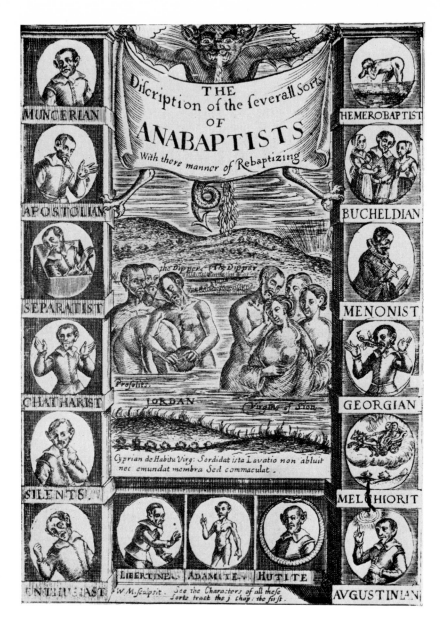

Anabaptists surrounded by representatives
of various Puritan sects

Thomas Fuller

Hugh Peters

RELIGIONS
ENEMIES.

WITH A BRIEF AND INGENIOUS
Relation, as by *Anabaptists*, *Brownists*, *Papists*,
Familists, *Atheists*, and *Foolists*, sawcily
presuming to tosse Religion in
a Blanquet.

The Anabaptist.　　　　　　The Brownist.

The Familist.　　　　　　The Papist.

Printed at *London* for *Thomas Bates* in the Old-baily. 1641.

Religion tossed in a Blanket

WILLIAM PERKINS

From the foregoing references to Puritans it might be supposed that the movement was dominated by ignorant bigots, and it is true that many Puritans were both uneducated and opinionated. Equal and direct access for all men to the fount of revelation was part of the central appeal of Puritanism. It was natural that men imbued with the urgent assertiveness of evangelical zeal should resent what they considered a merely fortuitous educational advantage of their enemies, and conclude that academic learning was used not to reveal, but to conceal, or to 'wrench' (a favourite word) the truth. It was an obvious next move to make a virtue of their limitations and a vice of their enemies' attributes. The grapes were not merely sour, they were poisoned. As late as the middle of the century John Webster was glorifying lack of learning in the saints as a badge of holy innocence, for 'Arts, sciences, Launguages etc., are Idols, Antichristian, the smoke of the botomless pit'.[1] By which route, accordingly, tests of intellectual sufficiency were conveniently despatched to join painting, music and drama among the anathemized vanities in the charnel house of Idolatry.

This was a phenomenon of the extreme left of the Puritan confluence; but from the centre to the right there were to be found in the universities scholarly Puritans of the highest intellectual standards (Cartwright and Preston were prominent examples), who were separated from the Calvinism of Archbishops Abbot and Usher by little more than the system of the episcopacy.

Such a one was William Perkins,[2] a Cambridge scholar destined to exert a strong influence on the thought of Massachusetts and other American puritan settlements. His claim on our attention here is the special interest he took in the current problem raised by the increasing incidence of witches.

Examination of the evidence proves less reassuring.[3] The mythology

1. *The Saints Guide*, 1654. Cf. *Academiarum Examen*, 1654.

2. In *Armila Aurea* (Cambridge, 1590; in English, 1591) Perkins gave thanks for the benefits he had enjoyed from an academic education.

3. Since its publication in 1941 Lynn Thorndike's *History of Magic and Experimental Science* has been a standard work of reference. In the area it covers, Lea's *History of the*

of post-Reformation diabolism and the train of atrocities it set in motion, far from being the relic of a dying past, was a seething ferment which raged in unprecedented virulence to climaxes of collective hysteria both in Catholic and Protestant communities.[1] Methods of investigation and trial form a pattern which has since become again hideously familiar in the twentieth century. The demoralization of the accused was effected by indefinitely prolonged interrogation, sometimes with the use of torture to extremity; then, to complete the godly process, the yielding of the donation obligatory for atonement, without which there could be no relief from torment: the naming by the condemned of other 'witches'. Thus the ravening lunacy, fed fresh victims by the victims it devoured, was self-perpetuating. The most disturbing aspect of the obscene picture is that men of otherwise enlightened character and even high intellectual distinction were found among the accusers, as well as the accused. In Bamberg and Würzburg, notorious black spots of persecution during the reign of the Prince–Bishop John George II, lawyers, including judges, priests, scholars, noblemen, were dragged to the stake to be burnt along with children of 10 and old women;[2] and Jean Bodin, the supreme political thinker of the century and author of the dialogue in praise of religious tolerance, *Colloquium Heptaplomores de Abiditis Rerum Sublimium*, was also the author of *De la Démonomanie des Sorciers*, in which he prescribes death by fire, not only for witches, but for anyone who denies their reality, or even a particular of the approved teaching concerning them.[3]

Inquisition in Spain is unlikely to be superseded; and there is also his useful *Materials towards a History of Witchcraft*, edited by Arthur C. Howland (1957) best read in association with a valuable new contribution to the subject, the essay *Witches and Witchcraft*, by Professor Hugh Trevor-Roper (published in his *Religion, Reformation and Social Change* (1968)), to which I wish to declare my general indebtedness. Older books still worth attention are Michelet's *La Sorcière* and Thomas Wright's *Narratives of Sorcery and Magic* (1852).

1. The two centuries of most rabid witch mania may be said to have begun, as Professor Trevor-Roper observed (op. cit.) with the promulgation by Innocent VIII, at the instance of two Dominican inquisitors, of the papal bull, *Summis Desiderates Affectibus* in December, 1484. The same Dominicans, Sprenger and Kramer (Institor), were the authors of the much-employed handbook and guide to demonology and to methods of interrogation to be used upon witches, *Malleus Malificarum* (1489).

2. See Hauber's *Bibliotheca Magica*, a translation of which may be found in Wright, op. cit. Subsequently, as late as 1681, the Marshal of Luxembourg was tried for sorcery.

3. It was a dangerous matter to question belief in witches. The humanist Johann Weir said as much as he dared in the premature enlightenment of *De Praestigiis Daemonum* (1564) and drew upon his head the thunderous reproofs of Bodin in *De Magorum Daemonomania* (1579). A Dutch Protestant pastor, Balthasar Bekker, ventured in *De*

In England the discovery of witches was never pursued with the relentless concentration found in the Alps and the Pyrenees, or in Germany, Flanders and Scotland,[1] although the subject did hold a dreadful fascination for James I. But it had its ugly part to play here too. In Perkins's sermon on Witches we see how easy, once the premise of diabolical as well as divine presence in the world is accepted, becomes the graduation into justifying acts of cruelty against the infective servants of the fiend. Perkins is here earnestly concerned to teach his congregation that, in the case of a suspected witch, a record of benevolent actions need not be a sign of innocence. For there are 'good' as well as 'bad' witches, the former seeming to do no harm, and even manifestly doing good; but both are equally contracted to Satan, equally damnable, and the good witch, if there be a distinction, the more deserving of death.

At the time when Perkins preached, England was the most compassionate country in Europe in the treatment of witches. They were hanged, not burned. But the commonwealth brought a rise in persecution, especially in ultra-Puritan East Anglia, and the 'witch-finder general', Mathew Hopkins, who terrorized the counties he toured accompanied by an assistant and a female 'searcher', was responsible for the hanging in 1644 of sixty women in Essex alone. One of the last victims of this period was John Lowes, the old vicar of Brandeston in

Betroverde Wereld (1691–3) to reject all belief in sorcery and witchcraft, and even to doubt the existence of the devil, for which he was lucky to have been only deposed and excommunicated. Reginald Scott, a pioneer of rational scepticism in this field, attracted with his Discovery of Witchcraft (1584) the indignation of James VI of Scotland in Daemonologie (1597) for his 'damnable opinions', being 'not ashamed in public print to deny there can be such a thing as witchcraft'.

1. The history of witchcraft in Scotland is exceptionally vicious and unrestrained, due to the clergy's right to interfere in every corner of life in the name of morality, and the victims included a number of eminent people. Sir Michael Scott of Balwearie, and William, Lord Soulis, of Hermitage Castle, 'notable sorcerers', were boiled to death; Lady Glamis was executed in 1537 for making an attempt by witchcraft upon the life of the king, James V. Dr. Fian, the master of the school at Saltpans in Lothian, charged with conspiracy to drown James VI, had his nails torn from his fingers, and his legs were crushed by the Boot till the marrow was squeezed out of his bones, before he was at last permitted to end his life in the fire. While Alesoun Balfour, before she was sent to the stake at Kirkwall in 1596, was tormented on the caschielawis (a kind of grill) while her husband and son were tortured before her eyes and her seven-year-old daughter was put in the pinnywinkles (finger and toe screws). See Pitcairn's Criminal Trials in Scotland from 1484 to 1624 (1830–3); R. Wodrow's Analecta (1842–3); and J. D. Dalyell's Darker Superstitions of Scotland (1834).

Suffolk, who was induced under torture to confess to having employed two imps to sink a ship.[1]

The Good Witch Must Also Die[2]

A Discourse on Kinds of Witches
and their Necessary Punishment

The *good Witch*, is he or shee that by consent in a league with the deuill, doth vse his helpe, for the doing of good onely. This cannot hurt, torment, curse, or kill, but onely heale and cure the hurts inflicted upon men or cattell, by badde Witches. For as they can doe no good, but onely hurt: so this can doe no hurt, but good onely. And this is that order which the deuill hath set in his kingdome, appointing to seuerall persons their seuerall offices and charges. And the good Witch is commonly tearmed the *vnbinding Witch*.

Now howsoeuer both these be euil, yet of the two, the more horrible & detestable Monster is the good Witch, for look in what place soeuer there be any bad Witches that hurt onely, there also the deuil hath his good ones, who are better knowne then the bad, beeing commonly called *Wisemen*, or *Wise-women*. This will appeare by experience in most places in these countries. For let a mans childe, friend, or cattell be taken with some sore sicknes, or strangely tormented with some rare and vnknowne disease, the first thing he doth, is to bethink himselfe and inquire after some Wiseman or Wisewoman, & thither he sends and goes for helpe. When he comes, he first tells him the state of the sicke man: the Witch then beeing certified of the disease, prescribeth either Charmes of words to be vsed ouer him, or other such counterfeit meanes, wherein there is no vertue; beeing nothing els but the deuills Sacraments, to cause him to doe the cure, if it come by Witchcraft. Well, the meanes are receiued, applied, and vsed, the sicke partie accordingly recouereth, and the conclusion of all is, the vsuall acclamation; Oh happie is the day, that euer I met with such a man or woman to helpe me!

*

Men of learning haue obserued, that all Witches through Europe, are of like cariage and behauiour in their examinations, and conuictions: they use the same answears, refuges, defenses, protestations. In a word, looke what be

---

1. See Baxter, *Certainty of the Worlds of Spirits* (1691); c.f. *A Magazine of Scandall* (1642).

2. *A Discourse of the Damned Art of Witchcraft* (Cambridge, 1608).

the practises and courses of the Witches in England, in any of these particulars, the same be the practises of the Witches in Spaine, Fraunce, Italie, Germanie, &c. Wherefore the case is cleare, they are not deluded by Sathan, through the force of humour, as is auouched; for such persons, according as they are diuersly taken, would shewe themselues diuersly affected, and varie in their speeches, actions, and conceits, both publike and priuate. Fourthly, our Witches are wont to communicate their skill to others by tradition, to teach and instruct their children and posteritie, and to initiate them in the grounds and practises of their owne trade, while they liue, as may appeare by the confessions recorded in the Courts of all countries. But if they were persons troubled with melancholie, their conceits would die with them. For conceits, and imaginarie fancies, which rise of any humour, cannot be conueyed from partie to partie, no more then the humour it selfe. Lastly, if this sleight might serue to defend Witches vnder pretence of delusion through corrupted humours, then here were a couer for all manner of sinnes. For example: a fellon is apprehended for robberie or murther, and is brought before the Iudge: Vpon examination he confesseth the fact, beeing conuicted the law proceeds to condemnation. The same mans friends come in, and alledge before the Iudge in this maner; This man hath a crazie braine, and is troubled with melancholy, and though he hath confessed the fact, yet the truth is, it was not he, but the deuill, who himselfe committed the murther, and made him thinke he did it, when he did it not, & hereupon he hath confessed. Would any man thinke, that this were a reasonable allegation, and a sufficient meane to mooue the Iudge to acquite him? Assuredly if it were, vpon the same ground might any sinne be laid vpon the deuills backe, and all good lawes and iudiciall proceedings be made voide.

Therefore howsoeuer the patrons of Witches be learned men, yet they are greatly deceiued in fathering the practises of Sorcerie vpon a melancholike humour.

But for the further ratifying of their assertion, they proceed, and vse this argument: They which confesse of themselues things false, and impossible, must needs be parties deluded, but our Witches doe this, when they be examined or consulted with, as that they can raise tempests, that they are caried through the aire in a moment, from place to place, that they passe through keyholes, and clifts of doores, that they be sometimes turned into catts, hares, and other creatures; lastly, that they are brought into farre countries, to meete with Herodias, Diana, and the Deuill, and such like; all which are mere fables, and things impossible.

Ans. We must make a difference of Witches in regard of time. There is a time, when they first beginne to make a league with Sathan, and a time also after the league is made and confirmed.

When they first beginne to grow in confederacie with the deuill, they are sober, and their vnderstanding found, they make their match waking, and as they thinke wisely enough, knowing both what they promise the deuill, and vpon what conditions, and therefore all this while it is no delusion. But after they be once in the league, and haue been intangled in compact with the deuill (considerately as they thinke, for their owne good and aduantage) the case may be otherwise. For then reason and understanding may be depraued, memorie weakened and all the powers of their soule blemished. Thus becomeing his vassels they are deluded, and so intoxicated by him that they will run into thousands of fantasical imaginations, holding themselves to be transformed into the shapes of other creatures, to be transported into the ayre into other countries, yea, to do so many strange things which in truth they do not.

*

Touching the manner of Examination, there be two kinds of proceeding; either by a single Question, or by some Torture. A single question is, when the Magistrate himselfe onely maketh enquirie, what was done or not done, by bare and naked interrogations. A torture is, when besides the enquirie in words, he vseth also the racke, or some other violent meanes to vrge confession. This course hath beene taken in some countries, and may no doubt lawfully and with good conscience be vsed, howbeit not in euery case, but onely vpon strong and great presumptions going before, and when the partie is obstinate. And thus much for Examination: now followeth Conuiction.

Conuiction, is an action of the Magistrate, after iust examination, discouering the Witch. This action must proceed from iust & sufficient proofes, and not from bare presumptions. For though presumptions giue occasion to examine, yet they are no sufficient causes of conuiction. Now in generall the proofes vsed for conuiction are of two sorts, some be lesse sufficient, some be more sufficient.

The lesse sufficient proofes are these. First, in former ages, the partie suspected of Witchcraft, was brought before the Magistrate, who caused red hoat iron, and scalding water to be brought, and commaunded the partie to put his hand in the one, or to take vp the other, or both; and if he tooke vp the iron in his bare hand without burning, or endured the water without scalding, hereby he was cleared, and iudged free, but if hee did burne or scalde, he was then conuicted, and condemned for a Witch. But this manner of conuiction, hath long agone beene condemned for wicked and diabolicall, as in truth it is, considering that thereby many times, an innocent man may bee condemned and a ranke witch scape unpunished.

*

But some witches there be that cannot be conuicted of killing any: what shall become of them? *Ans.* As the killing witch must die by another Law, though he were no Witch: so the healing and harmlesse Witch must die by this Law, though he kill not, only for a couenant made with Satan. For this must alwaies be remembered, as a conclusion, that by Witches we understand not those only which kill and torment: but all Diuiners, Charmers, Iuglers, all Wizzards, commonly called wise men and wise women; yea, whosoeuer doe any thing (knowing what they doe) which cannot be effected by nature or art; and in the same number we reckon all good Witches, which doe no hurt but good, which doe not spoile and destroy, but saue and deliuer. All these come vnder this sentence of *Moses*, because they deny God, and are confederates with Satan. By the lawes of England, the thiefe is executed for stealing, and we thinke it iust and profitable: but it were a thousand times better for the land, if all Witches, but specially the blessing Witch might suffer death. For the thiefe by his stealing, and the hurtfull Inchanter by charming, bring hinderance and hurt to the bodies and goods of men; but these are the right hand of the deuill, by which he taketh and destroieth the soules of men. Men doe commonly hate and spit at the damnifying Sorcerer, as vnworthee to liue among them; whereas the other is so deare vnto them, that they hold themselues and their countrey blessed that haue him among them, they flie vnto him in necessitie, they depend vpon him as their god, and by this meanes, thousands are caried away to their finall confusion. Death therefore is the iust and deserued portion of the good Witch.

WILLIAM CRASHAW[1]

New-found Virginia was prominent in the news at the beginning of the sixteenth century, but reports of the place were already mixed and confusing. There was the natural appeal to the adventurous and the acquisitive of a distant land of virgin opportunity. John White's report on the charms and resources of the region was full of praise and encouragement. On the other hand, the mysterious disappearance of an entire community of colonists at Roanoke was an eerie event which might make the boldest ponder; and there were other reports, less favourable than White's, which suggested that life in the New World was far from comfortable, but dangerous and unhealthy.

William Crashaw's sermon, preached before a carefully assembled concourse, was, in intent, a recruiting address, aimed to attract cash investments of all kinds and volunteers of the *right kind*; they had already had too many of the wrong kind—men under one or another kind of necessity to leave England—and Crashaw is at pains to refute the slanderous suggestions that Virginia is already the resort of fugitives and rogues. Gentlemen of substance are particularly welcome because the colony needs development; but there is room for all honest, able-bodied men, who are not afraid of hard work and the wholesome challenge of an active life. This regulation, he explains, necessarily excludes actors. Crashaw had already complained bitterly of plays and players in a sermon preached at Paul's Cross, on February 14th, 1608, at 6 a.m. ('they know they have no calling, but are in the state like warts on the hand and blemishes in the face').

Crashaw would have liked to suppress what he disrelished. He was neither the first nor the last with a pious ambition to play censor. That dispensation was not to be vouchsafed him, but his sermon, a good (structurally a model) one, was responsible for the translation to Virginia at a critical moment of additional Anglo-Saxon stock, which might not otherwise have left the shores of England.

1. William Crashaw, 1572–1626. St. John's College, Cambridge: B.A., M.A., B.D. 1603. Second Prebend at Ripon, 1604.

A New Yeere's Gift to Virginia

A sermon preached in London, on February 21st. 1609
before the Hon. the Lord Laverre, Lord Governor and
Captain General of Virginia and others of His Majesty's
Counsel for that Kingdom, by W. Crashaw, B. D.,
Preacher at the Temple

All I haue to say I will reduce to two heads, namely,

to lay downe truly
{ The encouragements.
{ The discouragements
{ in this businesse.

For in 'this or any other action to be vndertaken, if the encouragements *to it*,
and discouragements *from it*, be both of them truly & justly laid down, and then
weighed in the balance of wisedome, it will easily appeare to men of vnderstanding, whether the businesse be fitter to be undertaken, or relinquished:
Answerably let vs deal in the present action, and so proceed accordingly.

And first let vs truly and impartially propound the *discouragements* that
seeme to attend this present intendment of *plantation of an English Colonie in
Virginea.*

The first and fundamentall is the *doubt of lawfulness of the action*, the question
being moued by many, and some not out of curiositie, nor other sinister, but
conscionable and Christian respects: and this keepes many from assisting it;
for how may they put their helping hands to that which they are not resolued
in conscience, to be lawfull and warrantable in it selfe. For these mens sakes,
and not for such as make it but a shelter of their couetous and carnal respects,
we will giue passage to this obiection.

And for answere hereunto; first, we freely confesse an action cannot be
good, excellent or honorable, and much lesse can it be necessarie, vnlesse
it first of all appeare to be lawfull: secondly, for the present action, we also
confesse and yeeld to this as to a principle of Iustice. A Christian may take
nothing from a Heathen against his will, but in faire and lawfull bargaine:
Abraham wanted a place to burie in, and liked a peece of land: and being a
great man, and therefore *feared*, a iust and meeke man, and therefore *loued* of
the heathen, they bad him *chuse where hee would, and take it:* No, saith
Abraham, but *I will buie it*, and so he paide the price of it: so must all the

children of *Abraham* doe. Thirdly, it is most lawfull to exchange with other Nations, for that which they may spare, and it is lawfull for a Christian to haue commerce in ciuill things euen with the heathen: vnlesse they be such of whom God hath giuen a plaine and personall charge to the contrarie, *as he did to the Israelites of the cursed Canaanites*, whom they were commaunded to kill, and haue nothing to doe withall: But we haue no such commaundement touching the *Virginians*.

Vpon these grounds, which I hope are vndeniable, I answere more particularly to the present occasion: that first we will take nothing from the *Sauages* by power nor pillage, by craft nor violence, neither goods, lands nor libertie, much lesse life (as some of other Christian nations haue done, to the dishonour of religion.) We will offer them no wrong, but rather defend them from it: and this is not my bare speech, but order is so taken both in our *Pattents* and *Instructions*, and such is the resolution of our *Gouernours*.

Secondly, we will *exchange* with them for that which *they may spare*, and we doe neede; and they shall haue that which we may spare, and they doe much more need. But what may they spare? first, *land and roome* for vs to plant in, their countrey being not replenished by many degrees: in so much as a great part of it lieth wild & inhabited of none but the beasts of the fielde, and the trees that haue growne there it may be 1000. yearse (whose antient possession to disturbe, we holde no great offence:) and who knowes not, but as the present state of *England* stands, we want roome, and are likely enough to want more?[1]

Againe, they may spare vs *Timber, Masts, Crystall* (if not better stones) *Wine, Copper, Iron, Pitch, Tar, Sassafras, Sopeashes*, (for all these and more, we are sure the Countrey yeeldes in great abundance) and who knowes not we want these, and are beholden to some for them, with whom it were better for vs if we had lesse to doe?

These things they haue, these they may spare, these we neede, these we will take of them. But what will we giue them? first, we will giue them such things as they greatly desire, and doe holde a sufficient recompence for any of the foresaide commodities we take of them: but we holde it not so; and therefore out of our humanitie and conscience, we will giue them more, namely such things as they want and neede, and are infinitely more excellent then all wee take from them:

and that is $\left\{\begin{array}{l}\text{1. } \textit{Ciuilitie} \text{ for their bodies,} \\ \text{2. } \textit{Christianitie} \text{ for their soules:}\end{array}\right\}$

The first to make them *men*: the second *happy men*; the first to couer their *bodies* from the shame of the world: the second, to couer their *soules* from the wrath of God: the lesse of these two (being that for the bodie) will make

1. English population in 1600 was under five million (*Whitaker's Almanack 1970*).

them richer then we finde them. For he that hath 1000. acres, and being a *ciuill* and *sociable* man knoes how to use it, is richer then he that hath 20000. and being a sauage, cannot plow, till, plant nor set, and so receiues no more profit then what the earth of it selfe will yeelde by nature: so that we are so farre from disinheriting them of their possessions, or taking any thing from them, that contrariwise we will make them much richer, euen for matter of this life, then now they are, as they themselues will hereafter confesse. Whereby appeares the vanitie of this obiection, for when they are *ciuilized*, and see what they haue receiued from vs, I dare say they will neuer make this obiection against vs that these men now doe. And now if the smaller and baser part of our paiment be better worth then all wee take from them, then it seemes the second, which is the chiefe of all, namely, *religion*, they haue from vs for nothing: and surely so it is, they shall haue it freely for Gods sake, and for their soules sake: and yet we know the holy ghost hath tolde vs, that *if we communicate vnto them our spirituall things, it is but a small thing if they impart vnto vs their temperall:* then how much smaller is it if they impart vnto vs their temporall, when we communicate vnto them both spirituall and better temporall then we receiue from them. And this may suffice for the lawfulnesse of the action, especially seeing whosoeuer would be satisfied more particularly, may haue recourse to a learned and godly *Sermon*, and to a short, but a iudicious and sincere declaration, well pend, both set out by authoritie for that end, and the truth whereof will be iustified both by the Authors, and the whole bodie of the Counsell for that king-dome. This discouragement troubled the conscience, the rest are rather grounded on politike and humane reasons, wherein therefore I will bee the shorter, and commit them to those whose element it is to consider and determine of such matters.

The second discouragement, is the *difficultie of Plantation*, for that the countrey is *farre off*, and the *passage* long and dangerous, the *climate* hot and disagreeing with the state and temper of our bodies. For answere, if these obiections proceede from malice, they are to be reiected; if from ignorance, as we rather suppose, let them then know for satisfaction, that first for the *distance*, it is nothing to speake of: a two moneths voyage, and wee hope wee shall shortly bee able to say a moneths: compare it with other voyages that are of name, and it is the neerest of all. Secondly, for the *passage*, it is the easiest, fairest and safest that hath been discouered to any place: we come not neere the *Sunne*, nor vnder the Æquinoctiall *line*, to distemper our bodies: wee haue no *straites* to passe through, we come neere no *enemies countrie*; no *rocks, shelues, sands,* nor *vnknowne Ilands* lie in our way: we are not in danger of the *Turkes gallies*, nor other enemies of Christian religion (who neuer yet did peepe out of the straits of *Gibraltar:*) we feare no congealed seas nor mountaines of *Ice*, to immure vs: But after we are out of our owne dores (the narrow Seas) wee keepe a faire course, betwixt the *Sunne* in the South on the left hand, and the *Ice* in the North on the right, vpon the maine Ocean, where we haue sea roome enough: And it is hard to name any other great voiage from this land, but the passage is subiect either to the vntemperate heate of the *Sunne* on the one side, or the danger of the *Ice* on the other side; witnesse the voyages to the *East Indies*, and others into the south, and to *Moscouie*, *Danske*, and others into the North and East: onely this passage into *Virginea*, being into the West Southwest, or thereabouts, is in that true temper so faire, so safe, so secure, so easie, as though God himselfe had built a bridge for men to passe from *England* to *Virginea*.

And let no wise man obiect that our last fleete was dispersed and sore shaken by *a storme*; for he cannot but know that such as saile by sea must as well expect *tempests of winde*, as trauellers on the land *shewers of raine*, and as he on the land is but *a simple swaine*, as the prouerbe is, that lets his businesse *for a shewer of raine*, no lesse is he that feares to saile on the sea for a tempest of winde: but our comfort is, that as the heauens *cannot giue raine of themselues, but it is the Lord:* nor the windes can rise of themselues, but *at Gods word the stormie winde ariseth, and lifteth vp the waues of the Ocean:* So neither Sea nor winde are in the hand or power of the diuell nor the Pope, for if they were, we should neuer plant nor land at *Virginea*.

As to the third, which is the *Climate*, let vs not abuse our selues by ignorance or vaine reports, but examine the trueth, looke into the *Mappes* and *Cards*, or, if thou hast not skill in them, looke into our *Patents*, or if thou canst not reade, or hast them not, aske and inquire of trauellers by sea or land, if the land that lieth betweene the 34. and 45. degrees of Northerly latitude from the Æquinoctiall line, be not farre enough from the *Torrida Zona*, and from the distempering heate of the Sunne: and though the middle of *Virginea* seeme to be in the same position with the heart and middle of *Spaine*, as *Toledo*, or thereaboutes: yet it falles out (for reasons not yet fully discerned) it is not so hot as *Spaine*, but rather of the same temper with the South of *France*, which is so temperate and indifferent, as if our owne were something neerer vnto it, we would be well content with it. And a further euidence that all this is true, we haue from the experience of a *Virginean*, that was with vs here in *England*, whose skinne (though hee had gone naked all his life, till our men persuaded him to bee clothed) was so farre from a *Moores* or East or West *Indians*, that it was little more blacke or tawnie, then one of ours would be if he should goe naked in the South of *England*. And to that experience adde a better, namely of *our brethren in Virginea*, who some of them haue been there many yeeres, and doe not complaine of any alteration, caused by distemper of the Climate.

The third *discouragement* is, that it hath so poore and small a beginning, and is thereupon subiect to the mockes and floutes of many, who say it is but the action of a few priuate persons, and they send but poore supplies, but handfuls of men at a time, and one good ship would beate them all.

For answere, I say, many greater States (then this is like to proue) had as little or lesse beginnings then this hath: The *Israelites* went downe into Egypt, *being but seuentie soules*, and were there but about two hundred yeeres, or little more, and most of that time vnder miserable bondage, yet did they grow to six hundred thousand men, beside children, and soone after to one of the greatest kingdomes of the earth: looke at the beginning of *Rome*, how poore, how meane, how despised it was; and yet on that base beginning grew to be the *Mistresse of the world*.

Oh but those that go in person are rakte vp out of the refuse, and are a number of disordred men, vnfit to bring to passe any good action: So indeed say those that lie and slander. But I answere: for the *generalitie* of them that goe, they be such as offer themselues voluntarily, for none are pressed, none compelled: and they be like (for ought that I see) to those are left behind, euen of all sorts better and worse. But for many that goe in person, let these obiecters know, they be as good as themselues, and it may be, many degrees better. But as for *mockers* of this businesse, they are worthie no answere: yet I could *tell them a tale*, not vnfitting them, but I will spare this place and audience, not them. But I will repeate them *a true storie*, and leaue it to themselues to make application. When God had moued the heart of *Artaxerxes* to send *Nehemiah*, and a few with him, to restore *Ierusalem* and build the walles, the text tels vs that as that poore people were at their worke, presently certain, who thought themselues no meane men, namely, *Sanballat the Horonite*, and *Tobiah an Ammonite*, were not a little stirred, *and mocked the Iewes, and spake in the hearing* of their companions, *What doe these weake Iewes? will they fortifie? will they sacrifice? will they finish it in a day? they build*, saith another; *but if a fox goe vp he will break downe their stonie wall*: and are not the like scornefull words muttered against vs and this present voyage? But what were these mockers? euen *Horonites and Ammonites, and such as had no portion, nor right, nor memoriall in Ierusalem*: I wish better to *our mockers*, though they wish so euill to vs: but let them take heede, though they care not for hauing *portions* with vs *in this aduenture*, that yet they haue their *right and portion and memoriall in Ierusalem*, or else they will proue mockers of vs in *iest*, and of themselues in *earnest*. But what saith *Nehemiah* and the Iewes that thus were flouted? *Heare O our God, for wee are despised, and turne their shame vpon their owne head, giue them vnto a prey in the land of their captiuitie, couer not their iniquitie, nor let their sinne be put out in thy presence, for they haue prouoked vs before the builders*[1]. Farre be it from me and vs all thus to say of ours: but contrariwise I pray God this curse be farre *from our mockers*, but I also pray they may be as farre *from deseruing it*.

1. Nehemiah 2 and 4: (ante 'Authorised Version').

But if any with no mocking spirit nor ill mind, doe only for his owne satisfaction further obiect that we send men that cannot liue here, men that are in debt, men of base fashion: Indeed thus said *Nabal* the churle, of *Dauid* and his companie reprochfully, terming them *a rout of vnruly seruants that runne away from their masters, and base fellowes of whom I know not whence they are*, 1.Sam.25.10,11. But hoping that these doe obiect out of better mindes, I answere, first, this is true for some, not all, and so it is in euery towne in England. Secondly, wee doe and must send such as we can, not such as we would. Thirdly, if they were all, or the most, such as is obiected, it is no more then wee haue obserued to be the beginners of great and noble actions: Remember who and what they were that came to *Romulus* and *Remus*, and were the founders of the Romane Citie & State, euen such as no man can without impudencie compare ours with them.

*

If any doe yet further replie and say: But it can neuer doe well to send such fellowes, such loose, leaud, licentious, riotous, and disordered men, they that cannot bee kept in compasse at home, how can they be ordered there? I answere, this obiection is much in *shew*, but the least of all in *substance:* for to say nothing that *there* is not that meanes nor occasions, to offend in many kindes that be *here* in abundance, we are further to know that as long as we haue wise, couragious, and discreete *Gouernours*, together with the preaching of Gods word, we much care not what the generalitie is of them that goe in person; considering we finde that the most disordered men that can bee raked vp out of the *superfluitie*, or if you will, the very *excrements*, of a full and swelling State, if they be remoued out of the fat and feeding ground of their *natiue countrey*, and from the licentiousnesse and too much libertie of the States where they haue liued, into a more bare and barren soile, as euery countrie is at the first, and to a harder course of life, wanting pleasures, and subiect to some pinching miseries, and to a strict forme of gouernement, and seuere discipline, doe often become new men, euen as it were cast in a new mould, and proue good and worthie instruments and members of a Common-wealth: Witnesse the companions of *Romulus* and *Remus*, that were the founders of the Romane State. And if you will haue a more infallible testimonie, looke into the Scriptures, call to minde the *men that came to Dauid*, qualified as you heard before, men *in danger of law*, men in *debt*, and *discontented* persons. Our base churles would roundly answer like *Nabal*, Are these *Dauids companions?* are these his partakers? such fellowes as these, that bee the scumme and skouring of the streetes, and raked vp out of the kennels, are like to be the founders of a worthie state. But see the shallownes of these mens conceits: for when those men had liued a while in *Dauids* fashion, and been trained vp vnder his discipline, they were so altered and refined, that many of them, all being some foure hundred (no more then a Virginean fleete) became worthie to bee of the honorable order of *Dauids Worthies*, or *Mightie men*, and proued great statesmen in the Common-wealth, and all of them did *Dauid* hold so well to haue deserued, that when God gaue him peaceable possession of his owne, *he brought vp all those men euery man with his household, and they dwelt in the Cities of Hebron*, where they proued good members, nay rather gouernours of the Common-wealth, and raised their families to greater honour then euer they had before. Now if those men so basely giuen, and ill qualified (as we heard afore) notwithstanding by sharpe and godly discipline proued so well; how much rather may wee hope the same, of our brethren gone and going to *Virginea*? many of whom are of good descent, of noble and generous spirits, vertuous, and valorous, and fearing God, and many waies as worthie as many of their ranke that are left behinde them. And to conclude, it is well enough knowne to them that know any thing, that there are good reasons, whereupon it comes to passe that such as liue licentiously in a State of *long continuance*, which is ripe and rotten for want of reformation, will easily be brought into order in a *new gouernment:* and no lesse good reasons are there why there is and will be better gouernment, and better execution of lawes in a *little territorie*, then in a great and populous *kingdome*, and in a new begun rather then in an old and setled State: the truth whereof many of you (right Honorable and beloued) doe better conceiue then I can expresse.

*

The next *discouragement* is, that the Countrie is ill reported of by them that haue been there. I answere, it is not true, in all, nor in the greater or better part; for many there be and men of worth who haue been there, and report so well of it, that they will not be kept from going thither againe, but hold it and call it, their home, and habitation, nor can all the pleasures, ease, delights and vanities of *England* allure them from it. But that *some*, and it may be *many* of the vulgar and viler sort, who went thither only for ease and idlenesse, for profit and pleasure, and some such carnall causes, and found contrariwise but cold entertainment, and that they must labour or else not eate, and be tied within the bounds of sharp laws, and seuere discipline; if such base people as these, doe from thence *write*, and here *report*, all euill that can be of that countrie, we doe not maruell, for they do but like themselues, and we haue euer found that all noble exploites haue been so maligned and misreported by the greater part (which generally is the worse part) of men.

*

The next *discouragement*, is the hard and miserable conditions of them that goe and stay there, their fare, their diet, their drinke, their apparell, their houses, their bedding, their lodging, are all so poore so pitifull, that no English men are able to endure it.

I answere, first, doe we purpose to attempt and atchieue, to begin and to perfect any noble exploite, in such fashion of life as wee liue in *England?* Let vs not deceiue our selues. Stately houses, costly apparell, rich furniture, soft beds, daintie fare, dalliance and pleasures, huntings and horse-races, sports and pastimes, feasts and banquets are not the meanes whereby *our forefathers* conquered kingdomes, subdued their enemies, conuerted heathen, ciuilized the Barbarians, and setled their common-wealths: nay they exposed them-selves to frost and colde, snow and heate, raine and tempests, hunger and thirst, and cared not what harnesse, what extremitie, what pinching miseries they endured, so they might atchieue the ends they aimed at: and shall wee thinke to bring to passe a matter of this honour and excellencie, which the ages to come shall stand amazed to beholde, and not to endure much corporall hardnesse? What was there euer *excellent* in the world that was not *difficult?* Nay euen therefore more excellent and more esteemed because *difficult:* they therefore were misaduised that went to *Virginea* with purpose to liue for the present, as they liued in *England,* and vnworthie are they to be counted *Fathers* and *Founders* of a new *Church* and *Common-wealth,* that resolued not to vndergoe and endure all difficulties, miseries and hardnesse that flesh and blood is able to beare.

Secondly I answere, this obiection yeeldes no cause of mislike of this action more then others (seeing there neuer was noble action that was not subiect to these miseries:) but it discouers the pusillanimitie, the basenesse, the tendernesse and effeminatenesse of our English people: into which our nation is now *degenerate,* from a strong, valiant, hardie, patient and induring people, as our forefathers were: which comes to passe not by our peace & plentie (as some causelesly cauill) but by the abuse of them, that is, by want of exercise of armes and actiuitie, want of trades and labour, by our idlenesse, lazinesse and lasciuiousnesse, where in *Cities* haue laboured to match the *Court,* and the *Countrey* enuies the Cities, and so now at last all turne after state and pompe and pleasures: and if any occasion fall out that men should be put to any hardnes, in cold or heate, by land or sea, for diet or lodging, not one of 100. is found that can indure it: but when other people can indure winter and summer, winde and weather, sunne and showers, frost and snow, hunger and thirst, in campe or garrison, by land or sea, and march on foote through snowe or waters, then our men for the most part are consumed and dead, or else got home againe to the fire side in *England.* But it was another kinde of life that made our *forefathers* fearefull to other nations, and terrible to their enemies: had they been such *mecocks*[1] *and milksops,* as we are now, they had neuer expulsed the *Danes,* nor ouercome the *French;* we had neuer

1. 'Mecock', more often 'meacock': an effeminate poltroon.

quartered the armes of *France*, nor crowned our kings in *Paris:* we had neuer taken so many forraine *Kings* in the fielde, and sometimes on their *owne ground:* we had neuer made the mightiest *Emperours* seeke alliance and marriages with vs, and some of them to come in *person* into our land, and fight vnder the banners and pay of our *Kings.* Thus they with *labour* wonne, what we with *idlenes* haue lost: for what is there that industrie, labour, paines and patience will not winne, and yet all those cannot winne so much, as idlenesse, dainties, and effeminatenesse will easilie lose: witnesse for proofe hereof, *our selues* and our neighbours of the *lowe countries:* who can but wonder that will obserue, what the *Hollanders* were an hundred yeares agoe, how dull, how base, how poore and seruile? But since they shaked off that dull and lazie humour, put themselues to paines & labour, to indure all hardnesse, and vndergoe any extremities, are they not become for their valour, their gouernement, their wealth, their power and their policie, euen the *wonder of nations?* Let some ascribe this to a fortunate Constellation, others to other causes, but all wise men may easily perceiue that this grew only from these two rootes, of Industrie and Vnitie: both of them being perfected with a valour and *resolution* of heart to endure any thing, so they might attaine the honorable *ends* they proposed to themselues: (which whether they haue not now attained, and that in so braue a fashion as is to the worlds admiration, I can say but little, but let wise men iudge.) The premisses considered, were it not good for vs if our people were inured to more hardnesse, and brought vp vnder obedience of sharper discipline, and accustomed to lesse daintinesse & tendernesse then heretofore? And are not those to be commended, which shew by their resolute vndertaking of an action so honorable in the ends of it, and yet accompanied with so many difficulties, that the ancient valour of English blood is not yet extinguisht? And canst not thou, who, like a Churle or an Epicure, sitst at home by the warme fire, and saiest, it is good sleeping in a whole skin; and that drinkest thy *wine in boles*, and stretchest thy selfe vpon the bed of lazinesse, and followest nothing but pleasure after pleasure; canst not thou, I say, be content to see others take in hand noble enterprises, but thou must depriue them of their due praises, and bring them vnder the compasse of thy base censure? If the action be honorable and excellent, then either do thou attempt it, notwithstanding the difficulties; or if thou darest not, at least honor them that dare. This should be my answere if the voyage were attended with as many difficulties and miseries as these men doe, or any can imagine.

But now I answer more particularly, that if our men there haue been at any exigents in this kind, it grew not from any necessitie that must needes accompanie that plantation, or that countrey: but proceeded plainly from the want of *gouernement*, and absence of our Gouernours, which was caused by the *hand of God*, and force of tempest, which neither humane *wit* could foresee, nor *strength* withstand. Or suppose something was miscarried by negligence, haste, or other humane infirmitie; shall *one staine* blemish the *beautie* of so faire a businesse? shall one *particular miscariage*, ouerturne the frame, or condemne the substance of the whole action? Surely wisedome and good reason will not admit it. And to conclude, seeing it is knowne to all, that know any thing in this matter, that the principal (if not the only) wound in this businesse hath been the *want of gouernment*, there is now care taken, that (by the blessing of God) there neuer shall bee want of that againe: which being once setled, we doe very well know that there will nothing else be wanting (in a short time after) needfull for the comfort of mans life: In the meane time wee care not (I speake in their names who goe in person, of whom out of my owne heart I could wish to be one my selfe) I say we care not what we indure, as long as we go forward in comming neerer to those high and excellent *ends*, which in the beginning wee proposed to our selues.

The next *discouragement* is, the vncertaintie of profit, and the long time that it must be expected, it be certaine. But I will not wrong you nor my selfe, in seeking to say much to so *base an obiection*. If there be any that came in only or principally for profit, or any that would so come in, I wish the *latter* may neuer bee in, and the *former* out againe. If the planting of an *English Colonie*, in a good and fruitfull soile, and of an *English Church* in a heathen-countrey; if the conuersion of the *Heathen*, if the propagating of the *Gospell*, and inlarging of the *kingdome* of Iesus Christ, be not inducements strong enough to bring them into this businesse, it is pitie they be iń at all. I will discharge my conscience in this matter: If any that are gone, or purpose to go in *person*, do it only that they might liue at ease and get wealth; if others that *aduenture their money* haue respected the same ends, I wish for my part *the one* in England again, and *the other* had his money in his purse; nay it were better that euery one gaue something to make vp his aduenture, then that such *Nabals* should thrust in their foule feete, and trouble so worthie a businesse. And I could wish (for my part) that the proclamation which God inioyned to bee made before the *Israelites* went to battell, were also made in this case: namely, that *whosoever is fainthearted. let him returne home againe, lest his brethrens hart faint like his*: for the *Coward* not only betraieth himself, but daunts and discourageth others. *Priuate ends* haue been the bane of many excellent exploits, and *priuate plots* for the gaine of a few, haue giuen hindrance to many *good and great* matters. Let vs take heed of it in this present businesse, and all ioyntly with one heart aime at the generall and publike ends, lest we finde hereafter to our shame and griefe, that this *one flye hath corrupted the whole box of oyntment*, though neuer so precious. Let vs therefore cast aside all cogitation of profit, let vs looke at better things: & then I dare say vnto you as Christ hath taught me, that *if in this action we seeke first the kingdome of God, all other things shall be added vnto vs:* that is (applying it to the case in hand) if wee first and principally seeke the propagation of the *Gospell* and conuersion of *soules*, God wil vndoubtedly make the voiage very profitable to all the *aduenturers* and their *posterities* euen for matter of this life: for the *soile* is good, the *commodities* many, and necessarie for England, the *distance* not farre off, the *passage* faire and easie, so that there wants only *Gods blessing* to make it gainfull: now the high way to obtaine that, is to forget our own affections, & to neglect our own priuate profit in respect of Gods glorie; and he that is zealous of Gods glorie, God will be mindfull of his profit: and he that seekes only or principally *spirituall* things, God will reward him both with those *spirituall and temporal* things. And as, though we may not do wel *to be wel spoken* of, yet if we do wel, God will *make vs* wel thought of, and spoken of, of all good men: so though we do not intend our profit in this action, yet, if wee intend Gods honor, and the conuersion of *soules*, them together, for I would gladly separate them, but they will not: for who but the *Diuell*, and *Papists*, and *Players* doe mocke at religion, and abuse the holie Scriptures? that the *Diuell* doth, who doubts? that the *Papists* doe, their many bookes doe witnesse, especially their damnable and hellish *Pruri-tanus*: that *Players* doe, too many eyes and eares can witnesse, some to their content, and many to their hearts griefe. Seeing then they will not be separated, let them goe together: the rather seeing they bee all enemies to this noble action.

The *Diuell*: and who can blame him? for we goe to disherit him of his ancient freehold, and to deliuer from out of his bondage the soules, which he hath kept so many yeeres in thraldome: wee therefore expect that hee will moue all the infernal powers against vs, and that we shall want no hurt nor hindrance that he is able to effect. But let him and all his partakers know, wee haue *him* on our side, who was promised in the beginning to be *the breaker of his head*, and who accordingly trampled him vnder his feete, *triumphed ouer him on the crosse*, and ouercame him in the graue (his owne denne): we goe to preach the faith, *against which all the gates of hell shall not preuaile.* And for his pleading of possession, wee care not: the possession is his, but the *right is Christs*, and we are for him, and therefore doubt not but to bring from heauen such an *Iniunction* out of the highest Court of *Equitie*, as shall remoue him out of possession, maugre his malice. Wee know his force, his furie, his malice, his wit and subtletie: and, as the Apostle saith, *we are not ignorant of his practises.* But when wee remember that he cannot enter into a *hogge*, but by Gods permission: when we remember that the windes and seas are not his, nor doe obey him, *but him that we serue:* when wee remember how the *Apostles* ouerthrew him, euen by the preaching of the *Gospell*, which wee carrie to *Virginea*; these and such like considerations make vs that wee feare not him, and all his angels so much, as hee feares the *prayers* of the poorest *Christian* in the world. And yet we will not countermine against him by charmings and inchantments, we will not *cast out diuels by the prince of diuels*, but wee will onely assault him with *the sword of the spirit, which is the word of God:* for we know that when the *Apostles* were to giue him the great ouerthrow, and his deadly wound, by recouering the whole world from *heathenisme to Christ*, this was that onely weapon with which they ouercame him: and though wee be not so skilfull *fencers*, nor can handle this weapon so well as they, yet wee know it hath not lost his force, but is the *sharpe two edged sword*, in whose hand soeuer it is vsed. And as long as our end is to plant and preach the Gospell, hee may for our sinnes, and sinfull cariage, *hurt* and *hinder*, but hee can neuer *ouerthrow* the worke, but contrariwise it shall be *his ouerthrow*, and the ruine of his kingdome in that countrey.

For the *Papists*,[1] wee know they approue nothing that *Protestants* vndertake; but wee vndertook not this to be approued by them: they would haue all the glorie to themselues of conuerting the Heathen; and if they did *conuert* them indeed, wee would commend and imitate them: but let them not enuie vs, for doing that which they extoll in themselues. If they seeke the *Popes* and *their owne* glorie, why should not wee seeke *Gods*? If they seeke *Gods glorie*, wee haue cause to seeke it more then they: in such workes as these wee will neuer breake from them, we will neuer forsake them: wee would ioyne with them to *conuert the Heathen*, wee would ioyne with them to *vanquish the Turke*. But their blinde guides the *Iesuites* tell them that wee are cursed, and all that partake with vs, and that they had better suffer *Heathen and Turkes* then ioyne with vs. And hence is it that they maligne and depraue this voyage, and wee are well assured that they haue filled all corners of this kingdome, with all base reports and slanders of this action, that mans wit can deuise. But let them goe on, wee little regard it, the more they hate it, the more we loue it; the more basely they speake of it, the more honourably doe wee hold it. Oh but the *Pope* will curse vs. Let him doe so, when hee would haue God the more to blesse vs: for what *Protestant* or any other did hee euer curse, but God blest them the more? *Leo* the 10. cursed *Luther*, and all men expected when he should haue died some horrible death: but hee liued to die in his bed, and proued the confounder of the Pope in his life and death. . . .

As for *Plaiers:* (pardon me right Honourable and beloued, for wronging this place and your patience with so base a subiect,) they play with *Princes* and *Potentates, Magistrates* and *Ministers*, nay with *God* and *Religion*, and all *holy things:* nothing that is good, excellent or holy can escape them: how then can this *action?* But this may suffice, that they are *Players:* they abuse *Virginea*, but they are but *Players:* they disgrace it: true, but they are but

1. The preacher did not live to see his son, Richard, the poet, become a convert to the Roman Catholic Church.

Players, and they haue *played* with better things, and such as for which, if they speedily repent not, I dare say, vengeance waites for them. But let them *play* on: they make men laugh on earth, but *hee that sits in heauen laughes them to scorne*; because like the flie they so long play with the candle, till first it singe their wings, and at last burnes them altogether. But why are the *Players* enemies to this Plantation and doe abuse it? I will tell you the causes: First, for that they are so multiplied here, that one cannot liue by another, and they see that wee send of all trades to *Virginea*, but will send no *Players*, which if wee would doe, they that remaine would gaine the more at home. Secondly, as the *diuell* hates vs, because wee purpose not to suffer *Heathens*, and the *Pope* because we haue vowed to tolerate no *Papists*: so doe the *Players*, because wee resolue to suffer no *Idle persons in Virginea*, which course if it were taken in *England*, they know they might turne to new occupations.

Thus the *Diuell, Papists, and Players,* (the enemies of this action) single them asunder, or let them ioyne their forces, wee care not for their malice, wee seeke not their fauour: nay wee had rather haue them all three against vs then with vs: and against them all, and all other that shall maligne vs whosoeuer, we say no more but this: *he hath set vs on worke that will maintaine vs:* and for our selues no more but this; *If God be on our side, who can be against vs?*

And thus with an indifferent vnpartiall eye we haue obserued, and laid downe all the *discouragements* that seeme to be incident to this businesse: and all, which I euer heard, either *friend* to feare, or *enemy* to obiect, and haue answered them all out of the grounds of truth.

Now let vs accordingly consider of the *encouragements* which God hath giuen vs, to proceede in the prosecution of this enterprise.

The first *encouragement* is, the consideration of the *excellencie of the action in it selfe:* this excellencie consists of these three degrees:

It is
{ a most *lawfull*,
an *honorable*, and
a *holy* action.

1. The *lawfulnesse of this enterprize* hath been, I hope, sufficientlie declared alreadie, and more may be said, if any thing be further obiected against it.

Secondly, the honour of this action is extraordinarie, 1. in regard of the Ends, being of a more high & excellent nature then are in other voiages, which for the most part bee profit and pleasure. 2. It is more honourable in regard of the vndertakers. Where was there euer voiage that had such a King and such a Prince to bee the Patrons and protectors of it? the one to begin, the other to second it. What voiage euer was there which had so many honourable vndertakers, and of so many sorts and callings, both of the *Clergie* and *Laitie, Nobilitie, Gentrie,* and *Commonaltie, Citie* and *Countrie, Merchants* and *Tradesmen, Priuate persons* and *Corporations?* as though euery kinde and calling of men desired to haue their hands in so happie a worke. All which considered, giue me leaue to affirme (with due respect to other, and without disparagement to any) that of all voiages euer attempted in this Nation, *The Virginean voiage is the most honourable*.1

1. Crashaw preached this sermon at a critical moment in the history of Virginia. Expeditions dispatched in 1606 by the Virginia Company had foundered, as he admits (p. 140, lines 12–13); other, earlier miscarriages had been satirised on the stage (p. 148, 149), perhaps in the lost play, *The Conquest of the West Indies* (1601); Crashaw himself was still smarting from the mockery of *The Puritane or the Widow of Watling Street* (1606). Reports of a state of lawless violence in Virginia had been reaching England: 1609 had been the 'starving year' and in June 1610 the sixty-five survivors of the original five hundred settlers had started to abandon the colony and return to England. Their departure was narrowly prevented by the arrival of Delaware who, having been invested with sweeping powers to amend disorder, persuaded them to return and continue the struggle against crime, disease, hostile Indians, crop failure, and polluted water. It was to the members of Delaware's expedition, on the eve of their departure, and to all other acceptable persons, who might be persuaded to subscribe, that Crashaw preached the incentive of a familiar Puritan formula (p. 146–7): temporal profit must not be made a primary objective, but prosperity may be expected to follow, as the reward for faithfully seeking to fulfil God's will.

ROBERT MILLES[1]

The reign of James I brought a marked increase in the picaresque to the English scene. Novel varieties of 'gentlemen Barabases', with matching doxies, abounded, and the least dangerous was the old-fashioned ruffian who would rob you of your purse by stealth or menace. He would only take what you had about you, but if you fell into the hands of a band of kind-faced confidence tricksters, all affectionate goodwill and flattery, you might sign away your inheritance in the space of a few days, believing that you were doubling it. The streets of London swarmed with pickeers of both sexes in quest of prey, and the spoor of the well-heeled rustic squire on a visit to the capital was the favourite of all. Every place of assembly was a hunting ground for such light-fingered and light-tongued, the church, the fair, the market, the ordinary, where travellers dined, and, most rewarding of all, the playhouse.

The stage, the traditional rival of the pulpit, had always been the object of severest Puritan censure. Thirty-five years previously a preacher had complained that, even on the Lord's day, 'the better parte of it is horribly prophaned by deuillish inuentions as with the Lords of misrule, Morice dauncers, Maygames, inasmuch as in some places they shame not in any time [of] divine service to come to daunce about the church and without to have men dauncing in nettes, which is most filthie.'[2] Closing the playhouses had been an imperfect remedy for actors were shameless and incorrigible ('Let them say what they will, we

1. Disappointingly little is known of this other unrelenting enemy of the theatre. He was probably the Robert Milles who Matriculated pensioner from St. John's College, Cambridge, in Lent 1582-3. We know that he was Preacher at Gedney-senne and Sutton St. Edmonds in Holland, Lincolnshire, in the first decade of the 17th century and that the local magnate, Sir William Welby, sent his eldest son and heir, William, to the same college in April 1603. The choice may have been made on the advice of Milles, for preacher and patron were evidently on closer terms than their social disparity might suggest. In his 'Epistle Dedicatory, addressed to Sir William, Milles describes him as not only 'auditor', but 'adiutor' (helper) in respect of the sermon, and appeals to him for protection. The preacher's attack on the theatre had provoked rough treatment from the satirical playwrights and Milles complains of his sermon being 'injuriously handled by prophane Philistines' (Sig A6ᵛ).

2. John Stockwood, *A Sermon preached at Paul's Cross on St. Bartholomew's Day, being the 24th August (1578)*.

will play . . .'), would perform on improvised stages, 'euen after the manner of the old heathenish Theatre of Rome, a shew place of all beastly and filthie matter, to the which it cannot be chosen that men should resort without learning there much corruption. For he that beheld but the filthie picture of Jupiter in a shower of golden raine descending unto Diana[1] could thereby encourage himself into filthinesse.' How much less can 'flocks of wyld youths of both sexes resorting to Enterludes where both by lively gesture and voices there are allurements into whordom . . .' come away 'always pure and not inflamed with concupisence'. In the next breath the preacher asks a rhetorical question, to which he has already received a disagreeable answer. 'Who is there that is so euill as to affirme two hours spent in hearing a bawdie play, which should be spent in hearing a sermon to be the redeeming of tyme . . .?'

Imminent strokes of divine retribution are predicted, for were not the 'Children of Israel led into captivity because they kept not the Lord's Saboth; and what became of him that gathered sticks on that day. I doubt not that you will remember, we, notwithstanding on the Lord's day must haue Fayres kept, must have Beare Bayting, Bul bayting (as if it were a thing of necessity that Beares of the Paris garden to be bayted on the Sunnedaye) must have baudie Enterludes, silver games, dicing, carding, tabling, daunzing.'

But a decade later Puritans were asking the same question with mounting indignation.

'. . . I have heard some hold opinion that they (plays) be as good as sermons and that many a good example maie be learned out of them.'
'O Blasphemie intolerable. Are filthie playes and Bawdie Enterludes comparable with the word of God . . . ?'[2]

A substantial part of the world seemed to think that they were, and by 1611 the view from the Puritan pulpit revealed more iniquity than ever.

---

1. A libel upon almost the only continent goddess in classical mythology. Danae, not Diana, was the favoured recipient of Jupiter's golden embrace.
2. Philip Stubbs, *The Anatomy of Abuses* (1583).

Abraham's Suite to Sodom

A Sermon preached at Paul's Cross
on August 25th, 1611[1]

Notwithstanding *Longæsunt Regum manus*, that Magistrates haue long armes, and many eares: yet *latet anguis in herba*, when *Moses* was on the Mount, *Israel* playd the wanton: and euen in this Citie (though not in the heart) yet in close back wings and obscure angles therof, there be many nests full of idle birds, which the carefull Magistrate seldom findeth out. *Ignauum fucos pecus a præsepibus arcent*, There is in the regiment of Bees an intrusive & troublesome Droane, which eateth vp the sweete hony, for which the poore painefull creatures haue laboured for long before. And in the curious Bee-hiue of this commonwealth there are foure sorts of idle Bees, much like the foure Sects of Philosophers, which sometimes flourished in *Athens*, the *Academicke, Epicure, Peripatetique*, and the *Stoicke*. The first were greatly giuen to studie and contemplation, and these are your idle gamesters, who are all night in speculation, deuising new tricks, and inuenting strange conueyance by Cards and Dice, which next day they put in practice. God sayth, *In the sweate of thy face thou shalt eate thy bread*, and these idle Bees liue by the sweate of other mens browes, onely by playing. *Dauid* with on(e) smooth stone out of his bag discomfited the whole hoast of the Philistines: And this idle Gamester with a blind bone out of his iugling boxe, with the actiuity of a Polupragmaticall finger, can in one howre vndoe many a hopefull heire: I had almost sayd, many an honest Tradesman. Of the second Philosopher the *Epicure*, I spake before in fulnesse of bread, and therefore I leaue him to his pleasure, which is his *Summum bonum*. The third is the *Peripateticke*, who vsed to dispute walking, and in this order are Cunny-catchers, who like the Diuell are alwayes compassing the Earth, and still going vp and downe seeking whome they may deuoure. These cunning Philosophers walke from Inne to Inne, from East to West, from Towrehill to Tyburne, (and there I leaue them) and with Sathan can turne themselues into an Angell of light, full of good words, and with *Iudas* embrace a man with a courtly boonecongee, and at parting cut a mans throate, and empouerish many a plaine dealing countrey guest with cousenage in copartnership.

The fourth idle Bee, or sect of Philosophers is the *Stoike* who vsed to

1. Published 1612.

keepe their acts and disputations standing. And these I call your mimicall Comædians, and apish actors, who with *Thraso* thunder out *sesquipedalia verba*, a heape of inkehorne tearmes to the tenour of a poore Colliar, and with a ridiculous *Tu quoque*, moue many a foole to laugh at their owne follies. And further the licentious Poet and Player together are growne to such impudencie, as with shamelesse *Shemei*, they teach Nobilitie, Knighthood, graue Matrons & ciuil citizens, and like Countrey dogs snatch at euery passengers heeles. Yea, Playes are growne now adayes into such high request (*Horrosco referens*) as that some prophane persons affirm, they can learne as much both for example and edifying at a Play, as at a Sermon. *O tempora, O mores*, O times, O manners, tremble thou Earth, blush yee Heauens and, speake O head, if euer any *Sodomite* vttered such blasphemie within thy gates. Did the diuell euer speake thus impiously in this conflict with the Archangell? To compare a lasciuious Stage to this sacred Pulpet and oracle of trueth? To compare a silken counterfeit to a Prophet, to Gods Angell, to his Minister, to the distributer of Gods heauenly mysteries. And to compare the idle and scurrile inuention of an illiterate bricklayer, to the holy, pure and powerful word of God, which is the foode of our soules to eternal saluation. Lord forgiue them, they know not what they say.

THOMAS ADAMS[1]

At the time when Robert Milles preached his sermon, the 'illiterate bricklayer' was in the middle of one of his most productive periods. *The Silent Woman* and *The Alchemist* had followed each other in quick succession and now *Cataline* was in production and the shape of *Bartholomew Fair* would have been forming in his mind. But the achievements by which the age would above all else be celebrated in centuries to come, meant, for a small, vociferous part of Jacobean society, only vice and vanity, 'the smoke of the bottomless pit'. The paradox is complicated by the dramatic nature of the talent of certain of the best Puritan divines, which in other circumstances might have found its most fruitful expression in the abominable activities they stood to denounce. This applies to a singular degree in the case of Thomas Adams, who is divided from other Puritan clergy by a wide difference in *literary* quality. He would have agreed with Sibbes and Ames and Perkins and the rest of his reforming brethren in radical particulars of Genevan doctrine and practice, including reprobation of the theatre; yet he himself was endowed with the equipment to have made a playwright of distinction, and, when he went into the pulpit, the forces with which he was charged could not be suppressed. His sermons engage as a play does, or should do, by alchemy of psychological transference, whereby *they* presently become *us*, and a spectacle an experience. This, of course, is an effect far more difficult to produce from the pulpit than the stage, and we have no evidence of how far Adams's own personality was an asset to his sermons; but in the role of author he was well sufficient. His preoccupation with human depravity is reminiscent of Webster, but his imagery is more colourful and ingenious. What the structure of a conjectured play of his might have been it is difficult to conceive, but it is evident that the force of the

1. Thomas Adams, fl. 1612–53. 1612 preacher at Willington, between Bedford and St. Neots. 1614 Vicar of Wingrave, Buckinghamshire. 1618–23 Preachership of St. Gregory's under St. Paul's Cathedral, and preached occasionally at St. Paul's Cross and Whitehall. Published sermons include *The White Devil*, 1612; *The Gallent's Burden*, 1612; *The Diull's Banket*, 1614; *England's Sickness*, 1615. See Newcourt's *Repertorium*; Walker's *Suffering of the Clergy*; Joseph Angus in Nichol's *Puritan Divines* (3 vols.), 1862.

dialogue would have been an important factor in the product, and he demonstrates that, in telling a story, he can move with swift economy when he wishes, and he can bring the briefest of thought to a climax, in which sound and meaning are united.

'Every man is borne a pharisee, well conceited of himselfe; and if he miss scandalous impietie he presently blesseth his own happy disposition.'[1]

And again:

'Many will not name the devill without defyance yet serve him with all diligence. They spit him out of their mouthes, but he is lower, they should conjure him out of their hearts,'[2]

In a number of important respects Adams departed from the practice and limitations of contemporary Puritan preaching. In the first place his evocations of sin were lurid and stark, without a figleaf's concession to decorum, especially in respect of sexual sins, with which he seemed so preoccupied that he retained their imagery as metaphor in which to describe other sins. Then, he had no bashful doubts of using his classical scholarship as paint. Most interesting of all, he reverted to the old medi-aeval habit, offensive to most Puritans, of using *exempla* from popular field sports and wanton pastimes. Nicholas Bozon, the fifteenth-century Franciscan, exhorted young men to 'flee minstrelsy as the hare flees the sound of the huntsman's horn'; and the pre-Reformation preacher was prone to see Christ as 'the great huntsman the wiche over al lovithe huntyng of soules'. Adams, among many illustrations, sees death, in his pursuit of a man, playing with him like 'the greyhound with the badger; sometime he follows fair and far off, keep aloof out of sight. Anon he takes his career and is at his heels. Sickness is the neighing of his nostrils, after which, though he allows us some breath, yet in the end overtakes us and is upon us in an instant.'[3]

Southey did him no service by likening him, in a brief beam of attention, to Shakespeare, but it is not an exaggeration to describe Thomas Adams as one of the more considerable buried literary talents of the seventeenth century. I have no hesitation in placing him close behind

1. *Meditations on the Creed. Works* (1629), p. 1188.   2. Ibid.
3. Ibid., p. 201. Unfortunately, although his intentions were excellent, his knowledge of field sports was not. The greyhound never has been, nor could be, used to hunt the badger. One good reason is that the badger is a nocturnal mover and the greyhound can only chase what he sees. Another and better reason from the greyhound's point of view is that, if a greyhound did by some chance confront a badger, and was foolish enough to engage the most resolute fellow in England's wild life, he would be lucky to escape with nothing worse than a lacerated muzzle. How did Adams get the notion? Could one of his parishioners have been pulling his leg?

the other two high masters of the narrative sermon in the second part of the period we are covering, John Donne and Jeremy Taylor. His is not a peculiar genius like Taylor's, nor an exhaustively polished virtuosity like Donne's; but neither is it blemished, like Donne's, by the conceits of indulgent self-regard, nor refined, like Taylor's, by arcane distillations to a state when the hermeneutic purpose of the operation is left behind. In effect, Adams is more functional than either because, with all the richness of his resources, he is never for a moment what Taylor and Donne in their different styles not infrequently give the impression of being, eminent soloists dispensing eloquence, like music, for its own sake.

There is evidence in a sermon of 1612 that Adams may himself have been the subject of criticism by other Puritan clergy (and perhaps laity) for his liberal attitude towards learning, and he says
'There have been some, niggardly affected towards learning, calling it a man's wisdome: they thrust out the use of the artes, as if with Julian they would shut up the school doores and send all human knowledge into banishment.' But, he asserts, everything is admissible to serve as 'the handmaids of divinity'. As for the condemners of learning, they only object to others having what they lack.
'They wrong us. We make not the pulpit a philosophy, Logicke, Poetry and Schoole, but all these are so many stairs to the pulpit . . .'.
If they could beat down learning they might escape censure for their own ignorance:
'For shame let none that hath borne a book dispraise learning; she hath enemies enough abroad though she be justified of her own children at home: Let Barbary disgrace Arts not Athens.'

In the middle of the nineteenth century the works of Adams came to the notice of non-conformist thought (probably through the praise of Southey) for the first time for two hundred years. It needed some courage for a man in Dr. Joseph Angus's position to underwrite with his approval their publication, and he protects himself with a general monition concerning Adams's serious 'lapses of taste'[1] and 'grave faults'. This purported to be a literary judgement but it is not difficult to imagine the disquiet induced in mid-nineteenth-century minds by, for instance, the following sally:
'We preach the same Jesus to you that Gabriel did to Mary. O that our

1. Joseph Angus, 'Memoir of Thomas Adams', in *Works of Thomas Adams* (Edinburgh, 1862), Vol. III.

sermons had such success in your ears as his did in hers that you might all depart pregnant of the Lord Jesus.'[1]

Nor by Adams's fascinated scrutiny of the more scandalous misdemeanours on Jesus's maternal side of the family:

'Tamar is the first; and she stole from her father-in-law an incestuous copulation. . . . Yet is this incest pardoned and this woman royally chronicled. Rahab is the next and she was in every way contemptible . . . by trade a hostess, by conversation a harlot . . . her body being as common as her house. Hostess and harlot were held convertible terms; if a guest wanted lodging her own bed was public. Yet she became a mere chaste convert, honest and honourable . . . and the holy line of Jesus is not ashamed to admit her into that happy pedigree. Bathsheba is the last . . . one that ambitious to be a queen, leaped into the bed of her husband's murderer. She first lies with an adulterer and then marries a homicide. . . .'[2]

To Adams, all this, being biblical, qualifies for unreserved ventilation, and of course ends on a triumphant note for the hero of his story. 'Yet from these came the Lord Jesus, from such unholy loins the most holy saviour. . . .'

If anything more had been needed to persuade his Victorian descendants that their spiritual ancestor, for all his gifts, was a dangerous asset, they would find sufficient passages like the one at the beginning of *The White Devil*[3] where Adams explains that anything is permissible, indeed righteous—adultery, fornication, rapine, plunder—so long as the Lord decrees it.

You haue read him commanding the brother *to raise up seed to his brother* (Deut. XXV. 5) notwithstanding the law, *Thou shalt not commit adultery* (Math. XII. 24) commanding the Israelites to rob the Egyptians (Exodus XI. 2) without infringing the law of stealth; all this without wrong, for *the earth is His and the fulness thereof.*[4]

In homely terms it is as if 'Thou art the father of many children: thou sayest to the youngest, "Sirrah, wear you the coat today, which your brother wore yesterday."[5] Who complains of wrong?'

The Antinomianism that all things were permissible which were authorized by God, and that His instructions would be communicated express to the heart of his elect, had, in effect, no sinister temptation for a man as unworldly as Adams; but the same notion could produce, when the opportunity arose, very different effects upon ambitious men with an appetite for power.

1. Adams, op. cit., p. 1123.   2. Ibid., p. 244.
3. *The White Devil* (1611), pp. 10–11.   4. Ibid.   5. Ibid.

The Rich Man[1] (c. 1612)

Luke XII.20. *But God said unto him, 'Thou fool, this night they soul shall be required of thee: then whose shall those be which thous has provided?'*

Comes his Riches ill his credit is the Common curse. *Populus sibilat*, the world rails at him liuing: and when he dies, no man sayes It is pitty, but it is pitty he died not sooner. *They shall not lament* for him, with Ah Lord, or Ah, his Glory. *But hee shall be buried with the burial of an Ass, that hath lived the life of a wolf.* His glorious Tombe erected by his enriched heyre shall bee saluted with execrations and the passengers by will say Here lyes the Devil's Promoter. Come his wealth well, yet what is credit, of how may we define a good name? Is it to have a Pageant of crindges, and faces acted to a taffaty[2] Iacket: To be followed by a world of hang-byes, and howted at by the reeling multitude, like a bird of Paradise, stuck full of py'd feathers: To be daub'd over court-morter, flattery, and set up as a Butt for whores, panders, drunkards, cheaters to shoot their commendations at? To be licked with a sycophants rankling tongue and to have poor men crouch to him, as little dogges use a great mastiffe? Is this a good name? Is this credit? Indeed these things may give him a great sound, as the clapper doth a bell, but the bell is hollow. They are empty gulls whose credit is nothing else but a great noyse, forced by these lewd clappers.

A rich worldling is like a great Cannon, and flatterers praises are the powder that charge him; whereupon he takes fire and makes a great report, but instantly goes off, goes out in stench. He may thinke himselfe the better, but no wise man, no good man doth; and the fame that is derived from fools is infamy. . . .

For Sinne, what vice is euacuated by riches? Is the wealthy man humbled by his abundance? no, hee is rather swelled into a frothy pride; conceiting himselfe more then hee is, or at least imagining, that hee is eyther (τìȝ) or (ó) the man or some body. And as pride is *radix omnes peccati*; the roote of all sinne; so riches is the roote of pride, *Diuitiarum vermis superbia*, saith Saint Augustine. When the sunne of prosperitie heates the dunghill of riches, there is engendered the snake of pride. Wealth is but a quill; to blow vp the bladder of high-mindednesse. Saint *Paul* knew this inseparable consequence, when hee charged *Timothy*, to *Charge them that are rich in this world, that they bee not high-minded.* And doe wee thinke that the heate of malice will bee slaked by riches? no, it is fired rather into combustion; and now bursts foorth into a

1. From *The Cosmopolite or, Worlds Favourite. Works* (1629), pp. 688–92.
2. Made of silk, or rich cloth.

flame, what before was forced to lye suppressed in the embers of the heart. Is any man the more continent for his abundance? No, *Stat quæuis multo meretrix mercabibilis auro*: Whores are led to hell with golden threds. Riches is a warme nest, where lust securely sits to hatch all her vncleane brood. From fulnesse of bread, the Sodomites fall to vnnaturall wantonnesse. *Ceres et Liber pinguefaciunt Venerem.* Oppression is not abated by multiplication of riches; but rather *Longiorem & magis strenuam reddit manum*; giues it a longer and stronger arme. For as the poore cannot withstand, so the rich will not restraine the tyranny of great oppressors. *They couet fields, and take them by violence*: how? *Because their hand hath power.*

For Punishment, what security is in money? Doth the Deuill balke a Lordly house, as if hee were afraid to come in? Dares hee not tempt a rich man to lewdnesse? Let experience witnesse, whether hee dares not bring the highest Gallant both to sinne and shame. Let his food bee neuer so delicate, hee will bee a guest at his table; and perhaps thrust in one dish to his feast, drunken-nesse. Bee his attendance neure so complete, yet Satan will waite on him too. Wealth is no charme to coniure away the Deuill: such an amulet and the Popes holy-water, are both of a force. Inward vexations forbeare not their stings, in awe of riches. An euill conscience dares perplexe a *Saul* in his Throne, and a *Iudas* with his purse full of money. Can a silken sleeue keepe a broken arme from aking? Then may full barnes keepe an euill conscience from vexing. And doth hell-fire fauour the Rich mans limbes more then the poores? Hath hee any seruant there, to fanne cold ayre vpon his tormented ioynts? Nay, the namelesse *Diues* goes from soft linnen to sheetes of fire, from purple robes to flames of the same colour, purple flames; from delicate mor-sels, to want a droppe of water. *Herod*, though a King on earth, when he comes to that smoky vault, hath not a cushion to sit on, more then the meanest Parasite in his Court. So poore a defence are they for an oppressed Soule.

Nor from the body can riches remooue any plague. The lightning from heauen may consume vs, though wee bee clad in gold: the vapours of earth choke vs, though perfumes are still in our nostrills: and poyson burst vs, though wee haue the most virtuall Antidotes. What iudgement is the poore subiect to; from which the rich is exempted? Their feete doe as soone stumble, and their bones are as quickly broken. Consumptions, Feuers, Gowtes, Dropsyes, Pleurisies, Palseys, Surfets are houshold guests in rich mens families, and but meere strangers in cottages. They are the effects of superfluous fare and idlenesse; and keepe their Ordinarie at rich mens tables. Anguish lyes oftner on a Downe-bed, then on a pallet: diseases waite vpon luxurie, as close as luxurie vpon wealth. These Frogges dare leape into King *Pharaohs* chamber, and forbeare not the most sumptuous pallace. But money can buy medicines: yet what sicke man would not wish, that hee had no money, on condition that hee had no maladie. Labour and moderate diet are the poore mans friends, and preserue him from the acquaintance of Master Doctor, or the surfeted billes of his Apothecary. Though our worldling heere promiseth out of his abundance, meate, drinke and mirth: yet his body growes sicke, and his soule sadde: hee was before carelesse, and hee is now curelesse: all his wealth cannot retaine his health, when God will take it away.

But what shall wee say to the Estate? Euils to that are pouertie, hunger, thirst, wearinesse, seruilitie: Wee hope wealth can stoppe the invasion of these miseries. Nothing lesse: it rather mounts a man, as a Wrastler does his combatant, that it may giue him the greater fall. Riches are but a sheeld of Waxe, against a sword of power. The larger state, the fairest marke for misfortune to shoote at. Eagles catch not after flies: nor will the *Hercules* of ambition lift vp his clubbe, but against these Giants. There is not in pouertie that matter, for a Great mans couetous fire to worke vpon. If *Naboth* had had no Vineyard to preiudice the command of *Ahab's* Lordship, hee had saued both his peace and life. Violent windes blow through a hollow willow, or ouer a poore shrubbe, and let them stand: whiles they rend a peeces Oakes and great Cedars, that oppose their great bodies to the furious blasts. The tempests of oppressing power meddle not with the contemptible quiet of poore Laboures, but shake vp rich men by the very rootes; that their blasted fortunes may bee fit timber for their owne building. Who stands so like an eye-sore in the tyrannous sight of Ambition, as the wealthy? Imprisonment, restraint, banishment, confiscation, fining, and confining are Greatnesses Intelligencers; instruments and staires to climbe vp by into rich mens possessions. Superabundant wealth hath foure hinderances from doing good to the estate.

1. God vsually punisheth our ouer-louing of riches with their losse. Hee thinkes them vnworthy to bee riualls with himselfe: for all height and strength of loue is his due. So that the ready way to lose wealth, is to loue it. *Et delectatio perdet.*

2. The greatnesse of state, or of affection to it, opens the way to ruine. A full and large saile giues vantage to a Tempest: this pulled downe, the danger of the gust, and of shipwracke by it, is eluded: and it passeth by with onely waues, roring as if it was angry for being thus peruented. Hee that walkes on plaine ground, either doth not fall, or riseth againe with little hurt. Hee that climbes high towres, is in more danger of falling; and if hee fall, of breaking his necke.

3. Wee see the most rich Worldlings liue the most miserably; slaued to that wealth, whereof they keepe the key vnder their girdles. *Esuriunt in popina,* as wee say, they starue in a Cookes shoppe. A man would thinke, that if wealth could doe any good, it could surely doe this good; keepe the owner from want, hunger, sorrow, care: No, euen these euills riches doe not auoide,

but rather force on him. Whereof is a man couetous, but of riches? when these riches come, you thinke hee is cured of his couetousnesse: no, hee is more couetous, though the desires of his minde bee granted, yet this precludes not the accesse of new desires to his minde. So a man might striue to extinguish the Lampe, by putting oyle into it; but this makes it burne more. And as it is with some, that thirstily drinke harish and ill-brewed drinkes, haue not their heate hereby allayed, but inflamed: So this worldlings hote eagernesse of riches is not cooled, but fired by his abundance.

4. That which makes a man easie to hit, makes also his wound grieuous. The Poet[1] tells vs, that when *Codrus* his house burnes, (a little cottage in the Forrest) hee stands by and warmes himselfe at the flame: hee knoews that a few stickes, straw, and clay, with a little labour, can rebuild him as good a Tabernacle. But if this accident light vpon the Vsurers house, distraction sieseth him withall: he cryes out of his Chamber, and that chest, of his closet and cabinet, of his bonds and morgages, money and plate; and so much the more impatient, as hee had more to lose.

In a word, here is all the difference bewixt the rich and poore: the poore man would bee rich whiles he lives, and the rich man would be poore when hee dies. For it is small greefe to leave hunger, cold, distresse, bondage, hard lodging, and harder fare: but to forsake full barnes, full purses, musicke, wine, iunkets, soft beds, beauteous women, and these lust-tickling delights, and to go with death to the land of forget-fulnesse, this is the terrour. I end then as Paul concludes his council to rich men, *Lay up for your selves a good fonndation against the time to come that you may lay hold on eternal life.*

The White Devil[2]

... What? thy master, that honored thee with Christianity, graced thee with Apostleship, trusted thee with Stewardship, wilt thou denie him this courtesie, and without thine own cost; thy Master, *Iudas*, thy friend, thy God, and yet in a sweeter note, thy Sauiour, and canst not indure anothers gratiutall kindnesse towardes him? shall he powre forth the best vnction of his blood, to bath and comfort thy body and soule, and thou not allow him a little refection?[3] hath Christ hungred, thirsted, fainted, sweat, and must he instantly bleed and die, and is he denied a little vnction? and dost thou, *Iudas*, grudge it? it had come more tolerably from any mouth: his friend, his follower, his professor, his Apostle, his Steward! vnkind, vnnaturall, vniust, vnmercifull *Iudas*.

1. Juvenal, *Satires*, 4.   2. Preached 1612, published in *Works* (1629), pp. 38–56.
3. Refreshment.

Nay he termes it no better than waste and a losse: εἰς τί ἡ ἀπωλεια αὕτη *ad quid perditio hæc? Why is this wast?* What, lost and giuen to *Iesus?* can there be any waste in the creatures due seruice to the Creator? no: *pietas est proprietate sumptus facere.*[1] this is godlinesse, to be at cost with God: therefore our fathers left behind them (*deposita pietatis*) pleadges, euidences, sure testimonies of their Religion, in honoring *Christ* with their riches: (I meane not those in the dayes of popery, but before euer the locusts of the papal sea made our nation drunk with that inchanted cup:) they thought it no waste either (*noua construere, aut vetera conseruare*) to build new Monuments to Christs honour, or to better the old ones: we may say of them, as *Rome* bragged of *Augustus Cæsar: que inuenerunt lateritia, reliquerunt marmorea:* what they found of bricke, they left of Marble in imitation of that precedent in *Esay,* though with honester hearts: *The bricks are fallen downe, but we will build with hewen stones: The Sycomores are cut downe, but we will change them into Cedars.* In those dayes, charity to the Church was not counted waste: The people of *England,* deuout like those of Israel, cryed one to another (*afferte) Bring yee into Gods house;* till they were stayed with a statute of *Mort-maine;* like *Moses* prohibition, *the people bring too much*: But now they change a letter, and cry, (*Auferte*) take away as fast as they gaue, and no inhibition of God or *Moses,* Gospell, or statute, can restrain their violence: till the Alabaster-box be as empty of oile, as their owne consciences are of grace. We need not stint your deuotion, but your deuoration: euery contribution to Gods seruice is held waste: *ad quid perditio hæc?* now any required ornament to the Church, is held wast: but the swallowing downe (I say not, of ornaments, as things better spared, but) of necessary maintenance, Tythes, Fruits, Offrings, are all too little: Gentlemen in these cold countries haue very good stomacks, they can deuoure (and digest too) three or foure plumpe Parsonages; in *Italy, Spaine,* and those hot countries, (or else nature and experience too lies) a Temporall man cannot swallow a morsell or bit of a spirituall preferment, but it is reluctant in his stomacke, vp it comes againe: surely these Northerne countries, coldly situate, and neerer to the *Tropicke,* haue greater appetites: the *Affricans* thinke the *Spaniards* gluttons, the *Spaniards* thinke so of the *French-men, French-men,* and all thinke and say so of *English-men;* for they can deuoure whole Churches: and they haue fed so liberally, that the poore seruitors (ashamed I am to call them so) the Vicars, haue scarce enough left to keepe life and soule together: not so much as (*sitis & fames & frigora poscunt*)[2] the defence of hunger and thirst and cold requires: your fathers thought many Acres of ground well bestowed, you thinke the Tythe of those Acres a wast: oppression hath plai'd the *Iudas* with the Church, and because he would preuent the sins incurable by our

1. Paraphrase, Tertullian, *Apolog. Adversus Gentes,* cap. 39.
2. Juvenal, *Satires,* 14.

fulnesse of bread, hath scarce left vs bread to feed vpon, *Daniels* diet among
the Lyons, or *Elias* his in the wildernesse. I will not censure you in this, ye
Citizens; let it be your praise, that though you *dwell in sieled houses* your
selues, you *let not Gods house lie waste*: yet sometimes it is found, that some
of you so carefull in the Citie, are as negligent in the Country,[1] where your
lands lie; and there the Temples are often the ruines of your oppression; your
poore vndone, bloud-sucked Tenants, not being able to repaire the windowes
or the leades, to keepe out raine or bird.[2] if a leuy or taxation would force
your beneuolence, it comes maleuolently from you, with a *Why is this waste?*
Raise a contribution to a lecture[3] a collection for a fire, an almes to a poore
destitute soule, and lightly there is one *Iudas* in the congregation to crie *ad
quid perditio hæc? why is this wast?* Yet you will say, if Christ stood in need of
an vnction, though as costly as *Maries*, you would not grudge it: nor think
it lost: cosen not your selues, ye hypocrits: if ye will not do it to his Church,
to his poore ministers, to his poore members, neither would you to Christ: if
you cloth not them, neither would you cloth Christ if he stood naked at
your doores. Whiles you count that mony lost, which Gods seruice receiueth of you, you cannot shake away *Iudas* from your shoulders. What
would you do, if Christ should charge you, as he did the yong-man in the
Gospell *Sell all, and giue to the poore*, that thinke superfluities a wast? *oh,
durus sermo!* a hard sentence! *Indeed a cup of cold water* is bounty praised and
rewarded, but in them that are not able to giue more: *the widowes two mites*
are accepted, because all her estate. If God thought it no wast to giue you
plenty, euen all you haue: thinke it no wast to returne him some of his own.
Thinke not the *Oile* wast, which you poure into the *Lampe* of the *Sanctuary*:
thinke not the *bread* wast which you *cast* on the *waters of aduersity*: thinke
nothing lost, wherof you haue feoffed God in trust. But let me teach you
soberly to apply this, and tell you what indeed is *waste*.

1 Our immoderate diet: indeed not diet, for that contents nature, but
surfet, that ouerthrowes nature: *this is waste*. Plaine Mr. *Nabal* made a feast
like a *Prince*. *Diues* hath no other armes to proue himselfe a gentleman; but

---

1. A dual disturbance of notable proportions was then observable in the English scene:
while city and mercantile men of commerce were buying country estates as an indispensable qualification for admission to the gentry, a number of ancient land-owning families
were neglecting their properties, or racking them to meet the rising expenses of life at
an extravagant court.

Professor Lawrence Stone gives deserved emphasis to the conflict between court and
country interests in *The Crisis of the Aristocracy*, 1956: cf. for a lead to a variety of useful
views: Trevor-Roper, Hexter and others, *The Origins of the English Civil War* (ed.
P. A. M. Taylor) (1960); also Ivan Roots, *The Great Rebellion 1642–1660* (1966).

2. Canescunt turpi tecta relicta situ. Ovid, *Amores* 1. 8. 52.

3. Approval of endowments for 'lectureships' was already a clear indication of
Puritan sympathies.

a scutchion of these 3. colours: first he had mony in his purse: *hee was rich*: secondly, he had good rags on his back, *clothed in purple*: thirdly, dainties on his table; *he fared deliciously*, & that *euery day*: this was a Gentleman without Heraldry. It was the rule: *ad alimenta, vt ad medicamenta*: to our meate, as to our medicine: man hath the least mouth of all creatures: (*malum non imitari, quod sumus*). Therefore it is ill for vs, not to imitate that which we are: not to be like our selues: there are many shrewd contentions between the appetite and the purse: the wiseman is either a Neuter, or takes part with his purse: to consume that at one banket, which would keepe a poore man with conuenient sustenance all his life, *this is waste*. But alas our slauery to *Epicurisme* is great in these daies, *mancipia seruiunt dominis, domini cupiditibus*: seruants are not more slaues to their masters, then their masters are slaues to lusts. *Timocreons Epitaph* fits many:

Multa bibens, & multa vorans, mala plurima dicens, &c.[1]

he eate much and drunke much, and spake much euill: we sacrifice to our palates as to Gods: the rich feast, the poore fast, the dogs dine, the poore pine: *ad quid per ditio hæc*? Why is this wast?

Our vnreasonable ebrieties.————*Tenentque*
Pocula sæpe homines, & inumbrant ora coronis.[2]

They take their fill of wine here, as if they were resoulued with *Diues*, they should not get a drop of water in Hell: *Eate drink, play: quid aliud sepulchro bouis inscribi poterat*? what other Epitaph could be written on the sepulcher of an Oxe? *Epulonum crateres, sunt Epulonum carceres*: their boules are their bolts: there is no bondage, like to that of the Vintage. The furnace beguiles the ouen: the Celler deceiues the Buttery: we drinke away our bread, as if we would put a new petition into the Lords prayer, and abrogate the old: saying no more with *Christ giue vs this day our daily bread*, but *giue vs this day our daily drinke: quod non in diem, sed in mensem sufficit*: which is more then enough for a day, nay would serue a moneth. *Temperance* in the iust Steward, is put out of office: what place is free from these Ale-house recusants? that think better of their drinking-roome, then *Peter* thought of *Mount Tabor bonum est esse hîc: it is good being here: vbi nec Deus, nec Dæmon*: where both God and the Deuill are fast a sleepe. It is a question, whether it be worse to turne the image of a beast to a God, or the image of God to a beast: if the first be Idolatry, the last is impiety: a voluptuous man is a murderer to himself, a couetous man a theefe, a malicious a witch, a drunkard a deuill: thus to drinke away the poores reliefe, our own estate: *ad quid perditio hæc*? *Why is this waste*?

3 Our monstrous pride, that turnes hospitality into a dumbe shew: that which fed the belly of hunger, now feeds the eye of lust: akers of land are metamorphosed into trunks of apparell: and the soule of charity is trans-

1. Athenaeus, *Deipnosophists*, Bk x. 415.   2. Lucretius, 3, 913.

migrated into the body of brauery: *this is wast*: we make our selues the compounds of all Nations: we borrow of *Spaine, Italy, Germany, France, Turkie*
and all: that death when he robs an Englishman, robs all countries: where lies
the wealth of England? in three places: on Citizens tables, in Vsurers coffers,
and vpon Courtiers backes: God made all simple, therfore wo to these compounded fashions: God will one day say, (*hoc non opus meum, nec imago mea
est*), this is none of my workmanship, none of my image. One man weares
inough on his backe at once, to cloath two naked wretches all their liues: *ad
quid &c. Why is this waste?*

4 Our vain-glorious buildings, to emulate the skies, which the wise-man
cals, *the lifting vp of our gates too high.* Houses built like pallaces: Tabernacles,
that in the Masters thought, equall the Mansion of heauen: structures to
whom is promised eternity, as if the ground they stood on, should not be
shaken. Whole townes depopulate to reare vp one mans walles, chimnies
built in proportion, not one of them so happy as to smoak: braue gates, but
neuer open: sumptuous parlours, for Owles and Bats to flie in: *pride* begun
them, *riches* finished them, *beggery* keeps them: for most of them moulder
away, as if they were in the dead builders case, a consumption. Would
not a lesse house, *Ieconiah*, haue serued thee for better hospitality? our
Fathers liued well vnder lower roofes: this is waste, and waste indeed, and
these worse then the Deuill: the Deuill had once some charity in him, to
turne stones into bread, but these men turne bread into stones: a tricke
beyond the Deuill: *ad quid perditio hæc? Why is this waste?*

5 Our ambitious seeking after great alliance: the *sonne of the Thistle must
match with the Cedars daughter*: The father teares deare yeeres out of the Earths
bowels, and raiseth a banke of vsury, to set his son vpon, and thus mounted,
he must not enter saue vnder the noble roofe: no cost is spared to ambitious
aduancement: *ad quid &c. Why is this waste?*

Shall I say? our vpholding of *Theaters*, to the contempt of *Religion*: our
maintaining Ordinaires to play away our patrimonies: our foure-wheeled
Porters: our Anticke the fashion: our smoky consumptions: our perfumed
putrefaction: *ad quid perditio hæc?* Why are these wastes? experience will
testifie at last, that these are wastes indeed: for they waste the body, the
blood, the estate, the freedome, the soule it selfe, and all is lost, thus laied out:
but what is giuen (with *Marie*) to Christ, is lost like sowne graine, that shall
be found againe at the haruest of *Ioy*.

We haue heard *Iudas* censuring *Mary*: let vs now heare God censuring
Iudas: and that first negatiuely: *he cared not for the poore.* For the poore he
pleads, but himselfe is the poore he meanes well to: but let his pretence be
what it will, Gods witnesse is true against him: *he cared not for the poore.*

Obserue: doth Christ condemne *Iudas* for condemning *Mary*? then it
appeares he doth iustifie her action: he doth, and that after in expresse tearmes:

Let her alone, &c. Happy *Mary* that hast *Iesus* to plead for thee: blessed Christians for whom *Iesus Christ is an aduocate. Hee is neere mee, that iustifies mee, who will contend with me? verse 9. behold the Lord will helpe me, who is hee that can condemne me?* hence *Dauid* resignes his protection into the hands of God. *Iudge me, oh God, and defend my cause against the vnmercifull people.* And *Paul* yet with greater boldnesse, sends a franke defiance and chalenge to all the actors and pleaders that euer condemnation had, that they should neuer haue power to condemne him, since *Iesus Christ iustifies him.* Happy man whose cause God takes in hand to plead. Here is a *Iudas* to accuse vs, a *Iesus* to acquit vs: *Iudas* slanders, *Iesus* cleares: wicked men censure, the iust God approues: earth iudgeth euill, what is pronounced good in heauen! oh then doe well, though (*fremant gentes*) greate men rage, though peruersenesse censures, impudence slanders, malice hinders, tyranny persecutes: there is a *Iesus*, that approues: his approbation shall outweigh all their censures: let his spirit testifie with me, though the whole world oppose me.

Obserue: It is the nature of the wicked to haue no care of the poore. *Sibi nati, sibi viuunt, sibi moriuntur, sibi damnantur*: they are all for themselues, they are borne to themselues, liue themselues, (so let them die for them selues, and go to Hell for themselues. The fat Buls of *Bashan*, loue *the lambs from the flocke, and the Calues from the stall, &c. But thinke not on the affliction of Ioseph.* Your gallant thinks not the distressed, the blind, the lame to be part of his care: it concernes him not: true, and therfore heauen concernes him not: it is infallible truth, if they haue no feeling of others miseries, they are no members of *Christ*: goe on now in thy scorne, thou proud Royster: admire the fashion and stuffe thou wearest: whils the poor mournes for nakednesse: feast royall *Diues*, whiles *Lazarus* can get no crums: Apply, *Absolon* thy sound, healthfull lims to lust and lewdnesse, whiles the same blind, maimed, cannot deriue a penny from thy purse, though he moue his sute in the name of *Iesus*; thou giuest testimonie to the world, to thy own conscience, that thou art but a *Iudas*. Why, the poorest and the proudest haue, though not *Vestem communem*, yet *cutem communem*: there may be difference in the fleece, there is none in the flesh: yea perhaps, as the gallants perfumed body is often the sepulcher to a putrified Soule: so a white, pure, innocent spirit may be shadowed vnder the broken roofe of a maimed corps. Nay, let me terrifie them: not many rich, not many mighty, not many noble are called: It is *Pauls* thunder against the flashes of greatnesse: he sayes *not any* but *not many*[1]: for *seruantur Lazarus pauper, sed in sinu Abrahami Diuitis: Lazarus* the poore man is saued,[2] but in the bosome of *Abraham* the rich. It is a good

1. Not *no* rich men, but *not many*. '. . . non multi sapientes, non multi potentes, non multi nobiles. 1 Cor 1: 26.

2. An allusion to Augustine, *Enaratio in Psalmum*, VI, 6, where the saint refers to Luke xvi:23–31.

saying of the son of *Sirach: The affliction of one houre will make the proudest stoope*, sit vpon the ground, and forget his former pleasure; a piercing miserie will soften your bowels, and let your soule see through the breaches of her prison, in what need distresse stand of succour. Then you will be charitable or neuer, as phisitians say of their patients, *take whiles they be in paine*; for in health nothing will be wrung out of them: so long as health and prosperitie cloth you, you recke not the poore: *Nabal* lookes to his sheepe, what cares he for *Dauid*? if the truth were knowne, there are many *Nabals* now, that loue their own sheepe better than *Christs* sheepe: *Christs* sheepe are faine to take coats, their own sheepe giue coats. Say some that cauil, if we must care for the poore, then for the couetous; for they want what they possesse, and are indeed poorest: no, pitie not them, that pity not themselues; who in despite of Gods bountie will be miserable: but pitie those, whom a fatall distresse hath made wretched.

Oh, how vnfit is it among Christians, that some should surfet, whiles other hunger? one that should haue two coats, and another be naked, yet both one mans seruants? Remember that God hath made many his stewards, none his Treasurer: he did not meane thou shouldst hoord his blessings, but expend them to his glory: he that is infinitely rich, yet keepes nothing in his own hands, but giues all to his creatures: at his owne cost and charges he hath maintained the world, almost 6000. yeares: he will most certainly admit no hoorder into his kingdome: yet, if you will needs loue laying vp, God hath prouided you a coffer: the poore mans hand is Christs treasury. The besotted worldling hath a greedy mind, to gather goods, and keepe them; and loe, his keeping loseth them: for they must haue either (*finem tuum*, or *finem suum*) thy end, or their end: *Iob* tarried and his goods went; but the rich man went, and his goods tarried, *Si vestra sunt, tollite vobiscum*: if they be yours, why do you not take them with you? no, *hic acquiruntur, hîc amittuntur*: here they are gotten, her lost. But God himselfe being witnesse (nay he hath past his word) what we for his sake giue away here, we shall find againe hereafter; and the charitable man dead and buried, is richer vnder the ground, than he was aboue it. It is an vsual song, which the Saints now sing in heauen:

> *That we gaue;*
> *Thet we haue.*

This riddle poseth the worldling, as the Fishermens did *Homer: Que cepimus, reliquimus: quæ non cepimus, nobiscum portamus: what we caught, we left behind vs; what we could not catch, we carried with vs.* So, *what we loose, we keepe; what we will keepe, we shall loose, hee that looseth his goods, his lands, his freedome, his life for Christs sake, shall find it.* This is the charitable mans case: all his almes, mercies, relieuings are (wisely and without executorship) sowne in his lifetime; and the haruest will be so great, by that time he gets to heauen, that he shall receiue a thousand for one: God is made his debtor, and he is a sure paymaster. Earth hath not riches enough in it to pay him; his requitall shall be in heauen, and there with no lesse degree of honour than a kingdome.

Iudas cares not for the poore: Iudas is dead; but this fault of his liues still: the poore had neuer more need to be cared for: but how? there are two sorts of poore, and our care must be proportionable to their conditions, there are, 1. some poore of Gods making, 2. some of their own making: let me say, there are Gods poore, and the Deuils poore: those the hand of God hath crossed; these haue forced necessitie on themselues by a dissolute life. The former must be cared for by the compassion of the heart, and charity of the purse: Gods poore must haue Gods almes; a seasonable reliefe according to thy power; or else the Apostle fearefully and peremptorily concludes against thee: *the loue of God is not in thee.* If thou canst not find in thy heart, to diminish a graine from thy heape, a penny from thy purse, a cut from thy loafe, when *Iesus Christ* stands at thy doore and calls for it, professe what thou wilt, the loue of earth hath thrust the loue of heauen out of thy conscience. Euen *Iudas* himselfe will pretend charitie to these.

For the other poore who haue pulled necessity on themselues with the cords of Idlenesse, riot or such disordered courses, there is another care to be taken; not to cherish the lazie bloud in their vaines by abusiue mercy; but rather chafe their stunted sinewes by correction, relieue them with punishment, and so recouer them to the life of obedience. *The sluggard lusteth,* and hath an empty stomacke: he loues sustenance well, but is loth to set his foot on the cold ground for it. The lawes sanction, the good mans function saith, *if he will not labour, let him not eate.* For experience telleth that where slouth refuseth the ordinary paines of getting, there lust hunts for it in the vnwarranted pathes of wickednesse, and you shall find, that if euer occasion should put as much power into their hands, as idelnesse hath put villany into their hearts, they will be ready to pilfer your goods, fire your house, cut your throats. I haue read of the king of *Macedon,* descrying two such in his dominions, that (*alterum e Macedonia fugere, alterum fugare fecit*). He made one flie out of his kingdome, and the other driue him. I would our magistrates would follow no worse a precedent: indeed our lawes haue taken order for their restraint; wheresoeuer the fault is, they are rather multiplied; as if they had bin sowen at the making of the statute, and now (as from a haruest) they arise ten for one: surely our lawes make good wils, but they haue bad lucke for executors: their willes are not performed: nor their legacies distributed; I meane the legacies of correction to such children of sloath: *Impunitas delicti inuitat homines ad malignandum:* Sinnes chiefe incouragement is the want of punishment: fauour one, hearten many. It is fit therefore, that (*pœna ad paucos, metus ad omnes perueniat*) penalty be inflicted on some, to strike terrour into the rest.

It was *S. Augustines* censure: *Illicita non prohibere, consensus erroris est*[1] not to restraine euill, is to maintaine euill. The Common wealth is an instrument, the people are the strings, the Magistrate is the Musitian: let the Musitian looke that the Instrument be in tune, the iarring strings ordered; and not play on it to make himselfe sport, but to please the eares of God. *Doctores*, the Ministers of mercy, now can doe no good, except *Ductores*, the Ministers of Iustice put to their hands. We can but forbid the corruption of the heart; they must prohibit the wickednesse of the hand.[2] Let these poore be cared for, that haue no care for themselues: runnagates, renegates, that will not be ranged (like wandring Planets) within the Sphere of obedience: *yet a little more sleepe*, sayes the sluggard: but (*modicum non habet bonum*) their bunch will swell to a mountaine, if it be not preuented and pared downe. Care for these ye Magistrates, lest you answere for the subornation of their sinnes: for the other, let all care, that care to be receiued into the armes of *Iesus Christ*.

Obserue: *Iudas cares not for the poore*; what? and yet would he for their sakes haue drawne comfort from the Sonne of God? what an hypocrite is this? could there be so deepe dissimulation in an Apostle? yes, in that Apostle, that was a Deuill. Loe still I an haunted with this *white Deuill, Hypocrise*: I cannot saile two leagues, but I rush vpon this rocke; nay, it will encounter, incomber me quite thorow the voyage of this Verse. *Iudas* said, and meant not, there is Hypocrisie: *he spake for the poore*, and hates them, there is Hypocrisie: *he was a priuie theefe, a false Steward, &c.* all this not without Hypocrisie: shall I be rid of this Deuill at once, and coniure him out of my speech? God giue me assistance, and adde you patience, and I will spend a little time, to vncase this *white Deuill*, and strip him of all his borrowed colours.

Of all bodily creatures, man (as he is Gods image) is the best: but basely deiected, degenerated, debauched, the (simply) worst: of all earthly creatures a wicked man is the worst, of all men a wicked Christian, of all Christians a wicked professor, of all professors a wicked Hypocrite, of all Hypocrites a wicked, warped, wretched *Iudas*. Take the extraction or quintessence of all corrupted men, and you haue a *Iudas*: this then is a *Iudas*: a man degenerate, a Christian corrupted, a professor putrified, a guilded Hypocrite, a *white-skind Deuill*. I professe I am sparingly affected to this point, and would faine shift my hands of this monster, and not incounter him: for it is not to fight with the *Vniocrnes of Assyria*, nor the *Bulles of Samaria*, nor the *Beasts of Ephesus*: neither absolute Atheists, nor dissolute Christians, nor resolute ruffians: the hornes of whose rapine and malice are no lesse manifest, than malignant; but at once imminent in their threats, and eminent in their appearance. But to set vpon a Beast, that hath with the heart of a *Leopard*, the face of a man, of a good man, of the best man; a starre placed high in the

1. Ep. 182, to Boniface.
2. The Puritan prescription: ministry enforced by magistracy.

Orbe of the Church, though swooped downe with the Dragons taile, because not fixed; a darling in the mothers lap, blessed with the Churches Indulgence, yet a bastard: a brother of the fraternity, trusted sometimes with the Churches stocke, yet no brother, but a broker of treacheries, a brocher of falshoods: I would willingly saue this labour, but that the necessity of my Text ouer-rules my disposition.

I know, these times are so shamelesse and impudent, that many strip off the *white*, and keepe the *Deuill*; wicked they are, and without shew of the contrary: men are so farre from giuing house-roome to the substance of religion, that they admit not an out-roome for the shew: so backward to put on Christ, that they will not accept of his liuery: who are short of *Agrippa*, scarce *perswaded to seeme Christians*, not at all to be: these will not drinke hearty draughts of the waters of life, nay scarce vouchsafe (like the Dogs that run by *Nilus*) to giue a lap at *Iacobs Well*: vnlesse it be some as they report, that frequent the signe of it, to be drunke: they salute not Christ at the Crosse, nor bid him good-morrow in the Temple, but goe blustring by, as if some serious businesse had put haste into their feet, and God was not worthy be staid and spoke withall: if this be a Riddle, shew me the day, shall not expound it by a demonstratiue experience. For these I may say, I would to God they might seeme holy, and frequent the places, where sanctimony is taught: but the Deuill is a nimble, running, cunning Fencer, that strikes on both hands, *duplici ictu*, and would haue men either (*non sanctos, aut non parum sanctos*) not holy, or not a little holy, in their owne opinion, and outward ostentation: either no fire of deuotion on the earth, or that that is, in the top of the Chimney: That subtile *winnower* perswades men that they are all Chaffe, and no Wheat, or all Wheat, and no Chaffe: and would keepe the soule either lancke with ignorance, or rancke with insolence: let me therefore wooe you, win you to reiect both these extreames, betweene which your hearts lie, as the graine betwixt both the Milstones.

Shall I speake plainly? You are sicke at *London* of one disease (I speake to you setled Citizens, not extrauagants) and we in the Country of another: (a Sermon against Hypocrisie in most places of the Country, is like Phlebotomy to a Consumption, the spilling of innocent bloud) our sicknesses are cold Palsies, and shaking Agues: yours in the Citie are hotter diseases, the burning Feuers of fiery zeale, the inflammations and imposthumes of Hypocrisie: we haue the frosts, and you haue the lightnings: most of vs professe too little, and some of you professe too much, vnlesse your courses were more answerable: I would willingly be in none of your bosomes: onely I must speake of *Iudas*. His Hypocrisie was vile in three respects.

1 He might haue beene found: I make no question but he heard his Master preach, and preached himselfe, that Gods request is the heart: so Christ schooles the *Samaritane* woman: so prescribed the *Scribe*. *Thou shalt loue the*

Lord with all thy heart, &c. corde, Iudas, with the heart, which thou reseruest like an equiuocating Iesuite: nay, (*toto corde, for it is not tutum, except it be totum*) with the whole heart, which thou neuer stoodest to diuide, but gauest it wholly to him, that wholly killed it, thy masters enemies, and none of thy friend, the Deuill. Thou heardest thy master, thy friend, thy God, denounce many a fearefull, fatall, finall woe against the Pharisies: (*hac appellatione, & ob hanc causam*) vnder this title, and for this cause; Hypocrites, and because Hypocrites. As if his woes were but words, and his words winde, empty and aiery menaces, without intention of hurt, or extention of a reuengefull arme, behold thou art an Hypocrite: thou art therefore the worse because thou mightest be better.

2 He seemed sound: *spem vultu simulat, premit altum corde dolorem*, nay, (*dolum* rather) craft rather than griefe, vnlesse he grieued, that out of his cunning, there was so little comming, so small prize or booty: yet like a subtle gamester, hee keepes his countenance, though the Dice doe not fauour him. And as *Fabius Maximus* told *Scipio*, preparing for *Africa* concerning *Syphax: Fraus fidem in paruis sibi praestruit, vt, cum operæ pretium sit, cum mercede magna fallat*. 1. Livy, *Annals*, Bk XXVIII. xlii. 7. *Iudas* creepes into trust by his iustice in trifles, that he might more securely cheate for a fit aduantage. Without pretence of fidelity, how got he the Stewardship? perhaps if need required, hee spared not his owne purse in Christs seruice; but he meant to put it to vsury: he carried not the Purse, but to pay himselfe for his paines, thus (*iactura in loco, res quæstuosissima:*) a seasonable dammage is a reasonable vantage: in this then his vilenesse is more execrable, that he seemed good.

If it were possible, the Deuill was then worse than himselfe, when hee came into *Samuels* mantle. *Iesabels* paint made her more vgly: if euer you take a Fox in a Lambes skin, hang him vp , for he is the worst of the generation: a *Gibeonite* in his old shoes, a *Seminary* in his haire-cloath, a Ruffian in the robes of a *Iacobine*, flie like the plague: these are so much the worse Deuils, as they would be holy Deuils: true Traitours that would fight against God with his owne weapons; and by being out-of-cry religious, runne themselues out of breath to doe the Church a mischiefe.

3 He would seeme thus to his Master; yet knew in his heart that his Master knew his heart: therefore his hypocrisie is the worst. Had he beene an Aliant to the Common-wealth of *Israel*, and neuer seene more of God, than the eye of nature had discouered, (yet saies euen the heathen, ἔχει Θεὸς ἔκδικον ὄμμα: *God hath a reuenging eye:*) then no maruell, if his eyes had beene so blinde, as to thinke Christ blinde also, and that he, which made the eye, had not an eye to see withall: but he saw that *Sonne of Dauid* giue fight to so many sonnes of *Adam*, casually blinde, to one naturally and borne blinde; *miraculum inauditum*, a wonder of wonders, and shall *Iudas* thinke to put out his eye, that gaue them all eyes? oh incredible, insensible, inuincible ignorance?

You see his hypocrisie: me thinks euen the sight of it is disswasion forcible enough, and it should be needlesse to giue any other reason than the discouery: yet whiles many censure it in *Iudas*, they condemne it not in themselues, and either thinke they haue it not, or not in such measure. Surely, we may be no *Iudasses*, yet hypocrites: and who will totally cleare himselfe? let me tell thee, if thou doest, thou art the worst hypocrite, and but for thee we had not such need to complaine. He that cleares himselfe from all sinne, is the most sinner; and he that sayes, he hath not sinned in hypocrisie, is the rankest Hypocrite: but I doe admit a distinction. All the sonnes of *Adam* are infected with this contamination, some more, some lesse: here's the difference; all haue hypocrisie: but hypocrisie hath some: *aliud habere peccatum, aliud haberi a peccato*. It is one thing for thee to possesse sin, another thing for sin to possesse thee. All haue the same corruption, not the same eruption: in a word, all are not hypocrites, yet who hath not sinned in hypocrisie? Doe not then send your eyes like *Dinahs* gadding abroad, forgetting your owne businesse at home: straine not courtesie with these banquets, hauing good meat carued thee, to lay it liberally vpon another mans Trencher; be not sicke of this plague and conceale it, or call it by another name: hypocrisie is hypocrisie, whatsoeuer you call it: and as it hath learned to leaue no sinnes naked, so I hope it hath not forgot to cloath it selfe: it hath as many names as *Garnet*[1] had, and more *Protean* shapes than the *Seminaries*: the *white Deuill* is in this a true Deuill; *multorum nominum, non boni nominis*: of many names, but neuer a good one. The vilenesse of this *white Deuill* appeares in six respects.

1 It is the worst of sinnes, because it keepes all sins: they are made sure and secure by hypocrise. Indeed some vices are quarter-masters with it, and some Soueraignes ouer it: for hypocrisie is but another sinnes pander: except to content some affected guest, we could neuer yeeld to this filthy *Herodias*. It is made a stawking-horse for couetousnesse, vnder long prayers many a *Pharisie* deuoures the poore, houses, goods, and all. It is a complexion for lust, who, were she not painted ouer with a religious shew, would appeare as loathsome to the world, as she is indeed. It is a sepulchre of rotten impostures, which would stinke like a putrified corps, if hypocrisie were not their couer. It is a maske for treason, whose shop full of poysons, pistols, daggers, gunpowder-traines, would easily be spied out, had hypocrisie left them barefaced. Trechery vnder this vizard thrusts into Court-reuels, nay, court counsels; and holds the torch to the sports, nay, the bookes to serious consultations; deuiseth, aduiseth, plots with those that prouide best for the Common-wealth. Thus are all sins beholding to hypocrisie: she maintaines them at her own proper cost and charges.

2 It is the worst of sinnes, because it counterfeits all vertues: he that counterfeits the Kings Coyne, is liable to death: if hypocrisie finde not death, and

1. Henry Garnet S. J. 1555–1606.

(*mortem sine morte*) death without death, for counterfeiting the King of Heauens Seale manuall of grace, it speeds better then it merits. *Vice* is made *Vertues* Ape in an hypocrites practise. If he see *Chusi* run, this *Ahimaaz*[1] will out-run him: he mends his pace, but not his path; the good man goes slower, but will be at heauen before him: thus thriftinesse in a Saint, is counterfeited by niggardlinesse in an hypocrite: be thou charitable, behold he is bountifull, but not except thou may behold him: his vaine-glorious pride shall emulate thy liberality: thou art good to the poore, hee will be better to the rich: he followes the religious man a farre off, as *Peter* did *Christ*, but when he comes to the Crosse, he will deny him. Thus hypocrisie can put bloud into your cheeckes, (like the *Aliptæ*)[2] and better your colours; but you may be sicke in your consciences, and almost dead at the heart, and (*non est medicamen hortis*) there is no medicine in this Drugsters shop can cure you.

3 An hypocrite is a kinde of honest Atheist: for his owne *Good* is his *God*: his heauen is vpon earth, and that not the *Peace of his Conscience*, or that *kingdome of heauen, which may be in a soule liuing on earth*, but the secure peace of a worldly estate: he stands in awe of no iudge, but mans eye; that he obserues with as great respect, as *Dauid did the eyes of God*; if man takes notice, he cares not, yet laughes at him for that notice, and kils his soule by that laughter: so *Pigmalion* like, he dotes on his owne carued and painted peece: and perhaps dies *Zeuxis*[3] death, who painting an old woman, & looking merrily on her, brake out into a laughter that killed him: if the world do not praise his doings, he is ready to challenge it, as the Iewes God, *wherefore haue we fasted, and thou seest it not?* he crosseth Christs precept: the left hand must not be priuy to the right hands charity: he dares not trust God with a penny, except before a whole congregation of witnesses, lest perhaps God should deny the receit.

4 An hypocrite is hated of all, both God and man: the world hates thee, *Iudas*, because thou retainest to Christ: Christ hates thee more because thou (but) onely retainest, and doest no faithfull seruice. The world cannot abide thee, thou hypocrite: because thou professeth godlinesse; God can worse abide thee; because thou doest no more than professe it. It had beene yet some pollicy, on the losse of the worlds fauour, to keepe Gods: or if lost Gods, to haue (yet) kept in with the world: thou art not thy owne friend, to make them both thy enemies: miserable man, destitute of both refuges,

1. Ahimaz, son of Zadoc, who outran the Chusite to bring news of victory to King David, but omitted to report the death of Absolom. 2 Sam. 18:19–23.

2. The Aliptae, the managers of the Roman wrestlers, used to have their charges anointed with cosmetic unguents before a contest, to tone up their muscles and make them look more impressive. 'utque aliptae virium et coloris rationem habere,' Cicero. *Epist. Fam.* I. 9. 15.

3. Celebrated Greek naturalistic painter of the 5th century B.C., the fiction of whose manner of death was given currency by Festus, *De Verborum Significatione*, 3. See 'Pictor'.

shut out both from Gods and the worlds dores. Neither God nor the Deuill loues thee, thou hast been true to none of them both, and yet most false (of all) to thy selfe. So (this *white Deuill*) *Iudas*, that for the Pharises sake betrayed his Master, and for the Deuils sake betrayed himselfe, was in the end reiected of Pharises and Master; and like a ball, tost by the rackets of *contempt* and *shame*, bandied from the Pharises to Christ, from *Christ* to the *Pharises*, from wall to wall, till hee fell into the Deuils hazard; not resting like a stone, till he came to his center, εἰς τὸν τόπον τὸν ἴδιον *into his owne place.* Purposeth he to goe to *Christ?* his owne conscience giues him a repulsiue answere: no, thou *hast betrayed the innocent bloud.* Goes he to the *chiefe Priests and Elders?* cold comfort: *what is that to vs? see thou to that.* Thus (your *ambodexter* proues at last *ambo sinister*) he that playes so long on both hands, hath no hand to helpe himselfe withall. This is the hypocrites misery; because he weares Gods liuery, the world will not be his mother; because his heart, habit, seruice, is sin-wedded, God will not be his father: he hath lost earth for heauens sake, & heauen for earths sake; and may complaine with *Rebeccaes* feare of her two sons; *why should I be depriued of you both in one day?* or as sorrowfull *Iacob* expostulated for his, *Me haue you robbed of my children: Ioseph is not, and Simeon is not, and will you take* Beniamin *also? all these things are against me.* This may be the hypocrites mournfull Dirge: *My hypocrisie hath robbed me of all my comforts: my Creator is lost, my Redeemer will not owne me; and will ye take away* (my beloued *Beniamin*) *the world also? all these things are against me.* Thus an open sinner is in better case than a dissembling Saint. There are few that seeme worse to others then they are in themselues: yet I haue both read and heard of some, that haue with broken hearts, and mourning bowels sorrowed for themselues, as if they had been reprobates; and not spared so to proclaime themselues, when yet their estate was good to God-ward, though they knew it not: perhaps their wickedness and ill life hath beene grieuous, but their repentance is gratious: I may call these *blacke Saints.* The hypocrite is neate and curious in his religious out-side, but the linings of his conscience are as *filthy and polluted rags:* then I say still, a *blacke Saint* is better than a *white Deuill.*

5 Hypocrisie is like the Deuill, for he is a perfect hypocrite: so he begun with our first parents, to put out his apparant hornes in Paradise: *non moriemini, ye shall not die:* yet he knew this would kill them. An hypocrite then is the child of the Deuil, and (quoth *Time* the midwife) as like the father as it may possible looke: he is the *father of lyes*; and there is no lyer like the Hypocrite, for as *Peter* said to *Annanias*, *thou hast not lyed to men, but to God.* Nay, the hypocrite is his eldest son. Now, the priuiledge of primogeniture by the law, was to haue a *double portion*; wretched hypocrite in this eldership: (*Mat.24.51.*) Satan is called a Prince, and thus stands his monarchie, or rather Anarchie. The Deuill is King, the hypocrite his eldest sonne; the Vsurer his

yonger; Atheists are his viceroyes in his seuerall prouinces, for his dominion is beyond the Turks for limits, Epicures are his Nobles: persecutors his Magistrates: Heretikes his Ministers: traytours his executioners: sin his law: the wicked his subiects: tyrannie his gouernment: Hell his Court, and damnation his wages. Of all these the Hypocrite is his eldest Sonne.

6 Lastly, an hypocrite is in greatest difficultie to be cured. Why should the Minister administer physicke to him that is perfectly sound? or why should Christ giue his bloud to the righteous? Well may he be hurt and swell, swell and rankle, rankle and fester, fester & die, that will not bewray his disease, least he betray his credit.

Stultorum incurata pudor malus vlcera celat.[1]

A man of great *Profession*, little *Deuotion*, is like a body so repugnantly composed, that he hath a hot liuer, and a cold stomacke: that which heates the stomacke, ouer-heats the liuer: that which cooles the liuer, ouercooles the stomacke: so, exhortations, that warme his conscience, enflame his outward zeale: disswasiues to coole his hypocrisie, freese his deuotion: he hath a flushing in his face, as if he had eaten fire: zeale burnes in his tongue, but come neere this gloeworme, and he is cold, darke, squallid. Summer sweats in his face, winter freeseth in his conscience: March, many forwards in his words, December in his actions: pepper is not more hot in the tongues end, not more cold at heart: and (to borrow the words of our worthy Diuine and best Characterer) we thinke him a Saint, he thinkes himselfe an Angell, flatterers make him a God, God knowes him a Diuill.

This is the *white Deuill:* you will not thinke how glad I am, that I am rid of him: let him go; yet I must not let you go, till I haue perswaded you to hate this monster, to abhorre this Deuill. Alas! how forget we (in these dayes) to build vp the Cedar worke of pietie, and learne onely to paint it ouer with vermillion! we white and parget[2] the walles of our profession, but the rubbish and cobwebs of sin hang in the corners of our consciences: take heed; a Bible vnder your armes will not excuse a false conscience in your bosoms: thinke not you fadome the substance, when you embrace the shadow: so the fox seeing sweet-meats in the violl, licked the glasse, and thought he had the thing: the ignorant sickman eats vp the physitians bill, in stead of the receipt contained in it. It is not a day of 7. nay any houre of 7. daies, the grudged parting with an almes to a fire, the coniuring of a paternoster (for the heart onely prayes) or once a yeare renewing thy acquaintance with God in the Sacrament, can priuiledge or keepe impune[3] thy iniuries, vsuries, periuries, frauds, slanders, oppressions, lusts, blasphemies. Beware of this *white Deuill*, lest your portion be with them in hel, whose society you would defie on earth. *God shall smite thee, thou painted wall*; and wash off thy

1. Horace *Epist.* I. 16. 24.   2. Plaster.   3. Unpublished.

vermillion dye with the riuers of brimston. You haue read of some that heard Christ preach in their pulpits, feasted at his communion table, cast out deuils in his name, yet not admitted: whiles they wrought miracles, not good works, cast out deuils from others, not sinnes from themselues, they misse of entrance. Goe then and solace thy selfe in thy bodily deuotion, thou hearest, readest, receiuest, relieuest; where is thy conscience, thy heart, thy spirit? God asks not for thy liuery, but thy seruice: he knowes none by their confession, but by their conuersation. Your lookes are the obiects of strangers eyes, your liues of your neighbours, your consciences of your own, all of Gods. Do not *Ixion*-like take a cloud for *Iuno*, a mist for presumption of a sound and solide faith: more can say the Creed, than vnderstand it, than practise it. Go into your grounds in the dead of winter, and of two naked and destitute trees, you know not which is the sound, which the doted: the summer will give Christs marke: *By their fruits you shall know them.*

I speake not to discourage your zeale, but to hearten it, but to better it. Your zeale goes through the world, ye worthy Citizens: Who builds hospitals? the Citie. Who is liberall to the distressed Gospell? the Citie. Who is euer faithfull to the Crowne? the Citie. Beloued: your works are good; oh do not loose their reward through hypocrise. I am not bitter, but charitable: I would faine put you into the *Chariot* of grace with *Elias*, and onely wish you to put off this *Mantle*. Oh that it lay in my power to preuaile with your affections, as well as your iudgements: you loose all your goodnesse, if your hearts be not right: the ostentation of man shall meet with the detestation of God. You loose your attention now, if your zeale be in your eye, more than heart. You loose your praiers, if when the ground hath your knee, the world hath your conscience; as if you had two gods: one for Sundayes, another for worke daies; one for the *Church*, another for the *Change*. You loose your charity, whiles you giue glosingly, illiberally, too late: not a window you haue erected, but must beare your names: but some of you rob *Peter* to pay *Paul*: take *Tenths* from the Church, and giue not the poore the *Twentiths* of them. It is not seasonable, nor reasonable charity, to vndo whole townes by your vsuries, enclosings, oppressions, impropriations; and for a kind of expiation, to giue three or foure the yeerely pension of twenty marks: an Almeshouse is not so big as a village, nor thy superfluitie wherout thou giuest, like their necessity whereout thou extortest: he is but poorely charitable, that hauing made a hundred beggars, relieues two. You loose all your credite of pietie, whiles you loose your integrity: your solemn censuring, mourning for the times euill, whiles your selues are the euill cause thereof: your counterfet sorrow for the sins of your youth, whiles the sins of your age are worse; your casting salt and brine of reproofe at others faults, whiles your own hearts are most vnseasoned; all these artificiall whitings, are but thrifty leasings, sicke healths, bitter sweetes, and more pleasing deaths. Cast then away this bane of Religion, hypocrise; this candle with a great wicke and no tallow, then often goes out quickly, neuer without stench: this faire, flattering *white Deuill*. How well haue we bestowed this paines, I in speaking, you in hearing, if this Deuill be cast out of your consciences, out of your conuersations? It will leaue some prints behind it in the best, but blesse not your selues in it, and God shall blesse you from it: *Amen*.

The *affirmative* part of Gods censure, stands next to our speech: Describing his 1. meaning 2. meanes 3. maintenance. His *meaning* was to be a theefe, and sharke for himselfe, though his pretence pleaded (*forma pauperis*) in the behalfe of the poore. He might, perhaps, stand vpon his honesty, and rather than loose his credit, striue to purge himselfe by his suspectlesse neighbours: but there need no further Iury passe vpon him, God hath giuen testimonie, and his witnesse is beyond exception, *Iudas is a theefe*. A theefe: who saw him steale? he that hath now condemned him for his paines. Indeed the world did not so take him his reputation was good enough: yet he was a theefe, a crafty, cunning, cheating theefe.

There are two sorts of theeues: publike ones, that either with a violent hand take away the passengers mony, or rob the house at midnight: whose Church is the highway: there they pray (not to God, but) on men: their dwelling, like *Cains*, very vnsure: they stand vpon thornes; whiles they stand vpon certainties: Their refuge is a wood, the instrument of their vocation a sword: of these some are landtheeues, some sea-theeues: all roaue on the sea of this world, and most commonly suffer shipwracke, some in the deepe: some on a hill. I will say little of these, as not pertinent to my Text, but leaue them to the Iury: And speake of theeues like *Iudas*, secret robbers, that doe more mischiefe with lesse present danger to themselues. These ride in the open streets, whiles the other lurke in close woods. And to reason, for these priuate theeues are in greater hazard of damnation: the graue exhortations of the Iudge, the serious counsell of the assistant Minister, together with the sight of present death, and the necessity of an instant account with God, workes strongly on a publike theeues conscience, all which the priuate theefe neither hath, not hath need of in the generall thought. The publike theefe wants but apprehension, but this priuate theefe needs discouery: for they lye close as Treason, dig low like Pioners, and though they be as familiar with vs, as Familiars, they seeme stranger than the *Indians*.

To define this manner of theeues: A priuate theefe is he, that without danger of law robs his neighbour; that sets a good face on the matter, and hath some profession to countnance it: a faire Cloake hides a damnable fraud; a trade, a profession, a mystery, like a *Rome*-hearted Protestant, hides this Deuilish *Seminary* vnder his roofe without suspition. To say truth, most of our professions (thankes to ill professors) are so confounded with sinnes, as if there went but a paire of sheeres betweene them: nay, they can scarce be distinguished: you shall not easily discerene between a hot, furious professor, and an Hypocrite; betweene a couetous man and a theefe; betweene a Courtier and an aspirer; betweene a gallant and a swearer; betweene an officer and a bribe-taker; between a seruitor and a parasite; betweene Farmers and poore-grinders; betweene Gentlemen and pleasure-louers; betweene great men and madde men; betweene a tradesman and a fraudesman; betweene a monied man and a vsurer; betweene a vsurer and the Deuill. In many Arts the more skilfull, the more ill-full: for now adayes; *armis potentior astsu*; fraud goes beyond force: this makes Lawyers richer than Souldiers, vsurers than Lawyers, the Deuill than all. The old Lyon (saith the Fable) when his nimble dayes were ouer, and he could no longer prey by violence, kept his den with a feined sicknesse: the suspectlesse beasts drawne thither to a dutifull visitation, thus became his prey: *cunning* serued his turne, when his *canning* failed.[1] The world, whiles it was young, was simple, honest, plaine-dealing: Gentlemen then delued in the ground, now the soles of their feet must not touch it: then they drunke water, now wine will not serue, except to drunkenesse: then they kept sheepe, now they scorne to weare the wooll; then *Iacob* returned the money in the sackes mouth, now we are ready to steale it, and put it in. *Plaine-dealing* is dead, and what we most lament, it died without issue. Vertue had but a short raigne, and was soone deposed: all the examples of sinne in the Bible are newly acted ouer againe, and the interest exceeds the principall, the counterpane the originall. The Apostacy, now, holds vs in our manner: we leaue God for man, for *Mammon*, Once, *Orbis ingemuit factum se videns Arrianum*; the world gronaed, seeing it selfe made an *Arrian*: It may now groane worse, *factum se videns Machiauellum*, seeing it selfe made a Machiauell: *nisi Deus opem præstat deperire mundum restat*. Grieued deuotion had neuer more cause to sing, *Mundum dolens circumiui*; *fidem vndique, quæsiui, &c.*

> *The world I compassed about,*
> *Faith and honesty to finde out:*
> *But Country, City, Court, and all,*
> *Thrust poore deuotion to the wall:*
> *The Lawyer, Courtier, Marchant, Clowne,*
> *Haue beaten poore deuotion downe:*
> *All wound her; till for lacke of breath,*
> *Fainting Deuotion bleeds to death*

But I am to deale with none but theeues, and those priuate ones: and because *Iudas* is the precedent, I will begin with him, that is most like him: according to the prouerbe, which the Grecians had of *Philo Iudæus*: (ἢ Πλάτων Φιλωνίζει: ἢ Φίλων Πλατωνίζει: *aut Plato Philonem sequitur, aut*

---

1. This instance of Adams employing his favourite trope of *paronomasia* uses *canning* in the sense, now obsolete, of *ability*, in contrast to *cunning*.

Platonem Philo.) Either *Plato* followed *Philo,* or *Philo* imitated *Plato.* Let me onely change the names: *Either* Iudas *played the Pope, or the Pope playes the* Iudas. This is the most subtle theefe in the world, & robs all Christendome vnder a good colour: who can say he hath a black eye, or a light finger? for experience hath taught him, that *cui pellis Leonina non sufficit, vulpina est as-suenda*: when the Lyons skin cannot threat, the Foxes skin can cheat. Pope *Alexander*[1] was a beast, that hauing entred like a *Fox,* he must needs raigne like a *Lyon,* worthy he was to dye like a dog: for, *vis consily expers, mole ruit sua,* power without pollicy, is like a peece without powder: many a Pope sings that common Ballad of hell: *Ingenio perij, qui miser ipse meo: Wit, whither wilt thou? woe is me: my wit hath wrought my misery.*

To say truth, their Religion is nothing in the circumstance but craft: and pollicy maintaines their *Hierarchie*; as *Iudas* subtilty made him rich. *Iudas* was put in trust with a greate deale of the Deuils businesse; yet not more than the Pope. *Iudas* pretended the poore, and robbed them: and doth not the Pope thinke you? Are there no almes-boxes rifled and emptied into the Popes treasury? Our Fathers say that the poore gaue Peter-pence to the Pope, but our grand-fathers canot tell vs that the Pope gaue Cæsar pence to the poore: did not he sit in the holy Chaire, (as *Augustus Cæsar* in his imperiall Throne) and cause the whole Christian world to be *taxed*: and what? did they freely giue it? no, a taxation forced it; what right then had the Pope to it? iust as much as *Iudas* had to his Masters money? was he not then a theefe? yet, what need a rich man be a theefe: the Pope is rich, and needs must, for his com-mings in be great: he hath Rent out of Heauen, Rent out of Hell, Rent out of Purgatory: but more sackes come to his mill out of Purgatory, than out of Hell and Heauen too; and for his tolling let the world iudge: therefore saith Bishop *Iewel, He would be content to loose Hell and Heauen too, to saue his Purgatory.* Some by pardons he preuents from Hell; some by Indulgences he lifts vp to Heauen; and infinite by ransomes from Purgatory: not a iot with-out money: *cruces, altaria, Christum*: he sells Christs crosse, Christs bloud, Christs selfe; all for money.[2] Nay, he hath Rent from the very Stewes, a Hell aboue ground, and swels his Coffers by the sinnes of the people: he suffers a price to be set on damnation; and maintaines lust to goe to Law for her own;

1. Alexander VI.
2. This outburst, the vehemence of which does not evaporate on the printed page, displays clearly one of the deep underlying fears which Protestant reformers at this time felt for all suggestion of 'free will'. A doctrine of free will tended ultimately to validate comparative degrees of human merit; human merit pointed to acts of supererogation as aids to salvation, and this was only a step from accepting the reinforcement of episcopal (to a Puritan, in effect, *papist*) intercessory privilege, and therefore, *power.* The emotional lather, which this thought is the cue for working up in the next passage, should be noted. 'A doctrine laden with storm and havoc', said Acton (*A Lecture on the Study of History*) of the revolutionary force at the core of Protestant Puritanism.

giues whoredome a toleration vnder his seale: that *Lust*, the sonne of *Idlenesse*, hath free accesse to *Liberty* the daughter of *Pride*.

Iudas was a great statesman in the Deuils Common-wealth; for he bore foure maine offices: either he begged them shamefully, or he bought them bribingly, or else *Belsebub* saw desert in him, and gaue him them *gratis*, for his good parts: for *Iudas* was his white boy, he was, 1. an hypocrite, 2. a theefe, 3. a traytor. 4. a murderer. Yet the Pope shall vie offices with him, and win the game too for plurality. The Pope sits in the holy Chaire, yet a Deuill: Periury, Sodomy, Sorcery, Homicide, Patricide, Patricide, Treason, Murder, &c. are essentiall things to the new Papacy. He is not content to be *Steward*, but he must be *Vicar*, nay, indeed Lorde himselfe: for what can Christ doe, and the Pope cannot doe? *Iudas* was nobody to him. He hath stolne Truths garment, and put it on Errors backe, turning poore Truth naked out of dores: he hath altered the Primitiue institutions, and adulterated Gods sacred lawes; maintaining *vagas libidines*: he steales the hearts of Subiects from their Soueraignes, by stealing fidelity from the hearts of Subiects: and would steale the Crowne from the Kings head, and all vnder the shadow of Religion. This is a theefe; a notable, a notorious theefe, but let him goe: I hope he is knowne well inough, and euery true man will blesse himselfe out of his way.

I come to our selues: there are many kinds of priuate theeues in both the houses of *Israel* and *Aaron: in soro et choro*, in change and Chancell: Common-wealth and Church. I can taxe no mans person: if I could, I would abhorre it, or were worthy to be abhorred: the Sins of our Times are the Theeues, I would arraigne, testifie against, condemne, haue executed: the persons I would haue saued *in the day of the Lord*.

1 If there bee any Magistrates (into whose mouthes God hath put the determination of doubts: and the distribution of right into their hands:) that suffer popularity, partiality, passion to rule, ouer rule their iudgements, these are priuate theeues: they rob the poore man of his iust cause, and equities reliefe, and no law can touch them for it: thus may causes goe, not according to right, but friendship: as *Themistocles* boy could say, *As I will, the whole Senate will:* for as I will, my mother will; as my mother will, my father will; as my father will, the whole Senate will. Thus a as Groome of a Chamber, a Secretary of the Closet, or a Porter of the Gate will, the cause must goe: this is horrible theft, though not araignable: hence a knot is found in a bulrush:[1] delay shifts off the day of hearing: a good paint is set on a soule pastboord: circumstances are shuffled from the barre: the Sunne of truth is clouded: the poore confident plaintife goes home vndone: his moanes, his groanes are vented vp to Heauen: the iust God sees and suffers it: but he will one day iudge that iudge. Who can indite this theefe? what law may passe on him?

1. *Nodum in scripo quaerere*: to find difficulties where none exist.

what Iury can finde him? what Iudge can fine him? none on earth: there is a
barre he shall not escape: if there be any such, (as I trust there is not) they are
theeues.

2 If there be any Lawyer, that takes fees on both hands, one to speake,
another to hold his peace: as (*Demosthenes* answered his bragging fellow
Lawyer) this is a theefe, though the law doth not call him so: a mercenary
tongue, and a money spel'd conscience, that vndertakes the defence of things
knowne to his owne heart to vniust, is onely proper to a theefe: he robs both
sides: the aduerse part in pleading against the truth, his owne Client in
drawing him on to his further dammage. If this be not, as the Romane
complained, *latrocinium in foro*, theeuery in the Hall, there is none: happy
Westminster Hall if thou wert freed from this kinde of Cut-purses. If no
plummets, except of vnreasonable weight can set the wheeles of their tongues
a going, and then if a golden addition can make the hammer strike to our
pleasure: if they keepe their eares and mouths shut, till their Purses be full:
and will not vnderstand a cause till they feele it: if they shuffle difficulties
into plainnesse, and trip vp the Lawes heeles with trickes: if they Surgion-
like keepe the Clients disease from healing, till hee hath no more money for
salue: then to speake in their owne language, *Nouerint vniuersi, Be it knowne
to all men by these presents* that these are theeues: though I could with rather,
that *Nouerint ipsi*, they would know it themselues, and reforme it.

3 If there be any officer, that walkes with vnwashen hands, I meane; with
the foule fingers of bribery, he is a theefe: be the matter penall or capitall, if a
bribe can picke Iustices locke, and pleade innocent, or for it selfe, being
nocent, and preuaile, this is theft. Theft? who is robbed? the giuer? doth not
the freedome of his will transferre a right of the gift to the receiuer? no; for
it is not a voluntary or willing will: but as a man giues his purse to the ouer-
mastring theefe, rather than ventures his life: so this his bribe, rather than
indanger his cause: shall I say the theefe hath as much right to the Purse, as
the Officer to the bribe: and they are both, though not equally palpable, yet
equally culpable theeues. Is the giuer innocent or nocent? innocent, and shall
not innocence haue her right without a bribe? nocent, and shall gold conceale his fault or cancell his punishment? Dost thou not know whether, and
wilt thou blinde thy selfe before hand with a bribe? for bribes are like dust
throwne in the eyes of Iustice, that she cannot without paine looke on the
Sun-shine of truth. Though a second to thy selfe receiue them, wife or friend,
by thy allowance, they are but stolne goods, coles of fire put in the roofe of
thy house: *for fire shall deuoure the houses of bribes.* And there haue bcene
many houses built by report, the first stone of whose foundation was hewen
out of the quarry of *bribery.* These are theeues.

4 There is theeuery too among Tradesmen: and who would thinke it?
many (they say) rob vs, but we rob none: yes, but they thinke that (*verba*

lactis will countenance *fraudem in factis*) smooth words will smother rough deeds. This web of theft is many waies wouen in a shop or ware-house, but three especially.

By a false weight, and no true measure, whose content or extent is not iustifiable by law; or the cunning conueyances in weighing or meating: such as cheat the buyer: are not these pretty trickes to picke mens purses? the French word hath well exprest them: they are *Liegerdumaines*. Now had I not as good loose my purse on *Salisbury plaine*, as in *London Exchange*? is my losse the lesse, because violence forbeares, and craft pickes my purse? The high-way theefe is not greater abomination to God, than the shop-theefe: and for man, the last is more dangerous: the other we knowingly fly; but this laughes vs in the face, whiles he robs vs.

By insufficient wares, which yet with a darke window and an impudent tongue, will appeare good to the buyers eye and eare too. Sophistry is now fled from the schooles into shops: from disputation to merchandizing: he is a silly Tradesman that cannot sophisticate his wares, as well as he hath done his conscience; and weare his tongue with protestations, barer than trees in Autumne, the head of old age, or the liuings of Church-men. Oathes indeed smell too ranke of infidelity; marry, we are Protestants, and protest away our soules: there is no other way to put off bad wares, and put vp good monies: are not these theeues?

By playing, or rather preying vpon mens necessities: they must haue the commodity, therefore set the dice on them: *vox latronis*: the aduantage taken of a mans necessity is a tricke beyond *Iudas*: Thou shouldest rather be like *Iob*, *a foot to lame necessity*, and not take away his crutch: or perhaps God hath put more wit into thy braines, than his, thou seest further into the bargaine: and therefore takest opportunity to abuse his plainnesse: thou seruest thy selfe in gaine, not him in loue: thou mayest, and laugh at the law: but there is a law thou hast transgressed, that, without Iesus Christ, shall condemne thee to hell.

Goe now, applaud your selues ye sonnes of fraud, that Eagle-eyed scrupulosity cannot finde you faulty, nor the Lyon-handed law touch you, please your selues in your securitie. You practise belike behind the hangings, and come not on the publike stage of Iniury: yet you are not free from spectators: *testante Numine, homine, Dæmone*: God, Man, Angels, Deuils shall witnesse against you: *ex cordibus, ex codicibus*: by your hearts, by your bookes God shall iudge you. Iniury is often in the one, periury in the other: the great iustice will not put it vp: they shall be conuicted theeues.

5 There are theeues crope into the Church too; or rather they incroach on the Church; for Ministers cannot now play the theeues with their Liuings, they haue nothing left to steale: but there are secret *Iudasses*, can make shift to doe it. *Difficilis magni custodia census*. The Eagles flocke to a carkeis, and theeues hanker about rich doores: at the dispersion of Church liuings, they

cryed as the *Babylonians, to the spoile, to the spoile.* The Church was once rich, but it was (*diebus illis*) in the golden time, when honesty went in good cloathes; and ostentation durst not giue religion the checke-mate: now they plead prescription, and proue them their owne by long possession. I doe not taxe all those for priuate theeues, that hold in their hands, lands and possessions that were once the Churches: but those that with-hold such as are due to Church-men. Their estates were once taken away by (more than) Gods (meere) sufferance, for a iust punishment for their idlenesse, Idolatry, and lusts: sure there is some *Achanisme* in the Campe of the *Leuites*, that makes this plague-sore to run still: there is some disobedient and fugitiue *Ionasses* that thus totter our ship. I complaine not that *claustra* are turned into *castra*: Abbies into Gentlemens houses: places of monition, to places of munition: but that men rob (*aram dominicam*) Gods house to furnish (*haram domesticam*) their owne house:[1] this is theft; and sacrilegious theft: a succession of theft: for the fingers of the sonnes are now heauier than the loynes of their fathers: those were (*improbi Papistæ*) wicked Papists, and these are (*improbirapistæ*) vngodly robbers.

This is a monstrous theft, and so exceeding all thefts, as (*non nisi in deum fieri potest*) it can be committed against none but God. When *Scipio* robbed the Temple of *Tholossa*, there was no a man, that carried away any of the gold, who euer prospered after it: and I pray you tell me, how many haue thriued with the goods of the Church? they goe from man to man without rest, like the Arke among the *Philistines*, which was remoued from *Ashdod* to *Gath*, from *Gath* to *Ekron*, as if it coulde finde no place to rest in, but vexed the people that kept it, till it returned to the old seat in Israel: oftentimes these goods left by Gentlemen to their heires, prooue gangrenes to their whole estates; and *house is ioyned to house* so fast, Gods house to their owne, that the fire, which begins at the one consumes the other: as the Eagle, that stole a peece of meat from the Altar, carried a cole with it that set her nest on fire. I am perswaded many a house of bloud in *England,* had stood at this houre, had not the forced springs of Impropriations[2] turned their foundation to a quagmire. In all your knowledge, thinke but on a Church robbers Heire, that euer thriued to the third generation: yet alas! horror to my bones, and shame to my speech! there are not wanting among our selues, that giue incouragement to these theeues: and without question, many a man, so well otherwise disposed, would haue beene reclaimed from this sinne, but for their distinctions of competencies: I appeale to their consciences, there is not an humorist[3] liuing, that in heart thinkes so, or would forbeare their reproofe, were he not well prouided for. These are the Foxes, that content not them-

1. From the time when Henry VIII took to wearing the great jewel from Becket's shrine on his finger, church looting had been an intermittently repressed Protestant sport.
2. See above, p. 16, fn. 1.
3. Person of perversely fantastical mind.

selues to steale the Grapes, but they must forrage the Vine: thus yet still *is Gods house made a den of Theeues*: without enuy or partiality they are theeues.

6 There is more store of theeues yet: couetous Land-Lords, that stretch their Rents on the Tenter hookes of an euill conscience, and swell their Coffers by vndoing their poore Tenants: these sit close, and stare the Law in the face, yet by their leaue they are theeues: I doe not denie the improuement of old Rents, so it be done with old mindes, I meane, our forefathers charity: but with the Deuill, to set right vpon the Pinacles, and pitch so high a prize of our Lands, that it straines the Tenants heart bloud to reach it, is theft, and killing theft. What all their immoderate toyle, broken sleepes, sore labours can get, with a miserable dyet to themselues, not being able to spare a morsell of bread to others, is a prey to the Land-Lords rapine: this is to rob their estates, grinde their faces, sucke their blouds. These are theeues.

7 Ingrossers: that hoord vp commodities, and by stopping their community raise the price: these are theeues. Many blocke-houses in the Cittie, Monopolies in the Court, Garners in the Country, can testifie, there are now such theeues abroad: we complaine of a dearth: sure the Heauens are too mercifull to ys, that are so vnmercifull one towards another: scarcity comes without Gods sending: who brings it then? euen the Deuill and his brokers, engrossing misers. The Common-wealth may often blow her nailes, vnelsse she sit by an engrossers fire: her limbes may be faint with hunger, vnlesse she buy graine at an engrossers price. I confesse this is a sinne, which the Law takes notice of, but not in the full nature, as theft. The pick purse (in my opinion) doth not so much hurt, as this generall robber; for they rob millions. These doe not with *Ioseph*, buy vp the superfluity of plenty, to preuent a dearth; but hoord vp the store of plenty, to procure a dearth: rebels to God, trespassers to nature, theeues to the Common-wealth: if these were apprehended and punished, neither Citie nor Country should complaine as they doe. Meane time the peoples curse is vpon them, and I doubt not but Gods plague will follow it: if repentance turne it not away: till when, they are priuate theeues.

8 Inclosers;[1] that pretend a distinction of possessions, a preseruation of woods, indeed to make better and broader their owne territories, and to steale from the poore Commons; these are horrible theeues. The poore mans beast is his maintenance, his substance, his life; to take food from his beast, is to take the beasts food from his belly: so he that incloseth Commons is a monstrous theefe, for hee steales away the poore mans liuing and life; hence many a Cottager, nay, perhaps Farmer, is faine (as the Indians doe to Deulis) to sacrifice to the Lord of the soyle, a yearely bribe for a *ne noceat*. For though the law forbids such inclosures: yet (*quod fieri non debet, factum valet*) when

1. Latimer's grievance, the abuse of enclosures (see above p. 16), remains a grievance seventy years later.

they are once ditcht in, say the Law what it will, I see no throwing out: force beares out, what fraud hath borne in: let them neuer open their mouthes to pleade the Common-wealths benefit: they intend it as much as *Iudas* did, when he spake for the poore: no, they are theeues, the bane of the common good; the surfet of the land, the scourge of the poore: good onely to themselues; and that in opinion onely: for they doe it, *to dwell alone*, and they dwell alone indeed, for neither God nor good Angell keepes them company, and for a good conscience it cannot get thorow their quicksets. These are theeues, though they haue inclosed their theft, to keepe the law out, and their wickednesse in: yet the day shall come, their lands shall be throwne out, their liues throwne out, and their soules throwne out: their lands out of their possessions, their liues out of their bodies, their soules out of Heauen; except repentance and restitution preuaile with the great Iudge for their pardon: meane time, they are theeues.

9 Many Tap-house-keepers, Tauerners, Victuallers, which the prouident care of our worthy Magistrates hath now done well to restraine: if at least this *Hydraes* heads doe not multiply. I doe not speke to annihilate the profession: they may be honest men, and doubtlesse some are, which liue in this ranke: but if many of them should not chop away a good conscience for money, drunkennesse should neuer be so welcome to their dores. The dissolute wretch sits there securely, and buyes his owne sicknesse, with a great expence; which would preserue the health of his poore wife and children at home, that lamentably mone for bread, whiles he lauisheth all in drinke. Thus the pot robs him of his wit, he robs himselfe of grace, and the Victualler robs him of his money. This theft might yet be borne: but the Commonwealth is here robbed too. Drunkennesse makes so quicke riddance of the Ale, that this raiseth the price of Mault: and the good sale of Mault, raiseth the price of Barley: thus is the Land distressed, the poores bread is dissolued into the drunkards cup; the Markets are hoised vp, if the poore cannot reach the price, the Mault-master will, he can vtter it to the Tap-house; and the Tap-house is sure of her old friend drunkennesse: thus theft sits close in a drinking roome, and robs all that saile into that coast. I confesse they are (most of them) bound to suffer no drunkennesse in their houses, yet they secretly acknowledge, that if it were not for drunkennesse, they might shut vp their dores, as vtterly vnable to pay their rents. These are theeues.

10 Flatterers, that eate like Moths into liberall mens coats, the bane of Greatnesse, are theeues, not to be forgotten in this Catalogue. These rob many a great man of his goodnesse, and make him rob the Common-wealth of her happinesse. Doth his Lord want money? he puts into his head, such fines to be leuied, such grounds inclosed, such rents improued. Be his maintainers courses neuer so foule, either he furthers them, or he smothers them: sinne hath not a more impudent bawd, nor his master a more impious

theefe, nor the Common-wealth a more sucking horse-leach. He would raise himselfe by his Great one, and cannot contriue it, but by the ruine of others. He robs the flattered of his goods, of his grace, of his time, of his freedome, of his soule: is not this a theefe? *beneficia, veneficia*: all their good is poyson. They are *Dominis arrisores, reipublicæ arrosores*:[1] their Masters Spaniels, the Common-wealths Wolues; put them in your Pater-noster, let them neuer come in your Creed: pray for them, but trust them no more than theeues.

11 There is another nest of theeues more in this Citie, Brokers, and breakers:[2] I conioyne them in my description, for the likenesse of their condition; Brokers, that will vpon a good pawne lend money to a Deuill: whose Extortion, by report is monstrous; and such as to finde in men is improbable, in Christians impossible: the very Vermin of the earth. Indeed man had a poore beginning; we are the sonnes of *Adam, Adam* of dust, dust of deformity, deformity of nothing; yet made by God: but these are bred like Monsters, of the corruption of nature, and wicked manners; and carry the Deuils cognisance: for Breakers, such as necessity compels to it, I censure not: if they desire with all their hearts to satisfie the vttmost farthing and cannot: God will then accept votall restitution for totall restitution: that which is affected for that which is effected: *the will for the deed*: and in those, debt is not (as the vulgar speech is) deadly sin: a sore it may be, no sin. But they that with a purpose of deceit, get goods into their hands in trust, and then without need hide their heads, are theeues: for the intent to steale in their minds, directed their iniurious hands. The Law arraigns them not, the iudgement seat of God shall not acquite them. These steale more quickly and with more security, than a high-way robber, who all his life time is in perpetuall danger: It is but passing their words, allowing a good price, conuaying home the wares, and on a sudden diue vnder the waters: a close concealement shall saue them fiue hundred pound in a thousand. They liue vpon others sweat, fare richly vpon others meat, and the debter is often made a Gentleman, when the Creditour is made a beggar.

Such false *Gebeonites* inrich Scriueners:[3] their vnfaithfulnesse hath banished all trust and fidelity. Time was, that *Nouerint vniversi* was vnborne, the Lawyer himselfe knew not what an obligation meant. Security stood on no other legs, but promises and those were so sound, that they neuer failed their burden: but *Time* adulterating with the harlot *Fraud*, begot a brood of

1. Imitation of Seneca's paronomasia on the words *arrisor* (a flattering smiler) and *arrosor* (a consumer): 'stultorum divitum arrosor et (quod sequitur) adrisor, et quod duobus his adjunctum est, derisor.' *Epist.* 27.
2. 'Breaker', in the sense of defaulting debtor.
3. Scriveners received a commission from money-lenders for introducing clients.

... usurers
that share with scriveners.

Webster, *The White Devil* iv, 1.

Nouerints:[1] and but for these shackles, debt would often shew credit a light paire of heeles. Therefore now (*plus creditur annulis, quam animis*) there is more faith giuen to mens seales, than to their soules. *Owe nothing but loue*: saith the Apostle: all owe this, but few pay it; or if they do, it is in crackt money, not currant in Gods Exchequer: for our loue is dissimulation, and our charity is (not cold, but) dead. But these bankrouts, of both wealth and honesty, owe all things but loue, and more than euer they meane to pay, though you giue them time till Domes-day. These are Theeues.

12 The twelfth and last sort of theeues (to make vp the iust dozen) are the vsurers. This is a priuat theefe like *Iudas*, and for the bag like *Iudas*, which he steales from Christ like *Iudas*, or rather from Christians, that haue more need, and therefore worse than *Iudas*. This is a man made out of wax: his *Pater-noster* is a *Pawne*: his *Creed* is the condition of this obligation: his religion is all religation: a binding of others to himselfe: of himselfe to the Deuill: for looke how far any of the former theeues haue ventured to hell, the vsurer goes a foot further by the standard. The Poet exclaimes against this sinne.

Hinc vsura vorax, auidumque, in tempore fenus, &c.[2]

Describing in that one line, the names and nature of vsury. *Fænus, quasi fætus*: it is a teeming thing, euer with child, pregnant, and multiplying: money is an vnfruitfull thing by nature, made only for commutation: it is a *præter-naturall* thing, it should engender money: this is *monstrosus partus*, a prodigious birth. *Vsura, quasi propter vsum rei*. The nature of it is wholly deuouring: their money to necessity is like cold water to a hot ague, that for a time refresheth, but prolongs the disease. The vsurer is like the worme we call the timber-worme; which is wonderfull soft to touch, but hath teeth so hard, that it eats timber: but the vsurer eats timber and stones too. The Prophet hedgeth it in, betweene *Bribery* and *Extortion*: *In thee haue they taken gifts to shed blood: thou hast taken vsury and increase: and thou hast greedily gained of thy neighbours by Extortion; and hast forgotten me, saith the Lord Therefore I haue smitten my hands at thy dishonest gaine, &c.* You heare Gods opinion of it. Beware this dishonest gaine: take heed least this casting your money into a *Banke*, cast not vp a *Banke* against you: when you haue found out the fairest pretexts for it, Gods iustice shall strike off all: *let no man deceiue you with vaine words for, such things Gods wrath will fall on the Children of disobedience.* Infinite colors, mitigations, euasions, distinctions are inuented, to countnance on earth, heauen-exploded usurie. God then shall frustrate all, when he poures his wrath on the naked conscience. God *saith Thou shalt not take vsurie*. Go now and study paintings, excuses, apologies, dispute the matter with God: hell fire shall decide the question.

1. Writs.

2. Lucan, I. 181.

JOHN DOD

We must interpolate here an example of Dod's authentic preaching to redress the parody by which he became known in popular anecdote. More prosaic in style than Adams, his influence on academic thought was considerable.

On Apostasy[1] (*c. 1612*)

Nothing doth so prouoke the vengeance of God against men, as this wretched *apostasie* doth. For a man to fall from riches to pouertie, from promotion to debasement, &c. it is a matter of nothing; God loues him neuer the worse: but to fall from profession to prophanenesse; from God to the Diuell; from heauen to hell; from life to death; this is a lamentable thing indeed. *Dauid* did not sustaine the fal of his house, but had onely sometimes, and a part of the roofe blowne off: yet was that a greater losse then if he had been depriued of his kingdome: neither would that haue so rent his soule, and crusht his bones, and grownd his heart to pouder, as the committing of those offensiue euils did: nay, if he had been set vpon a steepe rocke with a milstone about his necke, and from thence had been cast headlong into the sea, it had been but a trifle in comparison of the other. Oh then how fearefull must their case be that do vtterly forsake the liuing God? If his deadnesse and hardnesse of heart, and inability to do duties to God and men, were more bitter then the most violent death vnto him; if I say, the very decay in grace did bring with it such torture; what must they expect either in this world, or in that which is to come, or both, who doe not onely part, but wholly lose that taste of good things which once they had? and doe not onely in a passion, as *Peter* did, deny Christ, but quite and cleane forsake him?

Now the reasons to proue that this fall is the greatest, are these.

1. Because the things which they lose are most precious, being spirituall things.

2. The ruine in the soule, which is the more excellent part.

1. 'The second sermon upon the sixth of Luke', in *Seven Godlie and Fruitful Sermons* (1614), pp. 75–78.

And furthermore, the effects wil proue as much, which are,

1. Monstrous shame; for when any one falles from profession, all the world sees hee was but an hypocrite at best: and then prophane persons will insult and triumph; These are your professors; these are they that will heare Sermons; they are as bad people as any liuing; I will trust none of them all for such a ones sake: and thus they purchase infamy and disgrace vnto themselues, as *Achitophel* and *Iudas* did.

2. And not only so, but also euerlasting paines, as we see in *Iudas*; who did not only die a base kind of death, being his owne executioner, and hauing his filthy bowels, that had been so full of couetousnesse and cruelty, gushing out: but also seeking to exempt himselfe from the paines and gripings of an euill conscience, hee cast himselfe into the torments of hell, which are easelesse and endlesse.

For instruction, that wee should labour to set sure in the things of God: for better is it to haue any decay, then a decay in the conscience: and to haue any losse and hurt, then those which are in the soule.

Now if we would not haue a great and shamefull fall, let vs take the direction of *Iude*, which he giues as a preseruatiue against apostacie. *But ye, beloued* (saith hee) *edifie your selues in your most holy faith.* That is the first thing, that wee must still bee building vp of our selues, and striue to bee better and better: for we are like a boate that goes against the streame; if wee labour not with might and maine to rowe vpward, we shall be carried violently downeward.

A second thing is, that we must *pray in the holie Ghost.* Many will bragge that they say their praiers morning and night: but doe they pray their praiers? A parrot may say a praier, but Christians must pray in the holy Ghost, that is, with such petitions as the Spirit warranteth, & with sighes & groanes which it worketh in the heart. These two things whosoeuer can practise, namely, to build vp himselfe daily, and offer vp faithful prayers vnto God, he shall be sure to stand fast and firme.

Secondly, this is for comfort to those on whom the Lord hath bestowed his good Spirit: for if it be the greatest fall to fall from religion, then it is the greatest rising to rise vnto grace: and if they be cursed that fal away, then blessed are those that draw neare vnto God, and with full purpose of heart cleaue vnto him, growing daily in humilitie, and in contempt of the world, in conscience towards God, and in care to leade a good and holie life before men. This is indeed the greatest promotion: and therefore *Iames* saith, *Let the brother that is of low degree, reioyce in that he is exalted.* Exalted (might some say:) what exaltation is that, when they are as poore as euer they were? A maruellous great exaltation it is; for they are made Christians, and so consequently kings, both in respect of grace and glory. *Caine* and *Nimrod*, and many other reprobates, went beyond ten thousand of vs for outward things:

but al that aduancement was to their greater shame and confusion. For earthly promotion is nothing else but an high stage, and if one be an idiote, it were better for him to play his part on the ground: if those that are in eminent places haue not power to master their owne lusts and carnall affections, they are but great fooles vpon an high stage. Therefore let vs seeke for spirituall things more then for earthly, and bee more thankfull and ioyfull when we find grace in our hearts, then if we should find many mines of gold, which none could lay claime vnto but our selues.

THOMAS ADAMS

Dining with the Devil[1] (c. 1613)

————Nec enim lex æquoir ulla est
Quam necis artifices, arte perire sua.

No iuster Law can be devis'd or made,
Then, that sinnes agents fall by their owne trade.

The order of Hell proceeds with the same degrees; though it giue a greater portion, yet still a iust proportion of torment. These wretched guests were too busie with the *waters* of sinne; behold now they are in the depth of a pit, *where no water is. Dives*, that wasted so many Tunnes of wine, cannot now procure water, not a pot of water, not a handfull of water, not a drop of water, to coole his tongue. *Desideravit guttam, qui non dedit micam:*[2] A iust recompence! He would not giue a crumme; he shall not haue a drop. Bread hath no smaller fragment, then a crumme; water no lesse fraction thên a drop. As he denied the least comfort to *Lazarus* liuing, so *Lazarus* shall not bring him the least comfort dead. Thus the paine for sinne, answeres the pleasure of sinne. Where, now, are those delicate morsels, deepe carowses, loose laughters, proud port, midnight reuels, wanton songs? Why begins not this fellow-guest with a new health? or the Musicke of some rauishing note? or, if all faile, hath his foole-knauish Parasite no obscene iest, that may giue him delight? Alas! Hell is too melancholly a place for mirth. All the Musicke is round-ecchoing groanes: all the water is muddy with stench: all the food anguish.

Thus damnable sinnes shall haue semblable punishments: and as *Augustine* of the tongue, so we may say of any member: *Sinon reddet Deo faciendo quæ debet, reddet ei patiendo quæ debet. If it will not serue God in action, it shall serue him in passion.* Where voluntary obedience is denied, involuntary anguish shall bee suffered. Know this thou swearer, that as thy tongue spits abroad the flames of Hell, so the flames of Hell shall be powred on thy tongue. As the Drunkard will not now keepe the Cup of satietie from his mouth, so God shall one day hold the Cup of vengeance to it, and he shall drinke the dregges thereof. As the Vsurers are tormentors of the Commonwealth, on earth; so they shall meet with tormentors in Hell; that shall transcend them, both in

1. From *The Fatall Banket, Works* (1629), pp. 223-7.   2. Augustine, *Homilies*, 7.

malice and subtilty: and load them with bonds and executions; and (which is strangely possible) heauier then those, they haue so long traded in. The Church-robber, incloser, ingrosser, shall finde worse prolling[1] and pilling[2] in Hell, then themselues vsed on earth; and as they haue beene the worst Deuils to their Countries wealth, so the worst of Deuils shall attend them. The vncleane adulterer shall haue fire added to his fire. And the couetous wretch, that neuer spake but in the Horse-leaches language, and carried a mouth more yawning, then the graues, is now quitted with his *nunquam satis*, and findes enough of fire *in the depth of Hell*.

The Deuill hath feasted the wicked, and now the wicked feast the Deuill: and that with a very chargeable *Banket*. For the Deuill is a dainty Prince, and more curious in his diet, then *Vitellius*. He feedes, like the Caniball, on no flesh, but mans flesh. He loues no venison but the *Heart*, no fowle but the *Breast*, no fish but the *Soule*. As the *vngodly haue eaten vp Gods people as bread*; so themselues shall be eaten as bread: it is iust, that they be deuoured by others, that haue deuoured others. As they haue beene Lions to crash the bones of the poore; so a *Lion* shall crash their bones: they are *Satans* Feast, *he shall deuoure them*. Thus they that were the guests, are now the *Banket*: as they haue beene feasted with euils, so they feast the Deuils.

Make a little roome in your hearts, ye fearelesse and desperate wretches, for this meditation. Behold, now, as in a speculatiue glasse, the Deuils hospitality. Once bee wise: beleeue without triall, without feeling. Yeeld but to be *ashamed of your sinnes*, and then I can (with comfort) aske you, *what fruit they euer brought you?* Let mee but appeale to *Philip of Macedon*, when hee is drunke, to *Philip of Macedon*, when he is sober; from your be-witched lusts, to your waked consciences; and you must needs say, that *brevis hæc, non vera voluptas*. All *the workes of darkensse are vnfruitfull*, except in pro-ducing and procuring *vtter darknesse*. Sinne is the Deuils earnest-penny on earth, in Hell he giues the Inheritance. Temptation is his presse-money: by rebellion, oppression, vsury, blasphemy, the wicked like faithfull Souldiers fight his battels: When the field is wonne, or rather lost (for if he conquers, they are the spoile) *in the depth of hell* he giues them pay. Who then would march vnder his colours; who, though he promise *Kingdomes*, cannot performe a *Hogge*? Alas poore beggar! he hath nothing of his owne but sinne, and death, and hell, and torment. *Nihil ad effectum, ad aefectum satis*. No positiue good, enough priuatiue euill.

Euen those, that passe their soules to him by a reall Couenant, he cannot enrich: they liue and dye most penurious beggars, as they doe pernicious villaines. And they, vpon whom God suffers him to throw the riches of this world (as a snare ouer their hearts) which he cannot doe, but at second hand; haue not enough to keepe either their heads from aking, or their consciences

---

1. Prowling.   2. See above, fn. p. 60.

from despairing. Thus, though God permit them, to helpe the *rich man* to *fill his barnes*, the Vsurer to swell his Coffers, the luxurious to poison his blood, the malicious to gnaw his bowels, the sacrilegious to amplifie his revenewes, the ambitious to aduance credit; yet there is neither will in God, nor willingnesse in the Deuill, that any of these should be a blessing vnto them. All is but borrowed ware, and the Customers shall pay for day: the longer they abuse them, the larger arrerages[1] they must returne. Onely here, I may say, that *bona sunt, quæ dona sunt*, they are goods, that are gifts. God giues his graces freely, the Deuill his Iunkets falsly: for the guests must pay; and that dearely; when the least *Item* in the bill, for paines, is beyond the greatest dish of the Feast, for pleasures.

Solomons Sermon spends it selfe vpon

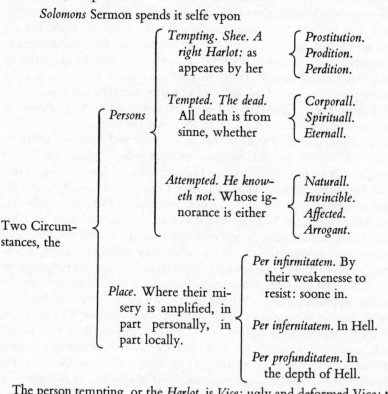

Two Circumstances, the

Persons

Tempting. Shee. A right Harlot: as appears by her

- Prostitution.
- Prodition.
- Perdition.

Tempted. The dead. All death is from sinne, whether

- Corporall.
- Spirituall.
- Eternall.

Attempted. He knoweth not. Whose ignorance is either

- Naturall.
- Invincible.
- Affected.
- Arrogant.

Place. Where their misery is amplified, in part personally, in part locally.

- *Per infirmitatem.* By their weakenesse to resist: soone in.
- *Per infernitatem.* In Hell.
- *Per profunditatem.* In the depth of Hell.

The person tempting, or the *Harlot*, is *Vice*; ugly and deformed Vice; that with glazed eyes, surphuld cheekes, pyed garments, and a *Syrens* tongue, winnes easie respect and admiration. When the heat of tentation shall glow vpon concupiscence, the heart quickly melts. The wisest *Solomon* was taken and snared by a woman: which foule adutery bred as foule an issue, or rather *progeniem vitiosiorem*, a worse, Idolatry. Sathan therefore shapes his

1. Arrears.

Temptation in the lineaments of an *Harlot:* as most fit and powerfull, to worke vpon mans affections. Certaine it is, that all delighted vice is a spirituall adultery. The couetous man couples his heart to his gold. The Gallant is incontinent with his pride. The corrupt Officer fornicates with bribery. The Vsurer sets continuall kisses on the cheeke of his security. The heart is set, where the hate should be. And euery such sinner spends his spirits, to breed and see the issue of his desires. *Sinne*, then, is the Deuils *Harlot*, which being tricked vp in tempting colours, drawes in visitants, *præmittendo suavia, promittendo perpetua*, giuing the kisses of pleasure, and promising them perpetuall. We may obserue in this *Strumpet*.

1 *Prostitution.* Pro.7.13. *So Shee caught him, and kissed him, and with an impudent face said vnto him, &c.* Shame now-a-dayes begins to grow so stale, that many vices shall vie impudent speeches and gestures with the *Harlot*. *Come, let vs take our fill of loue:* as *Potiphars* wife to *Ioseph*, without any preparatory circumlocutions or insinuations; *come lie with mee*. Sinne neuer stands to vnty the knot of Gods interdiction, but bluntly breakes it; as the Deuill at first to the rootes of mankinde, *yee shall not die*. The Vsurer neuer looseth so much time, as to satisfie his conscience: it is enough to satisfie his concupiscence. A good Morgage lies sicke of a forfet, and at the Usurers mercy. It is as surely damned, as the Extortioner will be, when he lyes at the mercy of the Deuill. These are so farre from that old *Quære* of Christians, *quid faciemus, what shall we doe?* That they will not admit the nouell question of these toyte[1]-headed times, *What shall we thinke?* They will not giue the conscience leaue, after a tedious and importunate sollicitation, to study of the matter. But are more iniurious and obdurate to their owne soules, then that vniust Iudge to the widdow.

A Cheate is offred to a Trades-man, an Incloser to a Landlord, an vnder-hand Fee clapt in the left hand of a Magistrate; if they be euill, and corruption hath first Marshalled the way, the field is wonne. They neuer treat with sinne for truce, or pawse on an answere, but presently yeeld the fort of their conscience. No wonder then, if the Deuils *Harlot* be so bold, when she is so sure of welcome. It is our weaknesse, that giues Sathan encouragement: if we did resist, he would desist. Our weake repulses harten and prouoke his fiercer assaults. He would not shew the worldling his apparant hornes, if he did not presume of his couetous desire to be horsed on the backe of *Mammon*, and hurried to Hell. Hence sinne is so bold as to say *in the wicked heart, Non est Deus, there is no God:* and so peremptorily to conclude to it selfe, *I shall not be moued; for I shall neuer be in aduersity*. Hence euen *their inward thought is, that their houses shall continue for euer, &c.* This is presumptuous and whorish prostitution, to set out Iniquity bare-faced, without the Maske of pretexts, to hide her ugly visage. An impetuous, a meretricious Impudence,

1. Giddy, unsteady.

that not with a feminine rapture, but rather with a masculine rape, captiues the conscience. You see *Follies* prostitution.

2 Prodition is the rankling tooth that followes her rauishing kisses. *Iudas* kissed his Master with the same heart. Iniquity hath an infectuous breath, if a faire countenance. All her delights are like faire and sweet flowers, but full of Serpents. The vanquished concludes with a groane.

Sic violor violis, oh violenta tuis.

Thy soft flowers haue stung me to death. For indeede it is most true, *Nemo ipsum peccatum amat, sed male amando illud quod amat, illaqueatur peccato.* No man loues sinne for its owne sake, but by an irregular and sinister loue, to that he doth loue, hee is snared with sinne. The Deuill knowes, that his *Ephesian Harlot, Vice,* would want worshippers, if treason and death were written vpon the Temple-dore: therefore health and content are proclaimed, and as on the Theater presented; but there is Hell vnder the Stage, there is treason in the vault.

Thus *Temptation* misleades the Nauigatours with a Pyrates light; deceiues the liuing soules with a dead bird; a *Syren,* a *Iudas,* a Iebusite[1], a Iesuite. For were the Iesuite to play the Deuill, or the Deuill the Iesuite on the stage of this world; it would be hard to iudge which was the Iesuite, which the Deuill; or which played the part most naturally. As Iniquities are *Sathans Harlots* to corrupt the affections; so Iesuites are his Engines to peruert the braines: for if the new guest here be heart sicke, so their Proselite is braine-sicke. Both are made so dissolute, till they become desolate, robbed and destitute of all comfort.

Sinne deales with her guests, as that bloody Prince, that hauing inuited many great States to a solemne Feast, flattered and singled them one by one, and cut off all their heads. As fatall a successe attends on the flatteries of sinne. Oh then, *fuge exulceratricem hanc:* Fly this *Harlot,* that carries death about her. Goe a loofe from her doore, as they say, the Deuill doth by the Crosse: but (let that sauour of supposition, nay of supersition) doe thou in sincere deuotion flee from sinne, *quasi a facie colubri,* as from a Serpent. Shee hath a *Syrens* voice, a Mermaides face, a *Helens* beauty to tempt thee: but a Leapers touch, a Serpents sting, a trayterous hand to wound thee. The best way to conquer Sinne, is by *Parthian* warre, to runne away. . . .

1. A member of the small mountain tribe which, in the first centuries of Israel's occupation of Canaan held Jerusalem until David captured the Citadel: also, in the 16th and 17th centuries, a nickname for a Jesuit.

HENRY GREENWOOD[1]

In the Middle Ages volcanoes were accepted as irrefutable proof of the existence and nature of hell;[2] an authority as reliable as Gregory the Great supplied a warm account of the region in his *Dialogues*.[3] The reformation did not change the ancient concept of the terrain of damnation, but did somewhat enlarge the recruitment of the damned by including religious enemies. It was the practice in preaching to issue at intervals a graphic reminder of what lay in store of the contumacious, as much to cheer the elect as to abash the wicked. A favourite view of hell was the lake of Tophet, which is here depicted in some detail.

Tormenting Tophet[4]
A View of Hell

A sermon preached at St. Paule's Crosse on the
14th June, 1614

Ut per hortum voluptatis, Paradisi scilicet, sedes beatorum figuratur: ita per hunc locum terroris, Tophet, fcilicet, infernus describitur: that is: As by the garden of pleasure, namely Paradise, the place of the blessed is figured: So by this place of terrour, namely, Tophet, the dungeon of hell is described.

1. Probably the Henry Greenwood who matriculated as a sizar at Pembroke College, Cambridge, in 1598; B.A. 1601–2; M.A. 1605; ordained deacon October 12th, 1602. If so, we know no more about him than that by 1628 he was vicar of Great Sampford and was still alive in 1650 when he dedicated a revised work to 'his very good Friends Sir Lestange Mardavnt (Bt) of Massingham Hall, Norfolk and to his vertuous Lady, the Lady Frances Mordavnt, his loving bedfellow.'

2. *Gesta Romanorum*, EETS, p. 177.

3. '. . . et quia poenas damnatorum non vident oculo corporali, ideo minus eas credunt. Propter talis ergo Deus aliquando poenas infernales visibiliter ostendit, sicut in partibus Cecilie patet, ubi ignem infernalem de lacis illis eructantem ostendit'. Quoted by John Bromyard in *Summa Predicantium*, 'Damnatio', see Owst, op. cit., p. 173.

4. *Tormenting Tophet, or a terrible Description of Hel, able to breake the hardest heart, and cause it to quake and tremble* (1615).

From which fearfull Metaphor we may justly make this our observation: namely, that Hell is a most lamentable and wofull place of torment, where (in regard of the extremeity of torments imposed upon the damned) there shall bee screeching and screaming, weeping, wayling, and gnashing of teeth for evermore: and this is Tophet.

Where torment shall be upon torment, each torment easelesse, endlesse, remedilesse; where the worme shall be immortall, colde intolerable, stench indurable, fire unquenchable, darkenesse palpable, scourges of Devilles terrible, and screeching and screaming continuall: and this is Hell.

In hell (sayth S. Austine) there is *vermis conscientiae, ignitae lachrymae,* and *dolor sine remedio*: that is, The gnawing worme, the burning teares, and sorrow that can never be eased.

And againe, hee sayth in this third Tom *de Spiritu et Anima: Ibi erit metus et moeror: luctus et dolor: tunc vere nihil lugere erit misi flere, quia poenitere tunc nulli poterit valere: ibi erit torter coedens, vermis corrodens, ignis consumens*: that is: In hell there is howling and horrour, sobbing and terrour: where weeping helpes not, and repentance bootes not: where is paine killing, worme gnawing, and fire consuming. *Vermis et tenebrae flagellum, frigus et ignis: Daemonis aspectus, scelerum, confusio, luctus.*

Tertullian in *Apologetico,* speaking of Hell, sayth thus: *Gehenna est ignis arcani subterraneus ad poenam thesaurus*: that is, Hell is a treasure of secret fire kept under the earth to punish withall. The truth of this heavy report Diues with the residue of the damned, doe finde by wofull experience, who still cries out, I am tormented in this flame.

This is miserable Tophet, prepared for all ungodly people of the world.

The meditation of these torments should breake our stony hearts in peeces, and strike us into such a dismall dumpe, as was Baltazar, when hee saw the hand writing on the wall against him: these should be of an extractius force and power, to draw grones from our hearts, teares from our eyes, and sinnes from our soules: *Gravia peccata gravia desiderant lamenta*: Great sinnes require great lamentations: Sweet meat must have sowre sawce: sinne must have mourning, eyther here by attrition Legall and centrition Evangelicall, or else hereafter wee shall be cast into Tophet, where wee shall lie screeching and screaming continually.

Plangite igitur plangenda: Bewayle your sinnes therefore that ought to be lamented: *Estote tam proni ad lamenta, sicut fuistis ad peccata*: Bee as prone to lamentation, as ever you were to transgression, as prone to lament them, as ever yee were to commit them.

In a booke inscribed *De natura rerum,* I read of a Byrd called *Avis Paradisi*: the Birde of Paradise: which is so called in regard of her splendid and excellent beauty: which Birde being taken in the snare of the fowler, doth *ingemiscere ac lachrymare dies noctesque* mourne and lament night and day, untill shee be restored to liberty[1]: So we that were once *Aves Paradisi*, Birdes of Paradise, but now captivated in the thraldome of sinne and Sathan, and lyable to this tormenting Tophet, should never cease mourning and wayling, untill wee bee restored to Grace againe.

Blessed are you that have grace thus to mourne, yee shall bee comforted: the Lord will wipe away, as all sinnes from your soules, so all teares from your eyes in the kingdome of salvation.

*

And in Samuel wee reade, That Kings are not exempted from the judgements of God: If yee doe wickedly, yee shall perish, and your King.[2]

In the first Epistle to the Corinths, we may read who they are that are threatned with Tophet: neyther fornicators, nor idolaters, nor adulterers, nor wantons, nor theeves, nor covetous, nor drunkards, nor extortioners shall inherite the Kingdome of God: This is spoken of Kings, as well as of others. And in the Rev. we finde, that the fearefull and unbelieving, the abominable, murtherers and whore-mongers, and sorcerers, idolaters, and all lyers shall have their part in the Lake that burneth with fire and brimstone: And this is spoken of the King as well as of the Begger: for the Lord in judgement freeth from hell, not according to place, but grace: not outward condition, but inward disposition.

Nay moreover, great men, Noble men, and mighty Princes, are not onely lyable to Tophet, but the greatest part of them shall to the devill: Not many wise men, not many mighty, not many noble are called: for as God would have all men saved, and come to the knowledge of the truth, some of all sorts, some Jewes, some Gentiles, some Kings, some Nobles, some Preachers, some Rich, some Poore: so of all these, the greatest summe goe downe to Tophet. Yet for all this, great men must not be reproved forsooth, the trueth that maketh against them, must not be imbraced of them.

1. Not in Lucretius.
2. The subjection of kings to God's judgement had never been in question; but the emphasis and reiteration with which this element of doctrine was treated by certain Puritan preachers from the beginning of the new century, was notably prophetic of the collision to come.

LANCELOT ANDREWES

In the 1920s, when T. S. Eliot was the most influential literary critic alive, he dispensed praise, as might be expected, sparingly and armoured with reservations.

Thus when he published an essay, in high praise of a long depreciated Anglican divine,[1] it caused curiosity as well as attention. The homage rendered was to the memory of Lancelot Andrewes, a theologian and preacher who was scarcely a name to any but students of Jacobean ecclesiastical history.[2] It would be interesting to know what proportion of Eliot's readers were intrigued enough to resort to the originals, and how many reached the conclusion that Eliot had produced a careful piece of special pleading. Why he should have chosen this labour it is not my purpose to pursue here, farther than the obvious contingency that his motives were not unconnected with the recent ascendancy of Anglo-Catholicism in his life.

'Andrewes' works', said Eliot, in delivering his judgement, 'rank with the finest English prose of their time, of any time.'

The pronouncement is a rare eccentricity from a critic who was normally consistent in submitting his propositions to thorough and rigorous tests. It is not that the observations made, taken separately, are by themselves untrue or undeserved; but they are such a small part of an entirety of very different aspect that, in edited separation, they serve to mislead. Andrewes could write a hard, disciplined, quick-marching prose, which did what it could do, with admirable despatch, and was never required to do more. His short, neat iambic clauses are when necessary given extension by the coupling device of repetition. Even without seeing enough of the rest to appreciate that they are judiciously

---

1. T. S. Eliot, *For Lancelot Andrewes* (1926).
2. Lancelot Andrewes, 1555–1626. Bishop of Winchester. Son of a London merchant and intended for the trade, was sent, after showing early promise, to Pembroke Hall, Cambridge. Fellow of Jesus College; ordained 1580. Declined two bishoprics because the crown wished to alienate the revenues; Dean of Westminster, 1601. Bishop of Chichester, 1605; Bishop of Ely, 1609; Bishop of Winchester and Dean of the Chapel Royal, 1619; Privy Counsellor in attendance at the Hampton Court Conference, 1603–4; participated in the preparation of the 'Authorised Version' of the Bible, 1607.

timed and placed, the merits of the passages quoted with approval by Eliot are manifest. But what is *not* manifest from the essay alone is that one must hunt long and deep to find them; they are neither frequent, nor characteristic; for most of the time Andrewes is not writing better or worse 'literature', he is not writing, or trying to write, literature at all. He is engaged in doing something quite other than that for which Eliot here praises him.

That Andrewes was a superlative scholastic orator, the most celebrated of his age, is a matter of undisputed record. He preached mainly in a very self-consciously intellectual court, presided over by the royal pupil of George Buchanan, where theological and philosophical disputation were favourite pastimes, and nimbleness of wit and ingenuity of argument prized as high as beauty and the arts had been at the court of Francis I.

Thus the auditory to which he habitually addressed himself was a body of men and women whose conversational exercise consisted of fencing with epigram and paradox, and who sought recreation in rebuses, acrostics, riddles, anagrams, quotation-matching, puns, conundrums and theological disputation.

In purpose he was, above all else, a *rhetorician*. Now, while there is rhetoric which is literature, there is also rhetoric which is a kind of anti-literature; that is, not complete in the written word, requiring for its consummation the skill in active play of its creator's living presence. There are speeches which are literature, and so, by definition, enduring, which could have been less effective, for the primary purpose they were created to serve, than speeches which were not literature and required fertilization by the speaker to whom they belonged, but, given that union of favourable circumstances, could produce a stronger intended effect upon a given audience, at a particular time.

It may be recognized, without detraction from Andrewes's ability to write good narrative prose, when he required it, that his aim was at another target. He was less a man of letters than a man of learning, with a sharpened wit practised in the special skill of contracting, almost to the form of notes, the largest number of ingenious variations upon a taken theme, and then expanding and projecting them into an interpretative performance. The process would employ dramatic pause, arsis, variety of inflection, selective emphasis, and all the technical resources of rhetoric, in support of the quickening vitality which every orator must be able to call up. Analogies tend to be specious rather than reliable, and are seldom to be trusted far; but I believe one would be moving roughly in the right direction if one thought of Andrewes, doing for his words something akin to what a dancer does for his choreography. To the university men of letters of the day Andrewes's thaumaturgic virtuosity represented everything most admirable in a preacher; to the Puritan, then, and for years to come, everything most detestable.

I have thought it best, in order to illustrate what I have sought to describe, to present in extended context the now celebrated passage on the coming of the Magi quoted by Eliot ('It was no summer progress. A cold coming they had of it . . .'[1]) which appears in the Nativity sermon of 1622. Preceding it is part of the earlier nativity sermon of 1614 where Andrewes is at his most typical, showering the congregation with a sparkling cascade of 'divisions'; and following it a tirade from a sermon on the *Gunpowder Plot*, where he is at his least typical, because he feels obliged, by the frightfulness of the danger recalled, to be relatively simple, plain and monitory. Considering the 'escape' is already ten years old, the emotion remains remarkably fresh. But if the alleged conspiracy—and there is much which remains mysterious about it—had been successful, Andrewes himself would have been among the select victims to ascend heavenwards with the explosion, a circumstance which, no doubt, helped to keep indignation in good repair. The same sermon is interesting as a measure of the exaltation (more than permitted, morally approved), of the reverend prelate, over the torture and mutilation of the convicted men. This is an element of seventeenth-century sensibility which should not be entirely forgotten during enjoyment of the age's more engaging aspects. In the previous reign Elizabeth and Burghley had felt constrained to explain and justify[2] (almost apologize for) the use of torture in exceptional circumstances.[3] That was part Tudor discretion, but also part scruples. James displayed neither discretion nor scruples, but, on occasion, a fair measure of unscrupulous cunning. Andrewes learnt when to say 'Amen'.

1. See below, p. 229.

2. *A Declaration of the favourable Dealing of Her Majesties Commissioners appointed for the Examination of Certain Traitours and of Tortures unjustly reported to be done upon them for matter of Religion*, 1583.

3. Ibid. '. . . there was a perpetual care had, and the queen's servants, the warders, whose office and act it is to handle the wrack, were ever by those that attended the examinations specially charged to use it in as charitable a manner as such a thing might be.'

We join the king and a luxurious congregation at Whitehall in the middle of the Christmas, 'Nativity' sermon. Andrewes has already dissected and analysed the etymological roots of each word of his text, and he now moves closer in, to interpret the meaning of the order and inter-relationship of the parts. Then, towards the end of this section (from 'And this is the proper *Immanu* of his name'), he begins to pull away from particulars and expand his resources in order to glorify the miracle of soteriology in its final and total effects. In this heightened emotional atmosphere he produces the anagnorisis of the theotechnic drama, a cartwheel of fireworks, blazing as it whirls in staccato bursts of amphimacer, and simulating the excitement of spontaneous discovery by virtue of the preacher's superlative skill in aposiopesis, which the serrated caesura, the epanodos, polyptoton, leading a firmly controlled battery of classical tropes, were carefully designed to serve. This was the kind of radiant *bravura* esteemed in oratory above all else by the Jacobean court wits to whom the discourse was addressed.

The Meaning of Immanuel

A Sermon preached before the Kings Majestie at White-hall on Sunday the XXV December A.D. MDCXIIII, being Christmas Day.[1]

Ecce virgo concipiet, et pariet Filium, et vocabitur nomen Eius Immanuel. (Isa. vii:14).

Behold a virgin shall conceive and bear a Son and she shall call his name Immanuel.

And, now, to looke into the *Name*. It is compounded, and to be taken in peeces. First, into *Immanu*; and *El*: Of which, *El*, (the latter) is the more principall by farre: for, *El*, is God. Now, for any thing yet said in *concipiet* and *pariet*, all is but *man with us*: Not, God *with us*, till now. By the name, wee take our first notice, that this Childe is God: And, this is a great addition, And here (loe) is the wonder: For, as for any childe of a woman, to *eat butter and honey* (the words, that next follow) where is the *Ecce*? But, for *El*, for God, to doe it; that, is worth an *Ecce* indeed.

1. Lancelot Andrewes, *XCVI Sermons* (1635, 3rd edn.), Sermon Nine.

El, is God: And, not God, every way; but (as the force of the word is) God, in his full strength and vertue: God, *cum plenitudine potestatis* (as we say) with all that ever He can doe: And that is enough, I am sure.

For the other, *Immanu:* though *El* be the more principal, yet, I cannot tell, whether it, or *Immanu,* doe more concerne us. For, as, in *El,* is might: So, in *Immanu,* is our right, to His might, and to all He hath, or is worth: By that word, we hold; therefore, we to lay hold of it. The very standing of it, thus before; thus, in the first place, toucheth us somewhat. The first thing ever, that we to looke for, is *Nos, Nobis,* and *Noster* the Possessives: For, they doe *mittere in possessionem,* put us in possession. Wee looke for it first; and loe, it stands here first: *Nobiscum,* first; and then, *Deus,* after.

I shall not need to tell you, that, in *nobiscum,* there is *mecum;* In *nobiscum* for us all, a *mecum,* for every one of us. Out of this generalitie, of *with us,* in grosse, may every one deduce his owne particular; *with me,* and *me,* and *me.* For, all put together make but *nobiscum.*

The Wise-man (*Prov.*30.) out of *Immanuel* (that is, *nobiscum Deus*) doth deduce *Ittiel,* (that is,) *Mecum Deus,* God *with me;* his owne private interest. And Saint *Paul,* when he had said to the *Ephesians,* of Christ, *Who loved us,* and *gave Himselfe for us:* might with good right, say to the *Galatians, who loved me, and gave Himselfe for me.*

This *Immanu* is a Compound againe: we may take it, in sunder, into *Nobis;* and *cum:* And so then have we three peeces. *El,* the mighty God: and *Anu,* wee, poore we; (Poore indeed, if we have all the world beside, if we have not Him to be *with us:*) And *Im,* which is *Cum,* And that *cum,* in the midst betweene *nobis* and *Deus,* God and Vs; to couple God and *us:* thereby to conveigh the things of the one, to the other. (Ours, to God: Alas, they be not worth the speaking of:) Chiefely then, to conveigh to us, the things of God. For, that is worth the while: they are (indeed) worth the conveighing.

This *Cum* we shall never conceive to purpose, but *carendo:* the value of *With,* no way so well, as by *Without:* by stripping of *Cum,* from *nobis.* And so, let *nobis,* (*us*) stand by our selves, without Him, to see, what our case is, but for this *Immanuel;* what, if this *Virgins Child* had not this day beene *borne* us: *Nobiscum* (after) will be the better esteemed. For, if this Childe be *Immanuel,* God *with us;* then without this Childe, this *Immanuel,* we be without God. *Without Him, in this World* (saith the *Apostle;*) And, if without Him, in this, without Him, in the next: And, if without Him there, if it be not *Immanu-el,* it will be *Immanu-hel;* and that, and no other place, will fall (I feare me) to our share. Without Him, this we are: What, with Him? Why, if we have Him; and God, by Him; we need no more: *Immanu-el,* and *Immanu-all.* All that we can desire is, for us to be *with Him,* with God; and He to be *with us:* And we, from Him, or He, from us, never to be parted. We were, with Him, once before, and wee were well: and when we left

Him, and He no longer *with us*, then began all our misery: Whensoever we goe from Him, so shall we be; in evill case: and never be well, till we be backe with Him againe.

Then, if this be our case, that we cannot be without Him; No remedie then, but to get a *Cum*, by whose meanes, *Nobis* and *Deus* may come together againe. And, Christ is that *Cum*, to bring it to passe. The parties are, God, and *We:* And now, this day, He is both. God, before eternally; and, now to day, *Man:* and so, both, and takes hold of both, and brings both together againe. For, two Natures here are in Him: If *conceived* and *borne of a woman*, then, a Man: If God *with us*, then, God. So *Esay* offered His *signe, from the height above, or from the depth beneath:* Here, it is. *From above, El; From beneath, Anu*; one of us, now: And so, His *signe*, from both. And, both these Natures in the Vnitie of one Person, called by one Name, even this name *Immanuel.*

Vocabit nomen: I told you, in His *Name*, is His *Vocation* or Office, to be *cum*, to come betweene, (that is) to be a Mediatour, to make Him, that was *contra nos, nobiscum* againe. A *Mediatour is not of one, but* God *is one.* God and Man, are two; and they were *two* (as they say:) Were two, and two will be, till He make them one; recapitulate and cast up both into one summe: to knit *Anu*, (that is, *We*) and, *El* (that is, God) with His *Im*, into one: One word, and one thing, *univoce*, againe.

So, upon the point, in these three peeces, there be three Persons; so, a second kinde of Trinitie: God, *We*, and Christ. *El*, is God: *Anu*, *We*: for Christ, nothing left but *Im*, that is *Cum*, or *With*. For it is He, that maketh the Vnitie in this Trinitie; maketh God *with us*, and us, with God: and both, in and by Him, to our eternall comfort and joy.

Thus is He *with us:* And yet, all this is but Nature still. But, the *nobiscum* of His *Name*, bodeth yet a further matter. For (indeed) the *With us*, of His Name, is more than the *With us*, of His Nature. If we make a great matter of that (as, great it is, and very great) behold, the *Ecce* of His Name, is farre beyond it. *With us* in His Nature, that is, *with us*, as Man; that is short: We are more; sinfull men: A wretched condition added to a Nature corrupt: Will He be *with us*, in that too? Else, this (of Nature,) will smally availe us.

What, in Sinne? Nay, *in all things, sin only except.* Yea, that is, in being *like us;* but not, in being *with us.* For, in being *with us*, except sin, and except all: The *ridding us of our sin*, is the only matter, (saith *Esay*, after.) Therefore, to be *with us*, in all things, *sin it selfe not except.* Saint *Iohns Caro factum est*, will not serve: Saint *Pauls Fuit peccatum*, must come too. In, *with us*, there too. I say it over againe: Vnity of *Nature* is not enough; He is to be *with us*, in Vnitie of *Person*, likewise. So, He was. The Debtor and Surety, make but one person, in Law. That, He was: and then, He was *cum*, *with us* throughly, as deepe in, as we.

And this is the proper *Immanu*, of His Name. And this, the *Immanu* indeed.

And, till He was thus *with us*, no name He had; He was *Christus anonymus*, Christ unchristned (as it were.) For, His Name came not, till He became one *with us* in person: Not, till His Circumcision: Not, till for us, and in our names; He became debtor of the whole Law; Principall, Forfeiture, and all. To the *hand-writing* He then signed, with the first fruits of His bloud. And then, name the childe, and give Him this Name, *Immanuel*. For, thus He was a right *Immanuel*; truly, *With us: With us*, as men: *With us*, as sinfull men: *With us*, in all things, sinne it selfe not excepted.

May I not adde this: It is said in the Text, *Shee shall call: Shee*, that is, His Mother. Why, *Shee?* To let us understand, that *shee* might give Him the Name, while Hee undertooke this for us. But, His Father, till all was discharged, and the *hand-writing cancelled*; till then, He suspended, He gave it Him not. His Mother, *She* did; when he dropped a little bloud, at the sealing of the Bond. But, He was faine, not to drop bloud, but to sweat bloud, and to shed His bloud, every drop of it, yer this *With us* were full answered. And then, His Father did it too; *Dedit illi nomen super omne nomen:* Then, and not before. His Mother, now: His Father, not till then. But then, He had proved Himselfe fully *with us, per omnia*, when neither Wombe nor Birth, Cratch nor Crosse, Crosse nor Curse could plucke Him away from us, or make Him not to be *with us*. Then, *vocabit illi nomen*, both She and *He:* Mother, Father, and all. *With us*, to *eat butter and honey*, seemeth much: And it is so, for God. What say ye, to *drinke vineger and gall?* That is much more, (I am sure:) yet, that He did: I cannot (here) say *with us*, but *for us*. Even, drunke of the cup with the dregs of the wrath of God: which passed not from Him, that is might passe from us, and we not drinke it.

This, this is the great *With us:* For, of this, follow all the rest. *With us*, once thus, and then, *with us* in His *oblation* on the Altar of the Temple; *With us* in His *sacrifice*, on the Altar of the Crosse: *With us*, in all the *vertues* and *merits* of His *life*; *With us*, in the *satisfaction* and *satis-passion* (both) of His *death: With us*, in His *Resurrection*, to raise us up from the earth; *With us*, in His *Ascension*, to exalt us to heaven: *With us*, even then, when He seemed to be taken from us: That day, by His Spirit; as, this day, by His flesh. *Et ecce vobiscum*, and loe, I am true *Immanuel, With you*, by the love of my *Man-hood; With you*, by the power of my *God-head*, still *to the end of the world*.

One more yet. He wonne it, and Hee weares this name; and, in it, He weares us. And it is both a comfort to us, and a glory, that so He weares us. That, Hee is not, cannot be named, without us: that when He is named, *Et nos una tecum Domine*, we also are named with Him. In *Immanu*, is *anu*, and that is we. This is not it; but this: That He hath set us in the fore-part of it; *Immanu* before *El*, *Nobiscum* before *Deus*. This note is not out of place, in this place, where precedence is made a great matter of: That *Immanu* is before *El:* That is, *Wee* first, and God last.

Good manners would, in a name compound of Him and us, that He should have stood before us, and it have beene *Elimmanu*, (at least,) *Deus nobiscum*, and *Deus* before *nobiscum*; Not, *Immanuel, Nobiscum*, before *Deus*: He, before us; He the prioritie of the place, in all reason: *Booz*[1], he placed them so (*Ruth* 2.) and so should we (I dare say) if it had beene of our imposing, *Elimmanu*: It had beene great arrogancie otherwise. But, He giving it Himselfe, would have it stand thus; *Vs* set before Him. There is a meaning in it. And what can it be but this? That, in the very name we might reade, that we are dearer to Him, than Himselfe; that He so preferred us; and that His owne name doth *præse ferre* no lesse, but give out to all the world, the *Ecce* of Saint *Iohns* Gospell, *Ecce quomodo dilexit!* the *Ecce* of his Epistle, *Ecce quantam charitatem habuit! See, how He loved them! Behold, how great love He bare to them!* See it, in His very name: We are a part of it; We are the forepart of it, and He the latter; He behind, and we, before: Before Himselfe, and that by order from Himselfe: He would have it *Immanuel*. O, whether was greater, humility, or charity in Him! Hard, to say whether, but both unspeakable. . . .

Andrewes preached regularly on the theme of the Gunpowder Plot as the anniversary came round. His 1615 'Fifth of November' sermon is his most violent, but not his most ingenious, or fanciful essay. The following year, exercised somewhat, perhaps, by the challenge not to be repetitious, he preached on the text, *venerunt filii usque ad partem*, likening the barrels of powder in the vault to children in *utero*, Guy Fawkes being the *obstetrix*; but 'there was no strength to bring forth!'

A Sermon of Thanksgiving for Deliverance
from the Gunpowder Plot 1605

Preached before His Majesty on the 5fth.
November 1615

Super omnia, above all examples (to begin with.) For, the like never seen, nor heard of. Nay, not to be raked out of any story, in any Age, of any Countrey, civil or savage, of the like. And *Super omnes*, over all it would have gone, not

---

1. Boaz.

spared any, no degree, high or low; no estate, Nobles or Commons; no calling, sacred or civil; no sex, King or Queen; no age, King or Prince; no Religion, their own, or others. This is but *super omnes*: Nay, *super omnia*, it was too: *Super, up* with lime, and stone, and timber, iron, glasse and lead: *up* with floor, windowes and walls, roof and all. Yet another *super omnia*: all bands of birth, countrey, allegiance, nature, blood, humanity and Christianity; tread upon them, trample upon them all, tear them all in pieces. Never such a *super omnia*, in all senses. So (indeed) a cruelty for the Devil himself: To make the opposition perfect, of God's *Mercy*, and *Satans Cruelty*. Of whom (to give each their due) it may be said, and no lesse truly said, *Crudelitates ejus super omnia opera ejus*, his *Cruelties* are above all his *works*: than of God, that *His Mercies are above all His*.

Super omnia opera ejus, it is; and *contra omnia opera Dei: Above all his own*, and *against all God's works*. The enemy of God he is, and so of all God's *works*; and of those *His works* most, that God most sets by (that is) mankind; And of that part of mankind most, *God* hath done most for, and so may be thought, most to favour (that is, *Christen men:*) And then of them, if there be a *Non taliter* in *His* mercy, a *Non taliter* too, in *his malice*, straight. If a *super omnes* with God, a *Super omnes* with him, *in sensu contrario*.

To any *creature* (only because it is a creature) is he cruel: he will into the *Hogstie*, to shew it rather than not to shew it at all.

But, to *man*, to one man, rather than to a whole heard of Swine.

And among men, his malice is most at *Christen men*: they are nearer to the Kingdom of God. To keep them from that, Himself hath irrecoverably lost (that is) Heaven; and to plunge them into eternal misery, whereinto himself is fallen, without all redemption.

And among Christen men, to the *best* sort; to publike persons, rather than to private mean men.

But, if he could get a whole *Parliament* together: A King, his Nobles, his Commons; that is, a King, Kingdom and all; and up with them all at once, all together: there were none to that: that (lo) he would over sea and land to compasse. For, that were indeed, with him, a *super omnia*: He never had done the like.

Of this their *Father*, were those ungodly men of this Day. Ungodly (I say:) For *Salomon* sets us this signe, to know *ungodly men* by; *Viscera impiorum crudelia*, if the *bowels be cruel*, then *ungodly*, certainly. No *pity*, no *piety*, with him. And we find, that *mercy* is a plant of our nature: So incident to the nature of man, as they are holden *inhumane*, that are without it. No *pity*, no *humanity*. Why then, *Satanitie*, it must be, if *God* and *man* disclaim it: : Even of him, *cujus crudelitas super omnia opera ejus*.

Now God cannot abide *cruelty* at any hand. By what He placeth highest, may we know, what He loves best (*mercy*:) and by that, may we know, what

He can worst away with (*cruelty.*) Nay, if once *he take his fellow by the throat, deal cruelly* with him: *never hear him* more. No *cruelty* can He endure, at all: specially, no such cruel cruelty, as this that passed all.

And in this case of ours, I make no doubt, *God* was moved both wayes.

One way, by *Mercy*: for us, that *our bones might not be scattered*, in every corner; as *when one heweth wood*, chips flye about. And again; for them, we should have left behind, that *Videns Jesus turbas, misertus est eis*, He looked upon them too, and saw, they should have been ἐσκυλμένοι and ἐρριμμένοι, *scattered all*, and *hurried up and down*, like a sort of poor masterlesse *sheep: His mercy* wrought with Him, in both these respects.

But on the other side, their *Cruelty* moved Him also. And (I am perswaded) *God*, looking upon those mercilesse bowel'd men, when in their hearts they hatched that monster of *cruelty*, even at the fight of that barbarous resolution (yea more than barbarous) His heart even turned against them, His very soul abhorred that devilish intention of theirs. They had thought to have had the Day; but, to the high praise of His *mercy*, and to the confusion of *Satan* and all his *cruelty*, He gave order, *Mercy* should have the day: and she had it, that there might be a *mercy, super omnia, above* this *Cruelty super omnia*: as there was. Their counsel brought to light; brought to nought; brought upon their own heads: and both counsel and counsellours brought to a shamefull end.

Nay, would they make mens bowels fly up and down the ayr? Out with those bowels: what should they do in, that have not in them that, that bowels should have. Would they do it by *fire*? Into the fire with their bowels, before their faces? Would they make mens *bones* flie about like *chips*? Hew their bones in sunder. Just is *Davids* prayer: *Their delight was in cruelty, let it happen to them: They loved not mercy, therefore let it be far from them.*

But, how now? We are gone now from *mercy* quite. No no: there is *mercy* even in this severity. In the *Psalm of Mercy* (*CXXXVI.*) *Slaying* is made a *work of mercy; Slew the first-born of Ægypt: cruel Pharaoh, cruel Og, For his mercy endureth for ever: Mercy*, in ridding the world of such. For, they are not worthy to be *inter opera Dei*, among *Gods works*, that renounce that Vertue: that is, *super opera Dei*, over all *Gods works*.

And so now ye see that *Super*, I told you, we should come to at last; *Over hell*, and them there. The *Super Superantis*, the *Over* of an *Overcommer*; of *Mercy* a *Conquerer. Above His* other *works*, with the *Super* of a *Soveraign*, to protect them: *Upon* the *devil* and devillish men in their *works*, with *Super Aspidem & Basiliscum*, to tread upon them, to *make His enemies His foot-stool*, and so a *Super, Over* them too.

JOHN HALES[1]

Violence was an element which had never been lacking in the English social scene. To live quietly, peaceable men had to be circumspect and guard their tongues, for blows and drawn weapons followed hard upon hard words. Latimer and Gilpin both condemned the incidence of affrays in daily life and how relevant were such monitions, and the regular homily on *Contention*, may be inferred from the issue of a statute to punish fighting in church.[2] He who struck the first blow in church with a naked weapon should lose his ears, 'or if he wants ears' be branded on the face. But although there was abundant wounding and killing in brawls and *chaud mêlée*, the 'duel', single combat by challenge and appointment, conducted under agreed rules and conditions, was unknown in England, until the fashion was introduced from France in the last years of Elizabeth's reign. By then it was already endemic in France. Four thousand gentlemen were recorded killed in 'affairs of honour' in the first years of the reign of Henry IV alone. The corollary of the duel was, of course, the growth of fencing as an important part of a prudent, 'gentle' education, and the appearance in England of a number of foreign fencing masters, like the famous Saviolo, who would teach, either with rapier and dagger, or rapier and cloak, how to 'kill any man, bee it with a thrust *punta*, a *stocada*, with an *imbrocadda* or a changing blow, be it with the edge, with the back, or with the flat'. Public displays of swordsmanship became a popular spectacle and, as early as 1602, one fencing master called Dun was accidentally killed by another called Turner when his eye was pierced in the course of a professional demonstration. The moral pressure to accept a challenge was becoming a social force so strong that the practice threatened to grow out of all authority but its own, as it had done in France.[3]

1. A biographical note on John Hales will be found on p. 335.

2. Statute 5. 6 E 64. *Abridgement of all Statutes from Magna Carta until 1641* (1666), p. 228.

3. That it never gained in England, even temporarily, the undisputed ascendancy which it achieved and held in France, is in a large measure due to the independence and influence of the commercial and professional elements of English society, who from the very beginning reacted to it with the steady disapproval which Manningham showed

In 1614 a Star Chamber prosecution was brought against two men, Priest and Wright, for conspiring to provoke a duel, Priest by issuing a challenge, Wright by delivering it; and Francis Bacon, then Attorney General, made the proceedings the occasion of some official observations upon 'the causes and remedies of this mischief, that prevaileth so in these times . . .'.[1]

Bacon reflects upon the social danger of the quarrels of individuals being perpetuated by duelling into feuds involving whole families and factions in bloodshed without end, for, 'when every man shall bear the sword not to defend but to assayle, and priuate men beginne . . . to giue leave to themselves and to right their owne wrongs, noe man can foresee the dangers and inconueniencies that may arise and multiply there-upon'. He dwells on the 'miserable effect when young men full of towardness and hope . . . shall bee cast away and destroyed in such a vaine manner . . .' and the grievous waste when there is 'noble and gentle blood spilt upon such follies'. But after all these protestations it turns out that the thing most offensive to him in the present case is that the blood which would have been spilt was *not* 'gentle' or 'noble'. Priest, the challenger, was a barber–surgeon, and Hutchest, the challenged, a butcher; and the former, with his would-be second, Wright, had im-pudently presumed to ape the vices of their betters by seeking from Hutchest 'satisfaction' for a supposed wrong. Perhaps Priest's profes-sional activities with razor and lancet had stimulated dreams of triumph with sword and dagger. But, at all events, Hutchest's exercise with the cleaver had nourished no such delusions of grandeur in his breast; for he not only refused the challenge but reported his challenger and second to the magistrates.

Bacon deprecates the inferior status of the accused, wishing that he had 'some greater persons' as subjects for the censure of such an august assembly; but he suggests the incongruity of the situation may not be without its uses for 'I should think (my Lords) that men of birth and quality will leaue the practise, when it begins to bee vilified and come so lowe as to Barbers-surgeons and Butchers and such base mechanical persons.' He exhorts the superior personages in society to remember the responsibility borne by their examples, for 'the stream of vulgar opinion is such as it imposeth a necessity upon men of value

even for the accidental death at sword play of Dun. 'A goodly sport in a Christian state to see one man kill another.' (*Diary*, February 1602).

1. *The Charge of Sir Francis Bacon . . . touching duells* (1614).

to conform themselves or else there is no liuing or looking upon men's faces . . .'.[1]

As it turned out, the 'stream of vulgar opinion' taught itself the lesson that duelling was folly, without benefit of any aristocratic example, while 'men of birth' continued to puncture and slice each other's bodies with a measure of social toleration until well into the nineteenth century. The first phase of the vogue was at its height in 1619 when John Hales preached his sermon against duelling.

Of Duels

A sermon preached at the Hague in the year 1618

Numbers 35. 33.   *And the land cannot be cleansed of blood that is shed in it but by the blood of him that shed it.*[2]

. . . Combats betwixt subjects for private causes, till these latter ages of the world, was never allowed: yet, I must confess, the practice of it is very antient; for Cain, the second man in the world, was the first duelist, the first that ever challenged the field; the text saith, that Cain spake unto his brother, and when they were in the field, he arose and slew him. Gen. iv. 8. The Septuagint, to make the sense more plain, do add another clause, and tell us what it was he said unto his brother; 'Let us go out into the field,' and when they were in the field, he arose and slew him: 'Let us go 'out into the field,' it is the very form and proper language of a challenge. Many times indeed our gallants can formalize in other words, but evermore the substance, and usually the very words are no other but these of Cain, 'Let us go out 'into the field.' Abel, I persuade myself, understood them not as a challenge; for had he so done, he would have made so much use of his discretion, as to have refused it; yet can we not chuse but acknowledge a secret judgment of God in this, that the words of Cain should still be so religiously kept till this day, as a proeme and introduction to that action, which doubtless is no other than what Cain's was. When therefore our gallants are so ready to challenge

1. Here Bacon's high moral tone proved too much for one contemporary reader of the copy which, three hundred and fifty-four years later, has been in use to me, and he inscribed the marginal annotation, '*But you was afterwards put out for bribery*'.

2. It is worth noting that seven years after the publication of the *Authorised Version,* Hales still makes his own translation direct from the Greek or Latin text. The *Authorised Version* reasd, *for blood it polluteth the land and no expiation can be made for the land for the blood that is shed therein, but by the blood of him that shed it.*

the field, and to go into the field, let them but remember whose words they use, and so accordingly think of their action.

Again, notwithstanding duels are of so antient and worshipful a parentage, yet could they never gain so good acceptance as to be permitted, much less to be counted lawful, in the civil part of the world, till barbarism had over-ran it. About five or six hundred years after Christ, at the fall of the Roman empire, abundance of rude and barbarous people brake in and possest the civiler part of the world; who abolishing the antient laws of the empire, set up many strange customs in their rooms. Amongst the rest, for the deter-mining of quarrels that might arise in case of doubtful title, or of false accusation, or the like, they put themselves upon many unusual forms of trial; as, to handle red hot iron, to walk bare-foot on burning coals, to put their hands and feet in scalding water, and many other of the like nature, which are reckoned up by Hottoman[1] a French lawyer: for they presumed so far on God's providence, that if the party accused were innocent, he might do any of these without any smart or harm. In the same cases, when by reason of unsufficient and doubtful evidence, the judges could not proceed to sen-tence, as sometimes it falls out, and the parties contending would admit of no reasonable composition, their manner was to permit them to try it out by their swords; that so the conqueror might be thought to be in the right. They permitted, I say, thus to do; for at the best it was but a permission to prevent farther mischief; for so this end sometimes some known abuses are tolerated: so God permitted the Jews upon slight occasions to put their wives away, because he saw, that otherwise their exorbitant lusts would not be bounded within these limits, which he in paradise in the beginning had set. And it is observed of the wise men which had the managing and bringing up of Nero the Emperor, that they suffered him to practise his lusts upon Acte, one of his mother's chamber-maids, 'Lest if he were forbidden that, he should turn his lust upon some of the noblewomen.'[2] Permission and toleration warrants not the goodness of any action. But, as Caiaphas said, 'Better one man die, than all the people perish;' John xi. 50. so they that first permitted duels seem to have thought, better one or two mutinous persons, and disorderly, die in their folly, than the whole commonwealth be put into tumult and combustion: yet even by these men it was never so promiscuously tolerated, that every hasty couple, upon the venting of a little choler, should presently draw their swords; but it was a public or solemn action, done by order, with inspection, either of the prince himself, or of some other magistrate appointed to order it. Now certainly there can be no very great

---

1. François Hotman, 1524–90; author of Anti-Tribonian (1567), Franco–Gallia (1573).

2. Ne in stupra foeminarum illustrium perrumperet, si illa libidine prohiberetur. Tacitus, Annal. xiii. cap. 12.

reason for that action, which was thus begun by Cain, and continued only by Goths and Vandals, and mere barbarism.

Yet that we may a little better acquaint ourselves with the quality of it, let us a little examine the causes and pretences which are brought by them who call for trial by single combat. The causes are usually two; First, disdain to seem to do or suffer any thing for fear of death: Secondly, point of honour, and not to suffer any contumely and indignity, especially if it bring with it disreputation, and note of cowardice. For the first, disdain to fear death; I must confess I have often wondered with myself, how men durst die so ventrously, except they were sure they died well: in other things which are learned by practising, if we mistake, we may amend it; for the error of a former action may be corrected in the next: we learn then by erring, and men come at length not to err, by having often erred: but no man learns to die by practising it; we die but once, and a fault committed then, can never afterward be amended, because the punishment immediately follows upon the error.[1] To die is an action of that moment, that we ought to be very well advised when we come to it; on that moment hangs eternity: you may not look back upon the opinion of honour and reputation which remains behind you: but rather look forward upon that infinite space of eternity, either of bliss or bale, which befals us immediately after our last breath. To be loth to die upon every slight occasion, is not a necessary sign of fear and cowardice: he that knew what life is, and the true use of it, had he many lives to spare, yet would he be loth to part with one of them upon better terms, than those our books tell us, that Aristippus a philosopher being at sea in a dangerous tempest, and bewraying some fear, when the weather was cleared up, a desperate ruffian came and upbraided him with it, and tells him, That it was a shame that he, professing wisdom, should be afraid of his life; whereas himself, having had no such education, exprest no agony or dread at all. To whom the philosopher replied, there was some difference between them two: 'I know,' saith he, 'my life may be profitable many ways, and therefore am I loth to lose it; but because of your life you know little profit, little good can be made, you care not how easily you part with it.'[2] Beloved, it may be justly suspected, that they who esteem thus lightly of their lives, are but worthless and unprofitable men: our own experience tells us, that men who are prodigal of their money in taverns and ordinaries, are close-handed enough, when either pious uses, or necessary and public expence requires their liberality; I have not heard that prodigals ever built churches. So these men that are so prodigal of their lives in base quarrels, peradventure would

---

1. In aliis rebus siquid erratum est, potest post modum corrigi, quia poena statim sequitur errorem. *Alluding to a saying of Cato recorded by Vegetius.* lib. i. cap. 13.

2. Diogenes Laertius, II, 71. (*Aristippus*). Cf. Gellius: *Aulus Gellii Noctes Atticae,* lib. xix, cap. 1.

be cowardly enough, if either public service, or religion did call for their help; I scarcely believe any of them would die martyrs, if the times so required it. Beloved, I do not go about to persuade any man to fear death, but not to contemn life; life is the greatest blessing God gives in this world, and did men know the worth of it, they would never so rashly venture the loss of it: but now lightly prizing both their own and others blood, they are easily moved to shed it; as fools are easily won to part with jewels, because they know not how to value them. We must deal with our lives, as we do with our money, we must not be covetous of it, desire life for no other use but to live, as covetous persons desire money, only to have it: neither must we be prodigal of life, and trifle it away upon every occasion; but we must be liberal of our lives, know upon what occasion to spare, upon what occasion to spend them. To know where, and when, and in what cases to offer ourselves to die, is a thing of greater skill than a great part of them suppose, who pretend themselves most forward to do it; for brutishly to run upon and hasten unto death, is a thing that many men can do; and we see that brute beasts many times will run upon the spears of such as pursue them: but wisely to look into, and weigh every occasion, and, as judgment and true discretion shall direct, so to entertain a resolution either of life or death; this were true fortitude and magnanimity.[1] And indeed, this prodigality and contempt of life is the greatest ground of this quarrellous and fighting humour. There is a kind of men, who, because they contemn their own lives, make themselves lords and commanders of other men's, easily provoking others to venture their blood, because they care not how they lose their own.[2] Few places of great resort are without these men, and they are the greatest occasioners of bloodshed, you may quickly know them; there are few quarrels wherein they are not either principals, or seconds, or some way or another will have a part in them. Might there be public order taken for the restraint of such men, that make a practice of quarrelling, and because they contemn their own lives, carry themselves so insolently and imperiously towards others: it will prevent much mischief, and free the land of much danger of blood-guiltiness.

The second cause which is much alledged in defence of duels, I told you was point of honour, a conceit that it is dishonourable for men of place and fashion quietly to digest and put up contumely and disgrace; and this they take to be a reason of that authority and strength, as that it must admit of no dispensation.

For answer, First, the true fountain and original of quarrel are of another

1. Nam impetu quodam et instinctu procurrere ad mortem commune cum multis; deliberate vero et causas ejus expendere utque suaserit ratio vitae mortisque consilium vel suscipere, vel ponere ingentis est animi. Pliny, *Epist.* lib. i. cap. 22.

2. Quisquis suam vitam contempsit, tuae dominus est, Seneca. Epist 4.

kind, and honour is abused as a pretence: the first occasioners of a great part of them are indeed very dishonourable; let there an inventory be taken of all the challenges that have been made for some time past, and you shall find that the greatest part by far were raised either in taverns, or dicing-houses, or in the stews: pardon me, if in a case of this nature I deal a little plainly; drinking, gaming, and whores, these are those rotten bones that lie hid under this painted sepulchre and title of honour.

Lastly, to conclude, It is a part of our profession, as we are Christians, to suffer wrong and disgrace. Therefore to set up another doctrine, and teach that honour may plead prescription against Christ's precepts, and exempt you from patient enduring of contumely and disgrace, you withstand Christ, and deny your vocation; and therefore are unavoidably apostates. But we lose our labour, who give young men and unsettled persons good advice and counsel; the civil magistrate must lay to his hand and pity them, who want, discretion to pity themselves: for as bees, though they fight very fiercely, yet if you cast a little dust amongst them, are presently parted: so the enacting and executing some few good laws, would quickly allay this greatness of stomach and fighting humour. How many have been censured for schismatics and heretics, only because by probable consequence, and afar off, they seemed to overthrow some Christian principle? But here are men, who walk in our streets, and come to our churches, who openly oppose that great point of Christianity, which concerns our patience, and yet for their restraint, no synod is called, no magistrate stirs, no church-censure is pronounced. The church of Rome hath, long ago, to the disgrace of the reformed churches, shut them out of the number of Christians, and pronounced them all excommunicated persons, who, upon what pretence soever, durst enter the field for duel and single combat.

Theodosius the Emperor enacted it for a law, and it is extant at this day in the Code, a book of laws, that if any man spake disgracefully of the Emperor 'from levity, it should be despised, if from madness, held worthy of pity, but if with an injurious intention, forgiven.[1]

So great a virtue is patience, that for the attaining of it, it is God's will we should suffer ourselves to be contemned as cowards.[2]

Christ is an example to us of suffering disgrace; let us as the Israelites look up to this serpent, and all the stinging of fiery serpents shall do us no harm. We must foresake and follow Christ; therefore honour and reputation too; if we be ashamed of this pattern of patience Christ will be ashamed of us.

---

1. Si ex levitate procefferit, contemnendum est, si ex insania, miseratione digniffimum, si ex injuria, remittendum. Cod. Theodos. 1. ix. Tom. 4. l. 1.

2. Summa virtus habenda patientia est, quam ut caperet homo justus voluit illum Deus pro inerte contemni. Lactantius, *Divinarum Institutionem Adversus Gentes Libri* VII. vi. 18.

JOSEPH HALL

The next sermon is a traditional set-piece on vanity, especially in apparel, notable because it is preached by Joseph Hall[1] who was, after Donne and the ageing Andrewes, the most accomplished court preacher of the times. Renowned as orator, classical scholar, and the most acute polemicist of the younger talents in the church, Hall leaned towards Calvinism, but without abatement of his loyalty to the episcopacy. He sought an ecclesiastical accommodation which would reconcile all reasonable men, which meant in effect that he was too moderate for his own good and roused the hostility of each opposing extreme by being willing to treat with the other.

1. Joseph Hall, 1574–1656. Bishop of Norwich. Born Ashby de la Zouche. His mother being a Puritan, he was sent, with the help of an uncle, to Emmanuel College, Cambridge, in 1589. B.A. 1592; M.A. 1596; B.D. 1603; Fellow 1595; graduated in all 'with great applause' and read the public rhetoric lecture in the schools for two years. His early poetry is lost, but he made a name with his Satires, in 1597, and Vigidemiarum in 1598. In 1599 Whitgift ordered his works, along with those of Marston and Marlow, to be burned for licentiousness, but Hall managed to obtain a reprieve for his, and soon after took holy orders, and held successively the livings of Halstead and Waltham in Essex. In 1605 he accompanied Sir Edmund Bacon to Spain dressed as a layman, and greatly impressed the Spanish clergy by his learning. Dean of Worcester 1612. Represented England at the Synod of Dort, 1618–19. Bishop of Exeter 1627. Bishop of Norwich 1641. In the same year, having questioned the validity of laws passed while the Bishops were forcibly prevented from going to the House of Lords, he was impeached and imprisoned, being released after seven months on the payment of a huge fine and the raising of even larger sureties. Laud's fall was now imminent; thereafter Hall's revenues were sequestered and he was ultimately ejected from his own house, his personal property was despoiled and he suffered vindictive persecution by the new Puritan masters of the church. He retired to a small rented farm at Higham, near Norwich, in 1647, and died there on September 8th, 1656. His published works include Contemplations, 1612; Christian Meditations, Episcopacy, Mundus Alter et Idem, The Discovery of the New World (which was described as 'scurrilous'). As a writer he was highly esteemed by his contemporaries. Fuller called him 'the English Seneca', and Pope paid him the extraordinary tribute of calling his work 'the best poetry and the truest satire in the English language'. His collected works were published in 10 volumes (ed. Josiah Pratt) in 1808, and in 12 vols. (ed. Peter Hall) in 1837–39. Biography: Autobiographical Tracts; Life by George Lewis (1868); Life of Archbishop Laud by Peter Heylin, 1668; Fuller's Worthies; Clarendon, History of the Rebellion in England; Hall's Kings Prophecie.

Righteous Mammon[1]

A Sermon preached on Monday in Easter Week, 1618

... Wealth is like vnto words, by imposition, not naturall; for commodities are as they are commonly valued; wee know, bracelets of glasse, and copper chaines, and little bels, and such like trifles, are good merchandise some-where, though contemptible with vs; and those things which the Indians regard not, Europe holds precious. What are coynes where their vse and valuation ceases? The Patars, and Souses, and Deniers, and Quart-d'escus, that are currant beyond the water, serue but for counters to vs: Thus it is with all our wealth: Consider, I beseech you, that all our Crownes, and Soueraynes, and Pieces, and halfe-pieces, and Duckets, and double Duckets, are currant but to the brim of the graue, there they cease; and we iustly laugh at the folly of those Easterne Pagans, which put coyne into the dead mans hand for his prouision in another world: What should we doe therefore, if we will be prouident Trauellers, but make ouer our money here, to receiue it by exchange in the world to come? It is our Sauiours counsell, *Make you friends of the vnrighteous Mammon, that they may receiue you into euerlasting habitations.* And as a father sayes sweetly, *If yee will bee wise Merchants, thrifty and happy vsurers, part with that which you cannot keepe, that you may gaine that which yee cannot lose;* Which that ye may doe, both in preparation of mind, and (when need is) in a charitable abdication, hearken to the Duties which God layes vpon you. The remoueall of euill must make roome for good; First therefore our Apostle would haue our hearts cleared of euill dispositions, then setled in good: The euill dispositions that do commonly attend wealth, are Pride and Misconfidence: Against these our Apostle bendeth his charge; *That they be not bye-minded; That they trust not in vncertaine riches.*

For the first; It is strange to see how this earthly drosse, which is of it selfe heauy, and therefore naturally sinkes downward, should raise vp the heart of man; and yet it commonly caries a man vp, euen to a double pitch of pride, one aboue others, the other aboue himselfe: Aboue others in contempt, aboue himselfe in oure-weening; The poore and proud is the Wise-mans monster, but the proud and rich are no newes: It is against all reason, that metals should make difference of reasonable men, of Christians; for as that wise Law giuer said, *A free man can be valued at no price:* Yet Salomon

1. *Works* (1628) p. 1,709.

noted in his time, *The rich rules the poore*; not the wife: and *Siracides* in his, *The rich speakes proudly, and what fellow is this?* and Saint *Iames* in his, The man with the gold ring lookes to sit highest. And not to cast backe our eyes, doe ye not see it thus in our times? If a man be but worth a foot-cloth, how big hee lookes on the inferiour passengers? and if he haue purchased a little more land, or title then his neighbours, you shall see it in his garbe; If he command, it is imperiously, with sirrah, and fellow; If he salute, it is ouerly, with a surly and silent nod; if he speake, it is oracles; if hee walke, it is with a grace; if he controll, it is in the killing accent; if he entertaine, it is with insolence; and whatsoeuer he doth, he is not as he was, not as the Pharise sayes, like other men. He lookes vpon vulgar men, as if they were made to serue him, and should thinke themselues happy to be commanded: and if he bee crossed a little, hee swels like the sea in a storme; Let it be by his equall, he cares more for an affront, then for death, or hell; Let it be by his inferiour, (although in a iust cause) that man shall be sure to be crusht to death for his presumption: And alas, when all is done, after these hye tearmes, all this is but a man, and (God knowes) a foolish one too, whom a little earthly trash can affect so deeply.[1]

Neither doth this pride raise a man more aboue others, then aboue himselfe; And what wonder is it if hee will not know his poore neighbours, which hath forgotten himselfe? As *Saul* was changed to another man presently vpon his anointing, so are men vpon their aduancement; and according to our ordinary Prouerb, Their good and their blood rises together; Now it may not be taken as it hath beene; Other cariage, other fashions are fit for them; Their attire, fare, retinue, houses, furniture displease them, new must be had; together with coaches, and lacquies, and all the equipage of greatnesse: These things (that no man mistake me) I mislike not; they are fit for those that are fit for them. Charity is not strait-laced, but yeelds much latitude to the lawfull vse of indifferent things; (although it is one of *Salomons* vanities, that seruants should ride on horse-backe; and hee tels vs it becomes not a swine to bee ring'd with gold) but it is the heart that makes all these euill; when that is puft vp with these windy vanities, & hath learned to borrow that part of the deuils speech, *All these things are mine*; and can say with him that was turned into a beast, *Is not this great Babel that I haue built?* or with that other patterne of pride, *I sit as a Queene, I am, and there is none beside me.* Now all these turne into sinne.

The bush that hangs out, shewes what wee may looke for within; Whither doth the conceit of a little inheritance transport the Gallants of our time? O God, what a world of vanity hast thou reserv'd vs to? I am asham'd to

---

1. In Lawrence Stone's *Crisis of the Aristocracy* useful attention is given to the turbulence of Jacobean social mobility and the manifestations of ambition and insecurity in strife, which Hall reprehends here. See pp. 199–233.

thinke that the Gospell of Christ should be disgraced with such disguised clients. Are they Christians, or Antickes in some Carnevale, or childrens puppets that are thus dressed? Pardon, I beseech you, men, brethren, and fathers, this is my iust and holy impatience, that could neuer expresse it selfe in a more solemne assembly (although I perceiue, those whom it most concernes, are not so deuout as to be present.) Who can without indignation look vp on the prodigies which this mis-imagination produces in that other sex, to the shame of their husbands, the scorne of Religion, the damnation of their owne soules? Imagine, one of our fore-fathers were aliue againe, and should see one of these his gay daughters walke in Cheape-side before him; what doe you thinke he would thinke it were? Here is nothing to be seene but a verdingale, a yellow ruffe, and a periwig, with perhaps some feather wauing in the top; three things for which he could not tell how to find a name: Sure, he could not but stand amazed, to thinke what new creature the times had yeelded since he was a man & if then he should run before her, to see if by the fore-side he might ghesse what it were, when his eyes should meet with a poudred frizle, a painted hide shadowed with a fan not more painted, brests displayed, and a loose locke erring wantonly ouer her shoulders, betwixt a painted cloth and skinne; how would he yet more blesse himselfe to thinke, what mixture in nature could bee guilty of such a monster? Is this (thinkes he) the flesh and blood? is this the hayre? is this the shape of a woman? or hath nature repented of her worke since my dayes, and begunne a new frame? It is no maruell if their forefathers could not know them; God himselfe that made them, will neuer acknowledge that face he neuer made, the hayre that hee neuer made theirs, the body that is asham'd of the Maker, the soule that thus disguises the body.[1]

Let me therefore say to these dames, as *Benet* said to *Totilaes* seruant,[2] *Depone, filia, quod portas, quia non est tuum*;[3] Lay downe that ye weare, it is none of your owne. Let me perswade them (for that can worke most) that they doe all this in their owne wrong. All the world knowes that no man will rough-cast a marble wall, but mud, or vnpolisht ragge: That beauty is like truth, neuer so glorious, as when it goes plainest; that false art, in stead of mending nature, marres it. But if none of our perswasions can preuaile. Heare this, ye garish Popingayes of our time, if you will not be ashamed to cloath your selues in this shamelesse fashion, God shall cloath

---

1. Cf. above, pp. 62–67, 79.

2. St. Benedict to Riggo, a member of King Totila's body-guard, masquerading, on orders, in his master's clothes to test the saint's powers of divination. Gregory the Great, *Vita S. Benedicti*, cap. xix.

3. Serious scholar though he was, by the standards of his day, even Hall flounders carelessly, and at times even ungrammatically when he quotes. Here he begins by making Riggo feminine: the authentic text reads, 'Pone fili, pone hoc quod portas: non est tuum.'

you with shame and confusion: heare this yee plaister-faced *Iezabels*, if you will not leaue your dawbing, and your high washes, God will one day wash them off with fire and brimstone.

I grant, it is not wealth alone that is accessary to this pride; there are some that (with the Cynicke, or that worse dogge, the patcht Cistertian) are proud of rags; there are others, that are rich of nothing but cloathes, somewhat like to *Nazianzens* country of *Ozizala*, that abounded in flowers, but was barren of corne; their cloaths are more worth then all the rest; as wee vse to say of the Elder, that the flower of it is more worth then all the tree besides; but if there be any other causes of our hye-mindednesse, wealth is one, which doth ordinarily lift vp our heads aboue our selues, aboue others, and if there be here any of these empty bladders, that are puft vp with the wind of conceit, giue me leaue to prick them a little; and first, let mee tell them they may haue much, and be neuer the better: The chimney ouer lookes all the rest of the house, is it not (for all that) the very basest piece of the building? The very heathen man could obserue (πολλοῖς ὁ δαίμων, &c.) That God giues many a man wealth for their greater mischiefe: As the Israelites were rich in Quailes, but their sawce was such, that famine had beene better; little cause had they to be proud that they were fed with meate of Princes, with the bread of Angels, whiles that which they put into their mouthes, God fetcht out of their nostrels. *Haman* was proud that he alone was called to the honour of *Esters* feast: this aduancement raised him fifty cubits higher, to a stately gibbet. If your wealth be to any of you an occasion of falling, if your gold be turned into fetters, it had beene better for you to haue liued beggers. Let me tell them next, of the folly of this pride; They are proud of that which is none of theirs. That which law and case-diuinity speakes of life, that man is not *dominus vitæ suæ, sed custos*, is as true of wealth: Nature can tell him in the Philosopher, that hee is not *Dominus*, but *Colonus*, not the Lord, but the Farmer. It is a iust obseruation of *Philo*, that God onely by a propriety is stiled the possessor of heauen and earth, by *Melchisedech*, in his speech to *Abraham*, we are onely the tenants, and that at the will of the Lord; At the most (if we will as Diuines) we haue *jus ad rem*, not *dominium in rem*, right to these earthly things, not Lordship ouer them; but right of fauour from their proprietary, and Lord in heauen, and that liable to an account. Doe we not laugh at the groome that is proud of his masters horse, or some vaine whissler, that is proud of a borrowed chaine? So ridiculous are we to be puft vp with that, whereof we must needs say, with the poore man, of the hatchet *Alas, Master, it is but borrowed*; and whereof our account shall be so much more great, and difficult, as our receit is more. Hath God therefore laded you with these earthly riches? be ye like vnto the full eare of corne, hang downe your heads in true humility towards that earth from which you came: And if your stalke be so stiffe, that it beares vp aboue the rest of your ridge, looke vp

to heauen, not in the thoughts of pride, but in the humble vowes of thankfulnesse, and be not hie-minded but feare.

Hitherto of the hye-mindednesse that followes wealth; Now where our
pride is, there will be our confidence: As the wealthy therefore may not be
proud of their riches, so they may not trust in them: What is this trust, but the
setting of our hearts vpon them, the placing of our ioy and contentment in
them; in a word, the making of them our best friend, our patron, our idoll,
our god? This the true and ielous God cannot abide, and yet nothing is
more ordinary; *The rich mans wealth in his strong City*, saith *Salomon*: & where
should a man thinke himselfe safe, but in his fort? He sees Mammon can doe
so much, and heares him talke of doing so much more, it is no maruell if hee
yeeld to trust him: Mammon is so proud a boaster, that his clients which
beleeue in him cannot chuse but be confident of him; For what doth he not
brag to doe? *Siluer answers to all*, saith *Salomon*. That we grant; although we
would be loath it could answer to truth, to iustice, to iudegment: But yet
more, he vaunts to procure all, to pacifie all, to conquer all; He saies, he can
procure all, secular offices, titles, dignities; yea (I would I might not say in
some sacrilegious and periured wretches) the sacred promotions of the
Church: and ye know that old song of the Pope, and his Romane trafficke,
Claues, Altaria, Christum: Yea foolish *Magus* makes full account, the Holy
Ghost himselfe may be had for money. He sayes he can pacifie all; *A gift in
the bosome appeases wrath*; yea, he sayes (looke to it ye that sit in the seats of
iudicature) hee can sometimes bribe off sinnes, and peruert iudgement: He
sayes hee can ouercome all, according to the old Greeke verse, *Fight with
siluer launces, and you cannot faile of victory*; yea, he would make vs beleeue he
thought this a bait to catch the Sonne of God himselfe withall (*All these will
I giue thee*). Briefly hee sayes according to the French Prouerbe, *silver does all*.

RICHARD HARRIS

By the second decade of the seventeenth century a moderate Puritan is showing signs of worry over the practical consequences of his party's general teaching. Things have gone far further than was ever intended by respectable Presbyterians. A change, not an abandonment, rather a tightening, of authority was what they had envisaged. But now artisans are neglecting their trades to bandy theology; the vulgar prefer to preach than to listen. Social disrespect and intemperate aspirations are in the air.

Richard Harris[1] had a reputation for avarice. As President of Trinity College, Oxford, he was noted for the exorbitant fines he imposed. He could preach heart-rendingly and was one of the six divines empowered in 1647 to invade any pulpit and preach where they thought fit. His wife suffered from religious mania.

Portents of Dissolution

God's Goodness and Mercie Laid open in a sermon
Preached at Paul's Crosse on the last of June, 1622 by
Master Robert Harris, Pastor of the church of God at
Hanwell, Oxfordshire.

... I blush, I bleed to speak it, able men are ready to hyre out themselves for bread, and excellent wits hang the head for want of watering, gasping like fishes out of the water, being out of all, both meanes and hopes. If there be any true bloud yet running in your veines, you that can feed Birds and

1. Richard Harris, 1581–1658. B.A. Magdalen Hall, Oxford, 1600; B.D. 1614. Presented to the living of Hanwell, Oxfordshire, by Sir Anthony Coke, 1614. Accused but not convicted of pluralism. Famous for his preaching at church of St. Paul and St. Saviour's, Southwark. President of Trinity College, Oxford, 1648, in place of ejected Hannibal Potter. Visitor to University, 1654–58.

Dogs, starve not Grace and Learning. Children might be Schollars, Schollars Preachers, Preachers Saviours, and that of thousands, did not dog eate the Childrens bread.

Secondly, you must ayme at the common good, for that is still the greatest good; and heere two rules, first, if you will be for the publicke, you must be good in private: beare your owne fruit, worke in your owne hives, man your owne oares, and make good your owne standing. Happy is that body, wherein the eye sees, the eare heares, the liver sanguifies, &c. Happy that house, wherein the Master rules, the man runs, the head leades, and the body followes: Happy that State, wherein the Cobler meddles with his last, the Tradesman with his shop, the Student with his booke, the Counseller with State, the Prince with the Scepter, and each Creature lives in his owne Element; but woe bee to the Heathens Army, when all will be Captaines, and none Souldiers, woe to that body that will bee all head; members misplaced are neither for vse nor ease.

Secondly, we must shoote at the common white, that is, though you be private in your standings, yet you must be publicke in your affections, and intendements.

For the first; I meane affections, as King *Richard* bestowed himselfe diversly at his death, so must we in life; *Bohemia* claimes a part in our love, the *Palatinate* a part, the *Churches* abroad, our *Brethren* at home a part: at home, in selling we must be buyers, in lending borrowers, in visiting patients, in comforting mourners; abroad, we must in our owne peace consider their warres, feele them panting, see them bleeding, heare them scriching; O *husband, O wife, O my childe, my childe, O mother, mother, mother, my father is slaine, my brother is torne, my legge is off, my guts be out, halfe dead, halfe alive, worse then eyther, because neyther,* O that we had hearts to bleed over them, and to pray for the peace of *Ierusalem.*

For the second, our thoughts must all meete in the common-good, like so many lines in a Center, streames in the Sea; Christ Iesus *pleased not himselfe,* saith S. *Paul*; *He dyed for us,* saith S. *Iohn,* therefore we must for our brethren; one member will dye for all, one Heathen for many; if we must dye for the common-good, must wee not live to it? If all must, must not the more publique persons? Yes you Lawyers (to instance) must be common blessings, and not seeke your owne, you must (with *Papinian*) reject bad causes, and ripen good; there goes but a paire of Sheares betweene a protracting Lawyer, and cheating Mountebanke, that sets his Client backward and forward like a man at Chesse, and proves a butcher to the filly sheepe, which ranne to him from the Drover. . . .

JAMES USHER

The Irishman, James Usher, Archbishop of Armagh, was left of centre in the church. Like James Hall, an Episcopalian Calvinist, but doctrinally more severe, he was esteemed one of the most learned men of his age, and, a prodigious bibliophile, he laid the main foundations of the great library of Trinity College, Dublin. Again, like Hall, he sought a middle-way resolution of modified episcopalianism, but the zealots on neither side desired a peaceful compromise.

Usher's stature and integrity were such that, although he was unswervingly loyal to Charles in the Civil War, Cromwell treated him with deference. By all accounts the Archbishop was of sweet and gentle nature, but there is little hint of this in the doctrine of his sermon on damnation, probably preached first in 1620, when he was Bishop of Meath.

In the Calvinists' hell, it seems, if that be our terminus, we need expect to reserve to ourselves no element of our character which might be of comfort. If in this life we had a measure of courage, or patience, or resolution—anything of fortitude or dignity—it will be taken from us, and nothing left but unrelieved, perpetual abjection in terror, anguish and agony. It is the ultimate expression of metaphysical anti-humanism. How a character can be radically modified and still be the character condemned to suffer is not justified or explained; but doubtless the question would present no difficulties to a philosophy of pre-destined damnation.

The Natural Man is a Dead Man[1] (c. 1620)

... Now all these excellent gifts and natural endowments which did adorn a wicked mans soul, before the soul is hurled into hell, must be taken away from him. There is a kind of degradation of the soul, it is depriested as it were, and becomes like a *degraded Knight* that hath his honour taken from him. All the rich talents, and all the rich prizes that were put into the fools

1. *Eighteen Sermons* (1660), pp. 138–144. Dated uniformly 1640 but probably not all of the same vintage.

hand, shall be taken from him. Is there any moral vertue? Are there any common graces and natural endowments in the miserable soul? it shall be stript of all, and packt to hell. You that have abused your learning and gifts that God hath given you, do you think that they shall go with you to hell? No such matter, you shall be very sots and dunces there. All your learning shall be taken from you, and you shall goe to hell arrant blockheads. He that had fortitude in this world, shall not carry one drachm of it to hell: all his courage shall then be abased, and his cowardly heart shall faint for fear. Fortitude is a great advantage to a man in distresse, but let not the damned soul expect the least advantage: his fortitude which he had whilst he was in the way, shall be taken from him. It may be he had patience in this world. Now patience is a vertue unfit for hell, therefore shall that be taken from him. A man if he were in most exquisite torments, yet if he had patience, it would bear it up with head and shoulders (as we say) but this shall adde to his torments, that he shall not have any patience left him to allay it. A man hath perhaps hope in this world, and, as the Proverb is, were it not for hope the heart would burst; yet even this too shall be taken away from him, he shall have no hope left him of ever seeing Gods face again, or of ever having any more tasts of his favour: And so what hath been said of some, may be said of all his graces and endowments: he shall clean be stript of all ere he be sent to hell.

I come now to speak of the place of torment it self, wherein the sinner is to be cast eternally, which is the second act. But think not that I am able to discover the thousandth part of it, no nor any man else: God grant that no soul here present ever come to find by experience what it is. What a woful thing is it, that many men should take more paines to come to this place of torment, then would cost them to goe to heaven, that men should wilfully run themselves upon the pikes, not considering how painful it is, nor how sharp those pikes are: And this I shall endeavour to my power to set forth unto you. This Text contains a Catalogue of that black Roll (though there are many more then are here expressed) but here are the grand crimes, the ring-leaders to destruction, the mother sins. And here we have in the first place the *Fearful*: whereby is not meant those that are of a timorous nature (for fear simply is not a sin) those that are simply fearful; but *such as place their fear on a wrong object, not where it should be*: that fear not God, but other things more then God. Such as if affliction and iniquity were put to their choise, will *rather choose iniquity then affliction*: Rather then they will have any cross betide them, rather then they will incur the indignation of a man, rather then they will part with their life and goods for Gods cause, will adventure on any thing, *choosing iniquity rather then affliction*; being afraid of what they should not fear, never fearing the great and mighty God: This is the fearful here meant. See how *Job* expresses it, *Job* 36.31. *This hast thou chosen. This* (that is) *iniquity rather then affliction: to sin rather then to suffer.* Christ biddeth us *not to fear poor vain man, but the omnipotent God, that is able to kill and to cast into hell.* The man that feareth his Landlord, who is able to turn him out of his house, and doth not fear God, who is able to turn him into hell, this dastardly spirit is one of the Captains of those that goe to hel, those timerous and cowardly persons, that tremble at the wrath or frowns of men, more then of God. . . . The greatest man that lives cannot shield himself from death, and from a covering of worms, and wilt thou *be afraid of a man, and forget the Lord thy Maker?* The more thou art taken up with the fear of man, the lesse thou fearest God; and the more thou remembrest man, the more thou forgettest thy Maker.

You have seen the main, the ring-leaders, which are these fearful, faithlesse, dastardly, unbelieving men.

Now see what the filthy rabble is that followeth after, and they are *Abominable, Murtherers,* &c. *Abominable,* that is, *unnatural,* such as pollute themselves with things not fit to be named, but to be abhorred, whether it be by themselves, or with others. They are the *abominable* here meant, such as *Sodome* and *Gomorrah,* who were *set forth to such as an example, suffering the vengeance of eternal fire,* Jude *v.* 7. such are *abominable,* being given up to unnatural lust. Let them carry it never so secretly, yet are they here ranked amongst the rest, and shall have their portion in the burning lake.

After these come *Sorcerers, Idolaters, Lyars:* Though these may be spoken fairly of by men, yet cannot that shelter them from the wrath of God, they shall likewise have their part in this lake when they come to a reckoning. If there be, I say, a generation of people that worship these, say what you will of them, when they come to receive their wages, they *shall receive their portion in that burning lake with hypocrites:* Those that make so fair a shew before men, and yet nourish hypocrisie in their hearts, these men, though in regard of the outward man they so behave themselves that none can say to them, *black is their eye,* though they cannot be charged with those notorious things before mentioned; yet if there be nothing but hypocrisie in their hearts, let it be spun with never so fair a web, never so fine a thred, yet they shall have their portion in the lake, they shall have their part, their portion, *&c.* Then it seems these of this black guard have a peculiar interest unto this place. And as it is said of *Judas,* Acts 1.25. *that he was gone* εἰς τὸν ἴδιον τόπον, *to his proper place.* So long as a man that is an enemy to Christ, and yeilds him not obedience, is out of hell, so long is he out of his place. Hell is the place assigned to him, and prepared for him; he hath a share there, and his part and portion he must have: till he come thither he is but a wanderer. The *Evangelist* tells us that the *Scribes and Pharisees* went about to gain Proselytes, and when they had all done, they made them *seven times more the children of hell then themselves, filios Gehennæ:* So that a Father hath not more right in his son, then Hell hath in them: He is a vessel of wrath fill'd top full of iniquity, and a child of the Devils: So that as we say, *the gallows will claim its right*, so hell will claim its due. But mistake me not, all this that I speak concerning Hell, is not to terrifie and affright men, but by forewarning them to keep them thence. For after I have shewn you the danger, I shall shew you a way to escape it, and how the Lord Jesus was given to us to deliver us from this danger: But if you will not hear, but will try conclusions with God, then you must *to your proper place, to the lake that burneth with fire and brimstone.*

A Lake 'tis, a River, a flaming River, as *Tophet* is described to be a *lake burning with fire and brimstone*, a Metaphor taken from the judgment of God on *Sodome* and *Gomorrah*, as in that place of St. *Jude* before mentioned, as also in 2 *Pet.* 2.6. where 'tis said *God turned the Cities of Sodom into ashes, making them an example to all them that should after live ungodly.* Mark the judgment of God upon these abominable men, the place where they dwelt is destroyed with fire, and the situation is turn'd into a lake full of filthy bituminous stuff called *Lacus Asphaltites*, which was made by their burnings. And this is made an instance of the vengeance of God, and an Embleme of eternal fire; therefore said he, *you shall have your portion with Sodome.* Nay, shall I speak a greater word (with Christ) and tell you, that though they were so abominable, that the Lake was denominated from them, yet it shall be *easier for Sodome and Gomorrah then for you*, if you repent not while you may, but goe on to despise Gods grace.[1] But can there be a greater sin then the sin of *Sodome*? I answer yes. For make the worst of the sin of *Sodome*, it is but a sin against *nature*. But thy impenitency is a sin against grace, and against the Gospels and therefore deserves a hotter hell, and an higher measure of judgment in this burning pit. . . .

1. An exemplary Calvinist mind, having repudiated the concept of human 'free will to good', appears constrained in practice to treat the same concept as an inescapable element of reality. Lines 25–29, p. 226, summarize the doctrinal anomaly.

LANCELOT ANDREWES

A Cold Coming[1]

A sermon preached before the King's Majesty at
Whitehall, on Monday, the XXV December A.D.
MDCXXII, being Christmas day.

Now, for *venimus*, their *comming* it self. And it follows well. For, it is not a
star only, but a *Load-star*: And whither should *stella Ejus ducere*, but *ad Eum*?
whither lead us, but to *Him*, whose the *star* is? to the *Stars Master*.

All this while we have been at *dicentes*, saying and seeing: Now we shall
come to *Facientes*, see them do somewhat upon it. It is not *saying* or *seeing*
will serve St. *James*: He will call, and be still calling for *Ostende mihi, shew me*
thy Faith by some Work. And, well may he be allowed to call for it, this
Day: It is the day of *Vidimus*, appearing, Being seen. You have seen His star:
Let Him now see your star, another while. And so, they do. Make your faith
to be seen: So it is: Their *Faith*, in the *steps* of their *Faith*. And, so was
Abraham's, first, by *comming* forth of his countrey; As, these here do, and so
walk in the steps of the faith of Abraham; do his first work.

It is not commanded, to stand *gazing into heaven* too long, Not *on* Christ
Himselfe ascending: much lesse on His *star*. For, they sate not still gazing on
the *star*. Their *Vidimus* begat *Venimus*; their *seeing* made them *come*; come a
great journey. *Venimus* is soon said; but a *short word*: But, many a wide and
weary step they made before they could come to say *Venimus, Lo, here we
are come*; *Come*, and at our journeyes end. To look a little on it. In this their
Comming, we consider, 1. First, the *distance* of the Place they came from. It
was not hard by, as the *shepherds* (but a step to *Bethlehem* over the fields:) This
was riding many hundred miles, and cost them many a dayes journey. 2.
Secondly, we consider the *way*, that they came: if it be *pleasant*, or plain and
easie: For, if it be, it is so much the better. This was nothing *pleasant*; for
through *desarts*; all the way waste and desolate. Nor (secondly) *easie* neither,
For, over the rocks and crags of both *Arabies* (specially *Petræa*) their journey
lay. 3. Yet if safe: But it was not; but exceeding dangerous, as lying through

1. Andrewes, op. cit., Sermon Fifteen (on Mat. II, 1, 2).

the middest of the *Black Tents of Kedar*, a Nation of *Thieves* and cut-throats; to passe over the *hils* of *Robbers*; Infamous then, and infamous to this day. No passing without great troops of convoy. 4. Last we consider the *time* of their *comming*, the season of the year. It was no *summer progresse*. A cold *comming* they had of it, at this time of the year; just the worst time of the year, to take a journey, and specially a long journey in. The wayes deep, the weather sharp, the dayes short, the sun farthest off in *solstitio brumali*, the very dead of *Winter*, *Venimus*, We are come, if that be one; *Venimus*, We are (now) come, come at this time, that (sure) is another.

And these difficulties they overcame, of a *weary-some, irk-some, trouble-some, dangerous, unseasonable* journey: And for all this, they came. And, came it cheerfully, and quickly; As appeareth by the speed they made. It was but *vidimus, venimus* with them; They *saw*, and they *came*: No sooner *saw*, but they set out presently. So, as upon the first appearing of the *star* (as it might be, last night) they knew it was *Balaam's star*; it called them away, they made ready straight to begin their journey this morning. A signe they were highly conceited of His *Birth*, believed some great matter of it, that they took all these paines, made all this haste, that they might be there to *worship Him*, with all the possible speed they could. Sory for nothing so much, but that they could not be there soon enough, with the very first to do it even this *day*, the *day* of His *birth*. All considered, there is more in *venimus* than shews at the first sight. It was not for nothing, it was said (in the first verse) *Ecce venorunt*; their *comming* hath an *Ecce* on it: it well deserves it.

And we, what should we have done? Sure, these men of the *East*, shall *rise in judgment against the men of the West*, that is, us: and their *faith*, against ours, in this point. With them it was but *vidimus, venimus*: With us, it would have been but *veniemus* at most. Our fashion is, to see and see again, before we stirre a foot: Specially, if it be to the worship of Christ. Come such a Journey, at such a time? No: but fairly have put it off till the spring of the year, till the dayes longer, and the wayes fairer, and the weather warmer: till better travelling to Christ. Our *Epiphany* would sure have fallen in *Easter-week* at the soonest.

But then, for the *distance, desolatenesse, tediousnesse*, and the rest, any of them were enough to mar our *venimus* quite. It must be no great way (first) we must come: we love not that. Well fare the *Shepherds* yet, they came but hard by: Rather like them than the *Magi*. Nay, not like them neither. For, with us, the *nearer* (lightly) the *furthest off*: Our Proverb is (you know) *The nearer the Church the farther from God*.

Nor, it must not be through a *Desart*, over no *Petræ*. If rugged or uneven the way; if the weather ill disposed; If any never so little danger, it is enough to stay us. To *Christ* we cannot travel, but weather and way and all must be fair. If not, no journey but sit still and see further. As indeed, all our Religion is rather *vidimus*, a *Contemplation*, than *Venimus*, *a Motion*, or stirring to be ought.

But when we do it, we must be allowed leasure. Ever, *veniemus*; never *venimus*: Ever *comming*; never come. We love to make no very great haste. To other things perhaps: Not to *Adorare*, the Place of the worship of God. Why should we, *Christ*, is no Wild-Cat.[1] What talk you of *twelve* dayes? And if it be *forty dayes* hence, ye shall be sure to find His mother and Him; She cannot be Churched till then: What needs such haste? The truth is, we conceit Him and His *Birth* but slenderly, and our haste is even thereafter. But, if we be at that point, we must be out of this *Venimus*: they like enough to leave us behind. Best, get us a new *Christ-masse* in *September*: we are not like to come to *Christ* at this *Feast*. Enough, for *venimus*.

1. This metaphor, which has appealed to many critics as bold originality, is, in fact, an entirely traditional employment of a received mediaeval antecedent. 'The cherche is non hare: there men leve it they may fynde it.' *Jacob's Well*, EETS, p. 141.

SAMUEL WARD[1]

Andrewes' sermons were not a digestible diet for the generality. The following sermon, preached in Suffolk, near Ipswich, represents staple fare. Its preacher, Samuel Ward, was not quite as priggish as he sounds. He kept a diary at Cambridge in which his own modest susceptibilities to temptation are recorded.

June 21st. 1595	My too much drinking after supper. . . .
September 15th. 1595	My too much gluttony at dinner time.
October 3rd. 1595	My immoderate eating of walnuts and cheese after supper.
February 1st. 1596	Oh, the Greevous sinne. Trinity College which had a woman which went from chamber to chamber in the night tyme. My adultrous dreams that night.
September 8th. 1596	. . . my goyng to the taverne with such lewd fellowes. How little grieved was I att ther swearing and otheese and wyld talk. . . .[2]

Ward's sermon, *Woe To Drunkards*, lived on after its author, to enjoy quite a vogue in the disrespectful dayso f the Restoration. The printed version has been modified and probably enlarged by the preacher.

---

1. Samuel Ward, 1577–1640. Born Suffolk. St. John's College, Cambridge, on the nomination of Lord Burghley. B.A. 1596; Fellow of Sidney, Sussex, 1599; M.A. 1600. Lecturer at Haverhill. 1603 appointed preacher at St. Mary-le-Tower, where he remained for thirty years (vacating his fellowship on marriage in 1604). In 1621 he was briefly imprisoned for drawing an anti-papist caricature which offended Count Gondomar. Afterwards he was occasionally, but, thanks to the tolerance of Archbishop Williams, never seriously, in trouble, until, in 1636, Laud caused him to be suspended from preaching and ordered to recant his pulpit condemnations of 'bowing' and *The Book of Sports*. Withdrew to Holland for a time, but in 1638 he was back in Ipswich, negotiating the purchase of a house. *Collection of Sermons and Treatises* published 1627–28, and 1636. Reprinted Edinburgh (ed. Rev. J. C. Ryle), 1862.

2. M. Knappen, *Two Puritan Diaries* (1933).

Woe to Drunkards (1622)[1]

Proverbs. 23. 29–32. To whom is woe? To whom is sorrow? To whom is strife?
etc.[2]

In the end it will bite like a serpent and sting like a cockatrice.

Seer, art thou also blind? Watchman, art thou also blind or asleep. Or hath a
spirit of slumber put out thine eyes? Up to thy watch tower! What decriest
thou? Ah, Lord, what end or number is there of the vanities which mine eies
are weary of beholding? I see men walking like the tops of trees shaken with
the winds, like masts of Ships reeling on the tempestious Seas. Drunkenesse,
I meane, that hatefull Night-bird; which was wont to wait for the twi-light,
to seeke nooks & corners, to avoid the howting and wonderment of boyes
and girles; Now as it were some Eglet to dare the Sunlight, to fly abroad at
high noone in every street, in open Markets & Faires without feare or shame,
without controle or punishment, to the disgrace of the Nation, the outfacing
of Magistracy & Ministry, the utter undoing (without timely prevention) of
health and wealth, Piety and Virtue, Towne and Countrey, Church &
Common wealth. And dost thou like a dombe dog hold thy peace at these
things, dost thou with *Solomons* sluggard fould thine hands in thy bosome,
and give thy selfe to ease and drowsines, while the envious man causeth the
noisomst & basest of weeds to overrun the choisest *Eden* of God? Vp &
arise, lift up thy voice, spare not and cry aloud. What shal I cry? Cry, woe
and woe againe unto the Crowne of pride, the drunkards of *Ephraim.* Take
up a Parable, & tell them, how it stingeth like the *Cokatrice,* declare unto
them the deadly poyson of this odious sin. Shew them also the soveraign
Antidot & cure of it, in the Cup that was drunke off by him, that was able
to overcome it: cause them to behold the brazen Serpent & be healed. And
what though some of these deafe Adders will not bee charmed nor cured,
yea though few or none of these Swinish heard of habituall drunkards, accustomed to wallow in their mire, yea deeply and irrecoverably plunged by
legions of devils into the dead sea of their filthines: what if not one of them
will be washed, and made cleane, but turne againe to their vomit, and trample
the pearles of all admonition under feet; yea, turne againe, & rend their re-
proovers with scoffes and scornes, making jests and songs on their Alebench:

1. Published 1627.   2. Geneva (1560 and 1586 edns.)

Yet may some young ones be deterred, and some Novices reclaimed, some
Parents & Magistrats awakened to prevent and suppresse the spreading of
this Gangrene: And God have his work in such as belong to his grace. And
what is impossible to the worke of his grace?

Goe to then now yee Drunkards, listen not what I, or any ordinary
Hedge-priest (as you stile us) but that most wise & experienced royall
Preacher, hath to say unto you. And because you are a dull and thicke eared
generation, he first deales with you by way of question, a figure of force
and impression. *To whom is Woe? &c.* You use to say, Woe be to hypocrits.
'Its true, woe be to such and all other witting and willing sinners, but there
are no kind of offenders on whom woe doth so palpably inevitably attend as
to you Drunkards. You promise your selues mirth, pleasure, and jollitie in
your Cups; but for one drop of your mad mirth, be sure of gallons, and tuns
of woe, gall, wormewood, and bitternesse here and hereafter. Other sinners
shall taste of the cup, but you shall drinke of the dregs of Gods wrath and
displeasure. *To whom is strife.* You talke of good fellowship and friendship,
but wine is a rager and tumultuous make-bate, and sets you a quarrelling,
and meddling. When wit's out of the head and strength out of the body, it
thrusts even Cowards and dastards unfenced & unarmed into needlesse
frayes and combats. And then to whom are wounds, broken heads, blue eyes,
maymed limmes? You have a drunken by-word. Drunkards take no harme,
but how many are the mishaps and untimely mis-fortunes that betide such,
which though they feele not in drinke, they carry as marks and brands to their
grave. You pretend you drinke healthes, and for health, but to whom are all
kind of diseases, infirmities, deformities, pearled faces, palsies, dropsies,
headaches? If not to drunkards.

Vpon these premises he forcibly inferes his sober and serious advise.
Looke upon these wofull effects and evills of drunkennesse, and looke not
upon the Wine, looke upon the blue woundes, upon the red eyes it causeth,
and looke not on the red colour when it sparkleth in the Cup. If there were
no worse then these, yet would no wise man bee overtaken with Wine: as
if he should say, What see you in the Cup or drinke, that countervaileth
these dreggs that lye in the bottome. Behold, this is the Sugar you are to
looke for, and the tang it leaves behinde. Woe and alas, sorrow and striefe,
shame, poverty, and diseases; these are enough to make it odious, but that
which followeth withall, will make it hideous and fearefull. For *Salomon*
duely considering that he speaks to man past shame and grace, senselesse of
blowes, and therefore much more of reasons and words, insisteth not upon
these petty woes; which they, bewitched and besotted with the love of Wine,
will easily oversee and overleape: but sets before their eyes the direful end and
fruit, the blacke and poysonfull taile of this sinne. *In the end it stingeth like
the Serpent, it biteth like the Cockatice,* (Or *Adder*) saith our new Translation.

... And why indeed (without a miracle) should any expect that one stung with this Viper should shake it off, and ever recover of it againe. Yea, so far are they from recovering themselves, that they infect and become contagious and pestilent to all they come neere. The Dragon infusing his venom, and assimulating his elfes to himselfe in no Sin so much as in this, that it becomes as good as meat and drinke to them, to spend their wits and mony to compasse Alehouse after Alehouse, yea, Towne after Towne, to transforme others with their Circean cups, till they have made them bruits and swine worse than themselves. The Adulterer and Vsurer desire to injoy their Sin alone, but the chiefest pastime of a drunkard is to heat and overcome others with wine, that he may discover their nakednesse, and glory in their foyle and folly. In a word, excesse of wine, and the spirit of grace are opposites, the former expels the later out of the heart, as smoake doth Bees out of the Hive: and makes the man a meere slave and prey to Satan and his snares, when by this poyson he hath put out his eyes, and spoyled him of his strength; hee useth him as the Philistines did *Sampson*, leads him in a string whither hee pleaseth like a very drudge, scorne and make-sport to himselfe and his Imps; makes his grind in the Mill of all kind of Sinnes and vices. And that I take to be the reason why Drunkennesse is not specially prohibited in any one of the ten Commandements, because it is not the single breach of any one, but in effect the violation of all and every one: it is no one Sin, but all Sins, because it is the In-let and sluce to all other Sins. The Devill having moystened and steeped him in his liquor, shapes him like soft clay into what mould he pleaseth: having shaken off his Rudder and Pilot, dashes his soule upon what rocks, sands, and Syrts hee listeth, and that with as much ease as a man may push down his body with the least thrust of his hand or finger. He that in his right wits and sober mood seemes religious, modest, chaste, courteous, secret; in his drunken fits sweares, blasphemes, rages, strikes, talkes filthily, blabs all secrets, commits folly, knowes no difference of persons or sexes, becomes wholly at Satans command, as a dead Organ to be enacted at his will and pleasure. Oh that God would be pleased to open the eyes of some drunkard, to see what a dunghill and carrion his soule becomes, and how loathsome effects follow upon this spiritual death, and sting of this Cockatrice, which is the fountaine of the other two following, temporall and eternall death.

An Ale-wife in Kesgrave, near to Ipswich who would needs force three serving men (that had been drinking in her house and were taking their leave) to stay and drinke the three Outs first (that is, Wit out of the head, Money out of the purse, and Ale out of the Pot) as she was coming towards them with the pot in her hand, was suddenly taken speechless and sick, her tongue swolne in her mouth never recovered speech, the third day after dyed. This Sir *Anthony Felton* the next Gentleman and Iustice, with divers other eye-witnesses of her in sicknesse related to mee; whereupon I went to the house with two or three witnesses, inquired the truth of it.

Two servants of a Brewer in *Ipswich*, drinking for a rumpe of a Turky, struggling in their drinke for it, fell into a scalding Caldron backwards: whereof the one dyed presently, the other lingringly, and painfully, since my coming to *Ipswich*.

Anno 1619. A Miller in *Bromeswell*, comming home drunke from *Wood-bridge* (as he oft did) would needs goe and swim in the Mill-pond: his wife and servants, knowing hee could not swim, disswaded him, once by intreaty got him out of the water, but in hee would needs goe againe, and there was drowned, I was at the house to inquire of this, and found it to be true.

In *Barnwell* neere to *Cambridge*, one at the Signe of the *Plough*, a lusty yong man, with two of his neighbours, and one woman in their company; agreed to drinke a Barrell of strong Beere; they drunke up the vessell, three of them dyed within foure and twenty houres, the fourth hardly escaped after great sicknesse. This is have under a Iustice of Peace his hand neere dwelling, besides the common fame.

A Butcher in *Hasling-field*, hearing the Minister inveigh against Drunken-nesse, being at his cups in the Ale-house, fell a jeasting and scoffing at the Minister and his Sermons. As he was drinking, the drink, or something in the cup quackled him, stuck so in his throat that hee could not get it up nor downe, but strangled him presently.

At *Tillingham* in Dengy Hundred in Essex, three young men meeting to drinke strong waters, fell by degrees to halfe pints: one fell dead in the roome, and the other prevented by company comming in, escaped not without much sicknesse.

At *Bungey* in Norfolke, three comming out of an Alehouse in a very darke evening, swore, they thought it was not darker in hell it selfe: one of them fell off the bridge into the water, and was drowned; the second fell off his Horse, the third sleeping on the ground by the Rivers side, was frozen to death. This have I often heard, but have no certaine ground for the truth of it.

A Bayliffe of *Hadly* upon the Lords day being drunke at *Melford*, would needs get upon his Mare to ride through the street, affirming (as the report goes) that his Mare would carry him to the Devill; his Mare casts him off, and broke his necke instantly. Reported by sundry sufficient witnesses.

Company drinking in an Alehouse at *Harwich* in the night, over against one Master *Russels*, and by him out of his window once or twice willed to depart; at length he came downe and tooke one of them, and made as if he would carry him to prison, who drawing his Knife, fled from him, and was three dayes after taken out of the sea with the Knife in his hand. Related to me by Master *Russell* himselfe, Major of the Towne.

At *Tenby* in Pembrokeshire, A Drunkard being exceeding drunke, broke himselfe all to pieces off an high and steepe rocke in a most fearefull manner, and yet the occasion and circumstances of his fall so ridiculous, as I thinke not fit to relate, lest in so serious a judgement I should move laughter to the Reader.

A Glasier in *Chauncery Lane* in London, noted formerly for profession, fell to a common course of drinking, whereof being oft by his wife and many Christian friends admonished, yet presuming much of Godd's mercy to himselfe, continued therein, till upon a time having surcharged his stomacke with drinke, he fell a vomiting, broke a Veine, lay two dayes in extreame paine of body and distresse of mind, till in the end recovering a little comfort, hee died: both these examples related to mee by a Gentleman of worth upon his owne knowledge.

Foure sundry instances of Drunkards wallowing and tumbling in their drinke, slaine by Carts, I forbeare to mention, because such examples are so common and ordinary.

A Yeomans Sonne in Northhamptonshire being drunke at *Wellingborough* on a Market day, would needs ride his Horse in a bravery over the plowed lands, fell from his Horse and brake his necke: reported to me by a Kinsman of his owne.

A Knight notoriously given to Drunkennesse, carrying sometimes pailes of drinke into the open field to make people drunke withall; being upon a time drinking with company, a woman comes in, delivering him a Ring with this Poesie, *Drincke and die*, saying to him, This is for you; which he tooke and wore, and within a week after came to his end by drinking: reported by sundry, and justified by a Minister dwelling within a mile of the place.

Two examples have I knowne of children that murthered their owne Mothers in drinke, and one notorious Drunkard, that attempted to kill his father; of which being hindered, hee fired his Barne, and was afterward executed: one of these formerly in print.

At a Taverne in *Breadstreet* in London, certaine Gentlemen drinking Healths to their Lords, on whom they had dependance; one desperate wretch steps to the Tables end, layes hold on a Pottlepot full of Canary Sacke, sweares a deepe oath; What will none here drinke a health to my noble Lord and Master? and so setting the Pottle-pot to his mouth; drinkes it off to the bottome, was not able to rise up, or to speake when hee had done, but fell into a deep snoaring sleepe, and being removed, laid aside, and covered by one of the servants of the house, attending the time of the drinking, was within the space of two houres irrecoverably dead: witnessed at the time of the printing hereof by the same servant that stood by him in the Act, and helpt to remove him.

In *Dengy Hundred*, neere *Mauldon*, about the beginning of his Majesties raigne, there fell out an extraordinary judgement upon five or sixe that plotted a solemne drinking at one of their houses, layd in Beere for the once, drunke healthes in a strange manner, and dyed thereof within a few weekes, some sooner, and some later: witnessed to me by one, that was with one of them on his death-bed, to demand a debt, and often spoken of by Master *Heydon*, late Preacher of *Mauldon*, in the hearing of many: the particular circumstances were exceeding remarkable, but having not sufficient proofe for the particulars, I will not report them.

One of *Aylesham* in *Norfolke*, a notorious drunkard, drowned in shallow Brooke of water with his Horse by him.

Whilst this was at the Presse, a man 85. yeares old, or thereabout, in *Suffolke*, overtaken with Wine, (though never in all his life before, as hee himselfe said a little before his fall, seeming to bewaile his present condition, and others that knewe him so say of him) yet going down a paire of staires, (against the perswasion of a woman sitting by him in his Chamber) fell, and was so dangerously hurt, as he dyed soon after, not being able to speak from the time of his fall to his death.

The names of the parties thus punished, I forebeare for the kindreds sake yet living.

If thou beest yet insensate with wine, voyd of wit and feare, I know not what further to mind thee of, but of that third, and worst sting of all the rest, which will ever be gnawing, and never dying: which if thou wilt not feare here; sure thou art to feele there, when the Red Dragon hath gotten thee into his den, and shall fill thy soule with the gall of Scorpions, where thou shalt yell and howle for a drop of water to coole thy tongue withall, and shalt be denied so small a refreshing, and have no other liquor to allay thy thirst, but that which the lake of Brimstone shall afford thee. And that worthily, for that thou wouldest incurre the wrath of the Lambe for so base and sordid a Sin as drunkenesse, of which thou mayest thinke as venially and slightly as thou wilt. But Paul that knew the danger of it, gives thee faire warning and bids thee not deceive thy selfe, expressly, and by name mentioning it among the mortall Sins, excluding from the kingdome of heaven. And the Prophet *Esay* tels thee, that for it *Hell* hath enlarged it selfe, opened it's mouth wide, and without measure; and therefore shall the multitude and their pomp, and the jolliest among them descend into it.

All this while, little hope have I to work upon Drunkards, ... my main drift is, to stirre up the spirits of Parents and Masters, who in all places complaine of this evill, robbing them of good servants, and dutifull children, by all care and industry to prevent it in their Domesticall education, by carrying a watchfull and restraining hand over them. Parents, if you love either soule or body, thrift or piety, looke to keepe them form the infection. Lay all the barres of your authority, cautions, threats and charges for the avoyding of this epidemicall pestilence. If any of them be bitten of this Cockatrice, sleepe not, rest not, till you have cured them of it, if you love their health, husbandry, grace, their present or future lives. Dead are they while they live, if they live in this sin. Mothers, lay about you as *Bathsheba*, with all entreaties; What my sonne, my sonne of my loves and delights, Wine is not for you, &c.

My next hope is, to arouse and awaken the vigilancie of all faithfull Pastors and Teachers. I speake not to such Stars as this Dragon hath swept downe from heaven with its tayle: for of such the Prophets, the Fathers of the Primitive, yea, all ages to complaine of. I hate and abhorre to mention this abomination: to alter the Proverbe, *As drunke as a Begger*, to a Gentleman is odious; but to a Man of God, to an Angell, how harsh and helish a sound is it in a Christians eares? I speake therefore to sober Watchmen, *Watch and be sober*, and labour to keepe your Charges sober and watchfull, that they may bee so found of him that comes like a thiefe in the night. Two meanes have you of great vertue for the quelling of this Serpent, zealous preaching and praying against it. Its an old received Antidote, that mans spittle, especially fasting spittle, is mortall to Serpents. Saint *Donatus* is famous in story for spitting upon a Dragon[1] that kept an high way, and devoured many passengers. This have I made good observation of, that where God hath raised up zealous Preachers, in such townes this Serpent hath no nestling, no stabling or denning. If this will not doe, *Augustine* enforceth another, which I conceive Gods and Mans lawes allow us upon the reason he gives: If *Paul* (saith hee) forbid to eate with such our common bread in our owne private houses, how much more the Lords body in Church assemblies: if in our times this were strictly observed, the Serpent would soone languish and vanish. In the time of an Epidemicall disease, such as the Sweating, or Neezing sicknesse, a wise Physician would leave the study of all other diseases to find out the cure of the present raging evill. If *Chrysostome* were now alive, the bent of all his Homilies, or at least one part of them should be spent to cry downe drunkennesse, as hee did swearing in *Antioch*: never desisting to reprove it, till (if not the feare of God, yet) his importunity, made them weary of the sinne.

... Who sees and knowes not, that some one needlesse Ale-house in a countrey Towne, undoes all the rest of the houses in it, eating up the thrift and fruit of their labours; the ill manner of sundry places, being there to meet in some one night of the weeke, and spend what they have gathered, and spared all the dayes of the same before, to the prejudice of their poore wives

---

1. St. Donatus of Arezzo A.D. 363: the dragon resided in and poisoned a wayside well and, when it emerged one day and wound its tail round the leg of Bishop Donatus, the saint 'smote him with his staff, or as some say spat in his face.' See 'Donatus' in *Golden Legends*, Caxton's translation of Jacobus de Voraigne's *Legenda Aurora* (1470). The reference is in vol. iv of the Temple Classics edition (1900).

and children at home; and upon the Lords day (after evening Prayers) there to quench and drowne all the good lessons they have heard that day at Church. If this goe on, what shall become of us in time? If woe be to single drunkards, is not a Nationall woe to bee feared and expected of a Nation overrun with drunkennesse? Had wee no other sinne raigning but this (which cannot raigne alone) will not God justly spue us out of his mouth for this alone? We read of whole countries wasted, dispeopled by Serpents. *Pliny* tels us of the *Amyclæ, Lycophron*, of *Salamis*; *Herodotus* of the *Neury*, utterly depopulate and made unhabitable by them. Verely, if this Cockatrice multiply and get head amongst us a while longer as they have of late begun, where shall the people have sober servants to till their lands, or children to hold and enjoy them. They speake of drayning Fens; but if this evill be not stopped, wee shall all shortly be drowned with it. I wish the Magistracy, Gentry, and Yeomanry would take it to serious consideration, how to deale with this Serpent, before hee grow too strong, and fierce for them. It is past the egge already, and much at that passe, of which *Augustine* complaines of in his time, that hee scarce knew what remedy to advise, but thought it required the meeting of a general Council. The best course I thinke of, is, if the great persons would first begin through reformation in their own families, banish the spirits of their bitterness, abandon that foolish and vicious custom as Ambrose and Basil[1] calls it.

If this helpe not, I shall then conclude it to bee such an evill as is onely by soveraigne power, and the Kings hand curable. And verely next under the word of God which is omnipotent, how potent and wonder-working is the word of a King? when both meet as the Sunne, and some good star in a benigne conjunction, what enemy shall stand before the sword of God and *Gideon*? what vice so predominant which these subdue not? If the Lyon roare, what beast of the forrest shall not tremble and hide their head? have we not a noble experiment hereof yet fresh in our memory, and worthy never to die, in the timely and speedy suppression of, that impudent abomination of womens mannish habit, threatning the confusion of sexes, and ruine of modesty? The same Royall hand, and care the Church and Commonwealth implores for the vanquishing of this poyson, no lesse pernicious, more spreading, and prevailing. Take us these little Foxes, was wont to bee the suit of the Church, for they gnabble[2] our Grapes, and hurt our tender branches: but now it is become more serious. Take us these Serpents, lest they destroy our Vines, Vinedressers, Vineyards and all.

---

1. Ambrose, *De Elia et Jejunio*, Liber Unus, cap. xiv. Basil, *Hom. Contra Ebrios*.
2. Nibble. Other contemporary terms of interest in this sermon are foyle (or foil): dishonour; syrts: quicksand (from Syrtis) see p. 235; and quackle (East-Anglian dialect): to choke, p. 236.

JOHN DONNE

John Donne has received wider acclaim than any other preacher represented in this collection. It was as a wit and a poet that he first gained renown among the few; it is as a wit and a poet that he is now remembered by the many. Even those who do not ordinarily read poetry may respond to 'Go and catch a falling Star', or, 'I wonder by my troth, what thou and I did till we loved'. But it was as a preacher that he won general celebrity in his own lifetime. If ever a man had preaching thrust upon him it was he. Not until he was forty-two and had striven for years without success to open every secular door to advancement, did he resign himself to holy orders. By then his precarious position, without secure employment, was becoming desperate, and the king, from whatever devious motives, had declared that Mr. Donne should find royal favour through ordination or not at all.

It says much for the buoyancy of his temperament that he was able to bring his creative talents to bear upon his enforced profession, with such effect that he succeeded Lancelot Andrewes as the most admired and prolific master of preaching at court.

The two preachers were as unlike as near-contemporary professionals can be. We have observed Andrewes, highly artificial in construction, but deeply serious in purpose, stalking his chosen words relentlessly, and operating upon their meaning with surgical exactitude. Donne, in contrast, invites us to share in a subjective adventure in transcendental experience. Under the gown of divinity the romantic impulse continues its career, and his spiritual transactions with God are as rapturous as his venereal ones formerly were with women. To T. S. Eliot, for whom emotion was only decent when under the subjection of discipline, Donne's sumptuous agonies lie under the suspicion of 'impure motives'.[1] It is natural that Eliot should feel no sympathy either for the 'sorcerer of the emotional orgy' or for his work—he uses Donne as a footstool for Andrewes—but his observation of Donne is acutely discerning. It is not, however, I think, in its conclusion, just. 'Impure

---

1. T. S. Eliot, 'For Lancelot Andrewes' (1928), in *Selected Essays* (1932), p. 345.

motives' imply a degree of insincerity, of wilful *deception*, and there is no evidence, internal or external, of Donne's being guilty of cynicism. His perception may be more intense than profound, but that is a distinction of quality, not a failure of sincerity. Again and again he shows himself incapable of modifying his daemon; his lyrical heart, and when he has to turn his attention to sin and damnation he continues to *sing*; it is black lyricism, but in his ecstasies of abjection he is lyrical still. There is, it is true, a voluptuous element of abandonment in his professions of anguished mortification; and sometimes the emotional agitation is vulgarized and devalued by promiscuity, like an organ *tremolo* turned on and left on; but, considering the history of Donne's ordination, it is remarkable that there are not more signs of psychological strain in his adjustments from profane to sacred objects. Somewhere there lay a defeating flaw in the relationship between Donne and the society in which he lived. It may be expressed in two questions unanswered, and, for that matter, usually unasked. Why, despite his widely recognized abilities, his energy, his attractive nature and charm, was he excluded for years from any kind of worthy employment, while men of less account passed him by? Why, once he was ordained, did he receive no further advancement than the deanery of St. Paul's, a respectable appointment which he made spectacular, but not a post of high honour or responsibility?

It is almost as if he never entirely lived down the social disaster of his rash wedding. To contract in secret an unauthorized marriage with the sixteen-year-old niece of one's influential employer was not a formula for success in the early seventeenth century. In consequence of which misconduct Donne suffered imprisonment, loss of livelihood, and was reduced to the insecurity of casual employment for a long time to come. It seems hardly conceivable that a romantic indiscretion of youth should have been held against his credit indefinitely, yet it is not possible to account for the frustrations of his career without the presumption of an exceptional force militating against him.[1] Was there, perhaps, in his brilliant nature, some quality which denied him the confidence and trust of the establishment, a hint of instability, of lack of weight or solidity, a latent recklessness?

In reconstructing the nature of Donne's success in the pulpit we should take into special consideration two factors: first, he brought to

1. His own view? '... culumnies and misinformations ... malice in great persons ...'
See below p. 274.

his sermons a public personality of ravishing charm; and second, a London Jacobean congregation came to church prepared to enjoy flesh-creeping thrills and theatrical rhapsodies as a legitimate part of a preacher's dispensation.

The Nature of Damnation

A sermon preached before the Earl of Carlile and his company at Sion in 1622[1]

That God should let my soule fall out of his hand, into a bottomlesse pit, and roll an unremoveable stone upon it, and leave it to that which it finds there, (and it shall finde that there, which it never imagined, till it came thither) and never thinke more of that soule, never have more to doe with it. That of that providence of God, that studies the life and preservation of every weed, and worme, and ant, and spider, and toad, and viper, there should never, never any beame flow out upon me; that that God, who looked upon me, when I was nothing, and called me when I was not, as though I had been, out of the womb and depth of darknesse, will not looke upon me now, when, though a miserable, and a banished, and a damned creature, yet I am his creature still, and contribute something to his glory, even in my damnation; that that God, who hath often looked upon me in my foulest uncleannesse, and when I had shut out the eye of the day, the Sunne, and the eye of the night, the Taper, and the eyes of all the world, with curtaines and windowes and doores, did yet see me, and see me in mercy, by making me see that he saw me, and sometimes brought me to a present remorse, and (for that time) to a forbearing of that sinne, should so turne himselfe from me, to his glorious Saints and Angels, as that no Saint nor Angel, nor Christ Jesus him-selfe, should ever pray him to looke towards me, never remember him, that such a soule there is; that that God, who hath so often said to my soule, *Quare morieris?* Why wilt thou die? and so often sworne to my soule, *Vivit Dominus*, As the Lord liveth, I would not have thee dye, but live, will neither let me dye, nor let me live, but dye an everlasting life, and live an everlasting

1. Carlisle was Ambassador in France from July 1621 till Summer 1622. In February 1623 he went to France and Spain. Syon was the house of his father-in-law, the Earl of Northumberland who was released from the Tower in 1621, after fifteen years' imprison-ment. The time when this sermon was preached at Syon was probably, therefore, Autumn 1622.

death; that that God, who, when he could not get into me, by standing, and knocking, by his ordinary meanes of entring, by his Word, his mercies, hath applied his judgements, and hath shaked the house, this body, with agues and palsies, and set this house on fire, with fevers and calentures, and frighted the Master of the house, my soule, with horrors, and heavy apprehensions, and so made an entrance into me; That that God should loose and frustrate all his owne purposes and practises upon me, and leave me, and cast me away, as though I had cost him nothing, that this God at last, should let this soule goe away, as a smoake, as a vapour, as a bubble, and that then this soule cannot be a smoake, nor a vapour, nor a bubble, but must lie in darknesse, as long as the Lord of light is light it selfe, and never a sparke of that light reach to my soule; What Tophet is not Paradise, what Brimstone is not Amber, what gnashing is not a comfort, what gnawing of the worme is not a tickling, what torment is not a marriage bed to this damnation, to be secluded eternally, eternally, eternally from the sight of God? Especially to us, for as the perpetuall losse of that is most heavy, with which we have been best acquainted, and to which wee have been most accustomed; so shall this damnation, which consists in the losse of the sight and presence of God, be heavier to us then others, because God hath so graciously, and so evidently, and so diversly appeared to us, in his pillar of fire, in the light of prosperity, and in the pillar of the Cloud, in hiding himselfe for a while from us; we that have seene him in the Execution of all the parts of this Commission, in his Word, in his Sacraments, and in good example, and not beleeved, shall be further removed from his sight, in the next world, then they to whom he never appeared in this. But *Vincenti & credenti*, to him that beleeves aright, and overcomes all tentations to a wrong beliefe, God shall give the accomplishment of fulnesse, and fulnesse of joy, and joy rooted in glory, and glory established in eternity, and this eternity is God; To him that beleeves and overcomes, God shall give himselfe in an everlasting presence and fruition, *Amen*.

JOSEPH HALL

As James I's reign advanced, tensions rose. The Roman Catholics, to whom James had made promises which he was unable to keep, felt bitterly betrayed. If he was looking for an excuse to deny them even a limited toleration, the Gunpowder Plot provided it. The Puritans, militant now and hungry for power, disregarded instructions from the bishops and set about imposing their concept of 'Righteousness', in and out of church, upon the country at large. The latter could be achieved by alliance between a Puritan minister and a Puritan magistrate, which could impose repressive measures (like any local government where the majority are unorganized and unled), so the active policy where such a compound governed was not only 'away with surplices and hats and tables used as altars', but 'away with the wicked maypole and sinful games on the village green'. The ballad singer lamented,

> But since the summer Poles were overthrowne
> And all good sports and merriments decayed
> How times and men are changed.[1]

As yet, Puritan social policies only prevailed in certain districts; in others summer sport went on in the old ways and in the height of the controversies, playful songs bubbled out of the country's youth, as careless as were ever made.

> Jone to the Maypole away let us on;
>> Tyme is swift and will soon be gone;
> See how the wenches hie to the Greene,
>> where they know they will be seene;
> Bess, Moll, Kate, Doll, these want no loves
>> to attend them
> Hodge, Dick, Tom, Nick, brave dauncers,
>> who can ammend them.
> Jone, shall we now have a Hay or a Rounde,
>> or some daunce that is new founde?[2]

It was certainly no part of the Establishment's intention that the Church of England should be made to appear repulsively severe to the laity, and

1. *Pasquil's Palinodia* (1619).
2. 'May day Ballad' (1630), *Roxburghe Ballads*, 7, 81.

the crown countered with the *Book of Sports*, which the clergy were ordered to read from their pulpits, declaring the right of the people to engage in lawful outdoor recreations after divine service on Sunday. Puritan clergy retaliated by refusing, or just omitting to read the offensive mandate. Some were reported, later tried and ejected, and took refuge in more sympathetic districts. The apprehension of disunity sharpened intolerance on both sides. In international relations there was an ominous breach between the policy of the crown to cultivate Spain and the traditional antipathy of the people for their old enemy. We know that Samuel Ward went to prison for drawing a cartoon which only a few years before would have been considered unexceptionably patriotic.

The situation is reflected in a nervous proclamation of 1620 censuring the 'greater opennesse and libertie of discourse, even concerning matters of state (which are no Theams or subjects fit for vulgar persons or common meetings), than hath been in former times used or permitted.'

The proclamation ends by inviting help from that most disreputable and false-faced of servants, the 'informer'. Violence, and the scent of violence, was in the air; and behind it lurked the fear which had haunted Englishmen of substance since the Peasant Revolt of 1381, that lawful controls might break down and the brutish rabble erupt in an anarchy which would engulf all.

In the same year as the proclamation was issued, Joseph Hall preached before the King at Theobalds.

The True Peace-maker

A Sermon preached before His Majesty at Theobalds,
on September the 19th, 1624

We speak of Justice first as a single virtue. Habits are distinguished by their acts as by their objects. The object of all moral virtue is good, as of all intellectual is true. The object of this virtue of Justice is the good of man in relation to each other. Other vertues order a man in regard to himself; Justice in regard to an other. This being either common or priuate, common of all, priuate of some, the acts and vertue of iustice must be sutable, either as man stands in habitude to the whole body, or as he stand to special limbs of the body. The former of these is that which Philosophers and Casuists call a legal and universal Justice. The latter is the particular Justice which we use to distinguish by *Distribution* and *Commutation*; the one consisting in matter of Commerce, the other in Reward or Punishment; both of them according to a meet though different equality. An Arithmetical equality in Commutation, Geometrical in Distribution; the former regarding the value, of worth, or things, the latter, regarding the proportionable difference of the person. The worke of all these three Iustices, is Peace.

First, the legall Iustice is the apparent mother and nurse of publique Peace: When Gouernors and subiects are carefull to giue each other their owne; when both conspire to command and obey for the common good; when men frame their liues to the wholsome lawes of their Soueraignes, not more out of feare than conscience; when respect to the community caries men from partiall reflections vpon themselues; As contrarily distractions, and priuate ends are the bane of any state. When the head and members vnite their thoughts and endeuours in the center of the common good: the head to deuise and command, the eies to see, the eare to heare, the palate to taste, the heart to moue, the bellowes of the lungs to blow, the liuer to sanguisie, the stomach to digest, the guts to export, the hands to execute, the tongue to talke for the good of this naturall Common-wealth of the body, all goes well and happily; but if any of these parts will bee gathering to themselues, and obstructions grow within; and mutinous distempers arise in the humors, ruine is threatned to the whole: If either the Superiors miscommand, or the inferiors disobey, it is an affront to Peace. I need not tell you that good lawes are the walls of the City, the sinewes of the politicke body, the rule of our life, the life of our state, without which men would turne brute, yea monstrous; the world were a Chaos, yea an hell. It is wisedome that makes lawes, it is Iustice that keeps them; Oh let this Iustice still blesse vs with a perpetual peace; as the those that doe not thinke the world made for vs, but our selues made for the world, let vs driue at an vniuersall good; let there be euer that sweet correspondence betwixt Soueraignty and subiection, that the one may bee happy in the other, both in peace.

Secondly, the distributiue Iustice is not lesse fruitfull of peace; when rewards of honors, and gracious respects are suited to the well-deseruing; when malefactors smart according to their crimes; This Iustice hath stocks for the vagrant, whips for harlots, brands for petty larzons, ropes for fellons, weights for the contumaciously silent,[1] stakes for blasphemous hereticks, gibbets for murtherers, the hurdle, and the knife, and the pole for traitors; and vpon all these engines of Iustice hangs the garland of peace. It was not for

1. *Peine forte et Dure*, the practice of pressing, if need be to death, anyone arraigned of a felony who refused to plead, persisted until 1736.

nothing that *Maximilian* the First, passing by the gallowes, salued it with *Salue Iustitia*. Ye neuer see Iustice painted without a sword; when that sword glitters with use, it is well with the publique; woe be to the Nation where it rusts. There can be no more acceptable sacrifice than the bloud of the flagitious. Immediately after *Garnets* execution, *Father Dauid* at *Ypre*, in a publike Sermon declared the miracles showne thereat; Amongst the rest, that a spring of oyle brake forth suddenly in the place where that Saint was martyred; In stead of a lie, let it be a parable; The bloud of Traitors shed by the sword of Iustice, is a well of oyle to fatten, and refresh the Common-wealth.

I know well how mercy befits the mouths of Gods Ministers: The soft tongue of a Diuine is no meet whetstone for the edge of seuerity; but withall, I dare say, that Iustice is a noble worke of mercy; neither need we wish to bee more charitable, than the God of mercy that saies, *Thine eie shall not spare the murtherer*, Numb.35.31. *The Tempter to idolatry*, Deut.13.6. The very sonnes of *Leui* were appointed to win an euerlasting blessing, by consecrating their hands to God in Israelitish bloud: The vniust fauour, and plausibility of Romish Doctors, towards capitall offenders, hath made their Sanctuaries (euen literally) a denne of theeues, an harbour of villany. It is memorable of *Lewis* of *France*, (stiled the Saint) that he reuersed a pardon wrought from him to a malefactor; vpon reading that verse in the *Psalme, Beati qui faciunt institiam in omnitempore; Blessed are they that doe iustice at all times*: No maruell if one of those foure things which *Isabel* of *Spaine* was wont to say, she loued to see, were, *A Theefe vpon the ladder*; Euen through his halter might she see the prospect of peace. Woe bee to them that either for gaine or priuate interest ingage themselues in the suit of fauour to maliciously bloudy hands; that, by the dam of their bribes labour to stop the due course of punitiue Iustice; these, these are the enemies of peace; these staine the land with that Crimson die, that cannot be washed out but by many wofull lauers of reuenge: Farre, farre be it from any of you, generous Christians, to endeuour either to corrupt, or interrupt the wayes of iudgement, or for a piruate benefit to crosse the publike Peace: Woe be to those partiall Iudges, that iustifie the wicked, and condemne the innocent; the girdle of whose equity sags downe on that side where the purse hangs: Lastly, woe to those vnworthy ones that raise themselues by fraud, bribes, symonie, sacriledge; therefore are these enemies to the State, because to Peace; and therefore enemies to Peace, because violaters of iustice, *And the worke of iustice is Peace*.

Thirdly, that commuatiue Iustice workes Peace; needes no other proofe than that all the reall brables and suits amongst men, arise from either true or pretended iniustice of contracts. Let me leade you in a terme morning to the spacious Hall of Iustice: What is the cause of all that concourse? that Hiue-like murmure? that noise at the Bar, but iniurious bargaines, fraudulent conueyances, false titles, disappointment of trusts, wrongfull detentions of money, goods, lands, coozenages, oppressions, extortions? Could the honesty and priuate Iustice of men preuent these enormities, silence and solitude would dwell in that wide Palace of Iustice; neither would there be more Pleas than Cob-webs vnder that vast roofe. Euery way therefore it is cleare, that the worke of Iustice is peace; In so much as the Guardians of Peace are called Iusticers. . . .

WILLIAM PROCTOR[1]

London's Iniquity

A sermon preached at Paul's Cross on September 26th., 1624

... If fearefull woes, or most heauy iudgements, may be vndoubtedly ready to fall on most renowned places and people, for their sinnes against God; yea the more renowned, the more they hasten on themselues most fearefull woes, and most heauy iudgements, as is plainly euident from this remarkable example of *Ierusalem* in my Text; then how shall ye escape the fearefull woes, or the most heauy iudgements of God? you are not priuiledged beyond *Ierusalem*; wherefore you must be content (with *Belshazar*) to bee weighed in the ballance, that so you may be tryed whether or no yee are found wanting. *Ierusalem* was the Citie where the King of *Israel* dwelt; or neere to *Ierusalem* on mount *Zion*, which bordered on *Ierusalem*, was the Pallace of that great King: So is *London* the Citie where the Kings of *England* usually dwell, or neere vnto this Citie, & in the borders thereof: As *Ierusalem* was, so is this the crowning Citie; now if you equall *Ierusalem* in iniquitie, as yee doe in worldly dignitie, you may and must expect the selfe same measure that was measured vnto it.

The Prophet (in the Chapter immediately going before my Text) de-nounceth a fearefull woe against two capitall sinnes, namely *Pride* and *Drunkennesse*, which were frequent in *Ephraim*, or in *Israel*: for so by *Ephraim* we are to vnderstand the people of *Israel*, or *Ierusalem*, which was the chiefe Citie in *Israel*, according to the vsuall phrase of the holy Prophets. *Woe* (saith the Prophet) *to the crowne of Pride, to the Drunkards of Ephraim*, verse the first of the former Chapter.

And is not this Citie guilty of these sins? I wish it were not: oh, but Pride is the raigning sinne, and if in time ye preuent it not, I feare it will be the destroying sin thereof; excessive Pride manifested both in your feeding and

1. All that is known of this preacher is that he delivered this sermon at Paul's Cross on the day given above, and that he published it the following year, 1625. He may have been the Proctor who was Rector of Over Bodlington, in Northamptonshire, at this time.

250

apparelling, like so many vaine-glorious rich men; ye are gorgiously ap-
parelled, and yee fare sumptuously euery day; we cannot by your apparrell
discerne a young Prentice from a young Gallant, a phantasticke Tradesman,
from a great landed Gentleman.

And as for that beastly sinne of Drunkennesse, like filthy *Sodome*, herein
you declare your sicknesse openly, by your frequent reeling two and fro
in the streets, and staggering like drunken men, for so the Psalmist disciphers
a drunken man. *Psal.*107.27.

Bodily vncleanenesse, that was another grieuous sinne in *Israel; How* (saith
God) *is the faithfull Citie become an harlot? Isa.*1.21. And when they were
fedde to the full, then they committed adultery, and assembled themselues
by troopes in the Harlots houses, they were as fedde Horses in the morning,
euery one neighed after his Neighbours wife. *Ier.*5.7.8.

And is this Citie exempt from the grossenesse of this sinne? how then are
brazen-fac'd strumpets suffered most impudently and vnnaturally, to intice
men as they passe in the open streets, and in the sight of the Sunne? I feare
there are too many of beastly *Polyphemus* his mind, who accounted the
Ramme happy, because he could haue his lustful pleasure of sundry Sheepe.[1]
Cruell Oppression, niggardly Couetousnesse, and treacherous dealing; these
also were the sinnes of *Ierusalem*, as you may see in the beginning of this
prophesie.

And are not these sinnes raigning in this Citie also? Oh how cruelly doe
many great rich men, breake the backs of many inferiour men? I meane of
many young beginners in trading, by their mercilesse racking of them? and
how commonly doe many among you make a profession of sinfull Vsurie?
And how doe the treacherous dealers, deale very treacherously, by deceitefull
Wares and Measures.

Common swearing, that was another crying sinne in Ierusalem; *Because
of swearing the Land mourneth*, saith the Prophet *Ier.*23.10. and too rife is this
sinne also. A true religious man can scarce passe through the streets, but his
eares will bee made euen to tingle, at the ordinary hearing of prophane and
blasphemous swearing. Yet indeede I am informed, & I cannot but take
notice of the piety of the supreame Officer of this Citie (in causes temporall)
for restrayning common swearing, as much as in him lyeth, by imposing on
such offendors, such punishment as the late Lawes haue prouided.

1. I am unable to provide any clue to the source of this embellishment, unless it be
Mr. Proctor's godly imagination. There is no such allusion in the *Odyssey*, nor in later
repositories of Cyclopic lore, like Euripedes' *Cyclops*, or Theocritus' *Eleventh Idyll*.

THOMAS LUSHINGTON[1]

During the reign of James the House of Commons had shown an increasing thin-skinned tenderness wherever its personal dignity and privilege was touched from without. Men could be summoned before the assembly, brow-beaten and punished for any quip about the House which happened to be offensively credible. This quick irritability was in part the product of the Commons' frustration in their relations with the Crown and it was not diminished at the accession of Charles, when all doubt was removed that the new king had no more intention than his father ever had of granting any part of their long-pressed appeals for a greater share of government. To parliament's irascible susceptibilities we owe the existence of one specially precious sermon, which otherwise almost certainly would not have been preserved and published. Many important Anglican divines published, if at all, only sermons prepared for state occasions. Thus, Richard Corbet, Bishop successively of Oxford and Norwich, though he preached from time to time, only published one sermon, and that a funeral oration in Latin. Like certain other poets, perhaps he thought that nothing of him was worth preserving except his verse, and, with the Puritans' tendency to identify themselves with the cult of preaching, a man like Corbet would have more enjoyed writing verses *about* preachers, like:

Am I mad, O noble Festus[2]
When zeal and God by knowledge
Have put me in hope
To deal with the Pope
As well as the best in the College?

1. Thomas Lushington, 1590–1661. Lincoln College, Oxford. B.D. 1627; D.D. 1632. Vicar of Barton Turf and Neatshead, in Norfolk, 1633, and of Felixstowe and Walton in Suffolk 1636. Presented by the King to the rectories of Burnham Wesgate in 1639, and of Burnham St. Margaret's and Burnham All Saints in Norfolk, in 1640. Deprived during the Civil War and lived thereafter in retirement. Like Hales he was suspected of Socinianism. Published work includes *Commentary on the Epistle to the Hebrews, translated from the Latin of Crellius; Commentary on the Galations* (1650); *Logica Analytica de Principiis, regulus et usus Rationis rectae* (1650).

2. 'But Paul saith I am not mad most excellent Festus.' *Acts,* 26: 25.

> Boldly I preach, hate a cross, hate a surplice,
> Miters, copes and rochets,
> Come, hear me pray nine times a day,
> And fill your head with Crochets.[1]

There were stories of Corbet singing ballads at Abingdon Cross on Market Days. He sang very well and Aubrey tells us that once when an itinerant ballad singer whom he met in a tavern complained of business being bad, 'the jolly Dr. putts off his Gowne and putts-on the Ballad Singer's Leather apron, and being a handsome man and had a rare full voice, he presently vended a great many and had a great audience'. On such expeditions it is possible that he was accompanied by his chaplain to be, Dr. Lushington. Thomas Lushington was more to Corbet than a chaplain. There was great love between the two wits and their unconsidered asides were the university's joy. 'Some dust, Lushington,' said Corbet, as he prepared to confirm a bald man, 'some dust or my hand may slip.'

Aubrey's account of their private carousels in the Bishop's cellars is not unfamiliar to print, but it will take no harm from a further airing. The Bishop and his chaplain were wont to go together to the wine cellar and lock themselves in and be merry. 'Then first he layes down his episcopal hood, "There lies the doctor." Then he puts off his gowne; "There lies the Bishop"; then 'twas "here's to thee, Corbett"— "Here's to thee, Lushington." '

Lushington was an early, almost archetypal, example of one of the most valuable contributions made to civilized manners by the English academic tradition. He was a man of vast learning which he carried with playful, almost negligent ease, unblemished by pedantry. Unlike Corbet, he seems to have been singularly lacking in ambition, and his disposition, as we shall see, was to tease, rather than court, the establishment. Advancement would probably have been thrust on him had it not been for the Civil War, and afterwards, he pleaded old age in declining high honours. At the time which concerns us, 1623 or 1624, Lushington, a celebrated figure at Oxford, preached at St. Mary's Church in April a sermon which was greatly admired by the university élite as a *tour de force* of wit and erudition, but which was considered scandalously blasphemous by more conservative or less sophisticated in the auditory. In the sermon Lushington first puts himself in the place,

---

1. 'The Distracted Puritan', *Poems*, ed. J. A. W. Bennett and H. R. Trevor-Roper (Oxford, 1955), p. 56.

and then speaks the part, of one of the Roman guards posted at Christ's tomb after the crucifixion, and, according to Serenus Cressy, who was present, 'descanting upon the whole life of our saviour, rendered him and his attendants objects of the utmost scorn and aversion, as if they, all of them had been nothing but a pack of dissolute vagabonds and cheats. But presently the preacher changed his stile and became a disciple of Christ and with such admirable force of reason answered all the Cavillations and Invectives made before, that the loudly repeated applause of his hearers hindered him a good space from proceeding. . . .'[1]

Lushington may have credited everyone present with as much knowledge of mediaeval traditions as he had himself, but it is unlikely. The method he was using, of first issuing a blasphemous challenge to piety and then refuting it, was one employed in the schools and universities of the Middle Ages. A French example, which found its way into English homily books of the thirteenth century, recounts how a friar, a master of the University of Paris, was called upon to preach a synodal sermon in the presence of the King and many Bishops. On entering the pulpit the preacher began his sermon by gazing around him and uttering in a loud voice three times the scurrilously insulting exclamation, 'St. Pere et St. Paule, Babimbaboo!' Which was simply to call St. Peter and St. Paul, in the then vernacular, a pair of contemptible fools. To enforce his words he followed them by spitting. On being required to explain this affront he boldly replied that the Bishops, with their caparisoned steeds and delicate dishes, their costly garments, their vices and delights, believe they will go to heaven. Therefore Peter and Paul, who suffered poverty and tribulation, hunger and thirst and cold, must be contemptible fools.[2] Then, among many others, there was the sermon of *The Devil's Letter*,[3] a friendly greeting from the Prince of Darkness to his friends the Princes of the Church thanking them for their good offices and the number of souls they were sending him; there was the legend of Nemo, the 'no-man' who learnt to do all that Christ could do, ascended to Heaven, where he defied the Almighty and became God.[4]

Even knowledge of these precedents from former 'papist' times would not have mitigated the shock to such as were liable to take

1. *Fanaticism* (1672), p. 13.
2. Erasmus, *Colloq*: See Meray, *La Vie au temps des Libres precheurs*, ii, 130. Cf. Odo de Cheriton, Arundel MS. 231, fol. 63b, and edition Hervieux, No. VIII, and Etienne de Bourbon, *Anecd. Hist.*, ed. Lecoy de la Marche; quoted in Owst, op. cit., p. 242. Cf. pp. 64 and 243.   3. Harl. MS., 268, fol. 10b.
4. *Pars Sermonis de Nemine*. MS. Caius College, Cambridge, 230, fol. 34 *et seq*.

offence. It is probable, from what we know of him, that Lushington couldn't resist trailing his doctor's gown occasionally, for the fun of it. Cressy says that great scandal followed and Lushington was compelled by William Pierce, Vice-Chancellor of the University, to preach a recantation sermon. Lushington did preach a recantation sermon, of which one may say that, while it is impossible to fault on paper, it was capable of being delivered as a derisive parody from beginning to end. However, Clarendon, who was also present when the sermon was preached, went into print to correct Cressy, who, he said, had got the causation of the events entirely wrong. Not blasphemy, but contempt of the House, was the inflammable content. Lushington had made a disparaging reference, oblique but hazardous, to the House and its belligerent intentions towards Spain; and Pierce, who was his friend, advised him to anticipate the consequences, and propitiate injured parliamentary dignity by preaching a recantation.[1] This, accordingly, Lushington did, though a perceptive member of the House might have felt more stung by the recantation than by the asseveration. It seems hardly possible that the irony of the comparison between the chamber of the Last Supper and the Chamber of the House of Commons would be missed, even by a Member of Parliament.

Lushington's prose, like an athlete's articulation, beguiles with an air of unconsidered spontaneity. The movement of the short, crisp sentences seems so unassumingly colloquial, that it is only after the literal *quantity* of information and interpretation, imparted in so few words, is added up, that the authority of his skill admits its force. His classical allusions never obtrude; they are too relevant and too apt to seem less than inevitable. Not a sentence, not a word is present here by accident or by compulsion. The theme is ancient and deathless: hope, defying mortality, breeds adventure. It is all we possess of Lushington, apart from his Latin gospel commentaries, and we must thank the 'scandal' for having even the 'Repetition Sermon'.[2]

1. Edward Hyde, *Animadversions upon Fanaticism* (1672).
2. Professor W. Fraser Mitchell who had read an allusion to the occasion in *The Diary of John Rouse* supposed that 'the sermon . . . was never printed'. *English Pulpit Oratory from Andrewes to Tillotson* (1932), p. 356.

Christ, Dead or Alive?

The 'Repetition' sermon[1] preached in St. Mary's
Church, Oxford, in April 1623 by Thomas Lushington.

*Matthew, XXVIII. 13. His Disciples came by night and stole him away while we
slept.*

What's the best news abroad? So we must begin. 'Tis the *Garb* (*Les Nouvelle*)
the Grand Salute and common preface to all our talk. And the News goes
not as Things are in themselves, but as Men's Fancies are fashioned, as some
lust to report, and others to believe. To some relation shall go for true or
false, according to the key wherein men's minds are turned; but chiefly as
they stand diverse in religion, so they feign and affect different News. By
their news ye may know their *Religion*, and by their *Religion* fore-know
their *News*. This Week the *Spanish Match* goes forward, the *Bethlem Gabor's*
Troops are broken[2] and the next Week *Bethlem Gabor's* Troops go forward,
and the *Spanish Match* is broken. The *Catholique* is of the *Spanish Match*, and
the *Protestant* of restoring the *Palatinate*; and each Party think that the Safety
of the *Church* and Success of *Religion* depends upon the Event of one or
other, and therefore they cross and counter-tell each others News. *Titius*
came from *London* Yesterday, and he says that the new Chappel at St. *James's*
is quite finished: *Caius* came thence but this Morning, and then there was no
such Thing on Building. False News follows true at the Heels, and oftentimes
outslips it.

Thus goes the *Chronicle*-News, the Talk of the *factious* and *pragmatick*; but
the *Christian* News, the Talk of the *faithful*, is spent in *Evangelio*, in hearing
and telling some good News of their *Saviour*: And now all the Talk is of his
Resurrection: The Christian Currant goes, News from *Mount Calvary*, the
sixteenth Day of *Nisan*, in the Year thirty four, *old style*; as the three holy
Matrons deliver it at the *eight verse* of this *Chapter*. But since, there are certain

1. Harl. MS. 4162. First recorded publication under the pseudonym of Robert Jones,
B.D., in 1659.

2. Reference to Charles's expedition as Prince of Wales, accompanied by the Duke of
Buckingham to Spain at this time, for the purposes, neither of which was achieved, of
gaining the hand of the Infanta and effecting the restitution of the Palatinate to his
brother-in-law. 'Bethlem Gabor': Gabriel Bethlen, Prince of Transylvania, the most
resourceful Protestant adversary of the Emperor Ferdinand II, to whose fortunes in the
field and devious diplomacy English Protestant partisans reacted with barometric
sensitivity.

Souldiers arrived, and they say there was no such Matter as the *Resurrection*, 'twas but a Gull put upon the World by his *Disciples*; for it fares with spiritual News as with temporal, it is variously and contrarily related, till the false controuls the true. And as our modern *News* comes neither from the *Court* nor the *Camp*, nor from the Place where Things are acted, but is forged in *Conventicles* by *Priests*, or in some, *Paul's-Assembly*, or such like Place; and the divulge committed to some vigilant and watchful Tongue: So it is with the *News* of the *Non resurrection*; it came not from *Mount Calvary*, but the *Priests* are the *Authors* of it, at the *eleventh* Verse; and at the *twelfth*, they frame and mould it to the Mouth of the *Watch*. The *Divulgers*, Men of double Credit, they *know* the Truth, for they are of the *Watch*, and they will not *lye*, for they are *Souldiers*; nay, they will maintain it, for they are *Knights*, *Milites*, *Knights of the Post*, they are hired to say, saying, and they did say, *His Disciples came by Night and stole him away whilst we Slept*.

The Words so plain, they need no opening. May it please you that I make *three Cursories* over them; One for the *Souldiers*, another for the *Disciples*, and the Third for our *Saviour*. In the Two former we will beat the point *pro* and *con*, and in the latter reconcile it, for that's the fashion also. No *Error* so absurd but finds a *Patron* nor *Truth* so sound but meets with an *Adversary*, nor Point controverted, but the opposite Tenent may be reconciled; be they distant as *Heaven* and *Hell*, as incompatible as *Jews* and *Christians*, yet they shall meet with a *Moderator*; and a *cogging Distinction* shall state the Question on the absurder Side. First then for the *Souldiers*, whose *Cursory* hath no Parts, that's not the *Souldiers* Manner, but yet is sprinkled with *Absurdities*, that's the Manner of the *Watch*. They speak partly as they fight, *voluntarily*, and partly as they watch, *supinely*, and thus they begin their Talk.

'Ye Men and People of *Judah* and *Jerusalem*, this *Jesus of Nazareth* was a very *Jugler*, a neat Compiler of *Impostures*, pretended Title to the Crown of *Judah*, made himself the *Messias* and the Son of God, brought such strange Opinions as would turn the whole World out of *Byass*; having no Proof from Sense or Reason for his *Novelties*, he would needs confirm them by *Miracles*; and in the World's Eye he seemed to do *Wonders*, though his Works were indeed but meer Delusions, wrought by Slight of Hand, *hocus pocus*. All which was so manifestly discover'd, that to stop the Current of such false Coin, my *Lord President* was forced to nail him to the *Cross* for a *Counterfeit*. His *Master-trick* was that of the *Resurrection*, whereof he forespake in his Life-time: For he was no ordinary Dealer, but would make his Cunning to survive his Person, and durst fore-say so. To put this Piece in Execution, he entertain'd a Rabble of *Ruffians*, whom he termed his *Disciples*, as all *Plotters* have *Partners*: These he instructed in the Game while he lived, and they were to play it when he was dead. The List of his *Disciples* consisted of Men and *Women*; for in all crafty Carriages, there lyes a *Woman's* Part. The

Men were to perform all Manner of *Fact*, and the *Women*, whose Activity lyes in their Tongue, were to report the *Miracle*.

'The *High-Priests* and some of the *Sanhedrim*[1] being wise to apprehend, and wary to prevent the dangerous Consequences hereof, procured a Warrant from the *President* to seal up the *Tomb*, and place a *Watch* there; and we were the parties appointed to guard it. The Charge we underwent required good Service; for his *Disciples* were common *Night-walkers* like their Master, notable *Cutters*,[2] and carried as much Courage as Cunning; such tall Fellows with their Weapons, that they made it but a Sleight, either to withstand or assault a whole Multitude, and durst do any thing in their Master's Behalf. The other Night, when we apprehended him in *Gethsemane*, we were most of the lustiest Fellows in *Jerusalem*, and pretty well appointed; yet they stood to it stoutly, made a tal Fray, and sometimes put us to the worst. At the first *On-set* we were all knock'd down, and at our *Recovery*, *Rabbi Malchus*, a Follower of the *High-Priests* Company, and our Captain, was singled out by one of their Side, a *Sailor* he seemed, who with his Whin-yard lopt off one of his Ears; and had the Blow lit right, it would have cleft him down to the Twist; Nay they, were all *Bravos*, and their bloody Mind was seen upon *Judas Iscariot*, one of their own Company, who because he was our Bloodhound to scent their Master out, they persecuted the poor Wretch till they had paunch'd him; for not far from their Walk he was found hang'd with his Guts about his Heels. And for their bloody Pranks that Way, the Place begins to bear the Name of *Aceldama*, the bloody Field.

'For the Exploit of his Resurrection, they had the Assistance of their *Fellow-she-disciples*, Night House-wives too; for they were hovering about the *Sepulchre* from the Dead of the Night till the Morning, and were as the *Counter-Watch*, to give Notice of some Advantage to the *Disciples*, who lay not far off, some where above Ground, while their Master was under it. All the Day-time they stir not for Fear of *Passengers* frequenting to and fro in the Gardens and Walks about *Mount Calvary*, it being both *Sabbath* and *Passeover*: But in the Night they took their Opportunity by this Means. We had been extreamly over-travell'd, both to apprehend and guard him; first, to the *High-Priest*, next, to the *President*; from him to *Herod*, and back again; then to his *Arraignment*, then to his *Execution*, and ever since at his *Grave*: So turbulent the Man was, that his very dead Body would not ly still, and be quiet. This *Over-watching*, seconded with the Darkness of the *Night*, and *Coldnesse* of the *Air*, cast us into a heavy *Sleep*; thereupon the *Women* gave the *Watch-word* to the *Disciples*, who immediately do *exhumate* his Body; and while they translate and bury it elsewhere, the *Women* trot into the *Town*, and bruit it abroad, that their Master is risen.

'And the credulous City is partly inclined to believe the *Legerdemain*; they

1. Or *Sanhedrin*, a Rabbinical supreme court.   2. Cutters: thieves, cut-throats.

are willing to frame their Faith, and build their Salvation upon a flying Gull, raised by three *Way-going* Women, *gadling*[1] *Gossips* that came from *Galilee;* one of them *notorious*, so devilish, that there came *seven* Devils out of her, how many staid behind, *God* knows: It is like she was so full, there was Room for no more; and by her ye may guess at her Companions. Consider of it; the Matter is of Moment, a main Point of State, that concerns your own Nation: We are but Strangers, and no farther interested than for the Truth's sake to speak it; and therefore be advised whether ye will rely herein upon the Word of a *Woman*, or upon the Faith and Reputation of a *Soldier*.'

Here the *Soldier* puts up, and sheaths his malicious and blasphemous Tongue, more sharp and deadly than his Sword, and gives our *Saviour* a Wound more mortal far than those upon the Cross; They did but put him in a Trance, suspend his Life for a Day or two, at the most but kill his *Humanity*; but This would murder his *Divinity*, and dead his *Immortality*; it would nullify the *Gospel*, and frustrate all our *Faith*: For, *if Christ be not risen* (saith St. *Paul*) *then is our Preaching vain, and your Faith is also vain*.[2] And therefore I come to my second *Cursory*: *For his Disciples stole him away by Night*.

Herein we will deal *Christianly* and civilly, not give the Lie to the *Soldiers*, or foul Words to the *Watch*: But yet we may say, that their Tale hath no Truth in any Point of it, but a meer *Saying*. *Saying*, say ye. They say not of themselves, but as the *Priests* taught them; they knew they said false; and therefore, our saying to the Contrary, will easily obtain. . . . The *Watch* there, termed Soldiers, were of a middle Nature between *Soldiers* and *Hangmen*; *Speculatores*, they carried a Spear in their Hands, but a Halter at their Girdles, always ready for any deadly Service. They were σωματοφύλακες, *Satellites*, a Guard to the *Governor*; and *Custodes, Goalers, Wardens* for *Prisoners*; and *Vigiles, Watchers* for their Bodies who suffered: The common *Executioners* of corporal Punishment, whether it reached only to Sense, or forward to Life. To express their *Roman* Nature home, the *Eastern* Nation borrowed Language from the *Western*, the *Greeks* from the *Latin*, *Custodia*; and the *Syriac*, as Master *Fuller* observes, from *Quæstionarii, Officers ad quæstionem & inquisitionem, Questioners* or *Inquisitors, Tormentors*, or *Serjeants of the Rack*, to extort *Confessions* in criminal *Examinations*. At the Peril of their Life it was, if the Party under their *Execution* did not endure the *Extremity* of

1. Gadling: gossiping on the move.
2. Lushington seems to have been under suspicion of Socinianism in some quarters (see *Walker Revised*, p. 270), due to his translating from the Latin Crellius' *Commentary on the Epistle to the Hebrews* (cf. H. H. McLachlan, *Socinianism in 17th. Century England* 1951). There could be nothing less Socinian than the emphasis laid in the present sermon; but the more enquiring minds (even cautious John Hales) did tend to speak with different voices in public and private; and this would be especially true of someone as playful and careless of consequence as Lushington.

the *Law*; If the *Prisoner* escaped with no Punishment, or with less, or *in ultimo supplicio* recovered by his Life, or his dead Body otherwise disposed than the *Laws* ordained or permitted, then were those *Soldiers* to take the room of the *Prisoners*, to be wasted and spent out upon the same Punishment whereto the *Prisoner* was liable; *Ejusmodi pæna consumendi*, the very Words of the *Law*. Could any Man now imagine the *Watch* could now be either so careless, or such Cowards as to let our *Saviour* to be stole away? Men durst as well have fetcht him from the *Cross* as from the *Grave*.

But say, that they were such maimed *Soldiers*, as that they had neither Eye to *Watch*, nor Heart to Ward; yet the *Sepulchre* it self was so impregnable, that it alone would secure the Body. There could be no Burglary, nor breaking it up, no undermining; the *Soil* was *Pick-ax* proof, a firm Rock spread out of the Roots of *Golgotha*, gabion'd[1] and rough-cast with Flint. No removing of the *Tomb-stone*; that beside its Weight and Sullenness to give way, was rib'd and clasped down with Iron Bars and Bonds; the Closure soulder'd with the Seal of the *Sanhedrim*. Their ἐσφαλίσαντο τὸν τάφον, and σφραγίσαντες τόν λίθον, their fortifying the *Sepulchre*, and sealing up the Stone, says it was so, in the latter Verse of the former Chapter. For though he should revive, yet the high *Priests* never meant he should rise more, either by his own, or by the Strength of others. The *Watch* was but a stale to Colour their Pretence, and to lead their Request to *Pilate*. The Womens, *Who shall roll us away this Stone?* was a Matter more than they imagined, a Task above the Strength of a Man. A whole set of Leavers could not lift it: No rolling it away but by the Force of an *Angel*.

And now look into the *Grave*, see the Remains of the *Resurrection*, the impartial Witnesses and silent Sayings, that he was not stole away. The *Linnen* and *Grave Clothes* wherein he was involved, lined and loaden with a compound of *Myrrh*, *Aloes* and *Mastick*, Gums and Spices of *Arabia*, Unguents and Balms of *Gilead*, a Seare-cloth both costly and massie, ὦσει λκπεας ἑκατὸν. to the worth or weight of an hundred Pounds, somewhat unwieldy to be handled: The *Kerchief* so wrapt and displeited, as though yet it had not been used; and yet so laid aside, as though he would have come again. What manner of Men would leave these Things thus? His Friends would not for shame have stript him, and carried him away naked. His Foes would have esteemed the *Linnen* and embalming *Compounds* far beyond his *Body*. *Friend* or *Foe*, or *Neuter*, they durst not stay to flea the glewy *Sear-cloth* from his Skin, and give a diligent Folding to the *Kerchief*. But if notwithstanding he was stollen away, Why was not Search made to recover his Body? No *Hue* and *Cry* to pursue the *Malefactors?* No *Proclamation* out for their Attachment? Why were not the *Women* apprehended, or taken upon Suspicion? Why not so much as questioned? Questioned! about what? The *Soldiers* knew well

1. Gabioned: protected by a wicker basket, or by a structure of similar design.

enough he was not stollen away; for they sate by, and markt it; they were the *Watch*, and they did *watch*; they were not asleep; which is my last Contradictory.

Hitherto they talk like *Soldiers*, of coming by Night, and stealing away; now like *Watchmen*, in saying they were asleep. So sottish and unreasonable is Malice, that to burn his Neighbour's House, he will set Fire on his own; to bring in an Accusation on *Christ* and his *Disciples*, they make Confession of a Crime in themselves: They gull and befool themselves, and say, that the *Watch* was asleep. It may be as *Watchmen* they durst sleep, 'tis ordinary; but they durst not so as *Soldiers*, their Discipline too strict, and the Penalty thereof too severe. He that forsakes the *Watch*, *capite punitur*, 'tis Death (saith *Paulus*)[1] in Law 9. *in Excubias*, §. *de re militari*; and some good Captains interpret Sleep equivalent to Absence; whatever were the Letter of the Law, Practice made it so. And *Polybius* tells us, it was so put in *Execution*. If any Man of the *Watch* be found asleep, (saith he) ξυλοκοπέι, he is put to the *Bastinado*, a *capital* Punishment, and reach'd to the Head: For the then *Bastinado* was *Fuste cæditur*; and as they now pass the Pikes,[2] a thousand to one but the Party died under it. A whole *Squadron* of Men being to do Execution, one Back-friend or other would dash out his Brains, as now one Pike or other would broach him through. The *Roman* Discipline extreme dogged, and so profess'd itself, especially toward the *Watch*. The *Ban-dogs of the Capitol*, because they bark'd not that Night when the *Gaules* surpriz'd it; had their Legs broken, and were split alive upon a two-fork'd Stake set up in Publick; and in Memory thereof, (saith *Livy*) some Dogs were yearly so used, for Examples sake to make *Watch-men* beware.

And the *Rounders* so impartial herein, that they would make Execution *ipso facto*. *Epaminondas* walks the *Round*, and finding one *Soldier* asleep, some of the *Corrounders* entreat for him: Well, saith he, for your sakes I will leave him as I found him, and therewithal he stakes him to the Ground with his *Halbert*: He found him in a dead Sleep, and so he left him. Some dim Prints of that *Discipline* are seen to this Day in our modern Wars, where sometime the *Rounder* will clap a *Musquet-shot* through a sleepy Head: But antiently they durst do no other; for to wink at the Fault, or delay the Punishment, was in the Governour, *Patrimonii & astimationis damnum*, a Loss of Lands and Honour; and in Under-Officers, *capitale supplicium*. They durst not then sleep wilfully, and they had no need to sleep, they were not over-watch'd. How the *Day-watch* stood I have not yet read; but for the *Night-watch*, all

1. Paulus Diaconus (Paulus Warnefridus), the chief Lombard historian of the eighth century who worked probably at Monte Cassino.

2. *Pass the Pikes:* a form of 'running the gauntlet', used as a military punishment in the seventeenth century: also known as the 'Loupegarthe', see R. Monro, *Expedition with the . . . Scots Regiment* (1637), pt. 1, p. 4.

the World knows it was divided into four equal Parts, each containing three Planetary Hours, or one Quarter of the Night, how long or short soever. And the Turn came about but every third Night; and then every third Hour they were relieved by putting in a fresh *Watch*. It was now past the *Vernal Æquinoctial*, no *one Night-watch* sate full three modern Hours; so three Hours over in above three-score would bring no *Over-watching*. Seeing then they neither durst nor did, Why yet do they say they were asleep? The Reason is, They are of the ragged *Regiment*, mercenary *Soldiers*, hired to it by the *Priests*, with a large Piece of Money. The *Provant-man*[1] will undertake to say any thing, yea to do any thing for Money; for ten Groats a Week tug at a Wheel-barrow, and for a Stiver more, serve the *Enemy*, and for a *Piece*, pistol a *Prince*; suffer any thing for Mony; for a *Dollar* take the *Strappado*; for a Brace, draw at a *Decimation*.[2] Thus the *Priest* dealt with the silly *Soldiers*, as they did with *Judas*, only put them upon hanging. An old Trick of the *Priests*, and much in Use at this Day, seeing that now they practise it one upon the other, and so let them; good Speed may they have.

*

His *Resurrection* the Pattern and Pledge of ours, the Tenure whereby we hold our Title to *Salvation*. But for their being asleep, we will not much contend: It is credible they were so, the contrary being neither implied, nor expressed in the Scripture. But yet their Sleep is no Proof of their Saying. They know the things were done just as they say, for they were asleep the while. A right *Roman* Reason, a Proof put from a *Priest* to serve a sleepy *Soldier*. If they were asleep, how could they say he was stollen rather than risen? Or, if they suppose him stollen, how knew they his *Disciples* did it rather than other Men? This must needs argue in them either Calumny to accuse a Party without Cause, or Levity to lay the Cause upon a wrong Party; either way Folly to alledge so senseless a Reason. All our Knowledge is either from Sense, or Reason: from Reason they could not have it, That hath made against them all this while; from any Sense they could not, for they were asleep. In Sleep all Sensation is intercepted. They could neither hear, see, smell, taste, nor feel the *Disciples* coming, or his stealing; if they did, they were not asleep.

If some one were awake, and perceived it, why did he not give an *Alarm* to the rest? If they understood it afterwards from others, why do they not produce authentick Witnesses? If the *Disciples* themselves confessed it, why were they not punished, and Order taken to stop the Rumour of the *Resurrection*? There is no Way now left, but to pretend the *Spirit*, as our *Enthusiasts*

1. Provant-man: a venal hireling to be purchased cheap for any service.
2. Roman disciplinary practice; Cromwell used the same general method to punish looting. See *Several Proceedings in Parliament* 2nd to 14th October, 1652, p. 2488.

do, and to say, that while they slept, they had it in a Dream by Revelation. But that is refuted by Retortion of the same, for by Revelation every Christian knows the contrary; God reveals it unto him.

But why did the *Soldiers* produce this Reason? The Reason is, they took it upon Trust from the *Priests*. It is an old Error (let us not contend for the Age) to believe that the *Priest* cannot err. But why are the *Soldiers* got thus to argue against themselves? The Reason is, no Body else durst do it. In those Times, the *Soldiers* bore all the Sway, assumed all Power to make *Kings* and *Emperors*. But first the *Priest* hath done the like, putting the *Soldier* by. And now the *Peasant* thinks 'tis come to his Turn, under Pretence of his Privilege in *Parliament:*[1] He would dispose of *Kings* and *Commonwealths*, and rather than return it to the *Priest* from whom he hath taken it, would cast the Course back again upon the *Soldiers*. Nothing now contents the *Commonalty*, but *War* and *Contention*; he hath taken a Surfeit of *Peace*, the very Name of it grows odious: Now to give the *Soldier* his Passport, we sum up four Exceptions against his Saying: First, it is not *Verisimile*, the Unlikelihood of it hath appeared in every *Conradictory*. Secondly, they were *ignari rerum*, had no Information of what they affirm; neither Eye, nor Ear-witness of what they say, for they confess themselves asleep. Thirdly, Their Saying is contrary to what they had said before; in the Morning they told another Tale, at the eleventh Verse of this Chapter; if that were true, this is false; if that were not true, why should we believe this? Or who will trust Men in contrary Tales? Lastly, the Parties were corrupted, hired with a large Sum to utter their Saying, at the twelfth Verse. These two latter lie without the Text, and therefore I wholly forbear them, especially for the Point of *Corruption:* 'Tis a crafty Crime, and commonly hard to prove. We also forbear the Lie to the *Soldier*, because he abhors it. But to the *Priests* who put this Lie in their Mouths, and to their *Disciple-Priests*, who at this Day practise lying, and allow it to be lawful, we would mend the old Saying, *A Liar should have a good Memory*, and rather require in him a good Wit. His Memory serves but to avoid *Contradictions* of himself, but his Wit to prevent the *Contradictions* of others, that an Untruth seem not also unlikely. If therefore the *Priests* would have lied wisely, and with Credit, like *Satan* himself, the *Serpent* whom they served, they should, as they did formerly, have laid our *Saviour* to *Satan's* Charge, and have said, that the foul *Fiend* came by Night, and fetch'd him away; leaving out, *whilst the Watch slept*, and instead thereof have argued from the Descent of the Angel, and the Earthquake: This could not so easily have been discovered; but it might even as easily, where *Faith* had a *Fortification*; *human Reasons* urged against it are but as *Paper-shot*. Carnal Wisdom working against God is but Dirt and Rottenness. Our Counsels are

---

1. One of the offending passages, and keenly prophetic.

confounded, when carried against Christ. And so I come to my third and last Cursory, upon the Word of our *Saviour*.

Hitherto we have cleared the *Disciples*, but we must also give the *Soldier* content. There is no such Difference, but the Matter may be reconciled, and the Question stated on the *Soldiers* side. Said I not, it was the Fashion? The *Soldiers* then are in the right, their Saying very sound and *Christian:* A *Disciple* of his did come by Night and steal him away, and the *Soldiers* were asleep. A *Disciple* of his, and his most beloved *Disciple*, his human Soul, came by Night, was united to his Body, raised it, and withdrew it from the *Sepulchre* by Stealth, while the *Soldiers* were so between Sleeping and Waking, that they perceived it not. Of this *Cursory* very briefly, as the Words lie in order, declining all emergent *Controversies*, for that our present Quarrel lay only with the *Soldiers*.

We term him a *Disciple*, who receives Knowledge and Chastisement from another. As our *Saviour* was *God*, his *Soul* was ὁ μαθητὴς, the truest and most proper Disciple that ever was: It had received both Knowledge and Chastisement, as never Man had; Knowledge of all Manner, both Divine and Human infused and acquired: But whether it had no *Ignorance*, we leave it to the *Catholics.* and All Manner of Chastisement, both exemplary and satisfactory, for all Mankind, the Chastisement of our Peace was upon it: But whether it satisfied for *Reprobates*, we leave it to the *Arminians.* His Soul came, it could move, for it was separate; the Soul was from the Body, though neither from the *Godhead*: As all the rest of the Disciples, it forsook him on the *Cross*, and now it came again: But it came not as it went, it went by Violence and foreign Force, the *Jews* expelled it from him, although he was also willing it should go; but it came purely voluntary, by a domestick Agent: But whether by Virtue of the *Godhead*, or its own motive Faculty, we leave to the *School-men.* It came then, not as poor *Lazarus's* Soul came to *Abraham's* Bosom, carried by *Angels*, but single upon its own Force, and without any Help of others: But whether attended and waited upon by Troops of Angels, we leave it to the *Fathers. For the Time*, it came by *Night*; not for fear of the *Jews*, as *Nicodemus* came to him, but for love of his Promise, that he might rise the *third Day*. He came the *second* Night, the Night *second* to his *Passion*, but third to the Day of his *Resurrection*, some time between Midnight and Morning; but at what Time we leave it to the *Chronologers.* The *Unde* of its coming was from somewhere else, from a distant *Ubi*, for it was not come before it came: From whence definitively, whether from *Heaven* or *Hell*, we leave it to the *Calvinists.* The *Quo* or *Term* of its coming was the *Grave*, he subsisted there; but the *End* of the *Comer*[1], was the *Re-union* to the Body, to make his real Presence there: But whether thereby he became *Omnipresent*,

---

1. The act of coming. There might also have been an audacious double play with this word, in its meaning (Cummer, Kimmer) of 'gossip.'

to be every where while he was in the *Grave*, we leave to the *Lutherans*. His final Intent, not to organize the Body, it was not dismembred, nor any way corrupted, not so much as *in fieri*, no not dispositively; but to animate those Members, and to raise the Body from the Grave; in which Action both the Body and the Soul had their mutual Efficiency, each co-elevating other to make up the *Resurrection*: But whether these two Agents imply several Operations really distinct, we leave it to the *Nominalists*.

The Manner of his Resurrection so miraculous and ineffable, that bad Words express it best. In a moral Relation to the *Jews*, it is here termed Stealing: Not to shew what our *Saviour* did in his Rising, but to intimate what the *Jews* had committed by their *Crucifying*. Things of a super-eminent Nature, are fain to borrow Words of an inferior Signification, when they are related to a low Capacity; so *God* gives himself Attributes, not as he is, but according to the Weakness whereby Man apprehends him. And here the Action of our *Saviour* is set down, not as it is done, but according to the Wickedness that the *Jews* had done. The active Signification of Stealing belongs to our Saviour, but the moral Evil of it reflected upon others. The *Law* saith, he steals who fraudulently takes away something of another's, with Intent to get the Thing itself, its Use or Possession. If this Definition be true, his Resurrection was Stealing. His Body was now *Cadaver puniti*, the Carcase of one that had publickly suffered, and thereby forfeit to the *State*; no Man might meddle with it father than to bury it, nor that without special Permission; it was now none of his, his Right and Possession of it both gone; *tradiderat*, he had made Delivery of it, dispensed and passed it away to *Pilate*: *Pilate* disposed his Right to bury it, to the *Watch* to detain it, and now it was theirs. When therefore he took it from the *Grave*, he stole it: His *Repossession* of it defrauded all the *Præ-detainers*. Said they not also he was a Deceiver? But whether the Angel that rolled away the Stone, was necessary or ministerial, we leave it to the *Hermonists*.[1] By natural *Relation* his Body was his *own*, as being the essential and proper Counter-part of his Soul, præ-coexistent with it in one Person; but morally it was not so, or if it were, yet he might steal it for all that. A Man may steal that which is his own, by interverting that Right in it which hath been transferred to another; and what kind of *Theft* this was, we leave it to the *Lawyers*. God forbid we should lay other *Theft* to our Saviour, than that he attributes to himself, in saying, *He came like a Thief in the Night*, (*i.e.*) secretly and unawares: So was his Conveyance from the Grave, close, without the Consent and Notice of those that were present; such a Carriage we commonly call Stealth. We steal away from a Room, when we depart without the Knowledge of the *Company*: But whether he could convey himself so closely, as to pass through the *Tomb-stone*, we leave it to the *Philosophers*.

1. Hermonist: used here as an alternative to hermeneutist.

Yet so close it was, that the *Watch* perceived it not, for they were asleep; they were set to watch it, but they did not. Not to watch, is all one with not to be awake, and that with to be asleep. We commonly call him sleepy that is negligent or careless of what passeth, as the contrary we term Vigilant: So the *Watch* was fast asleep, they never gave Heed to the *Resurrection*: That so far from their Belief, that they had no Opinion of it. But if Death be a Kind of a Sleep, he is soundly asleep that lies for Dead; and so did the *Watch* in the 4th Verse of this Chapter, ἐγένοντο ὡσεὶ νεκροί, for Fear of the *Angel* they fell a shaking, and became as dead Men. His Presence gave them a strong *Dormitive*, it wrought beyond Sleep. Sleep reacheth but only to a Ligation of Sense; but in them all Motion ceased, they were exanimate: But whether that Fit held them only by way of *Syncope*, or did determine in a *Cataphora*, or *soporiferous* Passion, we leave it to the *Physicians*. *Fearful and cowardish Soldiers, more womanish than women!* At the Presence of the *Angel* the *Women* stand upright, but the *Soldiers* fall in a Swoon. Help them good *Women*, unbutton the *Soldiers*, ye need not fear their *Halberts*. There's Work for you and your *Spices*, your Odours to comfort and recal their *Spirits*. Bestow that *Charity* on the dying *Soldiers*, which you intended on your dear *Saviour*; for he is risen, and needs them not, but they may benefit the *Soldiers*. The *Soldiers*, used to such Fits, they had one of them the other Night in *Gethsemane*; but whether these Dejections were Sins in the *Soldiers*, we leave to the *Casuists*. Thus they were κοιμώμενοι, laid as Men asleep; for it signifies rather the Reclination or Posture of one asleep, than the Affection of Sleep itself. He that lies still without Sense or Motion, whether he be in a Sleep, or Trance, or dead, we say κοιμώμενος; and we call the *Church-yard* κοιμητήριον, because the Dead lye there as if they were asleep, they stir not. And so we must all be laid; there's no *Dormitory*. Our Case somewhat like the *Soldiers*: We are appointed here to watch our *Saviour*; and as we do it, we are subject to the *Soldiers* Infirmity, apt to be cast asleep, and become as dead Men. Yet let us not be subject to their Fear, our Death is but like their Swooning, that's the worst. We are liable to rise again, and our *Resurrection* shall be like our *Saviour's*: His and ours make a mutual *Aspect*; his the *Specimen*, and ours the *Compliment*. What he practised on himself, he perfects in us: He will come again by Night, and steal us to Glory, while we lye sleeping in the Grave. *Even so come Lord Jesus.*

The Recantation Sermon

preached the following day.

THE PREFACE BEFORE THE SERMON

Personal Prefaces are commonly unpleasant, mine is to me: It is *nomine pœnæ*, it requires my *Patience*, it entreats *yours*. I never came here *sponte*, sometimes upon *Request*, but now upon *Command*, to which my Obedience is very voluntary, as willing to give Satisfaction as any to receive it. I never stood here to shew my self but now, and now not for Worth, or Wickedness, but yet for Weakness, in not discerning the three vital Circumstances of a well ordered Action, *Person*, *Time*, and *Place*. For it I am now Prisoner to *Censure*, the Spectacle of *Submission*, and Petitioner for *Pardon*. It is good to be humble, I like it very well, and use it more than some Men think I do. My present Business is not to repeat that Sermon which the Repeater condemned, and left unrepeated in the Forenoon. I call it that, for now it is none of mine: It hath been censured publickly and justly; and so let it suffer, the whole for some bad Parts: as usually the Pravity of one Member is destructive to the whole Body. If ye will please to let it die, I will substitute another in the room; whereto, (though enjoined by Authority) my self doth most willingly condescend. My Text was also imposed and delivered in these Words, ἦσαν ἅπαντες ὁμοθυμαδὸν ἐπὶ τὸ αὐτό. In Prosecution whereof, I humbly crave a fair Construction, and a favourable Acception. First, for my Offence past, that my *Readiness* to acknowledge it, may go for one Degree of *Satisfaction* and *sudden Recantation* for another. What it wants in Ripeness, is supplied in Sincerity, though in this the more mature, because the more timely. Secondly, For my present Memory, I have had no Time to furnish it: It is a dull and drowsy Faculty, a great deal a-do to make it ready: And besides, it is somewhat cowardly in Point of Danger. It dares not shew it self; the least Agitation makes it run away; and my self hath partly spared it for your sake and University. My present Sermon is but a Brief, I would desire you to hear it read. You may please to return to the Text; 'tis written,

Acts ii. 1. the latter Part, *They were all with
one Accord in one Place.*

Man ceaseth to be *Man*, if we conceive him *all sufficient*; God only is so, He only is *all-sufficient*, who is only *Almighty*. Man's Being and his Good, is

Indigency and Want: His chiefest Business is to contend against it, and his Happiness to abolish it. *Private Want* is an Occasion of *Difference* and *Dissent*; but *common Want* the common Cause of *Concord*, the *Parent* and *Procurer* of moral Unity and all humane Societies. So all our Assemblies are grounded upon Want, sometimes to give Thanks that the past hath been supplied, but commonly to supply the Wants present. The Reason is, that when a Plurality of Agents are united in their Efficacy, the Operation is far more effectual than if each wrought single; and what the single Members cannot obtain apart, they may acquire jointly, being incorporate into one Body. This also is the Case of Christ's Disciples, the Want of their Master collects and imbodies them in together. They want him twice; once in Mount *Calvary*; there they want his Soul: This gathers them close in *Jerusalem*, and the Door is shut on them, but the Place not specified.

The second Time, he forsakes them on the Mount *Olivet* at the 9th Verse of the former Chapter, then they want his Person; that puts them together again at the 13th Verse, in the upper Room; there they consider of another Want, Means to perform their Ministry.

*

In the same Place; Not the same Place numerically, but relatively, in the same Room. This Place was a high Place; it was an *upper Room* and comely. We should do all Religious Exercises in a decent Place; the paring away of *Ceremonies* doth but take away the *Churches Ornaments*. Then it was a *high Room*. At all spiritual Exercises we should ascend. Now it is called in Latine *Cænaculum*, a Room to Sup in: All religious Exercises should be begun with the *Supper of the Lord*, and that must be common too, not for one only: This Room (some say) was belonging to *Nicodemus*; yet this proves not for *Conventicles*: For if we have the like Authority we will release our Canon. What if we say, this is *Solomon*'s Porch? For there were six-score Persons, and it was noised about by and by, yea by nine of the Clock *Peter* was in his Sermon: This therefore is like not to be in a private Chamber: But were not this, yet the other was, *verse 46*.

God would have them join together to receive the Holy Ghost; for where the Hearts are together it is much, but where they are together, and their Body in one Place, there is all the good Place can afford. Thus we came from the Plurality to the Unanimity, and from the Unanimity to the Unipresence; the first without the second is but confuted, and the second without the third is but singularity; but these altogether make a compleat Parliament.

And now for Application of what hath been said to our Parliament; in the Disciples a spiritual Want was the Cause of their Assembly, in the Parliament a temporal Want. The Event in the one was Good; God grant it be so in the other. The Time of that was after the Resurrection, and so is it of this. The Persons are all alike, *Men* all, no *Women*, they are too talkative. The Number alike, *those*, all the *Primitive Church*; *these*, all the *Commonwealth*. Of them both our Opinions are alike; the one we honour, and the other too, as true Law-givers. They were unanimous and unipresent, and so also is the Parliament; they had one Counsel, so have we; their *Accord* was good, and so is ours; perfect, to cut off all bad *Accord*. Their *Accord* resolves a spiritual Welfare, and so is our Accord, to mantain ourselves by War. So of these our Opinions are alike; the one would be without War, were they not provoked thereto, but now 'tis needful: So is our War also. That was an upper Room, high and stately, so is the Parliament; that was in the Suburbs of *Jerusalem*, this of *London*. Now let us praise God for them, and pray for them, that there be not Opposition between them. Let the *King* be the *Head*, they the *Heart*, we the *Members*. Let it be like the Parliament in *Mount Sinai*, the King and Subjects as *God* and *Moses*, and we like the *Israelites*. Let God say to the King that he will *help him*, and *destroy his Enemies*: Let the King say to his People as *David* to the *Gibeonites*; and let the People say to him as *Israel* to *David*, *We will serve and obey thee only, and do what thou commandest us*: And let me pray for them, that they may stand fast in the Faith: And let's all say of them, all that be of *Israel*, as a Congregation of one Mind, that this Union may be ruled by Order, and that like this spiritual one, let's pray there may be *one God, one Mind, one Spirit*; and let all the People say, *Amen*.

*

Here remains as yet a personal Conclusion. If I heretofore seemed to deliver any Doctrine contrary to this I now deliver, I utterly renounce it. The last Time I had these Words, *Now the Peasant thinks, &c.* I had also these Words, *Nothing contents the Commonalty but War and Contention*. I confess there I did very ill, forgetting that of *Solomon*, *There is a Time for War, and a Time for Peace*. For any other erroneous Thing I require your Pardon. A Word once spoken cannot be recall'd, it may be stopt. In the same Place where the Blot was made I am come to wipe it out. My last Petition to you is for Patronage from further Trouble.

JOHN DONNE

The Chastisement of Love

A sermon preached at St. Pauls, on the Sunday after
the conversion of St. Paul, 1624

Christ, who in his humane nature hath received from the Father all Judgement, and power, and dominion over this world, hath received all this, upon
that condition that he shall governe in this manner, *Aske of me, and I shall
give thee the Heathen for thine inheritance*, sayes the Father; How is he to use
them, when he hath them? Thus, *Thou shalt breake them with a rod of iron, and
dash them in pieces like a potters vessell*. Now, God meant well to the Nations,
in this bruising and breaking of them; God intended not an annihilation of
the Nations, but a reformation; for Christ askes the Nations for an Inheritance, not for a triumph; therefore it is intended of his way of governing
them; and his way is to bruise and beat them; that is, first to cast them downe,
before he can raise them up, first to breake them before he can make them
in his fashion. *Novit Dominus vulnerare ad amorem*; The Lord, and onely the
Lord knowes how to wound us, out of love; more then that, how to wound
us into love; more then all that, to wound us into love, not onely with him
that wounds us, but into love with the wound it selfe, with the very affliction
that he inflicts upon us; The Lord knowes how to strike us so, as that we
shall lay hold upon that hand that strikes us, and kisse that hand that wounds
us. *Ad vitam interficit, ad exaltationem prosternit*, sayes the same Father; No
man kills his enemy therefore, that his enemy might have a better life in
heaven; that is not his end in killing him: It is Gods end; Therefore he brings
us to death, that by that gate he might lead us into life everlasting; And he
hath not discovered, but made that Northerne passage, to passe by the frozen
Sea of calamity, and tribulation, to Paradise, to the heavenly Jerusalem. There
are fruits that ripen not, but by frost; There are natures, (there are scarce any
other) that dispose not themselves to God, but by affliction. And as Nature
lookes for the season for ripening, and does not all before, so Grace lookes for
the assent of the soule, and does not perfect the whole worke, till that come.
It is Nature that brings the season, and it is Grace that brings the assent; but

till the season for the fruit, till the assent of the soule come, all is not done.

Therefore God begun in this way with *Saul,* and in this way he led him all his life. *Tot pertulit mortes, quot vixit dies,* He dyed as many deaths, as he lived dayes; for so himselfe sayes, *Quotidie morior, I die daily*; God gave him sucke in blood, and his owne blood was his daily drink; He catechized him with calamities at first, and calamities were his daily Sermons, and meditations after; and to authorize the hands of others upon him, and to accustome him to submit himself to the hands of others without murmuring, Christ himself strikes the first blow, and with that, *Cecidit, he fell,* (which was our first consideration, in his humilitation) and then, *Cecidit in terram, He fell to the ground,* which is our next.

I take no farther occasion from this Circumstance, but to arme you with consolation, how low soever God be pleased to cast you, Though it be to the earth, yet he does not so much cast you downe, in doing that, as bring you home. Death is not a banishing of you out of this world; but it is a visitaton of your kindred that lie in the earth; neither are any nearer of kin to you, then the earth it selfe, and the wormes of the earth. You heap earth upon your soules, and encumber them with more and more flesh, by a superfluous and luxuriant diet; You adde earth to earth in new purchases, and measure not by Acres, but by Manors, nor by Manors, but by Shires; And there is a little Quillet, a little Close, worth all these, A quiet Grave. And therefore, when thou readest, That God makes thy bed in they sicknesse, rejoyce in this, not onely that he makes that bed, where thou dost lie, but that bed where thou shalt lie; That that God, that made the whole earth, is now making thy bed in the earth, a quiet grave,[1] where thou shalt sleep in peace, till the Angels Trumpet wake thee at the Resurrection, to that Judgement where thy peace shall be made before thou commest, and writ, and sealed, in the blood of the Lamb.

The Alienation of God

A Sermon preached at St. Paul's, on January 29th., 1625

I aske not *Mary Magdalen,* whether lightnesse were not a burden; (for sin is certainly, sensibly a burden) But I aske *Susanna* whether even chast beauty were not a burden to her; And I aske *Ioseph* whether personall comelinesse

---

1. The concept of the 'quiet grave' was original neither to Donne nor to Shakespeare; it was a common metaphor in mediaeval preaching.

were not a burden to him. I aske not *Dives*, who perished in the next world, the question; but I aske them who are made examples of *Solomons* Rule, of that *sore evill*, (as he calls it) *Riches kept to the owners thereof for their hurt*, whether Riches be not a burden.

All our life is a continuall burden, yet we must not groane; A continuall squeasing, yet we must not pant; And as in the tendernesse of our childhood, we suffer, and yet are whipt if we cry, so we are complained of, if we complaine, and made delinquents if we call the times ill. And that which addes waight to waight, and multiplies the sadnesse of this consideration, is this, That still the best men have had most laid upon them. As soone as I heare God say, that he hath found *an upright man, that feares God, and eschews evill*, in the next lines I finde a Commission to Satan, to bring in Sabeans and Chaldeans upon his cattell, and servants, and fire and tempest upon his children, and loathsome diseases upon himselfe. As soone as I heare God say, That he hath found *a man according to his own heart*, I see his sonnes ravish his daughters, and then murder one another, and then rebell against the Father, and put him into straites for his life. As soone as I heare God testifie of Christ at his Baptisme, *This is my beloved Sonne in whom I am well pleased*, I finde that Sonne of his *led up by the Spirit, to be tempted of the Devill*. And after I heare God ratifie the same testimony againe, at his Transfiguration, (*This is my beloved Sonne, in whom I am well pleased*) I finde that beloved Sonne of his, deserted, abandoned, and given over to Scribes, and Pharisees, and Publicans, and Herodians, and Priests, and Souldiers, and people, and Judges, and witnesses, and executioners, and he that was called the beloved Sonne of God, and made partaker of the glory of heaven, in this world, in his Transfiguration, is made now the Sewer of all the corruption, of all the sinnes of this world, as no Sonne of God, but a meere man, as no man, but a contemptible worme. As though the greatest weaknesse in this world, were man, and the greatest fault in man were to be good, man is more miserable then other creatures, and good men more miserable then any other men.

But then there is *Pondus Gloriæ, An exceeding waight of eternall glory*, and that turnes the scale; for as it makes all worldly prosperity as dung, so it makes all worldly adversity as feathers. And so it had need; for in the scale against it, there are not onely put temporall afflictions, but spirituall too; And to these two kinds, we may accommodate those words, *He that fals upon this stone*, (upon temporall afflictions) may be bruised, broken, *But he upon whom that stone falls*, (spirituall afflictions) *is in danger to be ground to powder*. And then, the great, and yet ordinary danger is, That these spirituall afflictions grow out of temporall; Murmuring, and diffidence in God, and obduration, out of worldly calamities; And so against nature, the fruit is greater and heavier then the Tree, spirituall heavier then temporall afflictions.

They who write of Naturall story, propose that Plant for the greatest wonder in nature, which being no firmer then a bull-rush, or a reed, produces and beares for the fruit thereof no other but an intire, and very hard stone. That temporall affliction should produce spirituall stoninesse, and obduration, is unnaturall, yet ordinary. Therefore doth God propose it, as one of those greatest blessings, which he multiplies upon his people, *I will take away your stony hearts, and give you hearts of flesh*; And, Lord let mee have a fleshly heart in any sense, rather then a stony heart. Wee finde mention amongst the observers of rarities in Nature, of hairy hearts, hearts of men, that have beene overgrowne with haire[1]; but of petrified hearts, hearts of men growne into stone, we read not; for this petrefaction of the heart, this stupefaction of a man, is the last blow of Gods hand upon the heart of man in this world. Those great afflictions which are powred out of the Vials of the seven Angels upon the world, are still accompanied with that heavy effect, that that affliction hardned them. *They were scorched with heats and plagues*, by the fourth Angel, and it followes, *They blasphemed the name of God, and repented not, to give him glory*. Darknesse was induced upon them by the first Angel, and it followes, *They blasphemed the God of heaven, and repented not of their deeds*. And from the seventh Angel there fell hailestones of the waight of talents, (perchance foure pound waight) upon men; And yet these men had so much life left, as to *blaspheme God*, out of that respect, which alone should have brought them to glorifie God, *Because the plague thereof was exceeding great*. And when a great plague brings them to blaspheme, how great shall that second plague be, that comes upon them for blaspheming?

Let me wither and weare out mine age in a discomfortable, in an unwholesome, in a penurious prison, and so pay my debts with my bones, and recompence the wastfulnesse of my youth, with the beggery of mine age; Let me wither in a spittle[2] under sharpe, and foule, and infamous diseases, and so recompence the wantonnesse of my youth, with that loathsomnesse in mine age; yet, if God with-draw not his spirituall blessings, his Grace, his Patience, If I can call my suffering his Doing, my passion his Action, All this that is temporall, is but a caterpiller got into one corner of my garden, but a mill-dew fallen upon one acre of my Corne; The body of all, the substance of all is safe, as long as the soule is safe. But when I shall trust to that, which wee call a good spirit, and God shall deject, and empoverish, and evacuate that spirit, when I shall rely upon a morall constancy, and God shall shake, and enfeeble, and enervate, destroy and demolish that constancy; when I shall

1. Pericarditis: inflammation of the pericordium (the closed membrane sac enveloping the heart). Due to antibiotics and 'chemo-therapy' the condition has become rare. 'Fibrous pericarditis' is marked by fibrous exudate on the serous membrane which, to the eye of a seventeenth-century anatomist, would have resembled 'hair'. I am indebted for this diagnosis to my physician, Dr. J. M. Slattery.

2. A hospital for the poor.

think to refresh my selfe in the serenity and sweet ayre of a good conscience, and God shall call up the damps and vapours of hell it selfe, and spread a cloud of diffidence, and an impenetrable crust of desperation upon my conscience; when health shall flie from me, and I shall lay hold upon riches to succour me, and comfort me in my sicknesse, and riches shall flie from me, and I shall snatch after favour, and good opinion, to comfort me in my poverty; when even this good opinion shall leave me, and calumnies and misinformations shall prevaile against me; when I shall need peace, because there is none but thou, O Lord, that should stand for me, and then shall finde, that all the wounds that I have, come from thy hand, all the arrowes that stick in me, from thy quiver; when I shall see, that because I have given my selfe to my corrupt nature, thou hast changed thine; and because I am all evill towards thee, therefore thou hast given over being good towards me; When it comes to this height, that the fever is not in the humors, but in the spirits, that mine enemy is not an imaginary enemy, fortune, nor a transitory enemy, malice in great persons, but a reall, and an irresistible, and an inexorable, and an everlasting enemy, The Lord of Hosts himselfe, The Almighty God himselfe, the Almighty God himselfe onely knowes the waight of this affliction, and except hee put in that *pondus gloriæ*, that exceeding waight of an eternall glory, with his owne hand, into the other scale, we are waighed downe, we are swallowed up, irreparably, irrevocably, irrecoverably, irremediably. . . .

3

CAROLEAN AND CIVIL WARS

JOHN WILLIAMS[1]

The sermon at James's funeral service was preached by that worldly and formidable ecclesiastic John Williams, Bishop of Lincoln and future Archbishop of York. Tolerant and unbigoted in an age of rising intolerance and bigotry, he could be hard when he thought it necessary, and there were few scruples his agile mind could not overcome; but he was a master negotiator; he preferred conciliation and compromise to the pride of deadlock for the sake of preserving the virginity of an unfertile principle. If he was given to intrigue, it was usually intrigue for sane and peaceful ends, however incidentally profitable to himself. Like Hales and Chillingworth he represented the case for reason and restraint which, with the benefit of hindsight, we see had no hope of success, until the fever of reckless contention, which had seized and was pounding through the body of England, had run its course. In his busy career of high office Williams had time to preach only occasionally; but it was his accomplishment as a pulpit orator which first attracted the favourable attention of the king. He was also, as this sermon preached over James's coffin illustrates, a consummate courtier. It is perhaps the last sermon of its kind, untroubled, serene, ornamental without a hint of controversy or danger, to be preached at court in England until the Restoration.

1. John Williams, 1582–1650. St. John's College, Cambridge 1598. B.A. 1601. Fellow 1603. B.D. 1613. D.D. 1617. Dean of Salisbury 1619. Dean of Westminster 1620. Succeeded Bacon as Lord Keeper. Bishop of Lincoln 1621, Laud's principal rival, he was imprisoned during the middle years of the 1630s and, with eleven other Bishops including Pierce and Hall, was imprisoned again in the Tower in 1640. He advised the king against signing the bill taking away his right to dissolve parliament. Archbishop of York 1640. Survived the civil war to live in retirement in Wales.

Great Britain's Solomon

A sermon preached at the funeral of James I by the
Bishop of Lincoln, on the 5th. of May, 1625

Salomon was *twice crown'd*, and anoynted a King, 1 *Chron.* 29.22. So was King *Iames. Salomons* minority was rough through the quarrells of the former Soueraigne; So was that of King *Iames. Salomon* was learned aboue all the *Princes* of the East, 1 *Kings* 4.30. So was King *Iames* aboue all *Princes* in the vniuersall world. *Salomon* was a Writer in *Prose*, and *Verse*, 1 *Kings* 4.32. So in a very pure and exquisite manner was our sweet Soueraigne King *Iames. Salomon* was the greatest *Patron* we euer read of to *Church*, and *Churchmen*; and yet no greater (*let the house of Aaron now confesse*) then King *Iames. Salomon* was honoured with *Embassadors* from all the *Kings of the Earth*, 1 *Kings* 4. last *verse*; and so you know, was King *Iames. Solomon* was a maine Improuer of his *home* commodities, as you may see in his *Trading* with *Hiram*, 1 *Kings* 5.9. *verse*; and, God knowes, it was the daily study of King *Iames. Salomon* was a great maintainer of *shipping*, and *Nauigation*, 1 *Kings* 10.14. A most proper Attribute to King *Iames. Salomon* beautified very much his *Capitall Citie* with *Buildings*, and *Water-workes*, 1 *Kings* 9.15. So did King *Iames*. Euery man liu'd in peace vnder his *vine*, and his *Figge-Tree* in the daies of *Salomon*, 1 *Kings* 4.25. And so they did in the blessed daies of King *Iames*. And yet towards his End, K. *Salomon* had secret *Enemies*, *Razan*, *Hadad*, and *Ieroboam*, and prepared for a *Warre* vpon his going to his *Graue*, as you may see in the *verse* before my *Text*. So had, and so did King *Iames*. Lastly, before any *Hostile Act* we reade of in the *History*, King *Salomon* died in peace, when he had liued about 60. *Yeares*, as *Lyra* and *Tostatus*[1] are of opinion. And so you know did King *Iames*. You see therefore a Mould fitted for another *Salomon* in the *Bulke*, and *Generall*. . . .

And I must say lesse of the *Last of all*, præuented therein by the *Magnificence* of his *Maiestie*: Because, for any thing wee reade in the *Scriptures*, the *Funeralls* of the first, came nothing neare the Stately *Funerals* of our second *Salomon*. Shall I say therefore of my præsent *Master*, that he is a great, and a hopefull *King?* All that is true; but I leaue it to another, that hath time to enlarge it. I will onely say, as St. *Ambrose* said of *Theodosius, Summam votorum*

---

1. Nicolaus de Lyra, 1250–1314, Biblical commentator whose *Postiliae* received wide attention. Tostado Alphonso, 1400–1455, Spanish theologian, critic of Torquemada and author of commentaries on the Old Testament.

complexus est, pius est;[1] He hath shew'd himselfe, as we desir'd he should, a *pious Sonne* of a *most pious Father*. He layes, with all possible solemnity, the Bodie of his *Father* in the Sepulchre of the Kings, erected by *Henry the seventh* his great *Grandfather, Tanquam in Ciuitate Dauid Patris eius; Iust as this other Salomon* was, In *the Citie of Dauid* his *Father*. And yet, with due reuerence to his *Maiestie*, I must be bold to say, that all this is nothing to that *Honour*, which God hath done to the *Funeralls* of his *Father*. So *deare in the fight of the Lord is the Death of his Saints*. For God hath prouided another *Statue* yet to adorne the *Exequies* of our *Late Soueraigne*. I doe not meane this *Artificiall Repræsentation* within the *Hearse*; for this shews no more then his outward *Body*; or rather the Bodie of his Bodie, his cloathes and Ornaments. But I meane that *Statue* which (beyond all *former præsidents of Pietie*)[2] *walk't on foot* this day after the *Hearse*, one of *Myrons Statues, Qui pæne Hominu manimas effinxerit*, which came so neare to the *Soules* of Men, *A breathing Statue* of all his *Vertues*. This God hath done for *Him*, or rather for Vs. For as he hath made a liuely *Repræsentation* of the *Vertues of Salomon*, in the Person of King *Iames*: So hath he done a like *Repræsentation* of the *Vertues* of King *Iames*, in the Person of King *Charles* our Gratious *Soueraigne*.

I will therefore conclude these Exequies of *Salomon*, with a saying spoken by that imitator of *Salomon, Mortuus est Pater, & quasi non est mortuus, Similem enim reliquit sibi post se*. Though his *Father* be dead, yet is he, as though hee were not dead, for he hath left *One* behinde him most like himselfe. *Whom God long prosper, and præserue.*

The Grace of our Lord *&c.*

1. Williams offers the reference *Orat. Funebr. de Morts Theodos. Imperator*; which can only be *De Obitu Theodosii Oratio*, but the phrase he uses does not figure in this work.
2. Te ad sydra tollit humus. Pliny the younger. *Panegyric*.

WILLIAM LAUD

'Curse not the king in thy thought', Manwaring would say. It had not come to that, or anywhere near it; the king was treated personally with deep respect and deference, and to the end of his life many who abhorred the royal policies absolved the king himself from any blame, ascribing responsibility for them entirely to his principal advisers. Of these, until the withdrawal of the king from London and the opening of hostilities between the crown and parliament, the paramount in England was William Laud, the Archbishop of Canterbury. So much obloquy has been cast on his name, by Puritan writers from Prynne onwards, that it is desirable to recall what his policy represented. Laud believed that the Church of England required at its centre a fixed and authorized liturgy, which would give to church services a regulated form and dignity. He believed that officiating clergy should be distinguished from the congregation by wearing approved vestments; he believed that the communion table should be placed in observance of ancient tradition 'altarwise' north and south at the upper end of the chancels. On one occasion, a dog having run away with the consecrated bread, he authorized the building of rails to prevent future desecration, and, in general, he encouraged the beautifying of churches. Without these basic forms he felt there could be no secure continuity in the church, and he believed it his duty to try to restore a more respectful practice: ''tis superstition nowa-days for any man to come with more reverence into church, than a tinker and his bitch into an ale-house'. To discharge his duty he was prepared if necessary to invoke the machinery of severe penal laws. But in many ways Laud was an exceptionally tolerant man and went out of his way to protect the right of ordinary people to enjoy their social liberties. Unfortunately, both his regulations and his tolerations were abomination to the Puritans. The regulations were Idolatry to all and the games were sinful vanity to the more extreme. Unfortunately too, for any hope of peaceful success Laud might have had, his church policy became inextricably entangled with the king's political programme, and many people who might not otherwise have objected to his episcopalian design did so when acceptance of it was made a test of *political* loyalty. On the other hand, in the growing confusion of the contention which was about to develop a new dimension, to be religiously Puritan, was not necessarily to be politically Puritan, that is, what would emerge as Parliamentarian. There were Presbyterians without interest in the overt political issues of the king's right to levy unvoted taxes, who would have been perfectly happy to accept the 'divine right of the king', providing it could have been reconciled with the divine right of the Presbyterian church and the authority of the Covenant. The conflagration of all these elements still lay ahead in 1625, when Laud preached at the inauguration of Charles I. The pristine clarity of the language, and the total absence of scholastic ostentation from one of the most eminent scholars of the age, is specially worthy of note as a corrective against the falsifying simplifications which have persisted in circulation (since they were first issued, as a kind of party propaganda), concerning the distinctions of character between 'Puritan' and 'Prelatic' preaching.

Laud was at this time Bishop of St. Davids and already on the way to becoming first minister of the crown. If ever a man discerned trouble ahead, it was the preacher on this occasion.

The Dangers of Disobedience

A sermon preached at the Inauguration of Charles I in
1625[1]

Take heed, I heartily beg it of you. I say it againe, take heed I heartily beg it of you, that no sin of unthankfulnesse, no base detracting murmuring sin, possesse your soules, or whet your tongues, or soure your brests against the Lord, & against his Anoynted: but remember in that these two things.

First, remember, that it is as easie for God to take away any blessing (even the great blessing of a good King) as to give it, remember that.

And secondly, remember, that unthankfulnesse to God for so gracious a

1. Published posthumously in 1645.

King, is the very ready way to doe it, remember that too: and therefore looke to these things in time.

I, but what then, hath a King enough, when God hath given him justice, and judgement? May his prayers then cease for himselfe, as your prayers for him? hath he no more need of God, when God hath once given him judgement?

O God forbid; surely he hath, and it is to be presumed, that the King daily praieth; I am sure his dutie it is, to pray that God would ever please to continue, and increase the righteousnesse, and judgement hee hath given to him. Nor can I thinke, but that *David* was very oft at this prayer too: for he saith, *Psal.99. The Kings power loveth judgement.* And it is more then probable, that that he loved, he would pray for; hee prayed to have it, and to increase it. And he that prayes so oft, *psal.119.* I say so oft that God would keepe him *in the way of his Commandements, and cause him to make much of his Law*; he must of necessity be presumed to pray for justice, and judgement, which is the vigour of all Lawes, divine, and humane.

And Kings have great need oft to pray for this grace, and for the continuance, and increase of it too.

For Kings stand high, that is true; but the higher they stand, the more they are exposed to tempests, and wind-shakings, that passe over the lower vallies with lesse noyse, and danger.

And Kings are great. That is true too: but the greater they are, the stiffer are the blasts of all temptations on them to batter, at least to shake justice, and judgement. Therefore they have need of God still, when hee hath given them most: and doubtlesse hee that hath most, hath need to pray: for the greater the King is, hee must most be presumed to be carefull of this dutie, that he prayes to God more then once, and more then others.

Neither is this prayer for strengthening, and increasing of judgement only. *David* goes further yet, it is not *Give the King judgements O God, But give the King thy judgements.*

For none but *thine* O Lord will serve the King; nor none but thine will long preserve the people. I know worldly policie, and the Professors may flatter themselves too hot in it. They may think that any course of justice, that any Standard may serve to governe a kingdom without any eye at all to heaven, without any respect to Gods judgements; without principally ayming at the judgement that is given, and executed by the Lord, as it is, 2 *Chron.* 29. They may think this and more; but let no man deceive himselfe, and then most when hee would be wise: For certainly, there can be no kingdome rightly constituted, further then God himselfe comes in, in laying the foundation of it in true, impartiall judgement. When the foundation of a kingdome is perfectly laid (which is a blessing seldome perfect in all things in any kingdom whatsoever, yet) no kingdome can continue upon such a foundation, longer then it stands upright on it. If it sway on either side; it if fall not presently, it growes weaker still, the more it leans away from justice and judgement which is Gods.

Soon after, in the same year, Laud registered a heightened awareness of danger.[1] Here we find him no longer content to caution against weakening of authority; the spectre already before his eyes is dissolution if authority be deserted by those who should be its protectors.

A Kingdom Melting

A sermon preached by the Bishop of St. Davids at
Whitehall on Sunday, 29th June 1625[2]

Psal. 75. 23. When I shall receive the congregation (or when I shall take a conuenant time) I will judge according unto right. The earth is dissolved (or melted) and all the inhabitants thereof; I beare up the pillars of it.

This Psalme is accounted a kind of Dialogue between God and the Prophet. For David sometimes speakes in his owne person and sometimes in Gods.

And by this we haue found what and who it is that melts great and glorious kingdoms. In the text there is no more *liquefacta est*, the earth is dissolved, not a word by *whom* or for what. But it is express *vers.* 7 that it is by God. And it is too well known that it is for sinne, and for great *sinne* too. For as there goes *sinne* before God *heates* so there go great and multiplied sinnes before God makes his *fire* so hote, as to *melt*, or dissolue a Kingdome. The *sinnes* of the *Amorite* not yet full, therefore not yet cast into the *melting* pot. But so soone as their *sinnes* were *full*, their State *melted*. The fruit of it from aboue, and the root of it from beneath, all destroyed. And this was not the *Amorites* case onely; for all Stories are ful of it, That when States haue *melted* into wanton, and lustfull *sinnes*, they haue not long after *dissolued* into desolation. For (as S. *Ierome* obserues) that course God holds with impious, and impenitent Kingdomes, as-well as men, *absque discretione personarum*, without any difference of persons, or places.

Well, when t'is *Terra liquefacta*, when a Kingdome *dissolues* and *melts*,

1. The king's nationally detested marriage with the French, Roman Catholic, Princess Henrietta Maria had just taken place.
2. pp. 1, 9-17.

what then? What? why then no man is in safety, till it settle againe; not a man. For the Text goes on: *The earth is dissolued, and all that dwell therein.* All men then to seeke what to doe; the wisest to seeke, and the strongest to seeke, All. And it must needes be so. For so long as a State is *Terra,* like solide ground, men know where to set their footing; and it is not euery *Earth-quake,* that swallowes the place. But when it is once, *Terra liquefacta, molten* and *dissolued,* there is no footing, no foundation then. *I sticke fast in the myre, where no ground is, Psal. 69* and *myre* is but *terra liquefacta, molten* and *dissolued earth.* All foule then, and no foundation.

And when a Kingdome *melts* indeed, that is, both wayes, In *sinne,* and vnder *punishment,* there's great reason the inhabitants should *melt* with it into *feare,* into *danger,* into *ruine.* For God neuer puts his *fire* to the *melting* of a State, but for *sinne,* and sinne that is neuer committed by the dead State, but by the liuing. For when a *fruitfull land is made barren,* it is *for the wickednesse of them that dwell therein.* And therefore there is great reason, when the *earth dissolues,* that the *inhabitants* should all sweat, and *melt* too.

When *Dauid* came to the Crowne t'was thus. How is it now? Why, if you take the *earth* at large, for the Kingdomes about you, out of question there hath beene *liquefactio;* a *melting* in the *earth,* and many Kingdomes haue *swet blood.* But if you take the *earth* for the State at home, then t'is high time to magnifie God: First, for the Renowned, Religious, and peaceable Reigne of our late dread Soueraigne of blessed Memorie, who for so many yeeres together, kept this Kingdome in peace, and from *melting:* And secondly, that now in the change of Princes, (which is not the least occasion for a State to *melt*) wee liue to see a miracle, *Change* without *Alteration.* Another King; but the same life-expression of all the Royall and Religious Vertues of his Father; and no sinewes shrinking, or *dissoluing* in the State.

If you aske me the cause of this happinesse, I can direct you to no other but God, and God in mercie. For as for the Kingdome, that is made of the same *Earth* with others, and is consequently subject to the same *disolution.* And as for vs that dwell therein, I doubt our *sinnes* haue been as calmorous vpon God to heate his *fire,* and make it fall on *melting,* as the *sinnes* of them that *inhabit* other Countreys.

And though I doubt not but God hath the sure mercies of David in store for the king, and will neuer faile him, yet if *Habitatores in ea,* they that dwell in this good and happy soile, will burden it and themselves with *sinne;* it will not be in the power, or wisdome, or courage, or piety of a King to keepe the State from *melting.* For Dauid was all these, and yet *liquefacta est terra,* the *Earth* was as good as *dissolued* for all that. And therefore that this Kingdome is not a *melting* too, I can giue no firme reason, but God and his Mercy. For hee is content to giue longer day for repentance, and repentance is able to doe all things with God. And the time calles apace for repentance: The

Heauens they *melt* into vnseasonable weather; and the Earth *melts* and *dissolues* her Inhabitants into infectious humours; and there's no way to stay these *meltings*, but by *melting* our selues, in, and by true repentance.

Would you then haue a settled and a flourishing State? Would you haue no *melting*, no *dissolution* in the Church? I know you would, it is the honourable and religious designe of you all: Why, but if you would indeed, The King must trust, and indeere his people: The people must honour, obey, and support their King: Both King, and Peeres, and People must religiously serue and honour God;[1] shut out all Superstition on Gods Name, the farther the better; but let in no prophanenesse therewhile. If this bee not done, take what care you can, God is aboue all humane wisedome, and in some degree or other there will bee *Liquefactio terra*, a *melting*, or a waste, both in Church and State.

And this falls in vpon the second generall part of the Text; which is The *Remedy*, as it was then with the Iewes, The *Preuention*, as it is now with vs; which God and the King will vse to keepe the State and the Church from *melting*. This Remedy (and the Preuention is iust the same) is expressed first in the Execution of *Iustice*. And this God promises for the King; and the King promises vnder God. *I will iudge according vnto right*, saith God; and *I*, saith the King.

Now *Iustice* and *Iudgement* is the greatest binder vp of a State; The great bounder of Peace and Warre. And it is not possible to finde *dissoluing* sinews in a Kingdome, that is gouerned by *Iustice*. For if the King flourish, the Kingdome cannot *melt*: And the Kings Throne, that is established by *Iustice*. Nay farther; Nothing but *Iustice* can establish the Throne, and make it firme indeed. But when God blesses the King with a heart full of *Iustice*, when God strengthens the King in the Execution of *Iustice*, when the King followes God as close as hee can, with *Ego iudicabo*, I my selfe will looke to the administration of *Iustice*, with which God hath trusted me; there can bee no *melting* about the Throne of the King, none in the State, none in the Church.

But then this Iustice, which preserues the King, and blesses the people, must be habituall. To doe *Iustice* casually, though the thing done be *iust*, yet the doing of it is not *Iustice*. The State may *melt* for all that, because the *Remedy* is but casuall.

Again, since the whole State hath interest in the *Iustice* of the King, his *Iustice* must be spreading ouer all persons, and in all causes. And so 'tis plurall in the Text, *I will iudge, Iustitias*, for euery mans cause, so farre as it is *iust*.

Why, but then must the King doe all this himselfe? No, God forbid that burden should lye vpon him? *Moses* was not able alone for that. It was, and it is too heauy. What then? why then *Iethro's* counsell must bee followed.

1. Tene magis salvum populus velit an populum tu. Servet in ambiguo qui consulit et tibi et urbi Iuppiter. Horace, lib. 1, ep. 16.

There must bee inferiour *Iudges* and *Magistrates* deputed by the King for this: Men of courage, fearing God, and hating Couetousnesse.[1] These must quit *Moses* from the inferiour trouble, that he may be actiue, and able for the great affaires of State. For if they be suffered to *melt* and drop downeward, there can be no standing dry or safe vnder them.

And hence it followes, that, *Ego iudicabo, I will iudge according vnto right*, is not onely the Kings engagement betweene God, and the People; but it is the engagement of euery Iudge, Magistrate, and Officer betweene God, the King, and the State. The Kings power, that's from God. The Iudges, and the subordinate Magistrates power, that's from the King. Both are for the good of the people, *That they may lead a peaceable life in all godlinesse, and honestie.* . . .

1. The hatred which Laud and Wentworth both incurred in the same quarters was partly due to their scrupulous opposition to the growing system of jobbery and nepotism in reversions and sale of offices, monopolies, and other manipulations of privilege, upon which a new emergent oligarchy relied for its nourishment.

JOHN PRESTON

If one were restricted to the words of two churchmen to illustrate the differences of values and emphases, as well as the specific issues dividing the Anglican and the Puritan positions on the eve of the Civil War, it would be difficult to find a better matched pair of foils than John Preston and Humphrey Sydenham.

Preston was a devious and complex character, and reckoned so in his own time, although he could write with a deceptive semblance of simplicity and inevitability. The intellectual leader of the Puritan faction at Cambridge, in succession to Perkins and Ames, he was in some respects markedly deviant from the general Puritan pattern of ways and means, being, perhaps, the only leading Puritan academic who was a consummate courtier. Not that he was venal, or favoured the court party. But he did have the quick, bland opportunism of the courtier. He did not scruple to capture the admiration of James I, who loved polemical acrobatics—the perverser the better—for their own sake, by proving in disputation before his royal auditor, that His Majesty's pet dog was capable of executing a syllogism. Power, temporal power, fascinated him, and the feints and deceptions of political intrigue appealed as if to a congenital competence in his nature. He appears to have been unable, or unwilling, to approach any situation openly or directly. Once, when he purposed to cross the channel to visit the Dutch universities, he went to intricate lengths to conceal his intentions, setting off demonstratively for Kent, to 'take the waters at Tunbridge', and, on his return, met any suggestion that he might have been out of England with an air of astonished incomprehension. On this occasion, however, he was under surveillance of a fox even craftier than himself. His activities had not escaped the attention of Lord Keeper Williams, who tailed him with a spy, fellow-travelling in the same boat with him to Rotterdam, to report back every move he made.

Nothing Preston did was ever quite what it seemed. When he was Master of Emmanuel he wished to absent himself from Cambridge for longer than was permitted by the college regulations, except in cases of 'violent detention', or engagement in 'college business'. By his persuasion the fellows were wrought upon to admit 'moral violence' —the violent moving of his conscience—within the definition of 'violent detention'. *Litigation* was next agreed to be valid 'college business', and a law suit was then kept simmering for four years. He was, said Fuller, 'the greatest pupil monger at the university, having sixteen fellow commoners (most heirs to fair estates) admitted in one year in Queen's College'. He surprised the world by refusing high office, the Bishopric of Gloucester, when it was offered him; but he had another, more strategic, perch in view, for

He was a perfect politician and used (lapwing like) to flutter most on that place which was furthest from his Eggs, exact at the concealment of his intentions with that simulation which some make to lie within the Marches of things lawful and unlawful.[1]

The 'lapwing' simile, which gives this sardonic judgement its acid charge, is not original to Fuller, who borrowed it, ready-fashioned for this context, from other earlier writers.

The approach to religion which Preston and the Puritan communion-of-the-elect stood for was regarded by Sydenham as encouragement to the dangerous mischief of sciolism. To him the Puritans, under a disguising cant of holiness, were 'discontented Neotericks', impelled by destructive envy to subvert the foundations of religious, and therefore also of social, order and cohesion, there being 'nothing so furious as ignorant zeal' whose 'vanity must be noised'; and it was Sydenham's prayer that, 'he that strikes at the mytor, God grant he catcheth not the sceptre, and (if he could grasp it) the very Thunderbolt: no Bishop, no King, and so by consequence no God.'[2]

Sydenham was the most explicit, as well as, perhaps, the most richly endowed orator to represent the Anglican point of view in the uneasy decade which preceded the Civil War. A poet of preachers, he could unite learning and fancy in striking concentration. Raising a memorial of wonder to David's musical genius, he first extolls the gifts of Orpheus, the virtuoso of pagan mythology; then, having established their stature, he suddenly dwarfs them to a 'plausible hoarseness' in respect of the 'sweet murmers of that heavenly turtle'.[3] He was also a poet of satire

---

1. Fuller, *Church History* (1655), xi, pp. 119, 126, 131.
2. *Sermons* (1630), *Waters of Marah*, pp. 33, 35, 36.
3. Ibid., *The Well Tuned Cymbal*, p. 6.

and invective and could make words cut like whips. When the Puritan Richard Sibbes, published his widely read treatise *A Reed Shaken in the Wind*, Sydenham, alluding to the confused babbling on religion by 'mechanicks and captiv'd women', which he believed the Puritans encouraged, referred to 'a reed shaken in the wind: Yes a very reed shaken with every wind of Doctrine.'[1]

Sometimes, when he denounced a transgression before a country congregation, he found that his words had wounded more deeply than he had intended, and on at least one occasion he went into print to diminish the heat of a searing reproof he had delivered from the pulpit. ' 'Tis true, a native roughness and austerity of language I have pupilled from my youth. That's mine own, I confess, but I dote not on it. . . .' and, he protested, 'I am a Levite still, not a libeller, and what I preached was not invective but a sermon.'[2]

If it should be wondered what kind of fire burnt his auditors to a degree requiring after-treatment, one example should provide sufficient illustration. The nature of retribution visited upon a prominent delinquent is contemplated. 'Oftimes his *vine is barren* and there are no olive plants about his table; God doth shut up the wombe, or so emasculate his loynes that either the fruit of it is *abortive*, or none at all . . .'; or, if there are children, they 'may be the whip and sword of a declining house' or, 'arrows that stick fast and pierce the very ioints and marrow, the venome wherof drinketh up the spirits of a Name and Family when the light shall be put out and the sparkle of his fire shine no more'.[3]

Where corresponding circumstances of misfortune were presently and locally evident to all, the emotional impact of such a commination upon a rural society of interlocked family alliances and feuds could be violent. But whatever the consequences of the sermon they did not deter Sydenham from publishing it.

Leaving aside differences of doctrine, which were not as substantial as the vehemence of the conflict might suggest, the differences of *priorities* and *emphases* estranging the two main bodies, amounted to different concepts of spiritual reality. One picks up the scent of the quarry in two quotations of not more than a few words each, one from Preston, one from Sydenham.

1. Ibid., *The Waters of Marah*, p. 37.
2. Ibid., *The Royal Passing Bell*, Epistle Dedicatory.
3. Ibid., *The Royal Passing Bell*, p. 31.

'If thou be but willing, Christ desires no more.'[1]

'If I give my body to be burned and have not Charity it profiteth me nothing.'[2]

Preston here proffers a lulling soft-sell of what, when the contract (or covenant) is signed, and the small print is read, will turn out to be either a portentous sham, an empty confidence trick, or the most exacting and rewarding personal commitment in the history of human idealism. Our actions, Preston tells us, are not prime, not even strictly relevant, to the issue of salvation. If, being chosen, we are 'clinging to Christ' and, therefore inevitably, struggling and vexed with sin—our sins and the sins of others—that condition is sufficient and our actions will be justified. *Belief in Christ is the only justification.* Good actions may come from believing, but they are worthless for salvation in themselves.

Sydenham reverses the order and alters the emphasis. 'Look to your life', he says, 'For if your conduct is wrong, above all, *if you lack Charity, you are in a state of self-deception*, not of grace.'

Life dealt cruelly with these two redoubtable contestants. Preston died of tuberculosis at the age of forty-one a few years before his party's triumph, thus missing the main opportunities of grasping power and dominion which, had he lived a normal span, would have been presented to his adroit fingers. Sydenham lived on long enough to see his worst prophetic fears fulfilled; Church and State overthrown; his king defeated and killed; he himself, as a loyal 'king's man' deprived of all his benefices and appointments. He did not survive long enough to see the pendulum swing decisively back with the restoration of the king's son to the throne, or to enjoy the rewards and rehabilitation which would have been his by right. The circumstances of his end are unknown, but his last years could not have been happy ones.

---

1. See below, p. 296.   2. See below, p. 314.

Of Faith[1]

Romans 1. 17. For therein is revealed a righteousness
of God by faith unto faith: as it is written, But the
righteous shall live by faith.

The gate is open to all, we shut out none; but none will come in, but those
whom God inables. A Pardon may be offered to all, and yet none accept it,
but those whose mindes God hath inclined. Therefore that he is offered to
all it is without question. They that question it, doe it because they doe not
vnderstand the Doctrine of our Diuines; for we propound it no otherwise in
substance then they doe, only we differ in the method: but it will be your
wisdome to looke to that which will be of vse, and yeeld comfort when you
come to dye. As this you may build on, The Gospel is preached to euery
creature vnder heauen, & therefore I haue my share in it. If a Pardon be
offered to some, whose names alone are inserted therein, you cannot say on
any good ground, I am pardoned: but when the Pardon is generall, and
offered to all, then I can beleeue the Pardon belongs to me. Were it onely to
the Elect, whose names are written in the pardon, we should first enquire
whether we be elect or no, but that's not the method.[2] Build you on the
sure promise, they that are pardoned, shall take hold of it, they that take not
hold of it, shall be excluded.

The next thing a man will desire to know, is this. What qualifications are
expected? Doth not God require to finde something in vs, if he giue it vs?

I answer, that it is offered to all, and no qualification at all is required as
præexistent to be found in vs, but any may come and take it. God requires
no qualification as concerning our sinnes; he saith not, you shall be pardoned,
so your sinnes be of such a number, or of such a nature, but though they be
neuer so many, though of neuer so extraordinary a nature, though they may
be aggrauated with all the circumstances that can be, yet there is no exception
at all of you, the pardon runnes in generall termes, *This is the Lambe of God*

1. 'The Breast-Plate of Love', preached *c.* 1625 *Eighteen Sermons* (1630), First Sermon.
2. Preston is here juggling with doctrine, evidently to ease the naked rigour of Calvin's
teaching. Calvin is quite explicit that it is 'the result of the divine will that Salvation is
offered to some and others are prevented from attaining it.' *Institutes*, XXI, Works
(translated by John Allen, 1935). Cf. ibid. vol. ii, p. 140, ' . . . he (God) gives to some
what he refuses to others'.

that taketh away the sinnes of the world. And seeing it is in generall termes, why will you interline and restraine it? You see it runnes in generall, and so you may take it.

And as it is propounded generally, so is it generally executed: 1 *Cor.* 6. 9. you shall finde, the greatest sinnes that can bee named are there pardoned: *Be not deceiued,* you know how *no fornicator, nor adulterer, nor uncleane person, &c. shall enter into the Kingdome of God, and such were some of you: but now you are iustified, now you are sanctified, now you are washed.* Though they had committed the greatest sinnes, you see, it is generally executed, without exception.

But there is another sort of qualification. Is there not something first to bee done? I know that though I haue committed all the sinnes of the world, yet they shall not prejudice my pardon; but I must doe something to qualifie me for it. No, not any thing as antecedareous and precedent to the pardon; it is only required of thee to come with the hand of faith, and receive it in the middest of all thy unworthinesse, whatsoever it be, lay hold on pardon, and embrace it, and it shall be thine middest.

Many men complaine that they would beleeue, but they want that sorrow that they should haue, they want that repentance that they would haue, they thinke they are not yet fit, therefore they dare not apply the promises.

To these we say now, that there is a double kinde of complaint.

One is, when a man lookes vpon these things, as vpon things that make him fit, which if he haue, he thinkes God will respect him; and if he haue not, he thinkes that God will not looke after him. If thy complaint be thus, it is sinfull; for in this thou seekest something in thy selfe.

But if a mans complaint be this, that he is not yet awaked enough, that he is not yet sensible enough of his sinnes, the doctrine of the remission of his sinnes, and free Justification doth not affect him as it should. Indeed, here is iust cause of complaint; for these things are necessary before you can come to take Christ. Therefore that place in *Mat.* 10.11. will explaine this, and answer an objection that may be made against it, when the Apostles were sent out to preach the Gospell, when they came to any house, they were bidden to *Enquire who were worthy; If any man be worthy* (saith Christ) *your peace shall come vpon him*: but if he be not worthy, shake off the dust, &c. A man would thinke by this that there were some worthinesse required in the partie that comes to Christ, and that before hee can apply the first promise of Justification.

To this we answer, the worthinesse that is required here is nothing else but an ability to prize Christ, to set him at a high rate, to long after him, to hunger and thirst after his righteousnesse, *your peace shall come vpon such a man.* That is, if there bee a broken-hearted man that lookes after Christ

1. Ibid., Third Sermon, preached *c.* 1625

whose heart yeranes after him, that he is able to prize him aright, he shall be accepted: but if they bee such men as will not receiue you, such as will not set meat before you, such as will giue you no respect, *shake off the dust of your feete, &c.* So that I say, such a complaint we may make, If we finde a want of desire after Christ; for that is required; but if we looke vpon any thing as a qualification in our selues, such a worthinesse is not required, we must be driuen out of all conceit of it, or else we cannot take *Christ.* So much for the Vse, that seeing it is onely faith whereby wee lay hold of *Christs* righteousnesse, that then we haue no reason to be discouraged, in respect of any want; nay, we must finde a want of all things, before wee can be made partakers of this righteousnesse.

Againe, secondly, if it bee by faith onely, by which we are made partakers of this righteousnesse, and by which we are saued, then we should learne hence to reioyce onely in God, and not to reioyce in our selues; for this is the very end why God hath appointed this way of saluation: *Eph.* 1.6. *For he hath chosen vs to the praise of the glory of his grace, in his Beloued.* That is, that he might haue the praise of the glory of his grace, as it is in *Ephes.* 2. Therefore it is of faith, and not by workes, that no man should boast of himselfe: 1 *Cor.* 1.30. Therefore Christ *is made to vs wisdome, righteousnesse, sanctification, and redemption*, that no flesh should reioyce in it selfe. Now if that be Gods end, if that be his aime, why he will haue vs saued by faith, let not vs disappoint him of his aime, let vs not take from him the glory of his grace; but let vs glory in the *Lord*.

This point we should especially looke to, not to reioyce in our selues, but in God: For, my beloued, wee are all naturally exceeding apt to reioyce in our selues, wee would faine finde some excellencie in our selues, euery man is apt to respect vpon himselfe, and hee would faine see some worth there that hee might reioyce in; and if he be no body at all there, it is contrary to his nature to thinke that he shall be accepted: there is nothing in the world that we are so backward to as this. It was *Adams* fault in Paradise, whereas hee should haue trusted God, and haue beene wholly dependant vpon him for all, he would needes know good and euill, he would haue something of his owne; and this was it that lost him all, and brought the curse vpon him, because hee would not bee dependant.

Now in the Gospell, God comes by a second meanes of sauing men, and in this the Lord would haue the creature to haue nothing in himselfe to glory in, but man is hardly brought to this, but exalts and lifts vp himselfe, and would faine haue some worth and excellencie of his owne; but as long as wee doe thus, wee cannot bee saued: that is the argument that is used *Rom.* 6.4. why *Abraham* was iustified by faith; if there had beene any other way, *Abraham* had had wherein to reioyce in himselfe: but faith excludes this reioycing, and onely faith; wee should, I say, learne to do this in good earnest, to see that there is no worth in our selues, to haue Christ to be to vs all in all: *Col.* 3.11. is an excellent place to this purpose, saith the Apostle there, (in the matter of saluation) *There is neither Iew nor Gentile, bond nor free, but Christ is all in all.* That is, when we come to be iustified before God, when wee come to the matter of saluation, *God* lookes at nothing in a man, he lookes at no difference betweene man and man; one man is vertuous, another man is wicked; one man is a Iew, and hath all those priuiledges; another man is a Gentile, an alien from the Common-wealth of *Israel*; one man is circumcised, another man is uncircumcised; but all this is nothing: Why? For Christ is all in all. Marke it: First, he is all; that is, there is nothing else required to iustifie: Indeede, if wee were something, and he were not all, we might then looke at something besides; but he is all.

Againe, he is all in all: that is, goe thorow all things that you may thinke will helpe you to saluation, in all those things Christ is onely to be respected, and nothing but *Christ*, whatsoeuer is done without Christ, God regards it not; If you will doe any worke of your owne to helpe your selues in saluation, if you will rest vpon any priuiledges, Christ is not all in all; but Christ must be all in all in euery thing: and if onely Christ be all, then we must come onely with faith; for it is faith onely that layes hold vpon Christ.

Now a naturall man, hee will not haue Christ to bee all, but himselfe will bee something; or if Christ be all in some things, he will not haue Christ to be in euery thing, to haue Christ to be his wisdome, his righteousnesse, his sanctification; to doe nothing but by Christ; to haue Christ to be his redemption, not to be able to helpe himselfe without Christ, but that Christ must helpe him out of euery trouble, and bestowe vpon him euery comfort, this, I say, is contrary to the nature of man: therefore we must bee thorowly emptyed of our selues in this matter of reioycing, aswell as in the matter of taking: for in what measure any man sets any price vpon himselfe, so farre as he hath any opinion of himselfe that he is something, iust so farre he detracts from Christ: but when a man boasts not of himselfe at all, such a man reioyceth in God altogether, such a man will stand amazed at the height, and breadth, and length, and depth of the loue of God; such a man will be able to see that there are vnsearchable riches in Christ; such a man will be able to say with *Paul*, that he cares for nothing, he reckons all the things dung, *Phil.* 3. I haue all the priuiledges (saith he) that other men haue; I am a Jew, I am a Pharise; but I reckon all these things as dung; that is, I care for none of them, if I had an hundred more: It is true, I haue beene as strict as any man; yea, I went beyond others: for I was zealous in that course wherein I was, yet I haue beene taught thus much, that all these things are nothing, for God regards them not, he regards nothing but *Christ* and his righteousness, therefore I looke not after these things, but that I may be found in him, not hauing mine own righteousnesse, but that righteousnesse that God accepteth, which is *through faith in him*. Therefore, my brethren, learne thus to reioyce in Christ, and in God, and not in your selues; this is the most excellent worke that we can performe, it is the worke of the Saints and Angels in Heauen, wee should learne to come as neere them now as we can: In *Rev.* 7.11. they cryed with a loud voyce, saying, *Saluation commeth by our God, that sitteth vpon the Throne, and by the Lambe; and therefore, praise, and wisdome, and glory be giuen to God for euermore;* because saluation is from the Lord, and from the Lambe, and not from our selues at all: hence it is that they fell downe, and worshipped him; and for this cause they all cry, wisdome, and glory, and praise be to our God for euermore.

If saluation had been from our selues, if wee had done any thing to helpe our selues therein, there had not been ground of giuing all praise and glory to God; and if this bee the worke of the Saints & Angels, we should labour to performe it as abundantly as we can now: and let vs doe it in good earnest: for if men could be brought to this, to reioyce in God alone, their mouthes would bee filled with praise exceedingly, they would regard nothing else, and in the course of their liues they would make it euident to the world, that they were such as made no account of the World, so they might haue Christ, they would be content with any condition: for *Christ* is all in all to them.

Thirdly, if it be by faith onely by which we are made partakers of the righteousnesse by which we are saued, then it should teach vs to let other things goe, and principally to minde this matter, to labour to get faith, whatsoeuer become of other things; for it is that by which we haue saluation.

The Papists, they teach that workes are the maine, and many things they prescribe that men must doe: our Doctrine is, you see, that faith onely is required: Indeede, many things follow vpon faith, but faith is that you must onely labour for, and then the rest will follow vpon it.

This Doctrine of ours, you shall finde that it is deliuered cleerely in *Gal.* 5.5,6. *We waite, through the Spirit, for the hope of righteousnesse, which is through faith.* That is, we looke for nothing from the Law, we regard no workes at all in the matter of iustification; that which we looke for, is onely that righteousnes which is taken by faith: and why doe wee so? For, saith he, *in Christ Iesus, neither circumcision is any thing, nor uncircumcision, but faith, &c.* As if he should say, there is good reason why we should expect saluation onely by faith, because nothing else will helpe vs in that worke, *circumcision is nothing, nor vncircumcision is nothing*: by those two hee meanes all other things, that is, the hauing of all the priuiledges in the world, the doing of all the workes that can be done, faith is all in all; but it must be such a faith as workes by loue; though it be by faith onely, yet it is not an idle faith: therefore you are especially to labour for faith.

There are many other excellencies that we are capable of, many morall

vertues, such as *Aristotle* and *Socrates* haue described; but without faith, God
regards none of these: take one that is a wicked man, and take another, let
him be neuer so vertuous, as *Socrates*, and *Seneca*, that were the strictest in
morality of all the Heathen; nay, take any man that liues in the Church,
that liues the most strict and exact life, and yet is not iustified by faith, *God*
makes no difference betweene these men, the one is as neere to heauen as the
other, God lookes vpon them both with the same eye; for he regards nothing
without faith. He that is the most prophane and vngodly, if he come with
faith, he shall obtaine *Christ*; the other that hath all other morall Vertues in
the most exact manner, without faith, they shall doe him no good: therefore
we are to seeke for nothing in the matter of iustification, but how we may
be enabled to beleeue, we are principally to study this matter of faith.

Take such a one as *Socrates*, and such a one as Saint *Paul*, it may be *Socrates*
might bee outwardly as temperate, and as patient, and be indued with as
many excellencies, hee might appeare in his carriage as strict as Saint *Paul;*
but here is the great difference, The one doth what hee doth of himselfe, and
through himselfe, and for himselfe; the other doth what hee doth of Christ,
and through Christ, and for Christ: therefore faith mainely is requisite.

If we had all other excellencies, yet we shall finde this in them, that they
doe alway giue something to the creature.

Again, if you goe neuer so farre in them, yet you shall finde that there is
some imperfection in them.

But faith it emptieth the creature of all things, it leaueth nothing in a man,
it makes him leane and rest only vpon Christ, and vpon his righteousnesse
for saluation.

But you will say, I am willing to doe this, to part from my lusts, and to be
to Christ alone, but I am not able, my lusts are strong and preualent.

To this I answer, If thou bee but willing, *Christ* desires no more: I would
but aske thee this, Suppose that thou wert able to ouercome those lusts; take
a man that is strongly giuen to good-fellowship, (as they call it) to company-
keeping, that is giuen to fornication, to swearing, or whatsoeuer the sinne
bee, take any preualent lust that is in any man that now heareth me, I would
aske him this Question; Put the case thou wert able to get the victory ouer
thy lust, would thou be content to part with it, and to take Christ? If thou
sayest, No, I had rather enioy the sweetnesse of my lusts still, Art thou not
now worthy to be condemned? But if thou answer, I would, vpon condition
I were able to ouercome my lusts; I assure thee, God will make thee able,
God requires no more but a willingnesse to come, and take Christ, the other
is *Gods* worke.

I, but I haue tryed, and haue not found it so.

I answer, it cannot be, thou hast not yet resolued to part with thy lusts,
thou hast not yet set downe this peremptory conclusion in thy selfe, that

thou wilt forsake euery thing that you may haue Christ: If any man say he
is willing to take Christ, and to part with the sweetnesse, and the pleasant-
nesse, and the profitablenesse that his lust brings to him, if he could get the
victory, if hee were freed from the sollicitations of them: Let me tell thee,
thou must first resolue to take *Christ* vpon his owne conditions, and for the
other, God hath promised to doe that himselfe: 1. *Cor.* 8.9. *God will confirme
you, and keepe you blamelesse; for he is faithfull that hath called you to the fellowship
of his Sonne.* As if hee should haue said, Doe you thinke that God will call
men to Christ, that he will beseech men to take his Sonne, will he call you
to the fellowship of his Sonne, and will hee not keepe you blameles? he hath
promised it, and sworn it, if he should not doe it, hee should be vnfaithfull;
when God calleth you to come vnto *Christ,* he promiseth that the vertue of
Christs death shall kill sinne in you, and that the vertue of Christs Resurrection
shall raise you vp to newnesse of life; God hath promised that he will giue
the *Holy Ghost*: for he neuer giues his Sonne to any, but he giues them the
Spirit of his Soone too. Now, *Hee that hath called you is faithfull, and he will
doe it.* So that I say, if thou wilt come in, (that is) if thou wilt accept of Christ
vpon his conditions, it is certaine God will receiue thee; and if thou find
thy selfe troubled with the violence of any lust, or of any temptation, presse
vpon God, vrge him with his Word and promise, that he would assist thee
by his own strength, that he would enable thee to ouercome, that he would
giue thee the Spirit of his Sonne, and resolue as *Iob, Though he kill me, yet
will I trust in him*: for I haue a sure promise, *Heauen and Earth shall passe, but
not one tittle of his sure Word shall passe till it be fulfilled.*

Of Love[1]

Examine yourselves by this, for it is a sure rule, if you love the Lord you will
hate that which is evill.

You will say, 'I hope I doe that.'

It is well if you doe, but let us consider that it may be you may be angry
with sinne, but doe you hate sinne? That was the commendations that the
Lord gives the Church in Rev. 2 Thou hatest the works of the Nicholations
which I also hate. Therefore if you would know whether you love the Lord
Jesus, try it by this; doe you hate sinne?

You will say, How shall wee know whether we hate it or no?

1. Preston, op. cit., Fourth Sermon, preached *c.* 1625.

In these three things you shall finde wherein hatred differs from anger, and thereby you may examine your selves.

First, hatred is more of generalls; a man hates all drunkards, if he hate drunkennesse: hee hates all toads and all serpents, if hee hate poyson. A man is angry with this or that particular, but hatred is of all. I would aske thee, doest thou hate all sinne, every thing that is called sinne, all that belongs to sinne? If it be this or that sinne that you make against, you are but angry with sinne, you doe not hate sin: for hatred fals alwaies upon the generall. Examine therefore if you finde this disposition in your hearts, that you hate every sinne, that your hearts rise against every thing that is sinfull, whatsoever is contrary to the Lord, whatsoever you apprehend under the notion of sin, that you hate, and resist, and strive against; this is a signe that you love the Lord.

Secondly, hatred desires the utter destruction of the thing it hates, anger doth not so, anger desires but a revenge proportionable to the injurie: therefore we say there is a kinde of justice in anger, it would not have the party that it is angry with to be destroyed, but it would have him sensible of its displeasure, it would have something done that might answer the injurie that is offered; but hatred desires the destruction of a thing utterly. Now doe you doe so with your sinnes? doe you desire to have them wholly extirpate and rooted out of you? to have your lusts thorowly and perfectly mortified? are you willing to have sinne so cleane taken away, that you may have any no libertie to have dalliance with it in any kind? do you hate it so as that you cannot endure to come neere it, nor to have it within your sight? It is a signe you hate it indeed.

Lastly, hatred differeth from anger in this, that it is implacable: hatred comes from judgement, and it continues, and therefore hatred is not a passion, but we call it an affection; it is a beautie, and disposition, and frame of the will; anger is a passion that dies, and flittes away after a time; but hatred continues. Is your disposition such to your sinnes? examine your selves; nothing is more frequent, my brethren, than to be humbled for some sinne, which amazeth you for the present, but doth your hatred continue? If not, you doe but fall out with your sinnes onely, and grow friends with them againe. If you did hate them, as you should, you would never returne to amity with them more.

Many a man takes resolutions to himselfe, I will be drunke no more, I will be a gamester no more, I will not commit such, and such grosse sinnes, as I have done any more; perhaps some shame, or some feare hath followed him, some deepe apprehension of wrath and judgement, which set him vpon this resolution for the present; but if the heart be right that thou hatest sin as thou shouldest, thou wilt continue hating of it. Therefore consider, whether you love the Lord Iesus by this triall, whether your hearts hate sin, in your constant resolution or no. This was the disposition that was in *Lot, His righteous soule was vexed with the unclean conversation of the Sodomits,* that is, he did not onely abstaine from the actes that they did, but his soule wrought against them, he was vexed with them, as a man is vexed with a thing that is contrary to his disposition.

So it is sayd of *Moses, he stood in the doore of the Tabernacle,* and he wept as he stood, his heart was mooved in him. It is not enough to abstaine from sinne, but to hate sinne, and that is an argument of our love to the Lord Iesus: take this therefore for an other triall of your love.

Againe, there is one more which wee cannot leave out, though it be a thing knowne unto you, yet because the Scripture gives it as a peculiar signe by which we may judge of our love to the Lord, it must not be passed by, and that is our love to the Saints; and there is good reason given of it, if we consider it well, 1 *Iob.* 4.20. Wilt thou say thou *lovest God whom thou hast not seene, and yet lovest not thy brother whom thou hast seene?* The meaning is this, for a man to love the Lord who is immortall, invisible, who dwelleth in light inaccessible, is a more difficult thing than to love my brother whom thou seest. For why doe wee love the Lord, but because we conceive him under such a notion? we thinke of him as such a God having such and such attributes: Now, saith the Apostle, whatsoever thou conceivest of God, that very image and disposition is stamped on man like thy selfe, thou shalt see the very same disposition in a holy man that is in the Lord himselfe. Indeed it differeth in the degree exceedingly, there is but a glimpse of it, yet why is it said that the Image of God is renewed, but that there is in holy men a disposition like the nature of God? Now this is in a more remisse degree in man, and therefore more sutable to our weaknesse; as you know, difficulty comes from disproportion, it is a harder thing to love the Lord than a man like our selves. If therefore wee doe not love men like our selves, in whom is stamped a disposition like the nature of God, and his Image, in some degree, surely we cannot love the Lord who is so farre above us.

Againe, a man like our selves is visible, we see his actions, we heare him speake, we know more plainly the frame of his disposition; and therefore it is more easie to love a holy man than to love the Lord: For so is the Apostles argument. Doe not thinke that thou lovest the Lord whom thou never sawest, when thou doest not love thy brother whom thou seest daily. Therefore wee may conclude thus much, if we love not the Saints and holy men, it is certaine we love not the Lord.

I confesse every man is ready to say (in this case) he loves holy men.

I would put you to this tryall, and aske you but this question; you shall know it by this: Doe you love all the Saints? You shall finde that the Apostle *Paul* still in his Epistles puts in that caution, *Love to all the Saints.* If thou love grace and holinesse, thou wilt love it wheresoever it is. Many men will love some particular grace, especially when it suteth with their disposition, and is agreeable to them, and to their constitution, but to love all grace, to love all holinesse in all the Saints wheresoever it is found, it is an infallible signe that thou lovest the Lord Iesus.

Againe, doest thou love none but them; that, where grace is, thou lovest, and where it is not, thou withdrawest thy love?

But, you will say, would you have us to love none but the Saints? I answer, it is true, wee ought to love all others with a love of pitty, wee should shew abundance of this love to all mankinde; but then there is a love of complacencie and delight, and with this love we ought to love none but the Saints.[1]

Againe, thirdly, doe you love them as they excell in holinesse? many men can love one that hath but some degree of grace; but if it be one that hath more exactnes than ordinarie, that hath proceeded higher in holinesse than he thinkes requisite, here his heart is readie to quarrell, and to rise against him.

Lastly, doe you manifest your loue by delighting in their companie, and by the fruites of love towards them? You may professe much, and say much, but of all other things companie is the worst dissembled. Will you professe that you loue the Saints, and that you delight in them, and yet desire to be in any company rather than in theirs? that when you are among them, you are as if you were out of your element, you move as if you were out of your owne center? It is impossible but that those that are moved by the same spirit should be best pleased when they are in one and the same society. Put all these things together, and by these you may judge whether you love the Saints or no.

You will object, I doe love the Saints, but who are they? I love not hypocrites, and so it is made a notable excuse.

I will not wish thee to love hypocrites, onely take heede thou suffer not the impes and instruments of the Divell to paint out the true Saints unto thee in the colours of hypocrites: thou must consider that it hath beene the usuall manner to cast that aspersion upon all the Saints, upon all holy men in all ages, as the Apostle saith in 2 *Cor. We are as deceivers though true*: that is the common esteeme that the world hath of the Saints, they judge them to be deceivers, and to be men that professe themselves to be otherwise than they are. You know what was said of Iesus Christ, some said of him he was a good man, others said nay, he was a deceiver of the people. You know what was

1. This paragraph taken by itself is a complete statement of the Puritan presumption to a superior exclusivity. Christ's injunction to 'love one another' is circumvented by making a distinction between two kinds of love: one Love—as it were, with a capital l —'the love of complacancie', reserved for other 'Saints'; the other, a second-class remnant, 'the love of pitie', fit to be disbursed among the carnal and unregenerate. For the execution wrought upon this doctrine by Sydenham, see below, pp. 314, 316.

said of *David*, that he was a subtle man, one that went about to deceive others. *Paul*, you know, was reckoned the great impostor of the world; this was alwayes laid upon the Saints: therefore let not the Divells instruments deceive thee in that.

Besides, why are they hypocrites? Is it because there are some shewes of holiness in them? surely that is not argument enough.

Thou wilt say, because they doe not answer that which in their profession they make shew to be.

If that be the reason why dost thou not pitch thy hatred upon those that are found to be so? And to conclude this you must know that no man speaks against religion or hates religion under its own notions, under its owne name, but something else must be put upon it, the name of hypocrite, or the like.

The reference on page 297 to the Nicolations is interesting. They were a heretical sect, not yet excommunicated or separate in apostolic times, which flourished in two of the seven Churches of Asia, teaching 'the doctrine of Balaam . . . to eat things sacrificed unto idols and to commit fornication.' Rev. ii: 14. The reference to Balaam indicates that the fornication was of a religious kind. Until the return from Babylon the Jews were familiar with the practice; 'consecrated' women and even boys served in the Temple: 2 Kings xxiii: 4–7. A succession of prophets and kings strove to expel the cult: Deut. xxiii: 18: Hosea ix: 12–14. Eusebius (*Hist. Eccl.* iii. 29) says the heresy of the Nicolations did not last long. All this means is that the name changed; the doctrine recurred; see Tertullian, *De Praescr.* cap. xxxiii; Clement of Alexandria, *Strom.* iii. 2.; Justin Martyr, *Trypho* xxxv.

HUMPHREY SYDENHAM[1]

Prophecy was a favourite religious exercise of the Puritans. It was a group operation, an advanced version of preaching, undertaken when two or three of the elect were gathered together. The intention was to revive the authority of the Old Testament Prophets as the interpreters and spokesmen of God's word and will. Elizabeth had not been slow to detect the potential threat to unity and authority in these independent and unsupervised seminaries, or to lean against the practice with the full weight of the crown. But, after her death, prophesying began to burgeon aggressively, like other forms of dissent. It was this kind of 'prophesying', and the extreme Puritan denunciations of learning and the arts which commonly went with it, that provoked prophesying in its more popular sense of 'prediction', from the Anglican clergy.

In *The Athenian Babbler*, Humphrey, 'silver-tongued', Sydenham, examines the symptoms of current social unrest. We now have iconoclasm as a *political phenomenon*, although it was not yet clearly thought of as that. The anti-intellectualism of the Puritan left wing had provided a front of moral righteousness to lend a posture of propriety to impulses of destructive envy, evinced in rowdy and violent demonstrations against whatever the demonstrators could not themselves master or understand.

Considering that the date is only 1625 Sydenham is almost uncannily accurate in his foreboding. It was the uncomfortable fate of this man of discernment, to be able to recognize, without being able to prevent, the rabid virus which had already entered the country's blood-stream.

---

1. Humphrey Sydenham, 1591–1650, Royalist. Exeter College, Oxford. B.A. 1610, M.A. Fellow of Wadham 1613; Ejected from his various benefices by Parliamentary Commissioners. See Wood, *Athenae. Oxon.* ed. Bliss, iii, 274. Walker, *Suffering of the Clergy*, p. 76; F. W. Weaver, *Somerset Incumbents* (1889), pp. 157, 309, 323.

The Athenian Babbler (1626)

A sermon preached at the Church of St. Marie's Oxford
on the 9th. July, 1626, by Humphrey Sydenham M.A.,
Fellow of Wadham College.

Acts. 17. 18. Some said, *What will this babbler say?*

I neuer yet read that the true vse of secular Learning tooke from the glory
of that which was Diuine; I haue, that it hath added, nor that any thing
gleaned and pickt, and culled with a cleane hand was distastfull vnto God;
I haue that it was approued. I know there is a *Venomous eloquence* (as *Cyprian*
wrote of that of *Nouatus*[1]) and this perchance the *Babler* himselfe vses, when
hee leades silly Creatures captiue, but it is odious both to God and Man, and
hath beene the maine Engine in all Ages by which *Schismes* and *Heresies* haue
wrought. In those Sacrifices of old, *Leuit.* 4.5. You know whatsoeuer was
vncleane, *was abomination vnto the Lord*; the Offering it selfe must bee without
blemish, the Altar seuen dayes cleansed before it was layd on, the Priest too
washed before the Congregation, ere hee dared to immolate; and why not
so in this Holocaust and Sacrifice of the lippes? Why not the Offering without
blemish, the Altar cleansed, the Priest so in his Discourse too, that what is
kindled heere may burne as a sweet Incense vnto the Lord? smells that are
vnsauoury neuer touch his nostrils, sounds harsh and jarring, neuer his eares;
and therefore, the Bells of *Aaron* were of pure Gold,—*Ne subæratum aliquod
tinniat in Sacerdotio,*—saith *Gregory*.

It is a sullennesse, or rather policy, most in our age haue got, that what is
in a way of eminence and perfection, they censure as a piece of affectation or
curiositie, when (God knowes) it is but to colour some sinister pretence, and
for a fairer varnish of their owne weaknesses. You know the story of the
Painter and the Cocke, and the Boy that kept the liue ones from his shop
least comming too nigh, the vnskilfulnesse of that hand should bee discouered, which had drawne the other at so rude a posture.

There is a malicious ignorance possesseth many, by which they vnder-value
all things aboue their spheare, and cry downe that industry or Art in others,

1. Novatus: the presbyter in Carthage who promoted the Novation heresy and was
Cyprian's most persistent enemy. See Cyprian, *epist.* lii.

which is beyond the verge and fathome of their owne abilities. But why should Moles repine that other see? Or Cripples murmure that others halt not? *Tolle quod tuum est & Vade.* Yet loe how euen those last and gasping times keepe vp with the manner of those of old, both in their spleene and weakenesse. There bee (saith the Father[1] to his *Marcellinus*) that account inciuilitie of Manners and rudenesse of Speech, true Holinesse,—and with such,—*Quis non Vicus abundat?* Would I could not say,—*Que Academia?* These Cynickes are in euery Tub, these *Stoickes* heere at *Athens.* But why should the talke of such bee a burthen in our way? Learning vnto a Wise-man is as an ornament of Gold, and like a bracelet on his Arme, but Fetters about the feete, and Manackles about the hands; of whom? of him that (but now) was the burthen in the way, the *Foole,* whom least wee should leaue without his companion, *Syracides* brings home to the gates of the *Babler,* and I will leaue him there,—*As a house that is destroyed, so is Learning to a Foole, and his Knowledge is but talke without sense.*[2] The tayle of the Verse carryeth the sting; for much of our *Bablers* knowledge is little better then—*Sermo sine sensu,* Wordes without Salt, Speech without Ballace. And yet (good Lord) how these lampes burne in our Tabernacles, these Bells sound in our Sanctuary? They are the thunderbolts of our Congregations, the Hotspurres of our Pulpits. Against the sinnes of the time they clacke loude, and often, but it is like Mills driuen by a hasty torrent, which grinde much, but not cleane; And indeed it is not much they grinde neyther, in substance, but in shew, neyther is the labour so superlatiue, as the noyse. Some that haue been conuersant in the trade, say, that Corne that is cleane and massie, will lye long in the wombe and body of the Mill and requires all the industry of stone and water, and will not bee deliuered without some time and trauaile, when graines which are mixt and course, runne through with lesse difficultie, and more tumult. The *Babler* will apply. Thus wee see empty vessels sound much, and shallow streames runne swift and loude, but on barren grounds, when those deeper ones glide slowly, as with more grauitie, so more silence, yet on fat soyles, and so the neighbouring Fields grow fertile with their abundance. If all truth of Religion raigned in the Tongue, and the subduing of our manifold rebellions in the mortification of the Looke, there were no sanctitie but here.—But the heate of this mans zeale, is like that of Glasse, which will bee blowne into any forme according to the fancy of him that blowes it, sometimes into that of a Serpent, sometimes of a Doue, but more often of a Serpent, then of a Doue, not for the wisedome of it, but the venome. Euery word is a sting against the Church, her Discipline, truth of Gouernment, Hee *Babbles* shrewdly against each Institution of it, State, Ceremonies, makes them adulterate, the dresses of the Great whore, and sets all without the walls of reformation, which Wheele and Role not

1. Jerome.   2. Ecclesiasticus (Apocrypha) xxi. 18, 21.

Oh Sir Ime ready did you never heare,
How forward I have byn tis many a yeare,
T'oppose the practice dat is now on foote
Which plucks my Prethren up poth pranche and roote:
My posture and my hart toth well agree
To fight, now plud is up: come follow mee.

Archbishop Williams ready for war

A

DECADE

OF

GRIEVANCES,

Prefented and approved to the Right
Honourable and High Court of Parliament,
againft the Hierarchy or government of the
Lord Bifhops, and their dependant offices,
by a multitude of people,
Who are fenfible of the ruine of Religion, the finking
of the State, and of the plots and infultations of
enemies againft both.

The tottering Prelates, with their trumpery all,
Shall moulder downe, like Elder from the wall.

Printed in the yeare, 1641.

The fall of the Prelates

Cromwell as preacher
and as regicide

SQVARE-CAPS

TURNED INTO
ROVND-HEADS:
OR THE
BISHOPS VINDICATION,
AND THE
BROWNISTS CONVICTION.

Being a Dialogue between *Time*, and
Opinion: Shewing the folly of the one, and
the worthinesse of the other.
By *H. P.*

Time.   *Opinion.*

Time *doth* Opinion *call unto accompt,*
who turnes the Bishops downe *and* Round-Heads *mount:*
Vpon Her lofty Wheele their Noddels *are;*
But Her Camelion *feedeth on His aire.*

LONDON, Printed for *I. Gyles*, and *G. Lindsey*, 1642.

Square Caps into Roundheads

The Brownifts Conventicle:

Or an affemble of Brownifts, Separatifts, and Non-Conformifts, as they met together at a private houfe to heare a Sermon of a brother of theirs neere *Algate*, being a learned *Felt-maker*.

Contayning the whole difcourfe of his Expofition, with the manner and forme of his preaching, praying, giving thankes before and after Dinner and Supper, as it was lately heard and now difcovered by a brother of theirs who is turned out of their Society upon fome difcontent, to be buffeted by Sathan.

His Auditors were Button-makers, Tranflaters, Weavers, Box-makers, with divers other holy Brethren and Sifters.

Printed 1641.

The Brownists Conventicle

Hugh Peters preaching

THE QVAKERS DREAM:

OR,
The Devil's Pilgrimage in England:
BEING

An infallible Relation of their several Meetings,

Shreekings, Shakings, Quakings, Roarings, Yellings, Howlings, Tremblings in the Bodies, and Rumings in the Bellies : With a Narrative of their several Arguments, Tenets, Principles, and strange Doctrine : The strange and wonderful Satanical Apparitions, and the appearing of the Devil unto them in the likeness of a black Boar, a Dog with flaming eys, and a black man without a head, causing the Dogs to bark, the Swine to cry, and the Cattel to run, to the great admiration of all that shall read the same.

London, Printed for G. Horton, and are to be sold at the Royal Exchange in Cornhil, 1655. Aprill. 26.

The Quakers Dream

THOMAS VENNER,
ORATOR CONVENTICULORUM REGNI
MILLENARII ET LIBERTINORUM, SEDUCTOR
et CAPITANEUS SEDITIOSOR. ANABAPTISTARUM
ET QVACKERORUM IN CIVITAT. LONDINENS.
Decollatq in quatuor partes diffectus D. 19. Ian. Anno 1661.

Thomas Venner

with the giddinesse of his tenents. The Golden-mouthed *Homilist* in his fourth vpon the *Acts*, speaking of that miraculous way of the Holy Ghosts descent vpon the Apostles in the day of *Penticost*, obserues nimbly, thus;— There came a sound from Heaven,—*As it were*—of a Rushing and mightie winde, and there appeared to them Clouen tongues,—*As it were*—of Fire,— *Recte vbique additum est,—Velut—ne—quid sensibile de Spiritu suspicareris,*— sayes the Father.[1]—And indeed, in those phanaticke Spirits, though the Tongues bee fiery, and the voyce as the Windes, rushing; yet in themselues there is nothing sensible; For as those which appeared to the Apostles, were but—*Velut ignæ*,—and *Velut flatus*,—so this orall vehemency is but—*Velut Zelus*, and *Velut Indignatio*,—False fire, or, at best, but some hot exhalation in the braine set on fire by continuall motion and agitation of the Tongue, and there it burnes sometimes to the madnesse of the Professour, most times, of the Disciple. Againe, these Tongues are said to *sit* vpon the Apostles,— *Sedendi verbum, stabilitatem ac mansionem, denotat,* the same Father—sitting presupposes *Stabilitie* and *Mansion*, but most of these haue neyther, eyther in their opinion, or course of life, but as the contribution ebbes or flowes; so they hoyse, or strike sayle, eyther way, sometimes for the wide mayne, sometimes for the next harbour. Againe, the Apostles are sayd there, to bee *fitted* with the *Holy Ghost.—Recte repleti, non enim vulgariter acciperunt gratiam Spiritus, sed eosque vt implerentur,* the Father still.—Where the Spirit powres out it leaues no part emptie, it doth fill, fill vp euen to the brim, giues power of speaking roundly, and fully; where it doth giue power,—no Rhumaticke Enthusiasmes, no languishing ejaculations, but such as the Spirit indeed haue dictated, such as flow from lippes immediately touched with the true Cherubin, and a Tongue swolne with inspiration. Againe, the Tongues which sate vpon the Apostles were *clouen Tongues*, other tongues, *Vers.* 4. and S. *Marke* calls them *new Tongues*. They were not confined then to a single dialect to *Babling* meerely in our Mother tongue, but the Text sayes they had diuers Tongues, of the *Parthian*, and *Mede*, and *Elamite*, *Phrygian*, and *Pamphilian*, and of those of *Lybia* which is beside *Cyrene*, And in those and (other Tongues too) they *spake the wonderfull workes of God.* Act. 2.11. Lastly, this Vision they saw when they were in the Temple, not in a Cloyster, a Barne, a Wood, a Conuenticle, and they were in the Temple with one accord too, with one Office, one Spirit, one Minde, one Faith; not heere a *Separatist*, there a *Brownist*, yonder a *Familist*, neere him an *Anabaptist*, but as their Faith was one, so was their life, and (if brought to the test) their death too. That was not *Religion* with them which was deuided, nor that *not vnity of opinion*, which they would not burne for. Some *Heathens* haue shewed such resolution

---

1. Sydenham has gone astray here; perhaps he was trying to quote from memory. The Latin version of Chrysostom reads: 'Recte ubique additur illud tamquam ne quid sensibile de spiritu existimes. Homilae LX in *Acta Apostolorum*, IV, 1.

and truth euen in their *false Religion*; such were those—*Aruales Sacerdotes*[1]—
of olde amongst the *Romaines*, the *Solduni* amongst the *Aquitans*; the *Ægip-
tians* also had their συναποθνησυόντος, so called, because, promiscuously
enioying each others benefites, as in one *Religion*, so in one Loue, they would
dye together; such were the *Hunnes*, *Hyberi*, *Cantabri*, and others, which
were joynt-sharers of each others miseries, and fortunes;[2] and if one by
disaster or disease met with Calamitie, or Fate, the other sought it.—

　　　　—*Placidamque petunt pro vulnere mortem.*

　　If in matters therefore as well Morrall as Diuine, there was such reciproca-
tion of old; and not onely in *Religions*, which were tainted, and smelt not
of the true God, but in that too which hath beene touched and influenced by
the *Spirit of the Almightie*, there was such punctuall correspondence then, why
such combustion now? Why those dayly scarres and wounds both by the
Tongue, and Penne? Why so much gall in our Pulpit, such wormewood at
the Presse? Why those *Ciuill-warres* in our owne tenents? Such stabbings in
particular opinions? Such heart-burnings in our *Brethren*? to the great disquiet
of our Mother, Church, and her Sonne they so labour to disinherit, the
Protestant, the wounded *Protestant*, who hath beene now so long Crucified
betweene the—*non-Conformist* and the *Romanist*, that at length hee is inforced
to flye to *Cæsar* for sanctuary, and in the very rescue and *Appeale*, like the
poore man between *Jerusalem*, and *Jerico*, *hee falls into the hands of Thieues*,
two desperate cut-throates and enemies to the Truth, and him, the *Pelagian*
and the *Arminian*. But no more (beloued) of those Daggers and Stillettoes
to our owne brests by the cruelty of our owne *Tribe*; Know, dissention is
the very gate of ruine, and the breach at which destruction enters. Ciuill-
warres are as dangerous in matters of *Religion* as *State*, and proue the Earth-
quakes both of Church and Common-wealth. The story of the *Romanes
shafts* is both old, and troden, but very pertinent; *in the Bundle they neuer felt
injury of hand, one by one were the conquest of a finger*, and *Tacitus* speakes of
Apronius Souldiers;—*Satis validi si simul*, &c. as long as they marched in their
combined rankes they stood aloofe all danger, but, these deuided, they grew
the prey and slaughter of the Aduersary;[3] and thus—*Dum singuli pugnant*,

　　1. Fratres Arvales, the twelve priests charged with observances of the ceremonies
sacred to Dea Dei, an earth Goddess, or, alternatively, of Acca Laurentia. The *Arval
Hymn*, in which Mars is invoked as an agricultural deity, is one of the oldest surviving
expressions of the Latin tongue.
　　2. Caesar, *Gallic*, lib. iii, cap 22, '. . . ut omnibus in vita commodis una cum eis fruan-
tur, quorum se amicitiae dediderint, si quid eis per vim accidat, aut eundem casum una
ferant aut sibi mortem consciscant neque adhuc hominem memoria repertus est quis-
quam qui eo interfecto cuis se amicitiae devovisset, mori recusaret.'
　　3. To maintain discipline Appronius imposed brutal punishments, but morale was
never high in his legions. See Tacitus, *Annals*, IV, 21.

vniuersi vincuntur. A mutiny or rent in an Army *is the Souldiers passing bell.* Death followes, or dispaire of victory, when those which are knit-vp in one heart of courage and affection trample on distrust as if they had already worne the palme and glory of their Tryumph. And it speeds no better in a diuided Church, where *Scismes* and *Factions* like so many *rents* and *breaches,* haue hewed-out, a way to her ouerthrow and ruine. No more *struglings* then by vnnaturall *twinnes* in the *wombe* of our *Rebecca.* No more warre in her members, no more *Bablings* in their tongue, no more venome in their Penne, to the great aduantage of the *Aduersary,* whose artillery is ready, his bow bent, the arrow on the string and malice leuelling at the very bosome of the Church, (I pray God, not of the *State* too) and waites onely opportunity to loosen it. But *let vs with all humblenesse of mind, meeknesse, long suffering (supporting one another through loue) endeauour to keepe the vnity of the Spirit in the bond of peace, knowing there is one Body, one Spirit, one Lord, one Faith, one Baptisme, one God, and Father of all, who is above all, through all, and in you all.*

And now Pavl hath bin at *Athens,* past his bickerings with the *Epicure,* and the *Stoicke,* had their censure,—*Hee is a Babler.*—He is now rigged for *Corinth,* and by this time arriued there, where I leaue him—*In earnest Disputation with the Græcians in the Synagogue.* The *Stoicke* is returned to his *Porch* too, the *Epicure* to his *Garden.* But heere is an *Athens* too, though no Pavl, or at least no such *Paul*; and yonder sits a *Stoicke* and hee whispers to his *Epicure,* What will *this Babler* say? He sayes—*Glory to God on high, in Earth peace, goodwill towards men.* Hee sayes, hearty and true Allegeance to his Soueraigne,—wishes the budding and continuance of a temporall Crowne heere, and the assurance of an immortall one hereafter.—Hee sayes, florishing to his Church, his Common-wealth, his People; swift and fierce destruction to his Enemies foraigne, and (if hee haue any such) domestique.—Hee sayes courage to his Nobility, vnity to his Clergie, loue to his Gentry, loyaltie to his Commonalty. In fine; Hee sayes prosperity to *Athens* (heere) vnanimity,
true brotherhood, happie successe to your stu-
dies, to your designes; and *The grace of*
our Lord Jesvs Christ
to you all, and with you all.
Amen.

JOHN DONNE

Burial as a Preparation for Life

A sermon preached at the funeral of Sir William
Cockayne, Knight, Alderman of London, on December 12th., 1626

John XI. 21. Lord, if thou hadst been here, my brother had not died.

There is no form of building stronger than an Arch, and yet an Arch hath
declinations, which even a flat-roofe hath not; The flat-roofe lies equall in
all parts; the Arch declines downwards in all parts, and yet the Arch is a
firme supporter. Our Devotions doe not the lesse beare us upright, in the
sight of God, because they have some declinations towards natural affections:
God doth easilier pardon some neglectings of his grace, when it proceeds
out of a tendernesse, or may be excused out of good nature, then any presuming upon his grace. If a man doe depart in some actions, from an exact
obedience of Gods will, upon infirmity, or humane affections, and not a
contempt, God passes it over oftentimes. For, when our Saviour Christ sayes,
Be pure as your Father in heaven is pure, that is a rule for our purity, but not a
measure of our purity; It is that we should be pure so, not that we should be
so pure as our Father in heaven. When we consider that weaknesse, that went
through the Apostles, even to Christs Ascension, that they looked for a
temporall Kingdome, and for preferment in that; when we consider that
weaknesse in the chiefe of them, S. *Peter*, at the *Transfiguration*, when, as the
Text sayes, *He knew not what to say;* when we consider the weaknesse of his
action, that for feare of death, he renounced the Lord of Life, and denied his
Master; when in this very story, when Christ said that *Lazarus* was *asleepe*,
and that *he would goe to awake him*, they could understand it so impertinently,
as that Christ should goe such a journey, to come to the waking of a man,
asleep at that time when he spoke; All these infirmities of theirs, multiply
this consolation upon us, That though God look upon the Inscription, he
looks upon the metall too, Though he look that his Image should be preserved in us, he looks in what earthen vessels this Image is put, and put by

his own hand; and though he hate us in our rebellions, yet he pities us in our grievances; though he would have us better, he forsakes us not for every degree of illnesse. There are three great dangers in this consideration of perfectnesse, and purity; First to distrust of Gods mercy, if thou finde not this purity in thy selfe, and this perfectnesse; and then to presume upon God, nay upon thine own right, in an overvaluing of thine own purity, and perfectnesse; And againe, to condemne others, whom thou wilt needs thinke lesse pure, or perfect then thy selfe. Against this diffidence in God, to thinke our selves so desperately impure, as that God will not look upon us; And this presumption in God, to thinke our selves so pure, as that God is bound to look upon us; And this uncharitablenesse towards others, to think none pure at all, that are not pure our way; Christ armes us by his Example, He receives these sisters of *Lazarus*, and accomplishes as much as they desired, though there were weaknesses in their Faith, in their Hope, in their Charity, expressed in that unperfect speech, *Lord, if thou hadst been here, my brother had not dyed:* for, there is nothing, not in spirituall things perfect. This we have seen out of the Text we have Heard; And now out of the Text, which we See, we shall see the rest, That as in spirituall things, there is nothing Perfect, so in temporall, there is nothing Permanent.

I need not call in new Philosophy, that denies a settlednesse, an acquiescence in the very body of the Earth, but makes the Earth to move in that place, where we thought the Sunne had moved; I need not that helpe, that the Earth it selfe is in Motion, to prove this, That nothing upon Earth is permanent; The Assertion will stand of it selfe, till some man assigne me some instance, something that a man may relie upon, and find permanent. Consider the greatest Bodies upon Earth, The Monarchies; Objects, which one would thinke, Destiny might stand and stare at, but not shake; Consider the smallest bodies upon Earth, The haires of our head, Objects, which one would thinke, Destiny would not observe, or could not discerne; And yet Destiny, (to speak to a naturall man) And God, (to speake to a Christian) is no more troubled to make a Monarchy ruinous, then to make a haire gray. Nay, nothing needs to be done to either, by God, or Destiny; A Monarchy will ruine, as a haire will grow gray, of it selfe. In the Elements themselves, of which all sub-elementary things are composed, there is no acquiescence, but a vicissitudinary transmutation into one another; Ayre condensed becomes water, a more solid body, And Ayre rarified becomes fire, a body more disputable, and in-apparant. It is so in the Conditions of men too; A Merchant condensed, kneaded and packed up in a great estate, becomes a Lord; And a Merchant rarified, blown up by a perfidious Factor, or by a riotous Sonne, evaporates into ayre, into nothing, and is not seen. And if there were any thing permanent and durable in this world, yet we got nothing by it, because howsoever that might last in it selfe, yet we could not last to enjoy it; If our goods were not amongst Moveables, yet we our selves are; if they could stay with us, yet we cannot stay with them; which is another Consideration in this part.

The world is a great Volume, and man the Index of that Booke; Even in the body of man, you may turne to the whole world; This body is an Illustration of all Nature; Gods recapitulation of all that he had said before, in his *Fiat lux*, and *Fiat firmamentum*, and in all the rest, said or done, in all the six dayes. Propose this body to thy consideration in the highest exaltation thereof; as it is the *Temple of the Holy Ghost*: Nay, not in a Metaphor, or comparison of a Temple, or any other similitudinary thing, but as it was really and truly the very body of God, in the person of Christ, and yet this body must wither, must decay, must languish, must perish. When *Goliah* had armed and fortified this body, And *Iezabel* had painted and perfumed this body, And *Dives* had pampered and larded this body, As God said to *Ezekiel*, when he brought him to the *dry bones, Fili hominis, Sonne of Man, doest thou thinke these bones can live?* They said in their hearts to all the world, Can these bodies die? And they are dead. *Iezabels* dust is not Ambar, nor *Goliahs* dust *Terra sigillata*, Medicinall; nor does the Serpent, whose meat they are both, finde any better relish in *Dives* dust, then in *Lazarus*. But as in our former part, where our foundation was, That in nothing, no spirituall thing, there was any perfectnesse, which we illustrated in the weaknesses of Knowledge, and Faith, and Hope, and Charity, yet we concluded, that for all those defects, God accepted those their regilious services; So in this part, where our foundation is, That nothing in temporall things is permanent, as we have illustrated that, by the decay of that which is Gods noblest piece in Nature, The body of man; so we shall also conclude that, with this goodnesse of God, that for all this dissolution, and putrefaction, he affords this Body a Resurrection.

The Gentils, and their Poets, describe the sad state of Death so, *Nox una obeunda*, That it is one everlasting Night; To them, a Night; But to a Christian, it is *Dies Mortis*, and *Dies Resurrectionis*, The day of Death, and The day of Resurrection; We die in the light, in the sight of Gods presence, and we rise in the light, in the sight of his very Essence. Nay, Gods corrections, and judgements upon us in this life, are still expressed so, *Dies visitationis*, still it is a Day, though a *Day of visitation*; and still we may discerne God to be in the action. The *Lord of Life* was the first that named *Death; Morte morieris*, sayes God, Thou shalt die the Death. I doe the lesse feare, or abhorre Death, because I finde it in his mouth; Even a malediction hath a sweetnesse in his mouth; for there is a blessing wrapped up in it; a mercy in every correction, a Resurrection upon every Death.

ROGER MANWARING

On July 4th, 1627, Roger Manwaring, chaplain in ordinary to Charles I, preached a sermon at Oatlands in which he asserted absolute supremacy of the king by divine right. It is a sign of the sharpening hostility between the crown and parliament that the latter made a public issue of the offence given their constitution by this sermon, and extorted an abject apology before the House from Manwaring, after he had been charged by Pym with 'trying to infuse into the conscience of his Majesty the persuasion of a power not bounding itself by law'.[1] This was an all too correct estimate of what the king already had in mind as his divinely granted prerogative. Here is one of the first open exchanges of polemical fire in what would become a battle of physical fire. Manwaring was fined and imprisoned for his offence, but the king, although publicly ungrateful, later remitted his fine and released him.

The Divine Right of the King

A sermon preached before His Majesty, at Oatlands,
on the 4th. of July, 1627

Royalty is an Honour, wherein, Kings are stated *immediately* from God. *Fathers* they are, & who gaue *Fathers* Authority ouer their Families, but hee alone, from whom all the *Fatherhood in heauen and earth is named*? The *power* of *Princes* then, is both *Naturall*, and *Diuine*,[2] not from any consent or allowance of men. And hee that gaine-saies this, *transgreditur terminos quos posuerunt Patres, saith Antonine.*[3] Not therefore, in any *consent* of Men, not in *Grace*,

1. See Rymer, *Foedera*, xviii, 1025.
2. Here there is printed in the margin *Spalet.*, which I take to be a printer's error for the abbreviation of Spalatin, the German reformer of the sixteenth century and author of *Chronicon et Annales* (See *Scriptores rerum Germanicorum*, Leipzig, 1728–30).
3. St. Antonius (Antonio Pierozzi), 1389–1459, Archbishop of Florence; author of *Summa Confessionalis*,' Mondovi (1472), and *Summa Historialis*, 3 vols. (Venice 1480).

not in any *Municipall Law*, or *Locall custome*, not in any law *Nationall*, nor yet in the law of *Nations*, which, consent of men, and tract of time, hath made forcible; not finally, in the *Pope*, or any *People* is *Regall preheminencie* founded; for *Adam* had *Dominion* setled in him, before euer there was either *Pope*, or *People*: neither *Popes* nor *Populous Multitudes* haue any right to giue, to take, in this case. So that *Royalty* is a Prehemencie wherein *Monarches* are inuested, *immediately* from God; For *by him doe they raigne*. And likewise *Sacred* to God himselfe; *For hee who toucheth them, toucheth the apple of Gods owne eye*: and therefore, *Touch not mine anointed.*

Supreame also it is, and *Independent* vpon any *Man, Men*, or *Angels*; and for this saith he; *They are Gods*: whose glorious and dreadfull[1] *Names*, must not bee medled with by any wicked *tongues*, or *pennes*, nor mingled with any lewd peruerse or deprauing *thoughts*; and for this, *Curse not the King in thy thought.*

And yet notwithstanding this; they are to bee sustained, and supplied by the hands and helpes of men; for *The King himselfe is serued by the field; & Reddite quæ Cæsaris, Cæsari: Render as due*, not giue as *arbitrary*, for, *for this cause pay wee tribute*, saith the great *Apostle*. God alone it is, who hath set *Crownes* on their heads, put *scepters*, yea and reuenging *swords* into their hands, setled them in their *thrones*; for this, doe their *Royalties* render to God (as a due debt) that great *Care, Paines*, and *Prouidence* which they sustaine in the ruling ouer, and preseruing of their people in wealth, peace, and godlinesse: and for this, doe the people render, *as due*, to them againe, by *naturall* and *originall Iustice, tribute, to whom tribute, custome, to whom custome appertaineth.*

1. The preacher is being a trifle shifty here. Calvin in sect. 2, cap. 20. of the *Institutes*, to which the preacher is appealing, makes no reference to monarchy, but in the following section, 3, he enjoins respect for civil government.

HUMPHREY SYDENHAM

The Waters of Marah and Meriah[1] (1630)

... *If I giue my Body to be burned* (saith Saint *Paul*) *and haue not Charity, it profiteth me nothing, nay had I all faith, so that I could remoue mountaines, and haue not Charity, I am nothing*; Not, *Nullus sum*, but *Nihil sum*, Not so much, not a *Man*, as not a creature, *nothing*.

Hearken then, thou sonne of *Tumult, whose lips enter into contention, and whose mouth calleth for stroakes*; *Thou* which raiseth tempests in Religion, and sowest Thy *Tares* of *Faction* amongst the *multitude*; thou which bringest in the strange *Leauen* of *New Doctrines*, and colourest them with they probable allegations, whereby the Consciences of the *Simple* are intangled, and the peace of the Church disturbed, though otherwise perchance, thou art punctuall enough, both in thy *conuersation* and thy *Tenents*, hast the gifts of *Prophecy*, vnderstand'st all *Mysteries* and all *Language*, yet, because in some things thou hast made a *breach* of this *Harmony* in the Church, thou art a *Rebell* both to it, and thy Christ, and except by *Retraction* and *Submission* thou art recald to the *Fold* from which thou hast wandred, thou stand'st *out-law'd* and excommunicate to *Heauen* and neither *Imprisonment* nor *Death* can make atonement for thy *Misreadings*. Is this harsh? 'Tis Saint *Augustines*, and he will yet goe farther: A *Schismaticke* brought vnto the *stake*; not for that *Error* which did separate him from the Church, but for the truth of the *Word* and *Sacrament* which he doth else maintaine, suffering the *Temporall* flames, to auoyde the *Eternall*, and beares it patiently; though that *Patience* be commendable, and a gift of God, yet (because in part a *Schismaticke*) not of that kind of gifts which are imparted *filÿs Ierusalem*, but to those also which are *filÿ concubinarum* (saith the Father) which euen carnall *Iewes*, and *Heretickes* may haue; and concludes at length, that *This* suffering and patience nothing profits *Him* towards *Heauen*; but supposes that the great *iudgement* will be in this more tolerable to *Him*, *Quam si Chrisum negando tormenta mortemque vitasset*, Then if by denying Christ ho had euaded the cruelty of his Death and Torment: in his Booke *de Patientia*.[2]

1. Op. cit., pp. 29-38.   2. Augustine, *de Patientia*, cap. 26, 27, 28.

You haue heard what *primitiue* times haue done for the barke and out-side of *Religion*; the very skin and shell of *Christianity*; Let vs now compare them a little with our owne; and wee shall finde, that they haue not any-whit gone beyond vs in the *Externall* profession of sincerity, tho in their suffering and *Tortures* they haue much. We haue deceitfull workers as well as they, *Transforming themselues into the Apostles of Christ, which glory in appearance, and not in heart.*

We abhorre, *That Age* should out-doe ours, either in *Hypocrise* or *prophane-nesse*, wee haue our *Donatists* and *Catharists*, and *Anabaptists*, as plentifully as they; and some besides, *they* had not; the *Brownist*, the *Barrowist*, and the *Familist*, and one more that both fosters and incloses all these, (may he be whisper'd without offence, my *Brethren*) the *Puritan*; but he will not be Titled so; the very Name hangs in his Iawes, and the chiefe way to discouer him, is to call him so; That fires and nettles him, and so repining at the Name, he ownes it; and questionlesse'tis his, though he shrowd and vaile it vnder the word *Brethren* in the Text; whose *Purity* consists much in washing of the *cut-wardman*, whilst their *Tenents* looke towards a *Legall* righteousnesse, and a triumphant and glorified condition of man here vpon earth; professing by their open *Pamphlets*, that the *visible* Church, the *true* visible Church, is deuoid of *Sinne* and *Sinners*, and for *Manners* cannot *erre*; and therefore *Paradox* it, That the *Assemblies* of good and bad together, are no Church, but *Heapes* of prophane men; as if in one field, there were not as well *Tares* as *Corne*, in one house, vessels of wood and *earth, as of gold and siluer*; a Mixture of good and bad, in all *Congregations*; which as an *Embleme* of the Church visible, our *Sauiour* types-out in the parable of the *Sower*, the *Marriage*, and the *Virgins*; Nay his *Blessed Spouse*, of her selfe, freely professes her deformity, *Tho I am comely, I am blacke, O yee Daughters of* Ierusalem, *blacke as the Tents of* Kedar. And yet These will haue her all *cleane* and *louely*, like a face without spot, or wrinkle; when wee know a Mole or Wart (sometimes) beautifies a feature; and in this *Warre* of *opposites*, there is both gracefulnesse, and *Lustre*; and therefore I suppose the Church was first compar'd vnto the *Moone*, not so much for *change*, as *obnubilation*, being obuious to *clouds*, and Eclipses; and when 'tis at clearest, 'tis not without a *mole* in her cheeke neither, at least-wise, to an *ocular* apprehension or; if it were all faire and *Lucid*, yet, 'tis by way of *Influence*, beam'd from a greater *light*, borrowed, not her owne, so is this of the Church too; one *sun* of righteousnesse enlightens *Both*, and therefore, *Woe vnto them, that call Light, Darknes, & Darknes, Light*; make a Church of it selfe shine, which cannot, or not shine, which might, if they were not, by others; dogmatically, & peremptorily laying downe, that *where Errors are, there is no True Church* (when there was neuer any, nor will be, whil'st 'tis *militant*, without them,) But *They* are no more of the substance of our *Religion*, or any *Essentiall* part of our Churches *Doctrine*, then ill humours which be *in*, are of the *Body*, or Dregs in a vessell of wine, part of the wine, or vessell.

'Tis true, some *Ceremonies* we retaine yet, as matters of *Indifferency*, and not of *Substance*, and these (forsooth) are so hainous, that they are *Thornes* in their sides, and prickles in their eyes; matter of *Ceremony*, is now matter of *Conscience*, and rather then subscribe, *Silence, Suspension, Imprisonment*, they venture on, and sometimes suffer too; where *A Brethren-Contribution*[1] more fats them, then al the Fortunes they were masters of before; and this (beloued) cannot be *zeale*, but *Schisme*, or if it bee *zeale*, it wants *Eyes*, and *intellectuals*, 'tis not *according to knowledge*; For what *Iudgement* would expose our Body vnto prison? our Calling to the staine of *Separation*, and *Reuolt*, for a thing meerely of *indifferency* and *Ceremony*? No, there is more in it, then This; the *Rochet, Tippet*, and the *Surplesse* is not that they shoot at, but the thing call'd *Parity*; *Moses* and *Aaron* they like not for the *Ephod*, and the *Rod*; they speake *power*, and *command*, and so intimate *obedience*; But these struggle for *equality*, the *Ecclesiasticke Hierarchy* they would demonish, *Episcopall corruption* is the great Eye-sore; *Downe with it, downe with it, euen to the ground*. And yet I dare say, there are some subtle *Pioners*, and secret *Mutiners* in Common-wealth, pretending plausibly to the flourishing of *Religion*, which if they could once glory in that *Babel* they endeuour to erect, they car'd not, if *Ierusalem* were *An heape of Stones*; 'Tis impossible, that Ciuill Authority can euer subsist without the other; and if there be once a full rent & flaw in Church-policy, what can we expect from that of *State*, or either, but vast *Anarchy*, and *Confusion*?

Thus, he that strikes at the *Myter*, God grant he catch'th not at the *Scepter*, and (if he could graspe it) the very *Thunderbolt*; no *Bishop*, no *King*, and so by consequence no God; *He* proclaimes himselfe the God of *Order*, and These would make him the *Father* of *Confusion*; and so, in circumstance disgod him too, seeing his greatest glory consists in the *Harmony* of his Creatures; the *Peace* of his Church, and vnanimity of his *Saints* and Seruants; and therefore (brethren) let me beseech you in the words of the *Apostle, Marke them which cause Diuisions and offences, contrary to the Doctrine which you haue heard, and auoyd them. For they that are such, serue not our Lord Iesus Christ, but their owne Belly, and by good words, and faire speeches, deceiue the hearts of the simple, Rom. 16. 17, 18, ver.*

I haue yet but *Beseech't* you in the words of an *Apostle*; Let me warne you also in the Language of a *Sauiour, Beware of Those which come to you in sheeps clothing*, with such a Cast of *Mortification* and *Integrity*, as if their conuersation spake nothing but *Immaculatenesse, when within they are rauening wolues*: such as will not onely *tondere pecus*, and *deglubere*; but *deuorare* too; subuert whole houses for filthy lucre: *You shall know them by their fruite*; Their fruite

---

1. A lectureship financed by the feoffee system.

vnto the eye beautifull and glorious, but to the finger, *Dust* and *Smoake*; or if not by their *fruite*, by their *Leaues*, you may, a few wind-falne vertues which they piece and sowe together to couer their owne *Nakednesse*. Will you haue them in their full *Dresse* and *portraiture?* Take the draught and paterne, then from the *Pharisee, Mathew* 23. There the *character* is *exact*; where if you obserue, They are twice called *Blind Guides, Blindnesse* of *knowledge* brings on *Blindnesse* of *Heart*; and therefore twice also *Fooles*, and *Blind*; *ver.* 17. 19. To this *Blindnesse* of Heart, *Pride* is annex'd; *They make broad their Phylacteries, and inlarge the Borders of their Garments; ver.* 5. To this *Pride, vaine-glory; They loue greetings in the Market, vppermost roomes at feasts, and chiefe seates in the Synagogues; ver.* 6. 7. To this *Vaine-glory, Hypocrisie, They make cleane the out-side of the cup and platter, and for a pretence make long prayers; and all to be seene of men, v.* 14. 25. To this *Hypocrisie, Spirituall malice; They shut vp the Kingdome of Heauen against men, for they neither goe in themselues, nor suffer them that are entring, to goe in, ver.* 13. Lastly, to this *Malice*, there is *vnchartitablenesse; They bind heauy Burdens, and grieuous to be borne, and lay them on mens shoulders, but they Themselues will not moue them with one of their fingers, ver.* 4. Rare perfections, doubtlesse, for the *Sanctified* Child of God! Obserue the Catalogue, *Blindnesse of Heart, Pride, Vaine-glory, Hypocrisie, Malice*, and *Vncharitablenesse*: Let vs make it out, *Enuy*, and *all Vncharitablenesse*, and then *Libera a nos, Domine, Good Lord deliuer vs*; deliuer vs from all false-hood in his *Seruices*, and faction against his Church, that we may be his *Ministers* in *Sincerity*, and not in *shew*, as those false *Teachers* were of old, or our *Brainesicke* and discontented *Neotericks* at the present, whom Saint *Paul* discouers by a double *Attribute*, ματαιολόγοι, and φρεναπάται, *vaniloqui, & Seductores; vnruly and vaine-talkers*, and *Deceiuers, Titus* 1.10. They talke (it should seeme) They doe not *Teach*; and talke *vainely* too; and not onely so, but this *vanity* must be nois'd, *vnrulinesse* goes with it, and Those which in their *Doctrines* are vaine and vnruly too, sometimes proue *Deceiuers, Mentium Deceptres*, (as *Ierome* reades it on the Text) *Deceiuers* of *mindes*; of *weake* and *simple mindes, Mechanicks*, and *captiu'd women*, which haue beene the *disciples* of all *Schismes* and all *Heresies* in al *Ages*. And such indeed are the chiefest *Proficients* in their Schooles now: for none are so pinn'd to the strict obseruation of their *Precepts*, as these *Silly ones*. There is nothing so furious as an ignorant *zeale*, so violent as a factious *Holinesse*; and therefore when their *Doctrines* or their *practices* are touch'd vnto the *Quicke*, and made (once) the subiect of a Pulpit *Reprehension*; their Charity is presently on the Racke; the *Brasse* sounds loud, and the *Cymball* tinckles shrill, their *Censures* are full-charg'd, and come on like a peale of *Great shot*, thicke and terrible.

The *Cymball* (as *Caitean* obserues) was an Instrument of old, *Magis sonorum, quam musicum, not so musicall as loud* and of more noyse then melody, and such as *women* onely vsed, both in their times of *Triumph* and *Deuotion*. A pretty *inuention* for *weaknesse* and *child-hood* to play withall, and be it spoken without disparagement of some glories in that *Sexe*, a fit *type* of *women* and their *frailties*, who, for the most part are taken rather with the sound of things, then the things themselues, and are seldome without this Instrument of Noise about them. The *Tongue* is their proper *Cymball*, not the *well-tun'd Cymball Dauid* speakes of; but the *Loud Cymball*, with which they doe not so much praise God, as sometimes disparage men; Their *Morality*, and their *zeale* are neere one, a *shrilnesse* as well in their *Deuotion*, as their *Actions*, and their *practice* in both is a very *Tinckling*; Tinckling with their *Feete*, leade the *Daunce* to the next *Conuenticle*; *Tinckling* with the *tongue too*; Great *talkers*, in *Diuinity*; and if they could exchange a *Parlour* for a *Church*, or a *stoole* for a *Pulpit*, they would *preach too*, & ('tis thought) *Edifie* as much as their *zealous Pastor*. But *Away* with those *Ecchoes* in *Religion*, fitter for *Silence*, then *Reproofe*; and for *pitty*, then *confutation*; and therefore (once more) *I Beseech* you; and with the phrase of an *Apostle too, Bee not carried about with diuers and strange Doctrines*, Halt and limp not betweene *Innouation* and an *establish'd Discipline*. But (as *Peter* said to the *Cripple*) *In the Name of Iesus Christ of* Nazareth, *rise vp and walke*; Returne vnto the Church, whence ye are straggling; not *to your Stepdame*, but *your mother*, the *Mother* of whom you were borne and nurs'd; dry those teares she sheads for you; *peace* those sighs, and groanes, & complaints, which she wailes for you; Fall vpon those *Armes* which will embrace you, those *Bowels* which yearne for you, those *Paps* which gaue you sucke. *What went you to see? A Reed shaken with the wind?* Yes, a very *Reed*, shaken with euery wind of *Doctrine*; *A Reed* with a bruized *stalke* or broken *Eare*, no Corne in it; or if it haue, 'tis blasted with *Sedition*, fitter for the *Dunghil*, then the *Granary*.

Away then from *Lebanon* (my *Beloued*) from *Lebanon*; Looke from the *Den of Lyons*, and *Mountaines of the Leopards* (where the peace of *Religion* is blood-suck't and deuour'd) and *come hither to the mountaines of Myrrh; and hills of Frankencense; The Altars of the liuing God*, where the *Incence* of his Church flames cheerefully, with no lesse truth of *deuotion*, then vnanimity. *Loe*, her *golden vials, full of odours, Sacrifices* both *deuout* and *peace-able*, Such as the heart of his *people* offer, and not the hands, onely; *Calues* of our *lips*,[1] and groanes of the *Spirit*, which touch both the *eares* and *nostrils* of the *Almighty*. Let the *voyce* of *diuision*, then, jarre no more amongst you, which if there were nothing else to noise our frailties, were enough to speake bondage to the *flesh*, and not yet, our freedome to the *Spirit*. For whence are *strifes and enuyings? are they not from your lusts?* And whilst one saith, *I am of Paul, another, I am of Apollo*, are ye not *carnall? Christ is not deuided*, his Church is one; *My Doue, my vndefiled is but one, she is the onely one of her mother*, the *choice one of her that bare Her, Can.* 6.7.

The Church, (you heare) is Gods *onely one*, his *choice one*; He hath no more,

---

1. Words of prayer and praise as 'calves' (sacrifices); '. . . we will render the calves of our lips.' Hosea, xiv. 2.

and *we*, tho many, are but *one* neither, the *Churches one*, *Her choicest one*, *one Body*, nay, *one Bread*, 1 *Cor*. 10.17. Moreouer, *Christs Spirit* is but *one*; tho it bee in many, 'tis there still one *Spirit*, no *diuision* where that is, but all *peace*; and therefore 'tis call'd the *vnity of the Spirit*; and this *vnity* must be still kept in the *bond of peace*. Marke, here's no wauering, or *Temporary peace*; but this *peace* must be still kept, and not *slightly* kept, but there is a *Tye* on the keeping of it, *The Bond of peace*: and 'tis this *Bond* that makes the *vnity*, and this *vnity* that keepes the *peace*, and this *peace* that preserues the *Spirit*, so that 'tis still an *vnity of Spirit*, kept in the *Bond* of *peace*.

Come hither, then, my *Faithfull Brother in the Lord*, and let vs no more *censure*, but *expostulate*. Hast *Thou* the *true Faith* thou so much gloriest in? where is thy *zeale*? hast thou true *zeale*? where is thy *Charity*? hast thou true *Charity*? why art thou *Tumultuous*? *By this shall you know* (saith *Christ*) that *you are my Disciples, if you loue one another*. *Mutuall* agreement begets *Loue*, and this *Loue* make the *Disciple*, and this *Disciple* is *knowne to be Christs*, by a *Si diligeretis, onely, if yee loue one another*. And therefore in the first *Dawne* and *rising* of the *Christian Church*, the *chiefe* thing remark'd in it by the *Gentiles*, was the *Christian Loue: Vide vt inuicem se diligunt! vt pro alterutro mori sint parati!* as *Tertullian* stories it.[1] Lo how they *Loue!* the *Heathens* cry, How ready to *Dye* one for another! But this *Loue* of the *Brother* vnto *Death*, I presse not here; (for the very *Infidels* had their *Commorientes*, as well as *we*) but *Loue* vnto *Sincerity* and *Constancy*, of which he that is destitute, falls *short* both in *Religion*, and *Morality*. And therefore that *Text* in Saint *Peter* runs *Methodically*, *Feare God, Honour the King*, but first, *Loue the Brotherhood*; as if there could be no true feare of God, or honour of the King, except there be first *Loue* to thy *Brother*; to thy *Brother*? nay, the *Brother-hood*: την ἀδελφότητα, saith the *Greeke*, *Achava*, the *Hebrew*; *Brotherhood*, for the company and coniunction of *Brethren* in the Church; and in *this*, not so much a Coniunction of *persons*, as of *Mindes*, otherwise 'tis no Church. . . .

'Idolatry' could take many forms, including music. Organs and other musical instruments used by the Anglican clergy, in the course of religious service, would become, with the ascendancy of Puritanism, nearly as popular objects for destruction as stained-glass windows, carvings and sculpture. When Sydenham preached this sermon liturgical music and ecclesiastical art were still under Laud's protection, but Sydenham is in no doubt what his adversaries would like to do.

1. *Apologeticus* **39**: not 36 as given by Sydenham, op. cit., p. 38.

The Well-Tuned Cymball (1630)

A Vindication of the moderne Harmony and Ornaments in our Churches

Preached at the Dedication of an Organ lately set up at
Bruton in Somerset

Psal. 59.16 I will sing of thy Power; yea I will sing aloud of thy mercy in the Morning, because thou hast been my defence and my refuge in the day of my trouble.

The text, though but a verse, is a complete psalme, having in it all the properties of a spiritual song; where we may find the Parts, the Ground, the Descant, the Author or Setter of it, the time when it was sung and the occasion of the singing . . .

Tis then most happy with the affaires of God's People, when Kings are not only the patrons of the Church but ornaments such as can no lesse *beautifie* Religion, than *propugne* it. And this *Dauid* did in a double way, of Majestie and knowledge, being the *prime piece* in all *Israel*; for Harmony and Eloquence, exquisitely endowed with the perfections both of *Poetry* and *Musicke*; Insomuch, that some of the *Fathers* either to cry downe the *vaunts* of *Heathens* in their rarities that way, or else to rivall him with the fertile and richer Wits of their Times, have beene pleased to stile him *Simonides noster, Alecus, Catulus, Flaccus,* and *Serenus*; let me adde the Divine *Orpheus*, and *Amphion*, one that made Woods, and Beasts, and Mountaines; brutish, stony, and blockish dispositions to dance after his Harpe; and sometimes to sing with it in a *Laudate Dominum ipsi montes, ipsi arbores, ipsa jumenta, Praise the Lord ye Mountaines and little Hills, Trees, and all Cedars, Beasts and all Cattell, Psal.* 148. Herein personating Christ himselfe, who was that *Pæonius medicus* (as *Clemens Alexandrinus* stiles him) the *Spirituall Æsculapius, Ille Sanctus ægrotæ Animæ Incantator,*[1] The holy Inchanter of the sicke Soule, who first transform'd Beasts into men, reduc'd Savagees and Barbarisme into civilitie: *Qui sevos, ut Leones, ad mansuetudinem; Fallaces ut Vulpes, ad sinceritatem; obscenos ut sues, ad continentiem revocavit.* Cruelty, Craft, Obscænitie (Hieroglyphically shadowed under Lyons, Foxes, Swine) he translated to meeknesse,

---

1. Clement of Alexandria, *Pedagogus* lib. 1. cap. 2.

innocencie, temperance, causing the Wolfe to dwell with the Lambe, and the Leopard to lye downe with the Kid, and the young Lyon and the Fatling together, and a little childe leading them, *Isai.* 11.6. And although there be no Analogie between Truth and Fiction in respect of substance, let us make it up in respect of circumstance: They by their dexterity in Musicke, and cunning on the Harpe, redeem'd some of their from the Gates of Hell; our Prophet, though by his heavenly touch and warble, that way caus'd not the Redemption of any from below; yet on his ten-stringed Instrument, hee sung sweetly the Resurrection; For so Saint *Ierome* tells his *Paulinus*,[1] *Dauid Christum Lyra personat, & in Decachordo Psalterio ab inferis excitat Resurgentem.*

But lets us not so resemble small things to great, that wee should dare compare those Poeticke Rhapsodies with his sacred Harmony, their sensuall Elegies and Madrigals with his diviner Sonnets: *O procul hinc proculite prophani.* 'Tis true, his verses consisted of number and feet as well as theirs, and he was as criticall in their Observation as the daintiest Lyrick or Heroicke, yet there was a vast disparitie, both for sublimity of matter and elegancie of expression; Insomuch, that *Petrus Damianus*, the great adorer of *Humane Eloquence* (and one whose very soule was charm'd with their prophaner Sonnets) was inforc'd at length to his *Dulcius immurmurat filius Iesse.* The *Thracian* Harpe, and the *Mercurian* Pipe, and the *Theban* Lute, were but harsh and grating, when the Jewish Psaltery came in place; One touch of the sonne of *Iesse*, one warble of the Singer of *Israel*, was more melodious than all their Fabulous incantations, their *Syrenicall* fictions, which were but *Iucunda quædam auribus Rauca*, a kinde of plausible hoarsenesse, in respect of those sweet murmures of that heavenly Turtle. An Iliad of *Homer*, or an Ode of *Pindarus*, or a Song of *Anacreon*, or a Scene of *Aristophanes*, have not the juyce, and blood, and spirits, and marrow; the acutenesse, elegance, vigor, majesty, that one of his sacred Ditties are ballac'd and fraught withall: And God forbid that those *Ventosæ nugæ*, and *Expolita menditia*, those *Superbi errores*, and *Gacculæ Argutiæ*, (as Saint *Augustine* stiles them[2] to his *Memorius*) their garnished and beautiful lyes, their windy trifles, their vaine-glorious errours, their elaborate kick-shawes; their ingenious nothings should stand up in competition with one *Michtam*[3] of *David*, his Jewell, his golden Song, farre above their buskin'd raptures, their garish Phantasmes, their splendid vanities; the Pageants and Land-skips[4] (if I may so terme them) of prophaner wits: And yet there have been some Hereticks of old, *Gnosticks* and *Nicolaitans*, which have rejected the Psalmes as prophane Sonnets, the births of humane fancie and invention,

1. St. Jerome's disciple, the rich Roman widow, Paula.

2. Not in Epistle 131, as cited by Sydenham, which was addressed to the 'Lady Proba', but in Epistle 101, to Memor.

3. Michtam: Hebrew; exact meaning not known, but may carry some allusion to penitential psalms. See title of Psalm xvi.

4. A slightly earlier variant of 'landscape.'

without any influence or aspiration of the holy Ghost, whereas the very Spirit of God, our Saviour himselfe, and the Uni-vocall Consent of all the Apostles (nay the hallowed Quire of Heaven and earth, of Saints and Angels) have acknowledged, that God spake by the mouth of his servant *David*, that he was the sweet Psalmist of *Israel*, that his Word was in his tongue, he in Spirit calling him Christ the Lord, Mat. 22, 43.

However, there are amongst us some anti-harmonicall snarlers, which esteeme those *bellowings* in the Church (for so they have bruitishly phras'd them) no better than a windie devotion, as if it cool'd the fervor of their zeale, damp'd the motions of the Spirit, clogg'd the wheeles of their firy Chariot mounting towards Heaven, choak'd the livelihood and quicknesse of those raptures, which on a sudden they ejaculate; when, if they would but wipe off a little those wilfull scales which hang upon their eyes, they could not but see the admirable vertues and effects which *melody* hath wrought even in that part of man which is most sacred; Insomuch, that both *Philosophers* and *Divines* have jump'd in one fancie, that the *Soule* is not onely *naturally harmonicall*, but *Harmony it selfe*. And indeed, the whole course of nature is but a *Harmony*; the order of superiour and inferiour things, a melodious Consort; Heaven and Earth, the great *Diapason*; both Churches, a double Quire of *Hosannahs* and *Halleluiahs*, *Magnus Divinæ Majestatis præco, mundus est*, saith the loftie *Nazianzene*; the world is the great Trumpeter of *Divine* Glory, *Suave canticum*, as Saint *Bernard* hath it, a sweet Song; or else *Carmen pulcherrimum* (as S. *Augustine* will[1]), a golden Verse; as if in *Art* and *Consent* both, it resembled both a Verse and a Song. Now *Carmen* in most languages is nothing else but *laus*; and therefore that *Psalmodicall* Tract, which we call *Liber carminum*, the *Hebrews* call *Liber laudationum*; So that a Song is nothing else but a *Praise*; and therefore the whole world being a kinde of *Encomium*, or praise of the glory of God, we may not improperly call it a Song also.

And as the greater world is thus a Song, so is the lesser too: *Ipsius factura sumus* (saith Saint *Paul*) *wee are Gods workmanship*, which some from the Greeke render *Ipsius poema sumus*, wee are his Poeme, his Heroicke Poeme: All creatures, men especially, being certaine luculent Songs or Poems, in which divine praises are resounded, Nay some of the *Fathers* have call'd *Christ* himselfe a Song (for so *Clemens Alexandrinus pulcherrimus Dei Hymnus est homo, qui in justitia ædificatur*, the man of Righteousnesse is a most beautifull *Hymne* or *Song*, and so is his *Spouse* a Song too, and the love betweene both, *Canticum canticorum*, a Song of Songs, there being such a harmony betweene God and the World, and the World and the rest of his creatures there, that the one is like a well-set Antheme; the other as so many Singers and Choristers to voice and chant it: First, the Heavens, they sing, *Isai* 49.13.

---

1. Augustine, *De Civitate Dei*, lib. XI, cap. 18.

and then the Earth, that sings, *Psal.* 98.4. the Mountaines also they break forth into singing, *Isai.* 55.12. the Valleys they laugh and sing too, *Psal.* 65.13. the Cedar and the Shrub are not without their Song neither, *Isai* 14.8. (as well the In habitants of the Rocke, as those that dwell in the dust) nay, those creatures that cannot yet speake, doe sing, *The lame leapes as an Hart, and the tongue of the dumbe sings, Isai.* 35.6.

Seeing then, that the whole course of nature is but a Song, or a kinde of singing, a melodious concention both of the Creator and the creature: how can we conceive them to be lesse than prodigies, who as if they distasted this generall harmony, revile that particular and more sacred in our Churches, not considering what wonderfull effects and consequences *Musicke* hath wrought both in expelling of evill spirits, and calling on of Good.

Exagitabat Saul spiritus nequam, sayes the Text, *An evill spirit troubled Saul, and with one touch of Davids Harpe hee is refresh'd and the evill spirit departed from him,* 1 *Sam.* 16. *Elisha*, when he was to prophecie before the Kings of *Iudah* and *Samaria*, call's for a Musician, and as he play'd, *The Spirit of God fell upon him,* 2 *Kings* 3. *Mirum* (saith S. *Augustine*) *Dæmones sugat, Angelos ad adjutorium invitat.*[1] And yet 'tis not a thing so strange as customary with God to worke miraculous effects by creatures, which have no power of themselves to worke them, or onely a weake resemblance. What vertue was there in a few *Rammes* hornes, that they should flat the walls of *Iericho*? or in *Gideons* Trumpets, that they should chase a whole Hoste of *Midianites*? *Digitus Dei hic,* the finger of God is here, and this finger oftentimes runnes with the hand of the Musician: and therefore a moderne and learned Wit,[2] discoursing of the passions of the minde in generall, falls at length on those which are rais'd by *Harmony*, and dyving after reasons, why a proportionable and equall disposition of sounds and voices, the tremblings, vibrations, and artificiall curlings of the ayre (which in effect he calls, *The substance of all Musicke*) should so strangely set passions aloft, so mightily raise our affections as they doe, sets downe foure manners or formes of motion, which occurre to the working of such wonderfull effects.

The first is *Sympathia*, a naturall correspondence and relation between our diviner parts and harmony, for such is the nature of our soules, that *Musicke* hath a certaine proportionable Sympathie with them, as our tastes have with such varieties of dainties, or smelling with such diversities of odours. And Saint *Augustine* this way, was inforc'd to acknowledge, the *Omnes affectus spiritus nostri*, all the affections of our spirit, by reason of the variousnesse and multiplicity of them, had proper manners and wayes in Voyce and Song,

---

1. Psalmus daemones fugat Angelos ad adjutorium invitat. In *Librum Psalmorum, Prologus* (Migne, XXXVI, IV, 63).

2. The "wit" was Thomas Wright, whose popular book, *The Passions of the Mind*, Sydenham had been reading: see pp. 168–171 of the 1621 edition.

Quorum nescio qua occulta familiaritate excitentur,[1] which he knew not well by what secret familiarity or mysterious custome they were excited and rouz'd up.

The second, *Providentia,* Gods generall providence; which, when these sounds affects the eare, produceth a certaine spirituall qualitie in the soule, stirring up some passion or other, according to the varietie of sounds or voyces; For *The imagination* (saith hee) *being not able to dart the forms of fancies, which are materiall, into the understanding which is spirituall, therefore where nature wanteth, Gods providence supplyeth.* And as in humane generation, the body is from man, and the soule from God; the one preparing the matter, the other creating the form: so in *Harmony,* when *Men* sound and heare, *God* striketh upon and stirreth the heart; so that, where corporall musicke is unable of it selfe to work such extraordinarie effects in our soules, God by his Ordarie naturall providence produceth them.

The third, more open and sensible, is *Sonus ipse,* the very sound it selfe, which is nothing else but an artificiall shaking & quavering of the ayre, which passeth through the eares, and by them uno the heart; and there it beateth and tickleth it in such sort, that it is moved with semblable passions, like a calme water ruffled with a gale of wind: For as the heart is most delicate and tender, so most sensible of the least impressions that are conjecturable; and it seemes that *Musicke* in those Cells, playes with the animall and vitall spirits, the onely goades of passion; So that although we lay altogether aside the consideration of *Ditty* or *Matter,* the very murmure of sounds rightly modulated and carried through the porches of our eares to those spirituall roomes within, is by a native vigour more than ordinarily powerfull, both to move and moderate all affections; and therefore Saint *Augustine* would have this custome of *Symphony* kept up in the Church, *Vt per oblectamenta aurium infirmior animus in affectum pietatis assurgat.*[2]

The fourth, *Multiplicitas objectorum,* for as all other senses have an admirable multiplicitie of objects which delight them, so hath the eare: And as it is impossible to expresse the varietie of delights or distasts which we perceive by, and receive in them, so here varietie of sounds diversificate passions, stirring up in the heart many sorts of joy or sadnesse, according to the nature of Tunes, or temper and qualitie of the receiver. And doubtlesse in *Harmony* we may discover the misticke portraitures both of *Vice* and *Vertue,* and the mind thus taken with resemblances, falls often in love with the things themselves: insomuch, that there is nothing more betraying us to sensuality, than some kind of *Musicke;* than other, none more advancing unto God. And therefore there must be a discreet caution had, that it be grave and sober, and not over-wanton'd with curiositie or descant. The *Lacedemonians* banished *Milesius* their famous Harper only for adding one string to those seven which he was wont formerly to teach withall, as if innovation in Art were as

---

1. Augustine, *Confessions,* lib. 10, cap. 33.   2. Ibid.

dangerous as in Religion: Insomuch, that *Plato* would make it a *Law* in *Musicke* that it should not be *Multiplex & effeminata*, he using it to his Scholars, *non* ἔργα, *sed,* παρέργα; ἔδυσμα *non* ἔδεσμα; *ut condimentum, non quotidianum pabulum*; as sauce only, or a running banquet onely, not as a full meale.

The over-carving and mincing of the ayre either by ostentation or curiositie of Art, lulls too much the outward sense, and leaves the spirituall faculties untouch'd, whereas a sober mediocritie and grave mixture of *Tune* with *Ditty*, rocks the very soule, carries it into extasies, and for a time seemes to cleave and sunder it from the body, elevating the heart inexpressably, and resembling in some proportion those *Halleluiahs* above, the Quire and unitie which is in Heaven. And this glances somewhat at that story of *Ignatius* by *Socrates*[1] who tooke a patterne of his Church-melody from a *Chorus* of Angels; which (as the *Historian* testifies) he beheld in a Vision extolling the blessed *Trinity* with *Hymnes* interchangeably sung. Or if this perchance prove fabulous, that of Saint *Augustine* will passe for canonicall, where *he stiles this voycing of Psamles aloft, Exercituum cœlestium Spiritale Thymiama*, The Musicke of Angels themselves, the spirituall Incense of that cælestiall Army. And as it is a representation of the Unitie above, so is it of concord and charitie here below, when under a consonance of voyce, we find shadowed a conjunction of minds, and under a diversitie of notes, meeting in one Song a multiplicitie of Converts in one devotion, so that the whole Church is not onely one tongue, but one heart. And to this purpose Saint *Augustine* againe, *Diver sorum sonorum rationabilis mode, ratusque concentus, concordi varietate, compactam bene ordinatæ civitates insinuat unitatem*, in his 17. *De civitate*, 14 chapter.

And here I cannot but justle once more with those spirits of *contradiction*, which are so farre from allowing *Harmony*, an *Embleme* of *unity* in the Church, that they make it their chiefe engin of *warre* and *discord*: and that which doth as it were betroth others to those solemne services is their chiefe motive of *separation* and *divorce*. A Psalme by *Voyce* barely they can allow, but not by *Instrument*, as if *this* were abrogated by the *Ceremoniall Law*; the *other* not, and yet if one, why not the other? And herein they not onely destroy the nature and propertie of Psalmes themselves, but cry downe the authoritie of the *Psalmist* too, in his *laudate Dominium in Psalterie*, praise the Lord upon the *Psaltery*, an instrument first invented for the Psalmes, and used onely to it; and therefore call'd *Psalterium a Psallendo*: Insomuch that some of the *Fathers* have defin'd a *Psalme* to be nothing else but *Modulatio per Instrumentam musicum*, or *Sermo musicus secundum harmoniæ rationem ad Organam pulsatus*,[2]

---

1. Socrates Scholasticus, *Hist. Ecclesias*, lib. 6, cap. 8. According to this account Ignatius, the third Bishop of Antioch, introduced responsive singing after experiencing a vision of angels hymning, in alternate chants, the Holy Trinity.

2. *De Civitate Dei*, lib. 17, cap. 14.

(so the Translator gives it me both from Saint *Basil* and *Gregory Nyssen*.) And what is this but our Prophets *Laudate Dominum in chordis & Organo?* Praise the Lord upon stringed Instruments and the Organ. The word of the *Septuagint* there is ὄργανον; which, though it generally signifie any kinde of Instrument, yet that is most properly called so; *Quod inflatur follibus,* saith Saint *Augustine:*[1] And what other is that in use now in our *Cathedralls?* which like those of old is an Instrument of *Exultation, Iob.* 21.12. and had his original! (for ought I know) from the invention of *Iubal* himselfe, in the 4. of *Genesis* 21. But whether it had or not, doubtlesse in many it doth sublimate devotion, sets their contemplation a soaring, as having a neere affinitie with the voyce of man; which lifted as it ought, resembles that of Angels, *Et hoc fit modulatione quadam & delectabili Canore,* sayes that renowned *African*,[2] by a kinde of modulaminous and delightfull ayre, which insinuating strangely with the outward Sense, steales subtilely into the minde of man, and not onely invites but drawes it to a holy chastitie and immaculatenesse, and therefore 'twas the wisdome of the *Spirit* (seeing mans disposition somewhat refractary to good, and struggling naturally with the Lawes of vertue, his affections more steepe and prone to the wayes of pleasure than the untrodden paths of Righteousnesse) to mix the power of Doctrine with that of Tunes, *Vt dum suavitate carminis mulcetur auditus, divini Sermonis pariter utilitas inseratur,* that whilst the eare was charm'd with the sweetnesse of the *Ditty,* the minde also might be rapt with the divinenesse of the matter, and so whilst others sing, we not onely heare, but learne too; *O vere admirandi magistri sapiens institutum, ut simul & cantare videamur, & quod ad utilitatem animæ pertinet doceamur,*[2] the Father still. . . .

And how can Gods Name be better glorified than in his House? and how better in his house, than by singing of his *Power* and *Mercy?* his Mercy in so drawing us, that wee can live unto him; his Power, for inabling us to doe something for his Glory. And 'tis well, that Those whom God hath enabled to doe, will doe something for Gods Glory; for the Glory either of his Name or House. A President this way is but Miracle reviv'd; and the Thing done, doth not so much beget *Applause,* as *Astonishment.* 'Tis somewhat above Wonder, to see the One without Prophanation, or the Other without Sacriledge; I meane not (and I say I meane not to forestall the preposterous Comments of others, which sometimes injuriously picke knots out of Rushes) that *Sacrilege,* which fleeces the Revenewes, but the *Ribbes* and *Entrailes* of a Church; defaces Pictures, and rifles Monuments, tortures an innocent peece of Glasse for the limme of a Saint in it; Razes out a *Crucifixe,* and sets up a *Scutchion;* Pulls down an *Organ,* and advances an *Houre-glasse;*[3] and so makes

1. In *Librum Psalmorum Prologus.*   2. Ibid.

3. A dig at the Puritan preachers' addiction to the hour-glass, which they took with them into the pulpit, ostensibly to measure the passage of time, but also, commonly, by

an House of Prayer, a fit den for Theeves. And indeed, this malicious dis-
robing of the Temple of the Lord, is no better than a *Spirituall Theft*; and the
Hands that are guilty of it, are but the Hands of *Achan*; and for their Reward,
deserve the hands *Gehazi*. God is the God of *Decency*. And *Ornaments* either *In*
his House, or *About* it (as they are Ornaments) are so farre from awaking his
Jealousie, that they finde his Approbation. He that hath consulted with the
Iewish Story, cannot want instance this way, nor illustration. The Law of old
required the *Altar* cleane, the Priest wash'd, the *Sacrifices* without blemish;
and this, when there was yet not onely a Temple not built, but not projected;
but *this* once enterpriz'd, straightway stones must be choicely hewed from
the Mountaines, Artificers fetch'd from *Tyre*, Cedars from *Libanus*, Silver
from *Tharshish*, Gold from *Ophir*, Silver and Gold in no small proportion,
ten thousand talents at least, to overlay the walls of it; besides, the very
beames and posts and *doores* o'respread with *Gold*, Gold of *Parvaim* (no other
would serve the turne) garnisht within with *pretious stones* and *graved Cherubins*, Cherubins of *Gold* too, *pure Gold*: (so sayes the Text) vail'd over with
blue and *purple* and *crimson* and *fine Linen*, nothing wanting for lustre or
riches, for beautie and magnificence for the house of a God; the *King* would
have it so, *Salomon* the wise King, and he would have it so for *Ornament*, and
not for *Worship*, except for the worship of his God, and that his *God* approves
of *with a fire from heaven*, 2 *Chron*. 7.1.

And now, my Brother, what capitall offence in the Image of a Saint or
Martyr, historically or ornamentally done in the house of the Lord? It invites
not our knee, but our eye; not our Observance, but our Observation; or if
perchance our Observance, not our Devotion: Though we honour Saints,
we doe them no worship; and though sometimes wee sing of, we sing not
unto them; wee sing of their *Sufferings*, not of their *Power*; and in so singing,
we sing unto God; Sing first of his *Power*, that he hath made them such
Champions for Him; and then, Sing aloud of his Mercy, that they were such
Lights unto us. And here, what danger of Idolatry? what colour for Offence?
what ground for Cavill or exception? Our dayes of Ignorance and blind zeale
are long since past by, but (it seemes) not of Peevishnesse of Contradiction:
And certainely, if Fancie or Spleene had not more to doe here then Judgement,
this Quarrell might be ended without Bloud. We are so curious in Tything
of Mynt and Cummin, that we let goe the waightier matters of the Law; and
whilst we dispute the indifferencies of a painted roofe or window, we sometimes let downe the very walls of a Church: And I dare say, if a Consistory did
not more scarre some than a Conscience, *Temples* would stand like those
Ægyptian Monuments, I know not whether a Modell of Antiquity or Desolation. 'Tis a misery, when the life of Religion shall lye in the Tongues of men,

holding it up when it was empty, to invite a compliant congregation to press them to
reverse the instrument and 'take another glass', see illustration of Hugh Peters.

and not in their Hands; or if in their Hands, sometimes not in their Hearts. The times are so loud for Faith, Faith, that the noyse thereof drownes sometimes the very Motion of good Workes; and even there too, where Faith is either begotten, or at least strengthened in *the House of the Lord*; That stands *Naked*, and sometimes Bare-headed, as if it begged for an Almes; when our Mansions swell in pride of their Battlements, the beauty of their Turrets; and yet their Inhabitants still cry as the mad people did after the Floud, *Come, let us make Bricke, let us Build:* But all this while, No noise of an *Axe* or a *Hammer* about the House of the Lord; Their project is to lift their *Earth* unto *Heaven,* and it matters not though the *Heaven* here below lay levell with the *Earth,* they sing of a *City* and *a Tower to get them a Name*; They care not for a *Temple* to sing aloud in to the Name of their God: And hence it is, that this God makes that sometimes a way to their confusion, which they intended a meanes to their Glory. . . .

THOMAS HOOKER

Thomas Hooker was the kind of Puritan divine who collided head-on with Laud's policy. At Chelmsford, where he held a lectureship, he had a following among the younger non-conformists, but after complaints had been lodged against him, he was threatened with arraignment and in May 1629 withdrew from the parish. In June of that year he appeared before the Bishops in London, but he had friends as well as enemies and the proceedings were stayed by the intervention of Samuel Collins, vicar of Braintree, in Essex. In 1630 he was again complained of by Dr. John Browning, rector of Rowneth in Essex, but a petition was produced in his favour, signed by forty-nine beneficed clergy of Essex. Later in the same year he was cited to appear before the Court of Commissioners, but at this point he chose to forfeit his sureties and fly from England to America, by way of Holland.

The sermon, part of which is quoted, was the last he ever preached in England—unlike Hook he did not return—and was delivered on the eve of his departure. It has been included because it exhibits, within a small compass, most of the characteristics of the *central* Puritan position of the period.

The preacher protests his humility, but claims, notwithstanding, to be chosen of God to speak for Him and to be on remarkably intimate terms with Him. In the middle of the sermon he engages in a kind of wrestling, or tug-of-war, with God ('No, thou shalt not goe away ...'); but he generously offers to share with his congregation the confidential information he has elicited in the course of these rough-and-tumbles with the Almighty ('I deal plainly with you and tell you what God hath told me ...'). The news is not good. Doom and damnation are hovering overhead and may be expected to swoop at any moment; and London is due to join Sodom and Jerusalem on the smoking scrap heap of the condemned, with the bogey-man of the seventeenth century, the Spaniard, as God's probable executioner. It is worth comparing the prophetic foreboding of the style with the expository composure of Anglicans like Collins and Lushington.

The Danger of Desertion (1630)

A Puritan's Farewell to England

Brethren, cast your thoughts afar off. What is become of those famous Churches, *Pergamus* and *Thyatira*, and the rest? Who would have thought that *Ierusalem* should have bin made a heap of stones, and a vagabond people? *Hos.* 7.9. *Plead with your mother, and call her Loammi, ye are not my people, and I will not be your God.* Thus as I may say, he sues out a bill of divorcement, as it was in the old Law, those that had anything against their wives, sued out a bill of divorcement, and so doth God, *Hos.* 2.2. she *is not my people, nor my beloved, let her cast away her fornications and idolatry, lest I make her as at the first,* that is, in Egypt poore and miserable: as if he should say to England, plead with England my Ministers, in the way of my truth, and say unto them, let them cast away their rebellions, lest I make her as I found her in captivity in the dayes of bondage.

But how doth God depart from a people?

1. When he takes away his love from a people, and as his respect, so his means too.

2. When he takes away his protection by taking downe the wals, that is, these two great meanes of safety, Magistrates and Ministers.

3. When instead of counselling, comes in bribing, and in stead of teaching, dawbing, when God either takes away the hedges, or the stakes are rotten, then God is going.

4. When God takes away the benefit of both these helps, and they are signes of Gods departing.

May God cast off a people, and unchurch a nation? then let it teach us to cast of all security, for miseries are nigh by all probabilities. When we observe what God hath done for us, all things are ripe for ruine, and yet we feare it not, we promise safety to our selves, and consider not that England is like so to be harrowed, wee cannot entertaine a thought that England shall be destroyed; when there are so many professors in it, we cannot be perswaded of it, according to the conviction of our judgements, either it must not be, or not yet, as if it were impossible for God to leave England, as if God were a cockering father over lewd and stubborne children: God may leave a Nation that is but in outward covenant with him, and why not England?

Englands sinnes have been great, yea and their mercies great. England hath been a mirror of mercy, yet God may leave us, and make us a mirrour of his justice. Looke how he spake to the people in *Ier.* 7. that *bragged of the Temple of the Lord, Sacrifices and offerings:* And what may not God which destroyed Shilo, destroy thee O England? Goe to Bohemia, from thence to the Palatinate, and so to Denmarke. Imagine you were there, what shall you see, nothing else but as Travellers say, Churches made heaps of stones, and those Bethels wherin Gods name was called upon, are made defiled Temples for Satan and superstition to raigne in? You cannot goe two or three steps, but you shall see the heads of dead men, goe a little further, and you shall see their hearts picked out by the fowles of the ayre, whereupon you are ready to conclude that Tilly[1] hath been there. Those Churches are become desolate, and why not England? Goe into the Cities and Townes, and there you shall see many compassed about with the chaines of captivity, and every man bemoaning himselfe. Doe but cast your eyes abroad, and there you shall see poore fatherlesse children sending forth their breathes, with feare, crying to their poore helplesse mothers. Step but a little farther, and you shall see the sad wife bemoaning her husband, and that is her misery, that the cannot dye soone enough; and withall she makes funerall Sermons of her children within herselfe, for that the Spaniard may get her little ones, and bring them up in Popery and superstition; and then she weeps and considers with her selfe: If my husband be dead, it is well, happily he is upon the racke, or put to some cruell tortures, and then she makes funerall Sermons, and dyes a hundred times before she can dye. Cast your eyes afar off, set your soules in their soules stead, and imagine it were your owne condition, why may not England be thus, who knowes but it may be my wife, when he heares of some in torments? Ah! Brethren, be not high minded, but feare, as we have this bounty on the one side, so may we have this severity on the other; therefore prancke not up your selves with foolish imaginations, as who dare come to England, the Spaniards have enough, the French are too weake: Be not deceived, who thought Ierusalem the Lady of Kingdomes, whither the Tribes went to worship, should become a heap of stones, a vagabond people, and why not England? Learne therefore to heare and feare, God can be a God without England, doe not say there are many Christians in it, can God be beholding to you for your Religion? No surely, for rather then he will maintaine such as professe his Name and hate him, *he will raise up these stones children unto Abraham;* He will rather goe to the Turks, and say your are my people, and I will be your God. But will you let God goe, England? Why are

---

1. Jan Tserklaes, Count Tilly, general commanding the Roman Catholic armies in the Thirty Years War, who, in 1620 at the battle of Prague, had destroyed Protestant hopes in Bohemia, and whose Croat and Walloon troops had acquired, especially at the storming of Magdeburg, a reputation for atrocious cruelty.

you so content to let him goe? Oh! lay hold on him, yea hang on him, and say thou shalt not goe. Doe you thinke that Rome will part with her religion, and forsake her gods? nay, an hundred would rather lose their lives. Will you let God goe? Oh England plead with your God! and let him not depart. You should onely part with your rebellions, he will not part with you. *Leave us not.* We see the Church is very importunate to keep God with them still, they lay hold on God with words of argument.

Thou hope of Israel, doe not leave us: they beset God with their prayers, and watch him at the Townes end that he might not goe away. No thou shalt not goe away, thou shalt abide with us still, they are importunate with God not to leave them.

Hence note this Doctrine.

That it is the importunate desire of Saints to keep God with them.

*

I deale plainly with you, and tell you what God hath told me: I must tell you on pane of salvation, will you give eare and beleeve. I poore Embassador of God am sent to doe this message unto you, though I am low, yet my message is from above, he that sent me, grant that it may be beleeved for his sake. Suppose God hath told me this night that he will destroy England, and lay it waste, what say you brethren to it? It is my message that God bade me doe, he expects your answer, what sayest thou oh England, I must returne an answer to my Master that sent me to night, why speake you not an answer? I must have one. Doe you like well of it, would you have England destroyed? would you put the old men to trouble, and the young men to the sword? would you have your women widowes, and your maids defiled? would you have your children, your deare ones to be throwne upon the pikes, and dashed against the wals? or would you have them brought up in idolatry under the necessity of preaching which is worst of all? would you see those Temples wherein we worship God burnt, and your owne houses? will you see England laid waste without inhabitants? are you willing to it? are you content? God bade me aske, why doe you not answer me? I must not stirre without it, I must have it, I am an importunate Embassador, send me not away sad, speake comfortably and cheerfully unto me. Are you willing to have God with you still, you are, are you not? I am glad of it; but you must not onely say so, but use the meanes, plead with God: And though his hand be up, and his sword drawne; yet suffer him not to destroy, but to sheath it in the bloud of our enemies, God grant it, and I should be glad to see England flourish still, and so are you, are you not? you are. Now if it come to passe that England be not, but destroyed and laid desolate, thanke your selves, and not God, he delights not in it. We may take up the complaint of the Prophet, *Isa.* 64.7. *No man stirs up himselfe to lay hold upon God:* For this is our misery, if that we have quietnesse and commodity we are well enough, thus we play mock-holy-day with God, the Gospell we make it our pack-horse: God is going, his glory is departing, England hath seene her best dayes, and now evill dayes are befalling us: God is packing up his Gospell, because no body will buy his wares, nor come to his price. Oh lay hands on God! and let him not goe out of your coasts, he is a going, stop him, and let not thy God depart, lay siege against him with humble and hearty closing with him, suffer him not to say, as if that he were going, farewell, or fare ill England, God hath said he will doe this, and because that he hath said it, he will doe it, therefore prepare to meet thy God O England! *Amos* 4.12. least God complaine of thee as he did of Ierusalem, lest my soule depart from thee, and I make thee a desolate land not inhabited.

*

Are we better then the old world; the same sinnes that were found in them, are found in us: *Sodome and Gomorrah on whom God rained fire and brimstone,* are not our sinnes as great? and are there not as great sinnes in us as were in *Ierusalem,* that was carried away captive? are we better then other Churches, then our brethren that have drunk so deeply of the cup of Gods wrath? what are we? I will tell you we are a burthen to God, he cannot beare us, he will thinke his paines well over when he hath destroyed us. You know all men are glad when their paines are over: so it is with God, we are a paine and a trouble to him, and why should God goe continually in paine and trouble with us, who are worthy to be destroyed? If his decree once come forth, then shall *England* seeke peace, and shall not finde it. *God will not pitty us,* as in *Isa.* 7.25. Ah! Brethren, what a heavy case is it, when a mercifull God doth shew himselfe unmercifull? when a patient God will be impatient? O beloved! there is a hard time befalling us of England; yet we consider it not; lamentable is our time. God wept over Jerusalem a long time: *Oh that thou hadst known in this thy day the things that belong to thy peace, but now they are hid from thy eyes*: So may I say to *England,* their Lord hath wept over it in mercy and patience a long time, but it hath not been taken notice of, God hath hid it from our eyes, what shall we doe when his mercy is turned into fury? and his patience into frowning? what shall we doe when we have leasure to consider what once we did enjoy? we can never prize Gods patience till that we finde the great want of it. Thus then the poore soule will say: There was a time when we might have been at peace with this patient God, but now it is hid from our eyes: I might have had mercy, but now the gate is shut, and not onely shut, but locked and barred too. Thus when people refuse mercy, he sends the contrary judgement, and then it will grieve and wound our soules to thinke what once we did enjoy; but that man that will bid God welcome to his heart, may goe singing to his grave.

*

You must be importunate with him to stay, and to continue, and count it a great favour that he will yet be intreated, *Isa*, 37. *Iacob wrestled with God*, and thus must we doe if we meane to keep him. You that live under the means, and will not walk in them, what great condemnation will be to you, over to them that have not the meanes, as it is said of *Capernaum, Mat.* 18,[1] so say I to *England*: Thou *England* which wast lifted up to heaven with meanes shalt be abased and brought downe to hell; for if the mighty works which have been done in thee had been done in India or Turky, they would haye repented ere this; therefore *Capernaums* place is *Englands* place, which is the most insufferable lest torment of all; and marke what I say, the poore native Turks and Infidels shall have a cooler summer parlour in hell then you; for we stand at a high rate, we were highly exalted, therefore shall our torments be the more to beare. The Lord write these things in our hearts with the finger of his owne Spirit for his Christs sake, under whom we are all covered.

1. Not 18, but 4: 13.

JOHN HALES

John Hales, 'the ever memorable', was revered among the most distinguished men of his age for his sweetness of temper, humility of spirit, and superiority of mind. He graduated B.A. at Corpus Christi, Oxford, before he was twenty, and was elected Fellow of Merton College in 1605 when he was twenty-one, 'as a person of learning above his age and standing'. In 1612 he was appointed to the Chair of Greek, and the following year was admitted a fellow of Eton. His reputation might have opened any door; but he had no appetite for preferment and the only appointment he would accept from Laud, and that reluctantly, was to a canonry at Windsor. He was one of that small company of choice spirits, lovingly immortalized by Clarendon, who walked and talked together in 'a university of purer air' under the oaks and limes in the gardens of Falkland's estate at Tew, where Clarendon said of himself that he was never so proud or thought himself so good a man as when he was the worst in the company.

In 1618 Hales accompanied Sir Dudley Carleton to the Hague where his sermon on *Duelling*,[1] was preached. It was during this visit that, as he said, he 'bade John Calvin goodnight', following in the steps of Richard Hooker to reject the claim of any one body to a permanent monopoly of truth and the authority of absolute and unalterable dogma.

But on his return to England he found his own country too had caught the infectious continental fever of intolerant contentiousness. To Hales's subtle and enquiring mind the clamorous slogans and simplifications of contending parties and sects were repugnant in their naive intemperance, and in 1619 he withdrew to his beloved Eton and devoted himself to a life of private study, punctuated by the pleasures of friendship at Tew. The latter was an oasis of enlightenment and tolerance of a kind that must inevitably perish in the clash of vindictive bigots dedicated to the pleasures of destruction in the name of righteousness. During the turbulence of the civil war Hales remained in his sanctuary until, with the Puritan supremacy, he was ejected from his fellowship on suspicion of 'malignancy'.

1. See pp. 212–216 above.

From then until his death in 1656 he lived in poverty, and had to sell his celebrated library to buy necessities; yet somehow he found money to help other distressed victims of the new order. He died in the house of one of his former servants, depressed by the 'black and dismal times', and requesting at the end particularly that there should be no 'sermons' and no 'bell-ringing' over him. He is buried at Eton.

Several of Hales's friends have left affectionate memories of him, the best being Clarendon's. Hales himself published little[1] and, of that little, some, including the sermons preached at Eton, were not pudlished at his instance. He spoke, in private, what he did not write, and there is evidence to suggest that some of his most mature thoughts he deemed it wisest to keep to himself.[2] The quality and lingering effects òf his conversation are suggested in the short record of two widely separated occasions. Once, when Hales was still a youthful prodigy, Ben Jonson, talking to him as one savant to another, belittled Shakespeare for his ignorance of the classical writers of Greece and Rome. Hales observed that if Shakespeare had not read the ancients he had likewise not stolen anything from them. Years later, when religious hysteromaniacs were urging their rival claims to the kingdom of heaven, Hales said a few words which reverberate still: '. . . nobody would conclude another man to be damned if he did not wish him to be so'. For his part, he said, he would renounce the Church of England tomorrow if it obliged him to believe that other Christians should be damned.

---

1. Mainly *The Golden Remains* (1659) and *Works*, 3 vol. (1765).

2. 'He had, whether from his natural temper and constitution, or from his long retirement from all crowds, or from his profound judgement and discerning spirit, contracted some opinions which were not received, nor by him published, except in private discourses, and then rather upon occasion of dispute than of positive opinion; and he would often say his opinions, he was sure, did him no harm, but he was far from confident that he might not do others harm, who entertained them, and might entertain other results from them than he did, and therefor he was very reserved in communicating what he thought himself in those points in which he differed from what was received.' Edward Hyde, *The Life of Edward Hyde, Earl of Clarendon . . . written by himself* (Oxford, 1759), pp. 27–28.

Of Gluttony

A sermon preached at Eton at Shrovetide, c. 1635

I Cor. VI. 13. Meats for the Belly and the Belly for meats, but the Lord shall destroy both it and them.

I will not study out, as the manner is, any curious division of these words. The holy Ghost hath here joyn'd the belly and meats together, and God hath entail'd destruction unto them both. Those whom God and the holy Spirit hath thus tied, I will not go about to divide: *Pereant res perdita; Belly, Meats, and Destruction*, all here go hand in hand, and let them so go undivided. And no marvel, for to keep the belly within bounds, there is nothing of power sufficient but destruction. *The tongue* (saith St. *James*) *is an unruly evil*. Beloved, the tongue is not a more unruly evil then the belly; it is the fourth daughter of the Horse-leech, unsatiable, ever more crying, Give, give; a rigorous creditour, which every day receives, and every day demands a tribute of meats, and drinks, and pleasures, and the like: which way shall we go about to tame it? First, it is not reason that can rule it: It was the saying of old *Cato*, *Venter non habet aures*, The belly hath no ears; now it is a vain thing to endeavour to perswade with that which hath no ears. Secondly, it is not time that can over-master it; for *Vitia ventris non modo non minuit ætas, verum etiam auget*, The vice and evil of the belly, intemperance in meats and drinks, is no way moderated, it is exasperated and encreased by age. Thirdly, it is not the consideration of cost and large expence that can restrain it; for it is a solemn maxim in the schole of gluttony, A near and hard and hucking[1] chapman shall never buy good flesh. The belly and money easily part; *Esau* will forego his birth-right, his honour, rather then lose his dinner. *Paulus Jovius*[2] reports of a Captain, one *Hugucchio*, that lost two Towns, onely because he would not break his meal; for, being invited to a public Feast, and receiving tidings of a revolt intended, he neglected and let slip the occasion, onely because he was loth to lose his share of a liberal dinner. Fifthly, it is not policy nor wisdom that can over-reach it. *Solomon*, the most politick and wisest man that ever was, prostitutes his learning, wit, wisdom, and all, to that base and sordid appetite. Sixthly, it may be sickness and fear of death may seem to speak to the belly with some authority, and bear some hand over it. *Demades* the

1. Haggling.   2. Paolo Giovio.

Oratour was wont to say of the *Athenians*, that they never came to consult of peace, *nisi atrati*, but in blacks and mourning; by which he meant, that that people, till war had brought some extreme inconvenience upon them, and swept away their citizens, their friends, their kindred, would never think of peace. As the *Athenians* did by peace, so we do by temperance; we never bethink our selves, or consult of moderate diet, *nisi atrati*, but in blacks and mourning, when our folly and intemperance hath cast us into some disease, and affrighted us with fear of death and destruction. And yet even this, though it be the strongest cannot much prevail with the belly; for how many do we see that in the midst of their sickness and of death, yet cannot forget their trenchers? As they have been wont, *molliter valere*, to be dainty in the time of health, so will they endeavour *delicate ægrotare*, to be delicious in their sickness; *vinum aut frigidam concupiscunt, & deliciarum patrocinium in accusationem non merentis stomachi habent*,[1] saith *Cornelius Celsus*,[2] they desire to please their intemperance with meats and drinks which hurt them, and put off the fault of a wanton appetite with pretence of a weak stomach. When *Philoxenus* the *Epicure*[3] had fallen desperately sick upon glutting himself on a delicate and costly fish, perceiving he was to die, he calls for the remainder of his fish, and eats it up, and dies a true Martyr to his belly. By this time you see, I hope, why it pleased God thus to yoke the belly and meats with death and destruction. Other passions in us find something that can subdue them, and that root them out: Fear and Anger, they will yeild to time and reason; Lust will abate with age and abstinence, onely the incessant appetite to meats and drinks is unconquerable, except it be by death, or extreme sickness, which is the way to death. This is a devil which no fasting, no prayer can cast forth, not time, nor reason can extinguish.

*

The Scriptures point out two sins unto us, *Oppression* and *Lust*: Intemperate lust is the inseparable companion of intemperate eating; *Nunquam vidi continentem quem non vidi abstinentem*, Seldom have you seen one continent that is not abstinent. We have thus far surveyed one world, and the sins of it, and we have found that eating is the first sin, the next, the last; all thrive by the favour of intemperance in meats, or drinks, or both. But now

1. *De Mediciana*, Bk. I, 8, ii. There is a slight discrepancy between Hales's quotations and the classical text, which reads ' . . . vinum aut *frigidam aquam concupiverunt* deliciarum patrocinium', etc.

2. Cornelius Celsus: writer of excellent Latin prose, born about 25 B.C., may have produced in *Mediciana* a translation of an earlier Greek work. There is some internal evidence to suggest that Celsus was not himself a practising physician. Pliny puts him among the *autores*.

3. A synthetic character compounded of Philoxenus, son of Eryxis, Philoxenus of Cythera and others: see Athenaeus, *Deipnosophists*, 6. d., et passim.

we have a new world, clean wash'd; what is it which now brings sin upon *Noah*, the father of the second world? even the same in a manner which brought it upon *Adam*, the father of the first; *Adam* sinned by eating, *Noah* by drinking: *Eating, Drinking*, no great matter to chuse, both are *gula*, both are the intemperance of the mough, and taste, and belly; and both intended here by St. *Paul* under the name of *Meats*. *Verisimile non est ut quis dimidiam gulam Deo immolet, aquis sobrius, cibis ebrius*, saith *Tertullian*: As therefore *Tertullian* acknowledged a drunkenness in *meats*, so is there gluttony in *wines* and *drinks*, So then, as by the mouth and belly sin comes into the new world, so it goes on; for, the sin next specified in Scripture is that of *Sodom*, and the five Cities: Would you know what sins they were? the Prophet will tell you, *Idleness, and fulness of bread:* He adds not Lust, for he needs not; that follows naturally upon the former, *tanquam vara vibiam*. Idleness, Fulness, and Lust, they are a three-fold cord, twisted by the devil, and hardly untwined and severed by any man. *Mens enim otiosi nihil aliud cogitare novit nisi de escis & ventre*, saith *Cassianus;*[1] *The mind of an idle person runs upon nothing but his belly and meats.* No sooner were the *Jews* freed from the Egyptian bondage, and now began to be at leisure, but forthwith, *Agape in cacabis fervet, fides in culinis calet, spes in ferculis jacet*; All their meditations are fix'd upon the flesh-pots of *Egypt*, their devotion is spent upon Onions and Garlick, and those other Egyptian Deities. Now the belly once filled, you need not doubt what follows: *Repletus venter facile despumat in libidinem; A full belly easily dissolveth and dischargeth it self by lust.* *Xenophon*, disposed to trifle away some of his spare time, writes an idle discourse, which he calls his συμπόσιον, his Banquet; where, after much impertinent talk, for the close and upshot of the meeting, he brings in, for the farther chearing up of his company, two young Boys acting *Bachus* going to bed to *Ariadne;* which they did in so gross, so unseemly, so loose a manner, that by and by (saith my Author) all that were married hasted home to their wives, and the unmarried vowed they would not continue long so.[2] Lo here the true issue of intempestive comessation and compotation, for surfet and lust dwell never far asunder. And therefore the Apostle St. *Paul*, when he had forbidden the Romans[3] *rioting and drunkenness*, he immediately adds unto them, *chambering and wantonness; Appendices scilicet gulæ, Lasciviæ & luxuriæ*, as *Tertullian* upon those very words doth note; *Wantonness and luxury are the complement of riot and intemperance.* By all this which I have delivered, I suppose by this time that your selves can conclude, what care and watch we ought to hold

1. *Institutes* X. 6.

2. In this passage, at the end of the *Banquet*, Xenophon uses terms, not of reproach, but of admiration to describe the performance; and he adds that the married guests and some who were not, sped to Athens with lively intent. But Hales was preaching for the edification of little Etonians.

3. Romans, 13:13.

over our meats and drinks; for, if eating were the door which first admitted sin, if it hath been a perpetual fomenter and nourisher of sin, we can do no less than to *set a watch upon the door of our lips*, not onely to beware what goes out, but what likewise goes in there. Unskilful Fencers will be sure still to remove their ward there where they have once received a blow, though they suffer some other part to lie open: It were a great shame for us, if having so long combated with the Devil, and received so many blows by incautelous eating, we should not have so much wit as young and unskilful Fencers have, remove our ward thither.

*

Aristotle tells us, that those that delighted in pleasing smells, are not to be ranged among intemperate persons: I must confess, I think he was deceived; for to be over-indulgent, over studious to please any one sense whatsoever, I say not onely the Taste and Touch, but the Eye with gawdy shews, the smell with fragrant and costly perfumes, the Ear with delicate Airs in Musick, it truly vanity and intemperance. The reason of his errour was, that he measured vices by the sensible inconvenience that follows upon them. Divines distinguish the Sacrament; some there be, say they, *quæ imprimunt characterem, which leave a mark behind them*; others leave none at all. This distinction fits the vices well, but *Aristotle* knew it not: Some vices leave a character, a mark, by which you may easily discover them; others are more close, their way is like the way of a *serpent over a stone, or the way of a bird in the air*, they leave no track, no footstep behind them. Sin in meats is very often committed, but it is not often discovered; you cannot trace it, it many times leaves no character to betray it. Now, Beloved, (and this was the reason why I have spoken all this) by so much the more ought we to be wary in eschewing this vice, by how much it is retired and unespied; remembring what the Apostle hath told us, that *some mens sins are open before hand, going before into judgment; and some follow after*. Open sins, sins that leave a character, these go before unto judgment; but sins that are otherwise shall not be hidden.

Secondly, another reason perswading us to keep watch over the vice of eating, is, that we have no law to restrain it; for table, for diet, no man hath any law but his money or his credit. Let our excess be never so great, let the surfet be never so apparent, yet is their no Magistrate to chastise it. This neglect opens a way to the practise of the sin, and makes men believe that the vice is lawful. *Hippocrates* complained much, that there was no law to restrain the errours of Physicians πλὴν ἀστοξίης, excepting perchance some small disgraceful report when a fault was espied.[1] Errours of diet have not so much as this to restrain them; yet to make a law in this behalf there is cause and ground enough. *Interest reip. ne quis re sua male utatur*; It is a rule warranted by

1. See 'Hippocrates', *Law*, cap. 1.

all reason, that it concerneth the publick good of the Common-wealth, that no man make ill use of what is his. The want of laws is it which hath given entrance to such monsters of luxury and prodigality, of whom *Tertullian* spake, *Quibus deus venter est, & culina templum, & aquiliculus altare, & facerdos coquus, & sanctus spiritus nidor, & condimenta charismata, & ructus prophetia est:*[1] *Whose god is their belly, the kitchin is their temple, the dresser is their altar, the cook is their priest, &c.* What examples are extant every where of this kind of men? *Augustinus Chieffius,*[2] a Banker, a Money-merchant at *Rome,* at the Christening of his son, entertained *Leo* the Tenth upon the River of *Tibris,* and all the foreign Ambassadors, with the Nobles of the City, with all exquisite and curious fare, dish'd out in costly plate; and upon the change of every Service (and they were not a few) all the meats, plate and all, all was cast away into the River, and new and costlier still supplied in the room. But what need I seek so far as *Rome?* our own Kingdom will yield us examples. Search but our own Records, consult but with the Author *De præsulibus Angliæ,*[3] *Of the Prelates of England,* and see what a prodigious Dinner is there described, at the Consecration of one of the Archbishops of *Canterbury; & horum tamen nihil Gallioni curæ erat,* yet was there found none of the *Gallions,* none of the Magistrates of the times, that took it to heart, or once thought to chastise it.

*

The first stroke which is to be given in this our warfare against the flesh, is to be directed against the belly. *Cæsar* was wont to command his souldiers, *faciem ferire,* to strike at the face; the laws of our spiritual warfare give us another rule. Men by the light of nature have seen thus much; it was the counsel of *Pythagoras,* κρατεῖν δὲ ἐθίξεο τούτων, γαστρὸς μὲν πρώτιστα;[4] *First, and above all things,* saith he, *be sure to make your self master of your belly.*

1. De Jejuniis, cap. XVI.

2. Agostino Chigi, one of the most opulent magnates of the Italian Renaissance, patron of Bembo and Aretino, intimate of Pope Leo X, to whom he often played host, admitted to owning a hundred houses, as many ships, and employing twenty thousand men. Hales omits the end of this story, which would not have served his purpose, but deserves mention here. The gold plate was cast negligently into the Tiber after use; but there were concealed nets in the river, by means of which, when the entertainment was over and the guests had dispersed, all was salvaged and restored to the Chigi vaults in readiness for the next banquet. The fullest account of Agostino Chigi has been given by his descendant, Fabio Chigi, who, before his elevation to the pontificate as Alexander VI, wrote a number of literary monographs, mainly under the pseudonym, 'Ernestus de Eusobius'. The Latin manuscript of his biography was edited by Giuseppe Cugoni and published as *Agostino Chigi il Magnifico* (Rome, 1878).

3. Francis Godwin, *A Catalogue of the Bishops of England* (1615), pp. 166–168: describing the consecration of William Waring.

4. *Pythagoron,* xi.

See you not what men do in the besieging of Cities? they cut off all convoy of victual, and that done, they know the place cannot long hold out. He that intends a Leaguer, and purposes to make himself master of his body, let him be sure to cut off all unnecessary convoys of meats and drinks, and the siege cannot last long. Secondly, I told you, there was another thing observable in this action of God, and that is the time in which he gave this law. *Cæsarius*, brother to *Gregory Nazianzen*, had a conceit, that *Adam* remained in Paradise fourty days, and that the law concerning eating was not given till the very latter end of this time; and that that part of St. *Paul's* disputation, *Rom. 7. Once was I alive without the law, but the law came, sin revived, and I was dead*, was to be understood in the person of *Adam*, for that part of the fourty days wherein he supposed that the law concerning eating was not given. Beloved, I know no ground, no warrant for this conceit; the Scripture tells me that *Adam*, immediately upon his creation was brought into Paradise; that immediately upon his entrance into Paradise the Commandment concerning eating was laid upon him, no footstep any of longer date of time is allowed. It was the purpose of God, that *Adam* from his very beginning should be a subject of obedience; wherefore he leaves him not an hour to his own discretion, but resolves to make trial of his obedience in the very first action which in course of nature he was to do. Betimes, immediately upon his first creation, in his infancy, as it were, he thinks good to set bounds to his diet. Nature leads the hand to the mouth; and hence it is, that Infants, whatsoever you put in their hands, they presently put it to their mouths. This proneness therefore of nature God restrains at the very beginning; to leave us an example to do the like by those whose education is committed to our charge; for from neglect of this proceeds the greatest part of the miscarriage of youths in their luxurious and riotous courses. *Ante palatum eorum quam os instituimus*, We season their palats, and teach them to know delicate meats, before they can give plain accent to any syllable. From the liberty they see we take, they learn to be licentious; from our full tables they learn to riot; from our example they learn to love evil, before they know what good is. Hence is the world filled with complaints, Fathers of Children for their luxury, Children of Fathers for their ill example; for it is but just, that evil example should return upon the head of him that gave it. *Petrus Crinitus*,[1] a great Clerk in the days of our grandfathers, thought it fit (forsooth) when he was now old, to do as *Socrates* did, under colour of free teaching to converse with youths in the streets, in the Tennis-courts, in Taverns and Compotations. But this errour cost him dear; for being on a time in a youthful meeting, one of his petulant Convivators poured a cup of cold water on his head; which affront he took so heavily, that he went home and died. Let Parents and Tutors take heed what behaviour they use with those who are committed to their charge; for

---

1. Peter Haarer, secretary to the Elector of Palatine, Louis V.

let them make account they will *frigida perfundere*, first or last they will pour a cup of cold water upon their heads, to their grief and shame. To conclude then this point; find we no law made to restrain the vice of eating? let us remember what St. *Paul* saith, *A good man is a law unto himself:* let every man be his own Magistrate, and let him lay upon himself this law, *Omne superfluum vetitum esto*, Whatsoever is superfluous in meats and drinks, let it be taken as forbidden.

*

The world is apt upon all occasions to fall upon unnecessary commessation and compotations, the Church needs not strike in to set it forward, and make Feasting a part of Religion, and bring the Church and the Kitchin together. And yet we see it doth; for when we celebrate the memorial of any Saint, the birth or death of any Apostle or Martyr, do we not call this solemnity their Feast, and so accordingly solemnize it with excess of cheer? I have often wondred upon what discretion it is, that Christians have thought fit to celebrate the memorials of Saints with feasting: Why should times of greatest seriousness be managed with feasting, which is one of the greatest vanities? *Stultum est nimia saturitate honorare velle Martyrem, quem constat Deo placuisse jejuniis; It is a foolish thing*, saith St. *Hierom, for any man to think he honours the Saints with eating, who are known to have pleased God best by fasting*.[1] The ancient Ethnicks were wont to celebrate their νηφάλια, their feasts of sobriety and fasting in the honour of *Bacchus*, who was their god of riot and drunkenness. Upon the like fancy I think (else I know not whence it should come) have Christians enterprised to appoint feasts of excess in the honour of the Saints, who are known to be, I say, not God's, but presidents and examples of all temperance and abstinence. The Church of *Rome* is wont, even to this day, when she gets the reliques and ashes of any of the Saints, to lap them up in silk and costly stuff, and shrine them in silver and gold; whereas, when the Saints themselves were on earth, and their bodies the living Temples of the holy Ghost, they would have thought themselves much wronged if any such costly ornaments should have been employed about them. Shall we think we honour them, when we lodge their dead bones in stately Sepulchres, whose glory it was in their lifetime to dwell in poor Cells, and Grots, and Caverns of the earth? Since their departure from us to heaven, have they altered their judgment, and learned there to approve and admire that which here in earth they thought their chief vertue to contemn? *Scilicet nostros mores templis immittimus*, We think that God and the Saints are like ourselves, and taken with that which pleaseth us: For, whether or no to expend these things in honour of God, be a sign of our love to him, I know not; but this

1. Temperate language for Jerome, but again, Hales was addressing schoolboys. Elsewhere (Epist. LIV. 10.) the Saint says, *Quidquid seminarium voluptatum est, venenum puta*.

I know, that it is a most certain sign, and a betrayer of our love to those things. For, Beloved, if we had no love unto them, if we bare them no respect, would we think we honour'd God by offering that to him which we our selves contemn? *Macchiavel* writing the life of *Castruccio Castracano*,[1] a Gentleman of *Luca*, tells us, that he delighted himself much in often feasting; and being reproved for it by some friends of his, he gave them this answer, *If feasting were not a good thing, men would not honour God and the Saints so much with it.* Lo here, Beloved, the natural consequence of Church-feasts; they are nothing else but an Apology for luxury: For when the Ministers of God shall out of these and the like places reprove superfluity of diet, the people have their answer ready, If this were a fault, then why is Christ and his Saints thus honoured with it?

This splendor of feasting and eating in memory of the Saints hath a little dazled the eyes of some great persons; St. *Hierom*, although a great Clerk, and singular contemner of secular superfluities, yet wee see in what a strange passion he was when he wrote his Book against *Vigilantius*[2]. And what, think you, might be the cause of so much heat? Understand you must, that there was a custom in the Church, in sundry places, for men and women, young and old, of all qualities and conditions, upon the Vigils of the Martyrs, to come together by night, and meet in Church-yards, and there eat and drink upon the Tombs of the Martyrs. This corruption *Vigilantius* had reproved: and good cause I think he had so to do; *Nox, vinum, mulier*, when men, women, maids, shall meet together by night in Church-yards to eat and drink, I think your own discretion will easily suggest unto you what faults were like to come.

1. Unfortunately never finished.
2. *Epistola contra Vigelantium.* Nothing strange about Jerome being in a passion; he was seldom out of one. He was capable of quarrelling with his friends Rufinus and Augustine: Vigilantius was his enemy.

CORNELIUS BURGES

Fast days, days of public Humiliation, were proclaimed by parliament to mark the gravity of an occasion and to demonstrate the seriousness of members' approach to it. To assist them to a fitting state of mind, it became customary for a 'fast sermon' to be preached to the respective assemblies of the upper and lower Houses.

In 1640 the parliament which would be remembered as the Long Parliament was summoned. The king's policy in Scotland was failing and, threatened with the spread of dissidence to the south, he needed more money than he could raise without parliament. It was the chance that John Pym, the master mind of the Country Party, had been waiting for; and he began to put into operation his plans to make this parliament the lever to break the domination by the king and his advisers of the country's legislature. To this end radical blows must be struck at the resources of the crown. First, the Episcopalian order of the church must be broken, or at least disarmed, for it was an organization of political allegiance. (It must be remembered that the Puritan complex, due to energy and initiative, had obtained a higher representation in parliament than its total numbers in the country alone would have justified.) Second, the king's right to dissolve parliament must be made conditional upon the consent of parliament itself; third—and upon the achievement of this all else depended—the one natural leader who might make the King triumph, Thomas Wentworth, Earl of Strafford, must be eliminated. To effect these measures the mind of parliament had to be prepared, its opinions shaped and held to the design required by the 'great contrivers'. To appreciate the 'fast sermons', therefore, we must recognize them as urgent political operations, and consider them against their background as the final expression of long conference and discussion, of additions and amendments, and the preachers as men coming most carefully briefed into the pulpit to fire the first salvos in what would prove lethal engagements.

Pym and his friends had come together with the express intention of killing two men. The first fast sermon to the parliament, preached by Cornelius Burges, vicar of Watford,[1] on November 17th, was an attack upon the sins of the great ones of the church, in preparation for the forthcoming impeachment (now secretly under way) of Laud. Dreadful wickedness was rife in high places. What was it? Might it possibly be 'Idolatry'?

A Responsibility to Punish

A sermon preached by Cornelius Burges to the Honourable House of Commons assembled in parliament at their public Fast, on November the 17th., 1640

THE PROPHESIE OF JEREMIAH. Chap. 50, verse 5.

They shall ask the way to Zion with their faces thitherward, saying, "Come, let us join ourselves unto the Lord in an everlasting covenant that shall not be forgotten."

Consider I beseech you, that it is not without a speciall Providence that this your meeting was cast upon this very day (for, I presume, little did you think of the 17 of *November*, when you first fixed on this day for your *Fast*;) that, even from thence, one hammer might be borrowed to drive home this nayle of Exhortation; that the very memory of so blessed a work begun on this very day, might throughly inflame you with desire to enter into a *Covenant*; and so, to go forward to perfect that happy Reformation, which yet in many parts lyes unpolished and unperfect.

Oh suffer not that *doore of hope* by Her set open this day, to be again shut, for want of a *Covenant*. If you would indeed honour Her precious memory; yea, honour God and your selves, and not only continue the possession of what she (as a most glorious Conduit pipe) hath transmitted to us, but perfect the work; set upon this duty of *joyning your selves to the Lord in an everlasting Covenant that shall not be forgotten.* And so have you the *Motives*.

I shall now shut up all with some few *Directions* to help us in it. And here, passing by what hath been already spoken touching the *preparatives* to it, the *Substance* of it, and the *properties* required in it, I shall only give you these six subsequent *Directions*.

1. At this early stage Burges was himself a conspicuous target as a militant Puritan. Later he would considerably moderate his tone, but too late to avert the consequences of his earlier efforts. Burges graduated B.A. at Wadham, 1615; M.A. 1618; B.D. and D.D. 1627; died 1665.

Give a Bill of divorce to all your Lusts, or kill them out-right. This Covenant is a marriage-Covenant, and there is no marrying with God, so long as your former husband, your base corruptions, your swearing, riot, drunkennesse, uncleannesse, pride, oppression, and what ever else your soules *know to be the plague of your own hearts*, remaine alive and undivorced. *For the woman which hath an husband, is bound by the Law to her husband so long as he liveth;* but, if he be once *dead, she is free from that Law*, Rom. 7. Therefore send these packing, in the first place. A wise man will never marry a strumpet, nor with any woman, that hath another husband: his wife that shall be only his own, none else shall have interest in her. Much lesse then, will the Holy and Jealous God admit of any Spouse that is wedded to any lust, and so continueth. Say then, what wilt thou now do? wilt thou still keep thy darling lust? Hast thou been a swearer, and so thou wilt be? a drunkard, an uncleane person, an oppressour, a prophane *Esau*, and wilt be so still? Know, that God will none of thee, but abhorres all such as thou art. He will admit none into Covenant but such as *touch not the uncleane thing, but separate* from it. To them only it is, that he promiseth, *I will be their God, and they shall be my people.*

More especially purge out and cast away (as a *Menstruous cloth*) all *Idols* and *Idolatry* in particular. All our Lusts are lothsome to his stomach, but nothing is so abominable to his Soule, as *Idolatry*. This is that spirituall whoredome which meritoriously dissolves the marriage bond where it is already knit, and lies as a barre in the way to a Covenant with God, where yet it is not made This was it for which the Lord proceeded so severely, first against the ten Tribes, and then against the residue, as you all know. For this, the Land spewed them out. And where ever God promiseth to recall them, he usually premiseth this, (which should first be done) *From all your Idols will I cleanse you. Ezek. 36.25. Ephraim also shall say, What have I to do any more with Idols? Hos.* 14.8. and all shall cast them away with detestation, saying, *Get thee hence, I say.* 30.22.

Every Idol is that great *Image of Iealousy*, which the Lord can by no meanes endure, and which will certainly be the destruction of King and People, where ever it is entertained, especially if againe received in, after it hath been once ejected. A sad example whereof we have in *Iudah*, where, after *Iosiah had taken away all the abominations out of all the countries that pertained to Israel, and made all that were present in Israel to serve the Lord onely*, the Act of Resumption of Idols and Idolatry by the succeeding Kings (although it is probable they did it onely *secretly* like those in 2 *Kin.* 17.9.) became the ruine of those Kings, and Kingdomes.

Beloved, let me speake freely, for I speake for God, and for all your safeties. You cannot be ignorant of the grosse Idolatry daily encreasing among us, and committed not (as adultery) in Corners onely, but in the open light; people going to, and coming from the Masse in great multitudes, and that as

ordinarily, openly, confidently as others go to and from our Churches.
And I doubt not but some of you doe know the number of Masses to exceed
that of Sermons.[1]

Whose heart bleeds not over this prodigious growth of Popery and over
flowing of Popish Masses? Who knowes not, that in the Masse is committed
the most abominable Idolatry that ever the Sunne beheld in the Christian
world? Who remembers not with indignation and horror, how often that
insatiable Idol hath bathed it selfe in the bloud of many of our Ancestors and
Progenitors? And can any be so silly as to beleeve, that it will rest satisfied
till it swim againe in our bloud also; unlesse we will joyne with Idolaters, and
so perish in Hell? For what ever some men talke of the possibility of the
salvation of some persons in that Church, (as they call it) yet it is agreed on all
hands, among us, that, for those of our owne Nation and once of our owne
Church where the light hath so long shined in so much brightnesse, so as they
have both received & professed it; if they shall (whether to gratifie a Parent, a
wife, husband, friend, Master &c.) put out their owne eyes, and returne backe
to *Babylon* from whence they were once set free, their case is very desperate and
dismall, and *it had been better for them never to have knowne, the way of righteousnesse, then after they have knowne it to turne from the holy Commandement once
delivered unto them.* Therefore I beseech you to take care of these above others.

Nor speake I this, onely to prevent a publique toleration, which I hope,
through the care of our Pious King, and your diligence, our eyes shall never
see) but to put on Authority to the utter rooting out of that abomination,
although committed in secret; and with connivence onely. . . .

Execute true Iudgement and Justice. *Loose the band of wickednesse, undoe the
heavy burdens, let the oppressed goe free, and break every yoke* of the oppressor.
This is a maine part of an *acceptable Fast*, and therefore must be performed of
all that will enter into Covenant with God. And this was part of Gods Answer
to the Jewes enquiring of the Prophet whether they should continue their
solemne Fasts? *Zach.* 7. Therefore herein deale impartially and throughly,
for hereby the Throne it selfe is established. It is true, a difference must be put
between those that are only led on in evill wayes by others, and those that are
leaders of others: but it becomes not me to prescribe to you in this case, your
own wisdome will teach you that. Only I am to pray you, that if you shall
find any escapes to have been made in the Ordinary Courts of Justice, in the
condigne punishment of *Murder* and *Idolatry*, take notice of them, and there
be sure to strike home, as *Samuel* did where *Saul* himselfe had been too
indulgent. There is nothing makes you such faire Images of God (in the
relation you now stand) as due execution of Justice and Judgement. Therefore, if you will indeed enter into a Covenant, let this be done.

1. A notable Puritan point: the sermon equated as sacrament, with the eucharist;
in practice preaching being treated as of superior importance.

Do your best to draw as many others as you can the same way. Parents and Masters are bound to take care that their children and families do feare, and serve God, as well as themselves. And You who now appeare before him in behalf of the kingdome, as you must enter into a Covenant for them as well as for your selves, so must you do your utmost that they also for themselves may passe under the same Covenant, with you. The representative Body of Israel that stood before the Lord to make a Covenant, in *Deut.* 29.15. made it not only for themselves and such were present, but for all that were *absent* also. And *Iosiah* when he entred into a Covenant himselff, he not only caused *all that were present of Iudah at the house of the Lord*, to stand to it, 2 *Chron.* 34.32. But he *made all Israel to serve, even to serve the Lord their God*, vers. 33. that is, to strike a Covenant with him. Therefore take care that all others, when you returne home, may make a Covenant before the Lord to walk after him in all his Commandements: that God may be set up more and more, and the hearts of all men may be lifted up in the wayes of the Lord to take hold of his Covenant also. If you do not this, you do nothing: for more is required at your hands, than of private persons, who yet are bound to call upon others (as the men in my Text) saying, *Come and let us joyne our selves unto the Lord in an everlasting Covenant.*

Would you have this to be done, namely, that all should *appeare before God in Zion*, for this purpose? Then set up *Way-markes* to direct them thither. Take speciall care that the Ordinances of God be set up, and held up, in more puritie, and plentie. Down at once with all inventions and fancies of men, which corrupt and adulterate the pure worship of God. Let none but He be worshipped, and let no worship be thrust upon him which himselfe hath not prescribed. Herein especially (yet still within your bounds) be zealous, and quit your selves like men.

Above all, take better order for the more frequent, and better performance, and due countenancing of that now-vilified (but highly necessary) Ordinance of Preaching, which, albeit it be Gods own arme and power unto salvation, is yet brought into so deep contempt (and by none more than by those who should labour most to hold up the honour of it) that it is made a matter of scorne, and become the odious Character of a *Puritan*, to be an assiduous Preacher. Yea so farre have some men run mad this way, that it is held a crime deserving Censure in the highest Ecclesiasticall Court in this Kingdome, to tell but a few Clergy men out of a Pulpit, that it is an essentiall part of the Office of a Bishop, to Preach. Some of you know that I belye them not.

And is it not then high time to vindicate the honour of Preaching from those virulent and scurrilous tongues and pens, that have of late daies (more then ever) blasphem'd this Ordinance; and, to take more pitie of the many darke and barren parts of this Kingdome, where many scarce have a Sermon in seven yeeres; nay some (as divers of worth do credibly report) not in their whole lives?

I know the many pleas of many idle droanes and mercilesse men to excuse and defend an unpreaching, or seldome-preaching Ministry; but all their fig-leaves are too short to cover their own shame, and the nakednesse of those poore perishing people whom such men make naked, to their own destruction also.

To tell us, that preaching indeed is necessary for the planting of a Church, but not so afterwards: is nothing but to bewray their owne sottish ignorance. Is not the word preached, the *milk* and food whereby men are, and must be continually nourished *to grow* up in the body of Christ, as well as the *Seed* whereof they are first begotten unto Christ? And can men that are born, and living, live safely, or at all, without continuall supply of food convenient for them? ...

And yet, as many of our blind guides and Idol Shepheards care not to erect Preaching where there is none, so doe they all they can to cheat and defraud those of it who doe or would enjoy it, sometimes by pulling it downe where it is set up, and (to fill up the measure of their wickednesse) glorying in it, when they have done; sometimes by striking out the teeth of it, that if men will needes preach, yet it shall be to little purpose; onely a frigid, toothlesse, saplesse discourse, never piercing deeper than the eare. If the Preacher come home to convince the Conscience of particulars that need reformation, (which yet was the old course, and should be so still) the Preacher is either derided as worthy of nothing but contempt, or else censured as indiscreet, rash, factious, and seditious.

And least men should surfeit of preaching, how be all Sermons, in the afternoones of the Lord's dayes, cryed downe, as the markes of Iudaizing Puritanisme, and as a burden intolerable to the people! ...

SAMUEL KEM

Even as he spoke, Burges's rhetorical appeal for more preaching was receiving vigorous support in an unlikely quarter.

One of the most curious phenomena which war, and rumour of war, projects, is the 'fighting parson'. He is immediately distinguishable from the other chaplains who serve with the armed forces in time of war by the personal belligerence of his style. It is as if he regarded the prosecution of war not as a necessary evil, the effects of which it is his duty as far as possible to mitigate, but as in every way the most welcome and desirable of circumstances. In meeting him, it is sometimes difficult to imagine what he did, and how he conducted himself, before the outbreak of war brought him the opportunity to behave naturally. Of this kind was Samuel Kem, chaplain first to a troop of horse of the Earl of Essex, and later to a regiment of the Earl of Denbigh. Kem wore uniform, buff coat and scarf and carried arms; he swaggered, and blasphemed, and stole indefatigably; and, of course, he preached, with a brace of pistols on the pulpit-cushion before him. It was said that he preached in the morning and plundered in the afternoon, but it had to be conceded that he was at all times prepared to preach a funeral sermon, providing the deceased had not died a natural death.[1] He had 'the reputation', said Wood, 'as the most notorious lyor that ever wore long ears'. During the Civil War he became known as a lecher, a glutton and a considerable extortionist. But when we meet him, preaching to the soldiers exercising in the Military Gardens in 1640, these happy days of rapine and looting are yet to come.

Despite his fire-eating, he himself always managed to be at peace with the ruling party (though he had a narrow escape in corresponding with Major James Greenstreet, a proclaimed traitor, during the Protectorate) and he lived into the Restoration, installed in the living of Albury. Perhaps there is a hint of why he survived in an anecdote of the war. The Puritan troopers had been growing restive in disapproval of the long hair manifested by their courtly commander Lord Denbigh, and demanded of Kem whether this might not attract the wrath of

1. *History of the Trials and Troubles of Archbishop Laud* (1645), ixx, 210. Cf. Wood, *Athen. Oxon.*, ed. Bliss iii, 607–9.

God. Denbigh was Kem's patron. Their chaplain told the soldiers that there was a just prohibition against growing hair long; but my lord did not *grow* the long hair on his head; it was a wig, so no offence was committed. Kem had three wives.

The New Fort of True Honour Made Impregnable[1]

A sermon preached in 1640 before the soldiers exercising in the Military Gardens

Rebus semper pudor absit in arctis.

It being the longing desire of my soule that, you may retaine your bequeather, *Honour, and Dignity*: and *he word being given* to mee, *Watchman what of the night?* give mee leave to tell you, I discover the forces of Hell readie to besiege it; our many sinnes amongst our selves undermining it: wherefore give mee leave to *sound an Alarme*, that those that are asleepe in securitie may be rouzed; that those that are disarmed may bee provided; and that this *Pillar of your honour* may bee secured. Let our duty of holinesse bee daily practised: *Let none passe* though never so speciously pretending, unexamined: Let not any thought, word, action, which may prejudice thy Glory. To which end be exhorted,

First, *Every souldier to march as under his Command*, and as Gods souldiers, carry your selves suteably. How carefull was *Zabud* to deport himselfe nobly, that *Solomon* might have noe impeachment by him? so *march and fight*, worthy the honour of God, that hee *discard* thee not. What? Gods souldier, and prophane, and unclean, &c? Sute such carriage with such honour? Are these *colours* fit to bee *displayed* in Gods *Armie*? Consider, these disorders are the enemies advantages. O say that these are Gods souldiers! Thus honour if wee walke not suteable to it, addes to our shame, and not our shining: and indeed when the Lord confers worship, wee should maintaine it by worth: If the Lords souldiers, be valiant for your Captaine, and if you will taste the sweete of the dignity, be content with the sower, to practice your whole duty: your Antients set two vessels before *Iupiter*: The one of exceeding sweet liquor, the other as extreamely sower, and none could come to taste the honey unlesse hee first tooke downe the gall: The Romans had two Temples, one of Honour, the other of virtue, but there was no coming to

1. Or *The Martialist's Dignity and Duty*.

that of Honour, but by that of virtue: so if yee will maintaine your *dignity*, maintaine your *duty*.

Secondly, *Renounce not your Captaine*, and become *Transfuga's*:[1] Be trustie and true hearted to him: Bee in earnest his souldiers, practise the *Countermarch* of affection betwixt God, and you: if his benefits and blessings move *in the front* towards you in much mercy, and goodnesse; let your obedience *bring up the reare*, to meete him with thankefullnesse: To which end *observe but every one his Leading* Mercies and you cannot mistake in this practise: no more then in your ordinary practise you can fayle, if the *Leader* observe his *right hand Man*. For let but every mercy bee a *Leader*, and conduct you in this orderly manner; and then will every act of obedience *make up a File* of thankfullnesse, which will in true *place*, and *distance* follow with great care, and severity, which will make a comely *body* fit for the Lord to *march in the midst of you*.

Courtship and complement sute not well with souldiers, wherefore be really obedient to all *words of Command* from your *Captaine*, and *march* with him at all times.

Thirdly, *Be at unitie amongst your selves: Eadem velle & nolle firma amicitia &c.* Let that bee the Buckler of all your Armes, to knit you together as one man. In your Postures yee seeme to be one *face*, one *backe*, one *flanke*: Divided Arrowes are soone broken. Let your affections be like the *Leviathans soales, that no sword can pierce or divide*: a Company divided cannot stand: *for the divisions of Reuben are great thoughts of heart*: Unity is the portall at which God enters: Division the gate at which hee goes out from any *Society*. Where unity is, saith *Bernard*, there is God and all goodnesse, sweetnesse, and all profit. The blessing of it is set downe with a note of admiration: Divisions amongst the Primitive Christians, was the feare of the Apostle, as that which would prevent all successe in his labours: unity is the preparation for sanctification: when they were in one place, with one accord, then came the holy Ghost. This is the Churches glory: Division is the basis of its utter ruine: wherefore as the Apostle to the *Phil:* so I to you: *If there bee therefore any consolation in Christ, any comfort of Love, any fellowship of the spirit, if any bowells and mercies, fulfill yee my joy, bee yee like-minded, having the same love, being of one accord, of one mind. Let nothing bee done through strife, let us follow the truth of Holinesse, in Love, that wee may grow up in him in all things*[2]

1. Deserters.

2. This quotation comes from one of those Puritan 'little pocket Bibles with the gilt leaves' upon which Selden commented (see below, p. 436) and it is interesting for the omission of a significant phrase italicized below in the Authorised Version of the same verse.

If there is therefore any comfort in Christ, in any consolation of love, if any fellowship of the Spirit, if any tender mercies and compassions, fulfil ye my joy, that ye be of the same mind, having the same love, being of one accord, of one mind, doing nothing through faction or vainglory, *but in lowliness of mind each counting the other better than himself.*

Fourthly, *Have a care of any compactment with any of Gods Enemies*, closing with them, whether persons or things. *Zabud*[1] was Solomons friend: *Solomon* had three enemies, *Hadad*,[2] *Rezon*, and *Jeroboam*. This last *Solomon* sought to kill: now if *Zabud* would hold in with *Solomon*, it was no wisedome to hold intelligence with any of them; it had beene enough to have lost his friendship for ever; and therefore hee becomes a profest enemie to all of them. Take heede of closing with wicked persons; *ranke* nor *file* thy selfe with them. We know how *Iehu* pincht K. *Iehosaphat* when he made a league with *Ahab*. Take heed also of friendship with sinne.

Every lust is an enemie to God. Not an enemie, but enmitie it selfe: and if *the wisdome of the flesh bee an enemie*, what is the folly of it? Take heede of closing with any lust, for it is onely for this, that God will leave you, or forsake your Societie. In *Esay*, God had taken up his residence in Ierusalem, hee had this house and hearth there, resolved to winter, and summer with them; yet the degrees of sinning caused his glory, by degrees to depart, till *Ezechiel* seeth that the glory of God was cleane gone out of the Temple.[3] *Iosephus* reporteth, when *Titus* and *Vespasian* came, and besieged Ierusalem, the gates of the Temple flew open, a prognostick that their combining with sinne, had thrust God out of their Societies. The Poets affirme, Troys vices were Troys ruine; and therefore was it as *Austin* affirmes, that they fastned their Gods with chaines to their Altars.

Fiftly, *Take heede to thy Captaines orders*: doe not that which will vex him[1], that's the next way to lose him indeed. *But they rebelled, and vexed his spirit, therefore hee was turned to bee their enemie, and hee fought against them.* Many *souldiers* there are that would take it amisse, if I should say they were not Gods souldiers; and yet are *discharging whole volleyes* of oaths against him: To whom give mee leave to say, as *Absolon*[4] to *Hushai. Is this thy kindnesse to thy friend*? so, is this thy duty to thy *Captaine*, to stab him with oathes, and to *counterbar* all his words *of command* to thee?

Surely the Lord may say to such, *These are wounds I was wounded with, in the house of my friends*. Wherefore take heed of delighting in sinne; give no leasure to it. *Epaminond as* being told that one of his souldiers were sick; hee replyed, *hee admired it that any of his souldiers had time to bee sicke*: So God admires how any of his have time to vex him by sinne; having so many enemies to contest with, and exercise their whole strength and time upon.

Sixtly, *Take heed of discontinuance from thy Armes* and practise, it argues little delight, and makes them in time of need more burdensome, gives the enemie advantage, and makes thee come short of they fellow souldiers.

Wherefore once more be exhorted to *Arme* with *David* to your slings, with *Peter* to your *swords*, with *Ionathan* to your *Bow*, with *Samson* to his *Jaw-bone*,

---

1. Zadok. 2. Haggith. 3. Ezekiel makes no reference to the *Temple*.
4. Not Absolom: Shimei cursing David.

and *Shangar* to his *goade*: your enemies are in *Armes*, the Philistines in the field, *Goliah* daring, the combate prepared: see you not your foes? Let me make the *discovery*: The *Cananites* are in *the valleys*, the *Aramites* in *the mountaines*: the *sonnes of Anak*, are not all slaine: Sathan, as Generall to our enemies, with *Ichu* cries, *who is on my side, who?* And loe what an host follow him! This *Ahab* hath hundreds of false Prophets: this *Serpent* hath a brood, that like the Mole can creepe under the earth, swim the sea, to raise Molehills in our *Trenches* to stumble at; and undermine Princes, *blow up* the maintainers of the Gospell with *gunpowder*: Hee hath *Ishmael* to scoffe; and *Rabshekah* to raile; *Ahitophel* to counsell, *&c.*

Secondly, with my Captaines leave I might check such souldiers, as care never to bee acquainted, who are their enemies, How many such *souldiers* are there like to *Mephibosheth*, and *Adonibezek*, lame of feete and fingers, or as *Samson*, when they are to fight want their strength and weapons? Oh how doth Sathan lead many, as the Prophet in the *Kings*, did the people into *Samaria*, unto the land of captivity before their eyes bee opened, enemies discerned.

Thirdly, *Keepe your orders, and standing*: know thy place thou art to warre in under thy *Captaine*: nothing loseth the *field* but to presume above our place; to command when to bee commanded: some march in the *Front* should in the *Reare*, this bringeth confusion: many take too much upon them, and so like an overcharged *Cannon* recoyle and burst, they are of no other use.

Fourthly, *Get strength and courage: Bee strong in the Lord, and the power of his might: David* prayes for the *spirit of life, and power.* Paul a worthy warriour often commands it, want of this loseth the field. For power may warre, but without courage dares not.

Fiftly, *Get wisedome and policy. Simeon* and *Levi* must goe together to slay our *Sechemites*: and wee have need of this combate of wit, for our enemies are ancient, and subtill politicians. And blind men are unfit to fight under any Command, but the *Prince of darknesse.*

Sixtly, *Cast away all that hindereth. Love not the world*, saith Saint *John.* Such whose affections are at home, with wife, goods, children, &c. are unfit to fight the Kings battailes, and such whose hearts are bent on the things of this life, *the Lords battails*: for these will faint, and cause others also. Now courage becomes the Lords battailes. Such as can mock at feare, Swallow the ground for fiercenesse, meete with a harnessed enemy, and cry *aha, aha*: when his darts *rattle against him.*

Use.

Of incouragement. Though enemies many, if on Gods side, hee is your Captaine, and Christ, Angells, Saints, all fellow souldiers: bee of good courage, strike hard, *stand fast, and bee strong in the Lord, and power of his might.*

1. For what an honor is it to be slain in the field?

2. All thy wounds shall be cured: the sooner killed, crowned, for by death we overcome.

3. If any souldier bee *faint hearted*, let them like timorous Ladyes passing over a streame, looke at the faire landing place: looke to heaven, see what landing there is, hundreds of Angels to entertaine thee: Thinke with *Moses* of the reward. Wherefore say with the Apostle, Fellow souldiers *comfort one another*, to the practise of your *dutie*, to maintaine your *dignity*,[1] *with these words*. And now I lay the burthen of these *Columnes* on your shoulders, and beseech you to march out of this place forward with holinesse, which the
Lord establish in your hearts, till he
bring you to receive a crowne of
eternall happines, and deliver
you from all your
enemies. *Amen.*

1. No reference to "dignity" in the Biblical text.

WILLIAM HOOK[1]

News of serious political discord and rebellion in England was disquieting to the emigrants in distant American colonies. Whatever their allegiance, their feelings for England were strong and mixed.

William Hook of New England responded with a sermon of impassioned sympathy without, though he was a Puritan and a religious refugee, committing himself irrevocably to either side, for he had every intention of returning, when a favourable opportunity appeared.

The ties of sentiment and association linking the American colonists to the homeland were then of the strongest, and supplies of information from England slow and irregular. A sermon like Hook's provided an imaginative commentary upon the latest news to have arrived by boat.

New England's Tears

A Sermon preached on July 23rd., 1640 by William Hook, sometime of Axmouth in Devonshire, Now of Taunton, in New England.

When *Artaxerxes* said unto *Nehemiah*, *Why is thy countenance sad, seeing thou art not sicke?* Have you not read the answer? *Why should not my countenance be sad, when the City, the place of my Fathers sepulchres lyes wast, and the gates thereof are consumed with fire?* Why? *Nehemiah* was well enough at ease, he had honour, and power, and favour, and pleasure enough, and being the Kings Cup-bearer, he had Wine enough of all sorts at his command, which maketh glad the heart of man. But what is all this not to cloud his countenance, and to overcast it with griefe and sorrow, when the City of his Fathers was layd wast, and the gates thereof consumed with fire? Thus Beloved, if our comforts were treble to what they are this day, yet could it not but much abate

1. William Hook, 1600–1677. Trinity College, Oxford, M.A. 1623. Vicar of Axmouth, Devon. Emigrated to New England. Returned 1656 and died in Bunhill Fields, 21st March 1677.

356

the sweetnesse of them, to consider what distresses may lie at this time upon our native Countrey, for ought wee know, and have too just cause to feare. When the Arke and Israel and Judah abode in tents, and *Joab* and his men were encamped in the open fields, *Urijah* tooke no comfort in his beautifull wife, nor in his house, nor in his meate and drinke.

Let us therefore, I beseech you, lay aside the thoughts of all our comforts this day, and let us fasten our eyes upon the calamities of our brethren in old *England*, calamities, at least, imminent calamities dropping, swords that have hung along time over their heads by a twine·thread, judgements long since threatned as foreseene by many of Gods Messengers in the causes, though not foretold by a Spirit prophetically guided; heavy judgements in all probability when they fall, if they are not fallen already. And not to looke upon the occasions given on the one side or the other, betweene the two Sister Nations (Sister Nations? ah, the word woundeth,) let us looke this day simply on the event, a sad event in all likelihood, the dividing of a King from his Subjects, and him *from them*, their mutuall taking up of Armes in opposition and defence; the consequences, even the gloomy and darke consequences thereof, are killing and slaying, and sacking, and burning, and robbing and rifling, cursing and blaspheming, &c.

If you should but see Warre described to you in a Map, especially in a Countrey well knowne to you, nay dearley beloved of you, where you drew your first breath, where once, yea where lately you dwelt, where you have received ten thousand mercies, and have many a deare friend and Countreyman and kinsman abiding, how could you but lament and mourne?

Warre is the conflict of enemies enraged with bloody revenge, wherein the parties opposite carry their lives in their hands, every man turning prodigall of his very heart blood, and willing to be killed and to kill. The instruments are clashing swords, ratling speares, skul-dividing Holbeards, murthering pieces, and thundering Cannons, from whose mouths proceed the fire and smell and smoake and terrour and death, as it were, of the very bottomlesse pit. Wee wonder now and then at the sudden death of a man; alas, you might there see a thousand men not onely healthy, but stout and strong, struck dead in the twinckling of an eye, their breath exhales without so much as, *Lord have mercy upon us*. Death heweth its way thorow a wood of men in a minute of time from the mouth of a murderer, turning a forrest into a champion suddenly; and when it hath used these to slay their opposites, they are recompenced with the like death themselves. *O the shrill eare-piercing clangs of the trumpets, noise of drums, the animating voices of Horse Captains and Commanders, learned and learning to destroy! There is the undaunted horse whose neck is clothed with thunder, and the glory of whose nostrills is terrible; how doth he lye pawing and praunsing in the valley going forth to meet the armed men? he mocks at feare, swallowing the ground with fiercenes and rage, and saying among the trumpets, Ha, Ha, he smels the battell a far off, the thunder of the Captaines and the shouting.* Here ride some dead men swagging[1] in their deep saddles; there fall others alive upon their dead horses; death sends a message to those from the mouth of the Muskets, these it talkes with face to face, and stabbs them in the fift rib: In yonder file there is a man hath his arme struck off from his shoulder, another by him hath lost his leg; here stands a Souldier with halfe a face, there fights another upon his strumps, and at once both kils and is killed; not far off lyes a company wallowing in their sweat and goare; such a man whilest he chargeth his Musket is discharg'd of his life, and falls upon his dead fellow. Every battell of the warriour is with confused noise and garments rouled in blood. Death reignes in the field, and is sure to have the day which side soever falls. In the meane while (O formidable!) the infernall fiends follow the Campe to catch after the soules of rude nefarious souldiers (such as are commonly men of that calling) who fight themselves fearelessly into the mouth of hell for revenge, a booty, or a little revenue. How thick and threefold doe they speed one another to destruction? A day of battell is a day of harvest for the devill. All this while, the poore wife and tender children sit weeping together at home, having taken their late farewell of the harnessed husband and father (Oh it was a sad parting if you had seene it!) never looking to see his face againe, as indeed many and the most of them never doe; for anon comes *Ely's* messenger from the Camp, saying, *There is a great slaughter among the people; and your husband is dead, your father is dead, he was slaine in an hot fight, he was shot dead in the place and never spake a word more.* Then the poore widow who fed yet upon a crumb of hope, teares her haire from her head, rends her cloths, wrings her hands, lifts up her voice to heaven, and weeps like *Rachell* that would not be comforted, her children hang about her crying and saying, O my father is slaine, my father is dead, I shall never see my father more; and so they cry and sob and sigh out their afflicted soules, and breake their hearts together. Alas, Alas! this is yet but Warre thorow a Crevise. Beloved, doe but consider; There is many times fire without warre, and famine and pestilence without warre, but warre is never without them: and there are many times robberies without warre, and murthering of passengers, ravishing of matrones, deflouring of virgins, cruelties and torments and sometimes barbarous and inhumane practices without warre, but warre goes seldome or never without them.

Warre, it is *malum complexum,* a compound of Judgements, a mixt misery, *the cup in the hand of the Lord, the wine whereof is red, and it is full of mixture.* The wine is indeed as red as blood, and the ingredients are fire, famine, pestilence, murthers, robberies, rapes, deflourings, cruelties, torments, with many other miseries. The voice of melody ceaseth, relations that were lately the comfort are now become the griefe of the life of men; the *high wayes are*

1. Swaying unsteadily.

unoccupyed, the travellers walke thorow by wayes, the Inhabitants of the villages cease, and the noise of the Archers is heard in the places of drawing water. Warre, it is the immediate hand of such whose tenderest mercies are cruelties, commonly therefore the last of Gods strokes upon them that will take no warning. But yet there is difference in warres; a warre in the borders of an enemy is held better then a warre in ones native Countrey; for commonly, the land that is as the garden of *Eden* before an enemy, behind them is like a desolate Wildernesse; and it is very wofull when people and land shall be wasted together. Or if it be warre in our owne Land, yet a warre against a forreigne enemy invading, is far better then a civill warre. It is grievous, but not admirable, to see an Egyptian and an Hebrew contending, but to see, as the Prophet sayth, Egyptians against Egyptians, and every one fighting against his brother, and against his neighbour, City against City, and Kingdome against Kingdome; or to see, as the same Prophet sayth, *Manasseh* against *Ephraim*, and *Ephraim* against *Manasseh*, and both against *Judah*; O, this is both lamentable and wonderfull! The mad Souldier in the heat of his blood, and the depth of his Atheisme, may account it perhaps at first with *Abner* but a play, to see Israelites catching of Israelites by the beard, and thrusting their swords in one anothers sides: but of all warres none so bloody, neither hath any play such bitternesse in the end.

It is a sad play, wherein not onely mens goods and bodyes and soules doe commonly lye at stake, but wherein also even the very Conquerour is conquered, as one that played but for his owne money, and at such a desperate play whose very gaines are loosings. No warres so cruell, so unnaturall, so desolating, as civill warres. You have heard, Beloved, of the dreadfull German-warres; why, if there be any in our owne Countrey this day, I may call them German warres, because they are the warres of Germans, even the bloody contentions of brethren; and when relations turne opposites, nothing more opposite. A Kingdome at warres with a forreigne enemy may stand, but a Kingdome divided against it selfe, can never; there can never prosperitie within *Jerusalems* pallaces, if first there be not peace within her walls. Unity and peace are a bond, and where that is broken, there must needs follow dissolution.

When the Philistines went beating downe one another, the *multitude* (mark the word) *melted away*. A thing never consumes faster, then when it falls to melting: and how doe such weaken themselves for an enemy without, and fight for the conquest of some forreigne adversary? *Gedeons* men may stand still every man in his place, so long as Midianites turne their swords against Midianites. Neither needs *Jehosophat* strike a stroake, when the Moabites, Ammonites and Edomites his enemies, lye in ambush one against another; first *Moab* and *Ammon* fighting against *Edom*, and then *Moab* and *Ammon* one against another. And what was the issue of the eleven Tribes warres with their brother *Benjamin*, but lamentation, mourning and woe? And yet too among civill warres, some are worse then other. I have read, I remember, in *Lucan*, of warres betweene *Cæsar* and *Pompey* worse then civill: and such especially are mutining warres, when there is little trust to either side, and friends are are scarce knowne from foes, but all things are filled with conjurations, treacheries, distractions, factions, feares, suspitions, tumults, combustions, spoylings, &c. The Lord be mercifull to old *England*, as hitherto he hath been, yea more then to any Land this day under the Sunne, which indeed heightneth its sins above the Sunne, and makes it more sinfull then any Land at this time in the whole world, insomuch, that we cannot but yeeld that there are no warres that *Englands* sinnes have not deserved. Let us therefore feare the worst at this present in behalfe of our deare Countrey-men (confidening also what ill tidings we have heard thence) that nothing, as we doubt, but a miracle of divine power and mercy can preserve them from the miseries of the devouring sword. I remember what the Auxiliaries of Egypt said in their distresse, *Arise, and let us goe againe unto our people, and to the Land of our Nativity from the oppressing sword*; but if wee were now under that misery, I doubt it would be in vaine for us to say the like. But that which wee are now called unto, is Brotherly Compassion, and to doe the part of *Jobs* friends in my Text, to fit astonished, as at the crying sinnes, so at the feared sorrowes of our Countrymen, for in all probabilitie, their griefe is very great.

To this end, you may thinke a while upon these particulars.

Of our civill relation to that Land, and the Inhabitants therein. There is no Land that claimes our name, but *England*, wee are distinguished from all the Nations in the world by the name of *English*. There is no Potentate breathing, that wee call our dread Soveraigne, but King Charles, nor Lawes of any Land have civilized us, but *Englands*; there is no Nation that calls us Countrey men, but the *English*. Brethren! Did wee not there draw in our first breath? Did not the Sunne first shine there upon our heads? Did not that Land first beare us, even that pleasant Island, but for sin, I would say, that Garden of the Lord, that Paradise?

Withall, let us thinke upon our naturall relations to many in that Land. Some of you, I know, have Fathers and Mothers there, some of you have Brethren and Sisters, others of you have Uncles and Aunts there, and neare kinsfolke. All these sitting in griefe and sorrow, challenge our sympathize; and it is a fearefull sin to be voyde of naturall affections: nature wrought in *Abraham*, as well as grace, when his nephew *Lot* was taken captive by the foure Kings.

But which is more, let us remember, how (for many of us) we stand in a spirituall relation to many, yea very many in that Land. The same threed of grace is spun thorow the hearts of all the godly under heaven. Such a one there, is thy spitiruall Father, he begot thee in Christ Jesus thorow the Gospell;

and there thou hast spirituall Brethren and Sisters and Mothers. O there is many a sweet, loving, humble, heavenly soule in that Land, in whose bosome Christ breaths by his blessed Spirit every day, and such as I hope wee shall ever love at the remotest distance, were it from one end of the earth unto the other. Why, they are bone of our bone, and flesh of our flesh in Christ, nearer by farre then friends and kindred, oh let their sorrowes be our sorrowes, and their miseries ours.

... Alas, how have they kept on sinning upon our examples? Anothers drunkennesses have begotten many a drunkard there, as anothers spirituall cowardize many a Nicodemite, and anothers Lukewarmenesse many a *Laodicean*. Now, doe we feare that the Lord is gone forth this day to call that Land to an account, and to visite for these and the like abominations, and is this nothing unto us? Shall men be slaine for our sinnes, and we afford them no sorrow? What? shall the old Prophet in *Bethel* rise up in judgement against us? for when he had slaine the man of God by his lying and dissembling to him, he yet mourned and lamented over him, saying, *Alas my Brother*. Ah my friends and brethren, let us doe the like; our sinnes have slaine, perhaps by this time, a little Army of men, what can wee lesse then lament over them, saying, *Alas, Alas, our Brethren*. Surely, wee in this Land have great cause to doe as wee doe this day, if for no other respect, yet for this; for wee have done enough and enough to overwhelme old *England* with the wrath of God; that our hearts at this time could be but over-shadowed with a cloud of sorrow!

Againe; let us suppose that things were even now turned end for end, and that wee were this day in distresse, and those our brethren in peace; I am confident, that they would condole with us, yea and powre out many a prayer for us: for they did as much, I know, when this Land lay sometimes under dearth, another time when the Indians rebelled, a third, when the monstrous opinions prevailed. And how have they alwayes lissened after our wellfare, ebbing and flowing in their affections with us? How doe they (I meane all this while, multitudes of well affected persons there) talke of *New-England* with delight! How much nearer heaven doe some of their charities account this Land, then any other place they heare of in the world? Such is their good opinion of us! How have some among them desired to dye, if they might not be vouchsafed to live in this Land?[1] And when sometimes a *New England* man returnes thither, how is he lookt upon, lookt after, received, entertained, the ground he walks upon beloved for his sake, and the house held the better where he is? how are his words lissened to, laid up, and related

---

1. Hook is romancing. Englishmen's feelings for their colonial brothers were more sympathetic than envious. '... many of our brethern forsook their native countries ... to live in howling wilderness'. Cromwell, *Speech to Parliament*, January 22nd, 1655.

frequently when he is gone? neither is any love or kindnesse held too much for such a man.

Neither let this be forgotten, that of all the Christian people this day in the world, wee in this Land enjoy the greatest measure of peace and tranquilitie. Wee have beaten our swords into plough-shares and our speares into pruning hookes, when others have beaten their pruning hookes into speares, and their plough-shares into sword. And now, as *Moses* sayd to the Reubenites and the Gadites, *Shall your brethren goe to warre, and shall yee sit still?* So, shall our brethren goe to warre, and we sit still, and not so much as grieve with them? shall they be wounded with the sword and speare, and not we pierced so much as with brotherly sorrow? Surely then, if ever the Lord should bring the like houre of temptation upon us, as his people here have not been long hitherto without exercise, he might justly shut us out of the hearts of all our brethren in the world. And whereas too perhaps here and there one in our native Land, especially in their passions, may have had some transient thoughts, touching, it may be, some of us, as if the exorbitant spirit of *John* and *James* were in us, desirous that fire from heaven should fall upon them, as if, I meane, we would be glad to heare of Judgements upon our native Countrey (oh cruell, and unnaturall!) our fellow-feelings this day, I hope, shall wipe away all such prejudices. And truly, if Gods Justice might be satisfied with that Lands amendment without one drop of blood, though wee should shed store both of teares and blood to effect it, wee would greatly rejoyce, and soone turne this day of Humiliation into a day of gratulation, praise, and thanksgiving.

What shall I say? If there should be any one heart here digd out of a Marpelian rock, let such an one remember, lastly, that in the peace of that Land, we shall have peace, and therefore in the misery of that Land, we shall never be happie. You know, that God hath hitherto made that Land a blessing unto this; If Christ hath a Vine here, that Land hath as yet been the Elme that hath susteined it. Thence hath the Lord thus stockt this American part with such Worthies, there were they bred and nurst, thence hitherto have been our yearely supplies of men, and of many an usefull commoditie. If then they suffer, we may easily smart; if they sink, wee are not likely to rise. And this, at least, may be a perswasive to a sordide minde, that will not be wrought upon by more ingenuous Arguments.

The mercifull God stirre up all our affections, and give us that godly sympathy, which that Land deserveth at our hands, and teach us to expresse it upon all occasions of ill tydings coming to our eares from thence. Yea, let us sit at this time like old *Ely* upon the wayes side, watching, as he did, for the Arke of the Lord, with a trembling hand and heart. And let us be every day confessing of our old *England* sinnes, of its high pride, Idolatry, superstition, blasphemies, blood, cruelties, Athiesmes, &c. and let us never goe to our secrete without our Censors in our hands for old *England*, deare *England* still in diverse respects, left indeed by us in our persons, but never yet forsaken in our affections. The good God of Heaven, have mercy upon it, and upon all his deare people and servants in it, for Christ his sake, *Amen*.

WILLIAM PIERCE

In January 1641 several bishops, prevented by the hostile mob from reaching the House of Lords to vote, challenged the validity of all laws passed during their enforced absence and were imprisoned and threatened with High Treason for their pains. Of these, one already mentioned was Joseph Hall, another was William Pierce (or Piers) Bishop of Bath and Wells, who preached two sermons to an exclusive congregation of fellow prelates, during their incarceration in the Tower. He is the same Pierce who was Vice-Chancellor of Oxford during the Lushington incident, and one of the sermons treats the same subject that Lushington had glittered over, the resurrection of Christ. William Pierce, arch-enemy of "lecturers"[1] and all Puritans, "that Great Beast of Canterburie", so called for the zeal with which he prosecuted Laud's policy of conformity, was not perhaps the most endearing of characters, but he had a truly marvellous capacity for survival. Hated, and, from the Puritan point of view, guilty of oppression, he nevertheless managed to obtain his release from the Tower, while Mathew Wren, the zealous Bishop of Ely, remained in confinement throughout the Protectorate, and unlike Hall, whose discipline had been mild, he managed to withdraw and live quietly on an unsequestered estate until the Restoration, when he too enjoyed a 'restoration' to his bishopric, and lived on to a great age. A competent scholar and a vigorous administrator, his prime gift seems to have been what Wood calls 'a good secular understanding', which, especially in his later days, 'found a congenial field in amassing a fortune by means of fines and renewals, of leases and other sources of profit arising from episcopal estàtes, the greater part of which was wheedled away from him by his second wife, who was too young and cunning for him'.[2] In one of the two prison sermons we find him issuing a grave monition against the vice of 'avarice'.

1. The *lecturer* was a Puritan phenomenon; a divine, unbeneficed and not responsible for normal pastoral parish duties, but engaged and paid by a Puritan patron or parish only to preach. Lecturers were strongly disapproved of by Laud as uncontrolled and subversive, and Pierce was outstandingly successful on clearing them out of his diocese.
2. Wood, op. cit., iv, 839.

The World, the Flesh, and the Devil

A sermon on resistance to worldly temptation, preached
in the Tower of London, on Sunday, the 30th. of
January, 1641, by the Bishop of Bath and Wells, in
the presence of other imprisoned Bishops.

Sufficiency is a word of mediocrity betweene two extreames, want and
abundance; for where there is sufficient, there is neither too much nor too
little.

And here we may admire the wisdome of God, who is *liberimum agens*, a
most free agent, & doth not worke like a naturall agent, the sunne shines, the
fire burnes, the water moistens, *quoad ultimam sphæram activitatis*, according to
their uttermost abilities to bring forth their effects; but God giveth his grace
unto every one of us according to the measure of the gift of Christ, as seemeth
best unto himselfe, *Eph.* 4.7. bestowing such a proportion of Grace upon all,
as is sufficient for all.

For with God is an ocean of grace, there is grace enough for you, and for
me, and for us all, and for as many worlds of men as God can make.

And God doth give unto every one of his servants that sufficiency of his
grace whereby they shal be able to overcome all temptations and afflictions,
and save their owne soules.

Wherefore then let us not murmure against God, if we attaine not unto that
abundance of grace wherewith the Apostles, and many other Servants of
God have beene endued above us; they have had the plentifull showrs of
Gods graces; but we will be content with the dew of his grace, they have had
the full sheaves of Gods graces, but we will bee glad of the gleanings of his
grace; they have had the rich banquet of Gods graces, but we will thinke our
selves happy, if we may have but the crummes of his grace; for if we have
but sufficiency of grace here, wee shall have abundance of glory hereafter.

It is with Grace as it was with Manna, hee that hath much, hath nothing
over, and he that hath little, hath no lacke, because hee hath that which is
sufficient for him.

And every grace of God that is sufficient, is also effectuall, and the efficacy
of grace is from it self, not from the wil of man; & therefore God in his answer
here unto Saint *Paul*, doth not say, *gratia mea sufficit tecum*, my grace is sufficient with thee, but *gratia mea sufficit tibi*, my grace is sufficient for thee;

for we are not sufficient of ourselves to thinke any thing that is good, but our sufficienty is of God, 2 *Cor.* 3.5. and therefore we must take heed we doe not part stakes between Gods grace and mans will, as the Papists doe, but wee must ascribe all this sufficiency to the grace of God, for it is he which worketh in us both to will and to do of his good pleasure, *Philip.* 2.1.

And therefore let us be covetous after nothing but this sufficient grace of God, let us pray that we may have grace enough, and then we shall have all things enough. It is a true maxime in Divinity, there is nothing that can suffice the heart of man, but onely Gods grace; where shall you finde the man that saith truly and from his heart he hath enough: When he hath a house he saith, O that I had a little land to it: And when he hath that: He saith, O that I had a Lordship to it, and when he hath that, he saith, O that I had the Mannor that is next to it, or this Office, or that Honour, or one thing or other more; and still as the world growes upon him, his desires grow upon the world, his enough changeth alwaies, every yeare, nay every day, nay every houre he thinkes upon another enough; but let a man have grace enough, and he hath all things enough, for Gods grace is alsufficient.

This sufficient grace makes a penny seeme to be as big as a shilling, a cottage seem to bee as faire as a Pallace, a prison seeme to be as large as a Country, want seeme to be abundance, and nothing to bee all things: This sufficient grace makes us rich in poverty, patient in adversity, strong in weaknesse, merry in affliction, and hopefull in despaire.

And this grace is sufficient for us against all the assaults of the world, the flesh and the divell, against all troubles and afflictions whatsoever: and although God could let his sufficient grace overcome all our temptations, all our afflictions at first in a moment, yet he will not have it so, for God will have his graces to be exercised in us, *tolle pugnam & non erit victoria, tolle victoriam & non erit corona,* saith Saint *Ambrose,* if there were no conflict betweene our temptations, and Gods grace, there would be no victory, and if no victory, no price: sometimes *Amaleck,* that is afflictions and temptations prevaile, and sometimes *Israel,* that is grace prevaileth.

Victores victique cadunt, victique resurgunt.

But in the end grace alwayes hath the upper hand, and we are more then conquerors through him that loved us, *Rom.* 8.37.

Be not then dismaid, O thou Christian soule, whosoever thou art, be not disquieted within thy selfe, because thou art fallen into a sore temptation, because thou art under an heavy affliction! what, wouldest thou be better then St. *Paul?*

Vide Apostolum patientem & noli te facere desperantem, saith Saint *Austin,* behold the Apostle suffering, and despaire not; nay behold Christ himselfe,

who was tempted and afflicted, that hee might succour us when we are
tempted and afflicted, *Heb.* 2.18. let us behold him then with a lively faith
and sure confidence, and hee will so succour us with his sufficient grace, *Vt
nec caro cum omnibus oblectamentis, nec mundus cum omnibus tormentis, nec
Diabolus cum omnibus tentamentis, &c.* as Saint *Bernard* speakes,[1] that neither the
flesh with her all her allurements, not the world with all its persecutions, nor
the Divell with all his temptations shall ever be able to separate us from the
love of God which is in Christ Jesus our Lord.

1. This 'quotation', if authentic, eludes me. It might be a synthetic paraphrase of
fragments from *Sermones in Cantica* XI. 7–8.

STEPHEN MARSHALL

The House of Commons, February 1641; Laud is in the Tower. The time has come to attempt the most difficult and imperative part of the project—the destruction of Strafford—and the fiercest pulpit voice, Stephen Marshall's, is given the commission to work the members into a condition of fear and anxiety and hatred, when they will, if necessary, break through the frame of law, in order to take the life of the adversary Pym most fears.

The Antinomianism that all is permissible, that nothing may not be *obligatory*, under the will of God as revealed to his prophets, is now showing the kind of purpose it can be put to if the old testament and present desires are set to ignite together. Now it is not merely *permissible* to kill, but 'cursed is everyone that witholds his hand from the shedding of blood'.

Meroz Cursed was Marshall's favourite sermon. He delivered it many times in the years to come, as an *obbligato*, long after the occasion of its delivery had passed away.

Meroz Cursed

A Fast Sermon Preached before the House of Commons on February 23 rd, 1641

Judges V. 23. Curse ye, Meroz, said the angel of the Lord, Curse ye bitterly the inhabitants thereof; Because they came not to the help of the Lord, To the help of the Lord against the mighty
All people are cursed or blessed according as they do or do not joyne their strength and give their best assistance to the Lords people against their enemies.
I beseech you see how cleare this is, not only in this *verse* (God laid nothing else to *Meroz* charge but only this, they came not out to help the Lord against

the mighty) but in other passages of this *Chapter*. *My heart is toward the Governors of Israel, that offered themselves willingly among the people. Hallelujah, Praise the Lord.* They are not so much as named without an *Euge*[1]. The *Princes of Issachar are blessed* for being with *Barak*. *Zebulun and Nepthali were a people that jeoparded their lives to the death in the high places of the field.* These are blessed also. *Blessed above women was Iael the wife of Heber the Kenite.* What made *Jael* such a *blessed woman?* Even this, *she put her hand to the naile, and her right hand to the workmans hammer, and with the hammer she smote Sisera, she smote off his head, when she had pierced and smitten through his temples.* On the other side see the *displeasure* that there is against the Tribes who came not out to helpe in this *expedition*. *Ruben* had businesse of his own, his flocks were to be attended. *Gilead* could plead that the River *Jordan* divided him, from *Barak* and his company: *Asher* had his own breaches to make up, and the Sea coasts to looke to. A man might think, these were faire *excuses*. But God had *great thoughts of heart against them all.* And wo to him, or them, against whom *God* hath *great thoughts*. The whole Chapter runs in this straine, they are cryed up, they are honoured and *blessed*: not only the heart of *Gods people*, but the soule of God himselfe (as I may say) tooke pleasure in them, who appeared on the Churches side; his *displeasure, indignation, wrath* and *curse* did rise against all, who came not to the helpe.

This is most plaine in many other Scriptures. I shall cull out but thee among three hundred, *Jer.* 48. 10. That whole Chapter containes the *doome of Moab*. Gods curse was now to be executed upon *Moab*, and you may read of *Moab*, that the Lord once sent to him when his people were in distresse. *Let my outcasts dwell with thee Moab, be thou a shelter to them in the time of a storme.* But *Moab was too proud* to listen to Gods counsell. *Moab* was alwaies an ill enemy to *Israel.* Now God comes to reckon with him for it. Now for spoyler shall come upon all his Cities. And to *them* who were to *execute* this vengeance of God against them, marke what a *charge* is given in the tenth verse, *Cursed is he that doth the worke of the Lord negligently*, or fraudulently, or deceitfully, as the word signifies; Now what was the worke which was to be done? the next words will tell you, *Cursed is every one that withholds his hand from shedding of bloud:* the strangest reason of a curse that ever was read of, if ever a man might have pleaded (with *Peter* when the voice said unto him. *Arise Peter kill and eate*) *not so Lord.* I have not beene accustomed to this, here were roome for such a *plea*, when his worke was to go and *embrew* his hands in the *bloud of men*, to spill and *powre* out the *bloud of women* and *children, like water* in every street. But he is a *cursed man that withholds his hand from this*, or that shall do it *fraudulently*, that is, if he do it as *Saul* did against the *Amalekites*, kill some and save some, if he go not through with the work: he is a cursed man, when this is to be done upon *Moab* the *enemy of Gods Church*. So that *whatsoever*

---

1. 'Euge': Latin exclamation of approval and praise.

imployment men are put to, they are cursed men, that take not part with God in his worke. Another place you shall find in *Psal.* 137.*v*.8,9. The daughter of *Babylon* was there to be destroyed, observe now the epithete which God gives to the *executioners* of his *wrath* against *Babylon*. *Blessed is the man that rewardeth thee, as thou hast served us. Blessed is the man that makes Babylon drinke the same cup, which Babylon had made Gods people to drinke.* Now he that reades the booke of the Lamentations, may finde how *Babylon* had used the Church of God, they had *broken* their *bones* as a *Lion* breakes the bones of a Lamb, brought their *necks* under *persecution*, made their *skin blacke like an oven, hang'd up their Princes by the hand,* and which is most of all cruell, had *dashed their children against the stones.* Now saith the Spirit of God, *Blessed is the man, that thus rewards Babylon, yea, blessed is the man that takes their little ones and dashes them against the stones.*[1]

1. Stephen Marshall (1594–1655); B.A. Emmanuel College Cambridge 1618; M.A. 1622; B.D. 1629; vicar of Finchingfield in Essex; was noted for the violence and volume of his pulpit delivery. He was known to pray aloud sometimes for two hours at a stretch and was one of three divines appointed in October, 1647, to prepare the 'shorter Catechism'. While he was chaplain at Holmby Hall during the king's captivity there, it was said that Charles sat down and began to eat while Marshall was still in full spate pronouncing Grace. (See *The Godly Man's Legacy* (1680), p. 20.)

SAMUEL FAIRCLOUGH

The trial of Strafford did not run smooth for the prosecution. He defended himself magnificently and the judges were unable to resist the conclusion that no treason had been proved against him. This put the house into intense anxiety. Did they dare let him go, who might again become their master, having shown their intentions so far? It was too dangerous; well-nigh suicidal, some thought. So it became necessary to resort to breaking through the fences of the law as they stood to reach him with the headsman's axe. The breach was made by substituting a bill of attainder for impeachment, which was a way of declaring to be treason what could not be proved to be treason. St. John was the most honest of the "inflexibles" and said, "We give the law to hares and deer as beasts of the chase, but knock foxes and wolves on the head, as they can be found, because they are beasts of prey."

But first the majority of the Lords had to be brought to approve the course. It was an uncomfortable decision, governed not by law or justice, but by fear. Some were moved by fear of Strafford, some by fear of those who feared Strafford. Wavering peers were threatened and intimidated in their houses and coaches by the rabble whom Pym had incited. In the streets members were under pressure from a desperate lobby while the pulpit thundered warnings of the atrocious consequences which would attend a guilty failure to execute Achen, and execute him quickly. The chosen preacher for the occasion was Samuel Fairclough,[1] the incumbent of a Suffolk living in the patronage of Sir Nathanial Barnardiston, a crony of Pym's. This hitherto undistinguished country parson, who till lately dared not appear in Strafford's presence with his head covered—nor dared his patron for that matter—

1. Samuel Fairclough, 1594-1677. B.A., 1615, Queens' College, Cambridge, where his strict principles were first noted when he refused to play the woman's part for which he had been cast in *the Comedy of the Ignoramus*, to be performed before James I. Subsequently as lecturer at Lyme Regis and then Clare in Suffolk a noted preacher, but called before the High Court of Commission as a factious man. In 1629 Sir Nicholas Barnardiston gave him the living of Kedington at Haverhill. He managed to dodge the *Book of Sports*, but in the Civil War was not noticeably sympathetic to the parliamentary army, and refused the engagement. At the Restoration, refusing to take the oath, he was ejected.

was now bold enough to stand before the House of Commons and make peremptory demand for the immediate execution of death upon "Achitophel", the treacherous and vaunting counsellor of "King David", while Strafford's case was still *sub judice* before the Lords and he, therefore, innocent in law.

It is unthinkable that a Fairclough would have had the temerity to speak as he did, without positive instruction and secure protection from his masters.

A Call for Blood

The Troublers Troubled, or Achan Condemned and Executed

A Fast Sermon preached before the House of Commons on 4th April, 1641.

Joshua 7. 25. And Joshua said, Why dost thou trouble us? The Lord shall trouble thee this day.

... If Gods haste move not, yet let *Achans* haste effect it, for the more daies *Achans* are permitted to stay, after discovery; the more doe they infect us; is the iniquity of *Peor* too little for us saith the people, but wee must have more? so say I, is it not sufficient that their sins have troubled us, but their continuance must infect us, and destroy us, *Deut.* 21. there is a law made, that the dead body of an executed malefactor should not be suffered to hang on the tree till to morrow *Junius*[1] out of *Epiphanium*[2] gives the reason, because the sight of them above the earth was execrable to the Lord:[3] till they were wholly abolished they would infect; now, if the bodies of our *Achans* infect spirituall as well as corporall, why should they stay above the ground till to morrow; which much like as is said of the Basilisk, *spectando, & dum spectantur,* both by our seeing them, and their seeing of us, they slay us.

1. 'Junius': François du Jon, *Sacrorum Parallelorum libri tres* (1558). Liber Secundus. Parallelus LII.

2. Epiphanius Scholasticus.

3. Fairclough does not find it convenient to quote du Jon's New Testament *parallelus,* Galatians. 3 : 13, 14. 'Christ redeemed us from the curse of the law, having become a curse for us: for it is written, Cursed is everyone that hangeth on a tree: That in Christ Jesus the blessing of Abraham might come upon the Gentiles that we might receive the promise of the Spirit through faith.'

First so long as they are seene, they slay us, because they keepe the fountaine of life from us, God will not come one moment to us till they be gone; censures and judgment, without execution, no more brings comfort to the body of a State, then promises of payment without satisfaction paies debts: while the debt is not paid the suite goes on, and while the life of the male-factor is in him, by unjust and unnecessary procrastinations; Gods justice for all our censures and purposes are still in force against us.

Secondly, and much more *spectando* while they live do they actually hurt, when they are questioned & condemned, the Law of Man against these *Achans* doth as the reviving of the Law of God in the consciences of wicked men, make them desperately evill, more then before, *me pereunte, ruat mundus*, saith *Achan*, oh that seeing I must die or *Israel*, that I might destroy *Israel* before I die. *Baalam* when he cannot curse from his Altars, undoeth *Israel* by his secret counsells to the King *Balacke* against *Israel*; had not *Absolon* beene spared, he had never driven his Father out of his Kingdome; this *David* and all the faithfull of *Israel* have got, by hearing the Woman of *Tekoah* for his reprievall; I may say of all *Achans* as our Saviour of *Judas*, it had beene good for them and the Kingdome where they live, they had never beene borne, but that they had perished before they had done either good or evill; but having done so much evill, and mischiefe to the lives and welfare of whole Kingdomes, why should life be further granted to them whose very life brings death to all about them?

Thirdly, in procrastinating their execution you hinder the joy, the com-fort, the Jubilee of the Church, for the returne of its praise; as long as these sonnes of *Belial* live, the Kingdomes peace and comfort cannot be established, onely when these are cast downe, will the Church lift up its head, and say exaltation, and shouting. Oh what joy was in *Israel* when *Moses*, *Aaron*, and *Miriam* saw the *Egyptians* dead upon the shore, then they sung and danced, when *Debora* and *Baruck* saw *Sisera* beheaded, then all but *Meros* that did not helpe the Lord, rejoyced: when *Mordecai* and *Hester* saw *Haman* hanged; then they kept the feast and daies of *Vrim*; and when *England* shall see these *Achans* executed, then shall they rejoyce in the Lord, and in the returne of his presence into his Temple, ordinances, and judicatures; *higaudia nostra morantur*: while these Froggs and Jesuits of *Rome* be extirpated, wee shall not sing the song of *Moses* and the Lambe. Oh therefore hast their ruine, and your owne triumph; though *Rome* were not built in one day, yet may it be, nay it shall be destroyed in a day, *Revel.*18.8. *her pangs shall come in one day*, nay in one houre, verse 10. *in one houre is thy judgment finished*; our Church hath long time beene in travaile to be delivered of these Vipers, and long travails are perilous, especially if so; and that the spirit and strength of pregnant begin to wast: the Dragon and false Prophet, labours with all their might to make the birth abortive, or destroy the issue in the Wombe, oh do you afford such helpe that shall be quick and lively, and be delivered before such Midwives come at her, then shall she forget all her sorrow, and immediately shall follow the Church *Hallalujah*, even the day that others have desired to see and could not, but by your expedition, in *Achans* destruction, your eyes shall immediately behold truth, and peace in your daies, and joy in all the *Israel* of God.

Fourthly, nor shall you by this expedition bring greater joy, to the Church then blessing to your selves. Consecrate your selves to day, saith *Moses*, to the sons of *Levi*, that God may bestow a blessing upon you; teaching us, the blessing that God will reward this service withall, should quicken their indeavours therein. Never any service that you shall doe unto God, or your Kingdome, shall be better rewarded, then this shall. *Levi* did all the services of the Temple, yet for his speedy extirpation of the abominable things had he the blessing; by this *Levi* got off the temporall guilt of the *Shechonites* bloud; by this their scattering in *Israel* was turned to a blessing, the temporall blessings of God assured, the blessing of immunitie from the sinnes of the Land obtained, the acceptation of the sacrifice of the people of *Israel* from their hands promised, as their hereditary blessing: so shall you by this worke of expedition of *Achans* judgment free your selves from the sinnes of all *Achans* of the times, as *Ioshua* here; turne away the wrath of God from your selves, and others, as *Phineas* elsewhere; you shall be sure that God that rewarded *Jehues* extirpation of *Iezebels* idolatry, with reward of a Kingdome, in the fourth Generation, though done in hypocrisie, will not be forgetfull of this your labour, to recompence it foure-fold more then to *Iehu*, if you doe it speedily and in sincerity: and that God of blessing, that blessed *Phineas* and all his posterity, saying, I impute his zeale, his speedy cutting off two execrable persons, for righteousnesse, and give him therefore the covenant of peace, and he shall have it, and his Sonnes after him from Generation to Generation, will certainly impute your speedy extirpation of many *Achans*, for righteousnesse, unto you and your Sons and heires, thereby inrouled in a Covenant of peace, and they shall have it from Generation to Generation when you are dead and gone.

Fifthly, to conclude all, and put an end to the exhortation, remember this one thing, that execution of justice upon *Achans* is the end and perfection of all other your paines, and labour spent, in the inquisition, examination, conviction, and sentencing, of *Achans*. All these are wholly directed to this, as to their end and scope, without which it is in vaine to rise up early and sit up late, and spend whole Weekes, and Moneths from your houses and families, to discover and bring them to light; to what end is this waste, if being found out, sentence is not executed, execution being the end & perfection of all censures & uncorrupt judgments? how can it appeare that the grounds, intentions, and rules of your sentences were pure, and uncorrupt, except

after they be pronounced they haste more then ever to their execution? for
this is the difference betweene naturall, and violent motions, violent, the
further they goe the fainter they grow; but naturall, make so much the more
haste, by how much they draw neerer to their end and center; therefore that
it may appeare to all the world, that this Assemblies aimes was the peace of
the Kingdome, and removeall of unjustice and unrighteousnesse from it, and
was carried thereto by the rules of wisdome and naturall affection to truth
and holinesse, being now so neere the end, make haste to the center, to wit,
execution of *Achans*, without unnecessary delaies, and needlesse procrastra-
tions. . . .

THOMAS GRANTHAM

While the conflict of stratagems and intrigues was moving the country closer to the brink of civil war, in quiet rural parishes all over England men carried on with the weekly round of work and play and worship; and humble clergymen preached sermons which were neither incitement to shed blood nor warnings of God's impending fury against those who suffered idols to stand unbroken. One unexalted, though far from ordinary, member of the clergy was Thomas Grantham, curate of High Barnet. He was also a schoolmaster. He taught at various addresses in London, in Bow Lane, in Migwell Street, in Holborn 'at Master Bull's' and at the Barbican, at the sign of the Horseshoe; and he was one of the most enlightened and independent educationalists of the century. In an age when a lavish use of the rod was considered indispensable to respectable instruction as well as discipline, Grantham banished all corporal punishment from his régime. His method was to teach by kindness, and if a boy did not respond to that he sent him away. He refused to teach more than fourteen boys at a time; they worked only five hours a day; the rest of the time they played, but they played in Latin. He developed a system of rapid teaching of Hebrew which seems to have achieved results remarkable enough to have provoked the boys of St. Paul's School to violence after they had lost a contest with his pupils. Naturally, orthodox adults were not behind schoolboys in being scandalized by his dangerous eccentricities. The sermon he preached on making the best of an imperfect marriage also gave offence; it was deemed to be disrespectful of Jacob, and an encouragement to polygamy and immorality, and he was ejected from the curacy of Barnet on the grounds of 'insufficiency' after complaints laid by certain 'ignorant lying men of the parish'. Like the rest of Grantham's record, the sermon is eminently sane, compassionate, tolerant, and sometimes funny. He did not give much care to correcting it before it went to the printers. The construction rambles sometimes into incoherence, as in the paragraph that ends 'cosin me of all'. Slovenly punctuation does not help; but his thoughts are studded with curious little fancies borrowed from the medieval pulpit, like 'the

Virgin Mary paid her fine in milk, but He in blood . . .' and the married man 'a fish in a net, he comes merrily in, but he is mighty perplexed when he cannot get out'. Altogether the gentle humanism of his spirit is a rare bloom to find in the hot intolerance of the time, to which, in the end, it falls a prey.

A Wife Mistaken, or a Wife and No Wife

A Sermon on being reconciled to marital imperfection

by Thomas Grantham, curate of High Barnet, 1641

Gen. 29. verse. 25.

And it came to passe that in the morning behold it was Leah. *And he said unto* Laban, *What is this thou hast done unto me? did not I serve with thee for Rachel? wherefore then hast thou beguiled mee?*

In the text you may observe a Conjunction and a division: a Conjunction, here are two together that should be asunder, *Iacob* and *Leah*. And in the morning behold it was *Leah*. A division, heere are two asunder that should be together, *Iacob* and *Rachel*: and first of the Conjunction as fittest for this season, and opportunity; you have seene the quality of this conjunction, it was an ill Conjunction, a great deale of deceit in it, and where is there a Conjunction, a Marriage, but there is deceit in it, and least this deceit should cause a separation, the Church bindeth them together before God and man, for better for worse, for richer for poorer. And unlesse this course were taken, how soone would there be a partition, their qualities being almost as different as heaven and hell, as the good Angels and the bad. *Nabal* and *Abigail*, *Nabal* a fool and churle, and of so base a disposition, such a man of *Belial*, that his own servants said a man could not tell how to speak to him: and she a kinde complementall woman, she fell at *Davids* feet, and offered to wash the feet of his servants. *David* and *Michal*, *Michal* a scoffing woman, deriding *David* for dancing before the *Arke*, and he a man after Gods own heart; *Socrates* with *Xantippe*, she is like a *Quotidian Ague*, or at the best she is like *Sauls* evill spirit that comes too often upon him. *Moses* and *Zipporah*, she a terrible firie woman, Thou art a bloudy husband to me, saith she, and *Moses* the meekest man above all the men of the earth. The learned distinguish a fourfold deceit in Marriage, the first is *error persona*, when *Leah* is given in stead of *Rachel*, one party for another, as to *Iacob*, and this mistake doth hinder and nullifie Mariage: for in Mariage there is a mutuall love and consent One to another, but this is not where *Leah* is given in stead of *Rachel*, and therefore no Mariage. But will some say, is it possible that *Iacob* (who was so subtill a man) should be so deceived, he was noted for a supplanter by his Brother *Esau*; Is he not rightly called *Iacob*, for he hath supplanted me these two times of my birthright and blessing. He was so grave, so arch a supplanter, that he could deceive his father although his voyce betraied him, and although his father told him it was the voyce of *Iacob*, yet he pressed him to blesse him in stead of his brother *Esau*. We say that man is an excellent *Hocus-Pocus*,[1] excellent in legerdemaine, and slight of hand that can deceive one that looks upon him. But he that can deceive the hearing, and the feeling, he is far more excellent: my sight may be deceived for I may take that which is Pictured to be lively and real, but my hearing, my feeling cannot be so easily deceiv'd. *Thomas* would not beleeve his seeing, his hearing, but when he came to feeling to lay his hand in our Saviours side, then he cried out, My Lord and my God. And now I suppose you are ready to ask, how this Subtil man was deceived? The deceit was thus: In those dayes the Brides came veiled and Masked to their Marriage Beds, for modesty sake, and it was a signe of Modesty to be silent. And thus much for the first deceit, which is *error personæ*, a mistake of the person, as this text represents to you. There is another deceit, which is *error qualitatis*, when a man takes as he thinkes he hath, one thrifty, honest, faire, and she proves a painted whorish, liquorish slut. And this deceit is generall, for many women shew like the Egyptian Temples, very beautifull without and built, and adorned with precious stones, saith, *Lucian*, but if you seek what god they worship within, you shall finde him to be a Cat, or a Goat, or an Ape, or some such ridiculous ill favoured creature: so, many women, although they be faire and beautifull without, are full of many vanities, fickle, unconstant, lascivious affections: many a man thinks he hath a saint, when he hath a Devill, a faire woman, when she is a painted plaistered faced *Iesabel*; I will not speak of these painted tombes and sepulchres, beautifull without, but loathsome within, these Apples of Sodom, that seeme faire to the sight but at the least touch they fall to dust: so the least approaching discovers the corruption of these creatures, so great is their corruption it corrupts the sweetest perfumes, and makes them loathsome as themselves: but I will not rake any longer in this unsavory dunghill. There are two other

---

1. A term to which hot offence was taken by his Puritan auditors, who later used it as a ground for ejecting him.

errours, or deceits in Marriage, as *error Conditionis*, and *error fortunæ*: but I let them passe, for feare I should run into the errour of being tedious to this assembly. I come now to the division, or separation; there is discovery of an ill Conjunction, therefore I will cast my meditations a little upon this appearance, or discovery of this Conjunction. In the morning behold it was *Leah*. There is many a man sleeps with *Leah* and thinks it is *Rachel*, there is many a man so blinded in his love & affection that he is as much or more mistaken in the qualities of his wife then *Iacob* was in the person of *Leah*: many a man thinks he hath a wife that loves him, when she cares not for him, and hee may think that she is sighing and sorrowing in his absence, when she is Revelling and Dancing. You may read *Pro.* 7.18. there's a woman speaks to a man in her husbands absence to take his fill of love with her: he (may be) thinks, she is weeping in his absence, when she is tumbling in her perfumed bed, as you may read there, verse 17. *I have perfumed my bed with Myrrhe, Aloes and Cynamon; I have decked it with coverings of tapestry, and fine linnen of Egypt*: no question this woman embraces her husband when he comes home, and he discovers nothing: for the way of an whorish woman, (as *Solomon* saith) *is like the flight of a Bird in the aire, like the passage of a ship upon the sea, like a serpent creeping into a rocke*: no signe of the birds flying, of the serpents creeping, of the ships passage.

Look upon *Ioseph's* Mistresse, she hath his coat to shew for honesty, *Ecce signum, Behold the coat of this Hebrew*: did *Sampson* thinke those hands would have clipped his lockes, that had so often embraced his body? Some rash men do maintain, that the reason why men thinke there are so many good women, is, because they are so blinde and ignorant themselves; if they had but the eyes of the Wife, to see with *Solomons* eyes, may be they would say, There was not one good of a thousand, and he had told them one by one. And how does *Solomon* define a good woman? just as the Philosopher does, *Vacuum ex supposito quod detur*; if there be a *Vacuum*, it is *Locus non repletus corpore*; if there be, or shall ever be such a thing in the world as a good woman, then she is this and that, she is like a merchants Ship that bringeth her food from far: and what of greater value! she is like to precious jewels, she is like to them, but there is none like to her, none of equal value with her. *Solomon* saith, *She is a crowne to her husband, she is the glory of her husband*, saith Saint *Paul*, the very skarlet she cloathes her servants in does shew her honourable, God himselfe cals her an helper, and such a helper she is, that man could not have been capable of that blessing, *Increase and multiply*, without her, then it was *The Seed of the woman that brake the Serpents head*: she was *Deipora*, she brought forth a God, and here I will be bold to say out of the due honour to that Sexe, that there have been women have deserved these praises of *Solomon*: What was that *Ester*? that Cherubin of the Church under whose wings it was safe: the Papists call the Virgin *Mary*, *Regina Cœli*, Queen of

Heaven, and they pray to her to command our Saviour, *Mater impera Filio*, Mother command thy Son; She hath more Churches dedicated to her than our Saviour, than all the Trinity, although she paid her Fine in milke, but He in blood, (as a great Divine saith.) How happy hath this Kingdom been under a Queen, there are many eyes now living that have seen it, and not a man but knowes it; I need not instance in particulars the elect Lady and her sister, to whom Saint *Iohn* writ, *Priscilla* able to informe a learned man *Apollos* in the Scripture: these women were highly honoured by that Apostle called from Heaven, *Greete Priscilla and Aquila, Rom. 16.3. Aquila and Priscilla salute you.* 1.Cor.16.19. *salute Priscilla and Aquila,* 2.Tim.4.19. *Priscilla went with him into Syria, Act.*18.18. and thus much for the discovery, how long may a man sleep before he knowes with whom, or what she is he sleeps withall, before he knows whether it be *Leah* or *Rachel.* I am come now to the division or separation, and you see it is a high and great division, *Iacob* begins to word it, to fall to termes with *Laban* (who was his Master) What is this thou hast done unto me; did not I serve with thee for *Rachel?* wherefore then hast thou beguiled me? And indeed the inconveniences were very many that befell *Iacob* by this wicked act of *Laban*: first of all he made his daughter a whore,[1] and a whore is odious to the children of God, she was either to be burnt, or to be stoned. Then the wrong done to *Rachel*, being deceived of her expectation, was enough to make her weepe her selfe blear ey'd like *Leah*, then he brought an inconvenience upon *Iacob*, having more wives then one; some say it was a sin, some hold it a great Inconvenience to have one, therefore much more to have two.

The married man is intangled like a fish in a net; he comes merrily in, but he is mightily perplext when he cannot get out; then this action of *Laban* was enough to set the sisters at variance, and what joy could *Iacob* have when his wives were devided, it was enough to devide his heart: then the desire of rule, and jealousies, and distrusts that one hath of the other; then the charges to maintaine two, whereas *Iacob* if he had had but one, he would never have sought further. God made but one for *Adam*, and *Lamech* was the first that had two Wives, and he had no more then two, and he was of the posterity of *Cain*, and condemned by the fathers: and from *Adam* to *Abraham*, none of the posterity of *Seth* had more then one wife (that we read of) they two shall be one flesh, and how can that be if a man have many wives. God made onely male and female, and he took but one rib, and made of one rib, One Woman, not many. I will not say, it was a sinne to have many wives, for I finde it in the Law, *Deut.*21.15. *If a man have two wives, one that he loveth, and another that he hateth,* and there the Law speaks of both their sons as

---

1. Grantham has lost his way here. Laban may have tricked Jacob, but he did nothing dishonourable to his own daughter Leah in sending her to Jacob before her sister Rachel. In any case, in the end Jacob had them both.

legitimate, *Deut.* 17.17. The Law does forbid the King to have many wives which may draw away his minde, and Saint *Augustine* (upon that place) saith, *permissum & Regi habere plures uxores non plurimas*, he may have more then one or two, but not many, and *Iehoiada* that was a most holy Priest, took two wives, for King *Ioash*, 2.*Chron.* 24.3. But me thinks I hear some say, *Laban* is unjustly condemned for dealing so strictly with *Iacob*: was it not a great kindnesse in *Laban* to take *Iacob*, *Iacob* that had cosined his Father, his Brother, and to trust him with his flock? And then it was a kindnesse that he gave him his daughter, and for ought I know the better of the two, the fairest is not alwaies the best. Beautifull *Rachel* sold *Iacob* for Mandrakes, whereas blear eyed *Leah* bought him and went out to meet him, *Gen.* 30.16. Tender eyed *Leah* will be weeping at my misfortunes, when beautifull *Rachel* will be laughing with another: *Abraham* went in danger with beautiful *Sarah*, but *Iacob* liveth secure with tender eyed *Leah*, *Rachel* stole her fathers gods, and could see her Father and husband quarrel the while, when *Leah* was continually weeping. *Rachel* will be impatient if she have not what she desires (give me Children or else I dye) and what is beauty with such disquiet-nesse, but like a faire house haunted with sprites, or a bed of violets with a serpent. But look upon *Leah* she is more moderate, tender eyed, she will be weeping in stead of scoulding, *Rachel* will be subject to be wandering like *Dina*. *Leah* is tender eyed, and the winde will hurt her, *venium spectantur ut Ipse*, they delight to be looked upon. What are these many fancies in their dressings but so many signes to invite a man to Inne there if he please, whereas the Passenger else had gone on his way? What does the fowler whistle for but to catch the Bird, and such is the end of their enchantments. Thus you see the danger of beauty, there is more danger in it then in the most unruly Elements. The fire hath no power of a man if he do not touch it; nor the water; but if a man look but upon beauty, it will endanger him, and it is kept with a great deale of danger and care, as the Apples of the *Hesperides* with a watchfull *Dragon*. But will some say, why doe you main-taine bleare eyed *Leah* against beautifull *Rachel*? *Leahs* fault was great in lying with *Iacob*. To this I answer, fornication was held no sin amongst the Gentiles, and the Church of *Rome* holds, *fornicationem non vagam*, that if a man keep constantly to one woman it is no sinne: and heer let no man be harsh against *Leah*, for she is tender eyed, and can weep teares enough to wash away her sin, tears enough to wash our Saviours feet. Alas, be not harsh against her, she is blear-eyed already & too much weeping will make her blinde. What if *Leah* have a blemish in the eye of her body, yet her understanding, the eye of her soule may be cleare, and beautifull; and if men consider rightly, the greatest deformity and blemish in a woman is, to be bleare eyed in her understanding, to mistake a mans actions, not to see them clearly. If her husband be sociable, then he is given to drunkennes, if silent, then he hath no discourse in him, if merry, not that gravity that becomes him, if he put not himselfe upon hard adventures to raise his fortunes, she is disquieted, and if he doe, and be foyled, then she contemnes him; give me the eye of the understanding, let the other eye be as cleare as Christal, if this be blemisht there is no joy. For ought I know, this *Laban*, this Idolater, shall rise up against many Christians. How usuall is it for many a man to make faire promises, to promise a man *Rachel*; he shall have this and that, and any thing his heart can desire if he will serve them; but when a man hath done all he can, they will put *Leah* upon him, some bleare eyed unhandsome thing, upon which so soon as a man can but look, he shall finde it to be *Leah*. It's plaine enough to bee seen (behold it was *Leah*) it is a hard thing for a man to get a *Rachel* of his Master, to get any thing that hath any delight or pleasure in it, great men will not part with their *Rachels*. And still I say, this *Laban* had more honesty and goodnes then many a Christian, for although he had done *Iacob* a little wrong, yet he had so much mildnes, and Gentlenes, and Gentility, as he did suffer *Iacob* to speak to him and to tell him of it (why hast thou beguiled me thus?). Now there are rich men, if they have done a man a displeasure, will not be told of it. Nay if a poore man trust a rich man with money, if he be not disposed to give it, or is unwilling, will be angry if the poore man ask it, and doe him all the mischiefe that may be, and what is this but like theeves that doe not onely rob a man, but binde a man too, and gag him that he shall not speak, or like Rogues that murther a man because they shall not betray them? God send me to deale with *Laban*, with an Idolater; I shall finde a man that I dare speak to, I shall find a mate that will give me *Leah*, that will give me something and cosin me of all.

God complained of his vinyard, that when he had taken a great deal of pains with it, it brought forth wilde grapes, *ecce Labruscus*, behold wilde grapes plaine enough to be seen. And heer if I should shew to the world with an *Ecce*, the wilde grapes, the Basest actions of men, I make no question but men would passe the same judgement that *David* did upon the rich man that tooke the poor mans Lambe. And heer let every man be exhorted not to deceive his servant or his kinsman or his friend. *Iacob* for deceiving his brother & his Father, was paid in his own Coyn, & enjoyed not the blessing twenty yeers after: *Laban* deceived him in his wife, *Laban* for deceiving *Iacob*, was deceived by *Iacob*, with the rods he laid. *Rachel* stole *Labans* gods for deceiving her of her husband at first. *Iacob* deceived his Father with Goats skins, and he himselfe was deceived with the blood of a Goat. *David* cut off the lap of *Sauls* coat, and his clothes would not keep him warme in his old age. *Sampsons* eye lusted after a Philistine, and *Sampsons* eye was put out, *Ieroboams* hand reached to the Prophet, and that hand withered. Thus you see how God punisheth sin in the same act, in the same part, in the same kinde. Time will not give me leave heer to shew you how many a man sleeps with

Leah, with some ugly deformed sin, and being blinded in sin and darknesse, thinks it is *Rachel*, (very beautifull) and loves it entirely, till the morning light of Gods grace arise, and then he sees the deformity of his sin, how bleare eyed it is, how ill-favoured, and now let every man consider how we are all servants to God, and we serve him for *Rachel*, for some pleasant thing we delight in, as the Apostles dream't of a Kingdome, if it please God to give us *Leah*, in stead of *Rachel*, to give us that which pleaseth us not so well, let us be content with it and serve him on still, he will at the last give us *Rachel*, we shall be married to him in whom are all joys, such as eye hath not seen, nor eare heard, neither hath it entered into the heart of man to conceive. To which God of his mercy bring us: to God the Father, God the Sonne, and God the Holy Ghost be all honour, &c.

PETER MOOR

A number of preachers have now been observed over a period of a century, most of them eminent, or at least, prominent men. But what of the rest, the commonalty of preachers and the congregations? Many sermons, better and worse, were never written, much less published, and of those that were published the preponderance was, of course, ephemeral. The odd curiosity which one circumstance or another saved from the general oblivion tends to point a distinction which should already have emerged from the more literary examples. In the preaching of the academic, Episcopalian tradition, the separation of role between the preaching clergy and the receiving laity was ordinal and clear cut. In the Puritan complex, especially among Independents of one sort or another, the community tended to be one of vocationally active religious laymen, among whom the minister, or pastor, was just another member of the team who happened to have volunteered for special duties. Each man could claim individual and direct access to God, through scripture and through personal communication. There was internal contradiction and conflict, which was never entirely resolved, between the drive to total independence of conscience, found in the more extreme separatist groups, and the demand for a perpetuation of authoritarian control over conduct, found in the main Presbyterian movement. But whether Presbyterian or Independent, the English reformers were, in the words of a Victorian, 'preachers to a man'. Today's auditor might be tomorrow's preacher. The recurring pattern to evangelize—to broadcast their personal current transactions with God, to expose triumphantly their palpitating sins and their prophetic souls, which told them that, sins and all, they were redeemed, not by righteousness, but by faith alone; and, of course, to denounce the unconfessed sins of others—this pattern was the central characteristic of the Puritan spirit.

An eye-witness account of the execution of Anne Boleyn's brother, George, reported that 'he made a very Catholic address to the people, saying he had not come hither to preach.'[1] This was not a ghoulish

1. *Letters and Papers of the Reign of Henry VIII* (Gairdner), Vol. X, 1536, No. 911i,

joke, but a realistic observation upon his supposed conformity, because had he been, as his family was judged, Puritan-inclined, he would not have mounted a platform, least of all his own scaffold, without preaching. The dying addresses of 'Puritan' malefactors (and there were quite a number) are immediately distinguishable by the didactic sermonical fervour of the speeches made immediately before they were turned off by the hangman. In 1641 an apprentice, called Peter Moor, was hanged for poisoning his master Humphrey Bigood, apothecary, and his last words were "taken down" and published in a pamphlet. The product has been tricked out by the practised hand of a professional journalist as unmistakably as the biographical confessions of the infamous which are favourite features in today's popular Sunday press. But, however much it has been knocked into shape, it is a work of adaptation, not invention, and evidently what contemporary readers expected that kind of Puritan youth to say in the circumstances.

One is left rather wondering why he did not poison his mistress instead of his master, but there must have been a sufficient answer to that which went with the boy to his grave.

The Poisoner's Farewell[1]

Spoken from the ladder at the Gallows, at Exeter, 1641

All you good Christian people which are come hither to see me dye, let me desire you to give attention to what I shall now declare, who hath now scarce one quarter of an houre to live: my parents are scarce unknowne to any here present: but as for my unhappy master, (the more wretch I for making him so) he was better knowne to you. I was an Apprentice to Master *Humphry Bidgood*, Apothecary, too good a maister for so ungracious a servant; notwithstanding, for a time my service was not disliked of, neither had it still, had I not wanted grace. Being in the prime of my youth, the devill by his allurements and wicked inticing, made me partaker of each damned vice, so that my heart being puffed up with ambition, I began to

p. 382: "Execution Criminal hecha en Inglatierra el 16 de Mayo 1536" (Vienna Archives). Cf. *Rymer's Transcripts*; Record Office (145, No. 7.)

1. *The Apprentice's Warning Piece* (1641).

scoffe at Gods holy Ministers, prophaning Sabbaths, and taking Gods holy name in vaine. But yet still was I provoked further to evil courses, so much alas, that you could scarce name a sinne wherein I had not beene an actor. Pride waxed daily more and more strong in me, in so much that I beganne to kicke at service, my time seeming too long and tedious to me, wherefore in all haste I did run to my parents, that they out of hand might buy out my time, which they rebuking me denyed, saying, I made more haste then good speed, in so much as I had not skill enough as yet to manage a shop of any consequence. Then went I again to my master, seeming to be contented to serve out my Apprenticeship, and so had done, had not my mistresse beene too cruell toward me; never permitting me to remaine quiet; for daily she was cause of such strife, that I grew desperate, and as one weary of life which makes me now to pray that never any young man may have so bad a mistris as she was to me.

Dayly was my heart more and more filled with discontent, still meditating of nothing but mischiefe, which at length thus did worke my fatall over-throw, for being still greedy to bee freed from my Apprentiship, I acted a deed which now doth make each Artery to quake, and totall body to tremble: for I seeing a messe of pottage about dinner time provided for my Master, I most unnaturall servant put powdred white Mercury into it, so privately that no man could perceive me, which so soone as he good man had tasted, presently began to swel, and a while after died.

Thus *Iudas* like traterously did I betray my master unto death, but yet was not found out, but yet the Lord whose judgments are alwaies just and true, caused many towards me to have a great mistrust, and layd the fault to my charge, which I most impudently denyed, which so soone as my father and mother did heare, upon their knees weeping with brinish teares came and desired mee to confesse the truth, which I denied, notwithstanding my con-science told mee that I lyed; in the same minde I went to my fathers house and received the Sacrament, still denying the hainous murder committed upon my Master, but God at last revealed it, and I was sent to prison, to answer for the Death of my Master, where I thought my selfe to be secure from being found out, because I did the act unseene. All the while I lay in prison, I had the keies thereof in my owne custody, with which I might have both freed my selfe and others; the divell daily tempted me to runne away, but God hee would not have it so, for to goe thence I had not the least of power, untill such time as the Assizes did begin, that I should answer the death of my Master, where I was most justly judged to die, my conscience still telling mee no man did the deed but I. One there is in this City whom I pray that the Lord may forgive, God hee knowes that I speake nothing concerning him at this present for any malice I beare to him, but to cleare my owne conscience.

His name is *White* a Papist,[1] who did oftentimes seduce me to abuse God's Ministers, and to spend my time in that Diabolicall study of reading Magicke, in which I tooke too much delight, which now doth very much oppresse my soule: All young men which are here present, and did behold me drawne hither upon a sledge, take warning by me, and let your study be, first, to please your heavenly Master, and then your Masters upon earth.

Contemne the divell, despise the world, and abhore lust; Hence, hence, with pride which is the divels darling, away with lust which is the divells chiefe attendant, away with magicke spells which lead unto the divell.

When I am dead let the cause of my dying bee engraved upon a stone that all may know wherefore I did die, and thereby take example. Pray, pray for my soule good christian people, that notwithstanding my horrid offence, the gate of heaven may not be barred against me: Againe, againe, and againe I earnestly intreat your prayers.

Now farewell dear father, a thousand times farewell, O Mother, also farewell to all my dear friends and kinsfolks.

Wipe, wipe your eyes, and each one cease his mourning, for I am now exchanging a lump of mortal clay, for immortal bliss; which I may receive grant, grant most merciful father! O receive me, receive me into thy bosom, for behold I come, I come, I come, I come.

The witness who took down the words, here adds, 'So soon as the words were spoken he was turned off the ladder and so died.'

1. The papists were behind even a squalid provincial murder.

SECTARIES AT HOME

An Alleged Conventicle Sermon

The movement which novelty was taking would go further before it was checked. The fancy of every vulgar aspirant to special knowledge was aired and inflated wherever two or three were gathered together. Cobblers, felt-makers, button-makers, serving men, preached varieties of religious gibberish from brewers' carts, and a contemporary remarked, 'nothing can pass muster which proceedeth from their mouths which is not extravagant *ex tempore*. Nay, some most prophanely, I may say, blasphemously have been heard to say that they could make a better prayer than that which our saviour taught to his disciples.'[1] They rejected all hierarchical authority, all received knowledge, and, inevitably, claiming one kind of licence, they incurred the suspicion of using another.

'They persuade their auditory to contemn the prayers of the Church, and the preachers of the gospel; also avowing their own zealous prayers to have such power with God ... By which lewd persuasion they have drawne divers honest men's wives in the night times to frequent their Assemblies, and to become of most loose and wicked conversation, and likewise many chaste virgins to become harlots. ...'[2] Few sermons from the more zany reaches of sectarian Puritanism have survived, as they were seldom written down, but we do have a parodic report of the evening transactions of a conventicle from somebody who claims to have been present.

After a long address by the chosen 'brother' on the wickedness of reading prayers from a book and of observing Saints' days and fast days and feast days, it became time to eat, and saying grace itself became an occasion of preaching. 'Imagine their exercise done', says our informant, 'and high time to refresh themselves; this holy brother which preached ... was invited to another brother's house to dinner,

1. *The Brownists Conventicle* (1641), p. 3.
2. *A True Relation of a Company of Brownists* (1641).

which was there present, and being come, and meat set upon the table, and all the saints set a boord, he began to say Grace, which is to this effect, having first surveyed every dish, and in what order it was placed at the boord, he began his thanks giving as followeth.'

The Brownists[1] Conventicle

Corroborate these thy good gifts unto our use, I beseech thee good Father, and make us thankfull for all these thy bountifull blessings upon this boord to nourish our corrupt bodies. These are boyl'd Chickens (I take it) let this dish of Chickens put us in mind of our Saviour, who would have gathered Jerusalem together as an Hen gathereth her chickens, but she would not: but let us praise God for these chickens, which are set before us, being fiv(e) in number. Let this leg of Mutton call us to remembrance, that King David was once a Shepherd; and so was Christ the Son of David, that good Shepherd, who having an hundred sheep, and losing one, to find that left ninetie and nine in the wildnernesse. Here is an excellent Loyne of Veale, let that prompts us to remember the Parable of the Prodigall child, whom to welcome home, the Father caused the fat calfe to be killed, which I thinke could not yeeld a better rump and kidney than is now visable before our eyes. And by this cramm'd and well fed capon, let us be mindfull of the cock, which crowed, three times, when Peter has as often denyed his Master, for which he went out and wept bitterly. These Rabbets recollect us to think (having worne fur upon their backs) of the two wicked Elders, that lay in wait to betray the chastity of Susanna: but I feare I have too much over-shot myselfe in alleaging any example out of the prophane Apocrypha. What see I there? a Potato pye, and a Sallad of Sparagus,[2] these are flirting meats, and provocations to procreation, by which good God, wee desire thee that according to thy blessings to our first parents in Paradise, we may increase and multiply. And when that Gamond of Westphalia Bacon comes to be cut up, let us think of that herd of Swine, into which by the permission of our Saviour the Devils entered, and from an high rock hurried them headlong into the sea. And as for these thy good blessings that are from the land, so likewise make us thankfull for this thy bounty sent us from the sea, and first for this Bole

1. Derived from the name of Robert Brown, the Elizabethan dissenter. By the 1640s it was used as a general description for separatists.

2. 'Some report . . . that of Rammes hornes buried, or hidden in the ground, is brought forth an Herbe, called Asparagus, in English Sperage.' Bossewell, *Armorie* (1572), iii, 19.

of Sturgeon, and let it so far edifie in us, as to thinke how great that Whales head was, which swallowed the Prophet Jonas, and kept him three dayes and nights in his belly. And though these Lobsters seeme to be in red coats like Cardinals, having clawes like Usurers, and more hornes than the Beast of Rome, which is the Whore of Babylon; yet having taken off their Papisticall copes and, let us freely feed upon what is within; for God regardeth not the outside, but the inside of man. I conclude with the fruit, which may it by thy grace to fructifie in our hearts, that these Pippins may put us in mind of the Apple of the forbidden Tree, which our Grand mother Eve (by the temptation of the Serpent) tasted in the middle of the Garden. For had she not, vile wretch, eaton a forbidden apple, all our Crabs had bin very good Pippins, and all our Thistles had beene very good Harti-choaks. And these Carawayes call to our remembrance that Manna which was like Coriander seed, by which the children of Israel were fed forty yeares together in the wildernesse. Thus as briefly as I can, I have gone thorow every dish on the boord, for every sundry dish ought to have a severall blessing. And now let us fall too, and feed exceedingly, that after our full repast, wee may the better prophesie.

"Then, [says our informant] Falling to and feeding lustily, and dinner being ended, another began his grace after meat, as followeth."

We thank thee, good Lord, that thou has sufficiently satisfied these our bodies with the blessings of the earth, so thou hath the like care to feed our soules with the spiritual good of Heaven: And in this our thanksgiving, let us remember all the blessed Pastours and Professeners whether in Amsterdam or elsewhere: but especially the Ministers of the Church in New England, the New Jerusalem, as Master Samuel Eaton, lately come from thence, and the rest, with all our brethren and sisters, the Saints there, that little flock, of which our Saviour speaks in the Gospell, Feare not little flock, who forsaking, and utterly renouncing all the prophane and Papisticall ceremonies here at home, have left the Land, to professe the more pure and sincere truth and doctrine abroad; as also for the seperated Saints here amongst us, the Elders and Deacons of our Congregations wheresoever assembled, whether in any private houses within the city, or in any Cow-house, Barne, or Stable without the wals or whether in the fields, woods, or groves, wheresoever the holy Assembly is convented and gathered. As for the prophane Churches, in which Idols have been formerly worshipped, and Copes and Surplices (the garments of the great Babylonian Whore) are still worne, we utterly abhor them: Neither let us forget that holy and good mans precepts, who never spake unto us but with a great measure of the Spirit, I meane Master How the Cobler; nor these Christian admonitions which were broken unto us by the breath of Master Eaton, the Button-maker in Saint Martins: nor those godly instructions which issued from the mouth of Master Greene, the felt-maker, with all the rest of their sanctified Society: As also for all our fellow-labourers in this our holy and good work, I meane those blessed and fruit-bearing women, who are not only able to talk on any Text, but search into the deep sense of the Scripture, and preach both in their owne families and elsewhere. Whom though Saint Paul forbade to preach in the Church, yet he left them liberty to preach in the chambers: nay, we all therefore, both brethren and sisters, to use our Talents together, that the brethren may be daily regenerate and new borne, and the sisters to labour in their severall vocations, that it may be the encrease and multiplying of these thy Saints, Amen.

[*Now the main course of the spiritual feast was served by the principal preacher of the day. It consisted mainly of a triumphant thanksgiving for the delivery of the 'saints' from their arch-enemy Laud.*]

The 12 of the Revelation, the 7 verse: And there was a battell in heaven, Michael and his Angels fought against the Dragon &c. Grace and peace be multiplied. This Text dearly beloved brethren, and most dearly beloved sisters, may not unproperly be applyed to these present times, and to acts late in agitation, here is a combat spoken of betwixt Michael and the Dragon: now my deare brethren and sisters; first, to enquire who is personated in Michael and his Angels and who pointed at in the Dragon and his Angels. To save you men your looking and you women your longing, I will tell you both, and that briefly thus. By this Michael and his Angels in my Text, is meant one particular Church, and peculiar congregation: and you deare Saints of both sexes have bin sensible, you know many yeares we have most miserably suffered in all servitude and slavery: Now by the Dragon, the holy Ghost labours to delineate unto the great Dragon and Devill of Lambeth. I say unto you againe brethren, wicked Angels are the Bishops, Deanes, Arch-Deacons, Prebends, non-residents, which live without the care and charge of soules; I could have expressed it in Latin, but I hold it to bee the language of the beast of Rome, and therefore omit it as a Heathenish language: besides his other Proctors, Prosecutors, Pursuivants, Puriters,[1] and all other his Ecclesiasticall Ministers and Officers. I had almost forgot his Advocates, Surrogates, with the Judges of his spirituall and Prerogative Courts, all which (brethren) are abhomination in the eyes of the Lord & their very names stink in his nostrils: The Bishops function, deare brethren, is an anti-christian calling; & the Deanes & prebends are the frogs & the locusts mention'd in the Revelation: There is none of these Bishops but hath a pope in their bellies: I will tell you, deare brethren, they be papists in grain; they are all of them unleavn'd soules, & now, I say, we have turned them over to be buffeted by the ugly sin Satan. What then shall we say of all his toyes and popish trincats—his invention and innovations? Or what shall we think

1. Pariter: an intentional error.

of their Altars, Images, unhallowed hoods, Surpleces and Coaps, with their unchristian cornered caps: their Palls, Albs, Rochets, Crosiers, Miters, Crosses, with all their traditions, Ceremonies, and unsanctified Superstitions? What my brethren (my sisters not forgotten) are but as the very rags dropt from the whore of Babylons rotten garments: nay, their cleanest washt Surpleces are at the best but like Porters frocks, which they weare when they carry burthens; and they appeare in our eyes more slovenly and sluttish, than the very fulsome and foule smock she puts off when she shitts herselfe: nay deare brethren, there is another crosse which stands in our way, and is an eye-sore to our uprightnesse, that guilded idolatrous Crosse in Cheapside[1], which so many adore and reverence when they passe by it: then there is another crosse, which is our eare-sore, as well as our eye-sore, deare brethren, that is those pipes, or Organs, as the reverend Scots Ministers call them; which makes more noyse with their roaring, than all the Bulls of Bason did, when Og their King passed by them in triumph.

What further may we liken that dogmaticall Dragon to: this litigious Arch Priest of Lambeth, than to a tyrannicall Nimrod, a proud Pharoah, a politick Achitophel, a wicked Haman, a cunning Caiphas, a iugling Pilot, a bloody-minded Herod, a persecuting Saul, and though he were a Batchelour, yet for a long time bore him as proudly as that Apocallypticall Beast of Rome with seven heads of impietie and ten hornes of iniquity: for how hath he persecuted this little flock of ours—and when he would not be seene in it himselfe, he imployed his apostaticall agents to disturbe us in our Conventicles, and debar us the libertie of our Consciences: and my dear brethren & beloved sisters, was not this the very device of an old Dragon, nay of a venemous Dragon? and are not the Archbishops and Bishops the very Buls of Bashan, their superiour and inferiour Officials and Officers, the great and little foxes? Those that wait on them, are the Wolves that would worrie the sheep and lambs: and yet you see how in the end wee that may be called the Michaelists or Michaelitains, have in this great battalle late fought since the time of the Parliament, have subdued and overcome the Dragon and his Angels, so that their Court is no longer to be found at Lambeth: so it is (according to my Text) no more to be found in Heaven.

This Dragon. I say deare brethren, and beloved sisters, is that Nimrod of Lambeth, the great hunter, who with his blood-hounds hunted and chaced us from one place to another. This was that proud Pharaoh, who would have us deliver up to the task-masters the full take of Brick, and yet would not allow us straw nore stubble to burne it. This is that politick Achitophel, who having mist of his designes, would saddle his asse (if hee had it) and ride home to his house at Lambeth and hang himselfe. This is that wicked Haman,

---

1. A relic of England's Catholic past, acutely offensive to Puritans, especially as it remained, for many, an object of veneration. See below, p. 413.

that would make havock of all us poor Mordecais, and the whole Nation of us distressed Jewes: (for I know there be some Christians and Sabatarians amongst us) but as he hath Idolatriz'd in the high places, wee hope to see him, like that Haman, mounted upon something fiftie Cubits high. This is that cruell Herod, but more bloody-hearted: he only slew the Babes and Sucklings but this Dragon would make slaughters of all of you, deare brothers and sisters, for which hee shall bee eaten up with the wormes of his owne Conscience. This is that Caiphas, that would couzen us of our lives. That Pilot that would give partiall sentence against us; that Saul before he was *Paul*, that would bring persecution amongst us, who are taken for the Olive-branches of the House of the Lord.

And now where is their Starre-parlour, for Star-chamber I cannot call it: Chambers (as we all know) were made for rest and pleasure; but this was onely for rigour and punishment: and where is now their High Commission Courts, by which the Saints hearts could not rest quiet in their bodies, nor their eares safe upon their heads? But some of his servants report that he was cleare of all these; but deare brethren, and best beloved sisters, I will tell you of what he was cleare: cleare from all sinceritie, vertue, and piety; cleare from all charitie, veritie, and honestie: but he, with all the rest of the Archiepisco-pacy, much contaminated with gormundizing and hypocrisie: But where are his full and surfeting Tables, where hee sate plentifully feeding, with his Chaplins, gaping one at another; some gaping after fat bits, others after fat Benefices, they aspiring to the highest degrees after the Prelacy, and he alike ambitious after the Papacy.

But what is now (my deare brothers, and sweet sisters) become of their vehement Orations, their demonical disputations? their syllogistic examina-tions? their Logical Interpretations? their erronious Equivocations? their mentall Reservations? and their uniust Condemnations of us that are the flock of the faithfull, and the onely reserved to eternall Salvation? what I say, but that this great Dragon, and his Angels shall be precipitated to perdition, he hurryed to the inferior parts of the earth, which is also called Hell, and Gehimon, and the tormenting Tophet, to which we also leave them, with all their Prelaticall trash and popish trumperies. . . .

STEPHEN MARSHALL

The autumn of 1641 was a period of sudden, sunny optimism. Strafford, the supremely feared of parliament, had been cornered unarmed, and done to death. Peace in Scotland set the church bells rejoicing throughout the country and plans for further social reformations were cheerfully cultivated. Then, suddenly, with the approach of winter, the lull ended and the storm began to rise. Peace in Scotland had brought the king back to London with a new goodwill behind him which could be dangerous for parliament's ambitions. But in any case, whatever the king designed, Pym and his friends had never had any intention of leaving the main issue, the relationship between the king and parliament, unconcluded. Then, suddenly, like Strafford mocking them from the grave, a bloody massacre drenched Ireland, the turbulent island which only the dead autocrat had been able to keep in unprecedented peace and prosperity. Parliament was going to have to fight for its very survival and Pym knew it. If the Episcopalian hierarchy and royal prerogative were not to crush them, every spring of religious and political energy, however dangerous and fanatical, must be roused and provoked to serve their aims. The final open attack on the king's position was to be the impeachment of the Roman Catholic queen, and the reservoir of bigotry and violence in the city populace must be whipped up and channelled into a torrent of demonstrations, marches, protests and attacks upon the property of the ungodly. For this purpose every level of society, which could be reached and used, must be wound up and alerted with animosity and fear, in preparation for the coming clash. Once more, a day of 'humiliation' was the warning signal of things to come, and on December 22nd the 'Geneva bull', Stephen Marshall,[1] was chosen to bellow the call to battle in a speech of political incitement disguised as a religious exhortation.

1. See above, p. 368.

Reformation and Desolation

or

A sermon tending to the discovery of the symptoms of a people to whom God will by no means be reconciled.

Preached before the House of Commons on
December 22nd., 1641

There is one only proper use for the present occasion and that is this; you are met this day together to *Fast* and *Pray* and *mourne* before the *Lord*; and (as I touched before) *hereby* you acknowledge that the wrath of God is kindled, and that your selves are called to take a course to turn away Gods wrath: and I verily believe this is the very end you aymed at, in calling us the unworthy Ministers of Christ to your help this day, that wee might bee assistant to you in whatever might turn away the wrath of God from you. Now two things were at large pressed upon you in the morning, as well befitting the work of this day. The one was to *rent*, and *break*, and *teare* every one of your *hearts* in the *seame* of your *sins*, kindly and throughly to humble you in the sight of God. The other was to provoke you to a *strong resolution* to leave the waies of sin in time to come.

In which two things, *humilition* and *Reformation*, stands the very life of unfained repentance, and the spirituall part of a Religious Fast; without which all our abstinence and sackcloth, and bodily exercises in watching, hearing, &c. are meere abominations in the sight of God. I rejoyce that you had these things set so home in the morning, some of my work being thereby spared. But the bringing this lesson home, if God set it on to your hearts, may help to fasten the counsell given you in the morning, *as a nayle in a sure place*. I shall endeavour to further your humiliation and reformation from the meditation of the fearfulnesse and dreadfulnesse of the wrath of God.

I must therefore entreat you all, (Honourable and beloved) since you have vouchsafed to call for the labour of a poor man to help you, let mee be as free with you, as if you were so many meane people: my duty this day is to doe that which *Ieremy* did: *God* calls him in a *mourning time*, and saith, goe to the *King* and *Queen*, and say *come yee down*, sit in the dust, *humble your selves*: So I say to you, come down, forget that any of you are *Earles* or *Lords*,

Knights, or *Gentlemen,* lay for a while these thoughts aside; and give mee leave to ask you two or three Questions, and be so faithfull to your own soules as to think how you can answer them before the Lord. Are yee not children of *Belial?* (that is the very thing which you must answer in your own bosome) *that is,* are there not amongst you such as *refuse* to carry the *yoak* of *Christ?* who will not take Christ to be your Saviour as he offers himselfe to you in his Gospel? you will have him upon other termes than to make him your *King, Prophet,* and *Priest;* you would have him to deliver you from hell, but hee shall not bee your Lord, so, as for you to resigne up your selves to him, as a dutifull wife resignes up her selfe to her husband. And for your *conversations,* you will doe what is good in your own sight; if you have a minde to sweare you will sweare, you will lie, bee uncleane, dissemble, these things please you well and you will doe them. Now hear what I say, what thy outward quality or condition is I know not: but this I know, persons of your quality do not use much to be scared; men are affraid to speak any thing that may make you tremble: but you must be scared, or we shall doe no good to you. You are now called to have your hearts rent, I have that to say, might rent the very cawle of you heart, even this, oh thou miserable and wretched worme! *great is the wrath of God that is kindled against thee.* This *terrible Lyon roares* against thee, a dreadfull fire is kindled, a horrible tempest is ready to fall upon they head, showers and floods of fire and brimstone are even ready to be powred out upon thee: how are thou able *to live with everlasting burnings? how wilt thou dwell with devouring fire?* Thou that art crushed before a moth, *how can thy heart endure, or thy hands be strong in the day that God shall deale with thee?* Thou that dar'st not think of lying *one day* upon a *wrack,* that canst not endure for *two* or *three* dayes to be *wrung* with the *colick,* that art not able to beare the thoughts of lying under the tearing of a *Quartane Ague* from *Michaelmas* to *Easter;* how wilt thou bee able to stand under the fall of such a huge rock as the wrath of the Almighty God? which every moment is ready to break downe upon thee. How wilt thou doe when these rivers of fire and brimstone shall be powred out upon thee? and thou no more able to stand before them, than a few dry leaves are able to resist the hugh breaking in of many waters? Oh beloved, would you with due care apply these things to your own hearts, and present them to your souls as things present, how would they bring down the most stubborn spirit! how would they help to *break* the *hardest* of your hearts before the *Lord!*

But there are two things which keep most people from being affected with them. The first is, These things are looked upon as things *a farre off:* Now it is a rule in *Opticks,* That things farre off, though they be *marvellous great,* yet seeme *very little;* a Starre that is bigger than all the earth, seemes no bigger than a candle being many miles distant from us. So while men look at the wrath of God, as *they* did at the Prophets Vision, *the Vision that he sees is for many dayes to come, and he prophesies of the times that are farre off*: And put the evill day from them: All these threatnings are but light matters. Secondly, it fares with most men in this point, as with some men that have shrewish wives, though their businesse lie within doores, yet they have no heart to be there for feare of chiding: So though it be the most necessary work to think of these things; yet because their unquiet consciences upon the least serious meditation, are ready to gnaw and teare them, and make them sleep uncomfortably, they labour to drive off the thought of this thing as farre as they can, and will not think of Gods wrath due to sinne, from yeeres end to yeeres end. Whereas if men would bring it in *rempræsentem*, and keep their eyes open to behold it, as a thing which *unavoydably* will come upon them, how admirably would it work upon mens hearts?

. . . The maine question is to enquire what are the Tokens, the *gray haires*, the *flourishing of the Almond tree*, whereby wee may guesse at *mans going to his long home*.

I answer, Politicians, and some Divines will tell you of the fatall period of Kingdoms, that they have their youth, their strength, and after a time their declination; and shew by abundance of experience, that States seldome continue above five or six hundred years without some fatall change: But we must goe by a surer rule than this. It is not length of time, which makes God weary of shewing mercy; but, what *Solomon* saith of Kings, *for the transgressions of a land many are the Princes thereof*: so for the transgressions of a land, and the transgressions *only*, many are the ruines thereof. Now there is one rule which God hath always proceeded by in the dissolution of Churches and Kingdoms ever since the beginning of the world, and that is this. That whensoever the sins of any *Church, Nation, City, Family,* or *Person* (you may take it as large or as narrow as you will) are come to a full measure, then God infallibly brings ruine upon them. This is the rule which I shall make plaine to you: God hath set severall vessels to limit the sins of all Nations, beyond which they shall not goe; as once God said to the waves of the Sea, *hitherto thou shalt goe, but here thy proud waves shall be staied*: so God hath said of the sinnes of Nations, Families, Persons: thus farre I will forbeare thee, but farther thy wickednesse shall not exceed; then comes thy end. . . .

Now if by the way you desire to know why God defers so long, and rather cuts not off wicked men sooner. I answer, it should suffice us, that it is his *will* to do it; but further he doth it, partly that they may be for *exercise* to his people to *purge* and *humble them*, as *Ashur* was his rod to whip his people, before the rod was burnt. And partly to declare his long-suffering, and patience, thereby to leave them without excuse if they prove incorrigible. Thirdly, this is for salvation to some, who in the meane time are to be gathered in: and this I take it, the Apostle meanes, 2 *Pet.* 3.9. when he saith, the Lord defers his comming to judgement, because the Nation of the Jews is first to be gathered in. So that as the Angel staid till *Lot* was plucked out of *Sodom*: so God hath some brands to snatch out of the fire, for whose sakes he defers the execution of vengeance against them, whose sins call for it. For these causes, and it may be others not known to us, but secret to himselfe, doth God deferre the full execution of his wrath till sinne be ripe.

But how may wee judge when the sins of a people grow to the full? I answer (and but briefly, because I would not be burthensome to an attentive auditory; the spirit is willing, but the flesh is weak in the best;) to finde out sinnes fulnesse foure things must come into consideration. First, what kindes of sinnes they are which are land-destroying sinnes. Secondly, the *quantity* of these sinnes. Thirdly, the *aggravation* of them. Fourthly, which is the upshot of all, the *incorrigiblenesse* of them.

First, the kinds of them, I meane thus, there was never any Church or Nation without sin, but all sinnes are not Church-wasting sins, nor Land destroying sins: but there are sinnes which are called *abominations*, such as make *a land spue out the Inhabitants: such as make God drive them out*: And they are some against the first table, some against the second table. Against the first table, First, the sinne of *Idolatry*. Evermore, as Idolls come in, God goes out: when there was an *Image of jealousie set up*, *God goes farre from his sanctuary*. God likes no such neighbours. When *Ephraim offended in Baal*, *he dies for it*: when *the meane man bowes himself*, *and the great man humbles himself* to stocks and stones, God will spare them no longer. When the glory due to Jehovah, is communicated to dumb Idolls, this God will beare at no peoples hand. And the reason is plaine, this is as the *marriage bed* to God, this provokes his jealousie, *which is his rage*, then *he will accept of no ransome*: This therefore is the *abomination that makes all desolation*. . . .

THOMAS FULLER

Of all the attractive figures of seventeenth-century letters, none is more genial or more versatile in his contributions than Thomas Fuller.[1] Perhaps no one else so uncontroversial succeeded in being so interesting, or so unmalicious in being so witty. He was a natural profuse writer, and yet a writer's writer. For any understanding of the times he lived in, and those immediately antecedent, his *Worthies of England* is essential reading, and his other works are valuable, especially his reply, *The Appeal of Injured Innocence*, to Peter Heylin's bitter attack in *Examen Historicum* on his *Church History of Britain*.

Fuller's prose is so lucid and instantly engaging that it states everything about itself that need be said of it. All his sermons and his private endeavours during the Civil War were directed to conciliation. A staunch, but never bigoted, royalist, he was forced to leave London for his allegiance, only to come under the hostile suspicion of the ultra-Cavaliers at Oxford, for being too moderate.

No more need be said of 'Blessed are the Peacemakers' than that it was preached at the end of the first year of war, when all the moderating voices of restraint and reason, Chillingworth's and Falkland's and

1. Thomas Fuller, 1608–1661. Born at Aldwicke in Northamptonshire. Queens' College, Cambridge, 1621. B.A. 1625; M.A., 1628. Transferred to Corpus Christi College, from which he received the curacy of St. Benet's; later obtained the prebend of Netherbury. B.D. 1635. After 1640 he settled in London and became lecturer in the Chapel of St. Mary Savoy. His loyalty to the King being offensive to the Puritan zealots, he retired to Oxford and left Oxford in trouble with the extreme Cavaliers to retire to Exeter in 1644. In 1645 he returned to London after the fall of Exeter. When Charles I was executed Fuller preached, at considerable risk to himself, the sermon 'The Just Man's Funeral'. Hard times of the Protectorate were relieved by many loyal friends; the Earl of Carlisle appointed him perpetual curate of Waltham; 1655–1656, lecturer of St. Clements and St. Bride's. In 1655, he passed successfully through examination by triers. In 1660 he published an appeal for a free parliament, by 'a lover of his country'. He may have accompanied Berkely to the Hague and was appointed chaplain to Charles II. Died August 16th, 1661, in Covent Garden, of an infectious fever, probably typhus. Works include: *History of the Holy Warre* (1639); *Joseph's Parti-Coloured Coat* (1640); *Good Thoughts in Bad Times* (1649); *Church History of Britain* (1655); *Worthies of England* (1662).

Life and bibliography by J. E. Baily (1874) and *Life* by Rev. Morris Fuller (2 vols., 1884).

Fuller's among them, were raised in vain in the cause of restraint while there was still time.

Blessed are the Peacemakers

A sermon preached on Innocents Day, 28th December, 1642, at the Savoy Chapel, London.

... We use to end our Sermons with a Blessing; Christ begins his with the Beatitudes; and of the eight my Text is neither the last nor the least: *Blessed are the Peacemakers.*

Observe in the words the best worke and the best wages: the best worke, *Peace-makers*; the best wages, *They are blessed.*

I begin with the worke, which shall imploy my paines and your attention this day. Now the goodnesse of peace will the better appeare if we consider the misery of warre. It is said, Gen. 12. 11, *And it came to passe when* Abraham *was come neere to enter into* Egypt, *that hee said unto* Sarai *his wife, Behold, now I know that thou art a faire woman to looke upon.* Why Now *I know thou art a beautifull woman?* Did *Abraham* live thus long in ignorance of his wives beauty? Did he now first begin to know her handsomnesse? Learned *Tremelius* on the place starts and answers the objection:[1] *Now*, that is, when *Abraham* came into Egypt; as if he had said, When I see the tawny faces and swarthy complexions of the sun-burnt Egyptians, thy face seemeth the fairer, and thy beauty the brighter in mine eyes. I must confesse, I ever prized Peace for a pearle; but we never did or could set the true estimate and value upon it till this interruption and suspension of it. *Now* we know, being taught by deare experience, that peace is a beautifull blessing: And therefore we will consider warre, first, in the wickednesse, then in the wofulnesse thereof.

First, warre makes a Nation more wicked. Surely, swearing and Sabbath-breaking do not advance the keeping of the first Table. And as for the second Table, how hard is it in these distracted times to be practised! Yea, it is difficult to say the Lords Prayer, the Creed, or ten Commandements: The Lords Prayer for that Petitition, *And forgive us our trespasses, as wee forgive them that trespasse against us; the* Creed for that Article, *The Communion of Saints,* which doth tye and oblige us to the performance of all Christian offices and charitable duties to those who by the same Christ seeke salvation, and professe

1. *Tremellii et Juni Test. Veteris Bib.* (edn. 1607), p. 16.

the same true Christian Catholike faith with us; the ten Commandements for that precept, *Thou shalt not kill:* and though men in speculation and schoole distinctions may say that all these may be easily performed in the time of war; yet our corrupt nature, which is starke nought in time of peace, is likely to be far worse in warre; and if these times continue, I am afraid wee shall neither say the Lords Prayer, nor beleeve the Creed, nor practise the Commandements. And as hard it will be preparedly and profitably to receive the Sacraments, when wee shall drinke success of it.

Objection: But may some say, though we doe never so much desire peace, we shall not obtaine that blessing, which is pronounced in my text, for the Peace-makers are to be blessed. And it is to be feared, that our breaches are too wide to be cured, and Gods justice must have reparation upon us.

Answer: By Peace-makers, Peace-endeavourers are to be understood; not only the Effectours of Peace, but even the Affectours of Peace shal be blessed. *Rom.* 12. 18: *If it be possible, as much as in you lyeth, live peaceably with all men.* God out of his goodnesse measures mens reward not by their successe, but desires: 2 *Cor.* 8. 12, *For if there be first a willing minde, it is accepted according to that a man hath, and not according to that he hath not.*

And yet I am not out of heart, but that there is hope of Peace, and that as yet our sinnes are not swel'd so high, but that there is mercy with God for our nation. First, my hope is founded on the multitude of good people in this land, which assault and batter Heaven with the importunity of their prayers. We read of *Ptolomeus Philadelphus,* King of *Egipt,*[1] that he caused the Bible to be translated by seventy Interpreters; which seventy were severally disposed of in seventy severall Cels, unknown each to other; and yet they did so well agree in their several translations that there was no considerable difference betwixt them in rendering the text; an argument that they were acted with one and the same spirit. Surely it comforts me when I call to minde, what shall I say? seventy? nay seven times seventy, yea, seventy hundred, yea, seventy thousand, which are peaceable in Israel, which on the bended knees of their souls daily pray to God for peace. These though they know not the faces, no, not the names one of another; nay, have neither seen nor shall see one another till they meet together in happinesse in Heaven; yet they unite their votes and centre their suffrages, in the same thing, that God would restore Peace unto us, who no doubt in his due time will heare their prayers.

Come we now to consider what be the hindrances of Peace. These hindrances are either generall or particular. The generall hindrance is this: The many nationall sinnes of our kingdome being not repented of. I say, of our kingdome, not of one Army alone. Thinke not that the Kings Army is like *Sodome,* not ten righteous men in it; (no, not if righteous *Lot* himselfe be put into the number;) and the other Army like *Syon* consisting all of Saints. No;

1. See John Spencer *Things New and Old* (1658), p. 109.

there be drunkards on both sides, and swearers on both sides, and whore-mungers on both sides; pious on both sides, and prophane on both sides: like *Jeremies* figges, those that are good are very good, and those that are bad are very bad in both parties. I never knew nor heard of an Army all of Saints, *save the holy Army of Martyrs;* and those, you know, were dead first; for the last breath they sent forth proclaimed them to be Martyrs. But it is not the sinnes of the Armies alone, but the sinnes of the whole kingdome which breake off our hopes of Peace: our Nation is generally sinfull. The City complaines of the ambition and prodigality of the Courtiers; the Courtiers complaine of the pride and covetousnesse of the Citizens: the Laity complaine of the lazinesse and state-medling of the Clergie; the Clergie complaine of the hard dealing and sacriledge of the Laity: the Rich complaine of the murmuring and ingratitude of the Poor; the Poor complaine of the oppression and extortion of the Rich. Thus every one is more ready to throw durt in anothers face then to washe his owne cleane. And in all these, though malice may set the varnish, sure truth doth lay the ground-worke.

Of particular hindrances, in the first place we may ranke the Romish Recusants. *Is not the hand of* Joab *with thee in all this?* was *Davids* question, 2 *Sam.* 14. 19; but is not the hand, may we all say, of *Jesvites* in these distractions? *Many times from my youth up have they fought against me, may* England *now say; yea, many times from my youth up have they vexed me, but have not prevailed against me.* At last, the Popish party perceived that the strength of *England* consisted in the unity thereof; (*Sampson* is halfe conquered when it is knowne where his strength doth lye;) and that it was impossible to conquer *English* Protestants, but by *English* Protestants. Is this your spite and malice, O you *Romish* adversaries, because you could not overcome us with *Spanish* Armadoes, nor blowe us up with Gunpowder Treasons, nor undoe us with *Irish* Rebellions, to set our selves against our selves, first to divide us, then to destroy us? Well God knowes what may come to passe. It may be when we have drunke the top of this bitter cup, the dregs may be for your share; and we may all be made friends for your utter ruine and destruction.

It hath been a great curse of God upon us, to make a constant misunderstanding betwixt our King and his Parliament; whilest both professe to levell at the same end. I cannot compare their case better than to the example of *Ruben* and *Judah, Gen.* 37. There *Ruben* desired and endeavoured to preserve the life of his brother *Joseph,* and *Judah* desired and endeavoured to preserve the life of his brother *Joseph*; and yet these two imbracing different meanes, did not onely crosse and thwart, but even ruine and destroy the desires of each other; for *Ruben* moved and obtained that *Joseph* might not be killed, *verse* 22; *And* Ruben *said unto them, shed no blood, but cast him into this Pit that is in the wildernesse, and lay no hand upon him; that he might rid him out of their hands, to deliver him to his Father againe.* Judah also desired the same; but being not privie to *Rubens* intents, and to avoid the cruelty of the rest of his Brethren, propounded and effected that *Joseph* might be sold to the *Medianitish* Merchants, meerly so to preserve his life; and thereby he did unravell all the web of *Rubens* designes, and frustrated his endeavours. Thus when God will have a people punished for their sinnes, hee will not onely suffer, but cause mistakes without mending, and misprisions without rectifying, to happen betwixt brethren who meane and really intend the same thing; so that they speake the same matter in effect, and yet be Barbarians one to another, as either not or not right understanding what they say each to other. Thus, the maintaining of the Protestant Religion in the purity thereof; the vindicating of the lawfull Prerogative of the King; the ascertaining of the just rights and priviledges of the Parliament; the defending of the dues and properties of the Subject are pleaded and pretended on both sides as the ultimate ends they aime at. Well, as our Saviour said to the blinde man, *Mat.* 9. 29, *according to your faith be it unto you:* so, according to the sincerity and integrity of their hearts, whom God knowes means most seriously, be it unto them; *we wish them good victory in the name of the Lord:* and yet even herein a friendly peace were as much better then victory it selfe as the end is better then the means; for, *blesed are the Peace-makers.*

The second thing that comforts mee is, when I looke on Gods proceedings hitherto in our Kingdome, his judgements seeme to be judgements rather of expostulation then of exterpation: we read, *Exod.* 4. 24, that God being angry with *Moses* for not circumcising his Sonnes, *It came to passe by the way in the Inne that the Lord met him, and sought to kill him.* Sought to kill him? strange: did God seeke to kill him, and not kill him? Speake, Lord, speake to the Fire, and it shall with flashes consume him; to the Ayre, and with pestilent vapours it shall choake him; to the Water, and with deluges it shall overwhelme him; to the Earth, and with yawning chops it shall devoure him. Well, the meaning is this; God sought to kill him, that is, in some outward visible manner whereof *Moses* was apprehensive; God manifested his displeasure against him, that so *Moses* might both have notice and leisure to divert his anger, with removing the cause thereof. He that saith to us, *Seeke and yee shall finde*, doth himselfe seeke and not finde; and good reason too, for he fought with an intent not to finde. Thus I may say that for these last foure yeeres God hath still *sought* to destroy the Kingdome of *England;* manifesting an unwillingnesse to doe it, if in any reasonable time we would compound with him by serious repentance. Thus the loving Father shakes the rod over his wanton childe, not with an intent to beat him, but to make him begge pardon; and such hitherto hath beene Gode dealing with our Nation, that he even courts and woes us to repentance, as loath to punish us, if wee would understand the signes of his anger, before it breake out upon us.

But if all faile, yet those that are Peace-makers in their desires doe enter a caveat in the Court of heaven, That if warres doe ensue, yet for their part they have laboured against it. If a man slaine were found in the field, and it not knowne who slew him, God provided, *Deut.* 21. 7, 8, That the Elders of the next City should wash their hands in the blood of an Heifer, and say, *Our hands have not shed this blood, neither have our eyes seen it. Be mercifull, O Lord, unto thy people Israell, whom thou hast redeemed, and lay not innocent blood unto thy people of Israels charge; and the blood shalbe forgiven them.* So this one day will be a comfort to the consciences of godly minded men, that they may appeale to the God of heaven, how they have prayed heartily for peace, have petitioned humbly for Peace, have been contented to pay deerly for peace, and to their powers have endevoured to refraine themselves from sinnes, the breakers of peace; and therefore they trust that Christian *English* Protestant blood, which shall be shed, which hath beene and hereafter may be shed in these wofull warres, shall never be visited on their score or laid to their charge.

But if all faile, and if we must be involved in a finall desolation, then let us goe to the *Assurance Office* of our soules, and have peace of conscience with God in our Saviour. It was wont to be said *A mans house is his Castle;* but if this Castle of late hath proved unable to secure any, let them make their conscience their castle; if beaten from all our parapets and outworkes, let us retire to this strength for our defence. It may seem, be it spoken with all reverence, a blunt expression of the holy spirit, *Luke* 12. 4, *Be not afraid of them that kill the body, and that have no more that they can doe.* Yea, but one may say, they may kil me with torment and with torture, make me drop out my life by degrees; why, the totall some of their malice is but to kill the body, *and then they have no more that they can doe.* But they may forbid my body Christian buriall; herein they do not do but suffer, for the living will be more troubled then the dead, if thy corps be not committed to earth; so that this in effect is just nothing. Then let Drums beat, and Trumpets sound, and Banners be displaid; let swords clash, and pikes push, and bullets flye, and Cannons roare; warre, doe thy worst; Death, doe thy worst; Devill, doe thy worst; their souls shal be happy that sleep in the Lord, for they rest from their labours. However, if it be possible, and if so great mercy be stored up in God for us, we would rather have peace in this world; and on the promoters thereof let the blessing in the light and rest, *Blessed are the Peacemakers.*

A Sermon of Reformation

preached at the Savoy Chapel on Wednesday,
July 27th, 1643

... A Moderne Author[1] tels us a strange story, how the servants of Duke *D'Alva*, seeking for a Hawke they had lost, found a new country in the Navell of *Spaine*, not known before, invironed with Mountaines, and peopled with naked Savages. I should wonder if such a *Terra incognita* could be found in *England*, which (what betwixt the covetousnesse of Land-lords and the carefullnesse of Tenants) is almost measured to an Acre. But if such a place were discovered, I must allow that the Preachers there were the first planters of the Gospel, which in all other places of the kingdom are but the Continuers thereof. I hope Christ hath reaped much goodnesse long ago, where these, now, new pretend to plant it. And if *England* hath not had a true Church hitherto, I feare it will not have a true Church hereafter.

The second thing I commend unto you is this, That a perfect Reformation of any Church in this world may be desired, but not hoped for. Let *Zeno-phons Cyrus* be King in *Plato's* Common-wealth, and Batchelors wives breed maides children in *Mores Vtopia*, whilest Roses grow in their Gardens without prickles, as Saint *Basil*[2] held they did before the fall of *Adam*. These phansies are pleasing and plausible, but the performance thereof unfeisable; and so is the perfect reformation of a Church in this world difficult to bee described, and impossible to be practised. For besides that Sathan will doe his best, or rather his worst to undoe it, Man in this life is not capable of such perfection. Look not to finde that in man out of Paradise, which was not found in man in Paradise, continuance in an holy estate. *Martin Luther* was wont to say, he never knew good order in the Church last above fifteen yeares in the purity thereof; yea, the more perfect the Reformation is, the lesse time it is likely to last. Mans minde being in constant motion, when it cannot ascend higher, will not stand still, but it must decline. I speake not this to dishearten men from endeavouring a perfect Reformation, but to keep them from being dis-heartened, when they see the same cannot be exactly observed.

And yet there are some now adayes that talke of a *great light*, manifested in this age more then ever before. Indeed we Modernes have a mighty

1. James Howell, *Instructions for Forreine Travell* (1642).
2. *Homily V*. 'De Germiatione Terrae'.

advantage of the Ancients: whatsoever was theirs, by Industry may be ours. The Christian Philosophy of *Justin Martyr*; the constant Sanctity of *Cyprian;* the Catholick faith of *Athanasius;* the Orthodox judgement of *Nazianzen;* the manifold Learning of *Jerome;* the solid Comments of *Chrysostome;* the subtill Controversies of *Augustine;* the excellent Morals of *Gregory;* the humble Devotions of *Bernard:* All contribute themselves to the edification of us, who live in this later Age. But as for any transcendent extraordinary miraculous light, peculiarly conferred on our Times, the worst I wish the opinion is this, that it were true. Sure I am that this light must not crosse the Scripture, but cleere the Scripture. So that if it affirmeth any thing contrary to Gods written Word, or enforceth any thing (as necessary to salvation) not exprest in Gods Word, I dare boldly say, That such a light is kindled from Hell. As for the opinion of Christs corporall visible Kingdome, to come within few yeares, I will neither peremptorily reject it, nor dare absolutely receive it. Not reject it, lest I come within the compasse of the Apostles re-proofe, 2 *Peter* 2. 12, *Speaking evill of the things they understand not.* Confessing my selfe not to know the reasons of their opinions, who though citing for it much Canonicall Scripture, yet their interpretations thereof may be but Apocrypha. Nor dare we receive it, not being safe to be familiar with strangers at the first sight; and this Tenent is strange, as set commonly afoot with these few last yeares. I am afraid rather on the contrary of a general defection. Seeing the word is so slighted, and the guests begin to play with their meat, I feare lest God the Master of the feast will call for the *Voyder:*[1] that so when Christ comes to judgement, he shall *finde no faith on the earth.* But of things to come, *little* and *doubtfully.* If this opinion of Christs corporall comming very shortly be true, I hope if we live we shall have our share therein: if otherwise, *Moses* hath no cause to complaine if dying he commeth not into the Earthly *Canaan*, but into the Heavenly.

Meane time whilest we expect the personall comming of Christ, let us pray for the peaceable comming back of him, who sometimes is called Christ in the Scripture, *the Lords Annointed.* O the miserable condition of our Land at this time! God hath shewed the whole World that *England* hath enough in it selfe to make it selfe happy or unhappy, as it useth or abuseth it. Her homebred wares enough to maintain her, and her homebred warres enough to destroy her, though no forreigne Nation contribute to her Overthrow. Well, whilest others fight for Peace, let us pray for Peace; for Peace on good termes, yea, on Gods termes, and in Gods time, when he shall be pleased to give it, and we fitted to receive it. Let us with both King and Parliament so well as to wish neither of them better, but both of them best. Even a happy Accommodation.

1. Vessel into which fragments of food and used dishes were swept after the repast.

By 1643 the satires had broadened, for the bathos of the originals
was now almost beyond parody.

Some small and Simple Reasons

Delivered in a Hollow Tree in *Waltham* Forrest, in a
Lecture, on the 33. of *March* last.[1]

My Dear-beloved, and Zealous Brethren and Sisters here Assembled in this
holy Congregation, I am to unfold, unravell, untwist, unty, unloose, and
undoe to your uncapable understandings, some small Reasons, the Matter,
the Causes, the Motives, the Grounds, the Principles, the Maxims, the whyes
and the wherefores, wherefore and why, we reject, omit, abandon, contemne,
despise, and are and ought to be withstanders and opposers of the Service-
book, (called by the hard name of *Liturgy*) or Common-prayer, which hath
continued in the Church of *England* 84. yeares.

I have exactly examined and collected some Notes and observations out of
the Learned Hebrew translated volumes of Rabby *Ananias*, Rabby *Achitophel*,
Rabby *Iscariot*, Rabby *Simon Magus*, Rabby *Demas*, and Rabby *Alexander* the
Coppersmith, and all nor any of their writings doth in any place so much as
mention that Book, or any such kind of Service to be used all by them; I
have farther taken paines in looking over some *Caldean*, *Persian*, *Egyptian*,
Arabian, and *Arminian* Authors (of which I understood not one word) I also
(with the like diligence and understanding have viewed the Turkish *Alacron*,
and there I found not any syllable concerning either *Liturgie*, Common-
prayer or Divine Service. As for Greek Authors I must confesse I understand
them not (or negatively) for which Reason I leave them, as impertinnet, and
touching the Latine Writers, they are partiall in this case, the tongue being
Romanian, and the Idiome is *Babilonish*, which seems to me an Intricate
confusion.

I having carefully veiwed the Tomes and Tenets of Religion, and books of
all manner of Hierogliphicks, writings, Scrolles, Tallies, Scores and Characters, and finding nothing for the maintaining of that Booke or *Liturgie*, I
lookt into the Ecclesiasticall History, written by one *Eusibius*, and another
fellow they call *Socrates*, wherein I found many Arguments and Incitements

1. 1643.

to move men to such doctrine as is comprised and compiled in the *Liturgie*. After that I searched into the *Acts* and *Monuments* of this Kingdome, written by old *Foss* and there I found that the Composers of it were Bishops and Doctors, and great learned Schollers men of unfained Integrity, of Impregnable Constancy, who with invincible Faith suffered most Glorious Martyrdome by the Papall Tyranny, for the writing and maintaining that Book, with the true Protestant Religion contained in it.

Brethren, I must confesse that I was somewhat puzzled in my mind at these things, and I could not be satisfied till I had consulted with some of our devout Brothers our brother *How* the Cobler was the first I brake my mind to and we advised to call or summon a *Synod* to be held in my Lord *Brooks* Stable (the Reverend *Spencer*[1] the stable Groome being the Metropolitan there). At our meeting there was *Greene* the Felt-maker, *Barebones* the Leatherseller, *Squire* the Taylor, with *Hoare* a Weaver, & *Davison* a Bonelacemaker of *Messenden*, & *Paul Hickson* of *Wickham* Taylor with some foure or five Bakers dozzens of Weavers, Millers, Tinkers, Botchers, Broomemen Porters, of all Trades, many of them bringing notes with them fitting for our purpose, which notes they had taken carefully from the instructions of the demi-martyrs and round and Sound Confessors, St. *B*. St. *P*. and St. *B*. out of which (with our owne Capacities and ingenuities to boot) we have collected and gathered, these sound and infallible objections against the Book of Common-Prayer, or *Liturgie*, as followeth.

For our owne parts (my Brethren) it is for the Reputation and Honour of our Holy Cause and Calling to contest, maligne and cavill, where we are not able either to convince by Reasons or Arguments; therefore I having trac'd the Booke from end to end, and yet (upon the matter) to no end for such ends as we would conclude upon, I find nothing in it disagreeing to Gods word or agreeing with our doctrine. The first prayer called the Confession, is quite contrary to our appetites and profession, for to confesse that *Wee have erred and strayed like lost Sheep*, is to acknowledge our selves to silly horned Beasts and Cuckolds, our Children (by that reckoning should be *Lampes*, our Wives *Yewes* and we (their innocent husbands) must be *Ram(s)*[2]; and every Lay Preacher, or Preaching Treadesmen would be accounted a *Bellwheather* to the flocke or Heard.

Neither do we think it fit to make our selves appear so weak witted or Pusillanimious as to confesse that *We have left undone those things Which we ought to have done, & done those things which we ought not to have done.* . . .

---

1. Two of the more conspicuous itinerant lay-preachers of the time. John Spencer, a 'horse-rubber', was the author of *A Short treatise concerning the lawfulness of every man's exercising his gifts* (1641).

2. A pun on the name of Robert Ram, zealous Cromwellian preacher and author of *The Soldiers Catechism* (1643). See below, p. 520*n*.

WILLIAM CHILLINGWORTH

The brightest, as Hales was the loftiest, star of the Falkland constellation at Great Tew was William Chillingworth.[1] His major work, *The Religion of Protestants as a Safe Way to Salvation*, written in answer to a number of Roman Catholic controversialists, in which he proposed that reason and tolerance, as well as scripture, were concomitants of Christianity, made him even more hated by the Puritans than he was by the Papists. At the outbreak of hostilities in 1642, he joined the king's party without enthusiasm or illusions for what he saw as a battle of the 'scribes and pharisees' against the 'publicans and sinners'. He was noted for the sharpness of his mind and the equanimity of his temper, which no degree of provocation seemed able to disturb,[2] while the urbane tone in which his own caustic observations were delivered drove his wilder adversaries into frenzies of rage. When the popular doctrine of the 'renunciation of righteousness' and the facile emotionalism it encouraged was at its height, Chillingworth observed that 'this doctrine of renouncing their own righteousness has been generally found to be most agreeable to those who have no righteousness to renounce'.

1. William Chillingworth 1602–1644. Born at Oxford; godson of Laud; Trinity College, B.A. 1620. Briefly converted to Roman Catholicism, visited Douai; renounced the Church of Rome and returned to the Anglican Church through exertions of Laud and his own analysis of his position. He wrote little beside his *magnum opus*, a few sermons and Additional Discourses (published in 1687), but his influence, his concept of free enquiry, and tolerance, as a necessary part of Christianity, was great during, and even greater after, his short lifetime.

2. 'A man of so great subtlety of understanding, and so rare a temper in debate, that it was impossible to provoke him to any passyon, so it was very difficult to keep oneself from being a little discomposed by his sharpnesse and quicknesse of argument and insistences, in which he had a great faculty and a great advantage over all men I ever knew.' Hyde, *Characters and Episodes of the Great Rebellion*, ed. G. D. Boyle (Oxford 1889), p. 307.

Blind Zeal and Deserved Confusion

A Sermon preached before His Majesty, King Charles 1
at Christchurch, Oxford, 1644.

Where almost are the men that are or will be perswaded the Gospell of Christ requires of men *Humilitie*, like to that of *little Children*, and that under the highest paine of damnation? That is, that we should no more over-value our selves, or desire to be highly esteemed by others, no more under-value, scorn, or despise others, no more affect pre-eminence over others, then little children doe, before we have put that pride into them, which afterwards we charge wholy upon their naturall corruption: and yet our blessed Saviour requires nothing more Rigidly, nor more plainly then this high degree of humility; *verily, saith he, I say unto you*, he speakes to his disciples affecting high places, and demanding which of them should be greatest, *except ye be converted and become as little Children, ye shall not enter into the Kingdome of Heaven.*

Would it not be strange newes to a great many, that not onely *adultery* and *fornication*, but even *uncleanenesse* and *lasciviousnesse*; not onely *idolatry*, and *witchcraft*, but *hatred, variance, emulations, wrath*, and *contentions*; not onely *murthers*, but *envying*: not *drunkennesse* only, but *revelling*, are things prohibited to Christians, and such as if we forsake them not, we cannot inherit the Kingdome of Heaven? and yet these things, as strange as they may seeme, are plainely written; some of them by S. *Peter*, 1 *Epist.* 4. *chap.* But all of them by S. *Paul, Gal.* 5, 15. Now the workes of the flesh are manifest, which are these; *adultery, fornication, uncleanenesse, lasciviousnesse, &c. of the which I tell you before, as I have told you in timespast, that they who doe such things shall not inherit the Kingdome of God.*

If I should tell you that al *bitternesse* and *evill speaking* (nay such is the modesty and gravity which Christianity requires of us) *foolish talke and jesting* are things not allowed to Christians, would not many cry out these are hard and strange sayings, who can heare them? and yet as strange as they may seeme, they have beene written well nigh 1600 yeares, and are yet extant in very legible Characters in the Epistle to the *Eph.* the end of the 4. and the beginning of the 5 chap.

To come a little nearer to the businesse of our times, the chiefe Actors in this bloudy Tragedy, which is now upon the Stage, who have robb'd our

Soveraign Lord the King of his Forts, Townes, Treasure, Ammunition, Houses, of the Persons of many of his Subjects, and (as much as lyes in them) of the hearts of all of them: Is it credible that they know and remember and consider the example of *David* recorded for their instruction, *Whose heart smote him when he had but cut off the hemme of Sauls garment*?

They that make no scruple at all of fighting with His Sacred Majesty, and shooting Musquets and Ordnance at Him (which sure have not the skill, to choose a Subject from a King) to the extreame hazard of his Sacred Person, whom by all possible obligations they are bound to defend, do they know (think you) the generall rule without exception or limitation left by the Holy Ghost for our direction in all such cases, *Who can lift up his hand against the Lords Anoynted, and be innocent?* or doe they consider his Command in the *Proverbs of Solomon, My sonne feare God and the King, and meddle not with them that desire change?* Or his councell in the Booke of *Ecclesiastes, I councell thee to keepe the Kings Commandement, and that in regard of the Oath of God?* or because they possibly may pretend that they are exempted from, or unconcerned in the commands of obedience delivered in the Old Testament, doe they know and remember the precept given to all Christians by S. *Peter, Submit your selves to every Ordinance of man, for the Lords sake, whether it be to the King as Supreame, or unto Governors, as unto them that are sent by him?* or that terrible sanction of the same command, *They that resist shall receive to themselves damnation,* left us by St. *Paul* in his Epistle to the *Romans,* who then were the miserable Subjects of the worst King, the worst man, nay, I think I may adde truly, the worst beast in the world, that so all rebells mouths might be stopt for ever, and left without all colour or pretence whatsoever to justifie resistance of Soveraign power. Undoubtedly if they did know and consider and lay close to their hearts, these places of Scripture, or the fearefull judgement which befell *Corah, Dathan,* and *Abiram,* for this very sinne which now they commit and with a high hand still proceed in, it would be impossible but their hearts should smite them, as *Davids* did, upon an infinitely lesse occasion, and affright them out of those wayes of present confusion, and eternall damnation. And then on the other side they that maintain the Kings righteous cause with the hazard of their lives and fortunes; but by their oathes and curses, by their drunkennesse, and debauchery, by their irreligion and prophannesse, fight more powerfully against their partie, then by all other meanes they doe or can fight for it,[1] are not I feare very well acquainted with any part of the Bible; but that strict caution which properly concerns themselves in the booke of *Deut.* 23.9. I much doubt they have scarce ever heard of it, *When thou goest to Wars With thine Enemies, then take heed there be no wicked thing in thee,* not only no wickednesse in the cause thou maintainest, nor no wickednesse in the means by which

1. Cf. Jeremy Taylor, below, p. 505.

thou maintainest it, but no personall impieties in the persons that maintaine it. Beloved for the former two, we have reason to be full of comfort and confidence; For what is our cause? What is that which you fight, and we pray for? but to deliver the King and all his good Subjects out of the power of their Enemies, who will have no peace, but with their slaves and vassalls? and for the meanes by which it is maintained, it is not by lying, it is not by calumnies, it is not by running first our selves, and then forceing the people to universall perjury; but by a just war, because necessary, and by as faire and mercifull a Warre as if they were not Rebells and Traitors you fight against, but Competitors in a doubtfull Title. But now for the third part of the caution, that, to deale ingenuously with you, and to deliver my owne soule, If I cannot other mens, that I cannot think of with halfe so much comfort as the former; but seeing so many *Ionasses* imbarqued in the same ship, the same cause with us, and so many *Achan's* entering into Battel with us against the *Canaanites*, seeing Publicans and sinners on the one side, against Scribes and Pharisees on the other; on the one side Hypocrisy, on the other prophannesse, no honesty nor justice on the one side, and very little piety on the other; On the one side horrible oathes, curses, and blasphemies; On the other pestillent yes, calumnies, and perjury: When I see amongst them the pretence of reformation, if not the desire, pursued by Antichristian, Mahumetan, devillish meanes; and amongst us little or no zeale for reformation of what is indeed amisse, little or no care to remove the cause of Gods anger towards us, by just, lawfull, and Christian meanes; I professe plainly I cannot without trembling consider what is likely to be the event of these distractions; I cannot but feare that the goodnesse of our cause may sinke under the burthen of our sinns: And that God in his justice, because we will not suffer his Judgements to achieve their prime scope and intention, which is our amendment and reformation, may either deliver us up to the blind zeale and fury of our Enemies; or else, which I rather feare, make us instruments of his justice each against other, and of our owne just and deserved confusion. . . .

WILLIAM LAUD

During the first two years of civil war, the primate of the Church of England (till lately, with Strafford, one of the two most powerful men in the land) lay a prisoner in the Tower. For some time attention was diverted from his case by the pressure of dramatic novelities. But when the war did not end with a quick, conclusive victory for either side, different psychological needs began to assert themselves; above all the need to keep the people of the capital, whence most of parliament's money came, mindful of present danger and properly abhorrent of the wickedness of their enemies. They could to some extent be kept alert and aggressive by bouts of 'idol smashing'. The supply of unbroken painted windows and unmutilated statues had not yet given out, and there was from time to time a bumper outing, like the destruction, on May 2nd, of the great Cheapside Cross, once the pride of the city. But something more, human sacrifice, was required to complete a godly warlike diet. Was the arch-idolator himself, whom God had delivered into their hands, to be spared? But what to charge him with in law? It was the same problem as had impeded Strafford's case, and the same ugly, last resort was available if all else failed. All else did fail. Laud, tired and old, unaided and alone as he was, made his accusers appear jejune and clumsy. When they denounced him in the hackneyed invective of sectarian slogans, he observed: '. . . I little deserve from them the Name of This great Firebrand; for many of them have warmed themselves at me but yet I never fired any of them'.[1] There was no evidence of treason that would stand, and wherever one's sympathies, if any, lie, it seems difficult to withhold admiration for this brave, witty, indomitable little man during the last, lonely ordeal of his life. He had pressed, with more zeal than realism, the cause of what his conscience told him was a proper, lawful and wholly benevolent discipline in the form of public worship. The Puritan's conscience told *him* that the same cause was worse than oppressive and unlawful, it was idolatrous and damned. Never the twain should have met, and their meeting was fraught from first to last with relentless rancour and harsh reprisals unworthy of either party's pretensions to Christianity. If Henry, Prince of Wales, had lived to be king, it is possible that the country might have been spared bloodshed, by way of a modified

1. *History of Troubles and Trials* (1695), fol. p. 136.

episcopalianism.[1] Pym was no fanatic, and religious tolerance might have come to England two generations before it did. But the irreversible march of actual events had now made it politic to fan and exploit, instead of damp down and discourage, the harsh fanaticism of the extremists. Accordingly, not without some organization, the cry now went up for the old man's blood. In conformity to recent precedent, parliament expected to receive the cue of a godly exhortation to set in motion the ignoble performance to come; and this was duly provided. On October 22nd Edmund Calamy rebuked the House of Commons for 'all the guilty blood that God requires you to shed and you do spare'.[2] Then on October 30th Edmund Staunton, a Scotch Presbyterian, preaching before the House of Lords, extolled the virtuous conduct of Phineas, who did not wait for legal authority before he speared Zimri and the Midionite woman; he lamented Saul's culpable neglect to hew Agag in pieces.[3]

Next day saw the predictable translation of impeachment into a bill of attainder, in effect, simply the issue by parliament to itself of a licence to kill. Sentence of death was a formality, varied by the favour, grudgingly allowed, of the headsman's axe instead of the rope; and, on January 10th, 1645, the archbishop was brought to the scaffold on Tower Hill, where, before the assembled multitude, he spoke his last words. To the chagrin of his enemies he bore himself with gentle and fearless dignity and his wit gleamed even in the shadow of death. Spiteful sneers were published later that he could not 'preach', for he read his last sermon on the place of execution. Laud was one of the more accomplished extempore speakers of his time, but had he not written and read his last words, his friends could not have preserved and authenticated the evidence of what he said, and his utterance could have been travestied and falsified.

1. Mere conjecture, suggested by association. Henry was a much better social mixer than his younger brother and more sympathetic to 'advanced' thought than either Charles or their father. He cultivated the friendship of distinguished intellects, like Raleigh and Bacon, who were not favourable to the claims of what would later be called the 'High Church' party, and certainly the kind of men who would later sign or support the 'Grand Remonstrance' had placed great hopes in him. In the dark days of 1650, John Hacket, although a future bishop, ascribed England's misfortunes to the early death of James' eldest son. 'So much light was extinguished that a thick Darkness, nest to that of Hell, is upon our Land at this day. O matchless Worthy!' *Scrinia Reserata* (1693) p. 27.

2. Edmond Calamy, *England's Antidote Against the Plague of Civil War* (1644).

3. Edmund Staunton, *Phinehas' Zeal in Execution of Judgment* (1644).

The Last words of the Archbishop of Canterbury

Preached in a sermon from the scaffold on Tower
Hill, before he was he was beheaded, January 10th,
1645

Good People,

You'l pardon my old Memory, and upon so sad occasions as I am come to this place, to make use of my Papers, I dare not trust my self otherwise. This is a very uncomfortable place to Preach in, and yet I shall begin with a Text of Scripture, in the twelfth of the Hebrews,

Let us run with patience that race that is set before us, looking unto Jesus the author and finisher of our faith, who for the joy that was set before him, endured the Crosse, despising the shame, and is set downe at the right hand of the Throne of God.

I have been long in my race, and how I have looked unto Jesus the Author and finisher of my Faith, is best known to him: I am now come to the end of my race, and here I finde the Crosse, a death of shame, but the shame must be despised, or there is no coming to the right hand of God; Jesus despis'd the shame for me, and God forbid but I should despise the shame for him; I am going apace, as you see, towards the Red-sea, and my feet are upon the very brinks of it, an Argument, I hope, that God is bringing me to the Land of Promise, for that was the way by which of old he led his people; But before they came to the Sea, he instituted a Passeover for them, a Lamb it was, but it was to bee eaten with very soure Herbs, as in the Twelfth of *Exodus*.

I shall obey, and labour to digest the sowre[1] Herbs, as well as the Lamb, and I shall remember that it is the Lords Passeover; I shall not think of the Herbs, nor be angry with the hands which gathered them, but look up onely to him who instituted the one, and governeth the other: For men can have no more power over me, then that which is given them from above; I am not in love with this passage through the red Sea, for I have the weaknesse and infirmity of flesh and blood in me, and I have prayed as my Saviour taught me, and exampled me, *Vt transiret calix ista,*

That this Cup of red Wine might passe away from me, but since it is not that my will may, his will be done; and I shall most willingly drink of this

1. Variant spelling of the same word in one paragraph, or even one sentence, is not uncommon in 17th century publications.

Cup as deep as he pleases, and enter into this Sea, ay and passe through it, in the way that he shall be pleased to leade me.

And yet (Good People) it would bee remembred, That when the Servants of God, old *Israel*, were in this boistrous Sea, and *Aaron* with them, the Egyptians which persecuted them, and did in a manner drive them into that Sea, were drowned in the same waters, while they were in pursuit of them: I know my God whom I serve, is as able to deliver me from this Sea of Blood, as he was to deliver the three Children from the furnace, *Daniel* 3.

And I most humbly thank my Saviour for it, my Resolution is now, as theirs was then; their Resolution was, They would not worship the Image which the King had set up; nor shall I the Imaginations which the People are setting up, nor will I forsake the Temple, and the Truth of God, to follow the Bleating of *Jeroboams* Calves in *Dan* and in *Bethel*.

And I pray God blesse all this People, and open their eyes, that they may see the right way; for if it fall out that the blinde lead the blinde, doubtlesse they will both into the ditch: For my self, I am, (and I acknowledge it in all humility) a most grievous sinner many wayes, by thought, word and deed, and therefore I cannot doubt but that God hath mercy in store for me a poor penitent, as well as for other sinners; I have, upon this sad occasion, ransack'd every corner of my heart, and yet I thank God, I have not found any of my sins that are there, any sins now deserving death by any known Law of this Kingdom; and yet thereby I charge nothing upon my Iudges (I humbly beseech you I may rightly be understood, I charge nothing in the least degree upon my Iudges) for they are to proceed by proof, by valuable Witnesses, and in that way I or any Innocent in the world may justly be condemned: And I thank God, though the weight of the Sentence lye very heavie upon me, yet I am as quiet within, as (I thank Christ for it) I ever was in my life: And though I am not only the first Archbishop, but the first man that ever dyed in this way, yet some of my Predecessors have gone this way, though not by this meanes: for *Elfegus* was hurried away and lost his head by the *Danes*; and *Simon Sudbury* in the fury of *Wat Tyler* and his fellowes: And long before these Saint *Iohn Baptist* had his head danced off by a lewd woman; and Saint *Cyprian* Arch-Bishop of Carthage submitted his head to a persecuting sword. Many examples great and good, and they teach me patience, for I hope my cause in Heaven will looke of another dye then the colour that is put upon it here upon earth; and some comfort it is to me, not only that I goe the way of these great men in their severall Generations, but also that my charge (if I may not be partial) lookes somewhat like that against Saint *Paul* in the 25, of the *Acts*, for he was accused for the Law and the Temple, that is the Law and Religion; and like that of St. *Stephen* in the sixth of the *Acts*, for breaking the Ordinances which *Moses* gave us, which Ordinances were Law and Religion: but you'l say, doe I then compare my selfe with the integrity of Saint *Paul*, and Saint *Steven?* no, God forbid, far be it from me; I only raise a comfort to my selfe, that these great Saints and servants of God were thus laid up in their severall times; And it is very memorable that Saint *Paul*, who was one of them, and a great one, that helped on the accusation against Saint *Steven*, fell afterwards into the self same accusation himselfe, yet both of them great Saints and servants of God; Ay, but perhaps a great clamour there is, that I would have brought in Popery, I shall answer that more fully by and by; in the mean time, you know what the Pharisees said against Christ himself, in the eleventh of *Iohn*, *If we let him alone, all men will beleeve on him,* Et veniunt Romani, *and the Romanes will come and take away both our place and the Nation.* Here was a causelesse cry against Christ that the Romans would come, and see how just the Iudgement of God was, they crucified Christ for feare least the Romans should come, and his death was that that brought in the Romans upon them, God punishing them with that which they most feared: and I pray God this clamour of *veniunt Romani*, (of which I have given to my knowledge no just cause) helpe not to bring him in; for the Pope never had such a Harvest in England since the Reformation, as he hath now upon the Sects and divisions that are amongst us; in the meane time, *by honour and dishonour, by good report and evill report, as a deceiver and yet true*, am I now passing out of this world.

Some particulars also I think not amisse to speake of: and first this I shall be bold to speak of the King, our gracious Soveraigne, He hath been much traduced by some for labouring to bring in Popery, but upon my Conscience (of which I am now going to give God a present account) I know him to be as free from this Charge I thinke as any man living, and I hold him to be as sound a Protestant, according to the Religion by Law established as any man in this Kingdom, and that He will ventur His Life as farre and as freely for it; and I thinke I do or should know both His affection to Religion, and His grounds upon which that affection is built, as fully as any man in England.

The second particular is concerning this great and populous City, which God, blesse; here hath been of late a fashion taken up to gather hands, and then goe to the Honourable and great Court of the Kingdom, the Parliament, and clamour for Justice, as if that great and wise Court, (before whom the causes come which are unknowne to the many;) could not, or would not doe Justice, but at their call and appointment; a way which may endanger many an innocent man, and pluck innocent blood upon their owne heads, and perhaps upon this City also, which God forbid: and this hath been lately practiz'd against my self, God forgive the setters of this, with all my heart I begge it, but many well-meaning people are caught by it: In Saint *Steven's* case, when nothing else would serve, they stirred up the people against him, *Acts 6.* and *Herod* went just the selfe-same way, for when he had kill'd Saint *Iames*, he would not venture upon Saint *Peter* too, till he saw how the people tooke it, and were pleased with it, in the 12 of the *Act.* But take heed of having your hands full of blood, in the first of *Isaiah*; for there is a time best known to himselfe, when God among other sinnes makes inquisition for blood; and when Inquisition is on foot, the Psalmist tells us, *Psalme 9.* that God remembers, that is not all, *that God remembers and forgets not* (saith the Prophet) *the complaint of the poore*; and he tells you what poore they are in the ninth verse, the poore whose bloud is shed by such kind of meanes: Take heed of this, *It is a fearefull thing* (at any time) *to fall into the hands of the living God,* in the 12. of the *Hebrews*: but it is feareful indeed, and then especially, when he is making his Inquisition for blood, and therefore with my prayers to avert the Prophesy from the City, let me desire that this City would remember the Prophesie that is expressed, *Ieremiah* 26.15.

The third particular, is this poore Church of England, that hath flourished and been a shelter to other neighbouring Churches, when stormes have driven upon them; but alas, now it is in a storme it selfe and God knows whether, or how it shall get out; and which is worse then a storme from without, it is become like an Oak cleft to shivers with wedges made out of its own body, and that in every cleft, phophanesse and irreligion is creeping in apace; while as *Prosper* saith, Men that introduce prophaness are cloaked with a name of imaginary religion; for we have in a manner almost lost the substance, and dwell much, nay too much a great deale in Opinion; and that Church which all the Jesuites machinations in these parts of Christendome could not ruine is now fallen into a great deale of danger by her own.

The last particular (for I am not willing to be tedious, I shall hasten to goe out of this miserable world) is my selfe, and I beseech you, as many as are within hearing, observe me. I was borne and baptized in the bosome of the Church of *England*, as it stands yet established by Law, in that profession I have ever since lived, and in that profession of the Protestant Religion here established I come now to die; this is no time to dissemble with God, least of all in matter of Religion, and therefore I desire it may be remembred; I have alwayes lived in the Protestant Religion established in *England*, and in that I come now to die: What Clamors and Slanders I have endured for labouring to keep an Uniformity in the external service of God according to the Doctrine and Discipline of this Church all men knowe and I have abundantly felt: Now at last I am accused of high Treason in Parliament, a crime which my soul ever abhorred; this Treason was charged upon me to consist of two parts; an endeavour to subvert the Law of the Realm, and a like endeavour to overthrow the true Protestant Religion established by those Laws. Besides my Answers which I gave to the several Charges, I protested my innocency in both Houses. It was said, Prisoners protestations at the Barre must not be taken *de ipso*; I can bring no witnesse of my heart, and the intentions thereof, therefore I must come to my Protestation, not at the bar, but to my Protestation at this hour and instant of my death, in which (as I said before) I hope all men will be such charitable Christians as not to thinke I would die and dissemble my Religion, I doe therefore here, with that caution that I delivered before, without all prejudice in the world to my Judges, that are to proceed *secundum allegata & probata*, and so to be understood, I die in the presence of Almighty God and all his holy and blessed Angels, & I take it now on my death, That I never endeavoured the subversion of the Laws of the Realme, nor never any change of the Protestant Religion into Popish superstition: and I desire you all to remember this Protest of mine, for my innocency in these and from all manner of Treasons whatsoever.

I have beene accused likewise as an enemy to Parliaments; no, God forbid, I understood them, and the benefits that comes by them, a great deale too well to be so, but I did indeed dislike some misgovernments (as I conceived) of some few one or two Parliaments; and I did conceive humbly that I might have reason for it, for *corruptio optimi est pessima*: There is no corruption in the world so bad as that which is of the best thing in it selfe for the better the thing is in nature, the worse it is corrupted; and this being the highest and greatest Court, over which no other can have any jurisdiction in the Kingdom, if by any way a mis-government (which God forbid) should any wayes fall upon it the Subjects of this Kingdome are left without all manner of remedie, and therefore God preserve them, and blesse them, and direct them, that there may be no mis-conceit, much lesse mis-government amongst them. I will not inlarge my selfe any further, I have done, I forgive all the world, all and every of those bitter enemies, or others whatsoever they have beene which have any ways prosecuted me in this kinde and I humbly desire to be forgiven first of God, and then of every man, whether I have offended him or no, if he doe but conceive that I have; Lord, do thou forgive me, and I beg forgiveness of him, and so I heartily desire you to joyne with me in prayer.

When Laud's head fell from the block his Puritan enemies would have danced with joy, if dancing had not been sinful. But leaping was permitted.

Cause of leaping for joy: That his day is past and night is come, who darkend the Lord's day more than any day, and would have profaned it by a law. Cause to leape for joy, that we saw his head drunk in his own blood.[1]

1. E.W., *The Life and Death of Archbishop Laud* (1645), p. 40.

CHRISTOPHER LOVE

Christopher Love[1] was a fiery young man and no doubt would have
been a fiery old man if his waywardness had not been the early death
of him. He began his life of contention by quarrelling with his father
over religion and went to Oxford against his wishes. In New Inn Hall
in 1640 he was soon in trouble as a militant non-conformist and one of
the first to refuse Laud's new canons. In 1642 he was expelled. From
then on he was continuously at acrimonious variance with one side or
the other; even, as on the occasion marked by this sermon, with both
sides at once. At the beginning of 1645 the commissioners representing
both sides met at Uxbridge to investigate the possibilities of a negotia-
ted peace. On January 30th, the day before the conference opened,
Christopher Love, newly ordained, preached an angry sermon, charged
with prejudice, on the issues which were to be discussed, and denounced
all compromise with the ungodly. His indiscretion offended both
parties and he was confined to his house during the remainder of the
proceedings. He need not have worried; the conference at Uxbridge
came to nothing.

England's Distemper

A sermon preached at Uxbridge, on the
30th December 1645

What is it that causeth distempers in a Land?

I shall keep within the bounds of the Metaphor. What breeds distempers
in the body naturall, carries some resemblance to that which causeth distempers in the body Politique, as

1. Feeding on unwholesome and poysonfull food soone distempers the
body; so when poysonfull errors and opinions get within the bowels of the

1. Christopher Love, 1618–1651. Further details below, p. 474.

Church or Kingdome, it greatly distempers it. My soul is troubled to consider what an inundation of hurtfull doctrines and poysonfull errours have been preacht and spread up and down throughout our Land; what hurtfull doctrines have been preacht, intrenching upon the State by our rising (though now falling) Clergie men; who would scrue up Prerogative to the highest peg, (by which meanes they have crackt it, at least the credit of it) affirming that Kings might do what they list, that the lives, wives, liberties and estates of their subjects are to be disposed by the King according to his owne will; yea, have they not taught the people, that if the King require the life of any or all his subjects, they must lay their necks to the block, they must not defend themselves by force of Armes in any case, which hurtfull opinions have so intoxicated most of the inhabitants of this Nation, the sad events of which appeares in this; That the Parliament hath so many hollow friends and open enemies. If we look into poysonfull errors that creep into the Church, we may soone discern what hath also distempered us; Oh! the abominable errors which have been nourisht in the bowels of this Nation, touching Freewill, falling from grace, universall Redemption, the abolishing of the Morall Law, denying sorrow for sinne, or seeking pardon for it, with many more; oh this hath layen our Land under sad distempers at this day!

2. Surfeits on meat that is sweet and good, distempers the body as well as that which is poysonfull. Oh how hath the inhabitants of this Nation surfeited on the Gospell, they are even cloyed with Sermons, Sabbaths, Fasts! And what kind of nauseousnesse of spirit is in men, they relish not the Word? Their souls loath this Manna, though it be new and good, this shews what doth distemper; the Lord cure us that we dye not of our wounds.

3. Living in an infected aire breeds diseases in the naturall body. This infectious aire is a corrupt, scandalous, unpreaching, and superstitious Ministery; which is in every corner of the Land; and oh! what plague sores of blindnesse, superstition, and prophanenesse hath it bred in the people of this Nation.

4. A fourth cause that breeds distempers in the body naturall is by heats and colds; either by over-heating the blood which casts into a Feaver, or by catching of cold which breeds aches and palseyes in the body. The heats of mens spirits in some things, their coolenesse in others, hath grievously distempered our Land. How hot and violent were our Pompous Prelates and their ungodly Train, in promoting the offensive and superstitious inventions of their own brains, yet cold and carelesse in all matters that concern God, his glory, or the Churches edification? How zealous were they to have the Churches adorned, to have the walls and windowes beautified, yet never took care about the conversations of the people to have them holy? How violent were they to have all Ministers in their Canonicall Habits, Hoods, and white Surplices (as Emblems of their purity, as they made them) yet

never looking after the lives of the Clergy; whereby they grew such prophane sons of *Belial*, who like *Elies* sons made the people abhor the offring of the Lord? With what heat and bitternesse of spirit did they vex and persecute the most strict, godly and conscientious people of the Land, sharpening the edge of the Law against them, who differed only from them in circumstantials? Yet how cool were they in prosecuting of Papists, who differ from us in fundamentals? they were rather cherisht, countenanced, and kept from the stroke of the Law, then punisht by it: How exact were they in all their antick gestures, vestures, cringings, carriages, in all their outward acts of worship, yet never regarded the inward and spiritual part of Gods worship. Al which they look after, is an out-side worship, the spurious vanity of their own inventions they would tender to the people under the notion of Decency; yea, they so doated on their external and pompous manner of worship, that I may boldly say, they had rather have our garments rolled in bloud, then one spot or blemish to be cast on their Surplices; yea, that gashes should be made in our corps, then any rent in their golden Copes, and that all our houses should be battered down about our eares, and turned into an heap of stones, then that any Popish relique, superstitious monument, or idolatrous picture, should be taken from the wals or windowes of their stately Cathe-drals. Oh beloved! the heat & violence of their spirits this way, and their coolnesse in all matters which concern God, hath bred all these distempers that are among us.

When is a Land distempered?

As first, when either the head is divided from the body, or one member divided from another. A wound (saith *Hippocrates*) is nothing else but *discontinuatio partium*; when one part is divided from another, though it be the least member of the body, the whole body will be distempered; the more is our misery, this symptome is discernable in our Land at this day: Is not our King the Head, divided from his Parliament, the representative Body of this Kingdome, and is not one member divided from another: if you look into the publike affairs of State, oh what divisions are there! Is not Protestant against Protestant? Nobleman against Nobleman? Gentleman against Gentleman? Neighbour against Neighbour? Is it not with us, as Christ hath fore-told, That *Hee came not to bring Peace on earth, but rather division; The father shall be divided against the son, and the son against the father; The mother against the daughter, and the daughter against the mother?* If we look into spiritual matters, oh what difference of opinions! what opposition of judgements? what clashings, contradictions, and crossenesse of spirit is there among those that professe godlinesse? This is the first Symptome that we are distempered.

Seek truth rather then peace. Truth is the most soveraign ingredient. Promises are the guides and bounds of a Christians desires: now when God would bestow a great blessing on his Church, he promiseth peace and truth, yea, and more truth then peace, as *Isay* 48.18. *Oh that thou hadst harkned unto me, then had thy Peace been as a River, and thy Righteousnesse, as the waves of the Sea.* Marke, *Truth* is promised as the waves of the Sea, but *Peace* only as a River; this was the greatnesse of their blessing, they had more *Truth* than *Peace*, and they had such a *Peace* that did flow from *Truth*, as Rivers do from the Sea. It will never be well with us till our Spirits prefer the Truths of God before an outward Peace, and till we desire such a *Peace* that flows from *Truth*. 'Tis reported of the *Sybarites* who were a people that had an affluence and confluence of outward blessings, who sent unto the Oracle of *Apollo* to know how long their peace and prosperity should last: The Oracle returned them this Answer; So long as you prefer your Gods before your prosperity and Peace, these shall continue, but when you prefer these before your gods, you shall be destroyed. I may more truely say, so long as you prefer the truths and precious things of God before a *peace* or any thing dear to you, so long your *peace* and prosperity shall continue, but when you prefer these before the Truths of God, these will be blasted to you.

Take these Ingredients next your heart. Physick is taken fasting next the heart, not when the stomack is clogged with meats. Oh let *Peace* and *Truth* be taken next thy heart: Love a *Peace* with thy heart, be not like King *Saul* and his Courtiers, who *Though their words were smother then butter, yet war was in their hearts*: and love likewise and obey the Truth from the heart; do not in dissimulation desire either. Thus I have done with the Directions: but a word now of Application and so I shall draw to a Conclusion.

1. Is the abundance of *Peace* and *Truth* the Ingredients which God doth use, to heal a distempred Kingdome: Oh then be willing to be at any cost to buy these Ingredients, venture on any hazards, run on any difficulties, undergo any hardships, part with any thing that is pleasant or dear to you, to purchase these preservatives for our Nation.

2. Abate not one scruple of these Ingredients. There are some Statists who may think a *Peace* may give distaste to some Military men; that *Truth* would disturb Malignants, and that to be exact in matters that concern God, might beat off some of the moderate party; therefore a small pittance of *Truth* shall suffice, so much as Malignants or the Moderate Party can bear with, or swallow down; no more than will suite with every mans humour. Is not this like the practise of a foolish covetous man, of whom 'tis storied, That having bought a pair of shooes which were too short for his feet, because his shooes were not fit for his feet, he would therefore cut his Toes to make his feet fit for his shooes: They are little wiser who would clip or pare the *Truths* of God to have them suite with the humors of men. 'Twas an Heroick resolution of *Luther*; *Fiat justitia ruat cælum.* Let *Truth* have place, let this Ingredient *Truth* be applyed, no matter though it please not some palates, though it agree not with some constitutions.

3. Is *Peace* and *Truth* the Ingredients which must heal us; Oh then doate not too much on this Treaty of *Peace* (which is this day beginning) as if without all peradventure this Treaty must heal all our Distempers, Compose all our differences, remove all our burthens, and accomplish all our hopes. Alas, beloved! there is a great gulf between our Enemies and us: there are a generation of men that cannot endure such corroding corrasives, and purging Physick as God in my Text prescribes, men who are neither lovers of *Peace* nor *Truth*.

1. Not Lovers of *Peace*, but still carry blood and revenge in their hearts against us, making the well-affected of the Nation the Butt of all their malice; who do not onely hate our bodies but our soules, who in their cups drink an health to our damnation; Is it likely to have a *Peace* with such men as these? whiles they continue thus, we can as soon make fire and water to agree, yea (I had almost said) reconcile heaven and hell, as their spiritis and ours, either they must grow better or we must grow worse, before we can agree. Then secondly, not lovers of *Truth*: Will the blood-thirsty Rebels of *Ireland*? the Idolatrous Papists of *England*? the pompous Prelates? the rest of the corrupt Clergy, and the prophaner sort among the Nation, who joyn hand in hand together: Are these likely to be Patrons of *Truth*? Deceive not your selves, there is little likelihood of a *Peace* with such: what I said before I say again, Either they must grow better or we must wax worse, before we can agree. Although I do disswade you not to doate upon this Treaty; yet

4. Let me entreat all you who are favourites in the Court of heaven, that you would imploy all the interest you have in God in powring forth importunate requests unto him, that a good issue might come to this Kingdome by this Treaty, that God (who carries an overruling hand over the Spirits of men) would encline the hearts of our enemies, who are in Armes against us to be at *Peace* with us; and that God himself who is the wise Physician of Nations would undertake our cure, and restore health to this dying and distempred Kingdome, and *reveal to it the abundance of Peace and Truth*.

HUGH PETERS[1]

Once the testing climax of Naseby was over, Cromwell could turn his major resources to attacking the great Royalist strongholds like Donnington Castle at Newbury and Basing House at Basingstoke, which until now had defied all attempts to storm them and were grievous impediments to communications between London and the West. Basing House, in particular, was to the Roundhead rank and file an exasperating symbol of traditional tyranny, grandeur and contemptuous sinfulness and, of course, *idolatry*. A 'nest of idolatry' Hugh Peters called the old house when he came that autumn with a large force of artillery and several regiments to be in at the kill. At 6 a.m. on October 14th, 1645, Cromwell's forces, having made a breach in the walls, stormed the defences and proceeded to sack, smash and burn the great house which, Peters recounts with gloating satisfaction, had been 'in beauty and statliness . . . fit to make an emporour's court'.[2]

Reporting the action in a letter to William Lenthall, the speaker of the House of Commons, Cromwell reports, 'many of the enemy our men put the sword',[3] and then remembers to give thanks: 'God abounds in his goodness to us . . .'. In the same letter asking Lenthall for more infantry and money to pay the present levies he refers to the army as 'your army'; the same army that would one day take Lenthall himself into custody.

Peters enjoyed the proceedings enormously and wrote an account of the events which was printed and read from all pulpits the following Sunday. He was the army's most political preacher.

---

1. 'Peter,' is the correct original of the name. His contemporaries, almost without exception, called him 'Peters', and I propose to follow them. The end of Peters' career is described on pp. 537–8.

2. Joshua Sprigge, *Anglia Rediviva* (Oxford, 1854), Part iii, Ch, 3, p. 150.

3. *Oliver Cromwell's Letters and Speeches* (ed. Thomas Carlyle), 1897 edn. I, 233.

The Storming of Basing House (1645)

The rooms before the storm, in both houses, were all completely furnished, provisions for some years rather than months; 400 quarters of wheat, bacon divers rooms full, (containing hundreds of flitches,) cheese proportionable, with oatmeal, beef, pork, beer, divers cellars full, and that very good.

A bed in one room, furnished, that cost 1300*l*., popish books many, with copes, and such utensils, that in truth the house stood in its full pride, and the enemy was persuaded that it would be the last piece of ground that would be taken by the parliament, because they had so often foiled our forces that had formerly appeared before it. In the several rooms, and about the house, there were slain seventy-four, and only one woman, the daughter of doctor Griffith, who by her railing provoked our soldiers (then in heat) into a further passion. There lay dead upon the ground, major Cuffle, (a man of great account amongst them, and a notorious papist,) slain by the hands of major Harrison, (that godly and gallant gentleman,) and Robinson the player, who, a little before the storm, was known to be mocking and scorning the parliament and our army. Eight or nine gentlewomen of rank, running forth together, were entertained by the common soldiers somewhat coarsely, yet not uncivilly, considering the action in hand. The plunder of the soldier continued till Tuesday night. One soldier had 120 pieces in gold for his share, others plate, others jewels; amongst the rest, one got three bags of silver, which (he being not able to keep his own counsel) grew to be common pillage amongst the rest, and the fellow had but one half crown left for himself at last.

Also the soldiers sold the wheat to country people, which they held up at good rates a while, but afterwards the market fell, and there was some abatements for haste. After that they sold the householdstuff, whereof there was good store; and the country loaded away many carts, and continued a great while fetching out all manner of householdstuff, till they had fetched out all the stools, chairs, and other lumber[1], all which they sold to the country people by piecemeal. In these great houses there was not one iron bar left in all the windows (save only what was in the fire) before night. And the last work of all was the lead, and by Thursday morning they had hardly left one gutter about the house. And what the soldiers left, the fire took hold on; which made more than ordinary haste; leaving nothing but bare walls and chimneys in less than twenty hours, being occasioned by the neglect of the enemy, in quenching a fireball of ours at first.

1. Movable furniture.

We know not how to give a just account of the number of persons that were within; for we have not three hundred prisoners, and it may be an hundred slain, whose bodies (some being covered with rubbish) came not to our view; only riding to the house on Tuesday night, we heard divers crying in vaults for quarter, but our men could neither come to them nor they to us. But amongst those that we saw slain, one of their officers lying on the ground, seeming so exceeding tall, was measured, and from his great toe to his crown was nine foot in length.

The marquis being pressed by Mr. Peters arguing with him, broke out, and said, that if the king had no more ground in England but Basing-house, he would adventure as he did, and so maintain it to his uttermost, meaning with these papists: comforting himself in this disaster, that Basing-house was called *loyalty*. But he was soon silenced in the question concerning the king and parliament, only hoping that the king might have a day again. And thus the Lord was pleased in a few hours to show us what mortal seed all earthly glory grows upon, and how just and righteous the ways of God are, who takes sinners in their own snares, and lifteth up the heads of his despised people.

This is now the twentieth garrison that hath been taken in this summer by this army; and I believe most of them, the answer of the prayers and trophies of the faith of some of God's servants, the commander of this brigade having spent much time with God in prayer the night before the storm, and seldom fighting without some text of scripture to support him. This time he rested upon that blessed word of God written in the 115th Psalm, ver. 8, *They that make them are like unto them, so is every one that trusteth in them;* which, with some verses going before, was now accomplished.

Whereas the house had ordered that the country people should carry away those buildings, God Almighty had decreed touching that beforehand, nothing remained but a blast of wind to blow down the tottering walls and chimneys: doubtless this providence of God hath a double voice, the one unto the enemy, and the other unto us; the Lord help us with skill to improve it. I hope by this time the state hath a pennyworth for a penny, and I hope they will have full measure and running over.

I wish that the payment and recruiting of this army may not be slighted: it is an easy matter to grieve God in our neglects towards him; and not hard to weary one another. What if the poor soldier had some remembrance, though small, to leave as the acceptance of this service, which is already begun by a worthy member of this house, who hath appointed some medals to be made of gold to be bestowed upon those that ventured on the greatest difficulties.

On April 2nd of the following year a Thanksgiving sermon was preached before both houses of parliament for the recovery of the

West. It was not preached by one of the usual parliamentary Presbyterian divines, but by an even bolder and more assertive voice; which reminds us that during the course of the war the army had developed into a separate and distinctive entity, one which, while in principle the servant of parliament, was going to show signs of a will of its own, not always in accord with that of its masters.

A very ancient historical process was taking place. A legislative assembly, parliament, had called into existence a military body to subdue its enemies; the work having been accomplished, the military had outgrown parliamentary control and developed a taste for power; now it was parliament itself which was about to be subdued.

The preacher on this occasion is an army preacher representing the views and interests of the new order; and again it is Hugh Peters. His style, exalted to a theatrical vehemence, has been effective with the soldiers to whom he has preached before and after battle, and he is not slow to invite parliament to count the blessings which the victories of the army have conferred, and to reflect upon what their own case might have been if victory had gone to the enemy. The merciful deliverance they have enjoyed, he warns them, must continue to be deserved. Without the shield and sword of the army, worse could yet befall. Parliament presently take the hint and confer on Peters two hundred pounds from the forfeited estates of the Marquess of Worcester.

God's Doings and Man's Duty

A sermon of thanksgiving for the Recovery of the
West and the disbanding of the King's Horse etc.,
preached before both Houses of Parliament and the
Lord Mayor and Aldermen of the City of London and
the Assembly of Divines on Lent Thanksgiving Day,
April 2nd, 1646

You Saints, you faithfull ones, you that have and do feele mercies, that weare mercies clothes, lye in mercies bed, eate mercies bread, live in mercies ayr, injoy mercies Ordinances: of whom and to whom I may say as they did of *Dorcas* when they thought her dead, *These are the Garments Dorcas made:* These are the fruits of mercy, these be the paths mercy hath strawed with flowers and sweets; mercies deliverances, protections, preservations: it is all mercy, mercy, free-mercy. More particularly let us now looke back upon what hath been spoken as our own, God having made it so; and call these dayes by their due and just names: these certainly are the best times we ever saw, we commonly miscall them: Those former dayes we doated on were none of the best; they were a sad seed-time of our misery: for most true it is, that the seeds of the ruine of estates & common-wealths are sowen in the dayes of their greatest prosperity; and of these *Halcion*-times, we might say,

——*Longæ pacis patimur mala, saevior armis*
Luxuria incubuit, victumque ulciscitur orbem.[1]

We could never have suffered so much by a forraign enemy, as by our home-bred luxury and wantonnesse: Oh call these ill times, when a base messenger from a proud Prelate could shut up these doors, stop the mouthes of the most godly ministers, that the best noble-man here could not injoy the worship of God freely; and hardly his Bible without reproach: I am bold to say you have heard more of Christ within these last four yeers, then you have for forty before; call such dayes good; And more especially to improve what I have spoken in the Doctrinall part; truely the Lord hath rightly timed his favours even, when he might most advance his own wisdome, power, and mercy; when he might stir up his gifts and graces in you: if the enemy ask after our Prayers, Fasts, Tears, yea, our God (as they were wont to do) we have all these this day from *Edge-hill*, and before, even to this very hour; yea all these preservations have been so seasonable, that what time we our selves would have chosen, hath been Gods time; that we may say as *David* in this Psalm, *Our times have been in thy hands, O Lord.*

And, I humbly beseech you, give the Spirit of the Lord its praise, who hath done the work. The Lord is willing you should have the mercy, so he may have the praise. *Potiphar* lets *Joseph* have the use of all he hath, onely keeps his wife to himself: *Pharaoh* lets him have the Kingdom, but he will keep the Throne. Gods Spirit hath so appeared, as we conclude means can do nothing without him, but he can do all without means; and what means doth, is all done by him: he it is that hath quickned and succeeded your counsels and executions; he hath even gone against means, and beyond means, for you; he it is who hath spirited all your endeavours, in Counsels and Armies, raised help for you out of the very dust. External motive he hath had none from us, who are not the loveliest people in the world; he hath from himself over-awed men, poured contempt upon Princes, taking away the occasions of many evils; met the proud in their full carrere, and wither'd their arm; often kept them from us by strange diversions, fill'd the world with tumults, that you might not be a prey to strangers. Oh the riches of his grace! His

1. Juvenal, *Satires* VI, 292.

own righteousnesse and holinesse have thus perswaded him to do; the glory of his mercy hath been his argument; his wisedom and faithfulnesse have been glorious in preserving crums and clusters. The very Truths now profest, have been rak'd up in contemptible ashes, and now revealed to the world; and *they that are wise, shall see the loving kindnesse of the Lord* in all.

For the *proud doer* (so called, because a contemner of the faithful) you see how the Lord hath resisted him, and hath taken him (in his month) as the wilde Asse in *Job*) you may remember how the *Egyptian* King out-lived many miracles, but must perish in the Red-sea; whether Red from the sand thereof, or the blood of many he spilt, I will not dispute. You know how the Lord hath been provoked by the low price set upon his holinesse, and his image in his Saints, the peculiar sin of this Nation; for travell where you will, even from hence to the *Garamants*, you shal never find but the Zelots in other parts of the world are honored, only in England, *Ludibrium vulgo*; It hath long been a crime to be godly, and he hath been a lost man that trades that way, whilst a company of obsolete and beggerly rudiments and ceremonies have been billeted upon Gods ordinances, and eat out the very heart of them; double Service, and no Preaching. Nay you have lived to see Iniquity in the fulnesse of it, Oaths and blasphemies unparallel'd; yea when one of our Troopers reproved one of theirs in *Cornwal* for swearing, was answered by that profane mouth. He would sweare as long as he was on horse-back, he should have time enough to repent on foot; nay, they would serve the Devil now, that he might use them kindly when they came to hell; the very Sun might even blush, looking upon such miscreants. Of this fulnesse you have seen the magnitude, multitude, measure, strength, age, growth, dexterity, impudence; and the good God grant we may see the period. How the Lord hath paid them in their own coyn, you have many witnesses: They would have war, they have it: the sword must decide the controversie; let God, angels and men give the verdict, and let it be carried down to after-ages, that God plenteously rewardeth the proud doer, or, that a Parliament and faithfull Councel to a State may live in the midst of the fury of an implacable Prince and his eare-wigs. Adde this, that you have been eare and eye-witnesses of the proud mens disappointments after all their labour and travels; their inventions have been many for mischief, which have been cherished by affection, formed by consultations and Junctoes, and made ready for birth by many resolutions, which have held as high as *Brainford*; what inland and foreign conceptions of this kind have we met with? Plot upon Plot, designe upon designe. Speak *London*, hath it not been so?

Let us now remember, the time of travelling could not be prevented; Petition sent after Petition, Declaration after Declaration; nothing must prevaile, but the acceptance of such a remedy as would prove worse then the disease: And then before the birth, what throws & pains? Send to *Denmark*, run to *Holland*, fly to *France*, Curse *Digby*, imprison *Hamilton*, &c. and then all help called in for midwifery, intreat friends here and there, pawn jewels, break and close with *Irish* even in a breath; any thing for help; hazard posterity, ingage in marriage, & as she did, rore out, *Give me a child or I die!* and that miscarriage we are this day to praise God for, and wonder at. The summe totall of all these endevours of the proud comes to nothing but vanity and emptinesse, all these conclusions vanish into a lie: the Parliament is not destroyed, the City stands, the Gospel is preached; we do not yet heare the screeches of defloured damosels, nor the cries of abused matrons, we hear not the ratling of their arms, nor the neighing of their horses in our streets. Oh, my Lords, you are not at *Oxford*, led up and down as *Sampson*, to be looked at by children, nor are you crying as poor Belisarius, *Date obulum Belisario, date obulum*! Nor you Gentlemen of the other House, crying at a prison grate to some mercifull man for a penny; Nor you, my Lord Major and your Brethren, under a great ransome for your freedome; Nor You, that your teachers are forced from you, but you can yet look upon them: And you (my reverend Brethren) who have been part of the divided spoile, you feele that mercy that gives them a loud lie.

But to raise the ground-work of our praises, (Right honorable and beloved) let us a little go back, and suppose that some Messenger were come from *Bristol* when we lost it, or suppose you had *Iobs* messengers one after another, and every one crying——

Luxuriat Britano sanguine pinguis humus

Suppose you were again hearing the story of that sad March out of that City, with the breach of all Articles (which they are not used unto from us) and think your selves sitting (as old *Eli*) in expectation of tidings from the Army, and what befell us in *Cornwal* in 1644 were now brought unto you: Or if not so far back, say that now you were reading the Letters from poor *Leicester*, taken, plundered, abused beyond president: what do you now think of this dayes mercy? Do you beleeve what you enjoy to be reall, or are you in a dream? Remember, I beseech you, it is not above a yeare since, when we had thought to have hung our harps upon willow trees in some strange countries under some strange Princes, and there might have been called unto for our English songs; Alas, how would they have been mingled with teares, sighs, and grones! They say, he that in a dark night came over a high bridge only upon a slight board lying crosse, comming the next day to look upon his deliverance, could not beare the weight of the mercy, but died away in the contemplation. The good God give us skill to manage what we do enjoy, least our preservation be but a reservation of us to greater calamity. . . .

THOMAS FULLER

As the war gradually advanced in favour of parliament, and the danger of Episcopal victory seemed to recede, the relative solidarity of the Puritan complex behind the new establishment began to break up. The various independent groups and sects which had supported parliament when all had been united against a common threat to 'Liberty', now began to challenge what they saw as the unlawful successor to the old, overthrown, oppressive orthodoxy. 'Why are you today so hot for rigid Presbytry, being so zelous yesterday for rigid Episcopacy?'[1] The answer was that to Presbyterians, 'liberty', when they used the word, meant liberty to benefit by obedience to rightful authority: their own. Years later, when the painful issue was still unresolved, the opinion was thrust naked into print. *It was none of the Old Cause that people should have liberty.*[2] Like the king before them, the presbyterian parliamentarians had failed to appreciate the depth and force of the opposition to their will. They desired a king, under control, within a Presbyterian churched monarchy. But now men were appearing, especially in the army, vehement and opinionated, and habituated to the use of force, who wanted neither Monarchy nor Presbyterianism; and, while the main body of the Independents were as orderly as the Presbyterians, but usually more tolerant, there were some who were inspired by visions of anarchical chimera. The holiness of ignorance and the wickedness of academic education could become the occasion of hubbubs and strange tumults, when 'violent hands were laid on the minister, rending his M.A.'s hood from his back . . .'. One offending preacher was nearly torn in pieces while the psalm was being sung and he waited beneath the pulpit to ascend.[3]

1. *Vox Populi* (1646).
2. *Toleration Disaproved and Condemned* (1670).
3. Even Cromwell could not batter it into their heads, and he spoke hard enough. 'Al the money of this Nation would not have tempted men to fight upon such an account as they have here been engaged in, if they had not had hopes of Liberty of Conscience better than Episcopacy granted them, or than would have been afforded by a Scotch Presbytery —or an English either if it . . . had been as sharp and rigid as it threatend when first set up.' Speech to Parliament, September 12th, 1654.

The competitive harangues must have been deafening, and even frightening. 'Seek after quietness with a holy emulation', one much interrupted clergyman implored desperately.[1] 'Let the Naylor keep to his Hammer, the Husbandman to his Plough, the Tylor to his Shears, the Baker to his kneading trough, the Milner to his Toll, the Tanner to his Hides, and the Souldier to his Armes etc. They must not leap from the shop to the Pulpit and from the army to the ministry, from the blue apron to the black gowne. Let them keep to the bounds and limits of their particular calling. God hath set every calling its bounds, which none might passe.' Then he trod on crucial ground. 'Superiors must govern. Inferiors must be governed. Ministers must study and preach. People must hear and obey.'

They may have heard but they did not obey. Fuller preaches a quiet sermon—he seldom preached any other kind—warning people that the restraints of disciplined civility and respect for peaceful order, which were formerly taken for granted, have been subverted, and if they are allowed to fall, much destructive mischief may ensue before they can be restored.

Fear of Losing the Old Light

A Sermon of Reformation, preached at the Church of
St. Mary Arches, Exeter, shortly before the surrender
of the city (9th. April), 1646.

Rev. 2. 5. And will remove the candlestick out of his place except thou repent.

God commonly moves the candlestick before he removes it. The light seemes sicke and faint before it dyes. In Mines, before a dampe commeth, candles begin to burne blew, as by instinct mourning their owne funerall before hand. Some in such sad symptomes discover themselves in our Candle, in the preaching of the word, if seriously considered.

First, it is an ill signe that so many wantonly play with the Word. When children begin to try Conclusions with a Candle, sporting themselves *at in and*

1. Thomas Hall, *The Pulpit Guarded* (1650).

out with it, their Parents use to take it from them, leaving them to doe pen-
nance in the Darke for their wantonnesse. I am afraid God will serve us in
like manner: so many have dallied with the Scripture, producing it for the
maintenance of their upstart monstrous Opinions. Secondly, so many
Theeves in the Candle, such variety of Sects and Schismes, which wast and
mispend the light, is another ill boding Symptome. Yet whilst others wonder
that they are so many, I wonder they be no more; for untill a good Peace be
setled, (which God Speed,) and whilst the great *Bond of Discipline is broken,*
every stick in the Fagot will be absolute and set up for it selfe. Lastly, if the
wax be taken away from the candle, (as in many places it is, and Tithes
denied for the Ministers maintenance,) the light must decay; the five foolish[1]
Virgins having so much wisdome as to know that their Lamps could not
burne when they wanted oyle; except any doe thinke Ministers may be like
the miraculous[2] Bush, which did burne and not consume, that so they may
always worke, and yet never wast. Put these together, (and others I could
instance in,) and though Ministers, Gods Doves, delight not to be Ravens to
croake Funerals; though they, Gods fixed Stars, would not be Comets
presaging sad Events; though these Ambassadours, *praying you to be reconciled to God,*[3] are loath to bee Heraulds to proclaime war: Yet be these things
seriously considered, and may they not amount to make us *Iealous* over
England *with a godly jealousie* what for the future will become of us? And this
I will boldly adde, that an awfull feare of losing the Candlestick is the best
Hope we have to keepe it.

But I foresee a Posterne Doore ready to be opened, that escaping thorow
it my Auditors may decline whatsoever this Day I have delivered. Some will
say, what Josiah was promised, we presume on: *the Evill will not come in our
Dayes.* The Gospel will last my life in the Land; and if we are not to care for
to morrow, much lesse will wee carke for the Day after our Death. Besides,
if a generall Judgement should come in my Time, I shall beare but my share,
and shift as well as another.

Well, Beloved, tis true this inconvenience attends all generall discourses,
(such as this Dayes Sermon is,) that as *filius populi* hath no father, so publique
reproofes are seldome particularly applyed by any to themselves. But, that I
may catch some fish I must weave my net closer, and draw the threds
thereof neerer together. Bee it granted what we hope and thou believest,
that the light of the Gospel will last thy lief, yet how long or little time thy
life will last, there is the Question. Nor will it be any violence to my Text,
in a secondary Sense, to expound this *Candle,* of the Life of every man, which
how long since it hath beene kindled we know, but how soone it may bee
quenched God knows. Some wares in England, are usually set to sale *by the
candle;* that chapman carrieth them, who giveth the most before the candle is

1. Matt. 25 : 8.   2.   Exod. 3 : 8.   3. 2 Cor. 5 : 20.

burnt out. Such is all our condition at this time: Heaven now is to be had, Happinesse to be purchased; *Buy the truth, and sell it not,*[1] lose not a good bargaine, bid bountifully; be not body wise, and soule foolish; the candle weares, the candle wasts, casualty may, sicknesse will, Age must extinguish it. If once the light be out it is too late; there is *no worke, nor devise, nor knowledge, nor wisdome in the grave, whither thou goest.*[2]

1. Prov. 23 : 23.   2. Eccles. 9 : 10.

RALPH CUDWORTH

The popular view to prevail of each side in the Civil War was the view seen through the eyes of the other. On one hand were reckless, licentious, plundering Cavaliers; on the other canting, censorious zealots, real or feigned, fanatics or hypocrites who would as soon venture out without their bibles as without their breeches. Every dispute being reduced to a religious issue, they quoted endlessly from the Old Testament, which never failed to produce an insult, a threat, or a justification for whatever occasion. Nothing like this warfare by quoting from a book (with supporting violence when necessary) is to be seen again until, three hundred years later, the sayings of Chairman Mao are employed in much the same way by the zealots of the Chinese puritan movement of the 1950s and 1960s.

Superior people on both sides were much closer to their counterparts on the other side than they were to their own rank and file. We know with what distaste Chillingworth and Sheldon viewed the reckless, intemperate excesses of those who were pleased to call themselves the king's 'friends'. Parliament also had its uneasy, qualified allies among men of the highest intellectual distinction, men like Selden and Cudworth,[1] the scales of whose judgement had committed them marginally in the opposite direction to Chillingworth and Hyde, but without impairing the reluctant antagonists' liking for each other. In 1647, Selden, the celebrated jurist, was made a university visitor. It was now the turn of the Puritans to eject the Episcopalians and Royalists from university appointments and church benefices, and he used the weight of his prestige to moderate, whenever possible, the revengeful rancour and bigotry of his colleagues. He even silenced the bible-quoters with the crushing observation, preserved by Whitelock: *Perhaps in your little pocket bibles with the gilt leaves the translations may be thus, but the Greek and Hebrew signifies thus and thus.*[2]

As a most important liberal academic figure, leader of the 'Cambridge

---

1. Ralph Cudworth, 1617–1688. Emmanuel College, Cambridge, 1632, B.A. 1636; M.A. 1639. Author of *The True Intellectual System of the Universe*, 1678.
2. Bulstrode Whitelock, *Memorials* (1682), *fol. p. 71.*

Platonist' philosophers and theological latitudinarians, Cudworth was a showpiece who had to be exhibited. He had just been appointed Master of Clare College and Regius Professor of Hebrew by the new dispensation, and in a sermon, which he was invited to preach before the House of Commons in 1647, he did well by his patrons. Unlike his philosophical writing, the sermon is not encumbered by any excess of discursive speculation; it is lucid enough to anticipate Dryden, economical and very firm. It must have perplexed or offended his largely Calvinist auditory for it shines with a humanist asserveration of man's free will and responsibility for himself. After the bellowed melodrama of Marshall and the sanctimonious malice of Fairclough, it briefly lifted parliamentary preaching from the service of political expedients to a level of thought which was, and remains, universally relevant.

In publishing the sermon, Cudworth takes the trouble to write a preface addressed to the House, in which he stresses what he considers the Members' duty to be in respect of the universities; and, in case there should be any misunderstanding, or wilful misconstruction, he disavows the restriction of study to divinity alone, hoping 'that after your care for the advancement of Religion and the publick Good of the Commonwealth you would think it worthy of you to promote Ingenuous Learning, and cast a Favourable Indulgence upon it. I mean not that only which furnisheth the Pulpit, which you seem to be very regardful of; but that which is remote from such Popular Use . . . which are yet all of them very subservient to Religion and useful to the Commonwealth.'

Quintessence of the Gospel

A sermon preached before the Honorable House of
Commons at Westmonster on March 31st., 1647

1 John, ii, 3, 4. And hereby we do know that we know him, if we keep his commandments.

He that saith, 'I know him, and keepeth not his Commandments is a liar, and the truth is not in him.'

. . . There be many that speak of new glimpses, and discoveries of Truth, of dawnings of Gospel-light; and no question, but God hath reserved much of this for the very Evening and Sun-set of the World, for *in the latter dayes know-ledge shall be increased*: but yet I wish we could in the mean time see that *day to dawn*, which the Apostle speaks of, and that *day-starre to arise in mens hearts*. I wish whilest we talk of light, and dispute about truth, we could walk more as *children of the light*. Whereas if S. Johns rule be good here in the Text, that no man truly knows Christ, but he that keepeth his Commandments; it is much to be suspected, the many of us which pretend to light, have a thick and gloomy darknesse within over-spreading our souls. There be now many large Volumes and Discourses written concerning Christ, thousands of controversies discussed, infinite problems determined concerning his Divinity, Humanity, Union of both together; and what not? so that our bookish Christians, that have all their religion in writings and papers, think they are now compleatly furnished with all kind of knowledge concerning Christ; and when they see all their leaves lying about them, they think they have a goodly stock of knowledge and truth, and cannot possibly misse of the way to heaven; as if Religion were nothing but a little *Book-craft*, a mere *paper-skill*. But if S. Johns rule here be good, we must not judge of our knowing of Christ, by our skill in Books and Papers, but by our keeping of his Commandments. And that I fear will discover many of us (notwith-standing all this light which we boast of round about us) to have nothing but Egyptian darknesse within upon our hearts. The vulgar sort think that they know Christ enough, out of their Creeds and Catechismes, and Confessions of Faith: and if they have but a little acquainted themselves with these, and like Parrets conned the words of them, they doubt not but that they are sufficiently instructed in all the mysteries of the Kingdome of Heaven. Many of the more learned, if they can but wrangle and dispute about Christ, imagine themselves to be grown great proficients in the School of Christ. The greatest part of the world, whether learned or unlearned, think, that there is no need of purging and purifying of their hearts, for the right knowledge of Christ and his Gospel; but though their lives be never so wicked, their hearts never so foul within, yet they may know Christ suffici-ently out of their Treatises and Discourses, out of their mere Systems and Bodies of Divinity; which I deny not to be usefull in a subordinate way: although our Saviour prescribeth his Disciples another method, to come to the right knowledge of Divine truths, by doing of Gods will; *he that will do my Fathers will* (saith he) *shall know of the doctrine whether it be of God*. He is a true Christian indeed, not *he* that is onely *book-taught*, but he that is *God-taught*; he that hath an *Unction from the holy one* (as our Apostle calleth it) that teacheth him all things; he that hath the Spirit of Christ within him, that *searcheth* out the *deep things of God: For as no man knoweth the things of a man, save the spirit of man which is in him, even so the things of God knoweth no man but the Spirit of God.* Inke and Paper can never make us Christians, can never beget a new nature, a living principle in us; can never form Christ, or any true notions of spirituall things in our hearts. The Gospel, that new Law which Christ delivered to the world, it is not merely a *Letter* without us, but a *quickning Spirit* within us. Cold Theorems and Maximes, dry and jejune Disputes, lean syllogisticall reasonings, could never yet of themselves beget the least glympse of true heavenly light, the least sap of saving knowledge in any heart. All this is but the groping of the poore dark spirit of man after truth, to find it out with his own endeavours, and feel it with his own cold and benummed hands. Words and syllables which are but dead things, cannot possibly convey the living notions of heavenly truths to us. The secret mysteries of a Divine Life, of a New Nature, of Christ formed in our hearts; they cannot be written or spoken, language and expressions cannot reach them; neither can they ever be truly understood, except the soul it self be kindled from within and awakened into the life of them.

*

I speak not here against a free and ingenuous enquiry into all Truth, according to our severall abilities and opportunities, I plead not for the captivating and enthralling of our judgements to the Dictates of men, I do not disparage the naturall improvement of our understanding faculties by true Knowledge, which is so noble and gallant a perfection of the mind: but the thing which I aime against is, the dispiriting of the life and vigour of our Religion, by dry speculations, and making it nothing but a mere dead scheleton of *opinions*, a few dry bones without any flesh and sinews tyed up together: and the misplacing of all our zeal upon an eager prosecution of these, which should be spent to better purpose upon other objects. Knowledge indeed is a thing farre more excellent then riches, outward pleasures, worldly dignities, or any thing else in the world besides Holinesse, and the Conformity of our wills to the will of God: but yet our happinesse consisteth not in it, but in a certain Divine Temper & Constitution of soul which is farre above it. But it is a piece of that corruption that runneth through humane nature, that we naturally prize Truth, more then Goodnesse; Knowledge, more then Holinesse. We think it a gallant thing to be fluttering up to Heaven with our wings of Knowledge and Speculation: whereas the highest mystery of a Divine Life here, and of perfect Happinesse hereafter, consisteth in nothing but mere Obedience to the Divine Will. Happinesse is nothing but that inward sweet delight, that will arise from the Harmonious agreement between our wills and Gods will. There is nothing contrary to God in the whole world, nothing that fights against him but *Self-will*. This is the strong Castle, that we all keep garrison'd against heaven in every one of our hearts, which God continually layeth siege unto: and it must be conquered and demolished, before we can conquer heaven.

*

The great Mysterie of the Gospel, it doth not lie onely in *Christ without us*, (though we must know also that he hath done for us) but the very Pith and Kernel of it, consists in *Christ inwardly formed* in our hearts. Nothing is truly Ours, but what lives in our Spirits. *Salvation* itself cannot *save* us, as long as it is onely without us; no more then *Health* can cure us, and make us sound, when it is not within us, but somewhere at distance from us; no more then *Arts and Sciences*, whilst they lie onely in Books and Papers without us; can make us learned. The Gospel, though it be a Sovereigne and Medicinall thing in it self, yet the mere knowing and believing of the history of it, will do us no good: we can receive no vertue from it, till it be inwardly digested & concocted into our souls; till it be made *Ours*, and become a *living thing* in our hearts. The Gospel, if it be onely without us, cannot save us; no more then that Physitians Bill, could cure the ignorant Patient of his disease, who, when it was commended to him, took the Paper onely, and put it up in his pocket, but never drunk the Potion that was prescribed in it. All that Christ did for us in the flesh, when he was here upon earth; From his lying in a *Manger*, when he was born in *Bethlehem*, to his bleeding upon the *Crosse* on *Golgotha*; it will not save us from our sinnes, unlesse Christ by his Spirit dwell in us.

*

Let nothing be esteemed, of greater consequence and concernment to thee, then what thou doest and actest, how thou livest. Nothing *without* us can make us either happy, or miserable; nothing can either *defile us*, or hurt us, but what *goeth out from us*, what Springeth and Bubbleth up, out of our own hearts. We have dreadfull apprehensions, of the Flames of Hell without us; we tremble and are afraid, when we hear of *Fire and Brimstone*, whil'st in the mean time, we securely nourish within our own hearts, a *true and living Hell*,

——*Et cæco carpimur igni:*

the dark fire of our Lusts, consumeth our bowels within, and miserably scorcheth our souls, and we are not troubled at it. We do not perceive, how Hell steales upon us, whilest we live here. And as for Heaven, we onely gaze abroad, expecting that it should come in to us from without, but never look for the beginnings of it to arise within, in our own hearts.

GEORGE COKAYNE

The last lethal convulsion of the Civil War was still to come. In 1648 the Scots, disillusioned in their hopes of England's conformity to Scotch-style Presbyterianism, rose in support of Charles who, though now a captive in England, had been intriguing with them, as he intrigued with everybody who was prepared to be involved. This bloodshed washed away the last scruples which had restrained the army from treating the king as they would treat another man. The grim Remonstrance demanding 'justice' which the army set to parliament on November 20th, appalled that body. The bulk of the members stood for law and order in the old, clear sense of respect for rank and property. They had sought to modify the monarchy to their advantage; to subdue the king's claims to absolutism and to obtain a controlling share of the administration, but it had never been their intention to discredit Monarchy, an institution which they regarded as the citadel of their own security. The growing restive element of Republicanism in the army alarmed them, for there was now no hiding the ruling consequence of the war, that the force which parliament had willed into being, to serve it, had become its master in all but name. The House sought to delay replying to the Remonstrance, and on November 22nd the familiar machinery of the 'Fast Sermon' was set in motion once more to point the direction of their duty and warn them of the results of negligence. The preacher, proposed by a member connected with the army, was a young man called George Cokayne, minister of St. Pancras, Soper Lane. This, and the one that followed, were the last sermons which the House would hear as a free body. Members were being offered their last chance to submit voluntarily to the will of the army. By a majority of ninety they rejected it, resolving, after debate, that they would not take the army's Remonstrance into consideration, and subsequently, on December 4th, that they would reopen negotiations with the king on the basis of his concessions in the Treaty of Newport. Meanwhile, the king had been taken into custody by the army and moved from Newport to Hurst Castle, a fortified stronghold. On the 2nd, the army, after a day of prayer, the usual prelude for Puritans to an act of violence, marched on London without the consent of parliament, and, due to the carefully timed, unnerving appeals of the army's agents (including Stephen Marshall who had by now shifted his allegiance), was not resisted by the city. The trained bands guarding parliament were dismissed, and replaced by two of the army's regiments. Overnight the members found themselves no longer rulers, but virtual prisoners, subject to control. The fact that nothing could be called constitutionally lawful which was rejected by the House was dealt with by a method, primitive, but entirely effective. On December 6th, Colonel Pride excluded by force about a hundred members averse to the army's wishes; then, and only then, was the acquiescent remnant, known henceforward derisively as the 'Rump' parliament, allowed to go through the motions of voting. During the next few days the mutilated and shackled body of the once supreme legislative assembly was battered with words from the spokesmen of the army, in and out of the pulpit—Thomas Brookes, John Owen, Hugh Peters, John Cardell, and of course, the inevitable Stephen Marshall.

Most of these sermons were not printed. Perhaps an instinctive tremor of uneasiness in the preachers cautioned against it. Only Peters exulted openly in the grisly progress of a monarch to the scaffold.[1] During the king's trial he harangued the assembled troops outside Westminster Hall and led them, like a cheer-leader in a sports stadium, in thunderous chanting of 'Justice, Justice', and 'Execution, Execution', to drown any expressions of protest or dissent. The orthodox Presbyterian divines, representing the movement which had first initiated resistance to the king, watched with horror the relentless preparations to destroy him with whom they had only sought a profitable settlement. They protested against the proceedings; they repudiated all responsibility for them.[2] They might as well have prayed to their God to strike the army with lightning. He was also the army's God, and at this time it was upon the army's, and therefore, the country's, master, 'His servant Oliver Cromwell', that He seems to have looked with favour.

The small section of the panoramic preparations for killing the king,

---

1. But he did not publish. Brookes did: *God's Delight in the Progress of The Upright* (1648).

2. *Serious and Faithful Representation* (1648). Cf. *A Vindication of the Ministers of the Gospel in and about London* (1648).

which now appears, is a part of a sermon preached by Cokayne to the House of Commons, as it stood, on November 29th, on the verge of its ignominious degradation by the arm of the military which it had itself conjured into being.

Flesh Expiring and the Spirit Inspiring

A sermon preached before the House of Commons, on
the 29th. of November, 1648

Delay not to act for the peoples good who have instructed you, (we here propound no way or manner how you should act, but leave that to your Wisdoms:) but this we shall be bold humbly to speak to you, Act without delay, for the peoples good, as God shall direct you. It is a sad thing for you to make the people stay under their Burthens for that which is their Right: If *God* lead us about in the wilderness, we should be content to submit to him therein. But this will be a great sin in you, to be the unhappy Instruments of our long detention under Thraldom and Misery. If you should delay our Relief, your Judgment would not linger. It is a notable saying of the Wise man, *Eccles.* 10.16. *Wo to them, whose King is a Child, whose Princes eat in the morning:* There is another Scripture that explains this, in *Jerem.* 21.12. *O house of David, thus saith the Lord, execute Judgment in the morning, and deliver him that is spoiled out of the hand of the oppressor.* You may see by this what is the meaning of the other Scripture, which saith, *Wo to those, whose King is a Child, whose Princes eat in the morning.* It is not for them to be first in eating and filling *themselves*, but in doing Judgment in the *morning*: This is that which may possibly be in the spirit of Governors, yea in those that are godly; They may be afraid to give the People their Right, for fear the People should be about to intrench upon what is due to them, But if ye be Gods Vicegerents, and do act what he commands, ye need not be afraid of this.[1] It was very remarkable in *David*, wherein he did exceedingly fail. We read in 1 *Sam.* 20. 14, 15. that *David* made a Covenant to do good to *Jonathan* and his housbold, because of the kindness that *Jonathan* shewed to him in his distress. And you shall see in 2 *Sam.* 9. at the beginning, there he makes enquiry, whether any of *Jonathans* race were to be found? and search being

1. An attempt to allay parliament's fears of revolutionary forces. The army's Leveller revolt took place in April of the following year.

made, *Mephibosheth, Jonathans* son, was found out, and he performs the Covenant with him; but see after this, how he declineth, and falls off from that former spirit of sweetness, by reason of the false reports that *Ziba* made concerning *Mephibosheth*, as you may see in 2. *Sam.* 16. 4, 5. ... And so *David* brake the Covenant which he had made with *Ionathan*. Had *David* fulfilled his oath to *Jonathan*, God would rather have established then unsetled his Kingdom. I leave it to your Wisdoms to make the Application. This be assured of, That if the Magistrates did give the people their due, and act according to Gods mind, God would keep the people within their Bounds. ... But, above all, let me commend this to you, That you delay not to do Justice, (yet still, as I said at first, mingled with Mercy.) Think not to save your selves by an unrighteous saving of them, who are the Lords and the Peoples known Enemies. You may not imagine to obtain the favor of those against whom you will not do Justice; For certainly, if you act not like gods, in this particular, against men truly obnoxious to Justice, they will be like Devils against you. Observe that place, 1 *Kings* 22.31. compared with Chap. 20. It is said in Chap. 20. that the King of *Syria* came against Israel, and, by the mighty power of God, he and his Army were overthrown, and the King was taken Prisoner. Now the mind of God was (which he then discovered onely by that present providence) that Justice should have been executed upon him, but it was not; whereupon the Prophet comes with ashes upon his face, and *waited for the King of Israel in the way where he should return; and as the King passed by, he cryed unto him, thus saith the Lord, Because thou hast let go a man whom I appointed for destruction, therefore thy life shall go for his life.* Now see how the King of *Syria*, after this, answers *Ahabs* love: About three years after *Israel* and *Syria* engage in a new War, and the King of *Syria* gives command unto his Souldiers, that they should fight neither against small nor great, but against the *King of Israel*. *Benhadads* life was once in *Ahabs* hand, and he ventured Gods displeasure to let him go; but see how *Benhadad* rewards him for it, *Fight neither against small nor great, but against the King of Israel.* Honorable and worthy, if God do not lead you to do Justice upon those that have been the great Actors in shedding innocent Blood, never think to gain their love by sparing of them; For they will, if opportunity be ever offered, return again upon you; and then they will not fight against the poor and mean ones, but against those that have been the Fountain of that Authority and Power which hath been improved against them.

*

... Honorable Worthies, when ever your thoughts are, in the least, drawn forth against those whom God hath honored, to save you and the Kingdom from ruine, remember if on that day (for scarce a day in a year hath not been honored with some deliverance,) God hath not done somewhat, by them, for your preservation; and surely if you thus think of what God hath done for you by them, and be led forth to bless his name for the discovery of his power in weak means for you, you will be so busied about this work, that you will not remember to do any thing against Gods Instruments, unworthy of you. It may be these men, we now speak of, may do somewhat which may not concur with your spirits; and it maybe that which, in the judgments of many, God sets not his stamp upon: yet for all this you must take heed of bringing in a *Noahs* flood to allay a little dust that flies in your faces; to bring a flood and deluge upon all our mercies, because of some unwonted interruptions of your proceedings, which perhaps (if weighed in some ballance) would be found too light for God to own.

*

Right Honorable, The great noyse and cry hath been, that you are the godly and religious Parliament, and every one of you hath been accounted a *Solomon*; The Lord make you like him, while he was young, and walked with God; but never let you live to be like him, when old, back-sliding and deaf, that succeeding *Rehoboam* may not, in this we are now upon, (*viz.* hearkning to God,) or in any thing that is worthy, shame and go beyond you. But to return to the Exhortation we were upon, I beseech you hear God in his Providences. Now, amongst all the things which God therein speaks to you, this is most remarkably audible, *viz.* that you should continually live upon him alone. What doth God speak by all the Victories he hath given you, and in putting your enemies under your feet, if not this? that he would have you evermore to depend upon him. You have known what it hath been to be in straights and how God hath stood by you; now you are in straights again will you depend upon any thing or expect help from any thing but God?

. . . Be constant in your communion with God; in all your transactions be still near God, in fellowship with him: *Are you not afraid*, saith God *to speak against my servant Moses*? Why should they be afraid of Moses The Lord tells us in the next words where he saith *He is a man whom I have spoken with Face to Face*.

There was much communion and familiarity between God and Moses, and this did set a Majesty upon him, and this will make you appear in Majesty, when you are much in fellowship with God. The Judges of old were wont to sit at the entrance to the Temple, there to give judgment, and the temple was a type of Christ; therefore it shewed that they that are judges indeed must still in judgment sit near Christ. But I wish to God you would sit in the Temple in continual Union and Fellowship with Christ when you judge and pass sentence; and then power and majesty will shine gloriously upon you; people then would not scorn but honour you.

I have but one more thing to add which I shall speak last because it should have the deeper impression upon you; it is this, Take care how you oppose the Spirit of God and the spiritual Worship of God.

*

But to wind up all, let God arise in you and exult himself in your conversations; let God judge the earth in you all that is corrupt and vain; do not keep anything in your hearts that you would have subdued, let God inherit you, become his; let him have your obedience; subject yourselves to God, and all the people will be subject unto you: give up all your honours and estates to God, let him order them, and dispose of them to his glory, and then you shall see the people will be willing to give their estates to you, they will not complain of their taxes and burdens any more; let God have all your praises, honour not yourselves nor one another, but God, and then the people, instead of railing upon you will honor and bless you for all the pains you have taken for them; let him inherit all your joy, rejoyce in the Lord that he is glorified and that he is honoured and you shall see the people shall rejoice in you; you shall be those which the people shall joy in and continually make their boast of; and that all this shall be, let us turn all into the Psalmists prayer; Arise O Lord and Judge the Earth, for thou shalt inherit all nations.

HENRY FERNE

While the panic-stricken House of Commons was listening to Cokayne preaching his godly ordinance of death, the king himself, as yet uncharged and untried, but virtually condemned, was listening at Carisbrooke to a different sermon from his favourite preacher and chaplain, Henry Ferne:[1] the text was Habakkuk 2 : 3.

' . . . it hasteth forward to the end, and shall not lie: though it tarry, wait for it; because it will surely come'.

This pious sentiment may have seemed in retrospect wry consolation to Charles when, exactly two months after hearing the sermon, he had his life cut short on the scaffold at Whitehall.

Comfort in adversity[2]

A sermon on Habukkuk 2. 3., preached before the
King at Carisbroke, on the 29th. of November, 1648

He that in the work of creation made all things in due proportion for *number*, *weight*, and *measure*; doth so, and more, in works of the Judgment & Correction; weighing out, and measuring the proportion, not only by the scale

1. Henry Ferne, 1602–1662. Bishop of Chester. 1620, Trinity College, Cambridge, pensioner, later Fellow. M.A. probably 1617; B.D. 1633. Living of Midbourne, Leicester shire. Archdeacon of Leicester and Chaplain Extraordinary to the king, 1641. D.D. 1642. Author of controversial tract, *The Resolving of Concsience* . . . (Cambridge, 1642), denying the right of subjects to take up arms against the sovereign. Remained with the king throughout the war until the surrender in 1645 and later joined Charles at Carisbrooke. At the Restoration was appointed successively Master of Trinity College, Cambridge, and Bishop of Chester. See Walker's *Suffering of the Clergy*, Pt. ii, p. 43, and Wood, op. cit., iii, p. 534–536; according to the latter 'his only fault was he could not be angry'.

2. This was the last sermon heard by Charles I. In the king's hour of tribulation Ferne had gone for comfort to one of the darkest, but most lyrically celebrated, chapters of Jewish history. After the battle of *Carchemish*, at the beginning of the seventh century B.C., Israel was one of the incidental victims in the overthrow of Egyptian supremacy by the

447

of wisdome, as in the creation, but by the ballance of Justice too; apportioneth the weight of affliction, and the length of the time, with respect to our continuance in Sin. Punishment, or chastisement for Sin, looks first at sins past, the greatnesse of them, and the years or time spent in them: then at our present condition, whether we are made sensible, and sufficiently humbled. Lastly, at our disposition for the future, whether prepared, and firmly resolved for obedience in time to come. Now see the proportion; He usually appoints the weight of the affliction, according to former provocations and sins past, but the length, and continuance of our sufferings according to the effect they have upon us, for humiliation and obedience.

All the Comminations we hear denounced against a sinfull people, and all the promises we find made to an afflicted Nation, speak thus much, that repentance and amendment is the condition of removing the Judgment, as it is the end for which he afflicts it. And if so, then surely will he not cease till he has his end upon us, *for will a man take up a snare* (saith the Prophet) *having caught nothing?* and will the Lord take off his rod till it has wrought upon us?

For the continuance of the rod, see a reason, *Isay* 9. 12. *they returned not to him that had smitten them, therefore his arme was stretched out still*: And for the removall of the rod, *Isay* 10. 5. *Assur was the rod of his* anger, for the chastising of his people, *but when he had performed his whole work upon Mount Sion, Verse* 12. then he takes off the rod, and layes it upon the *Assyrian*. Upon his and their Enemies will it be, *virga non removenda, a grounded Rod*, as another Prophet calls it, a rod not to be taken off from rebellious and obstinate Sinners. Or take we affliction in that other similitude of a furnace, to purge away our drosse and corruption; We see the Lord *sitting as a Refiner*, to moderate the fire, both for the heat, and continuance of it, not suffering his pretious mettall to be longer in the Furnace then is meet.

But what then meanes that *duplum* of punishment? *Isay* 40.2. *She hath received double for all her sinnes:* As in receiving of reward, there is no *duplum* or exceeding in the merit, no supererogation on our part: so in the receiving of correction no *duplum* or *doubling* of the punishment above the desert of sin. In the point of reward, man cannot take God with an ὑστερεῖ, tha the is behind hand with him in the recompence; and in the businesse of correction, man shall finde that upon his amendment, οὐκ ὑστερήσει, God will not be behind hand with a deliverance. That *double received for all her sinnes*, if it be not meant of the abundant grace and favour wherewith God embraced his people after he had plagued them (as some will have it) but of the punishment,

armies of the young Chaldean, Nebuchadnezzar, King of Babylon. The prophet Habakkuk engages in gusty dialogues with the Lord of Hosts ('Why dost thou show me iniquity and look upon perverseness', etc.), and after some wrestling obtains the required reassurance that He would again 'march through the land in indignation. . . . for the salvation of thine anointed'.

they had suffered (as I rather conceive) then doth it not imply a proportion to the desert of sinnes past, but signifies the abundant Correction they had received, and that *double*; not to what they had deserved, but to what would have been, had they sooner repented; if they had speedily broken off the course of their sins, the time of their sufferings had been so much shorter.

And let not any of us (how eager soever in our desire of ease and deliverance) think we have received at Gods hands after that measure, *double for our sinnes*, we may thank our selves if the time of our sufferings has been double, to what it might have been if we had been sooner corrected and amended. *I should soon have put down their Enemies*, saith God, *Psal.* 81. It should not have *tarryed* on his part, the failing has been on ours. And therefore, if any will be still asking how *soon?* or (as they that in the Psalmist complained they saw no *come*, and requiring a signe; He tells them, *it comes not with observation;* Not our Saviour did the *Pharisees*, demanding *when the Kingdome of God would come*, and requiring a signe; He tells them, *it comes not with observation;* Not with the outward shew of worldly Pomp and Glory, *but the Kingdome of God is within you*, there you must look for it, and know the comming of it, by those beginnings of grace wrought in you.

So neither doth deliverance come *with observation*; Such observation as is made upon outward meanes, numerous Armes, present Successe, (from which we have been too ready to conclude of the end) but such as is taken from within; The judgement of it must be taken from your selves. Do you find your hearts humbled within you, cast down in the sense of former provocations? *then lift up your heads, for your redemption draweth nigh.* Are your hearts turned within you? then look for a conversation of things, a change of time. Have you *engaged your hearts* (as the Prophet saith) *to approach to the Lord*, to wait upon him, as in the expectation of his good time, so in a course of after obedience? then know he will engage his holy arme for your deliverance, *it will not tarry* after that time, yea, he will *make bare his holy Arme* for it, (as the Prophet speaks) shew it from heaven, divested of all outward humane helps and assistance, do the work himself.

And now, before we seal up the comforts of this Assurance, we must remove a double scruple, that may disquiet it. For if we apply what has been spoken of nationall Calamities and Deliverances (upon which the Text proceeds) to particular men, we find, that wicked men, who remain unamended, enjoy the benefit of such a national Deliverance, & many righteous men swept away, or cut off by death, see not the promised redemption. The one may seeme to question the necessity of our performing the condition of amendment, the other to weaken the certainty of Gods performing the promise.

True it is indeed, that righteous men are often involved in the punishment of a sinfull Nation, faring worse for those about them; and men still continuing wicked, meet with a Deliverance, faring better for those, that by Repentance, and turning from their evill wayes, have turned away the wrath of God from a Nation. As to the outward man, it often happens (as Saint *Austin* said) *Malis bene, Bonis male;* yet not that to the true advantage of those, nor this to the disadvantage of these.

For first, see you in a Nationall Deliverance all partaking of the peace and benefit of it: He that by carnall security has *drawn back* from God, and continues uncorrected, as well as he, that in humiliation and amendment of life has *waited* upon God for the Deliverance. Both of them indeed enjoy it, one with another, but not one as well as the other, not with that joy, comfort, and blessing from Him, that sends the Deliverance. Alas, their *bed is shorter, then that they can stretch themselves on it, and the covering narrower then that they can wrap themselves in it.* The ease they have by such a Deliverance is too short, too narrow to afford a content that may *reach unto the soul.* They may obtaine a temporall deliverance promiscuously with others, and that *fide aliena,* but to receive and enjoy it with true content and comfort of the *Vivet* promised to the just man, *Verse 4.* it must be *ex side sua.* So the Psalmist, *My heart trusted in him, and I am helped, therefore my heart greatly rejoyced, &c.* therefore rejoyced greatly, or danced for joy (as the other translation hath it) because it first trusted in him. A double motion of the heart, the first of Faith, which carryes it upon God for the help, the other of Joy, for the receiving it from him: not this truly and really without the former. Then is there true joy, and great joy upon a Deliverance, when it has been prayed for first, and *waited* for by faith and patience. He that would not *waite* any longer, 2 *Kings* 7. 2. saw the promised Deliverance, and plenty, but did not taste of it. And they that still *draw back* from God, if live to see the Deliverance, and taste of it, shall find it as the flesh of quailes in their mouthes, but *Leannesse withall sent into their soul;* which may pine away under all the affluence and abundance of an outward peace.

Take heed therefore, lest there be in any of you, *an evill heart of unbelief,* in *departing from the living God,* an heart that casteth away all patience and care of well-doing; and yet causeth a man to *blesse himself,* saying, *I shall have peace though I walk in the imagination of mine heart, and adde drunkennesse to thirst;* I shall fare as others do in the common calamity or deliverance. But as God declares, *His soul will have no pleasure in those that draw back;* so shall they find, their soul cannot have true pleasure in the Deliverance, he will bestow upon a repenting Nation. They may promiscuously with others, be made partakers of it when it comes; but not enjoy it with that comfort, joy, and blessing, as they shall do, who so *waite* for it, as ye heard above.

For the Second: We see in common Calamities, righteous and good men overborne among the rest by the Violence of the *overflowing scourge;* and *swept away* with that *besome of destruction,* wherewith the Lord sometimes cleanseth a Land. As to the outward man indeed, they often bear a part in the common sufferings with that People or Community, of which they are a part; but then consider that in these generall calamities a speciall hand of providence is over such for their comfort and preservation. Every particular just man hath his assurance for a *Vivet*, till the deliverance come; the promise of it is not far from this Text, the *just shall live by his faith:* Live comfortably, live safely, even during the present distresse. Yea, when such are cast out into a forraigne Land, *I will be to them* (saith the Lord) *a little Sanctuary*; or an hiding place, to which they may still retire for refreshment and protection. *And in the day when he makes up his Jewels*, they are remembred, *Mal.* 3.17. as out of the sweepings of our house we gather ends of Gold or Silver, or what is pretious, casting out the rest to be trod to mire in the streets: so shall he gather his Jewels, or pretious ones out of the common filth and dust, which *the besome of destruction* has hurried out. There is a *Vivet* for the just man, a speciall care and provision for his subsistence and comfort till a generall Deliverance of the Nation come.

Nay, but if that Deliverance *tarry* so long, that he be cut off by death before he sees it, how will this promise of a *Vivet*, or a *non tardabit* be made good unto him?

We must know, that Temporall promises are not alwayes made good in the same kind, and he that has not faith to look beyond the very thing assured by them, may misse of his desire and expectation: being like to him that fights a battell without a Reserve; if his first strength be defeated, he's utterly broken. But he that *against hope can believe in hope*, when his first hope (which rests upon outward Visible meanes, and expects a temporall deliverance) failes, has a Reserve, an hope *sure and stedfast, which entreth into that within the vail*. He knowes, and shall find, if the promise of a temporall blessing or Deliverance be not made good to him in the same kinde, it will in a better, nothing at all to his losse or disadvantage: To them that *left Houses and Lands, &c.* for Christs sake, Houses and Lands, and an hundred fold more were promised in this life, not in the same kind surely. We know they did not, they could not receive them so; for they were to receive them (as it is there added) *with persecutions*, which would drive them from Houses and Lands. It was therefore further made good unto them, by their receiving that inestimable treasure of the Gospel, which would replenish their hearts with such joy and content, that they would not part with it for an hundred times as much as they had forsaken. This hundred-fold in this life they should enjoy till they were put into possession of that Kingdom which infinitely transcends all earthly advantages *Adeo satis idoneus Patientiæ sequester Deus* (saith *Tertul.*) so sure a Trustee is God, so able to restore what is laid up for the reward of Patience and Innocency. And thus is it with every righteous man, *that waits*, and is cut off by death before he sees the wish'd-for Nationall deliverance; a *justus Vivet*, made good to him even in death it self, he has then his deliverance though the Nation has not; so far is it from *tarrying*, in regard of his particular, that it comes sooner then was expected, and after a better way, then that of an outward temporall deliverance. For he is taken from the evill present, and to come, as good *Josiah* cut off in his prime by the enemies Sword, and what is denied him in this life, is made good in a better, and for a temporall outward peace expected, presently enjoyes an heavenly, and eternall. So that Majesty it self cannot lose by such a change, when as the next life affords *A Crown of glory that cannot fade away, a Kingdom that cannot be moved.*

To conclude, thus stands the assurance of this promise, *non tardabit, it will not tarry.* To every just man, though cut off before he see the nationall Deliverance, there is a *Vivet* in death it self, which is not a *tarrying*, but an hastening of his Deliverance. And to a whole Nation, upon their remarkable and more generall repentance and amendment, there is a Deliverance assured: *It will not tarry* after they are so fitted for it. Thus, when he has wrought his work of Chastisement upon this Land, as he *did upon Mount Sion, Isay* 70. (oh may he hasten it, by our speedy and more generall amendment!) then will he turn his hand against every adversary, *will punish the fruit of the stout heart* of all violent men, will *put them in fear, that they may know themselves to be but men,* and how vaine all their thoughts and purposes have been.

Then shall all that waite for the Salvation of our God, hear him say, *Turne ye Prisoners of hope*, and *comfort ye, comfort ye my people, speak comfortably to Jerusalem, tell her, her warfare is accomplished.* And we shall with comfort say, *Loe, this is our God, we have waited for him, and he hath saved us; this is the Lord, we have waited for him, and will rejoyce in his salvation.* Even so, O Lord, *haste thee unto us; thou art our helper and Redeemer, make no long tarrying O our God:* Haste thee to the help of thine Anointed, and of thy People of this Church, and of this Kingdome; and *lead thy people againe like a flock, by the hand of Moses and Aaron.* We beg it for Jesus Christ his sake, who bore the chastisement of our peace, to whom with thee O Father, together with the blessed Spirit, be all Honour, Dominion, &c.

This was the time of darkest anguish and frustration for those loyal to the king, and, in the moment of climactic outrage, they turned their fury, less against the rabid executant monsters, as they regarded them, the army, than against the shocked and bewildered, and now also, helpless, presbyterian parliamentarians and London aldermen who, in their dispute with the king, had brought the nightmare of the military criminals into being. There could be no open preaching against the regicides by name but, what would, if it could, have been said in public, may be inferred from anonymous publications.

Nor can ye thank any but your selves yee pittifull *Citts*, for this present Affliction that's fallen upon you; nay the whole Kingdome must curse you for the sad calamity it now lies under; did not you first flesh this Army with Victualls, Money, Arms, Plate, Rings and Bodkins? did not you feast them from time to time, invite them to Thanks-giving dinners? have you forgotten those Cart-loades of meat, drink and clothes; from time to time, sent out from your Benevolence? did you not first Arme this *Sylla* against a *Marian* crue as you term'd them? And is it now fit to disband, *donec Sylla omnes suas Divitiis explevit*, till the Saints have fill'd their Snap-sacks: In a word, Did not you let in this *Trojan Horse*? Behold the just reward of your folly, Cowardize, Treachery and Rebellion. And now may the *Viper* you have nourish'd eat into your owne *Bowels*; May the Fate of *Acteon* fall on you all; may ye first be made *Stagges*, and then devoured by your owne *Dogges*.[1]

They were. The 'dogs' devoured a hundred votes in order that they might thereafter devour a king.

1. *Mercurius Pragmaticus* (Marchmont Nedham), Tuesday January 16th, to Tuesday January 30th, 1649.

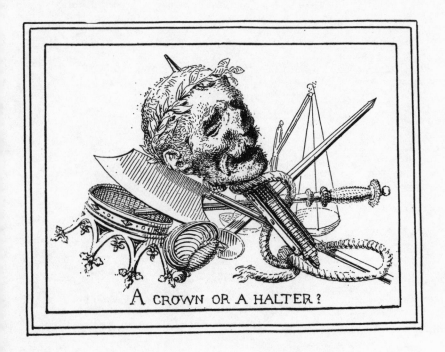

A CROWN OR A HALTER?

4

COMMONWEALTH AND PROTECTORATE

CROMWELL AND PSEUDO-CROMWELL

With the king's execution the entire scene was transformed, for with him disappeared the last uniting focal point of resistance. Now the sects and parties, which had been forming incipiently, could divide and give keener and more pressing attention to their several grievances and aspirations. The Levellers, the most radical of the army's political reformers, made their abortive effort and were crushed. Others bided their time. Meanwhile the 'preacher incitant', who had served parliament and the army in turn, became a superfluous weapon, and moreover one with a dangerous recoil. For who and what were now the natural targets of dissatisfaction but the army junta and its parliamentary rivals. The practice of regular fast sermons was promptly discontinued. Public sermons which tended to unsettle their auditors, especially sermons with political or quasi-political content, were not encouraged. But the kind of radical 'levelling' preacher who would preach such sermons needed no encouragement; he had much to say and many willing to hear him. Preaching he regarded as a sacred right, the legitimate means by which social communication and cohesion for action were properly effected. It was an embarrassing situation for the Rump parliament, with its own historical antecedents; but the members knew all too well that words could be cutting weapons, and they had to act. On July 9th, 1649, no doubt after a nudge from the army grandees who had been mopping up the Levellers, they did act; and the descendants of the men who achieved what they *had* achieved by force of preaching, and for whom preaching was a militant godly way of life, well-nigh a sacrament, did to others what previous governments had done to themselves; they passed an act restricting the right of preachers to criticize parliament's own proceedings.[1] The circle was completed.

At the centre of this circle stood the man who now bore alone the weight of power, responsibility, and hatred. He was hated with

1. *Resolves of the Commons concerning such ministers as shall preach or pray against the Present government* (July 9th, 1649).

competitive fervour by mutual enemies; by the Cavaliers for having despoiled them and killed their king; by the Presbyterians for having balked their parliament; and by the radical reformers for having frustrated their hopes of a thorough revolution. The Cavaliers, at least, pursued him into the grave, when, at the Restoration, his decomposed remains were dug up and hanged in public. Only a man of adamantine will could have carried this burden; Oliver Cromwell was such a man. He has been popularly deemed an arch-Puritan because he led a régime propelled by a Puritan movement; but in many important respects he was not a Puritan at all, and indeed incurred the disapproval of stricter Puritans because he took pleasure in such vanities as music, pictures and field sports. He was, however, a genuinely devout evangelical non-conformist—non-conforming equally to Episcopalian and Presbyterian decrees—and notably tolerant in religious matters. Preaching was, for him, the conduit of life; he himself preached in conventicles and, of course, in the field.[1] A sermon has survived in his name, said to have been taken down by one Aaron Guerdon, when Cromwell preached in the house of Sir Peter Temple, on April 30th, 1649. The last place in London where Cromwell would have been found at that time was the residence of Sir Peter Temple. Although he had served as a Colonel in the parliamentary army Sir Peter had violently opposed the trial of the king and, outraged by the execution, resigned his commission, expressing his disgust so forcibly that information had been laid against him in parliament for seditious speech. Cromwell might have been at the house of Peter Temple, the regicide, who had signed the king's death warrant, and he might even have preached there; but he would not have preached *this* sermon. The whole thing is a thoroughly unfriendly joke, full of veiled hints of indulgence in lust, avarice, cruelty, corruption and unctuous hypocrisy in general. How even Granger,[2] Archdeacon Nares[3] or anyone else could have hesitated to identify it outright as spurious is something of a mystery.

Who was Aaron Guerdon? Probably a pure invention of the author. But perhaps a study of the name would reveal a clue to a contemporary comic anagram. As for the authorship, one possible suggestion has been offered by Jasper Cross,[4] who thought it might have been John

1. At the time of the king's execution, a Dutch satire depicted him dressed in a preacher's gown, with an attendant wolf at his shoulder. (See illustration.)
2. *Harleian Miscellany*, iv, 176, fn. 2.
3. *Heraldic Anomalies*, 1, 59.
4. *Notes and Queries*, Series 1, Vol. 6, No. 158. November 6th, 1852.

Birkenhead. My personal preference inclines to Marchmont Nedham[1], whose style the sermon more resembles. Nedham died two years before the date of the publication, but it might have been found among his effects and thought worth airing by a friend who wished to remain unknown.

Whoever the writer, he has caught with malicious niceness the rambling, repetitive verbosity of the great Oliver, but, in the interests of communication, has made him, in parody, more coherent than he was in reality. It is interesting to compare this clever pseudo-Cromwell with authentic Cromwell, so I preface the 'sermon' with a passage from a speech delivered, as it happens, a few years later, when he was Protector. The speech does not purport to be a sermon; it is, in fact, an address to parliament, delivered on January 22nd, 1655. But, if it were presented to anybody unfamiliar with its identity, would it suggest any form of address as much as a sermon? The truth is, the lay-preacher was so deeply rooted in the man Cromwell that he seemed unable to open his mouth, or, for that matter, put pen to paper, without feeling the urge to preach. He preached when he exulted in the slaughter of his enemies; preached when he gave thanks for the preservation of his friends; he preached in triumph and he preached in adversity; and here he is talking to a captive congregation, parliament.[2]

These weeds, briers and thorns (*the ungodly, conspiring enemies* of the commonwealth)—they have been preparing, and have brought their designs to some maturity, by the advantages given to them . . . from your sittings and proceedings. But by the waking Eye that watched over the cause that God will bless, they have been, and yet are, disapointed. And having mentioned that Cause, I say, that slighted Cause,—let me speak a few words on behalf thereof; though it may seem too long a digression. Whosoever despiseth it, and will say, It is *non causa pro causa,* 'a cause without a cause,' the Allsearching Eye before mentioned will find out that man; and will judge him, as one that regardeth not the works of God nor the Operations of His Hands! For which God hath threatened that He will cast men down and not build them up. That *man who* because he can dispute, will tell us he knew not when the Cause began, nor where it is; but modelleth it according to his own intellect; and submits not to the Appearances of God in the World; and therefore lifts up his heels against God, and mocketh all his providences; laughing at the observations, made not up without reason and the Scriptures the quickening and teaching Spirit which gives life to these other;—calling such observations *enthusiasms* such men, I say, no wonder if they *stumble and*

1. See below, p. 461.   2. Speech to Parliament, January 21st, 1653.

fall backwards, and be broken and snared and taken by the things of which they are so wilfully and maliciously ignorant! The Scriptures say *The Rod has a voice, and He will make himself known by the judgements which He executeth.* And do we not think He will, and does, by the providence of mercy and kindness, which He hath for His People and their just liberties: *whom He loves as the apple of His eye?* Doth He not by them manifest Himself? And is he not thereby also seen giving kingdoms for them, *giving men for them, and people for their lives,*—as in Isaiah Forty-third?

So much for Cromwell speaking on a *political* occasion; thence to an impression of him, by someone, we may suspect, who had heard him speak, perhaps preach, in a private conventicle..

A most learned, conscientious, and devout Exercise, or Sermon

Held forth, the last Lord's-day of April, in the Year 1649, at Sir P. T.'s[1] House in Lincoln's-Inn-Fields, by Lieutenant-General Oliver Cromwell; as it was faithfully taken in Characters by Aaron Guerdon.[2]

ROM. xiii. 1.

'Let every Soul be subject unto the higher Powers; for there is no Power, but of God: 'the Powers, that be, are ordained of God.'

Dearly beloved brethren and sisters, it is true, this text is a malignant one; the wicked and ungodly have abused it very frequently, but (thanks be to God) it was to their own ruin: yet their abuse shall not hinder us from making a right use of it. Every thing is subject to be abused, be it never so holy or good: the men of God, the creatures of God, all are subject to injuries and abuse; the Council of State, the Parliament, the Army, the General, have been, and daily are abused; nay, even myself have not escaped the violence of those seducers, whose tongues are sharper than a two-edged sword. My

1. According to Oldy and Park (*Harleian Miscellany*, Vol. iv), these initials signify 'Sir Peter Temple', but, as I have explained, if this is so, it only confirms that nothing about the sermon was meant to be taken seriously.

2. Published London, 1680: thirty-one years after the alleged event: 'Mr. Guerdon', or somebody, was being very cautious.

very face and nose are weekly maligned and scandalized by those scribbling mercuries, Elencticus and Pragmaticus[1]; insomuch that, were it possible, they would raise a faction in my forehead, and make mutinies amongst my very teeth. It is true, I have a hot liver, and that is the cause my face and nose are red[2]; for my valour lies in my liver, not in my heart, as other men's; never any man could say my heart was stout: indeed the General's lie there, and that is the reason his face is pale. You all know, I never was a drunkard, although, when I was at the lowest, I had beer enough; for you know I had near relation to a beer-brewer; and I had always money to buy wine with, if I pleased, so that I might have been a drunkard, if I would; yet, you know, I am a temperate sober man, else I had never been so good a soldier. But, what is it the Malignants will not abuse, who let not to abuse themselves? I will warrant you, they would abuse our very wives too, if they durst; and I fear some of them do—you know what I mean;—but no more of that, at present. My text, you see, is scripture; and Scripture must be believed, next to our diviner revelations, be it what it will; but the Malignants, they would interpret it one way, and we, the Saints, interpret it another. Now let any body judge, whether they, or we, are to be believed: whether, I say, those ungodly Cavaliers, that sought to uphold tyranny and Antichrist; or we, that in the uprightness of our hearts, fought for liberty and freedom, and for establishing the kingdom of King Jesus. Surely, beloved, it is we that are in the right of it: I think none of you will deny it.

But now, that I spoke of kings, the main question is. 'Whether, by Higher Powers, are 'meant Kings, or the Commoners?' Truly, beloved, it is a very great question amongst those that say they are learned; but, I think verily, they make more stir about it, than needs: for may not every body, that can read, observe, that Paul speaks in the plural number, 'the higher powers?' Now, had he meant subjection to a king, he would have said, 'Let every soul be subject to the higher power;' that is, if he had meant one man: but, by this, you see, he intended more than one; for he bids us 'be subject to the higher 'powers,' that is, the Council of State, the House of Commons, and the Army. I hope I have cleared this point: so now then I will come closer to the words themselves, and shew you truly and plainly, without any gaudy rhetorick, what they signify unto us, that you be not deceived: and I tell you, this is not to be done by every spirit, but only by such, who are more than ordinarily endowed with the spirit of discerning. I confess there are

1. *Mercurius Elinctus*, Samuel Sheppard, and *Mercurius Pragmaticus*, Marchmont Nedham; the latter could, I think, be the author of the 'sermon'. It is the kind of thing he might have done and the style is like enough his known writing, except for one consideration which militates against the attribution: Nedham was usually coarse in his scurrility, even by the standards of the day; the author of this sermon is not.

2. Cromwell's nose was a favourite target of satirists.

many good men and women amongst you, that intend well, and speak well, and understand well; but yet cannot apprehend well all things that lurk in scripture-language, for lack of a sufficient measure of the spirit. They must be inwardly called thereunto, or else they are subject to errors and mis-constructions.

Well then, you see who are fittest to interpret, and I presume, you believe God hath abundantly supplied me: I do not boast of it, but I speak it to his glory, that hath vouchsafed to take up his lodging in so vile, contemptible, unswept, unwashed, ungarnished a room, as is this unworthy cottage of mine: but it was his will, and I am thankful for it.

Now the words offer themselves very naturally: they are plain, not difficult, but prostrate their sense in a most perspicuous manner.

For, first, beloved, by these words, 'Let every soul,' &c. we may under-stand, that every one of us have souls; whence I raise this doctrine: that it is an ungodly, irreligious, profane, and idle tenet amongst the wicked, to think, or say, that women have no souls. Mark, my beloved, to think, or say, &c. for there are many now-a-days, that think, and will not speak what they think; and others, that speak, and will not think what they speak: but we are none such—Dear sisters, it is a great abuse to your honourable sex.— And now, truly, I will turn to you only; for you have been our daily and nightly comforters: indeed, la, ye have! You have raised our drooping spirits, though never so much dejected; you have got us stomachs, when we had none, and furnished us with flesh, on all occasions; we never found you unwilling, or unready to help us, when we were the farthest from home. Believe it: when I lay before Pembroke-castle, my landlady, where I quar-tered, who had once been a Malignant, and then but newly crept into the state of grace; she, I say, had a good soul within her; she was brim-full of the spirit, and yet she was very handsome; which is strange: for seldom we find a perfection without an imperfection.—Commonly, women that are fair without, are either false or foul within; but to me she was neither. And yet I do not speak this to condemn beauty, for it is of a singular comfort and good use, and those that be fair, may be true and good. But this is *secundum majus & minus*, as the logicians cant; some are better than other some; that is, the English of the Latin: and, indeed, I have found great difference in women. Then again, when I came into Yorkshire, I met with Mrs Lambert,[1] the espoused of that honourable and valiant saint, Mr. J. Lambert: she, I say, is a woman, not very fair, I confess, but of as large a soul, and as full of the spirit, as any I ever yet met with. I profess, I never knew a woman more endowed with those heavenly blessings of love, meekness, gentleness, patience, and

---

1. Frances, wife of Cromwell's comrade in arms, General John Lambert, was a notably beautiful and attractive woman. There is no evidence of any amorous relationship between her and Cromwell. But he did admire her; his daughters did not.

long-suffering; nay, even with all things that may speak her every way deserving the name of a saint: and yet, I say, she was not very beauteous, or comely, for she is something foggy and sun-burnt, which is strange in that cold country. But what nature had denied her of ornament without, I found she had within her, a soul, a devout, sweet soul: and (God knows) I loved her for it.

Thus we find then both by scripture and experience, that all of us have souls, men and women. But then again, beloved, some have good souls, and some have bad; Mrs. Lambert hath a good soul, and no doubt, (nay, I know,) many of you that be here, are and have good souls within you. The Cavaliers and their queans are the bad souls; they serve, and are subject to bad and ungodly men: men did I call them? nay devils that would devour us, and drink themselves drunk with the blood of the saints.

By this then it is evident who have, and who are the good souls. Whence I raise this doctrine, or rather point of faith, That we are not to believe, or account any to have, or to be souls, but those that are of the family of *Saints*. (I would have said *Love*, but that it is a particular sect[1], something differing from ours.) Come on then: 'Let every soul be subject,' &c. Whereby we see, all souls, good and bad, are bound to be *subject*. All-Souls College in Oxford must be subject to the visitors; All-Souls day, though a superstitious holy-day, and strictly kept by the Papists, must be subject to labour and toil: your souls (brethren and sisters) must be subject to persuasion, to love, familiarity, and friendship; to all things that may increase or elevate the spirit; to kindle and take fire, like tinder, upon every spark and glance of our affections. O my dear brethren and sisters, Love! it is the fulfilling of the Law; what need we more then? It covers a multitude of sins; lo you there! it hides all our infirmities. Had one of us loved another, these differences and blood-shed had never happened. But some will object, and say, 'There is a lust, as well as love; and sometimes lust is falsely termed love.' I tell you, beloved, these nice and critical distinctions, are things that once had like to have undone us. Lust is nothing but a desire of any thing; and if, my beloved, we desire to enjoy one another, God forbid but we should help and comfort each other, and lay out ourselves, as far and freely as may be, to assist each other, in the embraces of the spirit: the laws of reason and nature require it of us.

But let us look yet a little further: 'Let every soul be subject to the higher powers,' &c. What those higher powers are, I have told you before; they are the Council of State, the House of Commons, and the Army; and God forbid but all men should obey them: that is, that the people be subject to the Council of State, the Council of State to the House of Commons, they to the Army, the Army to the General and the General to me. To me, I say, who have plotted, advised, counselled, and fought for both you and them these

1. The Family of Love.

seven years; and now at last purchased your freedom and liberty. Dear brethren and sisters, I speak it not in ostentation, but with thankfulness and glory to him, who made me so useful an instrument in this blessed work of reformation. For beloved, it was I that juggled the late King into the Isle of Wight: it was I dissolved the treaty: it was I that seized upon, and hurried him to Hurst-castle: it was I that set petitions a-foot throughout the kingdom, against the personal treaty, and for bringing the King and other capital offenders to justice: it was I that contrived, with the help of my son Ireton, the large remonstrance of the Army: it was I that prescribed the erecting of the high court of justice, and which brought the King to his trial: in a word, it was I that cut off his head, and with it all the shackles and fetters of the Norman slavery and bondage: it was I that cut off the heads of Hamilton, Capel, and Holland[1]: it was I that surprized the Levellers at Burford, and in Northamptonshire[2]: it was I that broke their design, destroyed Thompson[3] &c. dispersed and appeased the rest; and which have healed the late distempers of the Army, whereby the land is now restored to this blessed peace, tranquillity, and plenty. And therefore, I say, I may justly, and without ambition, style myself the author of all the kingdom's present and future happiness.

It is true, beloved, the General[4] is a stout and valiant man, and he hath great appearance of God in him; but fitter far to be passive than active in the affairs of state; he is fitter for a charge than a council: and the truth is, (as I may tell you under the rose) he wants brains to do any thing of moment. But indeed, this I may say for him, he is a man doth not seek himself; I never found him wilful, but willing always to submit to better judgments than his own. For when Sedgwick (that fast and loose priest) of Covent-garden, upon the King's trial, had writ to his lady to advise him to remit the execution of that sentence, and to wash his hands of his death; he, honest man, presently acquainted me with the business, and shewed me the arguments, given to persuade him against it; and freely referred all to my judgment. And the twenty-eighth of January, being the Lord's-day, at night I went to him in Queen's-street, attended with two troops of my own regiment, to remove the scruples he made upon that rascally priest's letter, or to secure him by force, in case he had contracted more, and would not be satisfied: but he, good man, gave

1. The Duke of Hamilton, Lord Capel and the Earl of Holland, prominent Royalists executed soon after the king.

2. The rising by the extreme left wing of army reformers, which Cromwell had put down rigorously that year in April.

3 William Thompson, the leader of the Leveller mutineers, was surrounded and shot to death in a wood in Northamptonshire; but not until the middle of May. Further evidence, if it were needed, of the fanciful origin of the composition.

4. Thomas Fairfax (third Lord Fairfax), commander-in-chief of the Parliamentary army.

me thanks for my pains, and told me I had fully resolved him. All this, beloved, I speak in honour of the man; but truly he is too great, to be so good as we must have a general, for you know he is a lord, and unless he be a lord, and no gentleman, (as I fear he will not acknowledge himself,) he is not for our turns: the rather, for that he is easily seduced, I have experience of him, and led away by every wind of doctrine; by mere appearances and shadows of reason. Truly, beloved, I think myself and my son Ireton may prove of greater use to the republick, than any other; and if we be but once the acknowledged governors thereof by the people, we believe we shall answer their expectations to a hair's-breadth; which if ever we be, then, beloved, it is I and my son who are the higher powers meant in my text, to whom subjection is commanded. For (as I told you before) it cannot be to one single man, must be to two or more; and truly, if the people shall think us (as we think ourselves) worthy of that trust, we shall discharge it faithfully, and study to merit it at their hands. But mistake me not; I do not mean by merit as the Papists do, that is, to deserve it at their hands, for the good works we have done: no, no, we will acknowledge it to be merely out of the free grace and mercy of the people; for when we have done all we can for them, we confess we are but unprofitable servants.

I thank them, they have made me general for Ireland; and you know I am upon the point of going thither, in great hopes of reducing those rebellious traitors to our obedience. But then, beloved, so many of you as go along with me, must be mindful of my text; that is, you must be *subject* to me, and my lieutenant-general. Whensoever we bid you go, you must run; when we bid you storm, you must do it, though it be against nothing but stone-walls. You owe us your lives and your limbs, and all that you have; whensoever we demand them, you ought to surrender, and that freely, not grumbling; for you must submit to the higher powers, &c.

The verity is, this expedition against Ireland is like to prove a very hard task, unless I can in policy engage Owen Roe,[1] if not to join with Jones, Monk, and Coot,[2] yet to keep off at a distance with Ormond.[3] I am, beloved, about it; and I shall do my endeavour too, to set Inchequeen and him at variance; and yet at that very instant will I lose no opportunity to re-oblige him to the Parliament: for you all know what Inchequeen is—I have him—I will not say how—but it is very probable an act of indemnity, tied in the strings of a five-thousand-pounds bag, may work a miracle. For he, good man, is but misguided; he stands not upon such punctilios of honour as Ormond doth.—

1. Owen Roe O'Neill, Irish patriot leader and military commander, who died suddenly (of poison, his Irish adherents believed) before he could try conclusions with Cromwell.

2. English military commanders in Ireland.

3. The Earl (later Duke) of Ormond: One of the king's most skilful and and tenacious supporters, who lived to enjoy the triumph of the Restoration.

In truth, beloved, this Ormond is a shrewd fellow, and were he not one of the wicked, a man highly deserving; not so much for his knowledge and experience in military affairs (which yet may challenge some proportion of honour), as for his diligence and faithfulness in the trust committed to him. Valour I will not allow him any; it is only desperateness, and that he wants not: but, remember we not how politicly he carried himself in the business of Dublin, after we had subdued the common enemy here the first time? How dexterously he avoided the messages and commands of the late King, which we extorted from him, for the surrender of that city? How shamefully he baffled our commissioners which were sent to treat with him about it; at what distance he kept them, still urging the captivity of the King to excuse his disobedience; and how often, and on what sleeveless errands, he sent them back to re-inforce their instructions; whilst all the while he was under-hand endeavouring to know the King's pleasure, by the hands of his own messenger? And when he was satisfied with the reality of the King's desires and condition, how notably he trucked with us, for his own security and satisfaction?—Nay more, when he stood upon the receipt of some thousands, before he would surrender, you shall hear how he there served us.—For notwithstanding that I caused the Parliament, by their letters, voluntarily to assure him the full double of the sum he demanded, upon condition he would quit the King's, and declare for our interest; and that hereunto he had re-turned a fine silver-tongued response in answer to the Parliament, and had thereupon returned him the authority of the Parliament, to indemnify him and his followers, for all things said or done in relation to the English or Irish wars, and four-thousand pounds in recompence for his losses: with this additional assurance, that he should, soon after the surrender, be re-invested with full power and government of Dublin, by commission from the Parliament: yet no sooner was Dublin delivered to us, upon the King's letters, and his passport sent him; but in contempt of all our fair and civil proffers, he transports himself for France, abruptly waving both our proffers and protection.—This, beloved, I instance not to justify him in his rebellious courses against the nation, (those I will use my utmost to destroy him for,) but, to let you see how gloriously even a wicked and ungodly man, as this Ormond is, appears in the eyes of the world, who but approves himself true to his trust, that scorns to be corrupted with gold, and continues so to the last; wherunto, beloved, you are all of you enjoined by the words of my text:—'Be subject to the powers,' &c.

Nor will I let to acknowledge him less formidable than faithful; for doubt less he hath gone very near to pacify all interests, and picked out of them a numerous army; over whom, he hath placed good officers. Good, said I? I do not mean, beloved, godly officers, for they are all of them prelatical or popishly affected; but tried soldiers: such as will not easily turn their backs on an enemy.—I must ingenuously confess too, they have a great strength by sea, and a number of wilful fellows for mariners; who are in great heart, by reason of the many and great prizes they have taken from us, and so forth. But, what of all this? Shall we therefore be discouraged? God forbid! The more numerous the enemy is, the greater shall be the victory over them; the more difficult the work is, the more our honour; the fuller their pockets are, the worse they will fight. You know, by experience, the plunder of Leicester gave us the victory at Naseby;[1] there you saw the Cavaliers choose rather to leave their King to his shifts, than shift from behind them their cloke-bags.—Believe it, brethren, we shall meet with many advantages against them—R. himself, I know, will do us some good, though it be but in crossing of proverbs: and hear I but once that Culpepper or Hyde is there,—doubt it not, all is our own.—I cannot recount a tithe of them. But this I am sure, the honest citizens have feasted us to good purpose; for, upon that occasion, we had their promise to advance monies a-fresh for Ireland.— *San nombre ou mesure:* that is French, beloved; the English whereof is, 'Without weight or measure.'[2]—Verily, they are of a stiff-necked generation, become very tractable and obedient servants; of a turbulent and mutinous, an exceeding meek and humble people.

And indeed, my beloved, it was no small work we had, to subdue those malignant spirits of the city; considering, how audaciously they once withstood our authority, and despised our government; how peremptorily they petitioned for a personal treaty with the King, and sent their servants into Colchester, Surry, and Kent, to force us thereunto; how bitterly they inveighed and railed against the honourable proceedings of the Parliament and Army; how largely they contributed to bring in a foreign nation to invade us, whilst, yet, they denied us the payment of our arrears, or to continue the necessary taxes, or excise, for our future maintenance; who had preserved them and their families, from the rapine and cruelty of a barbarous enemy. But, beloved brethren, I mean not to rip up all old matters. Let it suffice, that being thus warned by their mishap, you fall not into the like sin of disobedience to higher powers; there being no powers but of God; the powers that be, being ordained of God.

Object. But it may be, some here may object, and say, how shall we be secured, in your absence, from the malicious plots and contrivances of the Presbyterians, Malignants, and Levellers; since we cannot but expect, they will be complotting our ruin, especially Lilburn,[3] and the rest with him in

1. One of the contributory causes of the king's defeat at Naseby was the undisciplined dispersal of Royalist Cavalry in quest of plunder before the issue was resolved.

2. As may be seen from the foregoing extract of a parliamentary speech, Cromwell made heavy weather of the shortest quotation from a foreign language.

3. As the hero of the Levellers, a perpetual and eloquent thorn in Cromwell's side.

durance, whose spirits can never be quelled, but by a Cromwell; they being so implacable and desperate?

Answ. Truly, beloved, you that do, do very well to make these doubts: I like these doubting Christians, above all Christians, provided they be not jealous. And yet, my beloved, a man or woman may be jealous without cause, as that holy man of God, Major-general Lambert, is of his wife; which truly proceeds, not so much out of any corruption of judgment, as manners: yet the man was well bred, though not educated so well as we are in the South. But, as to this point, you shall hear how careful I have been to provide for your safety, and the peace of the nation, in my absencé. For supposing that Lilburn and his faction, and the rest of our enemies (as God knows we have too many), will strive to alienate the hearts of the people from me, and to usurp the rule and dominion to themselves, if a convenient strength, and some one or other were not left, fitted with policy and courage to restrain them; I have taken care, that my son Ireton shall stay amongst you, and that my corrival, noble Lambert, shall go in his stead, as my lieutenant-general, into Ireland: and my son, you all know, wants no spirit; if he did, he should never have married my daughter, that you may well think. As for his policy, I suppose you have as little reason to doubt of it, as I have of his fidelity. The large remonstrance renders him, as I take it, very clean-handed and subtle; and, with him, I will see a sufficient strength both of horse and foot be left; which, together with the city forces which we have engaged, and are as-certained, will stick to us: the General, so popular and valiant a man, staying here also to oversee them, shall (I warrant you) suppress all insurrections and tumults whatsoever. However, I have given such orders to my son Ireton, concerning Lilburn and the rest (if ever hereafter he observe him or them) to stir up the people to sedition, or scribble any thing, as formerly, against our lawful proceedings; that, forthwith, he shall execute justice upon them: and I think, dear brethren, you will judge it but necessary, since neither our mercy, nor the sense they have of the uprightness of our cause, will invite them to forbear bespattering the innocent robes of this infant state.

And now, beloved, as we must not conceal any thing from one another, I shall make bold to requite your ingenuity by the instancing one other doubt, with a danger, at the end of it; which although it may startle you at first sight, yet be of good courage, be faithful and strong; it admits of an easy solution: and that is the accord of the Scots with their new king.—Truly, I must confess my designs were never, till now, so diverted and confounded; for I must tell you, I have reverenced that short, but pithy precept of my father Machiavel, *Divide et impera*. So long as I could keep them at odds amongst themselves, I feared not but to order them, as I pleased. But now it is too true, that both the parliament and priests of that kingdom have attainted Argyle of high-treason; that is, for holding the hands of the Scots, until we executed that exemplary piece of justice on the King: and that therefore they intend to cut his head off; which if they do, then, beloved, they destroy our only friend in that kingdom[1] and the differences, on foot there, must needs expire with his breath: which being once done, they will have nothing left to do, but vie authority with us, and threaten a second invasion. For you must understand, the Scots are a warlike people, and that there is nothing will make them sooner rebel, than idleness and peace; so that, if this be so, we shall be sure to have them amongst us. Now, beloved, to preserve ourselves against them, in this great garrison of our English commonwealth. It is for our safety, that we quit those out-houses of Ireland; and, if they were burnt, it matters not, so we preserve but what we have already in possession. To which end I have resolved, if they cut off the head of Argyle, or otherwise disable him to prosecute our interest there, that then I will wave the war of Ireland; and, keeping the fore-door of this nation close shut, bend all powers to defend the back-door against that perfidious nation. And this I conceive to be the surest way, provided I can but make choice of able and trusty men to secure the ports, towns, and inland garrisons, without revolts or treachery.—And this will be easily done, considering the men and monies we have at our pleasure.—I tell you, brethren, our thousand shall slay their ten thousands, and, in a short space, make them a miserable little people; and, at length, root them out from off the face of the earth, and possess us of their lands, for an inheritance to us and our generations, for ever.

But I have strayed too far from my text. I will now come to the remaining words thereof, and so conclude:—'For there are no powers but of God,' &c. The Council of State, the House of Commons, the Council of War, and the High-Court of Justice, when it was, were all powers of God; and the following words of my text give you the reason: 'For the powers that be, are ordained of God.' Be they just or unjust, they are all of God, God ordained them; and so he did that tyrannical power of the late King, and those belly-gods the Bishops, to punish us for our infirmities. But now that he hath graciously removed those powers, he hath ordained ours, to preserve, cherish, elevate, comfort, and delight the saints, and to rule and govern the land in sincerity and in truth; to distribute justice, equally and impartially according to his will.—But the time is spent, and I must be marching.—I desire therefore, my dear brethren and sisters, that you daily pour out your prayers and supplications, for us; and for our success against the wicked and ungodly that are risen up against us; and that you cease not to comfort one another, with mutual embraces and spiritual kisses, to delight and sweeten your

---

1. A piece of whimsical hindsight. Argyll did not lose his head *then*, but he did later, at the Restoration, when, with the help of letters provided by Monk, his enemy, the Earl of Middleton, had him convicted of treasonable complicity with Cromwell.

passage through this vale of misery: and that you take especial care to strengthen and corroborate yourselves, with capon and cock-broth, that I may find oil in your lamps, at my return.

CHRISTOPHER LOVE

Redolent of malice as is the 'Oliver Cromwell' sermon, it is mild, gentlemanly stuff compared with the kind of missiles aimed at him from the pages of the political railers of the day, whose methods could give even a modern aspirant to 'satire' lessons in scurrility. In one he appears as the Town Bull of Ely, baited to provide entertainment for a party of sportsmen whose numbers include Lilburn, Overton and Walwyn.[1] The dogs set on him, all vicious, but each more cowardly and irresolute than the next, are former Puritan allies who have fallen foul of him, and whom the bull gores ferociously. Inevitably the game starts with a mock at Cromwell's unfortunate nose. Towzer, one of the dogs, succeeds in getting away with a piece of the bull's nose, which provokes a dialogue.

Lilburn What are those that creep with such black heads in his blood?

Overton An army of Maggots that took a pocksy delight to live in the warmth of his *Snowt*; and when he breathed out his Hypocricies and Blasphemies then these catel went to dinner. Foh, what a breath he has. T'will infect the whole kingdom with plagues and his nose set fire to it till it becomes more miserable than Sodom and Gomorah. . . .

Overton complains that 'he has' (by swerving from his principles) 'deceived him and thousands more' and therefore he'll 'have one more course at him, hit or miss.'

Overton A Dogge, a Dogge, a Dogge; a Kingdom for a good Dogge: Hy — day! Whose Crop-eared Curr is this?[2] O he was bred up at *Lincolns Inn*; I know him of old; they say his teeth be *poyson* by reason of a *Asp*, that lies under his tongue.

1. *A New Bull Bayting, or a Match Play'd at the Town Bull of Ely, by Twelve Mungrills* (1649).

2. William Prynne, the Puritan controversialist and lawyer, who in 1634 had lost his ears in the pillory, and three years later lost them again—what was left of them— and was branded on the face with the letters SL, seditious libeller, which Prynne construed as 'stigmata Laudis'. He hounded his enemy Laud to the scaffold, and sat in the Long Parliament as member for Newport, but quarrelled with Cromwell over the trial of the king, which he bitterly opposed, and was one of the members 'purged' by Pride's regiment.

Lilburn   No matter, so much the better; let him slip, Ha — looe — Crap;
A pox take him for a Curre, he has him by the *Genitals*; they'll
burn his *mouth*; pull him off by the *tayle*, and set him on fair;
Ha — looe — Crap for a second course, for they master Jack
Presbyter's credit: Alas, poor crap; he has him on his *horns*;[1] Save
him for pity. Foh, how he stinks!

The next dog to be loosed is the preacher, Cornelious Burges,[2] who
was by repute somewhat rapacious.

Overton   Here's another grizly Cur of the same *breed*;[3] set him on: This
Dogge was ty'de up in the pulpit in *Pauls* when the Army came
in; he looks as if he was got between a dog-fox and a Spannel
Bitch; a *Laodicean* whelp, neither hote nor cold; he looks as though
he were rather going to a hanging then to a match; sure he has
lost his 400 l. per annum:[4] draw him forward; Come along good-
Cole; how he fawns, as if he would suck Eggs; This *Tyke*, when
he percieves you *going*, will run at you as fierce as if he would eate
you; but stand but still, and he Retires back; run from him and
he will follow you, barking, bawling and snarling, and perchance
give you a bite behind.

Then comes another dog whom we have also met before.

Lilburn   . . . this is a lovely Dogge with a thin pair of chops; another of
Sir John Presbyter's breed, better to hand than to keep; how he
drivels out *Nonsence* and *Tautologies*; sure he has wasted his lungs
in confuting a May-pole, and entered into a *dispute* with the Maid-
marrian in a *Morrice-dance*, about the unlawfulness of that innocent
pastime; till the Hobby-horse confuted him with his *tayle*, and
returted *his rebuke* with his *heels*.

Walwyn   Stroke him and LOVE him; methinks 'twould make a pretty
foysting-hound for an *Alderman's daughter*:[5] he can turn after his
tayle; take a *Tythe-pigge*[6] by the *eare, fawn* on anybody, and bark
when his master bids him; stand up on *his* hind legs? or do anything
Sir John Presbyter will have *him*; he was once in request with the
Iuncto[7] though now *he* be out of service.

1. Prynne had been so obstreperous in resistance that soon after this he was imprisoned for nearly two years in Dunster, Taunton and Pendennis castles.
2. See above, p., 344.   3. Presbyterian, as opposed to Independent.
4. In 1644 Burges had obtained the Lectureship of St. Paul's, which carried with it
£400 a year, and the dean's house.
5. Perhaps a reference to the kind of scandal forming round his name to which Love
referred on the scaffold.
6. It was a common practice to pay tithes with a pig, and, as a Presbyterian, Love
was in favour of tithes.
7. The Army Grandees.

Overton Do they not *feed him*; *he* must do tricks or something for it: do ye think they'l keep a Doggee and *bark* themselves? or *maintain* a Dogge that will bark against themselves? that were the way to make People mistrust them for *Thieves*: he was counted a good *house* Dogge when he came from Vxbridge, but now *he fawns* not so much as formally, that makes him out of request, and miss of their LOVE.

Contentious as ever, Christopher Love had been unable to remain at peace with any ruling party for long. But in 1651 he went too far and obtained his *quietus*. He began to correspond with and raise money for the Cavalier conspirator, Massey, and his letters were intercepted. Cromwell was exceptionally tolerant of many offences, but seditious correspondence with the enemy was not one of them. Love was arrested and put on trial. He managed to quarrel with his judges before being convicted, on the evidence, quite properly.

His last sermon from the scaffold on Tower Hill was a long one, and consisted mainly of self-justification, not merely on the charges of which he had been convicted, but in respect of accusations of immorality which he admitted were in circulation.

The Sheriff, Titchburn, gave him great latitude, though reminding him, with brutal candour, that time was limited, and he and the headsman had another customer to serve before the light failed. At the end of his hectic life, Love is earnest, but evasive. He implies a state of 'innocence', without actually denying that he had done what he was convicted of doing, protesting that, 'for those things for which I am condemned neither God nor my own conscience condemns me'.

Having warned his hearers at length against mistaking old devils for new gods, he declares that he has 'lived in peace and would die in peace'.

We join the condemned man when he is already well into his stride.

Presbyterian Defiance

A last sermon preached by Christopher Love on
Tower Hill before his execution for treason on 16th
July, 1651

Beloved, I am this day making a double exchange, I am changing a Pulpit for
a Scaffold, & a Scaffold for a Throne; & I might add a third, I am changing
this numerous multitude, the presence of this numerous multitude on
Tower-hil, for the innumerable company of Saints & Angels in heaven, the
holy hill of *Sion*; and I am changing a guard of Souldiers for a guard of
Angels, which will receive me, and carry me into *Abrahams* bosome. This
scaffold it is the best Pulpit that ever I preached in; in my Church-Pulpit, God
through his grace made me an instrument to bring others to heaven; but in
this Pulpit he wil bring me to heaven. These are the last words that I shall
speak in this world, and it may be I shall bring more glory to God by this
one Speech on a scaffold, then I have done by many Sermons in a Pulpit.

Before I lay down my neck upon the block, I shall lay open my Cause
unto the people that hear me this day, that I might not die under all that
obloquy and reproach that is cast upon me; and in doing it, I shall avoid all
rancor, all bitternesse of spirit, animosity and revenge; God is my Record,
whom I serve in the spirit, I speak the truth and lie not; I do not bring a
revengefull heart unto the Scaffold. This day, before I came here, upon my
bended knees I have begg'd mercy for them that denied mercy to me, and
I have prayed God to forgive them who would not forgive me; I have
forgiven from my heart the worst enemy I have in all the world; and this
is the worst that I wish to my Accusers and prosecutors, who have pursued
my blood, that I might meet their souls in heaven.

I shall divide my Speech into three parts: I shall speak something concerning my Charge, and a word concerning my Accusers and touching my
Judges, without any animosity at all; and then something concerning my self
for my own Vindication, and then a word of Exhortation, and so I shall
commit my soul to God.

Concerning my Charge, it is black and hideous, many things falsly
suggested, hardly a line of it true, and nothing Capitall sufficiently proved
against me by any one Act that I am conscious to my self I did. The Charge
is high and full, but the Proof empty and low; though there were eight

Witnesses that came in against me, yet none of them did prove that ever I writ any Letter, or directed any man to write a Letter into *Scotland*, or into forraign parts; no man did prove that I sent away any Letter, that I received any Letter, that I collected or gave, or lent any money to assist or promote the Scottish War: This is all that is sworn against me, that I was present where Letters were read, and that I made a motion for money to give to *Massey*; so that (beloved) my presence at, and concealment of Letters that were received and sent from forreign parts, is that for which I must die.

As concerning my Accusers, I shall not say much; I do forgive them with all my heart, and I pray God forgive them also. Yet what the Evangelist said concerning Christ's Accusers, I may (without vanity or falshood) say of mine, That they did not agree amongst themselves: One Witnesse swears one thing, and another the quite contrary: Yea, not only did they contradict one another, but sometimes a single Witnesse contradicted himselfe. And though their Testimony did condemn my Person, yet I have condemned their Testimony. And truly there are many remarkeable circumstances that I might take notice of, either in, or before, or since the Trial, that might be worthy observation, but I will not insist upon it; only in the general (for I shall name none of my Accusers) some of them have sent to me, to pray me to forgive them the wrong they have done me: And one of them hath written to me under his own hand, to pray me to forgive him the wrong that he hath done me; and told me withall, that that day I should die a violent death, his life would be no comfort to him, because he was an Instrument in taking away of mine. Others of the Witnesses were some terrified before they would testifie; some were hired, some fined before they would bear Witnesse against me. But I will be off of this. As concerning my Judges, I will not judge them, and yet I will not justifie them: I will say but this of them, I beleive that what moved *Herod* to cut off *John* Baptist's head, that moved them to cut off mine; and that was for his Oaths sake: *Herod* to avoid Perjury would commit Murther; whereas if *John's* head had been upon his shoulders, he would have been guilty of neither.

I have something in the second place to speak concerning my self, and then I shall come briefly to a conclusion. Concerning my selfe, I have gone through various reports; there are many sons of slander, whose mouthes are as open Sepulchers, in which they would bury my Name, before my Friends can bury my Body; but my comfort is, there will be a Resurrection of Names as well as Bodies at the last day: God will not only wipe off all tears from my eyes this day, but he will also wipe off all blots and reproaches from my Name before many days be over; and though my body wil soon rot under ground, yet my hope is, my Name will not rot above it. I am not ignorant what Calumnies are cast upon me, and more likely to be after I am dead and gone. The very night before my intended Execution the last month, there was an insulting Letter written to me, to tell me, that after my death there should be something published against me to my shame. I hope you will have so much charity as not to beleeve reproaches cast upon a dead man, who will be silent in the grave, and not able to speak a word in his own justification. I am aspersed both as to my Practice, and as to my Principles. I shall begin with the first. There are five aspersions as to my Practice that are laid upon me, That I am a Liar, That I am an Extortioner, That I am an Adulterer, That I am a Murtherer, and That I am a Turbulent Person: Crimes scandalous in any man, but much more abominable in a Minister. Now I hope you will beleeve a dying man, who dares not look God in the face with a lie in his mouth: I am accused of lying, that what I denied before the High Court of Justice, that that afterwards I should confesse, or else was proved against me. Now in the presence of God I tell you, as I would confesse nothing that was Criminal, so I did deny nothing that was true; and that I may seal it to you with my blood, the same Protestations I made before the High Court, I shall make briefly now: 1. That I never writ Letter to the King, Queen, Church or State of Scotland, or to any particular person of the Scottish Nation since the Wars began to this day. 2. That I never received any Letter writ to me, either from the King, or from the Queen, or from the Church or State of Scotland, or from any particular person of the Scottish Nation, since the Wars began to this day. 3. That I never collected, gave or lent one peny of money, either to the King, Queen, Church or State of Scotland, or to any particular person to send into Scotland, to any person of the Scottish Nation to this day. It is true, I did confesse, though it was not proved (and haply upon that ground the mistake might arise) I did give mony to *Massey*, and I did also write a Letter to him, but he is of the English not of the Scottish Nation. That for which I come here, is only for moving for mony for him, and that not upon a military account, but meerly to relieve his personall necessities, and for being present where letters were read from him and others. And although man hath condemned me, yet I am so far from thinking that either God or my own conscience condemns me, as sinning in what I am condemned for, that both God and my own conscience doth acquit me: and what I said at the Bar when I received my Sentence, that I shall say upon the Scaffold, That for those things for which I am condemned, neither God nor my own conscience condemns me.

Again, I am accused to be an Extortioner; and this is in the mouths—I am loath to name them, because I will avoid all rancor: But I am charged as if I should be a grievous Extortioner, to receive Thirty pounds for the loan of Three hundred ponds, besides Eight pounds *per centum* for Interest; which in the presence of God and of you all, I do declare to you, is a most notorious and abominable falshood.

I am accused likewise to be an Adulterer, and this report is not in the mouths of mean men, but in the mouths of those that sit at the Stern: As if I were a debauched Person, and were guilty of Uncleannesse. Now I tell you, as *Luther* said of himselfe in another case, That he was not tempted to Covetousness, through the Grace of God I can say I was not tempted in all my life to uncleaness. It doth not much grieve me though their slanders lye upon me. I know my betters have been worse accused before me. Athanasius, he was accused by two harlots that he had committed folly with them, and yet the man was chast and innocent. Beza was charged not only with drunkeness but Lasciviousness.

In the middle of these spiritual preparations Love could not resist his last chance to aim a public kick at Cromwell and, without warning, he suddenly switched from resignation to rancour, much to the embarrassment of the Sheriff.

'Those who have gotten power into their hands by policy, and use it by cruelty, they will lose it by ignominy.'

Titchburn at once intervened to put an end to such prophecies.

'Sir, be modest. I am not able to endure this: indeed I am not'; and Love, recognizing that his voice could be silenced peremptorily, returned to the less inflammable topic of his own righteousness.

... I am now drawing to an end of my Speech, and to an end of my life together; but before I do expire my last breath, I shall desire to justifie God, and to condemn my self in all that is brought upon me. Here I come to that which you call an untimely end, and a shamefull death; but (blessed be God) it is my glory, & it is my comfort: I shall justifie God, he is righteous, because I have sinned; he is righteous, though he cut me off in the midst of my days, and in the midst of my Ministry: I cannot complain that Complaint in *Psalm* 44.12. *Thou sellest thy people for nought, and dost not encrease thy wealth by their price.* My bloud it shall not be spilt for nought; I may do more good by my death, then by my life, and glorifie God more in dying upon a scaffold, then if I had died of a disease upon my bed. I blesse my God, I have not the least trouble upon my spirit; but I do with as much quietnesse of minde lie down (I hope I shall) upon the Block, as if I were going to lie down upon my bed to take my rest. I see men hunger after my flesh, and thirst after my bloud, let them have it, it will hasten my happinesse, and their ruine, and greaten their guiltinesse: Though I am a man of an obscure Family, of mean Parentage, so that my blood is not as the blood of Nobles, yet I will say it is a Christians blood, a Ministers blood, yea it is innocent blood also: My body, my dead body, it will be a morsell, which I beleeve will hardly be digested, and my blood it will be bad food for this Infant-Commonwealth (as Mr. *Prideaux* call'd it) to suck upon: Mine is not Malignant blood, though here I am brought as a grievous and notorious offendor. Now beloved, I shall not only justifie God (as I do without a complement; for he were very just, if my Prison had been Hell, and this Scaffold the bottomlesse pit, I have deserved both; so that I do not only justifie God) but I desire this day to magnifie God, to magnifie the riches of his glorious grace, that such an one as I, born in an obscure Country (in Wales) of obscure Parents, that God should look upon me, and single me out from amongst all my kindred, to be an object of his everlasting love; that when as the first 14. years of my life I never heard a Sermon, yet in the fifteenth year of my life God (through his grace) did convert me. And here I speak it without vanity (for what should a dying man be proud of?) though I am accused of many scandalous evils, yet (I speak to the praise and glory of my God) for these twenty years God hath kept me, that I have not fallen into any scandalous sin: I have laboured to keep a good conscience from my youth up, and I magnifie his grace, that he hath not only made me a Christian, but a Minister, and judged me faithfull to put me into the Ministry: And though the Office be trodden upon and disgraced, yet it is my glory that I die a despised Minister; I had rather be a Preacher in a Pulpit, then a Prince upon a Throne; I had rather be an instrument to bring souls to Heaven, then to have all the Nations bring in Tribute to me: I am not only a Christian and a Preacher, but whatever men judge, I am a Martyr too, I speak it without vanity; would I have renounced my Covenant, and debauch'd my Conscience, and ventured my soul, there might have been hopes of saving my life, that I should not have come to this place; but blessed by my God, I have made the best choice, I have chosen affliction rather than sin and therefore welcome Scaffold, and welcom Axe, and welcom Block, and welcome Death, and welcome All, because it will send me to my Fathers House: I have great cause to magnifie Gods grace, that he hath stood by me during mine imprisonment, it hath been a time of no little temptation to me, yet (blessed be his grace) he hath stood by me and strengthened me; I magnifie his grace, that though now I come to die a violent death, yet that death is not a terror to me; through the blood of sprinkling, the fear of death is taken out of my heart; God is not a terrour to me, therefore death is not dreadfull to me; I blesse my God, I speak it without vanity, I have formerly had more fear in the drawing of a tooth, then now I have at the cutting off my head: I was for some five or six yeers under a spirit of bondage, and did fear death exceedingly; but when the fear of death was upon me, death was not neer mee; but now death is neer me, the fear of it is far from me: and blessed be my Saviour that hath the sting of death in his own sides, and so makes the grave a bed of rest to me, and makes Death, (the last enemy) to be a friend, though he be a grim friend. Further, I blesse my God, that though men have judged me to be cast out of the world, yet that God hath not cast me out of the hearts and prayers of his people; I had rather be cast out of the world, then cast out of the hearts of godly men. Some think me (it is true) not worthy to live; and yet others judge I do not deserve to die: but God will judg all, I will judg no man.

I have now done, I have no more to say, but to desire the help of all your prayers, that God would give me the continuance and supply of divine grace to carry me through this great work that I am now about: that as I am to do a work I never did, so I may have a strength I never had: That I may put off this body with as much quietnesse and comfort of minde, as ever I put off my clothes to go to bed: And now I am to commend my soul to God, and to receive my fatall blow, I am comforted in this, *Though men kill me, they cannot damn me; and though they thrust me out of the world, yet they cannot shut me out of heaven.* I am now going to my long home, and you are going to your short homes; but I will tell you, I shall be at home before you; I shall be at my fathers house, before you will be at your own houses: I am now going to the heavenly *Jerusalem*, to the innumerable company of Angels, to Jesus the Mediator of the New covenant, to the spirits of just[1] men made perfect, and to God the Judge of all, *In whose presence there is fulnesse of joy, and at whose right hand are pleasures for evermore.* I conclude with the speech of the Apostle, 2 *Tim.* 4.6,7. *I am now to be offered up, and the time of my departure is at hand; I have finished my course, I have fought the good fight, I have kept the faith, henceforth there is a crown of righteousnesse laid up for me; and not for me onely, but for all them that love the appearing of our Lord Jesus Christ,* through whose bloud (when my bloud is shed) I expect remission of sins and eternall salvation: And so the Lord blesse you all.

At the end of this fairly solid discourse, Love proceeded with panache to take over the stage-management of his own execution. He strode about the scaffold, scattering advice and exhortations as farewells to acquaintances in the crowd, chatting in a friendly way with the executioner (whom he tipped 3d wrapped in a piece of white paper), while Sheriff Titchburn became increasingly agitated at the duration of these activities. At last, Love announced his intention of praying

---

1. The reporter of the speech evidently thought it better to omit reference to an interruption here. Love had at first said 'the spirits of *all* men made perfect', but Titchburn, the Sheriff, could not let such a grave doctrinal error pass, and at once intervened with a correction.

before his departure. 'Yes, but consider the time', pleaded Titchburn. Love then embarked upon a prayer which lasted about six minutes, at the end of which, Titchburn, desperate by now, exclaimed, 'The House is risen, therefore. . . .'

'Ay, ay, sir', said Love, adding innocently, 'Is all in readiness?'

For Titchburn all had long been in readiness. Not so for Love, who now produced from some place of concealment, a red scarf which he directed to be disposed upon the block; then, after a conference with the executioner concerning signals, he knelt down and rested his head on the scarf.

On the signal, the executioner severed his head from his body at one blow; but Mr. Dun, 'the chyrugian', was in attendance to 'unite both together again.'[1]

Then the body of Christopher Love, silent at last, was placed in the black-draped coffin, which was waiting to convey the remains of this courageous and resolutely self-destructive man from the scene of his last preaching.

1. Perhaps to make his appearance more decorous at a lying-in-state.

JEREMY TAYLOR[1]

Cromwell, having pacified Ireland with measured severity, defeated and conciliated the Scots at Dunbar, and finally, at Worcester, on September 3rd, 1651, obtained 'the crowning mercy' of a conclusive victory over the resurrected arms of the Cavaliers, now applied himself to consolidating his military command with firm administration. The need, at least *his* need, for provocative, incitant public speeches was over, and, as Protector, he tightened his grip upon the preacher as upon every potential reviver of dissension. Not every voice could be silenced, but it could be subdued and contained by surveillance, if necessary by compulsion. The Puritan lay-preachers' dream of true revolution which would make them—the preachers, the *saints*—into rulers, still seethed in the breasts of men for whom the outcome of the Civil War was an evil compromise and a betrayal. Some of them, for what they said, would go to prison. Most of their words were never written down. What was written is of a limited interest to political historians, and of no literary merit. One or two Puritan divines of a pacific temper, like Howe and Bates, were allowed to make a contemporary impression, but it is doubtful whether the stiff prolixity of either will ever again be read for pleasure. There is Baxter to consider, but he was self-censored by prudence. In general the Protectorate was not a fruitful period for the English pulpit, or rather, the fruit was not notable for quality. But, as sometimes happens in indifferent vintages, there was an exception so important that it alone must qualify our evaluation of the whole.

1. Jeremy Taylor, 1613–1667; born Cambridge, son of a barber. Admitted sizar to Gonville and Caius College, 1626; B.A. 1630–1; ordination and M.A. 1633–4. His preaching attracted the attention of Laud, who translated him to Oxford by obtaining him a Fellowship of All Souls, 1636. Rector of Uppingham 1638 and successively chaplain to Laud and Charles I. D.D. 1642. Sequestered in 1644, he spent most of the Civil War protected by the second Earl of Carbury in the seclusion of Golden Grove, where *Liberty of Prophecying* and *Holy Living*, as well as the *Fifty-two Sermons* were written. Twice married, three of his sons dying in childhood. After the war he was rewarded in 1660 with the turbulent Irish bishopric of Down and Conner, from which he begged in vain to be recalled. Too gifted to be passed over, Taylor in England might have caused the restored Crown embarrassment, if his first wife was, as Reginald Heber asserts in his biography, the illegitimate daughter of Charles I. Taylor died of fever in Lisburn, on the 13th August 1667, and was buried at Dromore.

On a tranquil estate on the borders of Wales, far from the battles, the pillaging and burning, out of reach of the intrigues and betrayals and executions, the most richly gifted artist ever to apply his talents to the medium of preaching had taken refuge and was now composing his masterpieces.

Jeremy Taylor sometimes seems as if, intoxicated by the prodigality of his imagination, he is about to drown in his own words. But just as he is on the point of plunging under one foaming simile too many, never to surface more, he reappears, swimming, dolphin-like, with lyrical ease, and reminding us that, in his element of words, he is one of the great craftsmen, an artist of humbling authority. The flavour of his prose is unmistakable and unique, an exegetical amalgam of the general and the particular. Its imagery is never vivid, nor does it remain *hard* for long; but it produces haunting impressions. His words are spells and, at their utterance, eclectic myths take shape, vaporize, reform and dissolve, captivating the ear with the music of a kind of part-Christianized, pagan fairyland, where the satyr and the martyr, the sorcerer and the saint, contend for attention, and the unicorn lies down with the lamb.

One of the most interesting and distinctive characteristics of Taylor's prose is his use of falling and 'inconclusive' cadences, in which spondees and their auxiliaries are one of the devices used to prevent the words coming to a full stop, so that they can remain inviting and poised, at the end of each convolution, to glide into another progress. Just as any word he uses at once ceases to be its ordinary self when it joins his body of celebrants, and shares the ecstasy of the runes, so with persons and events; they are never the mortal, mundane actuality we meet in daily life. Not that there is evasion of the ugly, the harsh, the painful, the cruel; these are rather, as behoves a preacher, sought out in the course of duty; but, however vile their nature and effects, they are transmogrified and embalmed in the spices and fragrance of his poetry. He tells us, after his fashion, what they are, and the result is marvellously ornamented effigies which provoke wonder, more than dread. With Donne we cannot enjoy life above ground for long even on the most pleasant day, without the sweet stench of the grave rising to foul the fresh air. With Taylor we can pass through a charnel house and the prevailing quality of the experience will be aesthetic.

Such alchemy, of course, imposes limitations. The hermeneutical usefulness of Taylor's sermons must have been sometimes questionable, and the suspicion does arise that his monitions made the sins he depicted more alluring than repellent. There are worse visions of death than of the drunkards, going 'singing' to their grave; and his engaging description of the disgrace of eminent men 'fit to sit with princes and treat concerning peace and war . . .', who, victims of infatuation, 'fall at the beauty of a woman as a man dies at the blow of an angel', is an image which any aspiring gallant might profitably use to press his suit with almost any girl. His rustic auditory must have been a little bewildered at times by the treasures which the accidents of war had showered on them; and the thought of Taylor warning a Sunday assembly of Welsh agricultural labourers and estate servants against such temptations as coveting 'Galatian mules and fat Eunuchs from Tunis as their servants'[1] is an appealing one. He is never prudish, but, in treating subjects which a prude would not treat, he is rescued by the sheer superiority of his talent from being dainty. In reprehending incest he adjures you 'not to draw the curtain from your sister's retirement'. It is as if an emancipated, unworldly, but infinitely enquiring maiden aunt, had been touched by the breath of the muses[2]. Taylor was, above all, an *original*; there had been nothing quite like him before; he defied imitation, and, in any event, the future course of English literature would turn sharply away from the standards and influences which had informed his genius. In less than twenty years, Tillotson and Dryden, and a generation of new young writers, were honing down their prose to the taste of the Royal Society, and Taylor seemed an antiquated weird. But the gentle wizard was indestructible; he has continued to be rediscovered, again and again, long after most of his critics have been conclusively forgotten, or cut to a reduced stature. He was the grandmaster of the literary baroque, the late fulfilment and the end of the euphuist movement, a sublimation, florid but subtle, purged of all mechanical conceits and tricks. The subjects of his sermons are perfectly orthodox; but, beneath the general terms, they are full of references to events and misfortunes of the Civil War.[3]

1. To be exact, this admonition was not addressed to a congregation, since it comes from *Holy Living* (1650), but it is fairly representative of what he did say in the pulpit; i.e. he did exhort the rustics at Carbury to resist any predilection for 'Lavinian sausages and Cisalpine suckets, or gobbets of conditioned bulls flesh' (*House of Feasting*, Pt. 2.)

2. There was nothing 'maidenly' or 'auntish' about Taylor's own life. He was a handsome man and very popular with the ladies. He had a gentle and very pleasing voice, and, like all actively successful preachers, an attractive public personality.

3. See below, pp. 488, 490, 492, 493, 494, 496, 505.

Of Christian Prudence (1651)[1]

It is an office of prudence to serve God so that we may at the same time preserve our lives and our estates, our interest and reputation, for ourselves and our relatives, so farre as they can consist together. St. Paul[2] in the beginning of christianity was careful to instruct the forwardness, and zeal of the new Christians into good husbandry, and to catechize the men into good trades, and the women into useful employments, that they might not be unprofitable. For christian religion carrying us to heaven, does it by the way of a man, and by the body it serves the soul, as by the soul it serves God; and therefore it endeavours to secure the body and its interest, that it may continue the opportunities of a crown, and prolong the stage in which we are to run for the mighty price of our salvation: and this is that part of prudence which is the defensative and guard of a Christian in the time of persecution, and it hath in it much of duty. He that through an indiscreet zeal casts himself into a needlesse danger, hath betrayed his life to tyranny, and tempts the sin of an enemy; he loses to God the service of many years, and cuts off himself from a fair opportunity of working his salvation (in the main parts of which we shall find a long life and very many years of reason to be little enough) he betrays the interest of his relatives, (which he is bound to preserve) he disables himself of making provision for them of his own house[3]; and he that fails in this duty by his own fault 'is worse than an infidel:' and denies the faith, by such unseasonably dying, or being undone, which by that testimony he did intend gloriously to confesse; he serves the end of ambition and popular services, but not the sober ends of religion; he discourages the weak, and weakens the hands of the strong, and by upbraiding their warinesse tempts them to turn it into rashness or despair; he affrights

---

1. *Twenty-seven Sermons*, Sermon xx. The particular interest of this item is that it is in the nature of advice to distressed Cavaliers on how best to comport themselves under a hostile Puritan government.

This sermon, and the next six, are taken from *A Course of Sermons for all the Sunday of the Year*, comprising '*Twenty-Five Sermons* preached at Golden Grove, being for the Winter half year ...' (first published 1653); and '*Twenty-Seven Sermons*, preached at Golden Grove, being for the Summer half year ... (first published 1651): 2nd edition 1655, collated with 3rd edition 1667–1668, 4th edition 1673, 5th edition 1678, and the versions in Taylor, *Works*, edited by Reginald Heber 1822 (15 vols.), revised C. P. Eden, 1854 (10 vols.).

2. Titus iii : 14.   3. I Tim. v : 8.

strangers from entering into religion, while by such imprudence he shall represent it to be impossible at the same time to be wise and to be religious; he turns all the whole religion into a forwardnesse of dying or beggary, leaving no space for the parts and offices of a holy life, which in times of persecution are infinitely necessary for the advantages of the institution. But God hath provided better things for His servants:

Quem fata cogunt, ille cum venia est miser[1]

'he whom God by an inevitable necessity calls to sufferance, he hath leave to be undone;' and the ruin of his estate or loss of his life shall secure first a providence, then a crown.

At si quis ultro se malis offert volens,

Seque ipse torquet, perdere est dignus bona,

Queis nescit uti;—

'But he that invites the cruelty of a tyrant by his own follyes or the indiscretions of an unsignificant and impertinent zeal, suffers as a wilful person, and enters into the portion and reward of fools.' And this is the precept of our Blessed Saviour, next after my text, "Beware of men;" use your prudence to the purposes of avoiding their snare. Τῶν θηρῶν βροτὸς μᾶλλου ἀνήμερος; man is the most harmful of all the wild beasts. Ye are sent as sheep among wolves; be therefore wise as serpents: when you can avoid it, suffer not ment to ride over your heads or trample you under foot; that's the wisdom of serpents. And so must we; that is, by all just complyances, and toleration of all indifferent changes in which a duty is not destroyed and in which we are not active, so preserve ourselves that we might be permitted to live, and serve God, and to do advantages to religion; so purchasing time to do good in, by bending in all those flexures of fortune and condition which we cannot help, and which we do not set forward, and which we never did procure. And this is the direct meaning of St. Paul[2], "See then that ye walk circumspectly, not as fools but as wise, Redeeming the time, because the days are evil; that is, we are fallen into times that are troublesome, dangerous, persecuting, and afflictive; purchase as much respite as you can; buy or redeem the time by all honest arts, by humility, by fair carriage and sweetnesses of society, by civility and a peaceful conversation, by good words and all honest offices, by praying for your persecutors, by patient sufferance of what is unavoidable. And when the tyrant draws you forth from all these guards and retirements, and offers violence to your duty, or tempts you to do a dishonest act or to omit an act of obligation, then come forth into the theatre and lay your necks down to the hangman's axe, and fear not to die the most shameful death of the crosse or the gallows. For so have I known angels ascending and descending upon those ladders; and the Lord of glory suffered shame and purchased honour upon the cross. Thus we are to walk

1. Seneca, *Hippolytus*, Act 2, sc. 2, l. 442.   2. Eph. v : 15, 6.

in wisdom towards them that are without, redeeming the time[1]: for so St. Paul renews that permission or commandment; give them no just cause of offence; with all humility, and as occasion is offered, represent their duty, and invite them sweetly to felicities and vertue, but do not in ruder language upbraid and reproach their basenesse; and when they are incorrigible, let them alone, lest like cats[2] they run mad with the smell of delicious ointments. And therefore Pothinus[3] bishop of Lyons being asked by the unbaptized president, Who was the God of the Christians? answered Ἐὰν ᾖς ἄξιος γνώσῃ If you be disposed with real and hearty desires of learning, what you ask you shall quickly know; but if your purpose be indirect, I shall not preach to you, to my hurt, and your no advantage. Thus the wisdom of the primitive Christians was carefull not to profane the temples of the heathen, not to revile their false gods; and when they were in duty to reprehend[4] the follies of their religion, they chose to do it from their own writings, and as relators of their own records: they fled from the fury of a persecution, they hid themselves in caves, and wandered about in disguises, and preached in private, and celebrated their synaxes and communions in grots and retirements; and made it appear to all the world they were peaceable and obedient, charitable and patient, and at this price bought their time.

Lust for Revenge[5] (1651)

... What man can give a reasonable account of such a man, who to prosecute his revenge will do himself an injury, that he may do a lesse to him that troubles him. Such a man hath given me ill language; οὔτε τὴν κεφαλιὸν ἀλγεῖ, οὔτε τὸν ὄφθαλμον, οὔτε τὸ ἰσχίον, οὔτε τὸν ἀγρὸν ἀπολλύει;[6] My

1. Col. iv : 5.   2. Plutarch, *De Conjugalia Praecepta*, tom. vi.
3. Eusebius of Caesarea, *Historia Ecclesiastica*, 1, 204.
4. 'Represent' in the first two editions.
5. Taylor, op. cit., pp. 100, 101. The 'Deceitfulness of the Heart.' Sermon VIII.
6. Eden, in a footnote (Taylor, *Works*, 1854, iv, 427) corrects Taylor's faulty translation, 'the words refer not to the sufferer but the doer of the injury', and identifies the quotation as 'Arrian Epict. lib. ii. cap. 10. tom. iii, p. 154'. This is his way of indicating that it comes from the *Encheiridion* (the manual of Epictetus) by the Romanized Greek soldier, philosopher and historian, Flavius Arrianus, of Nicomedia in Bythnia, whose work, written in the second century A.D., was adapted for Christian use by St. Nilus of Constantinople in the fifth century, and first published, with a commentary by Simplicius, in Venice, in 1528. As usual Eden, although he cites a page number, does not think it necessary to divulge what edition he is using. The best modern edition is in Schweighauser's *Epicteteae Philosopheae Monumenta*, Vol. iii.

head akes not for his language, nor hath he broken my thigh, nor carried away my land. But yet this man must be requited. Well, suppose that. But then let it be proportionable; you are not undone, let not him be so. Oh yes; for else my revenge triumphs not. Well, if you do, yet remember he will defend himself, or the Law will right him; at least do not do wrong to your self by doing him wrong. This were but Prudence, and Self-interest. And yet we see, that the heart of some men hath betrayed them to such furiousnesse of Appetite, as to make them willing to die, that their enemy may be buried in the same Ruines. Jovius[1] Pontanus tells of an Italian slave (I think) who being enraged against his Lord, watched his absence from home, and the employment and inadvertency of his fellow-servants: he locked the doors, and secured himself for a while, and Ravished his Lady; then took her three sons up to the battlements of the house, and at the return of his Lord, threw one down to him upon the pavement, and then a second, to rend the heart of their sad Father, seeing them weltring in their blood and brains. The Lord beg'd for his third, and now his onely Son, promising pardon and libertie, if he would spare his life. The slave seemed to bend a little, and on condition his Lord would cut off his own Nose, hee would spare his Son. The sad Father did so, being willing to suffer any thing, rather then the losse of that Childe; But as soon as he saw his Lord all bloody with his wound, he threw the third Son, and himself down together upon the pavement. The story is sad enough, and needs no lustre and advantages of sorrow to represent it: But if a man sets himself down, and considers sadly, he cannot easily tell upon what sufficient inducement, or what principle the slave should so certainly, so horridly, so presently, and then so eternally ruine himself. What could he propound to himself as a recompence to his own so immediate Tragedy? There is not in the pleasure of the revenge, nor in the nature of the thing, any thing to tempt him; we must confesse our ignorance, and say, that The Heart of man is desperately wicked; and that is the truth in generall, but we cannot fathom it by particular comprehension.

1. In the original of Jovianus the place is Majorca and the slave a Moor, not an Italian. But the story was a popular one in the seventeenth century and Taylor might also have heard it in one of the several versions made up of rhymes like the following:

> With that he took her in his arms
> She straight for help did cry
> Content yourself, Lady (he said)
> Your husband is not nigh.
> The Bridge is down, the gates are shut
> Therefore come lie with me
> Or else I do protest and vow
> Thy Butcher I will be.

A Lamentable Ballad of the tragical end of a vertuous lady and Gallant Lord, with the untimely end of their children: the like never heard of (Bagford Ballads, 1, 220, 221).

For when the heart of man is bound up by the grace of God, and tied in golden bands, and watched by Angels, tended by those Nurse-keepers of the soul; it is not easie for a man to wander: And the evil of his heart is but like the ferity[1] and wildenesse of Lyons-whelps: But when once we have broken the hedge, and got into the strengths of youth, and the licenciousnesse of an ungoverned age, it is wonderfull to observe, what a great inundation of mischief in a very short time will overflow all the banks of Reason and Religion. *Vice* first is *pleasing*, then it grows *easie*, then *delightfull*, then *frequent*, then *habituall*, then *confirmed*, then the *man is impenitent*, then he is *obstinate*, then he *resolves never to Repent*, and then he is *Damned*. And by that time he is come half way in this progresse, he confutes the Philosophy of the old Moralists; For they, not knowing the vilenesse of mans Heart, not considering its desperate amazing Impiety, knew no other degree of wickednesse but This, That men preferred Sense before Reason, and their understandings were abused in the choice of a temporall before an intellectuall and eternall good: But they alwayes concluded, that the Will of man must of necessity follow the last dictate of the understanding, declaring an object to be good in one sence or other. Happy men they were that were so Innocent; that knew no pure and perfect malice, and lived in an Age, in which it was not easie to confute them. But besides that, now the wells of a deeper iniquity are discovered, we see by too sad experience, that there are some sins proceeding from the heart of man, which have nothing but simple, and unmingled malice; Actions of meer spite; doing evil, because it is evil; sinning without sensuall pleasures: sinning with sensuall pain, with hazard of our lives: with actuall torment, and sudden deaths, and certain and present damnation: sins against the Holy Ghost: open hostilities, and professed enmities against God and all vertue. I can go no further: because there is not in the world, or in the nature of things, a greater Evil. And that is the Nature and Folly of the Devil: he tempts men to ruine, and hates God, and onely hurts himself, and those he tempts: and does himself no pleasure, and some say, he increases his own accidentall torment.

Of Growth in Sin[2] (1651)

... It is a sad calamity, that there are so many millions of men and women that are entred into a state of sicknesse and danger, and yet are made to beleeve they are in perfect health; and they do actions concerning which

1. See Martial, lib. ii, epigr. 75.   2. Taylor, op. cit., Sermon XVI, pp. 199-201.

they never made a question whether they were just or no; nor were ever taught by what names to call them. For while they observe that *modesty* is sometimes abused by a false name, and called *clownishnesse*, and *want of breeding*; and *contentednesse* and *temperate living* is suspected to be *want of courage* and *noble thoughts*; and *severity of life* is called *imprudent* and *unsociable;* and *simplicity* and *hearty honesty* is counted *foolish* and *unpolitike*, they are easily tempted to honour *prodigality* and *foolish dissolution* of their estates with the title of *liberall* and *noble usages; timorousnesse* is called *caution; rashnesse* is called *quicknesse of spirit; covetousnesse*, is *frugality; amorousnesse* is *society* and *gentile; peevishnesse* and *anger* is *courage; flattery* is *humane* and *courteous*; and under these false vails vertue slips away (like truth from under the hand of them that fight for her) and leave vices dressed up with the same imagery, and the fraud not discovered, till the day of recompences, when men are distinguished by their rewards. But so men think they sleep freely when their spirits are loaden with a Lethargie, and they call a Hectick-feaver the vigour of a naturall heat, till nature changes those lesse discerned states into the notorious images of death. Very many men never consider whether they sin or no in 10000. of their actions, every one of which is very disputable; and do not think they are bound to consider: these men are to be pitied and instructed, they are to bee called upon to use religion like a daily diet; their consciences must bee made tender, and their Catechisme enlarged; teach them, and make them sensible and they are cured.

But the other in this place are more considerable: Men sin without observation, because their actions have no restraint of an express Commandment, no letter of the law to condemn them by an expresse sentence. And this happens, when the crime is comprehended under a generall notion without the instancing of particulars; for if you search over all the Scripture you shall never finde *incest named* and marked with the black character of death; and there are divers sorts of uncleannesse, to which Scripture therefore gives no name, because she would have them have no being; And it had been necessary that God should have described all particulars, and all kindes, if hee had not given reason to man. For so it is fit that a guide should point out every turning, if he be to teach a child, or a fool to return under his fathers roof: But he that bids us avoid intemperance for fear of a feaver, supposes you to be sufficiently instructed that you may avoid the plague; and when to look upon a woman with lust is condemned, it will not be necessary to adde, you must not do more, when even the least is forbidden: and when to uncover the nakednesse of Noah brought an universall plague upon the posterity of Cham, it was not necessary that the Law-giver should say, you must not ascend to your fathers bed, or draw the curtains from your sisters retirements. When the Athenians forbad to transport figs from Athens, there was no need to name the gardens of Alcibiades, much lesse was it necessary to adde, that Chabrias should send no plants to Sparta. Whatsoever is comprised under the generall notion, and partakes of the common nature, and the same iniquity, needs no speciall prohibition, unlesse we think we can mock God, and elude his holy precepts with an absurd trick of mistaken Logick. I am sure that will not save us harmlesse from a thunderbolt.

2. Men sin without an expresse prohibition, when they commit a thing that is *like* a forbidden evil. And when Saint Paul had reckoned many works of the flesh, he addes [*and such like*] all that have the same unreasonablenesse and carnality.[1] For thus, Polygamy is unlawfull, for it it be not lawfull for a Christian to put away his wife and marry another (unlesse for adultery[2]) much lesse may he keep a first and take a second, when the first is not put away; If a Christian may not be drunk with wine, neither may he be drunk with passion; if he may not kill his neighbour, neither then must he tempt him to sinne; for that destroyes him more: if he may not wound him, then he may not perswade him to intemperance, and a drunken feaver; if it be not lawfull to cozen a man, much lesse is it permitted that hee make a man a fool, and a beast, and exposed to every mans abuse, and to all ready evils. And yet men are taught to start at the one half of these, and make no conscience of the other half; whereof some have a greater basenesse then the other that are named, and all have the same unreasonablenesse.

3. A man is guilty, even when no law names his action, if he does any thing that is a cause, or an effect, a part or unhandsome adjunct of a forbidden instance; he that forbad all intemperance, is as much displeased with the infinite of foolish talk that happens at such meetings, as he is at the spoiling of the drink, and the destroying the health. If God cannot endure wantonnesse, how can he suffer lascivious dressings, tempting circumstances, wanton eyes, high diet? If idlenesse be a sin, then all immoderate mispending of our time, all long and tedious games, all absurd contrivances how to throw away a precious hour, and a *day of salvation* also, are against God, and against Religion. He that is commanded to be charitable, it is also intended he should not spend his money vainly, but be a good-husband, and provident, that he may be able to give to the poor, as he would be to purchase a Lordship, or pay his Daughters portion: and upon this stock it is that Christian religion forbids jeering, and immoderate laughter, and reckons *jestings* amongst the *things that are unseemly*, This also would be considered.

4. Besides the expresse laws of our Religion, there is an universall line and limit to our passions and designes, which is called *the analogie of Christianity*; that is, the proportion of its sanctity and strictnesse of his holy precepts. This is not forbidden, but does this become you? Is it decent to see a Christian live in plenty and ease, and heap up money, and never to partake of Christs passions: there is no law against a Judge, his being a dresser of gardens, or a

1. Gal. v : 21   2. Matt. xix : 9.

gatherer of Sycamore fruits, but it becomes him not, and deserves a reproof.
If I do exact justice to my neighbour, and cause him to bee punished legally
for all the evils hee makes mee suffer. I have not broken a fragment from the
stony Tables of the Law: but this is against the *analogie of our religion*; It does
not become a Disciple of so gentle a Master to take all advantages that he can.

The Righteous Cause Oppressed[1] (1651)

. . . That man knows nothing of *nature*, or *providence*, or *Christianity*, or *the
rewards of vertue*, or *the nature of its constitution*, or *the infirmities of man*, or *the
mercies of God*, or *the arts and prudence of his loving kindnesse*, or *the rewards of
heaven*, or *the glorifications of Christs exalted humanity*, or *the precepts of the
Gospel*, who is offended at the sufferings of Gods dearest servants, or declines
the honour and the mercy of sufferings in the cause of righteousnesse; For
the securing of a vertue, for *the imitation of Christ*, and *for the love of God*, or *the
glories of immortality*. It cannot, it ought not, it never will be otherwise, the
world may as well cease to be measured by time, as good men to suffer
affliction. I end this point with the words of Saint Paul,[2] *Let as many as are
perfect, bee thus minded, and if any man bee otherwise minded, God also will reveal
this unto you*, this, of the Covenant of sufferings concerning which the old
Prophets, and holy men of the Temple had many thoughts of heart; but in
the full sufferings of the Gospel, there hath been a full revelation of the
excellency of the sufferings. I have now given you an account of some of those
reasons, why God hath so disposed it, that at this time, that is, under the
period of the Gospel, judgement must begin at the house of God, and they
are either, πιμωείας or δοκιμαοίαι, or μδρτύειον, or imitation of Christs λυτρὸν,
chastisements, or trials, martyrdom, or a conformity to the sufferings of the
Holy Jesus.

But now besides all the premises, wee have another account to make
concerning the prosperity of the wicked: *For if judgement first begin at us?
what shall the end bee of them that obey not the Gospell of God?* that is the
question of the Apostle, and is the great instrument of comfort to persons ill
treated in the actions of the world. The first ages of the Church lived upon
promises, and *prophecies*; and because some of them are already fulfilled for
ever, and the others are of a continuall and a successive nature, and are
verified by the actions of every day: Therefore we and all the following

1. Taylor, op. cit., pp. 124–129. 'The Faith and Patience of the Saints, or The
Righteous Cause Oppressed'; Sermon X, Pt. 2.
2. Phil. 3 : 15.

Ages live upon *promises* and *experience*: and although the servants of God have suffered many calamities, from the tyrannie and prevalency of evil men their enemies, yet still it is preserved as one of the fundamentall truths of Christianity; That all the fair fortunes of the wicked are not enough to make them happy, nor the persecutions of the godly, able to make a good man miserable; not yet their sadnesses arguments of Gods displeasure against them. For when a godly man is afflicted and dies, it is his work and his businesse; and if the wicked prevail, that is, if they persecute the godly, it is but that which was to be expected from them: For who are fit to be hang-men, and executioners of publike wrath, but evil and ungodly persons? And can it be a wonder that they whose cause wants reason, should betake them-selves to the sword? that what he cannot perswade he may wrest? onely we must not judge of the things of God by the measures of men, τὰ ἀνθρώπινα the things of men have this world for their stage, and their reward, but *the things of God* relate to *the world to come*: and for our own particulars we are to be guided by rule, and by *the end of all*, not by events intermediall, which are varied by a thousand irregular causes. For if all the evil men in the world were unprosperous (as most certain they are) and if all good persons were tempor-ally blessed (as most certainly they are not) yet this would not move us to become vertuous: *If an angel should come from heaven*,[1] or *one arise from the dead*[2] and preach repentance, or justice, and temperance, all this would be ineffectuall to those to whom the plain doctrines of God, delivered in the Law and the Prophets will not suffice.

For why should God work a signe to make us to beleeve that we ought to do justice; if we already beleeve, he hath commanded it, no man can need a miracle for the confirmation of that which he already beleeves to be the command of God: And when God hath expressely bidden us to *obey every ordinance of man for the Lords sake, the King as supreme, and his deputies as sent by him*.[3] It is a strange infidelity to think, that a rebellion against the ordinance of God, can be sanctified by successe and prevalency, of them that destroy *the authority*, and *the person*, and *the law*, and *the religion*: The sin cannot grow to its height if it be crushed at the beginning; unlesse it prosper in its progresse, a man cannot easily fill up the measure of his iniquity: but then that the sin swels to its fulnesse by prosperity, and grows too big to be suppressed with-out a miracle, it is so far from excusing, or lessening the sin, that nothing doth so nurse the sin as it: It is not vertue, because it is prosperous, but if it had not been prosperous, the sin could never be so great.

> ——*Facere omnia sæve*
> *Non impune licet, nisi dum facis.*[4]

A little crime is sure to smart, but when the sinner is grown rich, and prosperous, and powerfull, he gets impunity.

1. Gal. i : 8.   2. Luke xvi : 31.   3. I Pet. ii : 13.4.   4. Lucan, viii, 492.

Jusque datum sceleri——[1]

But thats not innocence, and if prosperity were the voice of God to approve an action, then no man were vitious, but he that is punished, and nothing were rebellion, but that which cannot be easily suppressed, and no man were a Pirate, but he that robs with a little vessell, and no man could be a Tyrant, but he that is no Prince, and no man an unjust invader of his neighbours rights, but he that is beaten and overthrown. Then the crime grows big and loud, then it calls to Heaven for vengeance, when it hath been long a growing, when it hath thrived under the Devils managing; when God hath long suffered it, and with patience in vain expecting the repentance of a sinner: he that treasures up wrath[2] against the day of wrath, that man hath been a prosperous, that is, an unpunished and a thriving sinner: but then it is the *sin* that thrives, *not the man*: and that is the mistake upon this whole question: for the sin cannot thrive, unlesse the man goes on without apparent punishment, and restraint. And all that the man gets by it is, that by a continual course of sin, he is prepared for an intolerable ruine. The Spirit of God bids us look upon *the end of these men*; not the way they walk, or the instrument of that pompous death. When Epaminondas was asked, which of the three was happiest, himself, Chabrias, or Iphichrates, he bid the man stay till they were all dead; for till then that question could not be answered.[3] He that had seen the Vandals besiege the city of Hippo, and have known the barbarousnesse of that unchristned people, and had observed that S. *Augustine* with all his prayers and vows could not obtain peace in his own dayes, not so much as a reprieve for the persecution, and then had observed S. *Augustine* die with grief that very night, would have perceived his calamity more visible then the reward of his piety and holy religion.[4] When Lewis surnamed *Pius* went his voyage to Palestina upon a holy end, and for the glory of God to fight against the Saracens and Turks, and Mamalukes, the world did promise to themselves that a good cause should thrive in the hands of so holy a man: but the event was far otherwise; his brother *Robert* was killed, and his army destroyed, and himself taken prisoner, and the money which by his Mother was sent for his redemption was cast a way in a storm, and he was exchanged for the last town the Christians had in Egypt, and brought home the crosse of Christ upon his shoulder in a real pressure and participation of his Masters sufferings.[5] When Charles the fifth went to Algier to suppresse pirates and unchristned villians, the cause was more confident then the event was prosperous: and when he was almost ruined in a prodigious storme, he told the minutes of the clock, expecting that at midnight, when religious persons rose to Mattins, he should be eased by the benefit of their prayers: but the

---

1. Ibid., i, 2.   2. Rom. ii : 5.   3. Plutarch, *Apothegmata*, tom. vi.
4. Possidius, in *Vit. S. Aug.* cap. xxviii.
5. See *Histories of St. Louis*, by Joinville and Guillame de Nangis.

providence of God trod upon those waters, and left no footsteps for discovery: his navie was beat in pieces, and his designe ended in dishonour, and his life almost lost by the bargain. Was ever cause more baffled then the Christian cause by the Turks, in all Asia and Affrica, and some parts of Europe, if to be persecuted and afflicted be reckoned a calamity? What Prince was ever more unfortunate then Henry the sixt of England, and yet that age saw none more pious and devout, and the title of the house of Lancaster was advanced against the right of York, for three descents; but then what was the end of these things? the persecuted men were made Saints, and their memories are preserved in honour, and their souls shall reign for ever; and some good men were ingaged in a wrong cause, and the good cause was sometimes managed by evill men, till that the suppressed cause was lifted up by God in the hands of a young and prosperous prince, and at last, both interests were satisfied in the conjunction of two roses, which was brought to issue by a wonderful chain of causes managed by the divine providence: and there is no age, no history, no state, no great change in the world, but hath ministred an example of *an afflicted truth*, and *a prevailing sin*: For I will never more all that sinner prosperous, who after he hath been permitted to finish his businesse, shall die, and perish miserably: for at the same rate, we may envie the happinesse of a poor fisherman, who while his nets were drying, slept upon the rock and dreamt that he was made a King; on a sudden starts up, and leaping for joy, falls down from the rock, and in the place of his imaginary felicities, loses his little portion of pleasure, and innocent solaces, he had from the sound sleep and little cares of his humble cottage.

And what is the prosperity of the wicked? to dwell in fine houses, or to command armies, or to be able to oppresse their brethren, or to have much wealth to look on, or many servants to feed, or much businesse to dispatch, and great cares to master: these things are of themselves neither good nor bad; but consider: would any man amongst us, looking and considering before hand, kill his lawfull King to be heir of all that which I have named? would any of you choose, to have God angry with you upon these terms? would any of you be a perjured man for it all? A wise man or a good, would not choose it: would any of you die an Atheist that you might live in plenty and power? I beleeve you tremble to think of it. It cannot therefore be a happinesse to thrive, upon the stock of a great sin: for if any man should contract with an impure spirit, to give his soul up a at certain day, it may be 20. years hence, upon the condition he might for 20. years have his vain desires, should we not think that person infinitely miserable; every prosperous thriving sinner is in the same condition: within these twenty years, he shall be thrown into the portion of Devils, but shall never come out thence in twenty millions of years. His wealth must needs sit uneasie upon him, that remembers that within a short space he shall be extremely miserable; and if he does not remember it, he does but secure it the more. And that God defers the punishment, and suffers evil men to thrive in the opportunities of their sin, it may and does serve many ends of providence, and mercy, but serves no end that any evil men can reasonably wish or propound to themselves eligible.

Bias said well to a vitious person, *Non metuo ne non sis daturus pœnas, sed metuo ne id non sim visurus,*[1] He was sure that the man should be punished, he was not sure he should live to see it: and though the Messenians that were betrayed and slain by Aristocrates in the battle of Cyprus, were not made alive again, yet the justice of God was admired, and treason infinitly disgraced, when twenty yeers after, the treason was discovered, and the traitor punished with a horrid death. Lyciscus[2] gave up the Orchomenians to their enemies, having first wished his feet, which he then dipt in water, might rot off, if he were not true to them; and yet his feet did not rot till those men were destroyed, and of a long time after; and yet at last they did; *stay them not O Lord, lest my people forget it* (saith David)[3] if punishment were instantly and totally inflicted, it would be but a sudden and single document: but a slow and lingring judgement, and, a wrath breaking out in the next age, is like an universal proposition, teaching our posterity, that God was angry all the while, that he had a long indignation in his brest, that he would not forget to take vengeance: and it is a demonstration, that even the prosperous sins of the present age, will finde the same period in the Divine revenge when men see a judgement upon the Nephews[4] for the sins of their Grand fathers, though in other instances, and for sins acted in the dayes of their Ancestors.

We know that when in Henry the eight, or Edward the sixth dayes, some great men pulled down Churches and built palaces, and rob'd religion of its just incouragements, and advantages; the men that did it were sacrilegious; and we finde also that God hath been punishing that great sin, ever since,[5] and hath displaied to so many generations of men, to three or four descents of children, that those men could not be esteemed happy in their great fortunes, against whom God was so angry, that he would shew his displeasure for a hundred years together. When Herod had killed the babes of Bethlehem, it was seven years before God called him to an account.[6] But he that looks upon the end of that man, would rather choose the fate of the oppressed babes, then of the prevailing and triumphing Tyrant: It was fourty years before God punished the Jews, for the execrable murder committed upon the person of their King, *the holy Jesus*; and it was so long, that when it did happen many men attributed it to their killing S. *James* their Bishop and

---

1. Plutarch, *De Sera Numinis Vindicta,* tom. viii.   2. Ibid.   3. Ps. lix : 11.

4. Jeremy Taylor, 'The Entail of Curses Cut Off,' *Works,* ed. Eden, iv, 367. Cf. Horace, *Satires,* i, 2, line 37.

5. Spelman, *History of Sacrilage,* Ch. vii. *et seq.*   6. According to Baronius.

seemed to forget the greater crime,[1] but *non eventua rerum sed fide verborum stamus*: we are to stand to the truth of Gods word not to the event of things. Because God hath given us a rule, but hath left the judgement to himself; and we die so quickly, (and God measures all things by his standard of eternity, and 1000 years to God is as but one day)[2] that we are not competent persons to measure the times of Gods account, and the returns of judgement. We are dead before the arrow comes, but the man scapes not, unlesse his soul can die, or that God cannot punish him. *Ducunt in bonis dies suos & in momento descendunt ad infernum*,[3] thats their fate, *they spend their dayes in plenty, and in a moment descend into hell*: in the mean time they drink and forget their sorrow; but they are condemned, they have drunk their hemlock, but the poison does not work yet: the bait is in their mouthes, and they are sportive; but the hook hath struck their nostrils, and they shall never escape the ruine; And let no man call the man fortunate, because his execution is deferr'd for a few dayes, when the very deferring shall increase, and ascertain the condemnation.

But if we should look under the skirt of the prosperous and prevailing Tyrant, we should finde even in the dayes of his joyes, such allayes and abatements of his pleasure, as may serve to represent him *presently miserable*, besides his finall infelicities. For I have seen a young and healthfull person warm and'ruddy under a poor and a thin garment, when at the same time, an old rich person hath been cold, and paralytick, under a load of sables, and the skins of foxes: it is the body that makes the clothes warm, not the clothes the body: and the spirit of a man makes felicity and content, not any spoils of a rich fortune wrapt about a sickly and an uneasie soul. *Apollodorus*[4] was a Traitor, and a Tyrant, and the world wondered to see a bad man have so good a fortune; But knew not that hee nourished Scorpions in his brest, and that his liver and his heart were eaten up with Spectres and images of death; his thoughts were full of interruptions, his dreams of allusions, his fancie was abused with real troubles, and phantastick images, imagining that he saw the Scythians flaying him alive, his daughters like pillars of fire dancing round about a Cauldron in which himself was boyling, and that his heart accused it self to be the cause of all these evils: And although all Tyrants have not imaginative & phantastick consciences, yet all Tyrants shall die and *come to judgement*; and such a man is not to be feared, nor at all to be envied: and in the mean time can he be said to escape, who hath an unquiet conscience, who is already designed for hell, hee whom God hates, and the people curse, and who hath an evil name, and against whom all good men pray, and many desire to fight, and all wish him destroyed[5], and some contrive to do it? Is this man a blessed man? Is that man prosperous who hath stolen a rich robe,

1. Eusebius of Caesarea, *Historia Ecclesiastica* (English translation 1650), Bk. 2, Ch. 9, p. 23.

2. 2 Pet. iii : 8.   3. Job xxi : 13.   4. Plutarch, op. cit., tom. viii.   5. Cromwell.

and is in fear to have his throat cut for it, and is fain to defend it with the greatest difficulty and the greatest danger? Does not he drink more sweetly, that takes his beaverage in an earthen vessel, then he that looks and searches into his golden chalices for fear of poison, and looks pale, at every sudden noise, and sleeps in armour, and trusts no body, and does not trust God for his safety, but does greater wickednesse only to escape a while unpunished for his former crimes? *Aurobibitur venenum*, No man goes about to poison a poor mans pitcher, nor layes plots to forrage his little garden made for the hospital of two Bee-hives, and the feasting of a few Pythagorean herbeeaters.

Flesh and Spirit[1] (1653)

... *Nemo enim se adsuofacit ad vitandum & ex animo evellendum ea qua molesta ei non sunt!* Men are so in love with pleasure, that they cannot think of mortifying or crucifying their lust; we doe violence to what we hate, not to what we love. But the weaknesse of the flesh, and the empire of lust is visible in nothing so much, as in the captivity and folly of wise men. For you shall see some men fit to governe a Province, sober in their counsells, wise in the conduct of their affaires, men of discourse and reason, fit to sit with Princes, or to treat concerning peace and warre, the fate of Empires, and the changes of the world, yet these men shall fall at the beauty of a woman as a man dies at the blow of an Angell, or gives up his breath at the sentence and decree of God. Was not *Solomon* glorious in all things but when he bowed to *Pharoah*'s daughter, and then to Devils? and is it not published by the sentence and observation of all the world, that the bravest men have been softened into effeminacy by the lisping charms, and childish noyses of Women and imperfect persons? A faire slave bowed the neck of stout *Polydamas*,[2] which was stiffe and inflexible to the contentions of an enemy; and suppose a man set like the brave boy of the *King* of *Nicomedia*[3] in the midst of temptation by a witty beauty, tyed upon a bed with silk and pretty violences, courted with musick and perfumes, with promises and easie postures, invited by opportunity and importunity, by rewards and impunity, by privacy and a guard; what would his nature doe in this throng of evils and vile circumstances? The grace of God secur'd the young Gentleman, and the Spirit rode in triumph;

1. *Twenty-Five Sermons*, pp. 129-131. Sermon X, Pt. I.

2. Plutarch, *Moralia*, vi, De Garrulitate.

3. Jerome, in *Vita Sanctae Paulae*, tom. iv, pt. 2; Nicephorus of Constantinople, *Historia Ecclesiastica;* Migne (*Patrologie Cursus Completus, series Graeca*, tom. 108).

but what can *flesh* do in such a day of danger? Is it not necessary that we take in auxiliaries from Reason and Religion, from heaven and earth, from observation and experience, from hope and fear, and cease to be what we are, lest we become what we ought not? It is certain that in the cases of temptations to voluptuousnesse, a man is naturally, as the Prophet[1] said of *Ephraim*, like a Pigeon that hath no heart, no courage, no conduct, no resolution, no discourse, but falls as the water of *Nilus* when it comes to its cataracts, it falls infinitely and without restraint; And if we consider how many drunken meetings the Sunne sees every day, how many Markets and Faires and Clubs, that is, so many solemnities of drunkennesse, are at this instant under the eye of heaven; that many *Nations* are marked for intemperance, and that it is lesse noted because it is so popular, and universall, and that even in the midst of the glories of Christianity there are so many persons drunk, or too full with meat, or greedy of lust, even now that the Spirit of God is given to us to make us sober, and temperate, and chaste, we may well imagine, since all men have flesh, and all men have not the spirit, the flesh is the parent of sin; and death, and it can be nothing else.

And it is no otherwise when we are tempted with pain. We are so impatient of pain, that nothing can reconcile us to it; not the laws of God, not the necessities of nature, not the society of all our kindred, and of all the world, not the interest of vertue, not the hopes of heaven; we will submit to pain upon no terms, but the basest and most dishonorable; for if sin bring us to pain, or affront, or sicknesse, we choose that, so it be in the retinue of a lust, and a base desire; but we accuse Nature, and blaspheme God, we murmur and are impatient when pain is sent to us from him that ought to send it, and intends it as a mercy when it comes. But in the matter of afflictions and bodily sicknesse we are so weak and broken, so uneasie and unapt to sufferance, that this alone is beyond the cure of the old Philosophy. Many can endure poverty, and many can retire from shame and laugh at home, and very many can endure to be slaves; but when pain and sharpnesse are to be endured for the interests of vertue, we finde but few Martyrs; and they that are, suffer more within themselves by their fears and their temptations, by their uncertain purposes and violences to Nature, then by the Hang-mans sword; the Martyrdome is within; and then he hath won his Crown, not when he hath suffered the blow, but when he hath overcome his fears, and made his spirit conqueror. It was a sad instance of our infirmity, when of the 40 Martyrs of *Cappadocia*[2] set in a freezing lake, almost consummate, and an Angell was reaching the Crowne, and placing it upon their brows, the flesh fail'd one of them, and drew the spirit after it; and the man was called off from his Scene of noble contention, and dyed in warm water. . . .

1. Hosea vii : 11.   2. Basil, *Homilies*, xlx.

The Gluttons' Way (1653)[1]

1 Corinthians. 15. 32 (last part) *Let us eat and drink for tomorrow we die.*

This is the Epicure's Proverb, begun upon a weak mistake, started by chance from the discourse of drink, and thought witty by the undiscerning company, and prevail'd infinitely because it struck their fancy luckily and maintained the merry meeting; but as it happens commonly to such discourses, so this also; when it comes to be examined by the consolations of the morning and the sober hours of the day, it seems the most witless and the most unreasonable. . . . The old gluttons among the *Romans, Heliogabalus, Tigellius, Crispus, Montagnus, notæque; per oppida buccæ,*[2] famous Epicures, mingled their meats with vomitings; so did *Vitellius*, and enter'd into their baths to digest their Phesants, that they might speedily return to the Mullet and the Elese of *Syene*, and then they went home and drew their breath short till the morning, and it may be not at all before night,

Hinc subite mortes, atque intestata senectus.[3]

Their age is surprised at a feast, and gives them not time to make their will, but either they are choked with a large morsell, and there is no room for the breath of the lungs, and the motion of the heart; or a feaver burns their eyes out, or a quinzie punishes that intemperate throat that had no religion, but the eating of the fat sacrifices, the portions of the poor and of the Priest; or else they are condemned to a Lethargie if their constitutions be dull, and if active, it may be they are wilde with watching.

Plurimus hinc æger moritur vigilando: sed illum
Languorem peperit cibus imperfectus, & hærens
Ardenti stomacho[4] —

So that the Epicures *geniall* proverb may be a little alter'd, and say, *Let us eat and drink, for by this means to morrow we shall die;* but that's not all, for these men live a healthlesse life, that is, are long, are every day dying, and at last

1. Taylor, op. cit., pp. 191–201. 'The House of Feasting, or the Epicureans Measure': Pts. 1 and 2; Sermons XV and XVI.

2. Juvenal, *Satires*, iii, 35. Taylor has confirmed Tigellus Hermogenes, mocked by Horace (Satires I. 10. 80, 90, etc.), with Nero's crony Tigellenus.

3. Ibid., i, 144.   4. Ibid., iii, 232.

dye with torment. *Menander*[1] was too soft in his expression, —μόνος . . οὗτος φαίνεται εὐθάνατος— that it is indeed a death, but gluttony is a pleasant death,

—ἔχοντα πολλὰς χολλάδας κεῖσθαι παχὺν,
—μόλις λαλοῦντα, καὶ τὸ πνεῦμ' ἔχοντ ἄνω,
ἐσθίοντα καὶ λέγοντα, σήπομ' ὑπὸ τῆς ἡδονῆς·

For this is the gluttons pleasure, to breath short and difficulty, scarce to be able to speak, and when he does, he cries out, I dye and rot with pleasure. But the folly is as much to be derided as the men to be pitied, that we daily see men afraid of death with a most intolerable apprehension, and yet increase the evill of it, the pain, and the trouble, and the suddennesse of coming, and the appendage of an unsufferable eternity.

> *Rem struere exoptas cæso bove, Mercuriumque;*
> *Arcessis fibra —*

They pray for herds of cattell, and spend the breeders upon feasts and sacrifices. For why do men go to Temples and Churches, and make vowes to God and daily prayers, that God would give them a healthfull body, and take away their gout and their palsies, their feavers and apoplexies, the pains of the head and the gripings of the belly, and arise from their prayers and powre in loads of flesh and seas of wine, lest there should not be matter enough for a lusty disease?

> *Poscis opem nervis, corpusque; fidele senectæ.*
> *Esto age, sed grandes patinæ tucetaque, crassa*
> *Adnuere his superos vetuere, Jovemque morantur'*[2]

But it is enough that the rich glutton shall have his dead body condited and embalmed; he may be allowed to stink and suffer corruption while he is alive; These men are for the present *living sinners* and *walking rottennesse*, and hereafter will be *dying penitents* and *perfumed carcasses*, and their whole felicity is lost in the confusions of their unnaturall disorder. When *Cyrus*[3] had espyed *Astyages* and his fellowes coming drunk from a banquet loaden with variety of follies and filthinesse, their legs failing them, their eyes red and staring, cousened with a moist cloud, and abused by a doubled object, their tongues

---

1. Eden's footnote for this (Taylor, *Works*, iv, 187) is 'In *Piscat*, apud Athenaeus lib. xii, cap. 72 p. 1224'. No edition is cited. This is intended as an intimation that Athenaeus here alludes to a work of Menander's known as the *Fisherman* in which the Greek poet had described a glutton as 'a fat pig lying on his side' who dedicated himself so completely to the luxury that he could not live long to do so. 'But', Menander had said, 'This death seems to me the only happy one'. It is this conclusion that Taylor is questioning.

2. Persius, ii, 41.   3. Xenophon. *Cryopaedia*, i, 3, para. 10.

full as spunges, and their heads no wiser, he thought they were *poysoned*, and he had reason; for what malignant quality can be more venomous and hurt-full to a man then the effect of an intemperate goblet, and a full stomach? it poysons both the soul and body. All poysons do not kill presently, and this will in processe of time, and hath formidable effects at present.

But therefore me thinks the temptations which men meet withall from with-out, are in themselves most unreasonable and soonest confuted by us. He that tempts me to drink beyond my measure, civilly invites me to a feaver; and to lay aside my reason, as the *Persian* women did their garments and their modesty at the end of feasts: and all the question then will be, which is the worse evill, to refuse your uncivill kindnesse or to suffer a violent headach, or to lay up heaps big enough for an *English Surfeit. Creon* in the Tragedy said well,

κρεῖσσον δέ μοι νῦν πρός σ' ἀπεχθεσθαι, γύναι,
ἢ μαλθακισθένθ' ὕστερον μέγα στένειν[1]

It is better for me to grieve thee O stranger, or to be affronted by thee, then to be tormented by thy kindnesse the next day and the morrow after, and the *freed man* of *Domitius* the Father of *Nero*[2] suffered himself to be kild by his Lord; and the sonne of *Praxaspes* by *Cambyses*,[3] rather then they would exceed their own measures up to a full intemperance, and a certain sicknesse, and dishonour. For, (as *Plutarch*[4] said well) to avoid the opinion of an uncivill man, or being clownish, to run into a pain of thy sides or belly, into madnesse or a head-ach, is the part of a fool and a coward, and of one that knowes not how to converse with men *citra pocula & nidorem,* in any thing but in the famelick smels of meat and vertiginous drinkings.

PART 2, SERMON XVI

It is lawfull when a man needs meat to choose the pleasanter, even meerly for their pleasures; that is, because they are pleasant, besides that they are usefull; this is as lawfull as to smell of a rose, or to lye in feathers, or change the posture of our body in bed for ease, or to hear musick, or to walk in gardens rather then the high-wayes; and God hath given us leave to be de-lighted in those things which he made to that purpose, that we may also be

1. Euripides, *Medea*, 290.   2. Suetonius, *Lives of Caesars* (Nero: cap. v).
3. Taylor is here committing a pious fraud. According to Herodotus, whose account he purports to retail, the unlucky son of Prexaspes was given no opportunity of refusing or accepting a drink; he was not asked; he was not even in conversation with his slayer when he died. Cambyses took a bow and arrow and shot him through the heart, from some distance off, to demonstrate to the youth's rashly censorious father that wine did not impair his marksmanship. Lib. III (*Thalia*), cap. 35.
4. *De Tuenda Sanitate Praecepta*, tom. vi.

delighted in him that gives them. For so as the more pleasant may *better* serve for *health*, and *directly* to *refreshment*, so *collaterally* to *Religion*: Alwayes provided, that it be in its degree moderate, and we temperate in our desires, without transportation and violence, without unhandsome usages of our selves, or taking from God and from Religion any minutes and portions of our affections. When *Eicadastes* the *Epicure* saw a goodly dish of hot meat serv'd up, he sung the verse of *Homer*,

τοῦ δ' ἐγὼ ἄντιος εἶμι, καὶ ἐν πυρὶ χεῖρας ἔθηκε,[1]

and swallowed some of it greedily, till by its hands of fire it curled his stomach, like parchment in the flame, and he was carryed from his banquet to his grave.

Non potuit fato nobiliore mori:[2]

It was fit *he* should dye such a death; but *that death* bids us beware of *that folly*.

Let the pleasure as it came with the meat, so also passe away with it, *Philoxenus* was a beast ηὔξατό ποτε τὴν γεράνου αὐχένα ἔχειν,[3] he wisht his throat as long as a Cranes, that he might be long in swallowing his pleasant morsels: *Mæret quod magna pars felicitatis exclusa esset corporis angustiis,*[4] he mourned because the pleasure of eating was not spread over all his body, that he might have been an Epicure in his hands: and indeed, if we consider it rightly, great eating and drinking is not the greatest pleasure of the *taste*, but of the *touch*; and *Philoxenus* might feel the unctious juyce slide softly down his throat, but he could not taste it in the middle of the long neck; and we see that they who mean to feast exactly, or delight the palate, do *libare* or *pitissare*, take up little proportions and spread them upon the tongue or palate; but *full morsells* and *great draughts* are easie and soft to the *touch*; but so is the feeling of silke, or handling of a melon, or a moles skin, and as delicious too as eating when it goes beyond the appetites of nature: and the proper pleasures of taste, which cannot be perceived but by a temperate man. And therefore let not the pleasure be intended beyond the taste; that is, beyond those little naturall measures in which God intended that pleasure should accompany your tables. Doe not run to it beforehand, nor chew the chud when the meal is done; delight not in the fancies, and expectations, and remembrances of a pleasant meal; but let it descend *in latrinam*, together with the meals whose attendant pleasure is.

Let pleasure be the lesse principall, and used as a servant; it may be modest and prudent to strew the dish with Sugar, or to dip thy bread in vinegar,

1. Athenaeus. lib. vii, cap. 53.   2. Martial, lib. XI, ep. 79, line 12
3. Theophilus, apud Athenaeus, I, 10; Aristotle, *Nichomacean Ethics*, iii, 10.
4. The final word 'cessat' is missing from this quotation from Seneca, *Epist.* cxiv, which is also incomplete in other small particulars.

but to make thy meal of sauces, and to make the accessory become the principall, and pleasure to rule the table, and all the regions of thy soule, is to make a man lesse and lower then an Oglio, of a cheaper value then a Turbat; a servant and a worshipper of *sauces*, and *cookes*, and *pleasure*, and *folly*.

Let pleasure as it is used in the regions and limits of nature and prudence, so also be changed into religion and thankfulnesse. *Turtures cum bibunt non resupinant colla*, say Naturalists,[1] Turtles when they drink lift not up their bills; and if we swallow our pleasures without returning the honour and the acknowledgment to God that gave them, we may *large bibere jumentorum modo*, drink draughts as large as an Oxe, but we shall die like an Oxe, and change our meats and drinks into eternall rottennesse. In all Religions it hath been permitted to enlarge our Tables in the days of sacrifices and religious festivity.

> Qui Veientanum festis potare diebus,
> Campana solitus trulla, vappamque profestis.[2]

For then the body may rejoyce in fellowship with the soule, and then a pleasant meal is religious, if it be not inordinate. But if our festivall dayes like the *Gentile* sacrifices end in drunkennesse[3] and our joyes in Religion passe into sensuality and beastly crimes, we change the Holy-day into a day of Death, and our selves become a Sacrifice as in the day of Slaughter.

To summe up this particular, there are, as you perceive, many cautions to make our pleasure safe, but any thing can make it inordinate, and then scarce any thing can keep it from becoming dangerous.

> Habet omnis hoc voluptas,
> Stimulis agit fruentes,
> Apiumque par volantum,
> Ubi grata mella fudit,
> Fugit & nimis tenaci
> Ferit icta corda morsu.[4]

And the pleasure of the honey will not pay for the smart of the sting. *Amores enim & deliciæ mature & celeriter deflorescunt, & in omnibus rebus voluptatibus maximis fastidium finitimum est.*[5] Nothing is so soon ripe and rotten as pleasure, and upon all possessions and states of things, loathing looks, as being not far off; but it sits upon the skirts of pleasure. Ὅς δὲ τραπέζας ἐπορεξάμενος μελιχρῶν ἔθιγεν, ἦ μέγα κλαύσει πικρὰν μερίδα, τῶν ἀντίξων συνεφελκομένων· He that greedily puts his hand to a delicious table, shall weep bitterly when he

1. Pliny, *Historia Naturalis*, X, 52.
2. Horace, *Satires*, ii, 3, line 143.
3. *De Plantis*, Aristotle apud Athenaeus, ii, 11; cf. ii, 3.
4. Boethius, *De Consolatione Philosophiae*, lib. iii, metr. 7.
5. See Cicero, *Pro Caelio Oratio*, tom. vi, cap. 19.

suffers the convulsions and violence by the divided interests of such contrary juices: ὅδε γὰρ χθονίας θέσμος ἀνάγκας διχόθεν θνάτοις βίον οἰνοχοεῖ·[1] *For this is the law of our nature and fatall necessity; life is alwayes poured forth from two goblets.*

And now after all this, I pray consider, what a strange madness and prodigious folly possesses many men, that they love to swallow death, and diseases, and dishonor, with an appetite which no reason can restrain. We expect our servants should not dare to touch what we have forbidden to them; we are watchfull that our children should not swallow poysons, and filthinesse, and unwholesome nourishment; we take care that they should be well manner'd and civil and of fair demeanour; and we our selves desire to be, or at least to be accounted wise; and would infinitely scorne to be call'd fooles; and we are so great lovers of health, that we will buy it at any rate of money or observance; and then for honour, it is that which the children of men pursue with passion, it is one of the noblest rewards of vertue, and the proper ornament of the wise and valiant, and yet all these things are not valued or considered, when a merry meeting, or a looser feast calls upon the man to act a scene of *folly* and *madnesse*, and *healthlesnesse* and *dishonour*. We doe to God what we severely punish in our servants; we correct our children for their medling with dangers, which themselves preferre before immortality; and though no man think himselfe fit to be despised, yet he is willing to make himselfe a beast, a sot, and a ridiculous monkey, with the follies and vapors of wine; and when he is high in drinke or fancy, proud as a *Grecian* Orator in the midst of his popular noyses, at the same time he shall talk such dirty language, such mean low things, as may well become a changeling and a foole, for whom the stocks are prepared by the laws, and the just scorne of men. Every drunkard clothes his head with a mighty scorne, and makes himselfe lower at that time then the meanest of his servants; the boyes can laugh at him when he is led like a cripple, directed like a blinde man, and speakes like an infant, imperfect noyses, lisping with a full and spungy tongue, and an empty head, and a vaine and foolish heart: so cheaply does he part with his honour for drink or loads of meat; for which honour he is ready to die, rather then hear it to be disparaged by another; when himselfe destroyes it, as bubbles perish with the breath of children. Doe not the laws of all wise Nations marke the drunkard for a foole, with the meanest and most scornfull punishment? and is there any thing in the world so foolish as a man that is drunk? But good God! what an intolerable sorrow hath seised upon great portions of Mankind, that this folly and madnesse should possesse the greatest spirits, and the wittyest men, the best company, the most sensible of the word *honour*, and the most jealous of loosing the *shadow*, and the most carelesse of the *thing*? Is it not a horrid thing, that a wise, or a crafty, a learned,

---

1. Synesius of Cyrene, Bishop of Ptolemais (*c.* A.D. 406), Hymn iii, line 663 *et seq.*

or a noble person should dishonour himselfe as a foole, destroy his body as a murtherer, lessen his estate as a prodigall, disgrace every good cause that he can pretend to by his relation, and become an appellative of scorne, a scene of laughter or derision, *and all* for the reward of forgetfulnesse and madnesse? for there are in immoderate drinking no other pleasures.

Why doe valiant men and brave personages fight and die rather then break the laws of men, or start from their duty to their Prince, and will suffer themselves to be cut in pieces rather then deserve the name of a Traitor or perjur'd? and yet these very men to avoyd the hated name of *Glutton* or *Drunkard*, and to preserve their Temperance, shall not deny themselves one luscious morsell, or poure a cup of wine on the ground, when they are invited to drink by the laws of the circle or wilder company.

Me thinks it were but reason, that if to give life to uphold a cause be not too much, they should not think too much to be hungry and suffer thirst for the reputation of that cause; and therefore much rather that they would thinke it but duty to be temperate for its honour, and eat and drink in civill and faire measures, that themselves might not lose the reward of so much suffering, and of so good a relation, not that which they value most be destroyed by drink.

There are in the world a generation of men that are ingag'd in a cause, which they glory in, and pride themselves in its relation and appellative: but yet for that cause they will doe nothing but talk and drink; they are valiant in wine, and witty in healths, and full of stratagem to promote debauchery; but such persons are not considerable in wise accounts; that which I deplore is, that some men preferre a cause before their life, and yet preferre wine before that cause, and by one drunken meeting set it more backward in its hopes and blessings, then it can be set forward by the counsels and armes of a whole yeer. God hath ways enough to reward a truth without crowning it with successe in the hands of such men.[1] In the mean time they dishonour Religion, and make truth be evill spoken of, and innocent persons to suffer by their very relation, and the cause of God to be reproached in the sentences of erring and abused people; and themselves lose their health and their reason, their honour and their peace, the rewards of sober counsels, and the wholesome effects of wisdome.

> *Arcanum neque tu scrutaberis illius unquam,*
> *Commissumque teges, & vino tortus & ira.*[2]

Wine discovers more then the rack, and he that will be drunk is not a person

1. This and the following passages refer to the undisciplined conduct and debauchery with which too many of the Royalists, like Lord Goring and his company, were justly chargeable, and which were the cause of many critical miscarriages. See Hyde, *History of the Great Rebellion* (Oxford, 1826). Bk. vii, Vol. iv, p. 299.

2. Horace, epist. 18, line 37.

fit to be trusted: and though it cannot be expected men should be kinder to their friend, or their Prince, or their honour, then to God, and to their own souls, and to their own bodies; yet when men are not moved by what is sensible and materiall, by that which smarts and shames presently, they are beyond the cure of Religion, and the hopes of Reason; and therefore they must *lie in hell like sheep, death gnawing upon them, and the righteous shall have domination over them in the morning*[1] of the resurrection.

> Seras tutior ibis ad lucernas
> Haec hora non est tua, cum furit Lyacus
> Cum regnant rosa cum madent capilli[2]

much safer to go to the severities of a watchful and sober life; for all that time of life is lost, when wine and rage, and pleasure, and folly steale away the heart of a man, and make him go singing to his grave.[3]

Married Life (1653)[4]

... The Stags in the Greek Epigram, whose knees were clog'd with frozen snow upon the mountains, came down to the brooks of the vallies, χλιῆναι νοτεροις ἄσθμασιν ὠκὺ γόνυ',[5] hoping to thaw their joynts with the waters of the stream; but there the frost overtook them, and bound them fast in ice, till the young heardsmen took them in their stranger snare. It is the unhappy chance of many men, finding many inconveniences upon the mountains of single life, they descend into the vallies of marriage[6] to refresh their troubles,

1. Ps. xlix : 14.　　　　　　　2. Martial, lib. 2, ep. 19, line 18.

3. Taylor here gives a novel application to an old, familiar phrase, ordinarily used in approbation. Compare this with Thomas Hooker's conventional use of the same phrase, above, p. 332.

4. Taylor, op. cit., pp. 225-231. 'The Marriage Ring', Pt. 1, Sermon XVII.

5. Eden's footnote for this quotation (op. cit., Vol. iv, p. 213) reads, 'Appolonid Smyrn num xv in Anthology tom ii p 122'. I do not know which edition of the Greek Anthology he was using; not the one he might have been expected to use, the *Jacobus* (1817). At all events the reference would be unlikely to cause other than frustration to modern readers seeking to employ it. A practical identification is the *Palatinate Anthology*, Bk. ix (Declamatory Epigrams), no. 244. The poet was Appolonides of Smyrna.

6. Eden's footnote here (ibid.) also needs amendment. He writes, 'Lucilius num cxxxi in the Greek Anthology', but this bitter verse on the freezing by poverty of even paternal love is no. 388 in Bk. xi (Satirical Epigrams).
"Αχρις ἂν ῃς ἄγαμος, Νουμήνιε, πάντα δοκεῖ σοι
ἐν τῷ 3ῆν εἶναι τῶν ἀγαθῶν ἀγαθά·

and there they enter into fetters, and are bound to sorrow by the cords of a mans or womans peevishnesse: and the worst of the evill is, they are to thank their own follies; for they fell into the snare by entring an improper way: Christ and the Church were no ingredients in their choice: but as the *Indian* women, enter into folly for the price of an Elephant, and think their crime warrantable; so do men and women change their liberty for a rich fortune (like *Eriphyle* the *Argive*, Ἡ χρυσὸν φίλου ἀνδρὸς ἐδέξατο τιμήενται,[1] she prefer'd gold before a good man) and shew themselves to be lesse then money by overvaluing that to all the content and wise felicity of their lives: and when they have counted the money and their sorrowes together, how willingly would they buy with the losse of all that money, modesty, or sweet nature to their relative.[2] the odde thousand pound would gladly be allowed in good nature and fair manners. As very a fool is he that chooses for beauty principally; *cui sunt eruditi oculi & stulta mens* (as one said) whose eyes are witty, and their soul sensuall; It is an ill band of affections to tye two hearts together by a little thread of red and white.

Οὐδεμίαν (φησὶν ἡ τραγῳδία)
—ὤνησε κάλλος εἰς πόσιν ξυνάορν[3]

And they can love no longer but untill the next ague comes, and they are fond of each other but at the chance of fancy, or the small pox, or childe-bearing, or care, or time, or any thing that can destroy a pretty flower.[4] But it is the basest of all when lust is the Paranymph and solicits the suit, and makes the contract, and joyn'd the hands; for this is commonly the effect of the former, according to the Greek proverb,

᾿Αλλ᾿ ἤτοι πρώτιστα λέων γένετ᾿ ηὔγένειος,
Αὐτὰρ ἔπειτα δράκων, καὶ πάρδαλις, ἠδὲ μέγας σῦς[5]

At first for his fair cheeks and comely beard, the beast is taken for a Lion, but

---

εἶθ᾿ ὅταν εἰσ ἔλθῃ γαμετή, πάλιν εὐθὺ δοκεῖ σοι
ἐν τῷ ᣛῆν εἶναι πάντα κακῶν τὰ κακά.
᾿Αλλὰ χάριν τεκνίων: &c.

1. Homer, *Odyssey*, λ'. 326.
2.   Non ego illam mihi dotem duco esse, quæ dos dicitur;
        Sed pudicitiam, et pudorem, et sedatum cupidinem,
        Deûm metum, parentum amorem, et cognatûm concordiam.
Plautus, *Amphitrion*, Act ii, sc. 2, l. 209.
3. Euripides, apud Clement of Alexandria, *Stromata*, lib. iv, cap. 22.
4.   Tres rugæ subeant, et se cutis arida laxet,
        Fiant obscuri dentes, oculique minores,
        Collige sarcinulas, dicet libertus, et exi.
Juvenal, *Satires*, vi, 143
5. Homer, *Odyssey*, δ'. 456.

at last he is turn'd to a Dragon or a Leopard, or a Swine. That which is at first beauty on the face may prove lust in the manners.

αὐτοῖς δὲ τοῖς θεοῖσι τὴν κέρκον μόνην
καὶ μηρὸν, ὥσπερ παιδερασταῖς, θύετε

So *Eubulus*[1] wittily reprehended such impure contracts; they offer in their maritall sacrifices nothing but the thigh and that which the Priests cut from the goats when they were laid to bleed upon the Altars Ἐὰν εἰς κάλλος σώματος βλέψῃ τις, ὁ λόγος φησί, καὶ αὐτῷ ἡ σὰρξ εἶναι κατ' ἐπιθυμίαν δόξῃ καλή, σαρκικῶς ἰδὼν καὶ ἁμαρτητικῶς δι' οὗ τεθαύμακε κρίνεται, said St. *Clement*[2]. 'He or she that looks too curiously upon the beauty of the body, looks too low, and hath flesh and corruption in his heart, and is judg'd sensuall and earthly in his affections and desires.'. . .

Man and wife are equally concerned to avoid all offences of each other in the beginning of their conversation: every little thing can blast an infant blossome; and the breath of the south can shake the little rings of the Vine, when first they begin to curle like the locks of a new weaned boy; but when by age and consolidation they stiffen into the hardnesse of a stem, and have by the warm embraces of the sun and the kisses of heaven brought forth their clusters, they can endure the storms of the North, and the loud noises of a tempest, and yet never be broken: so are the early unions of an unfixed marriage; watchfull and observant, jealous and busie, inquisitive and carefull, and apt to take alarum at every unkind word. For infirmities do not manifest themselves in the first scenes, but in the succession of a long society; and it is not chance or weaknesse when it appears at first, but it is want of love or prudence, or it will be so expounded; and that which appears ill at first usually affrights the unexperienced man or woman, who makes unequall conjectures, and fancies mighty sorrowes by the proportions of the new and early unkindnesse. It is a very great passion, or a huge folly, or a certain want of love, that cannot preserve the colours and beauties of kindnesse, so long as publick honesty requires man to wear their sorrows for the death of a friend. *Plutarch*[3] compares a new marriage to a vessell before the hoops are on, κατ' ἀρχὰς μὲν ὑπὸ τῆς τυχούσης ῥᾳδίως διασπᾶται προθάσεως, every thing dissolves their tender compaginations, but χρόνῳ τῶν ἁρμῶν σύμπηξιν λαβόντων, μόλις ὑπὸ πυρὸς καὶ σιδήρου διαλύεται, when the joynts are stiffned and are tyed by a firm compliance and proportion'd bending, scarcely can it be dissolved without fire or the violence of iron. After the hearts of the man and the wife are endeared and hardned by a mutuall confidence, and an experience longer then an artifice and pretence can last, there

1. Apud Clement of Alexandria, *Stromata*, lib. vii.
2. Clement of Alexandria, *Stromata*, lib. iv, cap. 18.
3. Plutarch, *De Conjugalia Praecepta*.

are a great many remembrances and some things present that dash all little
unkindnesses in pieces. The little boy in the Greek Epigram,[1] that was creeping down a precipice was invited to his safety by the sight of his mothers
pap, when nothing else could entice him to return: and the band of common
children, and the sight of her that nurses what is most dear to him, and the
endearments of each other in the course of a long society, and the same relation is an excellent security to redintegrate and to call that love back which
folly and trifling accidents would disturb.

> —*Tormentum ingens nubentibus hæret*
> *Quæ nequeunt parere, & partu retinere maritos.*[2]

When it is come thus farre, it is hard untwisting the knot; but be carefull in
its first coalition, that there be no rudenesse done; for if there be, it will for
ever be apt to start and to be diseased.

   Let man and wife be carefull to stifle little things,[3] that as fast as they
spring, they be cut down and trod upon; for if they be suffered to grow by
numbers, they make the spirit peevish and the society troublesome, and the
affections loose and easie by an habituall aversation. Some men are more
vexed with a flie then with a wound; and when the gnats disturbe our sleep,
and the reason is disquieted but not perfectly awakened; it is often seen that
he is fuller of trouble then if in the day light of his reason he were to contest
with a potent enemy. In the frequent little accidents of a family, a mans
reason cannot alwaies be awake; and when his discourses are imperfect, and
a trifling trouble makes him yet more restlesse, he is soon betrayed to the
violence of passion. It is certain that the man or woman are in a state of
weaknesse and folly then, when they can be troubled with a trifling accident;
and therefore it is not good to tempt their affections when they are in that
state of danger. In this case the caution is, to subtract fuell from the sudden
flame; for stubble though it be quickly kindled, yet it is as soon extinguished,
if it be not blown by a pertinacious breath, or fed with new materials;
adde no new provocations to the accident, and do not inflame this, and peace
will soon return, and the discontent will passe away soon, as the sparks from
the collision of a flint: ever remembring that discontents proceeding from
daily little things, do breed a secret undiscernible disease, which is more
dangerous then a feaver proceeding from a discerned notorious surfeit.

   Let them be sure to abstain from all those things which by experience
and observation they finde to be contrary to each other. They that govern
Elephants never appear before them in white, and the masters of buls keep
from them all garments of bloud and scarlet, as knowing that they will be

---

1. Leonidas of Alexandria, No. xxix. in *Greek Anthology*.
2. Juvenal, *Satires*, ii, 137.
3. 'Quaedam parva quidem, sed non toleranda maritis', ibid., vi, 183.

impatient of civill usages and discipline when their natures are provoked by their proper antipathies. The ancients in their maritall Hieroglyphicks[1] us'd to depict *Mercury* standing by *Venus*, to sigifie, that by fair language and sweet intreaties, the mindes of each other should be united; and hard by them *Suadam & Gratias descripserunt*, they would have all deliciousnesse of manners, compliance and mutuall observance to abide.[2]

Let the husband and wife infinitely avoid a curious distinction of *mine* and *thine*; for this hath caused all the lawes, and all the suits, and all the wars in the world; let them who have but one person, have also but one interest. The husband and wife are heirs to each other (as *Dionysius Halicarnasseus* relates from *Romulus*) if they dye without children, but if there be children, the wife is a partner in the inheritance; But during their life the use and employment is common to both their necessities, and in this there is no other difference of right, but that the man hath the dispensation of all, and may keep it from his wife just as the governour of a Town may keep it from the right owner; he hath the *power*, but *no right* to do so. And when either of them begins to impropriate, it is like a tumor on the flesh, it drawes more then its share, but what it feeds on turns to a bile: and therefore the *Romans* forbad any donations to be made between man and wife, because neither of them could transfer a new right of those things which already they had in common; but this is to be understood only concerning the uses of necessity and personall conveniences; for so all may be the womans, and all may be the mans in severall regards. *Corvinus* dwels in a farm and receives all its profits, and reaps and sowes as he please, and eats of the corn and drinks of the wine, it is his own: but all that also is his Lords, and for it, *Corvinus* payes acknowledgement; and his patron hath such powers and uses of it as are proper to the Lords; and yet for all this, it may be the Kings too, to all the purposes that he can need, and is all to be accounted in the *census* and for certain services, and times of danger: So are the riches of a family, they are a womans as well as a mans; they are hers for need, and hers for ornament, and hers for modest delight, and for the uses of Religion and prudent charity; but the disposing them into portions of inheritance, the assignation of charges and governments, stipends and rewards, annuities and greater donatives are the reserves of the superior right, and not to be invaded by the under-posessors. But in those things where they ought to be common, if the spleen or the belly swels and drawes into its capacity much of that which should be spent upon those parts which have an equall right to be maintain'd, it is a dropsie

---

1. Plutarch, op. cit., tom. vi.
2. Hujus enim rari summique voluptas
   Nulla boni, quoties animo corrupta superbo
   Plus aloes quam mellis habet.
   Juvenal *Satires*, vi, 178.

or a consumption of the whole, something that is evill because it is unnaturall and monstrous. *Macarius* in his 32 Homily[1] speaks fully in this particular, a woman betrothed to a man bears all her portion, and with a mighty love pours it into the hands of her husband, and sayes, ἐμὸν οὐδὲν ἔχω, I have nothing of my own, my goods, my portion, my body and my minde is yours. All that a woman hath is reckoned to the right of her husband; not her wealth and her person only, but her reputation and her praise; So *Lucian*.[2] But as the earth, the mother of all creatures here below, sends up all its vapours and proper emissions at the command of the Sun, and yet requires them again to refresh her own needs, and they are deposited between them both in the bosome of a cloud as a common receptacle, that they may cool his flames, and yet descend to make her fruitfull; so are the properties of a wife to be dispos'd of by her Lord; and yet all are for her provisions, it being a part of his need to refresh and supply hers, and it serves the interest of both while it serves the necessities of either.

These are the duties of them both, which have common regards and equall necessities, and obligations; and indeed there is scarce any matter of duty, but it concerns them both alike, and is only distinguished by names, and hath its variety by circumstances and little accidents: and what in one is call'd *love*, in the other is called *reverence*; and what in the wife is *obedience*, the same in the man is *duty*. He provides, and she dispenses; he gives commandements, and she rules by them; he rules her by authority, and she rules him by love; she ought by all means to please him, and he must by no means displease her. For as the heart is set in the midst of the body, and though it strikes to one side by the prerogative of Nature, yet those throbs and constant motions are felt on the other side also, and the influence is equall to both: so it is in conjugall duties; some motions are to the one side more then to the other, but the interest is on both, and the duty is equall in the severall instances. If it be otherwise, the man injoyes a wife as *Periander* did his dead *Melissa*, by an unnaturall union,[3] neither pleasing, nor holy, uselesse to all the purposes of society, and dead to content.

1. Para. 9.   2. ῾ρητόρων διδάσκαλος. tom. vii, cap. 6.
3. Herodotus, Bk. v, cap. 92. Even the fleeting echoes of ancient scandals are not allowed to go to waste but, gathered into Taylor's catholic net, made to serve his exegesis. Cf. Nicolaus Damascenus, *Fragment 59*; Seneca, *de Ira*, ii, 36.

HENRY HAMMOND[1]

The death of Henry Hammond in 1660, at the early age of fifty-five, was the most severe loss suffered by the Church of England since the death of Richard Hooker with his *Ecclesiastical Polity* unfinished. Had he lived on, Hammond would certainly have become a leading bishop, if not archbishop, and he would have influenced the course of the Church as a whole, even more than Pearson did. He was in the latter's class as a scholar, but much superior in eloquence and literary grace, and, as an effective man of action, second only to Sheldon himself. Like Laud's unwavering followers, Cosin and Pearson, and most English Episcopalians, he incurred in Puritan quarters the reproach of Romanism but, like his friends, he demonstrated, especially during the interregnum, when the pressure from Rome was turned on supposed potential English converts, that on certain points he felt nearly as far removed from the current hermeneutics of the Papacy as he did on almost all points from the Calvinists.

It is ironic, but not surprising, that the keenest criticism of the abuse of learning—the exclusive reliance upon learning to fulfil human potential—should come, not from an ignorant fanatic, but from one of the most learned scholars in the country.

Satans Stratagems in the Heart (*c.* 1655)

And this is the *third ground* of *practical unbelief*, that *generalities* can be cheaply believed without parting from any thing we prize: The Doctrine of the *Trinity* can be received, and thwart never a *carnal affection*, as being an inoffensive

1. Henry Hammond, 1605-1660. Educated at Eton and Magdalen College, Oxford. B.A. 1622; M.A. and Fellow 1625; Rector of Penshurst 1633; D.D. 1638; 1649 Archdeacon of Chichester; chaplain to Charles I till 1647; subdean of Christchurch, deprived by parliamentary commissioners; retired to Westpool in Worcestershire where he died on April 25th, 1660. His most influential work was *Paraphrase and Annotations on the New Testament* (1653); *Collected Works*, 1674-84; biography by John Fell introduces his *Miscellaneous Theological Works* (4 vols. Anglo-Catholic Library, 1847-50).

truth. *Christ*'s sufferings and satisfaction for sin, by the *natural man*, may be heard with joy; but *particular application* is very difficult: That our *obedience* to every command of that *Trinity*, must be sincere; that we must forego all, and hate our own flesh to adhere to so merciful a *Saviour*, and express our love to the most contemptible Soul under Heaven, as he hath loved us; that we must, at last, expect him in *majesty* as a *Judge*, whom we are content to hug and embrace in his *humility* as a *Saviour*: This is a bloody word, as *Moses* his wife counted the *Circumcision*, too harsh and rough to be received into such pampered, tender, fleshy hearts.

The *fourth ground* is, a *general humor* that is gotten in the World, *To take care of nothing, but our reputations:* Nor *God*, nor life, nor soul, nor any thing can weigh with it in the ballance. Now it is a scandalous thing, a soul blot to ones name to be counted an Atheist, an arrant Infidel, where all are *Christians*; and therefore for fashions sake we will believe, and yet sometime the Devil hath turned this humor quite the contrary way, and made some men as ambitious of being counted Atheists, as others of being Christians. It will shortly grow into a gentile garb, and part of courtship, to disclaim all *Religion* in shew, as well as deeds. Thus are a world of men in the World, either profest Atheists, or Atheistical Professors, upon the same grounds of *vain-glory*; the one to get, the other to save their *reputation* in the World. Thus do many men stand up at the *Creed*, upon the same terms as gallants go into the field; that have but small maw to be killed, onely to keep their honor, that they might not be branded and mocked for cowards. And yet certainly in the truth, these are the veriest dastards under *Heaven*; no worldy man so fearful of death, or pious man of hell, as these are of disgrace.

The *last ground* I shall mention, and indeed the main of all, is, *The subtlety and wiliness of the Devil*. He hath tried all his stratagems in the World, and hath found none like this, for the undermining and ruining of Souls, to suffer them to advance a pretty way in *Religion*, to get their heads full of knowledge, that so they may think they have faith enough, and walk to hell securely. The *Devil's* first policies were by *Heresies*, to corrupt the Brain, to invade and surprize *Christianity* by force: but he soon saw this would not hold out long; he was fain to come from batteries, to mines, and supplant those Forts that he could not vanquish. The Fathers (and amongst them chiefly *Leo*, in all his writings) within the first Five hundred years after *Christ*, observe him at this ward, *Ut quos vincere ferro flammisque; non poterat, cupiditatibus irretiret, & sub falsa Christiani nominis professione corrumperet.* He hoped to get more by lusts, then heresies, and to plunge men deepest in an high conceit of their holy Faith. He had learned by experience from himself, that all the bare knowledg in the World would never sanctifie: it would perhaps give men content, and make them confident and bold of their estate; and by presuming on such grounds, and prescribing merit to Heaven by their

Lord, Lord, even *seal them up to the day of damnation*; and therefore it is ordinary with *Satan* to give men the teather a great way, lest they should grumble at his tyranny, and prove *Apostates* from him upon hard usage. Knowledg is pleasant, and books are very good Company; and therefore if the Devil should bind men to ignorance, our Speculators and Brain-Epicures would never be his Disciples; they would go away sadly, as the young man from *Christ*, who was well affected with his service, but could not part with his riches, *Mat.* xix. 22. So then you shall have his leave, to know, and believe in *God*, as much as you please, so you will not obey him; and be as great Scholars as *Satan* himself, so you will be as prophane. The heart of Man is the Devils Palace, where he keeps his state; and as long as he can strengthen himself there by a guard and band of lusts, he can be content to afford the outworks to God, divine speculation, and never be disturbed or affrighted by any enemy at such a distance.

Thus have you the grounds also whereupon *true Faith* (which is best defined a *spiritual prudence,* an application of *spiritual knowledg* to holy practice) should be so often wanting in men which are very knowing, and the fairest Professors of *Christianity.*

GEORGE LAWRENCE[1]

On the Death of Cromwell

Peplum Olivarii, or A good Prince bewailed by a good
People, represented in a sermon, Oct. 13 1658 upon
the death of OLIVER, Late Lord Protector, by George
Lawrence A.M., Minister of Crosses Hospital.

... *Octavian* and *Titus Vespasian* were not more lamented; of the former it was
said, Would to God he had not been born, or never died; and of the latter,
that he was the Love, Conquerour and delights of mankinde, to whom *Speed*
compares our *Henry* the fifth. And such was the lamentation of the Emperour
Severus, that the Senate of *Rome* said, he should either not be borne, or not
die. Our English Senate much laments his death, of whom it may be said, as
of *David*, Acts 13. 36. *After he had served his own generation, by the will of God
he fell on sleep.* I Chron. 29. 28. *He died in a good old age, full of dayes, riches and
honour, and Solomon his son reigned in his stead.* On whom the Criticks made
this Epitaph,

> *Here lies* David, *who when he was a boy*
> *Slew Lyons and Bears;*
> *In his middle age great* Goliah;

1. George Lawrence, 1615–1695; New Inn Hall Oxford, 1632; B.A. 1636; M.A. 1639.
Wood says of him (*Athenae*, IV, 783) 'a most violent puritan and a great admirer of the
Scotch covenant', in other words, a zealous Presbyterian, a description which, if true,
would not imply a favourable opinion of Cromwell. However, the religious mêlée was
by then displaying curious and ambiguous alliances, and perhaps, Lawrence expected
well from Richard, the new Protector, to whom the oration is addressed. The 'violent'
part of Wood's characterization is supported by the churchwardens' accounts for 'St.
George's' in Botolph Lane, where Lawrence had been engaged as Lecturer. He is 'desired
to preach no more, but will be paid his dues until 19th Nov 1641 if he will behave himself quietly.' After the Restoration 'he was', says Wood, 'silenc'd and ejected' but 'carried
on the trade of conventicling ... to the time of his death.' Other publications by
Lawrence include *Laurentius Lutherizans, or the Protestation of George Lawrence ... against
certain Calumnations asperged on him by the corrupt Clergie and their Lay Proselytes* (1642);
(Anon) *The debauched Cavaleer or English Midianite ...* (1642). See Palmer's *Nonconfor-
mists Memorial* (1802–3), iii, 516–517; Wood's *Fasti*, I, cols. 489, 508.

When he was a little older, great enemies,
The Philistins;
And in his old age, overcame himself.

In his fame, *Notum per fæcula nomen.* His memory as *of the just is blessed* Prov. 10. 4. *and shall be an everlasting foundation,* ver. 25. whence the Rabbins in their quotations of any eminent Author deceased, usually subjoyne this honourable commemoration, BENEDICTÆ MEMORIÆN. or such an one of blessed memory; *Memoria ejus sit in Benedictione. The righteous shall be in everlasting remembrance.* Psal. 112. 6. OLIVER of HAPPY MEMORY: this the second motive.

Consider your own sins. Our sins have hastned the Protectours removal; as unthankfulnesse, pride, animosities, avarice, formality and licentiousnesse. These were the ague fits which have expelled his breath, and our obduracy the stone which hath sunk him to the grave. And we may say, as *Bradford* said of the death of King *Edward* the sixth King of *England,* Our sins made holy *Oliver* die.

Consider our own losse. The losse of a General, is a general losse. The losse of him, is a complexion, or rather a complication of losses. We have lost a Captain, a Shield, the Head, an Heire of Restraint, the Breath of our Nostrils, an Healer, a Shepherd, a Father, and a Nursing Father, a Corner-Stone, a Builder, a Watchman, an Eye, a Saviour, a Steers-man and Rector, a Pilot, and a Common Husband.

Lastly consider our miseries which we deserve; even the miseries which befell *Judah* and *Jerusalem* after *Josiah's* death, in the dayes of *Jehoahaz, Jehoiakim* and *Zedekiah,* desolation of Cities, Temple, Families, and a Captivity stricter, and longer than a Babylonian; which the Lord in mercy turn from us, and turn us to him by true and unfeigned repentance. O *England* repent, repent.

And now considering all these incentives, who can refrain from weeping?

Quis enim tam tristia fando.
Myrmidonum, Dolopumve, aut Duri Miles Ulyxi
Temperet a lachrymis?[1]

And if any should ask me what is the cause of so much mourning? I answer with *Ambrose* telling the cause of his grief to a friend for the decease of an eminent person, demaunding the question, Because it would be a hard thing to finde one like to him. Saith God of *Solomon,* 1 Kings 3. 12. *There was none like him, neither after him should arise any like him.*

Anglia,
Nec primum similem visa es, nec habere sequentem.

1. *Aeneid,* I. 6–8.

He hath wonne the Palme, Victory, hath setled the Olive, Peace, and hath left his friends to hang their Harps upon the Willow.

Truly I may say his Deeds deserve a full, distinct, and faithful Chronicle, which were so superlative, that a succeeding generation of no little faith would scarce suppose them credible: yet of him I may dare say, as was said of the Royal Princesse, *Prov.* 31. 29. *Many Princes have done vertuously, but Renowned* OLIVER *hath excelled them all.*

But here an *Asthma* stops me; for with holy *Hierom*, if all the members of my body were converted into tears, yet in this short variety of words, I fear I should have silenced more than what is spoken; and with him of *Carthage*, better may I judge to say nothing more, than speak a little.

And therefore here die away my mourning pen, and let thy Manumitter sob the rest, τὰ δὲ λείψανα δι' ἅι, ἅι easing his heart-bound grief by weeping forth this Epitaph;

HIC JACET TOTIVS ANGLIÆ, SCOITÆ,

ET HIBERNIÆ INDVPERATOR,

ET

TOTIVS CHRISTIANISMI MIRACVLVM,

OLIVARIVS.

THE REDCOATS' CATECHISME

The death of Cromwell was the fall of the all-supporting pillar. Only the strength of the one man and the confidence he inspired, even in those who hated him, had held the new order up, and now, at his removal, the whole edifice tottered and began to crumble. The army had taken control of the country without a vestige of lawful right, but 'truly, by the Power of the Sword', as Peters had complacently told the indignant excluded members that fateful sixth of December. The arrogant violation of parliament and the killing of the king had introduced a traumatic new element of guilt and bitterness into the soul of the nation and split what had been the parliamentary party into railing factions. The English had had ten years to form an opinion of military dictatorship and they knew from the start they detested it.[1]

In the early years of the war it was the Cavaliers who had first gained a bad reputation for theft and terrorism. But the Roundheads had had years to catch up with and outstrip their adversaries in the uglier practices of military occupation, and it was *their* offences which were fresh in the minds of the people. The famous iron-side discipline which had been decisive in battle at Naseby and Dunbar did not survive long intact out of the field. From the end of the war onwards successive ordinances and statutes had been issued to try to protect civilians from molestation, and to curb at least the nocturnal disturbances of the peace by idle soldiers in pursuit of sport or gain.[2] At the death of Cromwell the grievances of the country at large sought expression more than ever in lampoons and songs of bitter invective. As for the Rump Parliament which returned, impudently hopeful, after the Protector's death, no parliament in English history—not even a modern one—has been held in such universal contempt and distrust.

1. This should not be taken to imply that Cromwell did not have his enthusiastic supporters. Every dictator has, and as quasi-dictators go he was a humanist.
2. i.e. *A statute against soldiers calling out to passengers and examining them (though they go peaceably and civilly along) and against playing at Nine Pins at unseasonable hours*, May 27th, 1651.

Make room for an honest Red coat
(And that you'll say is a wonder)
The gun and the blade
Are his tools—and his Trade
Is for to Kill and Plunder.
Then away with the Lawes
And the Good old Cause
N'er talk of the Rump or the Charter
Tis the cash does the Feat
All the rest is but cheat
Without that ther's no faith nor Quarter.[1]

The whole structure of government had been gaining in disrepute for more than ten years, not only the top layers of the Commons and the army, but all the proliferating local new-made jacks-in-office, 'the basest of people used for base ends',[2] extortionists, who 'trample magna carta under their feet, transgress all orders and ordiances of parliament . . . turn well affected men out of their freeholds and goods, imprison and beat their person without any known charge.'[3]

The mechanics of their corruption provoke wry memories. 'How frequently they levy one tax three or four times over and continue their levies often after the ordinances expire. How cruelly they raise the twentieth and fifth part upon the well affected, exercising an illegal, arbitrary, tyrannical power over their fellow subjects farre higher than ever Canterbury or Strafford durst advise the king to.'

Then when the money is extorted, what becomes of it? It 'runs through many muddy, obscure channels, through so many committees and officers fingers, both for collecting, receiving, issuing and paying it forth that it is impossible to make or balance any public account therof; and at least one half thereof is known to be devoured by the committees and officers, and those that for lucre protect them.'

Elsewhere the same writer sums up the general feeling, already in 1647, of disgust and outrage in the face of sanctimonious rapacity. 'But there never were more pretenders to truth than in this age, nor ever fewer that obtayned, or made care and conscience to use it in their words and deeds.'

It was inevitable that blame should be turned by their opponents upon the Puritans; for the Presbyterians had dominated the parliament that failed, and the Independents had dominated the army that trampled upon parliament; and it was at this period that the name of Puritan

1. *A New Ballad to an Old Tune, Tom of Bedlam*, 1659.
2. *Declarations of the Proceedings of the Commissioners*, 1647, p. 7.   3. Ibid.

consolidated the reputation for hypocrisy which it has never since been able to exorcize completely, even when undeserved.

Of the areas common to all varieties of the Puritan complex which offered a target to those who hated the movement, none was more conspicuous than the 'godly' practice of wholesale preaching which pervaded the Puritan way of life. The sermonical catechism was a form of godly disquisition in use at this time. It became of use also to the satirists.

The Redcoats' Catechism[1]

or Instructions to be learnt by every one that desires to be one of Parliaments Janizaries

Quest. *What is your name?*
Ans. Red coat.
Quest. *Who gave you that name?*
Ans. My God Fathers and God Mothers.
Quest. *Who were they?*
Ans. Severall. Necessity, Idleness, Murder, Rapine, Theft, principally the Devil and Parliament, the lust of the *Elders* the Parliament, and their *Caiaphas Cromwell.*
Quest. *Was this all they did engage for you?*
Ans. No. They did Promise and Vow three things in my Name. First, That I should utterly forsake God and all his Works, and shake of all Obedience to the Pomp and Vanities of King or House of Lords with whatsoever is consonant either to Law or Gospel. Secondly, That I should believe all the Articles of the Parliaments Faith, without Hesitation or Scruple. And Thirdly, To keep and observe all their Acts and Ordinances, and walk in the same all the daies of my Life.
Quest. *Dost thou not think that thou art bound to believe and do, as they have promised for thee?*
Ans. Yes Verily and by the Divels help and Sir *Arthurs*[2] I will, and I hartily thank our infernal Father *Belzebub*, that he hath called me to this state of

1. February 9th, 1659. Satire on R. Ram's *Soldiers Catechism.*

2. Sir Arthur Hesilrige (d. 1661). Originally a protégé of Pym's and one of the five members impeached by the king on January 3rd, 1642, but later sided with the army against parliament. During the Civil War he commanded a regiment of cuirassiers

Damnation, through his dear Child the Parliament. And I pray Satan to supply me continually with such Divelish intentions, as may continue me in it to my lives end.

Quest. Rehearse the Articles of thy belief?

Ans. I believe in the Divel the Father of Sectaries and sworn enemy to Religion or Reason, and in his dearly beloved Spawn the Parliament, which was conceived by the necessities of the King, born of the discontents of the people: suffered under *Oliver Cromwell*, was dissolved, cashiered and turned out, and for a while sent packing to Hell; but at last rose again, and ascended into its former place, and now sitteth on the right hand of *London* that Rebellious and stiffe-necked City; from whence it shall come to take vengance of them for their stubborn misdemeanours, I believe in Sir *Arthur Haselrigge* the whole number of Sectaries and Conventicles the Council of State, the Act of Oblivion, the resurrection of my Lord *Lambert*'[1] and the contriuance of our power to everlasting.

Quest. What dost thou chiefly learn by this thy belief.

Ans. First, I learn to believe in the Parliament, who hath made me and all the rest of my good brethren.

Secondly in General *Monke*[2] who hath redemed our Good old Cause from the jaws of the wicked.

Thirdly, In Sir *Arthur Haselrigge* who by his strenuous endeavours hath sanctified our interest.

Quest. You told me that your God-Father and God-Mother did promise for you, that you should keep and observe all the Parliaments; Commandments tell me how many there be?

Ans. Divers.

Quest. Which be they?

---

known, from their red tunics and breast-plates, as the 'Lobsters'. He fought at the capture of Malmesbury and Chichester and looted the communion plate of the latter. Subsequently he was much accused of extortion and corruption and he accumulated a great estate in the north of England by confiscation and speculation. (See Walker's *History of Independency* (1661); and for a denunciation of his activities, John Musgrave, *Sir John Hesilrige's Misgovernment* (1650), and his reply *Musgrave Muzzled* (1650); also John Lilburn, *A Preparation to a Hue and Cry after Sir John Hesilrige* (1649), and his reply, *An Anatomy of Lt. Col. John Lilburne's Spirit* (1649); etc.)

1. John Lambert; the best military commander produced by the Civil War, no Puritan, had quarrelled with Cromwell when he assumed the Protectorship, but on Cromwell's death, having overthrown the administration of the late Protector's son, Richard, he was enjoying the 'resurrection' of virtual dictatorship, assisted by what he called a 'committee of safety'. Monk and his army would frustrate Lambert's plan to establish a republic in England.

2. General George Monk: at this date he had not yet marched on London or declared himself in favour of a Stuart restoration. He commanded the largest part of the standing army and nobody knew which way he would jump.

Ans. These were given to us by our God the Parliament, when they assumed illegally the whole power and authority of these Nations into their hands, telling us. We are your only Lords and Masters that have redeemed you from the Tyrannical Government of a King or Single person, and brought you into the Freedom of a Lawless usurpation.

1. Thou shalt have no other Generals but us.

2. Thou shalt not set up any lawful Magistrate, King, Protector, or Single Person, or any thing in their likenesse. Thou shalt not subject thy self, to them nor truckle under them. For we your Lords and Masters are of so boundlesse spirits and so furious ambition, that whosoever shall offer resist to us, we shall punish them; sequester their Estates, and ruine their Families for ever; but those that will quietly submit their Ass-like backs to the intollerable slavery of our Lawlesse burdens, we will feed with the gracious Sugar-plums of *Kings Deans* and *Chapters* Lands for the maintenance of their Wives and Children.

3. Thou shalt not abuse our name with those ignominious terms of *Rump, Tail, or Fagg end* for we have deeply sworn, that his Arse shall make Buttons, who shall dare to affront us in that Nature.

4. Thou shalt remember to be present at the *Guard* day, the rest of the daies you may follow your lawful Vocations of Pimping, Picking of Pockets, Filching or the like; but that is wholly to be reserved to our service: thou shalt be sure then to give thy attendance with all due and careful preparation of Sword, Musket, and Bandeleers: for this is a day wherein you must be diligent, to preserve our security, lest we should be disturbed in our making those good Ordinances of Laws, Excise and such other Acts of Grace for your good & the ruine of this malignant Nation.

5. Have an awful and reverent fear in thy mind of us, that so thou mayest long enjoy thy place, without danger of being Disbanded or cashiered.

6. Thou shalt when Commanded, Commit what Murder or Slaughter, we shall think fit.

7. Thou shalt at all times hold it lawful and take all occasions to lye with the Citizens Wives, wich may be a means to provide you with Linnen and other necessaries, which your want of pay may cause your indigence of.

8. Thou shalt Plunder, Filch, and Steal any thing thou canst lay thy hands on, for herein you come nearest to our example, and similitude in our grand Robberies and Sequestrations.

9. Thou shalt not stick to Trapan, betray, swear, forswear any thing never so false which may conduce to our interest and advantage.

10. Thou shalt desire & covet above all things the Plunder of the City, the Ravishing of their wives, the Knocking down of their Prentices and taking from them all that they have for the inrichment of us and the Good Old Cause.

This effort proves satisfactory and the 'saint' receives confirmation and has a Red Coat laid on his shoulders.

As signs of dissension and disintegration were observed in the hated military junta the pent-up frustrations of years erupted in words, words of hope, of jubilation, of derision. Of all the hated members of the Committee of Safety, none was more hated than John Hewson. He had been a judge at the king's trial and signed the death warrant. Later he had been responsible for breaking up popular demonstrations against the régime with what was felt to be unnecessary brutality, and on one occasion several apprentices were killed. The beginning of the end of his power was celebrated with zest.

> Hewsons companions as scabby as coots
> Have infected him with the mange
> They have pist in his boots[1]
> He must cry roots[2]
> And TURNOUT[3] to turn up must change.[4]

Hewson had formerly been a cobbler in Westminster and he had lost an eye, so references to his trade and to the blind abound in all that features him.

1. A currently popular practical joke, favoured by the fashion of the day for wide-topped (waterproof), leather riding boots. If the jokers were in luck, the victim would come to his boots in a hurry and thrust one foot in before he apprehended the pleasantry.

2. I can offer no really satisfactory explanation for this expression. The most plausible suggestion has come from Mr. Sears McGee who thinks it may simply be an abbreviation of the Puritan reformers' slogan 'Roots and Branches'. Not a very apt cry for Hewson when he is himself being up-rooted; but this is verse, and many a word has found itself at the end of a line of doggerel for no other purpose but to make the rhyme.

3. A play on the military command summoning soldiers on parade.

4. *A New Ballad* (1659).

GOOD COUNSEL AGAINST COLD WEATHER

When a picture of Hewson was hanged from a gibbet at Cheapside and the Stuart Restoration became an increasingly probable resolution, the original took the hint and made his escape out of England.

> And now he's gone the Lord knows whether
> He and this Winter go together
> If he be caught he will lose his leather
>> Good people, pity the blind.

> Sing Hi Ho Hewson, the State n'er went upright
> Since cobblers could Pray, Preach, Govern and Fight
> We shall see what they do now you're out of sight
>> Good people, pity the blind.[1]

Hewson's fate inspired the most thoroughly developed—as well as perhaps the most scurrilous—example of the sermon form used as satire. In 1659, shortly before he fled the country, a sermon was 'published for the satisfaction of all those that have participated in the sweetness of public employment', allegedly preached by Hodg. Tubervil, chaplain to the Late Lord Hewson. All that is known for certain of its authorship is that it was *not* preached by Hewson's chaplain. It has been attributed to Edmund Cayton but the style bears no particular resemblance to *Will Bagnall's Ghost*. However, if we cannot identify the author, we do have the sermon, and it is worth having, for it is distinguished from most of the ribald outpourings in prose and verse of the time by its skill and control. Although it is, from beginning to end, an exercise of envenomed mockery, the author never for a moment betrays the convention in which he has chosen to work. It is structurally a perfect reproduction of a Puritan style of preaching down to the smallest details in the 'divisions' and the hilarious use of *et ceteras*, which preachers sometimes used as a lofty way out when they could not finish a quotation they had begun, or when the end of the quotation was inconvenient. The only inconsistency is the title, 'Walk Knaves Walk', which I suspect may not have been chosen by the

1. *A Hymne to the Gentle Craft* (1659).

524

author, and I have called the work here by its more appropriate sub-
title, 'Good Counsel Against Cold Weather'.

The sermon purports to be a warning by a Puritan preacher to his
army brethren that, with the approach of a severe 'winter', it behoves
them to protect themselves adequately against the rough weather to
come by obtaining a pair of stout boots, *waxed* boots (such as a good
cobbler makes) which are sufficiently waterproof to carry their wearer
far, and if need be fast, on uncomfortable and *wet* journeys, perhaps
over the sea.

The preacher does not insist that these all-important boots be *purchased*. That is not the way the brethren properly make their acquisitions.
There is another and a 'sweet' word to describe how they should go
about obtaining these all-important boots, and anything else they may
desire. The word is 'plunder'; 'therefore *plunder* ye waxed boots'.

The preacher goes on in a style of earnest and religious zeal to deal
separately and in strict order of correct progression with every problem and eventuality contingent upon obtaining 'waxed boots'. The
technic of 'divisions' requisite to Puritan preaching is used to define
boots in their kinds, functions, attributes and manufacture, and the
authentic note of sententious holiness is slyly applied in the advocacy of
infamous conduct. The inevitable didactic platitudes are perfectly
represented ('Bad times require good boots'), the repetitions, the
strained metaphors, are precisely hit, and, above all, the pervading
atmosphere, which perhaps most distinguishes Puritan preaching, of
private and privileged complicity.

Good Counsel Against Cold Weather
(Anon. 1659)

Beloved Brethren
   Though my profession of a cordwinder be something unsuitable to this
Teaching-Calling, yet my text is not, as I have served seven years apprenticeship in the one, and full as many in the other; so being a Journeyman, I hope
my words will deserve your attention and patience for whose sakes I have
travelled many a weary mile, and am now come hither purposely to instruct
you, making choice of these words of my Text, Hewson I. 2. Now because

the Times are bad and Winter draws near (as the old translation has it) therefore buy ye wax boots. But if we follow the new translation, according to that of our learned Monoculist, and noble commander, Colonel Hewson, who is known to be the best and ablest Translator of our profession now living, we shall find the foregoing part of the text more agreeing with the coherence of the words then the other: *Now because* (saith he) *the times are dangerous, and the Winter approaches, therefore &c.* Or as he hath it more elegantly in his learned Comment upon *Crispine de Acte Vampandi, Chap.* 18. *Now because the times are wavering, and the winter of our troubles steals upon us, therefore plunder ye,* [mark that beloved, 'tis a sweet expression. and full of comfort] *therefore plunder ye waxed Boots*; As if he should say, Now because the times are fickle, because the times are wavering, uncertain, perilous, inconstant and changeable as the Moon: And in the second place, Because the winter drawes near, because cold weather approaches (in which we are like to find cold comfort if we be not prepared beforehand against it) or rather (as in another place he hath it) because the Winter of our troubles steals hastily upon us, and the wicked begin to domineer over us, let us be even with the winter and the wicked too, and steal as fast from them as they do upon us, which is warranted by these words in the latter part of the text, *Therefore plunder ye*, &c. But we will follow the old translation of *Crispine*, who was too honest to plunder, therefore (saith he) *Buy ye waxed Boots*.

In which words observe these parts:
1. The time present.
2. The condition of the times.
3. The season of the times.
4. The benefit or use we should make of the times.
1. The time present, *Now*.
2. The condition of the times, *They are dangerous, uncertain, wavering &c.*
3. The season of the times, *The Winter approaches: Now because*, &c.
4. The benefit or use we should make of the times, *Therefore buy ye*, &c.

First of the time briefly, Now, now at present, now whilst it is time, whilst you have an opportunity to get money from the Malignant party; now (even now) before they rise up again, and force you to flye for refuge to some neighbour Nation; provide you of Materials to do it; take from them their Horses, Armour; nay such blessings as neither you nor your fathers before you could either purchase or enjoy, their waxed boots; and this leads me to the second thing considerable:

The condition of the times, *They are bad, dangerous, uncertain and wavering, &c.*

If the time be bad now, what will they be hereafter? Beloved, Man is a little world, the world is round, and so are we; the world is an hollow and empty thing, so are we; the world hath his times and seasons, his Winters and Summers, his Dayes and Nights, so hath man; he hath times of gettings, and his times of losings; his Sommers of pleasure, and his Winters of heaviness; his Dayes of joy, and his Nights of sorrow: Seeing then all these sublunary things are thus transitory and wavering, let us lay hold of whatsoever stands before us, let us take all things that comes in our way, furnishing our selves cape-a-pee, with the goods of the ungodly, implyed in these words, *Therefore plunder ye, &c.* and this brings me to the third Motive that should perswade, or rather invite us to do it, *Because the winter approaches.*

Now because the times are bad, and the winter approaches, therefore buy ye wax'd Boots.

Beloved, all creatures by natural instinct are taught to provide and lay up provision against Winter; the little Ant stacks up Corn; the laborious Bee layes up Honey against the cold Winter approaches; and will it not be a shame, nay a great shame beloved, for man who is a reasonable creature, and hath more strength and discretion then ten thousand Ants or Bees put them all together; I say, Will it not be a most abominable shame for him to be sent to the silly Ants and Bees for instruction, whilst he like the simple Grashopper hops and skips away the summer of his dayes in vanity and idleness, and afterwards in the winter of years is forced to perish and starve for want of food? O beloved, rather do any thing then starve; the Proverb saith, Poverty is the mother of misery, therefore it is good to provide & lay up something against a rainy day. Now what season is more rainy then the Winter season? and what is more seasonable at that time, what better sence in the world for our feet against the rain, wet and cold, then a pair of waxed Boots? therefore buy ye if ye have money, plunder ye if ye have none, (for it matters not how you come by them so you have them) waxed boots. So now I am come to the fourth and last thing, the benefit and use we should make of the times: Buy waxed boots, therefore buy ye waxed boots.

Where note, that the adverb *therefore*, is an adverb of connexion, for here it joins the winter and the boots together: Now beloved, since I have taken the boots in hand, give me leave to stitch them up in few words, telling you first how many sorts of boots there are; and next what manner of boots those be which are required here in my text. For the better explanation of which words, you are to take notice that there are eight several sorts of boots, I will run over them briefly, because I see the time hastens: I say beloved, there are several sorts of boots, First your Dutch boots, they are a people that will not put on a boot which is not as well liquored as themselves; from whence I gather this Observation, That drunken men love drunken boots. Secondly, there is your French boots; O defie them brethren, defie them, they are abominably contaminated with the disease of their countrey; how many whole congregations of ours have they already infected with it? Witness that lamentable snivelling and snuffling which of late hath spread it selfe through the bridge-fallen Noses of our ablest teachers, for which no other reason in the world can be given then their riding the Sisters in these French Pockey boots: Here by the way give me leave to tell you the several names of this Disease; Some call it *Morbus Neapolitanus,* and *Morbus Gallicus*: First, it is called the Neapolitan Disease, or the Disease of Naples; for it is observed by our wisest Physicians, that ever since Naples commidities came over into England, this disease hath been very busie amongst us. Others say it came by another Italian trick, and that it was brought over by advice of Nich. Machavil in a Florence silk Petticoat, under which device it hath continued ever since; therefore beloved have a care how you meddle with forreign Wenches Petticoats. *Latit Anguis in herba*: that is that Serpent the Devil lurks in their holes, and the Pox under their Petticoats.

Next it is called *Morbus Gallicus,* and not unfitly, for *Gallicus* signifies a Cock, and *Morbus* a Disease, that is, as much as to say, the Disease of the cock; and truly it is well known, that the cock is the first part that is infected with this disease: But some will say, What do you tell us a story of a cock and a bull? Why verily beloved, a good cock is a good thing; and bulls leather is good leather to make waxed boots of; which brings me to the third sort of Leather, your *Rusha* boots. Fourthly, there is your Spanish Leather boots. Fifthly, your Calves Leather Essex boots. Sixthly, your Slints[1] skin, or abortive Parchment boots. Seventhly, there is your Hell-cart, or Coach-boat. Eighthly and lastly, there is your right English Neats-Leather[2] boot, which is the boot intended here in my text for the Winter waxed boot: *Now because the times are bad, &c. therefore, &c.*

So now having shewn you how many several sorts of boots there are, give me leave likewise to shew you how to distinguish the good from the bad, (because I will not warrant all of our Profession to be honest men, since I know some who can stretch their consciences beyond their Last or their Leather) therefore that you may not be deceived in your choice of a perfect winter boot, you are to observe these four qualities.

1. The Grain
2. The length
3. The well joi- } of the Boot.
   ning & sowing
4. The waxing

First, the Grain of the boot; beloved, there are several sorts of Grains, there are your Grains of Corn, your Grains of Mustard-seed, your Beer and Malt Grains, &c. Next there is your good and Physical Grains. Thirdly, there is your *Granum vivens sensibile,* your living sensible Grains, (of which sort I fear here are too many in this Congregation) that is, your Knaves in Grain. And

1. 'Slint' or 'slent'; slanting, oblique; figuratively 'spurious'.   2. Ox-hide.

lastly, there is your Leather Grain, (the principal here intended) which if it be close and compact, stiff and shining, you may be assured (of the first thing observable) that your Leather is good.

The next thing considerable, is the joyning and well sowing of the boot; By joyning, you are to understand the even cutting and proportioning of the tops to the upper part, and the vampings to the lower part of the legs of the boots. This properly belongeth to the Master, but the other of sowing or stitching belongs to his Servant. Now in sowing or stitching, you are to take notice, that you are not to sowe boots as you sowe Corn, (in which he is accounted the best workman who scatters and disperseth his grain best) but you must sowe your stitches close together, first on the inside, next on the outside, if ever you mean to have your Boots go thorow stitch, and hold out water when the Winter comes, and the wayes are heavy and durty.

Thirdly, look to the length of your boots; Brethren, a long boot hath these commodities. First, it will keep warm, and cover that which hath covered many a Commodity. Next it will preserve you from fretting and galling between the legs, (a disease which many a dear Sister is troubled with, proceeding from the same cause though in a different manner) the man by hard riding, to the woman by being too hard ridden.

A third commodity belonging to long boots is this; that if the vampings fail, the leather shrinks, or the seames crack, yet they may be often mended, and the boots still do good service, which reason alone (if the two former are not prevalent) are enough to perswade you to buy long waxed boots.

Fourthly and lastly, you must observe the waxing of the boot, in which you are to take notice:

Bad times require good boots. I say bad times require good boots: because the times are bad, and the Winter, &c. therefore, &c. I shall explain my self to you brethren, briefly thus. I say, bad times require good boots; for verily beloved, the times are bad, very bad, and are like every day, for ought I see, to grow worse and worse; so as I fear, we must all of us e're long, be forced to fly for our Religion. Now beloved, whither shall we fly? Marry 'tis a Question worth your answering, but I doubt there are few or none here, that know how to resolve me in it; for verily I am as yet to seek my self, where to run or hide my head, should the malignant party prevail. But perhaps, some will cry out and say, we will fly to *New England*, another he is for *Geneva*, another he is for a nearer place then both these, he wil away to *Amsterdam*. Truely beloved, I must confesse, I cannot but approve of this place for the best, being it is not only the nearest, but the safest, and hath ever in former times, been found to be the only Nurse and Sanctuary, for all such as are like them, Dispisers of Royal Government, and Self-forms of Prayers.

But here will one object, and say. Is not this an Island wherein we now live, (I had almost said wherein we now dwell, but alas! if the times change, here will be no habitation for us:) and is not this Island encompassed round with a great Sea, will not all our shipping then be taken from us, how then shall we get over to *Amsterdam*; or what good then will our wax'd boots do us?

Beloved, this weak Objection, is easily answered thus. 'Tis true, that *England* is an Island encompassed with the Sea. 'Tis true, there will be no travelling out of it by Land, and it will likely prove as true, (if the wicked prevail) that our Navy will be taken from us. But O thou inconsiderate fool! whosoever thou art that raisest this idle objection,) hast thou not the more need of waxed boots to passe through this Sea? hast thou not great and rough Waters to wade over, before thou canst arrive at thy Journeys end? Now if thy boots be long enough, (which as I told you before, you must be sure to observe, before you buy them for this purpose) and the Seams strong and well-waxed, so as they will hold out water, which you ought first to make tryal of, by wading in them over the *Thames*, from the Parliament-stairs to *Lambeth*, or from *White Hall* to *Stangate*, (for one of these wayes we must all fly if the Cavaliers prevail) you need not be afraid afterward to go over with them, to any part beyond the Seas. So as methinks, this also should be another strong motive, to perswade us to buy strong and long waxed boots.

But here some incredulous and fearful brother, will make a scruple, and say: should we grant you, that it may be possible for us, to passe over the Sea in waxed boots; yet how shall we do now the Winter is come on, the days short, but the Night and our Journeys very dark and long? I say, how shall we doe in these dismal and obscure nights, to find our way, through so pathlesse and uncertain an Element as the Sea is?

O beloved be not dismayed, be not cast down with fear! take you no care for that. Have we not a good and glorious General gon before us, and with the beams of his bright shining Countenance, will like the Sun, disperse those dark shades that doth cover the Waters. He is our Leader, our Guide by day, and our Lamp by night, who hath carried a living fire in the Lanthorn of his beak; which neither the highest Winds can put out, nor the greatest Waves extinguish, because it will ever continue the same, so long as the Splendor of it endureth.

But we will leave generals, and come to particulars, for I fear I have been too tedious in illustrating this Doctrine, wherefore I will only passe to an use or two, and so conclude.

The first is an use of consolation or comfort. Is it so; That waxed boots will preserve us from the cold; is it so that with waxed boots, we may passe through thick and thin; Nay, through Seas of Troubles, why, what a great comfort and consolation is it, for all those who have occasion to travail through bad and sad ways, to be provided of waxed boots. Beloved, there are (as I shewed you before) your Summer and your Winter boots. In the one you may travail reasonably well, all the yeer long, provided your ways, and the journey be accordingly. As for example: If you have occasion to ride your *Newmarket* ways, your *Bansted Down* wayes, your *Tiptry Heath* wayes, or your *Salisbury plain* wayes, then these Summer boots will carry you through; these will preserve you well enough, provided no raine from above, or dust, mire, and waters from beneath, do not offend or molest you. But should you have occasion in the Winter time to travel, your *Essex* wayes, your *Dunmow* wayes, your *High Suffolk*, *Farningham Castle* wayes, or those most abominable dirty, miry, and watry *Wishbeech*, or *Ely Fenny* wayes; O in what a fine case would your Summer boots be, when they have been well washed in those filthy ways. How will they shrink together like parchment against the Fire. Therefore buy you waxed boots.

And this puts me in mind of a merry, but a real story, that I have heard from a credible person, who I am confident would not tell an untruth, of a certain young Gentleman, living not far from *Newmarket*, who was a Suiter to a fair Lady, dwelling at *Cholchester* in the County of *Essex*. Now this young Gallant, having never before, travelled five miles from his Fathers House, (imagined the same the Citizens Wife did, who having never in her life time been out of *London*, would needs perswade her Husband, that though she had but twenty miles to ride, and it was a rainy day, yet they two might ride safe and dry all the way, under the Penthouses:) So this spruce Blade, thinking all the World was heath ground, though it was in the depth of Winter, and his man perswaded him to put on his Winter boots, he would not go thither in any but a pair of thin Calves leather *Essex* boots, alledging this reason for it, That he new his Mistresse would love him the better, when she see he came to court her, in a pair of her own Country boots. Whereupon, he sets forward on his Journey; but mark Beloved what followed; he had not gone above half his way, before he took such an excessive cold on his Feet, that he was forced to alight at a poor blind Ale-house, at a place called *Black Chappel*, within three miles of *Dunmow*, where he had no sooner got a fire made, and his boots (which hung about him like Chitterlins, with much adoe pulled of) but he fell into a violent Ague, and was immediately compelled to take his bed, where he remained many days after. But I had almost forgot to tell you, that the poor Alehouse Keeper, where this Gentleman lay sick, did keep in his house a young water Spaniel, which he had newly taught to fetch and carry; this wanton unlucky Whelp, seeking about the house in the midst of the Night, for some bones to eat, lights upon the Gentlemans boots, which he no sooner meets with, but being desirous to put in practise, what his Master had so lately taught him, he takes first one boot, and afterwards another, and carryes them into the entry: where finding them wet and soft, instead of playing the Cur, falls to tearing them, and in short time pulled and knawed them into many peices. Now it chanced, that in the morning early, before it was light, the Old mans Wife (who also dressed tripes for to get a living) was called up by a Butcher, who brought her some inwards of a Beast for the same purpose, which she had no sooner received, but returning back through the entry, she unhappily stumbled upon the Gentlemans mangled boots, so as letting fall what she had in her hands upon them, groping in the dark, she took up all together, and carrying them into the Kitchin, (without lighting a Candle) first cut, and then washed and dressed them all together, and having afterwards well boyled the boots, amongst the rest in a Kettle, which over night she had set over the fire for the same purpose, she cast them into her sowcing Tub, where for a while we will leave them, and tell you what become of our sick Gentleman. Beloved, this Gentleman within few days after, began to recover, and waxed very hungry, so as calling his Landlord, to know what meat he had in the House; Truely Sir (quoth he) we have nothing but a dish of Tripes of my Wives one dressing, which if you please to have, they shall be made ready immediately. Well! well they are accepted of, and brought to the Gentleman, who sitting up in his bed, did feed heartily, till such time as taking up a piece of thin, long, lean Tripe (as he supposed) and finding a string jagged about the edge of one side of it, he called up his Landlady, and desired to know what part of the beast that was? the Poor woman searching it, and distrusting what it was, but not dreaming how it should come there, without speaking one word, runs down Stairs into the Kitchin, where she was no sooner come to search for the Gentlemans boots, she finds the puppy dog tearing of the Vampings, which he had lately transformed them into Slippers. In the mean time the Gentleman would not be satisfied, but calls for her again to answer his question, who as soon as she was come to him, he again demands of her, what part of the inside of the beast that was, he held in his hand. The poor woman, though fearful and trembling, yet wittily replyed, that she beleived it to be rather a part of the out-side, then the in-side of the beast, meaning the hide, and begging pardon for her carlesnesse, and the dogs wantonnesse, desired his worship to forgive them both, telling him plainly, that that peece he shewed her, was a peece of his worships boots, and that the threads, that looked like a purl or edging upon the tripe, was nothing but the jags of the Shoomakers ends which hung about it. The Gentleman at this accident, one while laughing, and another while fretting, caused the old man to ride away speedily to *Chelmsford*, for a strong pair of waxed boots, but what with his delay, (by reason of his sicknesse, and after-wards for want of boots) to visit his Mistris, whom he promised to have seen a week before;) she imputing his long stay, rather to a neglect and slighting of her, than his present misfortune, immediately contracted her self to another, who had formerly been a Servant to her, and at his coming discarded him, by which means he lost his Mistris, his labour, his boots, and had like to have lost his life too, had he not happily recovered.

O beloved! let this sad example be a Caveat for all you who have Mistresses, to have a care of wearing Tripes, when you ride a wooing, least you be served like this infortunate Gentleman, who for want of a pair of waxed boots, was first cast into an Ague, next had his boots cast into the Tripe tub; and lastly, was himself quite and clean cast out of his Mistresses favour. Therefore buy ye waxed boots; which brings me to the second use.

The second use is an use of Reproof; to reprove all those who are self-willed, and cannot fairly be perswaded to buy them waxed boots. But to such as these, examples move more than precepts, wherefore I will only give you one or two more, and so I will make an end, for fear of tiring your patience. I read of *Alexander* the Great, that passing over a River in *Alexandria*, without his Winter boots, he took such an extreme Cold in his Feet, that he suddenly fell sick of a violent Feaver, and within four dayes after dyed at *Babylon*. The like I find in *Plutarchs Lives*, of that noble Roman *Sextorius*, and also in *Homer* of *Achilles*, that leaving his boots behind him, and comming barefoot into the Temple of *Pallas*, whilest he was worshipping on his knees at her Altar, he was peirced into the Heel, with a venom'd Dart by *Paris*, (the part only of him which was vulnerable,) of which he suddenly dyed, which accident had never happened to him, (as *Alexander Rosse*, that little *Scotch* Mithologist observes[1]) had he not two days before, pawned his boots to *Ulisses*, and so was forced to come without them to the *Trojan* Sacrifice. He also further observes, that that *Achilles* (of whom *Homer* hath writ such wonders) was but a Shoomakers boy of *Greece*, and that when *Ulisses* sought him out, he at last found him at the Distaffe, spinning of Shoomakers thread; now this Boy was so beloved, that as soon as it was reported abroad, that the Oracle had chosen him to rule the *Grecians*, and conquer *Troy*, all the Journeymen in the Country, lifted themselves under him, and these were the Mermydons wherewith he got all his Honor, and overcame the *Trojans*.

But what need I mention forraign stores, being my self an Eye-witnesse of the lamentable ends many *Suffolk* men, in the Seige of *Cholchester*, who being forced to keep Centry in that wet and boggy Country, (during which Seige, it was generally observed for thirteen weeks, not a day passed, in which much rain did not fall) I say these poor Country Wretches, were forced to stand up to the knees day and night, in Cold, Dirt, Mire, and Wet; insomuch, that for want of waxed boots, many of them dyed suddenly, others had their Legs rotted off; many their feet gangreened, and after was cut off; and few or none, but had Ulcers, Boyls, and Iuflamamations, breaking out upon them.

1. 'Achilles was careless and secure of his feet, and therefore he was wounded there by Paris.' Alexander Ross, *Mystagogus Poeticus* (1653 edn.), p. 3.

Alas! alas! what would these poor Cripples do to run away, should the Times change, and the Malignants prevail over us? How must they be forced to bestir their Stumps for want of Legs, to escape the Enemy? This one comfort they will have above us, that whensoever they are taken by the Wicked, they will not find them stand complementing, or making legs for pardon; but they shall rather find them down upon their Knees, begging mercy and forgivenesse of them, whose persons they have turned out of their possessions, and whose houses these lame Creatures, have for these many yeers, converted into Spittles and Hospitals.

Thus I have shewn you what became of three great Princes, and of many poor *Englishmen*, who perish'd in these late Wars, for want of waxed boots. I should here give you an account, how and in what manner, you should know the right shape and fashion of a Winter boot: and likewise shew you, what manner of Heels are the best, the most suitable and serviceable for you against running or flying times, I shall only name them at present. Beloved, your Polony heel is good, your Wooden heels better, but those of Corke the best of all; for then will it be needful for you to make trial of a pair of High heels, and indeed you will then, and then only, have occasion to run, as though you ran for a wager; and for this use, your Corke heels are found by experience to be the best and highest in the World.

Lastly, I should have taught you the art of repairing, stitching, vamping, underlaying, and mending of your boots, and should likewise have shewed you how to choose the Soles of your boots; and also in a word have applyed these things to the good use of your bodies; but that I see the Glasse is run, and the time hath prevented me, I must be forced to make an end, concluding with the words of my Text, *Now because the times are bad, and Winter draws neer, therefore buy you Waxed Boots.*

5

THE RESTORATION

Derisive parody though it was, 'Hodg. Tubervil's sermon' contained sound advice, and Hewson took it. He got himself 'waxed boots' and he used them in the nick of time. On May 21st Parliament was informed that he had escaped overseas. On the 23rd Charles II was welcomed on the shores of England and subsequently parliament passed the Act of Indemnity, enabling the adversaries in the Civil War to bury past grievances, forgive and forget, and settle down to live in peace again together under the government of a united country. Of course it was too good to be entirely true. From the protection of this friendly Act were excluded a number of particular offenders whose crimes were considered too repugnantly gross for forgiveness. As a signatory of the late king's death-warrant Hewson was high on the list of wanted men, and machinery was put into motion to track him down and have him extradited. In his case the hunt did not succeed. It was reported that he died in Amsterdam in 1662; but in 1666 a travelling tobacco salesman was arrested in England on suspicion of being Hewson, and before he was released he said that he had known Hewson who died in Rouen. Not all the rest of the regicides were as fortunate, or, perhaps, as cunning. The surviving judges, including Harrison, Cook, Scott and Scroop were rounded up; also Francis Hacker, the captain of the king's escort to the scaffold, Captain Hewlett, the supposed executioner, and, perhaps the most damnable of all, in Royalist eyes, Hugh Peters, who had prominently exulted in public over the captive king, and led the Redcoats in their chant for death outside Westminster Hall during the trial. The account of his capture is from a hostile, not necessarily inaccurate, source, but it is unlikely that, whatever the truth, hatred of Peters would not have added at least some scurrilous embellishment. A sharp but inconclusive exchange of views on the subject between Virginia L. Ruland and J. Max Patrick may be found in the Huntingdon Library Quarterly XVIII (Feb. 1955) and XIX (August 1955).

Amongst the rest, their Baalam-like Prophet and Southsayer Hugh Peters, is close prisoner in the Tower of London. Some difficulty there was in the discovery of him; but upon Intelligence, that he privily lurked about Southwark, two Messengers were sent on Friday last to apprehend him; And entring the house of Mr. Broad a Quaker, in St. Thomas Parish, whose daughter then lay in; they searchd, but miss'd him, he being (according to his custom) crept into bed to the young woman, where the Messengers modesty forbad their search, she having bin delivered but two days before; And while they were searching at one Day a Cobler, Hugh the Firebrand escap'd from Childbed, leaving behind him his Cane with a Rapier in it, a Bible, and gray cloak. But on Sunday night they found him at one Mr. Muns in the Maze, who denyed himself to be Peters, and said his name was Thompson, threatning the Messengers with an Action at Law for offering to affirm he was Hugh Peters, and therefore refused to go with them, till at last being assisted by the Constable and others) they forced him; which he perceiving, desired he might speak privately with Mrs. Mun, which they denyed, unlesse he would speak in their hearing; after which he said, I will go, but I beg for the Lords sake that you will not call me Mr. Peters; for, said he, if it be known that I am Hugh Peters, the people in the street will stone me. But forcing him away, there was some tugging; and feeling his Skirts hard, they unript them, & found 5 pieces of Gold, some silver Medals, and out of his Pocket they took his Almanack, which he was very much troubled at. After which, they brought him to the Tower, & delivered him into the custody of the worthy Lieutenant Sir John Robinson; still avering his name was Thomson; till at last in private to Sir John he confessed who he was. This is St. Hugh, who when our Glorious Sovereign was led to Martyrdom, fell so heavy upon his righteous Soul, blaspheming him upon his then Text, (Psal. 149. To bind their Kings in Chains &c) and many other sordid Notions; too wicked and prophane to be here recited.[1]

In Peters' case the trial was a mere formality. When he tried to cite in mitigation some good actions of his, the Judge remarked dryly that he had not been brought there 'for anything good' he had done. Along with the other chief offenders he was condemned to be hanged, drawn and quartered, and on October 13th, 1660 the sentence was carried out with even more than usual barbarity. The crowd were incensed against him and nothing he might have said would have been heard above the raucous jeers and taunts, even if he had had the stomach to speak. But he preached in prison, shortly before his execution, a sermon which was published at his death.[2]

1. *The Speed and Confession of H. Peters . . . with the manner how he was taken* (1660).
2. *A Sermon by Hugh Peters Preached Before his Death As it was taken by a faithful hand and now published for publick Information* (1660).

RICHARD BAXTER

The long, exhausting, bloody ordeal was over; the darkness of bigotry was lifting, and a new day of sanity and goodwill was dawning. Such at least was the prospect which moderates of both sides strained to discern when, after a racking war and a spurious 'peace', they were united into Royalist alliance against the extremities of the ultra-republican elements of the 'Rump' and the Army.

Of these, 'the violent and the rigid'[1] a representative voice of the large and unified centre says:

'I must tell you plainly; you are esteemed but a kind of *Frantick*; and very paltry ones: in your policy pedantic, in your justice Narrow and Mechanical, Selfish in Conversation, Waspish in argument or debate, Perverse in business, Excentrick in your Motions, and true to no Principle ... the nations had hitherto seen little of you to enamour them. '

The more responsible optimists were cautious and chastened, especially the elders, who had seen too much evil to expect too much good; and former dogmatic partisans were taking generous draughts of the physic of self-criticism. The same, basically Royalist voice also says, talking to his own party,

'Gentlemen, it is too manifest that, in the first years of the war some of you (I mean the *Outrageous Royalists*) did more prejudice the king your master than the worst of his enemies.'

But the criticism most charged with resentment and blame is reserved for the political clergy, with the 'godly' laymen, given to preaching, close behind. For centuries the voice of the preacher had exhorted men to be 'religious', 'devout', 'holy'; but now, religious drives, real and affected, had been seen to produce consequences of ugly and destructive confusion; England had learnt at great cost that there could be religious perversions as well as religious vocations, and that the lusts of malice and envy and avarice and selfish ambition became peculiarly ravenous and shameless when they assumed the licence of religious zeal and divine inspiration.

Studiously addressing *all* churchmen, whether of the 'classical or

1. *A word in due season to the Ranting Royalists and Rigid Presbyterians* (1660).

Episcopal judgement' or of the rest, our probably secular spokesman is heard again.

'Remember you are ministers of the Gospel, not of the State; for which purpose our pious laws have provided you a peculiar maintenance to depend on no man, have both sequestered you from Publick Offices and exempted you from civil duties. Thrust not your sickles into any other harvest, Act not the part of Newes-mongers and Politicians. You no question struck the first stroke, for our *statesmen* turned not Preachers till our Preachers turned statesmen. It is surely high time you redeemed the credit you have so lost, whether as evangelists, Christians, or good citizens and stop their mouths who have too much colour to object that your blessings, and curses are like those of Balaam, and that indeed you deliver not your Christian ordinances but your own passions.'

Whether he believed he was prophesying, or merely expressing a pious hope, the writer was in fact predicting the essential nature of the Church of England to come, a national institution, but one mellowed into a flexibly inclusive tolerance, in which the clergy were relieved of the dangerous temptations of temporal power and the distracting responsibilities of secular politics: a constitutional Episcopacy, as it were; Laud's dream realistically modified and uncompelled. One day much of this would come to pass, when religion was no longer a white-hot issue; but the element of tolerance was not yet acceptable; too much rancour remained undispersed in too many breasts; unhealed wounds were still tender and would continue so for years to come. The Puritans had treated and punished a 'malignant' record, even reputation, for loyalty to the Episcopacy, as a political offence, a subversive association. Now the more unforgiving elements among the dominant Cavaliers were about to insist that any draught of religious uniformity should not be diluted to indulge the Puritans' scrupling palate, and that the non-conformity of these should be treated, in its turn, as political subversion.

All this was still part of 'tomorrow', though its lineaments were foreseen by some. As it dawns, we approach the end of our defined course with the sermons of four men, very different from each other, whom we leave, on the threshold of the Restoration, gazing from their several points of view, sorrowfully back to the past, and anxiously out to the future. The immediate past they know with a directness of experience which we can never imaginatively recreate; the imminent future they will also come to know in a sense which, again, we can never do; for they will help to make it and live into it; but, at the time when they are speaking to us, these events have not yet occurred, and what to them is still an ambiguous, unformed future, to us, from our observation post in time, is *history*, seasoned and irrevocable, perhaps most notable for its absentees. The Royal Society is not yet incorporated, the light of its *Philosophical Transactions* merely an osmosis of the thoughts of 'divers worthy persons'. The Slave Trade, which will taint us with the retributive social disease from which we are now suffering so feverishly, has not yet entered into its bestial secondary stage of development. Eighteen-year-old Isaac Newton has still to see the apple fall at Woolsthorpe. Young Samuel Pepys's diary is one year old; the great plague is a nightmare to come; London is not yet burning. It is, then, upon the omens of their own future existence that men in general, and our preachers in particular, gaze, on this 1660 spring of hope and rejoicing. The names of the four preachers are Richard Baxter, William Sheldon, John Bramhall and Isaac Ironside.

A moderate Puritan of Presbyterian leanings, Baxter suffered the temporal worst of both worlds. Anti-Episcopalian, but no regicide, he had been unable to reconcile himself to Cromwell's dispensation, and now, though he does not know it, he is about to have to reject the new order. Though his best work lies ahead, he is already esteemed one of the most eloquent Puritan preachers of the age, and his own piety is unquestioned. The *persona* of his sermon is the essence of Puritan idealism. The enthusiasm and the fervour of appeal, the earnest exclamations and apostrophes, the presumptions and allusions, the suggestion of intimate, private Revelation, the whole *method*, declares the position of the preacher as the paint on a canvas declares the position of a painter. Baxter is one of those who will be unable to yield himself to the terms of the Act of Uniformity, though tempted with a bishopric. Acceptance would have meant the end of all his hopes of an independent Presbyterian church—he must have already given up hope of an *exclusive* Presbyterian church in his time—and he will live to be prosecuted and harassed by his enemies, and, later, to be sentenced to imprisonment and threatened with the lash by Judge Jeffryes. But now, in high repute, and addressing an illustrious congregation this auspicious May day, he is full of hope of reconciliation and joy, although the veteran partisan in him cannot resist the opportunity to get in a dig or two at his old adversaries. He sees, of course, the possibility of the Restoration being used to indulge vengeance in the name of justice.

But it is the *hereafter* which he really has his eye on, and he gets everyone off there as quickly as possible, to enjoy the delights of contemplating the just man's everlasting communion with God.

There is a rather macabre likeness between the last quoted paragraph of Cokayne's exhortation to the House of Commons[1] (in God's Name to bring Charles I to Justice, which meant death) and Baxter's final paragraph in the following passage, exhorting the Lord Mayor, Aldermen and city magnates, in God's Name, to insist upon *his*, Baxter's, version of Church government on the return and accession of the dead king's son. In both instances the rewards offered are the same: the submission and obedience of the people to *their* temporal authority will be prescribed from the pulpits, if the magistrates, will but sustain the spiritual authority of the covenanted presbyters.

Right Rejoicing
or, The Nature and Order of Rational and Warrentable joy

A Sermon preached at St. Pauls before the Lord Mayor
and Aldermen and several Companies of the City of
London, in anticipation of the imminent return to
England of Charles 11, May 10th., 1660

How the Glory of God will make that face to shine for ever, that now looks too dejectedly, and is darkened with griefs, and worn with fears, and daily wears a mourning visage! No trouble can enter into the heavenly Jerusalem: nor is there a mournfull countenance in the presence of our King! Self-troubling was the fruit of sin and weakness, of ignorance, mistakes and passion, and therefore is unknown in heaven, being pardoned and laid by with our flesh, among the rest of our childish weaknesses and diseases. That poor afflicted wounded soul, that breaths in trouble as its daily air, and thinks it is made up of grief and fear, shall be turned into love and joy, and be unspeakably higher in those heavenly delights, then ever it was low in sorrow. O blessed face of the most Glorious God! O happy presence of our glorified Head! O blessed beams of the eternal love, that will continually shine upon us! O blessed work! to *behold* to *love*, to *delight*, and *praise*! O blessed company of holy Angels, and of perfect Saints, so perfectly united, so exactly suited, to concord in those felicitating works! where all these are, what sorrow can there be? what relicts of distress, or smallest scars of our

1. See above, pp. 445–446.

antient wounds! Had I but one such friend as the meanest Angel in heaven to converse with, how easily could I spare the courts of Princes, the popular concourse, the learned Academies, and all that the world accounteth pleasure, to live in the sweet and secret converse of such a friend! How delightfully should I hear him discourse of the ravishing love of God, of the Glory of his face, the better putting on our heavenly robes, and we are presently there. A few nights more to stay on earth; a few words more to speak to the sons of men; a few more duties to perform, and a few more troublesom steps to pass, will be a small inconsiderable delay. This room will hold you *now* but an hour longer; and this world but a few hours more; But Heaven will be the dwelling place of Saints, to all eternity. These faces of flesh that we see to day, we shall see but a few times more, if any; But the face of God we shall see for ever. That glory no dismal times shall darken; That joy no sorrow shall interrupt; No sin shall forfeit, no enemy shall endanger or take from us; no changes shall ever dispossess us of. And should not a believer then *rejoyce*, that *his name is written in Heaven?* and that every providence wheels him on, and whether the way be fair or foul, its *thither* that he is travelling? O Sirs, if Heaven be better then Vanity and Vexation; if endless joy be better then the laughter of a child that ends in crying; and if God be better then a delusory world, you have then greater matters set before you, to be the matter of your joy, then prosperity and success, or any thing that flesh and blood delights in. . . .

It is some matter of Thankfullness to me, that whereas to our perpetuall shame, we could not in so many years compose the disagreements in Church affairs among us, we are not altogether without hope, that agreement may be now more effectually procured; not only because that carnall advantages,[1] that hindred it with some, are taken from them, and suffering will dispose some more to peace; but because we are *perswaded* the *disposition*, and we are *sure* the *interest* of his Majesty standeth, for our reconciliation and unity. And verily we are the most inexcusable people in the world, if our own long and sad experiences do not resolve us to do the utmost in that work our selves, which if we are not horridly proud and wilfull, is easie to accomplish.

And its matter of Thanksgiving, that *God hath been all along so wonderfully seen in the work*; which makes us hope, that the issue will yet be for our good. The *first sparks* that set fire on the last foundation, are yet *much unknown*, but were *so little* as makes it the more strange. The wonderfull whirlwind that suddenly finished the subversion, was marvellous, though sad, because of the wickedness of men. The introducing of the remnant of the Members; *the* stop that was given them, when they had voted in a Committee, a liberty

1. The Episcopacy and its temporalities. At this stage Baxter seems confident that they will not return.

in Religion, that excepted not Popery:[1] the casting of them out, by those that set them up; the discoveries of the fallaciousness of some of their chiefs, that then were tempted into a compliance with the Army, and were fabricating a new form of a Commonwealth: the breaking of them and of the Army, in part by the returning Members:[2] the unexpected stop that was given first to their proceedings by his excellency in the North:[3] the expeditiousness, the constancy, the unanimity and strange successfullness of that attempt, that an Army that thought themselves only fit to be the Nations security for liberty and Religion, and were thought necessary to be entailed upon us to that end; that were so heightned in their own and other mens esteem, by their many and wonderfull successes, should in a moment (we scarce know how) fly all into pieces, as a Granado that's fired. That *Ireland* at the same time should be so strangely and easily reduced, and that by sober faithfull hands, and by so few, and with such speed! That this famous City should be so unanimously excited to concurre so eminently, and contribute so very much to the success: that his Excellency should conquer without any blows; and all be dispatched that since is done, with no considerable resistance; all this and much more, do make us wonder at the hand of God. And seldom is there so wonderfull an appearance of the Lord, but it holds forth matter that's *amiable* as well as *admirable* to his Church.

Lastly, That all this is done with little or no effusion at all of blood, when so much blood was shed in the foregoing changes, advanceth the wonder to a greater height. And I hope his Majesty and the two Houses of Parliament will take notice, how God hath gone before them in a tender and unbloody change, and will not hearken to them that protest against *revenge*, while they would use it under the name of *justice*. When the wheel of providence turneth so fast, if all that have the advantage of executing their wils under the name of justice, should *take* their advantage, you know what *names* and *sufferings* multitudes of the usefullest Members in such Nations, in the severall vicissitudes must *incurr*, to the detriment of the Commonwealth and Governours.

You see what cause we have of thankfulness: but I must tell you that this (as all inferiour mercies) are imperfect things, and being but *meanes* to greater *matters*, (the heavenly interest first treated on) they are no further significant or valuable, then they have some tendency to their end. And I must further tell you, that it's much committed into the hands of man, (under God) whether such beginnings shall have a happy or unhappy end. If *Christ* become to many *a stumbling stone*, and be *set for the fall of many in Israel*, (Luk.2.34.) and if the Gospel it self prove the *savour of death* to some, no

---

1. This disapproving reference is to Cromwell's tolerant religious policy.
2. The members of the Long Parliament excluded since 'Pride's Purge' who had at last returned to vote for a Restoration.
3. General Monk.

wonder if it be yet possible and too easie, for a sinfull Land, to turn these forementioned mercies and successes, into most heavy judgements, and to rob themselves of all the honour and the benefit. And therefore *above all*, for the Lords sake, and for a poor tired yet hoping Nations sake, and for the sake of the cause of Christ through the world, I beseech you, all from the highest to the lowest, that you will be awakened to an holy vigilancy, and look about you in your severall places, lest the enemy of Christ and you, should play his after-game more successfully then now you can foresee: and lest the return of a sinfull Nation to their vomit, should make the end yet worse than the beginning. It is not enough to have begun: the fruit of all is yet behind. I must here deal plainly with you, however it be taken, lest I be charged with unfaithfulness, at the dreadfull Tribunal to which both you and I are hastening. If these beginnings, through your neglects, or any others that have been the instruments, should now be turned to the reviveing and strengthening of prophaneness, and malignity against the holy wayes of God; to the introduction of meer formality in Religion; to the casting out, or weakening the hands of the faithfull Ministers in the Land; to the destruction of order and Discipline in the Churches, to the suppression of orderly and edifying meetings for mutuall assistance in the matters of salvation; or to the cherishing of ignorance or Popery in the people; it will blast the glory of all that you have done, and turn the mercy into gall. Believe it, the interest of Christ and holiness, will be found at last the surest ground, for any Prince to build his interest upon: And the owning of corrupt and contrary interests, that engage men in quarrels with the interest of Christ, is it that hath undone so many Princes and States already, that it should make the greatest learn at last, to account it their highest honour to be the servants of the King of Saints, and to devote their power to the accomplishment of his will. I need not tell you, that it's the sober, godly, conscionable sort of men, that know what they do, and why,[1] that will be the honour of their Governours, and the usefullest of their subjects, and not the barbarous malignant rabble, that understand not what belongs to the pleasing of God, the happiness of themselves, the good of the Commonwealth, or the honour of their King. And do you not think that remisness (to say no worse) of Magistrates that should restrain the insolencies of such, is not a great dishonour to our Nation, and a great temptation to many in the Countrey, that stand at a distance from the fountain of affairs, to continue their fears lest we have changed for the worse? Put your selves in their cases, and tell me whether you could with equall cheerfullness keep this day, if you were used as many able, faithfull Ministers and people are in the Cities and Countreys of the Land, who have their persons assaulted, their windows battered, their ministrations openly reviled, and that go in danger of their lives, from the bruitish rabble that

1. The Presbyterians.

were formerly exasperated by the Magistrates punishing them, or the Ministers reproof, or crossing them in their sins.[1] As Physicions are judged of, not so much by the *excellency* of their *remedies*, as by their *success*, and the people think of them as they see the patients *live* or *die*; so will they do by *your great-performances* which you mention before the Lord this day. Should they prove to the *suppression of serious godliness*, and the *setting up of the wicked of the Land*, I need not tell you *what a name it will leave unto the actors to all generations*. But if you vigilantly improve them (as you have given us abundant reason to expect,) and the issue shall be *the healing concord of the Churches, the curbing of profaneness, the promoting of a plain and serious Ministry, and of the diligent service of the Lord*; this is it that will make your Names immortall that have been the happy instruments of so blessed a work! How joyfully then will the subjects commemorate, the happy introduction of their Soveraign? With what love and honour will they hear his Name? How readily will they obey him? How heartily will they pray for him? How precious will *your* memory be? and this will be numbered among the wonderfull deliverances of *England*. If Godliness be persecuted or made a common scorn in the Land, the holy God will vindicate his honour, and make their Names a scorn and curse that shall procure it. But if you exalt him, he will exalt you: Protect his Lambs and he will be your Protector. He is with you while you are with him, 2 *Chron*.15.2. *Those that honour him he will honour; and those that despise him shall be lightly esteemed*, 1 Sam.2.30.

1. Baxter fails to appreciate the significance of these demonstrations which were expressions of popular resentment against meddlesome ministers.

WILLIAM SHELDON

Baxter and Sheldon make a classic study in contrast. To read in succession the 1660 'Restoration' sermons of the two men is to see in encounter the impulses which were, and would remain, unreconciled. For Baxter and his kind, this life was valueless save as a preparation for the glorious hereafter. All worldly activities other than religious, as interpreted by them, including the arts and science, were vanity. The ideal state was to be like Moses, in daily personal conference with God, praising his name and trampling on sin, the sin of others as well as one's own. This view was of course interpreted with greater and less severity from man to man, but it represented the guiding principles.[1]

Sheldon was a man of the world, but in his concept of the world, no less Christian by intent for that. To him the world was the place where God has chosen to put us. Our time in the world, therefore, was given us for *living*, not just for waiting impatiently to be removed to a better place. It was for us to serve God by making the best of life and all that could be done with it. All things performed in a Christian spirit were to the glory of God. The Church was the repository of traditions, received knowledge and revelation of our forefathers in God, and existed to provide a stable and enduring form of worship in accordance with the precedents of ancient and tested historical practice, and suitable to the language and understanding of the worshippers. The other important function of the Church was to recall people to Christian *practice* of their professions; to Sheldon, far more important than any presumed private discourses with God, was the duty to be an honest man and live a charitable, Christian life. It was not that there were not honest Puritans, nor that some Anglicans did not pray devoutly and

1. This attitude of the 'purest' Puritans may seem inconsistent in the light of the Puritans' general reputation for commercial initiative. It was a contradiction which the Puritan learnt to live with. His personal relationship with God was all that truly mattered, and in the interests thereof his relationship with Satan and all things carnal had to be kept continuously under attack. But there was deemed no better soil for Satan's seeds than idleness and 'vanity'; therefore arts, sport, pleasurable recreations were, broadly, to be discouraged. This as a start is not a bad foundation for commercial success. The zealous Puritan was never himself responsible for any prosperity achieved. Not he, but God working in him made the profit, and what God caused a saint to do was for His glory.

spontaneously in private; it was a matter of priority and emphasis, and of *climate*. Sheldon wished to cool religious emotion and bring the Church down to earth for a time, to receive literal and badly needed repairs. He had seen civil war and persecution fomented, his beloved master, Laud, and his king, murdered, and the country brought to the brink of ruin in a fever of religious frenzy. This of course is only one part of the picture, but it is the part which we must expect Sheldon, as a Royalist and an Anglican, to see with particular clarity, and to remember in his relations with these intemperate, hot-tongued evangelists who claimed to speak in God's name (with God's latest instruction personally delivered) on every aspect of national policy. The subliminary ideal of 'every man his own Moses' was to Sheldon impertinent and ridiculous; it could intoxicate the lower orders and the uneducated with delusions of grandeur, and subvert social discipline; it certainly would not do for a gentleman; for there was about its repulsive 'enthusiasm' something akin to indecent exposure.

When Sheldon preached this sermon of welcome to Charles II, he was standing on the springboard to power. He was not yet Archbishop of Canterbury, but he was already recognized as one of the leading counsellors of the new order. A survivor of Falkland's fellowship at Great Tew, and therefore, of course, a friend of Clarendon's, his superlative administrative abilities were never in dispute. He was shrewd, firm, prudent, persuasive. It was said of him that he was not truly religious. Certainly 'religion' did not mean the same thing to him as it did to his opponents.

Sheldon is important because his influence was great, and interesting because he bridged the smoking gap in the Church made by the civil wars. Producing new unmistakable echoes of Laudian wit, he yet also speaks already with the accents of a new voice, one that will prevail in literature and the arts, in the university and coffee house, in the theatre and the pulpit, for many years to come. Not himself primarily a man of letters, he displays the lineaments of the well-bred, deceptively careless-seeming simplicity, to be polished hereafter for the polite literate, by succeeding generations of Augustans; Tillotson, South, Glanvill, Spratt, Swift, and their company. Like Baxter, he takes the opportunity, in addressing a large concourse, to deal some resounding public blows upon the flanks of the enemy—not, of course, the same 'enemy' as Baxter's—as he embarks on the theme, odious to Puritan ears present, that this earthly life is meant to be enjoyed, addressing, no doubt, with special relish those present in conspicuously sombre clothes and with countenances 'sowr and severe'.

David's Deliverance and Thanksgiving

A thanksgiving sermon for the Restoration of the Monarchy preached before the King at Whitehall on June 28th. 1660

'Tis an excellent Rule of Life St. *Bernard* gives, *Do well, and be merry*; as merry as you will, the more the better; keep to the first, you cannot offend in the second. And let me tell you, that *Vertue and Religion* are the most *chearfull* things in the World, however some make them sowr and severe; they are, like God himself, all light and serenity, joy and comfort, especially in his service.

God loves the chearful Servant, and who does not? We may judge it by our selves. Who cares for him that goes to his *work* as if he went to the *Stocks* or a *Prison*? All parts of Gods service, even the sowrest and severest (had we time to shew it) are mixed with comforts, and should be performed joyfully; this of *Thanksgiving* above and beyond, and more then any: For here we swim with the stream. We are naturally chearful after a mischief avoided, a danger escaped;[1] and being so well prepared for it, should with all alacrity *sing* out our *thanks* and his *praise*, declare an exultation of mind in all innocent and decent expressions of joy and gladness.

'Twas ever the custome of all mankind to do it, in all Ages and places: Instances are infinite both within the Church and without. But in this hast we need go no further then the Prophet *David*, who in the Book of *Psalms*, for his several deliverances, is ever at [*I will sing*,] or [*O sing unto the Lord:*] either doing it himself, or calling others to do it, not coldly or faintly, but zealously and heartily; *Sing aloud, made a chearfull noise; Sing lustily unto him with a good courage.*[2] But this will not serve the turn neither, unless he call for Instruments, as well as men to assist; *Bring hither the Tabret, the merry Harp, and the Lute, blow the Trumpet too,*[3] all to incite, quicken and enflame his heart and affections, even to a transporting extatick joy of gratitude.

1. The danger escaped was a Puritan republic.

2. The Puritans were censorious of all liturgical music except the plainest of psalm singing.

3. Instrumental music in and out of church was abomination to strict Puritans. See above, p. 321 et seq.

We should indeed labour to foment it in us as much as may be, for the greater *joy without*, the greater *sense* and esteem of his *bounty within*; and the greater that is, ever the more, and the more sincere *Gratitude*; which if it be not *heard* in our *Tongues*, is certainly not *felt* in our *Hearts*, and therefore there it must be also.

And when this is done, the second part of Gratitude is performed; the *Tongue* hath done her part, but all is not yet done; this is but *Gratiarum dictio*, it reacheth no further then *words*, and something must be *done* as well as *said*.

The *thanks* of some are vocal enough, too much, because nothing else, nothing but sound and noise; and better a dumb heart then not sincere.[1] Words are a cheap way of payment,[2] and the world delights much in it; Gods benefits are not *words*, but *deeds*, and our Gratitude will be found short, if it reach not beyond words to *deeds*. Nay, Honesty and Reason require, that the compensation exceed the benefit received, that the return be made both in greater *measure*, and with greater alacrity (if it may be;) Because he that gave was *not obliged*; he that returns is; the one comes from a free and liberal *mind*, the other is a piece of *Justice*, and a Debt: And though we have paid what's due to *Justice*, in returning as much as we received; yet we are not upon even terms, unless we suffer one *kindnesse* to beget another, and return something over and above, and more then we received. A good man will do it when he can, and have a good mind, an earnest *desire* to do it when he cannot. And so should we to God, since 'tis impossible to make him answerable returns in *fact*, we must do it *in voto*, in desire. And though neither our *deeds* nor *desires* can in any degree equal his Bounty, but we must needs fall infinitely short in both; yet if we do what we can, and heartily wish we could do more, 'tis accepted with him.

And *something* (sure) we can do, and that *something* we must do. Now to learn what it is, we must consider; why we were *afflicted*, and why *delivered*? afflicted we were for our *sins*, delivered that we might *sin no more*. What those *sins* were that pulled down his *judgments* upon us, you heard before; how many, how great, how publick, how bold and daring; how our *provocations* multiplyed with and beyond his *judgments*. And now being delivered, we must remember, that *mercy* is ever shewed *propter spem*, in hope of amendment; and therefore take care to avoid those sins hereafter; at least to be sure to prevent their being publick and national any more. For if instead of improving this blessing of *Peace* to his glory, the good of others, and of ourselves, we abuse it to pride and vanities, pleasure and sensuality, excess and

1. The Puritans called clergy who preached what they thought insufficiently, 'dumb dogs'; Sheldon here beats them with their own stick, in the suggestion that a 'dumb', sincere heart is preferable to a preaching hypocritical tongue.

2. Preaching being to the Puritans almost a sacrament he uses 'words' by themselves to imply insincerity and insufficiency.

riot, we may be assured it will prove no blessing at all, but an *aggravation*, both of our *guilt* and *misery*, in bringing a worse War, and heavier judgments upon us, then we have yet felt.

But this is not all, we have more to do, to be thankful as we should, then this; then barely to *avoid sin*; we must *do good*[1] too. For the general end of all his blessings upon us, his mercies to us, and *deliverance* of us, of what kinde soever, is to lead us to a *holy*, *vertuous*, and *religious life*, St. *Luk.* 1.74,75. We are brought into danger and distress, because *bad*, delivered that we may be *better*. And this is the right *giving of thanks*, the best return we can make him, and the best esteemed by him: And so (you see) there is much more required to make up this duty, then *words*; much before, and much after, the *heart* before, and after the *hands*. If the first (the *heart*) be wanting, *words* are but *wind*, not better, nor so innocent as the pratling of a Parrat.[2] *Gratitude* is *heartless* without the one, and *lame* without the other. When either is wanting (the *heart* or *hands*) the *Tongue* is an *Hypocrite*, and gives *lies* instead of *thanks*; real thanks are good deeds, and they praise him best, that obey him best.

But now among those many duties a good life comprehends, and we in *gratitude* are obliged unto; some are more seasonable, more proper for this time and occasion. And to make the choice, we shall especially consider, that as *God hath done great things for us*, so it is necessary we *do something* again for him: As he hath *given* to us, so we *to give* to him.[3] Alas, how can that be! since our goods reach not to him, *he* needs them not. True indeed, but *His* do; the *poor* need, and by them our goods reach even to *Him* too. We relieve him in the *poor*, visit him in the *sick*, cloath him in the *naked*, redeem him in the *prisoner: For in that we do it to these, we do it to him*, Matth. 25.45. And no time more seasonable to do it in, none fitter then this: That at a *publick rejoycing* none may be *sad*, nor *fast* when others *feast*: And therefore, being cheered, refreshed, and comforted our selves, let us cheer, refresh, and comfort others; and being delivered our selves, let's deliver others from distress and want; those especially that have suffered in the late disturbances, the *sick*, the *maimed*, the *lame*, the *desolate Widows* and *Children* of such as fell in the Service. Let's be sure to make them (as well as ourselves) sensible of *Gods favors* to us: Let the *blessings* of *peace* distil from the *head* to the *skirts*, to the very meanest among us: *Works of Charity* are a proper *sacrifice* of *thanksgiving* at such a time as this.

But besides *giving*, there must be *forgiving* too, a duty at this time as season-able as the other, if not more; for it is the best part of our *Gratitude* to God, and the most acceptable to him, and we shall be without excuse, if we do it

1. Sheldon puts special emphasis on the importance of good works, knowing that any suggestion of good works as *justification* is anathema to Puritans, who, as a movement, depended upon election and faith.

2. That 'any Parrot can prattle', was a favourite Puritan reflection upon the saying of formal prayers. Sheldon is tossing it back to them with the cutting edge reversed.

3. Armenianism undisguised.

not. For shall God forgive us *Thousands of Talents*, sins many in number, great in weight? And shall we stick at a *few pence*, a few petty injuries of our Brethren, neither great, nor many; but such as for *number* or *weight* can stand in no comparison with ours against him? Shall *God*, so great, so glorious, after so high and many provocations, condescend to be at peace with us, and give us an assurance of it, by removing his *judgments*, and *crowning* him with many *blessings*? And shall *we* (poor worms) be at enmity among our selves for trifles, and that to the hazard of all the *comforts* of this life, and hopes of a better? Shall *we* retain the memory of former unkindnesses, and make a *Publick Act of Oblivion*, (which we expect) a *publick lye*; without either fear of God, of shame of the *World*? This is not to *have peace*, or enjoy it; but with great ingratitude to *throw* it at him again; it is but to change one war into another, the open into secret, hostility into treachery; and, by pretending *peace* and *kindness*, to smooth the way to *supplantation* and *injury*, the most *base, serpentine, unmanly thing* in the World.

And therefore I beseech you, take care that we strip our selves of all *unruly passions*, that we may have *peace within*, peace from turbulent, revengeful affections: For unless we have this, what's *outward peace* worth? Certainly no more to thee then health in the *City*, when the *Plague* is in thy *bosome*. Let's all seriously and sadly look back, consider, and bemoan one another: For what we have mutually done, and suffered-from-each-other; let's all be *sorry* for it, and all *mend*, perfectly *forgiving* what's past, and returning to as great a kindness as ever, and a greater then ever; that so, by all *mutual good Offices* we may make amends for our former *Animosities*.

It hath been our custom indeed (and more shame for us) to *forget benefits*, to write them in *sand*, but injuries in *marble*; we must now invert the order, write *Gods benefits* in marble, others injuries in sand, if we write them at all; never *forget* the one, never *remember* the other; that's the best, the most *Christian memory*, which (as *Cæsars*) *forgets* nothing but *injuries*: We should all do it, and *Princes* above all; for it becomes a *Publick Father*, to look upon all as *sons*, upon the *Prodigals*, with more kindness and tenderness, when they once come to themselves, acknowledge their errors, when he sees them *returning*, though *afar off*, to *run*, and *meet*, and *caress* them; to call for the *Ring* and the *Robe*; to set some marks of favour upon them more then ordinary, that may give assurance to the World and them, that the promises made them, were not the *effects of necessity*, but the *fruits* of a *gracious Princely minde*, inviolably resolved to outdo all his *Promises* and *Engagements*.

Lastly, and to conclude, Let every one of us (I beseech you) think upon these and the like duties, which this time and occasion call for, and continue them at all times. *Gratitude* is not the business of a day or year, but of our *whole life*.

JOHN BRAMHALL[1]

The problem of dealing appropriately with John Bramhall in the prevailing context baffled me; the combination of his abilities and their neglect deserved a book to itself and I was tempted to omit him altogether rather than do him less than justice. Finally I settled on offering one short passage—manifestly as a mere token of the untapped reservoir—from the rhapsody uttered in the hour of triumph for the Royal cause, after years of exile and poverty. He was by then 'in the declension of his age and health', but, said Jeremy Taylor, when he preached the Archbishop's funeral sermon, three years later, 'his very Ruines were goodly'.

A Sermon Upon His Majesty's Restoration
(1660)

Now we enjoy the sweet sauce of all temporal blessings, that is health. God knows how soon sickness may cast us upon our restless beds, and change our sweet repose into wearisome tossings. God knows how soon we may be choaked with the fumes of a vitious stomach or drowneed with hydropical humours, or burnt up with choleric distempers, or buried alive in the grave of melancholic imaginations. Now we sit in the beauty of peace, every man

1. John Bramhall, 1594–1663. Sydney Sussex College, Cambridge 1609; B.A. 1612; M.A. 1616; B.D. 1623; D.D. 1630; holy orders 1616, Rector of South Kilvington, Yorks; received Prebendary of Husthwaite from Neale 1633; Wentworth's chaplain in Ireland; Bishop of Derry 1634. Spent most of the Civil War on the continent, as a leader of the Anglican resistance movement to the Presbyterian church. Excluded, with Laud, by the Uxbridge Convention from the general pardon, and again in 1652 from the Act of Indemnity. Returned to England October, 1660. Archbishop of Armagh January 18th, 1661. His *Works* (Dublin 1677) are prefixed by a biographical memoir by John Vesey, Archbishop of Tuam; reprinted in the Library of Catholic Theology (Oxford, 1842–1845), 5 vols. See also William J. S. Simpson, *Bramhall* (1927); as good a starting point as any is T. S. Eliot's essay, *John Bramhall* (1927); a review of Simpson's book in *Selected Essays* (1951).

under his own vine and his own fig-tree. We know how soon our ringing of bells may be changed to roaring of cannons. It is the mercy of the Lord that these mischiefs do not overwhelm us.

GILBERT IRONSIDE

Gilbert Ironside (the younger) is already old when he preaches this sermon, an 'old man, plundered', he describes himself, 'of abilities as well as books by the Discouragements of our late confusions'. But he will live for another decade as a notably gentle and tolerant Bishop of Bristol. His life has spanned four reigns; in childhood an Elizabethan, he is now expressing the rejoicing of the county of Dorset at the accession of Charles II.

His sermon is an appeal for a little modesty and restraint in religious controversy to help heal the wounds of the nation. England has had a narrow escape from more bloodshed, perhaps from social disintegration. They have all seen fools with their follies strutting across the wastelands of a plundered society where 'everyone that could, made himself a king, and everyone that would made himself a priest' and where lay-preachers had 'made our church a babel'. It is time, he urges, to stop theological bickering and try to *live* a little more by the spirit of Christ's example.

We have observed a growing resistance to the prophetic, militant and incitant, sectarian preacher. But the forces which activated him were nowhere near exhausted; new civil war had been prevented, anarchy averted, but the struggle was not over.

1. Gilbert Ironside, 1588–1671. Trinity College Oxford 1604; B.A. 1608; M.A. 1612; Fellow 1613; B.D. 1619; D.D. 1660. An unusually rich man for a priest of the Church of England, probably partly by marriage. Rector of Winterbourne Steepleton 1618; rector of Winterbourne Abbas 1620; also rector of Yeovilton in Somerset: Bishop of Bristol 1661. By repute a generous and tolerant man, even managed to tolerate John Wesley (grandfather of the Methodist), who was one of those Puritans who did not wish to be tolerated, judging by the account given by Calamy (*Memorials*, pp. 438–47), not a man to be favourably predisposed towards a bishop.

God's Message to His People

A sermon preached at Dorchester, in the county of
Dorset, at the Proclamation of his sacred Majesty
Charles II, on May 15th., 1660, by Gilbert Ironsyde
B.D.

... We have had many days of solemn Humiliation and Thanksgiving, and
have been thought to have prospered even beyond our own present desires;
but we never I believe considered whether Gods Voice in his Word, and
his Voice in his Works went together; yet it was easily discerned, for did we
not fast to strife and debate, to say no worse? did we not fast to smite with
the fist? that is too soft a smiting; I am loth to name the Acts of Wickedness:
and when we gave thanks, was it not for Rapine, Violence, the shedding of
innocent Bloud, and other horrid consequences of War against our neighbour-
Nations, nay our own people? we should have hearkned to the voice of Gods
Word, forbidding our Barbarous Inhumanity, *Even the selling the Righteous
for silver, and the poor for shooes, Amos* 2.6,8. and not have hardned our hearts
from the Voice of his providence: take it for a Rule, When the voice of the
Word speaks one thing, and the voice of successes seems to speak another,
look upon it either as a Temptation or a Judgment, even a leading to a
reprobate sense, it is always so when God grants wicked men the wicked
desires of their wicked Hearts.

Not to trouble you much, it hath been a long time a praying time, the
Court of Heaven hath been solicited this many years *pro* and *con*, with much
Preaching, Fasting, and Crying to; and now let the world judge whose
prayers have been heard. Can it be denied that God did hear and grant the
prayers, sighs and groans, *hæ sunt ipsissimæ sanctorum Orationes*, of the now
instrument of his glory, and his peoples good, with all them that mourned in
secret with him, even when he seemed to others to be most deaf unto them?
and did he not reject all their Anti-suitors, even then when they thought and
proclaimed to the world that they had been heard because of their successes?
And the reason is evident, for were not their prayers contrary to the voice of
the Word, to oppresse the Fatherlesse and the Widow, a man and his house,
to subvert right, and pervert Justice, and rather to Sacrifice whole kingdomes
then their own Ambition and Lust? and were not those others according to
the Voice of the Word, that the yoke of every oppressor may be broken, that

God would judge the world in Righteousnesse, and at last require the bloud of his Servants? So that put the Voice of God speaking in his Word, and the Voice of Successe (as we see at this day) together, they make a full Answer from God the Lord out of heaven; and when God speaks so plainly, so distinctly, so with an Eccho, Voice answering Voice, can men or angels forbear their *Hosannahs, Blessed be he that cometh in the name of the Lord?* When we thus hearken what God the Lord will say, we need not fear, for he will, certainly *he will speak peace unto his people*; the next thing in the Text.

Peace in this place is the prosperous settlement of that Nation, and therefore we are to understand *his People*, not by way of distinction and separation, but the whole visible State and Church of the *Jews*: For that which is added, (*and to his Saints*) is onely expository, for what are his People but his Saints? and what are his Saints but his People? it is an Hebraism worth observing, affirming that to be which ought to be; to these he will speak Peace, therefore they wanted it for the present; he will speak Peace, therefore they shall not ever be without it; and he it is that will speak Peace, and therefore it can come from no other hand; and he will when it is best for them. The people of God do sometimes want Peace. The Moon hath her Wanes and Eclipses as well as her Light and Glory; and *Ecclesia habet sud tempora*, she is like the pole-Star, *Semper versatur; nunquam mergitur*, she is sometimes aloft, and anon you would think her falling into the Sea. In me, saith our Saviour, *you shall have Peace, but in the World tribulation*: What Peace had *Israel* in *Egypt* for near 200. yeares together, or in *Babylon* for 70 yeares? what Peace had the Primitive Christians in their 10. Persecutions near 400. yeares, and what our English Professors in those Marian dayes? I am sure our *Jerusalem* complaines, *that the plowers made long furrowes upon her back, more then once or twice, yea many times*, Psal. 129. and we our selves have lived to see, and feel, and smart under this Truth, conviction strong enough against Academicks and Scepticks themselves. And indeed, it is Gods wisdom to have it so, thereby to pluck his peoples Lips from the teats of this Earth: the Nurse puts Wormwood or some sharper thing to her Nipples to wean her child; and God doth imbitter our sweets, and blast our blessings, to take off our Affections from the things below, the better to fit us to walk with him, and have our converse in Heaven; for the want of Peace is the Mother of holy Wisdom, when we are quiet and at ease we are like the prodigall having his portion, minding nothing but travelling as far as we can from our Father into strange Countries, with Harlots and Riotous living; but the want of Peace, the sound of the Drum and Trumpet, the neighing and prancings of the mighty ones make us return to our selves, and think of home. Outward Peace also begets a kind of Spirituall lazynesse; and we say to our selves with him in the Parable, *Soul, eat and be merry, take thy ease*; but when Peace is gone, this lazy humour is gone, and we set our selves to work again. In a calm at Sea, the Mariners lie idle upon the decks: but when a storm is up, they also are up and are doing, some tend the Anchor, some guide the Ship, some dresse the Sailes, some pull the Ropes, and some stand at the pump; it is so with our Graces, in the time of Peace scarce one stirs, but when Peace is gone, every one is summon'd to his duty, Faith must steer, Hope must be the Anchor, Charity must dresse the Sailes, Patience must pull the Ropes, and Repentance stand at the Pump. Besides, we are apt to abuse Peace when we have long had it more then any other blessing whatsoever: We may truly invert the Apostles words, and say, *where (this grace) doth abound, there sin doth abound, even* Sodoms *sins,* Pride, Fullnesse of bread, Idlenesse, Drunkennesse, Uncleanness, Uncharitableness, Lukewarmness, Prophaneness; I cannot say they are the Effects of Peace, no more then the weeds in the Garden are the Effects of the Suns shining. No, they are the spurious brats of our own corrupt hearts, yet we know they are the companions and attendants of a long Peace; whereas Wars, Persecutions, Afflictions are Gods weeding knifes, to cut off these Evils even by the Rootes; therefore saith David, *it was good for me to be afflicted,* he means chiefly by the Wars made upon him by *Saul* and his Son *Absolom,* the Crosse of Christ saith a Father, was *Currus Triumphalis,* his Triumphant Chariot; so in its kind is the Cross of his Children, even Gods fiery Chariot in which he sets them to triumph over their spirituall Enemies, and so to ascend to his Throne of Glory: and if so, it is not onely Gods wisdom, but his infinite Goodness and Mercy, that his people have not alwaies Peace. I remember *St. Austin* against *Parmenion* but when?[1] There be two Adverbs which I had almost said are Antichristian when they interpose in holy things, the one is the *Quomodo dubitantis,* an How of doubting; the other a *Quando murmurantis,* the When of repining; the one is destructive of our faith, as in the Noble man, 2 *King.* 7. 7. as long as *Nicodemus* kept himself to his *Quomodo istud*? he could not enter into the kingdome of God: the other is destructive to our hope, as in *Jehoram, Should I attend any longer on the Lord?* the *Quomodo* hath almost spoiled us of all our Religion; for how many nice and needless, and therefore fruitlesse controversies hath it raised? We agree

---

1. To an editor accustomed to a burden of vague references and inaccurate quotations such ingenuous candour is endearing, and almost unique. 'Parmenion' is Parminianus, the Spaniard who succeeded Donatus the Great in the fourth century as the leader of the Donatists, the doctrinal ancestors of the Puritans, who required qualifications of absolute 'holiness' from members of the 'true church'—'the true bride of Christ'—and wished to exclude the rest of mankind from fellowship. The most potent reply to the lost books of Parminianus (and much used by Augustine) was that of Optatus, whose *De Schismate Donatistarum adversus Parmenianum,* written in 368, was first published in the edition of J. Cochlaeus (Mainz, 1549); a modern edition will be found in Vol. XXVI of *Corpus scriptorum ecclesiasticorum Latinorum* (Vienna, 1893).

upon Gods decrees, but whether they be *supralapsarian* or *sublapsarian*,[1] absolute or conditional, we defie one another as hereticks: that Christ is in the Sacrament all agree; but whether *Con*, or *Sub*, or *Tran*. or after Mr. *Calvins modo ineffabili*, (which sure must needs be best) the world will never agree: That Christ gave *Peter* the keys no man denies; but whether as he was an Apostle, or as a Pastor, or as a Believer, we most eagerly dispute. So for the *Quando*, it eats even into the marrow of the souls of Gods best people many times in their distresses; *Why art thou cast down, O my soul?* saith *David*; *why art thou so disquieted within me?* Not so much his sufferings as the *Quando* of his release tormented him: This cast down his soul, this disquieted his heart within him, for *hope that is deferred* (longer then we would or expect,) *makes the heart sick, Prov.* 13.12. Take heed therefore of the curiosity of the *Quomodo*, if you would preserve your faith; of the intemperance of the *Quando*, if you would not be sick at heart.

*

Many have spoken of the sinfullness of sin, and they have done well, few of the folly of sin; yet perhaps this is the more necessary Doctrine, and more instrumental to the conversion of a sinner. For tell a naturall man what grievous abominations his sins are, alas, the point is too high for him, or he hath wit and fancy at will to plead for his beloveds: But tell him that his sins make him a fool, unman him, so that now he doth but *insanire cum ratione*, he hath but reason enough to make himself a mad man, this will awaken him, because you deal with him upon his own principles. It were therefore worth the while to shew a sinner his folly, I mean the impenitent constant customer to Satan and his own lusts, otherwise *Stultorum omnia sunt plena*, we are all fools, for folly is bound up in the hearts of all the Children of *Adam*: But for the sins of weakness, *& quotidianæ incursionis*, the daily inrodes of frailties, if detested and resisted, they are not properly ours, though alwaies with us and within us; they be those other sinners that be the fools. I will give you but some few hints, which might occasion a larger Treatise.

A fool is a simple ignorant Creature, he hath but very little of the Light

1. *sublapsarian*: the milder school of Calvinism which teaches that God made man, having foreseen his fall and ready to proffer saving grace.

supralapsarianism: a variant Calvinist exegesis propounding that the mind of God conceived man without consideration of the fall, and later caused him to fall, the essence of the issue being whether God decreed rigid election and reprobation before or after the fall of Adam. Despite its not insignificant place in the history of Protestantism—it perpetuates Calvin's own teaching—the editors of the Protestant memorial, *The New Schaff-Herzog Encyclopedia of Religious Knowledge* (1911) may have found the *prima facie* moral monstrosity of superlapsarianism an intolerable embarrassment in the climate of early twentieth-century humanism; for they do not include the word in their twelve-volume work. As if by way of diversion, however, they offer a particularly brisk attack on the doctrine of *supererogation*.

that enlightens every man that cometh into the world; and *Aristotle*, a Heathen, could say, that *Omnis peccans est ignorans*, every evil doer is ignorant, I am sure the Apostle saith, *that his foolish heart is darkned*, and which is more, *that he is stark blinded by the god of this World*.

A fool is not only void of knowledg, but withall uncapable of any. Put him to School, let him converse with knowing men, except you can new make his soul, or new mould his braines, the fool will be a fool still: *O ye fools when will ye be wise?* The Interrogation implies a Negation, as much as never. The *Emblematist* tells you that if you, put an Asse amongst generous Horses, that he may learn to neigh as those Horses do, yet an Asse will bray as an Asse, as long as he is an Asse; and who can infuse goodness into a wicked heart? nothing but a new Creation can do it; it is that which *Solomon* teacheth in the 22. Pro. 17. *Though thou shouldest bray a fool in a mortar with a pestle as Wheat, yet will not his foolishness depart from him*: pound Wheat in a mortar with the heaviest pestle, you shall never separate the bran from the flowr; its the serch must do it. Its so with a wicked fool; nothing but the finest serch of Gods grace and Spirit can separate his folly from his soul. A Fool cannot make a good election of things set before him; any toy shall be preferr'd before that which is of excellent worth, and the greatest concerment; for a Fools head is a heap of fancies: No more can our spirituall fool discern things that differ, he will alwayes be speaking evill of good, and good of evill; set before him, as *Moses* and the Prophets use to doe, *life* and *death*, whih doe ye think he will choose? *Solomon* tells you that *the heart of a fool is in his left hand, Eccles.* 10.2. he had rather be standing on the left hand with the goats, then on the right hand with Gods sheep. Fools notwithstanding are wilfull in their choice, til they have wearied themselves with their bables, you shall not perswade them out of them: and are not wicked men as wilfull in their follies? neither parents, nor wife, nor children, nor friends, nor Sermons shall reform them, but *he that is filthy* will be *filthy still*. Much like the obstinate Jew, though he lay in a Jakes, yet none must help him out, because it was his Sabbath: and our wicked fool, though he wallow like the sow in the mire of his sensuality, none must help him out, because it is his Sabbath, his delight, he hath set up his rest there. Though a fool be thus obstinate, yet you may easily cheat him of any good thing he hath, to his very clothes: Such easie fooles are wicked men, they have most cheatable soules, pliable to any temptation, to any lust.

A Fool is a very contemptible creature, he makes sport to the very children in the streets; and our spirituall fool is the very off-scouring of all things, scorned even by those that are as bad as himself; its no news to hear one Drunkard upbrayd another with *Drunken fool*, or one unclean person to make himself merry with anothers uncleannesse. Put a fool into an Office, or Honour, what a ridiculous monster doth he appear? *As snow in summer, and rain in harvest, so honour is not seemly for a fool, Prov.* 26.1. Perhaps by this similitude of *snow, Solomon* alludes to the *white garments* which Princes and men of honour use to wear, compared to the *snow in Salmon Psal.* 68. or to the fading, melting nature of all earthly glory: be it so or so, Honour is not fit for a fool; nay its not onely his own, but the places punishment where he is. Snow in Summer, and Rain in Harvest are seldome blessings; it is so with the wicked and ungodly, when they rule, its not onely the same, but the punishment of a people.

Lastly, the Rod and House of Correction are commonly the Fooles portion; and what is the lot of our sinful fool but a rod, but a rod to some purpose? it hath but four twigs, but they be smart ones. Indignation, Wrath, Tribulation, Anguish; and a house of correction too to some purpose, even that Bridewell or Bedlam of hell, with the Devil and his Angels.

And now give me leave to speak freely unto you, Honored and Beloved. We are of this Nation have a long time been simple, sinfull, wicked fools. Those that have calculated will tell you that the year 41. was to be *Annus universalis insaniæ*; the first year of the universall madnesse of Christendome. I am sure then we began to plot, contrive, and act our follies, with an high hand, to break through all Laws both of God and Man, with the unjust Judge, neither fearing the one nor reverencing the other; nothing could restrain us, no not oaths themselves; then began Perjury to be the great sin, which all our nice and new-minted glosses will I fear never be able either to heal or plaister. We were also obstinate in our follies, nothing could take us off, not the voice of Gods word, not the perswasions of the wisest men, not the cryes of the people, nor the clamours of our own consciences. We were highly pleased with our wicked Chymera's, they were our Sabbaths, we had set up our rest in them. Let me adde what cheatable fools we have been, I doe not mean of our Estates, though this be true, but of those precious Gems, Laws, Liberties, Religion, Christianity, Humanity it self; such grosse fools have we been, and therefore God hath justly sent us to the house of correction of these late wars and oppressions; till now at last of his own free mercy and most infinite goodnesse, he hath released us, yet upon baile, even the caution of the Text, *But let them not &c.* It is both a caution and a threatning, and it looks more like a threatning then a caution, for it's a But with an Aposiopesis, *Let them not.* If they do—— The folly that is here spoken of is nationall, not personall; for when do we read that private men did draw down publick judgments upon a nation, except that nation made them its own by law or connivance? God will spare great wicked places for a few righteous, therefore he will not destroy great countrys for a few wicked sinners. Briefly, the sins of the Jews that brought this fury of *Antiochus* upon them, may be reduced to these two heads. First, the Tabernacle of *David* was let fall to the ground. Secondly, the publick worship and government of the Church, was quite changed from what God had established, the Priest-hood was taken from the Tribe of *Levi*, as the Scepter was departed from the Tribe of *Judah*: they might be necessitated perhaps to this latter, by the rising and breaking of the *Grecian* Monarchy, but the former must needs be from their own pride, faction and emulation, and this brought in *Antiochus*.

We have seen their follies, and in them we may see our own, which sure in generall was great and manifold, of the Court, City, Clergy, Country; we were generally a people laden with iniquity, yet he that drunk deepest of the Cup, was, I think, the most innocent person. Should I rake into the sink of all our follies, I should present you with a tedious and offensive inventory, lesse pertinent to my Pattern and Text; I will therefore keep close to both, and only say, as it was with them, so it was with us: *The Scepter was departed from Judas, and the Priest-hood from the Tribe of Levi; Every one that could, made himself a King, and every one that would, made himself a Priest.* The Roman Legendaries tell us of Pope *Innocent* the third, who in a Vision saw the two lay-Mendicant Preaching Fryers, *Dominick*, and *Francis* upholding his Latterane[1]; and our lay-gifted Brethren that did but think themselves so, or had the boldnesse to say they were so, made our Church a *Babell*, and upheld our confusion; by this I see two men running in opposition one from another, may meet at a point in the *Antipodes*, *Non est Sacri alicujus Ordinis prædicare Evangelium*. It belongs not to men in holy Orders to preach the Gospel, say some Papists, and the worst of Papists, the *Canonists*,[2] and *Non est Sacri alicujus Ordinis*; It belongs not to men in Holy Orders (Such are Anti-christian and *Baals*, Priests) to preach the Gospel, say some Protestants, but the worst of Protestants, the Sectaries;[3] therefore as it was with them, so you see it was with us, and then came in *Antiochus*; in a word, those two Staves which God had Erected among them, for his own Glory, and their Protection, the Staffe of Beauty, and the Staffe of Bands were broken, as it was with them, so it was with us, and then came in *Antiochus*.

Bands I am sure were broken by Faction and Schisme, Brotherly union in matters of Gods Service was quite gone, for there arose a generation of men, skilfull to speak Evil of Good, that branded whatever pleased them not, (though never so lawfull) for Superstitious and Idolatrous; little remembring

1. See Jacobus de Voraigne, *Legenda Aurora* (1470), 'Dominic'. Pope Innocent III sees in a dream St. Dominic—St. Francis does not enter the anecdote until later—sustaining the walls of the Church of Lateran when they seem about to fall.

2. Canonists: canon-lawyers, in the sense here of pedants concerned with artificial forms, at the expense of the spirit of Christianity.

3. On the other hand Ironside disapproves of sectaries as much as any Roman could wish. The catholicity of this position continued to prove influential in restoring the character of the Church of England.

that to condemn for such, which indeed is not such, is to make our selves Supersitious and Idolatrous.

Beauty was also broken, our government was shiver'd to pieces, we disliked what was present, and therefore made long Preparations, and strong Combinations for a Change, and a Change we must have, though by an honest Rebellion, which was the contradiction; To this purpose two things must be done, the one taught by *Machiavel* to bespatter our Governours, even to the slandering of the Footsteps of the Lords Anointed; the other was the Devils Sophistry, Liberty of Conscience must be pretended from all humane Laws: but who knows not that though humane Laws do not bind the Conscience, yet the Conscience is bound to humane-Laws; for he that hath said by S. *James*, *There is but one Law giver*, hath likewise said by S. *Paul*, *You must be subject not only for fear, but for Conscience sake:* Had humane Laws bound the Conscience, the one could not have said, *There is but one Law-giver*; and had not the Conscience been bound to humane Laws, the other could not have said. *Not only for fear but for Conscience sake*. Lastly, all this was fallaciously coloured over with the glorious Titles of Gods cause, and the Gospels purity. Our case you see was well like theirs, our Pride as great, our Emulation and heart-burnings greater, our Dissimulation both with God and Man greatest of all, and why might not *Antiochus* come in? These you will say were Cleargy sins, but those of the Layety were not inferiour, nay the very same; But what do I? I promised not to rake into the sink of these Follies, and surely I have gone no further then of necessity I must, to the satisfying of the Text, and my own duty; for had I not shewed our Follies, how could I have forewarned you, not to turn again unto them?

To return again unto our Follies, when we have not only seen them, but so lately and deeply smarted for them, is the greatest Folly in the World: Every child that hath been burnt will dread the fire, should not men do so? the reason of the difference is, the child continually sees the fire, and remembers its burning, but we forget the Judgements of God as soon as they are removed out of our sight; O Remember, remember that Gods quiver is full of deadly Arrowes, though these be gone, he hath heavier Judgements in store for us; if forgetting what is past, we return again to our former Follies. Christ you know told him so in the Gospel; *go sin no more lest a worse thing fall unto thee*, sin no more, not Absolutely, but Relatively; the same which now thou hast sinned; the sin of Unthankfulness to him that so graciously had forgiven thee: Briefly, therefore, the Folly of returning again appeares in these two things. First, in the guilt contracted, for if you believe the Schools, and you may, for its grounded on these words of Christ; a returning to sin past over and forgiven, puts new life into that very sin, and makes us doubly guilty in the sight of God, at least unto Temporal Judgements. Secondly, in the difficulty of a second pardon to be obtained, (for that such cannot be forgiven is the *Novatian* Errour,[1]) because by such returnings our minds are more darkned, the light of Gods grace is more diminished, the will is more depraved, the heart more hardned, the conscience nearer to be defiled and feared; such returnings must needs grieve Gods spirit, and if the greater care be not had, quench it: Therefore though God can easily forgive our greatest Follies, yet not our returnings again unto them. It is storied of a Grandee in *Rome*, that he barbarously slew his Servant even in the presence of the Emperour whom he entertain'd at a Feast, because he threw down unawares a Cubbord of his curious Glasses; it seems he esteemed more of his fine Glasses then of the precious bloud of a man: Our National Follies which you have heard were like curious new-fangled glasses, but will you esteem these glasses more then the bloud of men, of a Nation, of your own souls? Let me beseech you, as many be well-wishers to our peace, and this present solemnity, in Gods name and the Kings, in the name of the Church and State, for your own sakes, your wives and children, and your native Countries sake, turne not againe to your former follies, but lay aside all faction, dis-affection, all emulation and animosities, all envy, hatred, malice, uncharitablenesse, with all our former ungodly courses, else I must tell you, you have no part in the businesse and blessing of this day. Think not that our present peace is a new Patent for future wickednesse, or that if we can upbrayd some, insult over others, and drink the Kings Health, till with it our own sicknesse, that we are the Kings best friends and most faithful Subjects: No, we are his greatest enemies such as doe (what in us lies) betray both him and ourselves to our former miseries; and so I have done.

Nor can I conclude with a better Prayer than that of the first Text, which is both a Text and a Prayer.: *We pray thee save now O Lord, O Lord send now prosperity: Blessed be he that commeth in the name of the Lord.* Long may the King live, Long may he reign, Long may he be a father to the State, a Nursing Father to the Church. *Let all his enemies O Lord, be confounded, but upon himself let his Crown flourish* to be the joy of his people, and to the glory of God, and let all the people say Amen, Amen.

1. The word 'error' here stresses again Ironside's catholicity. 'Novatian Error': the denial by Novatian in the middle of the third century of the Church's power to grant absolution in certain cases (primarily the sin of apostasy) to make an example of Christians who had lapsed during the Decian persecutions of 249–250, and in principle to challenge the 'power of the keys'. The 'Novatian error' proved tenaciously recurrent and, of course, offered an encouraging precedent first to the principal bodies of Protestant reformers and later to sectarians.

EPILOGUE

Most Englishmen did echo the loyal preachers' welcome to the return-ing king with jubilation. The buoyancy was short-lived, but even disillusionment with the Restoration did not make a return to Puritan military dictatorship an attractive alternative to any but bigots or potential fugitives.[1] The Fifth Monarchists,[2] the most fanatical of the sectaries born of the Puritan complex, made one frantic effort to expel the loathed Anti-Christ, King Charles, and instal their own King Jesus in his place, which, if it had been as well organized as it was ferocious, would at least have thinned the ranks of the 'natural rulers'. In the early morning of January 6th, 1661, inflamed by a sermon preached by their leader, Thomas Venner, a renegade American cooper, who had somehow escaped from prison (where Cromwell had prudently confined him), a handful of godly desperadoes, fifty at the most, sallied forth from their lair, a meeting-house in Coleman Street, armed with words to preach to the convertible, and with swords to kill the rest, in particular, as they purposed, the king, the privy council and the entire magistracy of the capital. They scattered copies of a manifesto, which was a reproduction of what Venner had preached, exhorting the citizens of London to rise with them against the royal malignants and aid them to fulfil the destiny foretold in the seventh chapter of Daniel.[1]

I do Beleive all Governours, Governments, Laws and Constitutions to be Antichristian save Christ himself—his Deputies—his Visible kingdom with his Laws and Statutes; of which Laws his Saints shall be the Administrators

---

1. Complaints against military despotism imposed in the name of 'justice' abound in print, from the taking up of arms to the Restoration. As one writer put the sentiments of civilians at large (and indeed of many reluctant and uneasy military), 'No man knows what a bondange it is to be under the power of an army but they that feel it.' *The Copy of a Letter written from Northampton containing A true Relation of the Souldiers preaching and murdering of a woman* (1647), p. 8.

2. Fifth Monarchists believed that the Assyrian, Persian, Macedonian and Roman empires were the 'four great beasts' (Daniel vii : 3.) which had successively possessed the dominions of the earth, and that, they having passed away according to the prophecy, it was the duty of 'the saints of the most High' to proclaim and establish the fifth and last Kingdom of Christ upon earth.

(but without Literal Direction, for upon them shall rest the Spirit of Counsel and Wisdom). I do Beleive according to the Prophets that in the present year 1660 all Carnall Powers shall be Destroyed and that in the controversy lying between Zion and Babylon I am bound to Lift myself a Souldier to the Lamb and called to rise on God's behalf to Bind Kings in Chains etc.—To Raze and Root out all constitutions Antichristian whatsoever and never to sheath my sword till the Beast and Whore be destroyed, till Rome lie in Ashes and Babylon become a hissing and a curse etc. Wherefore let all that have lives to lay down for their King and Saviour come forth against the wicked with a sword and execute upon them the judgement written: As for the late King, he was a murtherer and a Tyrant and a Traytor: So is his Son and further an enemy and Rebell to Christ, and we owe no subjection to that bloody family.[1]

This handful of warriors for Jesus terrorized London for more than forty-eight hours; they seemed at first to be, as they claimed, super-naturally invincible,[2] repulsing with casualties the best regiments which could be deployed against them, including the King's Lifeguard. Such was the terror they inspired that General Monk (or the Duke of Albemarle as he was now styled) set about raising a force of ten thousand men to 'relieve' the capital. But the very panic the Fifth Monrachists excited was their weakness. The citizens bolted their doors and barricaded their windows; few ventured into the streets for fear of having their throats cut for the glory of Jesus, and there was no popular support for the insurrection. Loss of blood and loss of ammunition did for them one by one. Few surrendering, they were gradually killed or overcome by fatigue and numbers.[3] Venner himself was said to have nineteen wounds when he was finally taken. He and his lieutenant, Pritchard, were butchered—what was left of them—on a scaffold opposite their meeting-house. Venner went first and, while he was being dismembered, Pritchard preached such venomous scurrility against the king, that the public hangman had to interrupt his business to silence him by 'turning him off'. 'Thus ended a rebellion', observed

---

1. *The Fanatiques Creed* (1661); cf. *A Door of Hope, or a call and Declaration for the gathering together of the first ripe Fruits under the Standard of our Lord King Jesus* (1660).

2. They predicted that 'no weapons formed against them should prosper nor a hair of their heads be touched for one should chase a thousand, and two should put ten thousand to flight' (Cobbett's *State Trials*, VI, 67).

3. There were, no doubt, a few lucky ones. In Sewell's diary, written in Massachusetts, the following entry appears for January 31st, 1702: 'William Parsons of 88 years is buried. Was in the fifth monarch fray in London, but slipt away in the crowd.'

4. *The Kingdom's Intelligencer*, no. 3. Monday January 14th to Monday January 21st, 1661.

Echard, 'Of a very strange nature which was begun and carried out with such infernal rage, that if their numbers had been equal to their spirits they would have overturned the city and the nation, and the world, which in their imagination they had divided among themselves.'[1]

It was the last convulsion. The following year, the Act of Uniformity, requiring preaching clergy in particular to confirm to the Thirty-Nine Articles and the Book of Common Prayer, sentenced the entire Puritan complex of preachers to be involuntary 'dumb dogs'. Internicine hostility between the Presbyterians and rival sectaries now so far overrode all other considerations that loyal Presbyterians like Calamy and Ashe preferred to suffer inhibition themselves rather than see the mischief of 'toleration' accorded to schismatics and deviationists who had brought false doctrines disgrace to 'the Good Old Cause'.[2] Fire seemed to go out of the Puritan belly with bewildering suddenness. In Switzerland, Ludlow[3] would try to explain to his uncomprehending hosts—and for that matter to himself—with imperfect success, how the victorious saints had allowed their defeated enemies to insinuate themselves back into power and supplant them.

The outer crust, at least, of the answer is that, in their divisions, the Puritan congeries hated each other more than they hated their conventional adversaries. As for the latter, preaching had shown them what it could, and must not be allowed to do again; and the medium was put through a process of transmutation which subdued it to a decorous conformity, both of tone and content, to established order. The restraint and polished dryness and civility of a Tillotson; the cool elegance and acid disdain for 'enthusiasm' of a South, were to become the new criterions of merit. Preaching would continue, a socially prominent activity; indeed, an age of distinction was about to follow for the pulpit; but it would be a polite and discreet distinction. Henceforth the pulpit was to be accorded courteous deference; but the price it was to pay was *power*. The new spirit is refracted through Pepys (a modern man of the times if ever there was one) who, commenting on a sermon preached by an old-style combatant, remarked that it was 'too eloquent for a pulpit.'[4]

1. *State Trials*, 6, 70.
2. See letter signed by Calamy, Ashe and Manton, quoted in Robert Wodrow's *Sufferings of the Church of Scotland* (1721–22) I, lxiii.
3. Ludlow, *Memoirs* (Oxford 1894), I, viii.
4. *Diary*, March 1667. The 'too eloquent' preacher was Robert Mossum.

God had been withdrawn once more to a sacerdotally more decent elevation from the earth, and thereafter, a man claiming to be on terms of special familiarity with Him, would tend to incur general disrepute as a humbug, or something more dangerous. Everyone must worship, for such respect was due to the concept of 'superior powers', but extravagant devoutness had become suspect as pretentious hypocrisy, or worse, as *mischievous aspirations to superiority*. Preaching, once a turbulent heroism, was already on the way to becoming an insipid platitude. There would still be ups and downs, but more of the latter than the former. 'He that . . . preaches best will fight best', Cromwell had said.[1] Two centuries later, another preacher, in direct line of descent from Cromwell,[2] reaching the conclusion that there was nothing to fight about, observed, 'I like a silent church before the service begins better than any preaching'.[3] His own congregation agreed so far as to prefer a silent church to *his* preaching, and Ralph Emerson was ejected from his pulpit. It is a bold optimist who supposes that toleration, where it graces any scene, will prevail indefinitely without protection. There is a recurrent strain in human nature which does not welcome 'toleration', even of itself, seeming to prefer to be oppressed than to be tolerated; and it is a contingency worth remembering, that the 'saint', who patiently endures persecution, may, given the chance, cheerfully persecute others.

1. Cromwell to Colonel Hacker, December 25th, 1650.
2. Unitarian, out of Independent.   3. Emerson, *Essays; Self Reliance*.

FURTHER READING

A bibliography to match the contents of a diverse anthology, ranging over more than a hundred years, would be an impractical, as well as an inappropriate measure. But a short selection from a bibliography in progress, designed to serve the scope of a study complementary to this collection, may meanwhile conduct attention to some favourable routes for further investigation. The place of publication may be taken as London unless otherwise stated.

A Brief History of Preaching, by Y. T. Brilioth, translated by Karl E. Matson (Philadelphia, 1965) is a well-grounded work, the nearest to a comprehensive history of preaching which deserves attention. D. E. Dargan's *History of Preaching*, 2 vols. (New York, 1912) faithfully reflects popular literary taste of the time, and it may be worth dipping into for the sake of such intimations as 'Donne had real poetic talent and had he devoted himself to poetry could doubtless have attained high rank', while his preaching was 'marred by affectations and pedantry and straining for effect . . . .'.

Some knowledge of its antecedents is desirable as an introduction to post-Reformation preaching. Two books, the products of a lifetime of dedicated industry, offer a sound start: G. R. Owst's *Preaching in Medieval England* (Cambridge, 1926) and *Literature and the Pulpit in Medieval England* (Cambridge, 1933; reissued Oxford, 1961). These may be supplemented by the first part of C. H. Smyth's *The Art of Preaching* (1940), which contains an admirable account of a medieval academic sermon. The first part of the period under review may be approached through J. W. Blench's *Preaching in England in the Late Fifteenth and Sixteenth Centuries* (1964) a scholarly and accurate work. M. MacClure's *The Paul's Cross Centuries* (Toronto, 1958) is full of solid information. The most detailed books of reference covering the second phase remain W. Fraser Mitchell's *English Pulpit Oratory* (1932) and C. F. Richardson's *English Preachers and Preaching 1640–1670* (New York, 1928). Contemporary works on rhetoric and preaching should not be overlooked. One text-book of pervasive influence was Bartholomew Keckerman's *Rhetoricae Ecclesiasticae siue Artis Formandi et Habendi Conciones Sacras*,

Libri duo. Methodice Adornati per praecepti et Explicationes (Editio Tertia, Hanoviae, 1606). Subsequent and typical English publications include Thomas Hall's *Rhetorica Sacra* (1654); William Chappell's *The Preacher, or the Art and Method of Preaching* (1656); Thomas Blount's *The Academy of Eloquence* (1667); John Smith's *The Mysterie of Rhetorique Unveil'd*; and John Prideaux's *Sacred Eloquence* (1659). Useful references will be found in Ruth Beatrice Bozell's 'English Preachers of the Seventeenth Century on the Art of Preaching'; *Cornell University Abstracts of Theses for 1939* (1940). Studies considering particular aspects of preaching are A. F. Herr, *The Elizabethan Sermon: a survey and bibliography* (Philadelphia, 1940); Godfrey Davies, 'English Political Sermons, 1603–1646', *Huntingdon Library Quarterly*, III, no. 1 (October 1959); Ethyn Williams Kirby, 'Sermons before the Commons 1640–1642', *Amer. Hist. Rev.* XLIV, no. 3 (April 1939); James Spalding, 'Sermons before Parliament (1640–1649) as a public Puritan diary', *Church History*, XXVI (1967); John Sparrow, 'John Donne and Contemporary Preachers', *Essays and Studies*, Vol. XVI (1931); and, in particular, in the field of the Interregnum, Hugh Trevor-Roper, 'The Fast Sermons', first published in *Essays in British History presented to K. Feiling* (1957).

For general historical background only a few of the best recent works need be indicated. The first two volumes of W. K. Jordan's progressing study of the reign of Edward VI (1968, 1971); *Henry VIII* by J. J. Scarisbrick (1968) and *The Reign of Elizabeth* by J. B. Black (2nd edn., 1959). Two comprehensive studies of the first part of this complex and highly charged period are of distinguished merit: *The English Reformation* by A. G. Dickens (1964), and (from a Roman Catholic point of view) *The Reformation in England* by Philip Hughes (3 vols., 1950–4; reissued complete in one volume, 1964). The controversial subject of the circumstances leading to the Civil Wars are richly documented in *The Crisis of the Aristocracy* by Lawrence Stone (Oxford, 1965). *The Early Stuarts 1603–1660* by Godfrey Davies is a useful postscript to the magisterial works of Samuel Gardiner and Charles Firth, for which there are as yet no successors, and which are still indispensable. *The Origin of the English Civil War*, ed. P. A. M. Taylor (Boston, 1960), is a stimulating symposium of divergent views and includes contributions by Christopher Hill, J. Hexter and Hugh Trevor-Roper.

Church history, an account of the institution which alternately promoted and proscribed preaching, has been profusely, but seldom satisfactorily presented, owing to the residual violence of prejudice which the subject tends to awaken. (In this class, J. J. Perry's *History of the Church of England from the Death of Elizabeth to the Present Time*, 3 vols. (1861–4), and Stoughton's *History of Religion in England*, 8 vols. (1881) are mentioned as examples of how history should not be written.) High-Churchmanship-militant should not be missed in Jeremy Collier's *Ecclesiastical History of Britain*, and it is desirable to have the 9-vol. 1852 edition which carries an appendix containing the acrimonious correspondence the work provoked. Gilbert Burnet's *History of the Reformation* (1679–81, 1714) and *History of My Own Time* (1724–34) are the classic memorials to the Whig principles of judgement. The most delightfully readable, sometimes hilariously funny, account is from one of our men in the seventeenth century, Thomas Fuller himself; his *Church History of Britain*, ed. J. S. Brewer, 6 vols. (Oxford, 1845) is literature. Among modern works J. R. H. Moorman's *A History of the Church of England* (1953) is recommended. Authoritative studies on a narrower front are R. W. Dixon's *The History of the Church of England 1529–1570* (1878–1902), W. H. Frere's *The English Church in the Reign of Elizabeth and James* (1904) and W. H. Hutton's *The English Church from the Accession of Charles I to the death of Anne* (1903). William Shaw's *History of the English Church during the Civil Wars and under the Commonwealth 1640–1660*, 2 vols. (1900) is rather grey and pedestrian reading, but valuable for the author's intimate knowledge of contemporary records. Although R. G. Usher's statistics have been challenged in recent years, his *Reconstruction of the English Church* (1909) remains one of the more important works on the event. H. G. Alexander's *Religion In England* (London History Studies no. 4, 1968) is described as 'designed expressly for sixth-form students'. Some of its interpretations make uneasy companions, as if pronouncements of unreconciled judges have been mixed; but its concise chronological summary of events makes it of value to all with rebellious memories.

Devout tributes by later to earlier Puritans, which are naturally vehement in bias, but seldom dishonest, include Benjamin Brook's *Lives of the Puritans . . . from the Reformation to the Act of Uniformity in 1662*, 3 vols. (1813); J. B. Marsden's *History of the Early Puritans from the Reformation to . . . 1642* (1850) and *History of the Later Puritans 1642–1662* (1852); Daniel Neal's *History of the Puritans* (ed. J. O. Choules), 2 vols. (1848). For some of us, the above works, though informative, are only digestible, without ill effects, in small doses. In the event of real discomfort, Thomas Fuller is recommended as a hygienic remedy.

Some modern works on particular aspects of Church history and doctrine which will reward attention are George W. Addleshaw's *The High Church Tradition: a study in liturgical thought of the seventeenth century* (1941); Ronald A. Marchant's *Puritans and the Church Courts in the Diocese of York* (1960) [an exemplary study]; P. Collinson's *The Elizabethan Puritan Movement* (1957); M. M. Knappen's *Tudor Puritanism* (Chicago, 1939); J. F. New's *Anglican and Puritan, the basis of their opposition 1558–1640* (1964). The latter is particularly revealing in an area which has been strewn lately with diversionary *flora* to serve the purposes of popular ideologies.

The Revolution of the Saints: a study in the origins of radical politics by M. L. Walzer (1956) is an accurate title for a stimulating book. *Saints in Arms* by L. F. Solt examines part of the same field of seminal vitality. *Visible Saints* by H. Nuttal (Oxford, 1957) is an account, more sympathetic than critical, of the Independent movement. *The Economic Problems of the Church from Archbishop Whitgift to the Long Parliament* by Christopher Hill (1966) is a valuable guide to crucial but unpublicized issues. *God's Englishman: Oliver Cromwell and the English Revolution* (1970) by the same writer is a spectroscope of his subject's efforts and environment, fascinating to a reader already thoroughly familiar with the terrain, but perhaps discouragingly allusive to a new arrival. Mr. Hill does not disguise the fact that he is a Marxist and if the reader does not forget it either he need not be perplexed by the sometimes tendentious distribution of emphasis. William Haller's *Liberty and Reformation in the Puritan Revolution* (New York, 1955), continues to be the most convincing evocation of the Puritan climate-of-mind written in modern times. Robert S. Bosher's *The Making of the Restoration Settlement: the influence of the Laudians 1649–1662* (1951) is especially recommended to disentangle the mesh of faction and intrigue which, in the last phase of our cycle, ends in the Act of Uniformity. It also illustrates the severity of the lesson learnt by Anglican Royalists from the experience of having been overborne and ousted by the power of emotional, militant preaching. Edmund Calamy's *History of the Ejected Ministers* (1702), the Puritans' martyrology, and John Walker's *Sufferings of the Clergy* (1714) the Anglican counter-blast are inevitably instructive of the general conflict. They are best approached by way of A. J. Mathew's *Calamy Revised* (Oxford, 1934) and *Walker Revised* (Oxford, 1948), in which many murky corners are probed and illuminated.

In the turbulent war of ideas for which the pulpits provided the open cutting edges, the dynamics must be considered if *çasus belli* as well as *fortuna belli* is to be appreciated. Output in this field is vast. The following are a few works which I personally have found interesting:

Ed. T. Aston, *Crisis in Europe 1560–1660* (1965).

Charles Beard, *The Reformation of the 16th Century in its relation to Modern Thought and Knowledge* (1833).

Norman Cohn, *The Pursuit of the Millennium* (1957).

G. P. Gooch, *The History of English Democratic Ideas in the Seventeenth Century* (1898).

J. Hexter, *Reappraisals in History* (essays) (1961).

Philip Hughes, *The Theology of the English Reformers* (1965).

W. K. Jordan, *The Development of Religious Toleration in England 1603–1640* (1932–40) 4 vols.

P. E. More and F. L. Cross, *Anglicanism. The Thought and Practice of the Church of England Illustrated from the Religious Literature of the Seventeenth Century* (1935).

Christopher Morris, *Political Thought in England from Tyndale to Hooker* (1953).

Wallace Notestein, *The English People on the Eve of Colonization 1603–1630* (1954).

Robert Orr, *Reason and Authority. The Thought of William Chillingworth* (Oxford, 1967).

W. I. Trattner, 'God in Elizabethan England', *Journ. Hist. Ideas*, XXV (1964).

H. R. Trevor-Roper, *Archbishop Laud* (1940).
    Religion, the Reformation and Social Change (1967).

J. Tulloch, *Rational Theology and Christian Philosophy in England in the Seventeenth Century*, 2 vols. (Edinburgh, 1872).

Basil Willey, *Seventeenth Century Background* (1950).

B. H. G. Wormald, *Clarendon: Politics, History, Religion 1640–1660* (Oxford, 1939).

Francis Dunham Wormuth, *The Royal Prerogative 1603–1649* (Cambridge, 1951).

Perez Zagorin. *The History of Political Thought in the English Reformation* (1954).

Sixteenth- and seventeenth-century sermons up to 1662 are not readily obtainable, which is the principal reason for the production of this book. The works of a few of the more prominent preachers were assembled and reissued in the nineteenth century, under editorial direction of a quality they deserved, but such editions as these listed below are now themselves scarce.

Hugh Latimer, *Works*, edited by George E. Corrie, 2 vols. (1844) has not been superseded; but *Selected Sermons*, edited by Allen G. Chester (Charlottesville, 1968), will serve the reader who does not require the entire range of Latimer's preaching for study. Mr. Chester is also the author of the most thorough biography written to date, *Hugh Latimer* (Philadelphia, 1954).

Lancelot Andrewes, *Works*, edited by P. Wilson and James Bliss, 11 vols. (Oxford, 1841-54) again remains the standard collection. Books on Andrewes published since Eliot's enconium include John G. Bishop's *Lancelot Andrewes, Bishop of Chichester* (1963) and Paul Welsby's *Lancelot Andrewes* (1958); the latter contains a particularly good bibliography. Among the rest, since the turn of the century, H. B. Swęte's *Two Cambridge Divines* (1913) and Douglas Macleane's *Lancelot Andrewes* (1908) wear well. All biographers return to Henry Isaacson's *An Exact Narration of the Life and Death of Lancelot Andrewes* (1650).

An edition of the works of Richard Hooker, published in three volumes in 1888, contains Izaak Walton's *Life*.

Joseph Hall, *Works* (1625, etc.), was reissued edited by J. Pratt, 10 vols. (1808) and edited by P. Wynter, 10 vols. (Oxford, 1863). *The Life and Times of Joseph Hall* by John Jones (1826) looked like Hall's final obituary until the appearance of T. F. Kinloch's *The Life and Works of Joseph Hall* (1951), containing special reference to his quarrel with Milton.

Donne has been favoured with a recent edition of the whole body of his sermons: *The Sermons of John Donne* edited with introductions and critical apparatus by George R. Potter and Evelyn M. Simpson (Berkeley and Los Angeles, 1953-62). Studies appearing after this edition include Helen Gardner's *John Donne* (1962) and Robert C. Bald's *Donne's Influence on English Literature* (1965).

William Laud, *Works*, edited by G. W. Scott and James Bliss, 7 vols. (1847-60), contains his sermons. *Seven Sermons* (1651) was reissued edited by G. J. Hatherwell (1829). H. R. Trevor-Roper's biography has been noted above.

The Heber/Eden edition of the Works of Jeremy Taylor (1854) is cited above, p. 484. The sermons are in Vol. 4. Two modern studies of different aspects of Taylor's writing deserve notice: *The Rhetoric of Jeremy Taylor's Prose* by Mary S. Antoine (1946) and *English Casuistical Divinity during the Seventeenth Century, with special reference to Jeremy Taylor* by Thomas Wood (1952).

The Works of Thomas Adams, with a memoir by Joseph Angus, 3 vols. (Edinburgh, 1861–2) was the fruit of Adams' rediscovery earlier in the century: misdirection of pious industry (see above, p. 157); words and phrases altered to conform to Victorian usage; footnotes commonly vague or wrong.

INDEX